The Philip E. Lilienthal imprint
honors special books
in commemoration of a man whose work
at the University of California Press
from 1954 to 1979
was marked by dedication to young authors
and to high standards in the field of Asian Studies.
Friends, family, authors, and foundations have together
endowed the Lilienthal Fund, which enables the Press
to publish under this imprint selected books
in a way that reflects the taste and judgment
of a great and beloved editor.

The publisher gratefully acknowledges the generous support of the Philip E. Lilienthal Asian Studies Endowment Fund of the University of California Press Foundation, which was established by a major gift from Sally Lilienthal.

The Gender of Memory

ASIA PACIFIC MODERN

Takashi Fujitani, Series Editor

The Gender of Memory

Rural Women and China's Collective Past

Gail Hershatter

UNIVERSITY OF CALIFORNIA PRESS

Berkeley   Los Angeles   London

University of California Press, one of the most distinguished university presses in the United States, enriches lives around the world by advancing scholarship in the humanities, social sciences, and natural sciences. Its activities are supported by the UC Press Foundation and by philanthropic contributions from individuals and institutions. For more information, visit www.ucpress.edu.

University of California Press
Berkeley and Los Angeles, California

University of California Press, Ltd.
London, England

© 2011 by The Regents of the University of California

First Paperback Printing 2013

Library of Congress Cataloging-in-Publication Data

Hershatter, Gail.
    The gender of memory : rural women and China's collective past / Gail Hershatter.
        p.   cm. — (Asia Pacific modern ; 8)
    Includes bibliographical references and index.
    ISBN 978-0-520-28249-0 (pbk. : alk. paper)
    1. Rural women—China—Shaanxi Sheng—Social conditions.
    2. Rural women—China—Shaanxi Sheng—Economic conditions.
    3. Socialism—China—Shaanxi Sheng—History.   I. Title.
    HQ1769.S433H47   2011
    305.48'89510514309045—dc22   2010052235

Manufactured in the United States of America

20   19   18   17   16   15   14   13
10   9   8   7   6   5   4   3   2   1

For Gao Xiaoxian

CONTENTS

ACKNOWLEDGMENTS

A book fifteen years in the making marks a longish phase in a life. Since this one is, in part, a book about memory, finishing it seems to require at least a brief backward glance from the author. World events, the domestic time of my household, and the daily rhythms of work time in my university have all changed across the past decade and a half. I can name and arrange temporalities of all kinds: rupture, accretion, progress, decline, crisis, milestone, routine. When I try to imagine how I might give an account of this time span, how I might answer the sort of questions I blithely put to Chinese village women and men, the mind boggles, and I am impressed all over again with their narrative capacities and their patience. My first thanks goes to them.

The research for this book was only possible because of the intellectual acumen, curiosity, commitment, and endless competence of Gao Xiaoxian. I still marvel at my great good luck in finding her, and at her willingness to deal with the complications of taking me to Shaanxi villages over a ten-year period. Our research has been fully collaborative, and our discussions since 1992 have been one of the greatest pleasures and learning experiences of my life, but I take full responsibility for the ideas expressed in this book. I look forward to the book she plans to write based on our joint interviews, when her daily responsibilities to the organization she runs for Shaanxi women (www.westwomen.org) become less pressing. This book is dedicated to her.

Although I have spent thousands of solitary hours with the materials that undergird this book, the process of working on it has done away with any lingering notions I may have had that a historian works alone. In China, the Shaanxi Provincial Women's Federation was a generous host, and the Shaanxi Provincial Archives staff were helpful in locating materials. Ning Huanxia (1996), Wang Guohong (1997), Zhao Chen (1999), Yang Hui (2001), Yu Wen (2004), and Peng Jingping (2006) provided invaluable assistance on village visits recording and deciphering interview notes; Wang Guohong also conducted interviews of her own on our 1997 trip. Gao Danzhu accompanied me on a return visit to Village G in 2004. Zhao Yugong was an inexhaustible source of information about all matters of custom and local history stretching back to the Neolithic period, as well as pseudonyms for our interviewees. Jin Yihong helped arrange a visit to the Number Two Archives in Nanjing, and Yang Di and Li Yaqin assisted in collecting materials there.

Major grants from the Pacific Rim Research Program of the University of California (1994–96) and the U.S.-China Cooperative Research Program of the Henry Luce Foundation (1995–2001) enabled this research. A period of research and writing in 2000–1 was partially supported by a President's Research Fellowship in the Humanities, University of California; a fellowship from the National Endowment for the Humanities, an independent federal agency; and a Chiang Ching-kuo Foundation Senior Scholar Research Grant. Support for research assistance in 2000 was provided by a Special Research Grant from the Committee on Research, UC Santa Cruz. Fellowships from the John Simon Guggenheim Foundation and the Center for Advanced Study in the Behavioral Sciences (CASBS), Stanford University, in conjunction with sabbatical leave from UC Santa Cruz, made it possible for me to draft the book in 2007–8. CASBS provided a year in an incomparable setting with a wonderful community of scholars. I thank the colleagues who took time to recommend me for these fellowships: Timothy Brook, Paul Cohen, Susan Mann, Kenneth Pomeranz, and Anna Tsing. I was fortunate to participate in a writing group at CASBS with Paula Findlen, Sarah Maza, Katie Trumpener, and Julie Hochstrasser, although we were completely unsuccessful at weaning each other from our attachment to endless detail. Fred Turner and Tanya Marie Luhrman were also engaged and helpful interlocutors during that year of writing.

Much of the information collected for this book would undoubtedly have disappeared into unsorted piles had it not been for the software-writing genius of Randall Stross, creator of Notetaker, who also read the manuscript in its entirety and suggested eminently sensible changes. He was joined on my dream team of manuscript readers by seven other generous and intrepid souls: James Clifford, Harriet Evans, Emily Honig, Susan Mann, Kenneth Pomeranz, Lisa Rofel, and Anna Tsing. Collectively, they have reassured and pushed me, saved me from numerous misconceptualizations, and made a thorough rewrite possible. I alone had to decide what to do when they disagreed, and none of them is responsible for the choices I made, but I owe them all a serious scholarly and personal debt.

Charlotte Furth, Judith Zeitlin, Andrew Jones, Barbara Rogoff, and Sheila Namir directed me to sources in fields far from my own. I am rich in friends and colleagues who were willing to have conversations about and around this book during the years when it was taking shape, as well as reading early versions of some chapters. I particularly want to thank Wendy Brown, Judith Butler, Christopher Connery, Tony Crowley, Carla Freccero, Christina Gilmartin, Joan Judge, Rebecca Karl, Helene Moglen, David O'Connor, Mary Scott, Marilyn Young, and Wang Zheng.

This project went on for so long that many of the graduate students who worked for me as research assistants are now well into careers of their own. I thank Jin Jiang, Xiaoping Sun, Wenqing Kang, Lyn Jeffery, and Yajun Mo for their expert assistance. Alexander Day and Miriam Gross provided useful suggestions about sources. Former and current students Angelina Chin, Shelly Chan, Ana Candela, Nellie Chu, Alexander Day, Fang Yu Hu, Wenqing Kang, Sarah Mak, Yajun Mo, Amanda Shuman, Jeremy Snow, Xiaoping Sun, Jeremy Tai, Christina Wong, and J. Dustin Wright helped to shape my thinking about what to say and how to say it, and some of them read the entire manuscript and tried politely to let me know where it didn't quite work.

I have presented pieces of this work to thoughtful audiences on four continents, on occasions too numerous to mention. I hope that the many gracious hosts and helpful interlocutors I encountered will excuse the lack of detail provided in this collective thanks. I particularly benefited from the insightful commentary of Kathryn Bernhardt, Prasenjit Duara, Wilt Idema, Aihwa Ong, Elizabeth Perry, Carl Riskin, Charles Stafford, Mark Swislocki, and Harriet Zurndorfer.

For the maps in this book, which do not identify villages but do give a sense of their location, I thank Peter Bol, Guoping Huang, and especially the late G. William Skinner, whose spatial visions and cartographic passions have benefited so many of us.

At University of California Press, Takashi Fujitani recruited this book for his Asia Pacific Modern series, and my long-suffering editor, Sheila Levine, solicited and patiently waited for the completed work. Both swallowed their dismay at my delivery of an outsized manuscript (Sheila for the second time in her editorial work with me) and gently suggested ways to shorten it. Kate Marshall shepherded both book and author toward production; Jacqueline Volin took them through; Chalon Emmons made the final editing a pleasure.

For all the years of this work, my extended family supported, distracted, and challenged me in all the ways one could hope for. Many who share my Ellis Island–invented surname cheered me on: Evelyn, Richard, Mary Jane, Nancy, Bruce, and Andrea. The children in my family assemblage—Sarah Fang, Zachary Fang, Jordan Hauer-Laurencin, and Maya Hauer-Laurencin—were in elementary school when I started this work. Now, as young adults, they remain a continuing source of wonder and delight. I thank David Fang, Sankong Fang, and Sonia Garces for their familial friendship. Finally, Mercedes Grace Laurencin has sustained me with love, encouragement, and the profound pleasures of a shared life.

Parts of this book appeared previously in the following publications: "The Gender of Memory: Rural Chinese Women and the 1950s," *Signs* 28, no. 1 (2002): 43–70, © 2002 University of Chicago Press; "Local Meanings of Gender and Work in Rural Shaanxi in the 1950s," in *Re-Drawing Boundaries: Work, Households, and Gender in China*, ed. Barbara Entwisle and Gail E. Henderson, pp. 79–96 (Berkeley: University of California Press, 2000), © 2000 by the Regents of the University of California; "Making the Visible Invisible: The Fate of 'The Private' in Revolutionary China," in *Wusheng zhi sheng: Jindai Zhongguo de funü yu guojia (1600–1950)* [Voices amid Silence: Women and the Nation in Modern China (1600–1950)], ed. Lü Fang-shang, pp. 257–81 (Taipei, Taiwan: Zhongyang yanjiuyuan, Zhongguo jindaishi yanjiusuo [Institute of Modern History, Academia Sinica], 2003), © 2003 Institute of Modern History, Academia Sinica, Taiwan; "Virtue at Work: Rural Shaanxi Women Remember the 1950s," in *Gender in Motion: Divisions of Labor and Cultural Change in Late Imperial and Modern China*, ed. Bryna Goodman and Wendy Larson, pp. 309–28 (Lanham, MD: Rowman and Littlefield, 2005), © 2005 by Rowman and Littlefield Publishers, Inc.; "Birthing Stories: Rural Midwives in 1950s China," in *Dilemmas of Victory: The Early Years of the People's Republic of China*, ed. Jeremy Brown and Paul G. Pickowicz, pp. 337–58 (Cambridge, MA: Harvard University Press), © 2007 by the President and Fellows of Harvard College; "Forget Remembering: Rural Women's Narratives of China's Collective Past," in *Re-envisioning the Chinese Revolution: The Politics and Poetics of Collective Memories in Reform China*, ed. Ching Kwan Lee and Guobin Yang, pp. 69–92 (Washington, D.C., and Stanford, CA: Woodrow Wilson Center Press and Stanford University Press), © 2007 by the Woodrow Wilson International Center for Scholars; "Getting a Life: The Production of 1950s Women Labor Models in Rural Shaanxi," in *Beyond Exemplar Tales: Women's Biography in Chinese History*, ed. Hu Ying and Joan Judge (Berkeley: University of California Global, Area, and International Archive, 2011), http://escholarship.org, © 2011 by the Regents of the University of California.

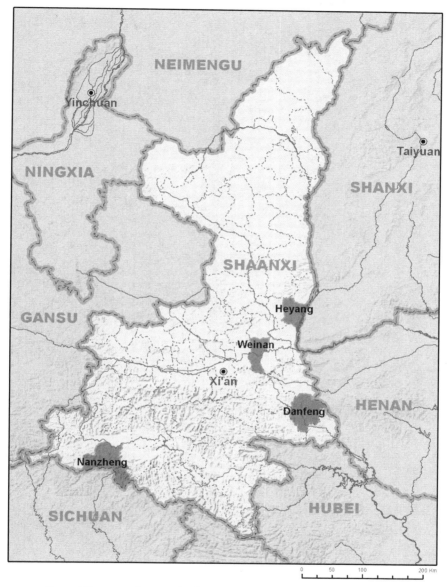

MAP 1. Shaanxi Province, showing the four major interview sites for this book. Digital elevation data from USGS (http://seamless.usgs.gov/); administrative boundaries and cities from China National Fundamental GIS (http://nfgis.nsdi.gov.cn). Cartographer: Guoping Huang, Harvard University Center for Geographic Analysis.

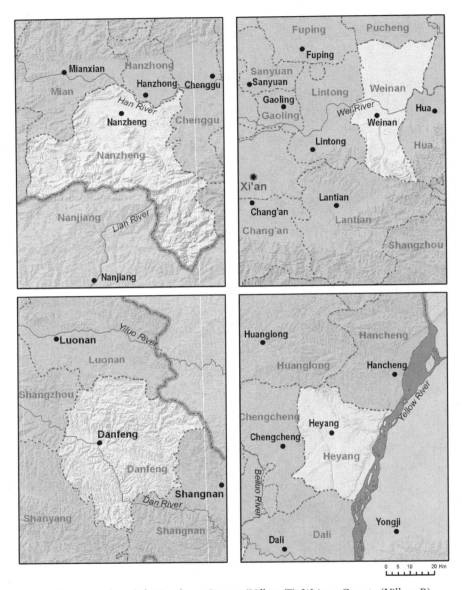

MAP 2. Clockwise from left: Nanzheng County (Village T); Weinan County (Village B); Heyang County (Village G); and Danfeng County (Village Z). Digital elevation data from USGS (http://seamless.usgs.gov/); administrative boundaries and cities from China National Fundamental GIS (http://nfgis.nsdi.gov.cn). Cartographer: Guoping Huang, Harvard University Center for Geographic Analysis.

Introduction

When Zhang Chaofeng was five years old, in 1938, her mother came back after a month away. Chaofeng lived with her parents and grandparents, famine refugees from neighboring Henan who had begged their way to Shaanxi. Chaofeng had an older brother, but her newborn sister had been given away. Then her mother had left to earn money working as a wet nurse for another family's child.

Chaofeng's mother was happy, carrying a month's wages in crisp new Nationalist government banknotes. She called the child over to her. Chaofeng took the pretty blue bills and held them up to the room's only oil lamp to have a closer look. Too close. With a whoosh, the banknotes caught fire.[1]

Chaofeng tells this story with great economy more than sixty years after the incident. As searing in its understatement as in its imagery, it opens out to an aftermath that the listener is left to imagine. Chaofeng does not linger over the details or comment on her own reaction when the money caught fire. Nor does she speculate about what her mother might have felt as the fruits of a month's labor, money she had been able to earn only by giving away her third child, turned to ashes.

In her narrative Chaofeng has already mentioned that three or four years after the bills burned up, her mother, unable to feed her, sold her to another family for about ten bushels of wheat, to be raised as a bride for their son. But she does not make a causal chain between the lost wages and her permanent departure for a distant county at age eight. The story stands alone, occupying slightly more than three lines of a twenty-two-page Chinese transcript: a mother's return, a glimpse of blue, a quick flame.

WHERE MEMORY LIES

Memory can be vivid, blazing—and ephemeral. This story haunts the listener with its sensuous immediacy and unspoken devastation. It is easy to imagine the burning banknotes as the central trauma of Chaofeng's childhood, the incident that determined her subsequent fate, the origin point for her narrative of her own life. And yet it was only by chance and in passing that we heard the story at all.

Chaofeng did not set out to talk about this incident. My research collaborator, Gao Xiaoxian, and I had gone to interview her because village leaders told us that she had been a *tongyangxi*, a "child raised to be a daughter-in-law," and that after Liberation in 1949 she had divorced, married a man of her own choosing, and been appointed head of the village women in 1958.[2] We had gone to hear the story of how a girl sold at eight grew up to become a revolutionary activist. She was telling that story when I interrupted, not very skillfully, with a factual question about how many people had been in her birth family. *Six, she said—grandfather, grandmother, father, mother, older brother, and me.* Then after a pause, as though suddenly remembering, *There was also a younger sister who was given away.* And then the burning banknotes.

What this story meant to Chaofeng remains obscure. She did not tell it with any particular affect, or stop to comment on it before she resumed her account of family poverty. Nor can a historian extract much about the broader economic context from this ephemeral memory. How much money was lost to Chaofeng's careless gesture? The child could have been holding a single bill or a roll of them; her phrasing does not make the distinction. Many blue banknotes from multiple banks might have circulated in late 1930s Shaanxi.[3] Chaofeng did not specify what she remembers seeing in the second or two before the bills caught fire. As a five-year-old, she would not have known the going wage for a wet nurse in 1938 rural Shaanxi, and no written record provides the answer for us.[4] And perhaps none of this detail, if we had it, would let us estimate how long Chaofeng's family might have survived on the lost wages.[5] At that time, the family had settled in an abandoned temple, in a village full of other Henan famine refugees. Chaofeng's grandfather and father sought work as short-term laborers, and her mother sometimes bowed cotton for others, earning four pieces of steamed bread for every *jin* of raw cotton she processed.[6] When there was no work, she would take the children out to beg. We would have to know how often the adults could find work, how much they paid to local authorities in miscellaneous taxes, how the local grain markets worked, and what sort of short-term credit a family of recently arrived outsiders could obtain. Chaofeng, a small child at the time and not much older when she was sold to be raised by others, probably never knew.

Chaofeng's memory does not let us recapture the child's lost world or the historian's lost society. It does something else, however: it surprises. Chaofeng introduces many themes provided by the 1950s Party-state, but her stories, recounted more fully in chapter 4, confound and complicate and sometimes derail them. She did become an activist and one of the first Party members in her village, for instance, but she hesitated for years before divorcing the abusive man to whom she had been married off as a child. She remembers her decision with pain, not because of the marriage—she spent little time with her husband, who worked away from home— but because of her close relationship with her mother-in-law. The Party-state stories of a straightforward move from oppression to liberation are not necessarily false or wrongheaded, but they are not enough.

Chaofeng's account of her life is what I call a good-enough story.[7] By this I mean a story that does not provide a complete understanding of the past, but instead surprises and engenders thought, unspooling in different directions depending on which thread the listener picks up. A good-enough story is available to reinterpretation; it can be woven into many larger narratives. Listening to Chaofeng's story and those of other rural Shaanxi women, paying attention to how rural women's accounts reinforce and contradict one another, does not by itself allow us to construct a history. But these good-enough stories do help us to think about how and where the history we tell about the early years of rural socialism in China is not good enough.

MISSING HISTORY

In 1996 Gao Xiaoxian and I began to collect the remembered life histories of elderly Chinese rural women in central and south Shaanxi villages. A lifelong resident of Shaanxi, Gao Xiaoxian was research office director of the Shaanxi Provincial Women's Federation and secretary-general of the Shaanxi Research Association for Women and Family. Since our first meeting at a conference in 1992, we had been talking about how little was known about life in the Chinese countryside under socialism, and how much of the emergent women's studies field in China was devoted to urban investigations. We wanted to elicit village women's accounts of the 1950s before advancing age and death silenced them.

For me, a historian of China based in the United States, this project was in part a response to a blank spot on a syllabus. Teaching the history of twentieth-century China, committed to including multiple voices and approaches, I would search each year for material to use in teaching about the 1950s. During that first decade of the People's Republic of China (PRC), ambitious state initiatives sought to reconfigure landholding, marriage, the organization of work, the very understanding of one's self, one's community, and one's past. Yet the official record provided mainly a mind-numbing list of initiatives: the Marriage Law, land reform, thought reform, Resist America Aid Korea, three-anti, five-anti, lower producers' co-ops, advanced producers' co-ops, Hundred Flowers, Anti-Rightist, communes, Great Leap Forward.

Official voices predominated in these sources, declaring that the space of the Chinese nation was finally to be stabilized: its borders fixed, mapped, and protected, its interior evenly governed by a Party-state with a comprehensive reach over the territory. These documents also posited a new temporality, one we might call "campaign time," cordoning off the pre-1949 past with the term "before Liberation" and measuring the present by state initiatives and popular participation in them.[8] Each of these campaigns was successively promulgated, propagandized, adumbrated, corrected, and superseded. But the record focused on campaign goals, rather than on their uneven implementation or unintended social effects. State-initiated campaigns were portrayed as more or less uniform, differing only in the local personnel, the specific sources of community friction, and (in more recent discussions) the degree of leadership error.

The effects of these campaigns outside the urban centers of power are still poorly understood.[9] Scholarship by social scientists writing outside of China, who sometimes used refugee interviews to supplement the official record, necessarily had more to say about urban than rural areas.[10] Eventually some extended memoirs by urban intellectuals joined the pile, detailing an initial guarded enthusiasm for the revolution, growing frustration, and ejection from the body politic as rightists in 1957. Even with the addition of their poignant voices, however, the 1950s outside the frame of these campaigns remained a largely featureless historical terrain. It was too easily seen, in retrospect, as mere warm-up for the disaster of the famine that began in 1959 and the eruption of the Cultural Revolution in 1966.

Farmers, although they constituted about 80 percent of the population, were relegated to walk-on parts in the grand drama of socialist construction.[11] Judging from the paper trail, they had divided the land of the rich with gusto in the early 1950s, then given it up with minimal resistance several years later in order to collectivize. They had resisted and blunted the effect of the 1950 Marriage Law. They had eagerly joined the activities of the early Great Leap Forward, smashing their own cooking stoves and contributing their woks to make backyard steel, only to starve in great numbers during the Three Hard Years. Far less accessible from the written record was any sense of how these state measures were understood at the time, particularly in areas far from the center of state enunciation, and particularly by women in farming communities.

Women in Shaanxi villages in the mid-twentieth century, as in much of rural China, were both objects and agents of revolutionary change. Following the 1949 Communist victory, the Chinese Party-state moved rapidly and forcefully to rearrange rural social relations and the categories through which they were understood. One of those categories was gender. When work teams redistributed land in the early 1950s, they counted women as full household members in making allocations. When the 1950 Marriage Law established new requirements for marriage and divorce, the Party-state announced an end to the purchase of child daughters-in-law and publicized the cases of women who broke off arranged engagements or left abusive marriages. State-sponsored literacy campaigns drew women into winter schools, and public health campaigns brought midwives trained in sterile childbirth techniques into rural homes. As agriculture was collectivized, larger work groups incorporated women as laborers. Early accounts of land reform, marriage reform, and collectivization emphasized women's active participation in these campaigns and suggested profound discontinuity, even incommensurability, in rural women's lives before and after Liberation. And yet, through all this reorganization and upheaval in the countryside, the voices of rural women, their responses to state initiatives, the degree to which their daily lives were affected by 1950s policies, remained muted. The figure of Woman as state subject was ubiquitous in the written record. Named women, however, with personal histories beyond the occasional expression of enthusiasm for Liberation and collectivization, were scarce.

Beginning in the 1970s, feminist scholars outside China looked critically at the revolution's consequences for women, including those in rural areas. Their work focused on the Party-state's limited conception of gender reform, centered mainly on Engels's dictum that women should be brought into paid labor outside the home. Scholars pointed to the Party-state's tolerance of patrilocal marriage, which kept women in a subordinate role in both their natal and marital villages; its willingness to downplay or postpone gender equality in the face of local resistance or in deference to other priorities; and its construction of collectives on the basis of male kin networks. These scholarly works about women, like the earlier accounts of campaigns, necessarily relied on state sources and tried to assess nationwide changes.[12] Even when the authors regarded such sources with skepticism, they could not help but take state policy pronouncements as the main subject. Rural women appeared mainly as targets of mobilization. As enthusiastic endorsers of particular state interventions (collectivization, the Marriage Law of 1950), they were audible as well, albeit in formulaic and routinized roles. Less accessible was a sense of how they engaged both government policy and local social practice, and in the process of engagement remade themselves.

The cultural and social history of the 1950s—the texture and nuance of life, the feel and meaning and local traces of the early years of state revolution—remained obscure. As a China historian who has drawn on oral narratives in books about the urban working class, women in the 1980s, and prostitutes,[13] I feared that possible sources for that history—the voices of people who remembered those years—were rapidly becoming irretrievable. The only way to find out what had happened to village women was to ask those who were still living at the time this project was begun, in the mid-1990s. The question of "what happened," then, was from the beginning entangled with the question of what women remembered from a distance of four decades or more, across intervening events that necessarily altered the meanings ascribed to the 1950s.

Gao Xiaoxian, my co-researcher, had overlapping but distinct concerns. Born in Xi'an in 1948, she knew the Shaanxi countryside well. She had spent part of her childhood in her grandmother's Shaanxi village, returning there as a "sent-down youth" during the Cultural Revolution. Trained in history and statistics, she had also become interested in oral history research. By the 1990s, her work for the Women's Federation and a new nongovernmental organization was involving her in the design of rural development projects centered on women. She quickly came to believe that for all the talk of a dramatic break with the Mao years, the first decade of rural reform in the 1980s had been profoundly influenced by the collective legacy of the 1950s. Community infrastructure, neighborhood dynamics, family relationships, residence and inheritance patterns, the gendered division of labor, individual desires: all had been reconfigured during the collective years in ways that shaped the subsequent possibilities of economic reform. Reasoning that good development policy could not be made without considering the environment it aimed to alter, she decided that a good place to start would be to ask how the collective years had shaped women's lives and labor. She also had questions, piqued but not answered during her undergraduate training in history, about the long-term role of women in home spinning and weaving.

Gao Xiaoxian and I are engaged in divergent writing projects for different audiences as a result of this research. She plans to use the material from our joint research trips to write a book for publication in Chinese: a history of rural women's labor and reproductive labor in Shaanxi over the past half-century. Our interests have converged around a core set of questions. If we placed a doubly marginalized group—rural women—at the center of an inquiry about the 1950s, what might we learn about the effects of Party-state policy and its permutations and appropriations at the local level? Viewed from the vantage point of a rural community, and recognizing that rural communities varied greatly, how was women's work affected by the state campaigns of the 1950s: land reform, cooperatives, collectivization, and the Great Leap Forward? What sort of work was considered respectable and desirable for women before Liberation, and how did it change during the 1950s? How did change in women's lives come about in rural villages? Who were the main activists, and how prominent were they in local events? What role did the Women's Federation play? How was local leadership developed? How did changes in women's work affect the household economy, domestic work, sexuality, marriage, and child rearing? What were the greatest sources of social tension? What changes transpired in the way women thought about themselves, their relationship to their family of origin, and their connection to their family of marriage? How did they compare their lives to those of their mothers and grandmothers? Looking back now on the 1950s, how do they compare the changes in their lives then to the changes that came later? The historian Joan Kelly once asked in a famous essay, "Did women have a Renaissance?"[14] If she had been writing about China instead of Europe she might have wondered, Did women have a Chinese revolution? If so, when, and in what ways?

THE PROJECT

These were the questions we set out to answer. In the decade between 1996 and 2006, Gao Xiaoxian and I collected life histories of seventy-two women.[15] All but one of the women were over the age of sixty at the time of the interview, and many were in their late seventies or older. They had been children or young adults when the People's Republic was established in 1949, and many had extensive memories of the 1930s and 1940s. A few had won acclaim in the 1950s and 1960s as national or regional labor models. Some had been local activists, village-level officials in charge of organizing women's labor, or midwives. Others had not participated actively in political life because of family circumstance or personal inclination or both. More than a few, like Chaofeng, had been transferred to the families of their future husbands years before marriage. Gao Xiaoxian did not know any of the women except for the labor models, whom she had met in the course of her Women's Federation work. But she and the village women we interviewed sometimes found that they had mutual acquaintances in the Federation network produced by half a century of work in rural Shaanxi.

Most of our interviewees lived in one of four villages. Village B, in Weinan County, and Village G, in Heyang County, were in the central Shaanxi region known as Guanzhong. Guanzhong—literally, "between the passes"—is the narrow belt of land along the banks of the Wei River, which bisects Shaanxi Province on a horizontal axis, with the city of Xi'an roughly at its center. Village T, in Nanzheng County, and Village Z, in Danfeng County, were in Shaannan (south Shaanxi), the lower third of the province (see Map 1). Shaannan lies on the other side of the Qinling mountain range from Guanzhong. Its crops and climate have more in common with areas of northern Sichuan than with the rest of Shaanxi. Both Guanzhong and Shaannan have areas of fertile soil and beauty, but in recent centuries the entire province of Shaanxi has been poor, and even in the early twenty-first century it is a world apart from the booming east coast cities of reform-era China.

Unlike the northern part of the province, where the Chinese Communist Party (CCP) made its wartime headquarters, none of the villages where we interviewed had a consistent aboveground Communist presence before 1949,[16] and their history in the decades before 1949 was very little affected by events in the central Party headquarters in Yan'an. Most villagers learned of the Communists only in mid-1949, when the Eighth Route Army (as it was still called locally) marched through their communities. Women in Yan'an had been mobilized for labor and political activity under Party direction in the 1940s, but change in women's labor in Guanzhong and Shaannan was a process that took place in the 1950s.

We visited two of the villages twice, reinterviewing women after three years in Village G and after a decade in Village B. In several villages we interviewed adult children of the older women. We spoke with urban women who had spent long periods in villages during the 1950s as organizers for the Women's Federation. In an effort to understand whether and how rural women's memories differed from those of men, we interviewed a smaller number of men who held local leadership positions in the same villages during the collective period. We found intriguing gender differences in everything from their sense of time and recitation of political events to their relationships with their mothers. The men with whom we spoke hewed much more closely to official terminology and periodization than the women, saying very little about themselves. But our sample of men was limited; in the villages where we interviewed, not very many rural men over the age of seventy were still alive and coherent, compared to the number of aging women. The absence of men reminded us of the ephemeral nature of our sources, lending further urgency to our project.

We asked about changes in women's field work, domestic labor, childbearing, and marriage, all noticeably gendered realms in which the remembered experiences of women differ from those of men. The gendered division of labor changed constantly in rural areas across the 1950s, with women being brought into ever broader spheres of activity, even as some of their original household economic activities were curtailed. And yet, while the specific content of gendered work kept shifting, gender difference itself remained a central organizing principle of rural life, accepted by officials and ordinary rural dwellers alike.[17]

This book asks what socialism was locally, and for whom, and how gender figured in its creation. Chapter 1, "Frames," introduces the importance of place, the inadequacy of archives, the unpredictability of interviews, and the plasticity of memory. Subsequent chapters trace out positions that rural women have inhabited across their lifetimes: refugee, leader, activist, farmer, midwife, mother, model, laborer, narrator. The chapters respect a rough chronology: "No One Is Home" is a pre-1949 story, "Widow" and "Activist" are set in the first few years of the People's Republic, "Farmer" in the mid-1950s, "Midwife" and "Mother" (the most difficult time frame to specify) from the 1950s through the 1970s, "Model" and "Laborer" in the late 1950s and early 1960s, and "Narrator" in the present of the interviews, from 1996 to 2006.

Childhood memories of the chaotic Republican period and the arrival of the Communists in 1949 are explored in chapter 2, "No One Is Home." Women spoke of their unprotected mobility as the children of the poor, as refugees, child brides, and farmers in a society that regarded women's appearance outside domestic space as scandalous. The chapter describes the picaresque adventures and terrible vulnerability of the refugee and future labor model Shan Xiuzhen, asking why the story of women's prerevolutionary confinement to the home has remained so enduring in spite of its obvious inaccuracy.

Chapter 3, "Widow (or, the Virtue of Leadership)," is set against the backdrop of the national land reform campaign and the formation of mutual aid groups in the early 1950s. It examines state attempts to develop local village leadership by assigning cadres, whom we might think of as state-sponsored community organizers, to reside in villages for long periods of time. The chapter explores the interaction between local women and young urban women organizers who conducted house-to-house mobilization of women while contending with their own problems of children left behind in the cities.

Along with chapters 4 and 8, "Widow" adapts Timothy Mitchell's discussion of what he calls the "state effect": the various kinds of work required to install the effect of an activist, transformational state standing apart from and above something called "society."[18] The chapter traverses the fuzzy, shifting, and constantly refigured boundary between what we conventionally divide into state and society, asking about the distinction between the state apparatus on the one hand and a more diffuse state presence, awareness of the state, and self-fashioning with state norms in mind on the other. In a period of generally acknowledged state expansion in rural China, where and how was awareness of the state produced, maintained, internalized, or broadened to encompass formerly unaddressed populations? We can take the state seriously, but not take it for granted, by exploring its contingency, its unevenness, the many kinds of incessant human labor and workaday practices required to make it seem natural and perduring. In the 1950s "the state" was no longer an external, peripheral presence, but often was embodied in a familiar neighbor such as a woman leader, activist, or labor model.[19] The chapter centers on the story of Cao Zhuxiang, a young village widow who was recruited by organizers to become a leader and labor model. Zhuxiang's status as a widow who declined to remarry, in accordance with village notions of virtuous behavior, enhanced her local prestige in complex and contradictory ways. In her account of herself, she drew on conceptions of the virtuous woman from a variety of prerevolutionary as well as revolutionary genres. Virtuous practices notwithstanding, however, she was subject to the hazards of leadership against the politically unstable backdrop of land reform and early collectivization.

Chapter 4, "Activist," considers stories told by younger village women about the extended campaign to implement the 1950 Marriage Law. Mobilized to become literate and politically conscious exemplars, women of marriageable age in the 1950s lived in a blurry zone where state goals, village practices, and kinship ties intertwined in ways far more intricate than written records convey. The chapter takes up the appeal of activism to these young women; the reconfiguration of village space they helped to effect through song, dance, and attendance at meetings; their investments in a Marriage Law campaign that often left their own household arrangements untouched; and the painful decisions to divorce taken by a small minority of women. Among those women was Chaofeng, the child who burned the banknotes, whose relationship with her mother-in-law proved much more difficult to sunder than that with her husband.

Chapter 5, "Farmer," inaugurates a discussion that continues across the rest of the book about the entry of women into full-time collective farming and the implications for individual women, families, and rural collectives. For Party-state authorities, the mobilization of women was a necessary component of socialist economic development. For women, the new organization of work brought a mixed experience: pleasurable sociality, economic and physical pressure, and a decline in the valuation of their spinning and weaving, which had been a crucial contribution to household welfare. Conflicts over how women should be remunerated, and women's remembered characterizations of what was fair and what was not, illuminate the persistence of a gendered division of labor even as the content of women's work changed.

Chapter 6, "Midwife," counterposes the Party-state campaign for safe, hygienic midwifery practices with a constantly refigured, actively circulating set of stories about the dangerous nature of childbirth. The training of new-style village midwives and the retraining of old-style midwives across rural China, sponsored by health bureaus and the Women's Federation, had dramatic effects on maternal and infant mortality rates. Less successful was the attempt to centralize childbirth in village "birthing stations." Well beyond the 1950s, the skilled village midwife who delivered babies at home remained a respected figure, sanctioned by political authorities and relied upon by childbearing women. But stories that exceeded and sometimes contradicted a straightforward tale of scientific progress continued to swirl around individual midwives. The midwife remained a liminal and often vulnerable figure at the border of life and death.

The rise in infant survival rates that midwives helped to achieve had unforeseen consequences, explored in chapter 7, "Mother." Behind women's entry into full-time field work lay a world of household labor, often discussed in late imperial writings but newly occluded by the language of the revolution. Women in rural households, now toiling in the fields for work points at least part of each day, were also responsible for preparing food, sewing clothing and shoe soles, and ensuring the safety of growing broods of children. The state paid a very narrow kind of attention to the domestic realm during the collective era. It campaigned for families to be harmonious, reject feudalism, and work for the collective. When women's labor was needed in the fields, state policy paid some attention to childcare groups during the harvest season. The only form of women's labor valorized by the state was collective labor; domestic labor became invisible, consigned to nighttime hours. This chapter asks what happens to a realm that dips below the horizon of history,[20] even as it undergoes profound transformations. If state discourse does not record those transformations except to applaud them as faits accomplis, then where else might we look for traces of them? Without a state-inflected language to describe much of the work they did, women turned to an older trope of virtue, the woman bent over her needlework late at night. Demands for household and maternal labor, unarticulable in the language of the collective era, survive in the contemporary memories of women. They describe their own virtue, fortitude, and suffering, offering both oblique statements and silences about maternal attachment. The childbearing and child-rearing experiences of this generation, which left them exhausted, meant that when the single-child family policy was announced in 1979, they were often its most enthusiastic proponents, responsible for mobilizing reluctant younger village women, who had come of age in a very different time, to terminate pregnancies.

Chapter 8, "Model," tells the dual story of how women became responsible for cotton cultivation and how a handful of nationally and regionally famous women labor models emerged into public view. Labor models were chosen and publicized by state authorities, and their activities were presented for emulation by a wider public. They were themselves a collective product: identified, trained, and written about by cadres of the Women's Federation, they participated actively in the making of their own careers. The painstaking process by which these exemplary figures were selected and publicized has left a rare archive of the lives of named individual rural women. Any attempt to understand the lives of these individuals in a biographical mode, however, founders on the lack of interiority recorded either in the archive or in individual memories. This raises two important questions: To what extent did women labor models come to understand themselves in the terms provided by the state? And is it appropriate to demand, as readers of the modern genre of biography conventionally do, that subjects have—and reveal—a distinct interior life?

Chapter 9, "Laborer," explores the entwinement of the campaign time of the state with the domestic time of the household during the Great Leap Forward and the subsequent famine. The Great Leap Forward aimed to reorganize every aspect of rural life, assigning villagers to construct reservoirs, smelt steel, and increase crop yields. Expansive utopian plans promised to relieve women of domestic tasks so that their labor could be devoted to these new projects. Ambitious documents envisioned children in daycare centers, food prepared and eaten in collective dining halls, grain milled and clothing stitched by machine, and childbirth and postpartum care removed from the home to well-staffed birthing clinics. Most of these initiatives did not get fully under way, and the one that did—the dining halls—came to be synonymous with hunger and the collapse of the Great Leap strategy. The Great Leap debacle has recently become the subject of detailed and impressive national and local studies,[21] but most of this material does not mention the feminization of agriculture that the Leap consolidated in Shaanxi and perhaps elsewhere as well. Well before the dramatic recent years of economic reform, many men left basic farming. Women's field labor from the late 1950s to the end of the collective era in the early 1980s, and the state accumulation of resources it enabled, were important components of the national economic strategy on which subsequent economic reform has been built.

The final chapter, "Narrator," turns to the retrospective recounting of life in the collective years by women in reform-era China, addressing an ongoing interdisciplinary and cross-geographical discussion about revolution, repudiation, and post-Communist nostalgia. It traces connections between eras that are conventionally studied separately: pre-Liberation (1949), socialist construction, and market socialism (or postsocialism), suggesting accretions, similarities, and transformations that do not easily map onto conventional historical markers. Women tell their stories in the wake of a disassembled state project. Most are widows or caregivers for invalid husbands, with complex relationships to grown children and to a new economic order in which they are superfluous. They are living their final years in villages where the able-bodied, capable adults have left to seek a living as migrant workers in the wealthier cities of the coast or abroad. In these hollowed-out villages, devoid of any monument or *lieux de memoire* except the occasional abandoned collective dining hall, women narrate the past in a time when no one around them wants to hear their stories and the world in which they once lived has left very little physical or discursive trace.[22] They have fashioned a narrative of progress, featuring themselves as paragons of womanly virtue, telling their stories in an era when the histories, memories, and institutions of the collective era are disappearing and devalued. Narrating their pasts, older village women make a compelling claim on the attention of the present.[23]

1

Frames

In rural Shaanxi in the 1950s, gender was everywhere an important axis of difference, and it remained so even as the content of normative gendered behavior shifted. Yet gender itself was entangled with specificities of locale and with generational differences. Other themes, too, crosscut and sometimes confound the neat sorting of women into specified roles and orderly progress through time. This chapter frames many of the stories that follow with attention to four of those themes: the importance of place, the limitations of the archive, the particularities of the listeners and speakers, and the gendered qualities of memory.

PLACE: "ALL SOCIALISM IS LOCAL"

In each of the places we interviewed, we aimed to understand the specific meanings of socialism, particularly for women who remembered the period before 1949 but whose adult lives were lived largely in the collective era. Local variations in size, gender ratios, crops, community norms, leadership, and accessibility (see Table 1) served as a constant reminder that the very term "China" is a convenient shorthand, a way of organizing our teaching, writing, and understanding of history and contemporary politics. In the long 1950s these villages were governed by a Party-state in the midst of a powerful drive to make "China" uniform, to produce in every village the presence of a state, even while institutionalizing differences between urban and rural life. This state was powerful in part because it managed to reach into rural areas, chiefly by involving local people rather than proclaiming from on high. But as the late Speaker of the U.S. House of Representatives Tip O'Neill once famously said, "All politics is local," and here our persistent habit of talking about

TABLE 1 A 1940 Republican government report gave the following population statistics
for the counties in which the four villages were located

County	Number of Households	Total Population	Number of Males	Number of Females	M:F ratio
Weinan	49,607	226,255	112,743	113,512	99
Heyang	32,942	143,627	72,840	70,786	100
Nanzheng	52,740	275,384	145,215	130,169	111
Shanyang*	31,226	140,151	75,901	64,250	118

*In the Qing and Republican periods, Village Z was part of Shanyang County. After 1949, when Danfeng County was
established, it became part of Danfeng. A 1951 report from Danfeng counted 163,141 people in the county: 85,451 men
and 77,690 women (MZT 198–381 [1951], Shaanxi Provincial Archives, 139–46). On the changing boundaries of
Weinan and Heyang counties during the Republican era, see Weinan diqu difang zhi bianji weiyuan hui 1996: 19–21.
SOURCE: Shaanxi sheng minzheng ting 1940: n.p.

Geography and weather also distinguished the villages from one another. In Guanzhong (central Shaanxi), where Villages B and G are located, dryland cultivation of wheat and cotton predominate, and drought is the main form of "natural" disaster. Shaannan contains both rice-growing areas (Village T) and mountainous districts (Village Z) and is more
prone to flooding, although drought can also be a problem. On flooding in the Village Z area during the period covered by this book, see Shaanxi sheng Danfeng xian shuili zhi 1990: 53–54, 58–62; on drought, see 70–73.

"China" obscures the extent to which all socialism is local. Even the most prescriptive
edicts of a centralized state must be implemented in widely varied environments,
by local personnel who interpret, rework, emphasize, and deflect according to particular circumstances. The working out of state policies was everywhere contingent
upon geography, prior social arrangements, and local personalities.

In Weinan County's Village B, for instance, located a few kilometers south of the
Wei River in the cotton-growing plains of Guanzhong (see Map 2), houses are close
together and neighbors know about goings-on in the next courtyard. By contrast,
in Village T, in Nanzheng County, a rice- and tea-producing district in Shaannan
not far from the Sichuan border, houses are spread among the paddy fields and
mountain paths.[1] In Guanzhong, where Village B is located, people used to say that
women in Shaannan, where Village T is located, were sexually loose, scattered as
they were where neighbors couldn't keep an eye on them. In Village Z, in southeast
Shaanxi's Danfeng County, near the Henan border, families who live on the main
street of the market town once looked down on those who lived in the mountains
(calling them "poor and backward"), and those who lived in the mountains looked
down on those in the town (calling them "sleazy merchants, not honest farmers").
Situated where the Dan and Yinhua Rivers converge at the eastern edge of Shaannan, Village Z has long been a trading center for mountain products such as tong
oil, walnuts, chestnuts, and medicinal plants.[2] In Heyang County's Village G, at the
northern edge of Guanzhong hard by the Yellow River, which divides east Shaanxi
from neighboring Shanxi Province, deep gorges in the friable yellow earth score

the landscape. Here the cultivation of cotton, the local practice of weaving, the ubiquity of local opera, and the persistent lack of water have all shaped household economies and modes of sociality.[3]

One additional group of interviewees was linked by organization rather than location: Women's Federation cadres who had been sent to work with village women in the 1950s. Now retired, they retain a keen sense of the importance of raising women's status, a goal formally espoused by all state agencies but pursued most passionately and consistently in Shaanxi by the Women's Federation. Unlike most of the village women we interviewed, Federation cadres worked in salaried positions and moved from place to place, often managing their own difficult family situations occasioned by long absences from home. Like village women, they speak of the past in terms that highlight their commitment and hard work. They redeem in memory an enterprise—establishing collectivization in general and expanding women's role in particular—that framed their adult lives but is now regarded with public skepticism or indifference.

In the early years of socialism, directives from a faraway national state authority, such as "Collectivize!" or "Don't treat marriage as a commercial transaction!" or "Give up sideline activities [such as weaving] and work for the collective!" were transmitted by a variety of Party-state actors, landing in myriad social environments and producing multiple effects. The state effect, with its rearrangements of space and recalibrations of time, was worked out through local relationships and practices and held in place by local understandings. The terms that come so easily to historians—"the rural," "the revolution," the names of individual government campaigns—are order-making devices imposed on an intractably varied landscape. Rather than presenting four distinct local studies, subsequent chapters draw material from all the villages where we interviewed, but the stories in each chapter retain the specifics of local geographies, relationships, and gendered work, reminding us that 1950s China was not a homogeneous place.

ARCHIVE

Historians do not write under conditions of our own choosing. When the time is long ago and the subjects are dead, we rely on written records and material artifacts. When a possibility exists of talking to those who witnessed or participated in past events, the project of "making the invisible visible" by simply asking and recording is seductive, but chimerical. Oral and written sources are both fragmented; neither is wholly reliable. Both are essential to this project, not because combining them offers a definitive account of the past, but because each type of source bears different traces of the circumstances under which it was generated. Different types of sources talk back to, ignore, or interrupt one another, and awareness of this is crucial to the crafting of a good-enough story that does not smooth over such dissonances.

The archival record on 1950s rural Shaanxi is seemingly wide and deep, but it is sobering to see how little it helps with the questions that concern us.[4] Published sources on the collective period—government announcements, press reports, and late twentieth-century compendia of local history known (like their historical predecessors) as gazetteers—offer much detail about the timing and content of state initiatives. They are most useful when we know something about how they were compiled. Talking to Women's Federation officials, for example, helped us understand how tales of the heroic deeds of labor models were developed for publication, with the assistance of Federation cadres who resided in villages for long stretches of time in the 1950s.

In using village, county, and provincial archives, we paid close attention to the classification and ordering of preserved materials: directives, exhortations, demands for reports, and stacks of internal memos. In the Shaanxi Provincial Archives, what the documents do most clearly is trace particular circuits of governmental activity.[5] Chronology is one principle of organization here, but it is trumped by hierarchy. If the subject is directives issued by government agencies about the Marriage Law, for instance, one is apt to find all central government documents at the beginning, then regional government documents,[6] then provincial, county, and so forth. The archives offer a clearer sense of the communications each government level generated than of what transpired when a communiqué hit the ground. As with all archives, any sense of interaction between the levels has to be assembled outside the logic of the file.

State classifications fragment the subjects they aim to govern, sometimes obscuring the workings of the Party-state itself. The Civil Administration Bureau was concerned with, among other things, the Marriage Law, but there is no discussion in the Bureau's files of the literacy classes conducted at the same time. No matter that literacy classes and the Marriage Law were, in combination, two of the most important institutions affecting the lives of young rural women in the early 1950s, and that the ability to read helped make awareness of the law possible. The Agriculture Bureau was in charge of the technical aspects of agriculture, so in its thousands of pages of documents about the Great Leap Forward one can learn how many tons of fertilizer were applied to each *mu* of cotton-growing land in every county. But there is nary a word about the communal dining halls, even though every farmer in the province was supposed to be eating in one at the time. No sustained account of social life emerges here, just a series of governmental prisms through which human activity is refracted. Although the same might be said of all archives, the absence is particularly surprising given the Party-state's explicit goals of creating and addressing new social subjects, such as peasants and women, and transforming the entirety of rural social and economic life through collectivization.

The fragmenting of social life into bureaucratic records becomes particularly striking when researching the three grim years that followed the Great Leap Forward. The desperation of China's farmers at that time has been well documented; the figure most commonly heard is that 30 million farmers died of hunger. Although by all accounts Shaanxi was not one of the provinces most devastated, the Civil Administration files from the years 1960–62 overflow with frantic activity occasioned by drought, flooding, and insect pests.[7] The quality of the paper on which these documents were written underscores the content: the smooth cream-colored stationery inscribed with the name of each government agency has been replaced by gray sheeting similar to that used for egg cartons. Most striking, however, is the lack of connection between the urgent distress that emerges from these pages and the upbeat accounts of meetings of cotton producers recorded in the contemporaneous files of the Agriculture Bureau. Scholars have explored at length the disconnect between central government decisions and local realities in this period. Here it appears that lateral in-state communications, even those required to provide relief, may have been ruptured as well, or at least not captured by Party-state archivists. The historian who enters the archive with questions about rural women will be made acutely aware of how Party-state agendas differ from her own.

LISTENER

Oral narratives are the only accounts we have for many aspects of early rural socialism in China, and this book would not be possible without them.[8] Just as we ask about the circumstances that gave rise to archival materials, we need to note the context in which these narratives were heard and collected.

Among many contextual factors, my status as a foreigner should not be forgotten. "It builds humility as well as impatience to contemplate what it took to get me here," reads the first line of my first fieldnote entry in August 1996. Prior to my arrival, Gao Xiaoxian and I would discuss the kind of place that we would like to visit: a place with a labor model, a place where women had played a prominent role in cotton growing or weaving, a place far from any urban center. Drawing on her intricate knowledge of rural Shaanxi, she would contact her counterparts in a district or county Women's Federation branch, and settle on a village in discussion with them. The local Women's Federation officials would then obtain approval from the county government, a process that usually went smoothly but could be derailed by unexpected concerns. During the summer of 1997, for instance, several counties were reluctant to host us because Hong Kong was being "returned to the ancestral nation," and local officials far from Hong Kong were unsure whether a foreigner's presence was appropriate at this moment of national celebration.

We never went from Xi'an directly to a village. We always passed through the district capital or the county seat (sometimes both), stopping to call on and be hosted by local officials, and picking up a Women's Federation cadre or two to accompany us to our introduction into the village. I came to think of this process as a cumulative accretion of legitimacy, so that by the time a carful of us arrived in a village, all the relevant people knew why we were there and what degree of responsibility they had for us.

Our arrival in a village was always put to local use. In Village T, the Women's Federation spent three hundred yuan to repair a rain-damaged road the day before our arrival.[9] In Village B, the village leadership welcomed us, partly because they regarded their resident labor model as an uncontroversial icon of local pride. They mobilized the residents to haul away a huge pile of garbage in honor of my arrival. They were exquisitely attuned to the pragmatic advantages of having the first-ever foreigner reside in their village for a few weeks. Wouldn't it be a good idea, they asked the county transportation department, to repair the road leading to the village before the foreigner had to ride on it? When we stopped for lunch with various officials in the county seat on our way to the village, I watched a woman from the county Women's Federation skillfully importune the county foreign affairs officer to make sure the electricity stayed on in the village during my stay. The officer promised to phone the generating plant and explain the "special circumstance" to them. Since the temperature averaged 100 degrees Fahrenheit during our stay, and the continuous power allowed everyone in the village to run their electric fans, I felt marginally useful.[10]

The ease with which people greeted and talked to us was a product of Gao Xiaoxian's standing in the Women's Federation, her many years of work in rural areas, and the fact that our arrival had received official permission. Contrary to the romance of the unscripted encounter that pervades much writing about China, had I shown up alone, or had Gao Xiaoxian escorted me without advance notice or approval, it is likely that people would have been more guarded about talking to us. In our rural interviews, we usually talked to women alone, occasionally in pairs or small groups. Interested neighbors, mainly children, sometimes loitered in the vicinity, more to get a look at me than to listen to the proceedings, but this curiosity abated within a day or so. I seldom led the questioning, although I intervened actively, conferred with Gao Xiaoxian during and between interviews, and spent most evenings walking with her while we puzzled over the day's conversations. At the beginning of an interview, it was not just my limited dialect competence that made me hang back. We wanted the old women with whom we spoke to be comfortable, and it seemed more prudent (although I was there in plain sight and far from silent) not to remind them incessantly how unprecedented the occasion was. Usually, after an hour or so, my foreign face seemed not to matter anymore.

Not that it was forgotten. Well into one interview, we were asking a woman we will call Qiao Yindi about several years she had spent with her husband in the far northwestern territory of Xinjiang in the early 1950s. Did you have many encounters with Uighurs, I asked her in Chinese. Clearly she understood me, because she replied directly to me in Chinese: *I did. But we didn't understand each other's lan-*

guage. There was a Han person nearby who understood, and who translated for me. We would meet and I would smile, he would smile, we would just greet each other. I didn't understand what they said, and they didn't understand what I said. We needed someone to translate. Just like when you talk.[11] More than once I returned to a village after several years' absence to find my photo enshrined next to those of close family members under glass on a cabinet. And in 2006 at Cao Zhuxiang's house, we saw an April 26 story in the county newspaper about her and Shan Xiuzhen. It reported that Cao Zhuxiang's fame was so great that in 1998 an American reporter came to interview her and subsequently wrote about her in a book called *Chinese Women*. That would be me, in 1996, working on the book you hold now. (As Gao Xiaoxian commented, one can see how archives mislead people.)

So I never forgot that I was a foreigner heavily dependent on my collaborator and on a host of others: local officials; a series of note takers recruited by Gao Xiaoxian from among her co-workers in Xi'an (including, on one trip, her oldest daughter), who wrote while we talked and taped and spent hours going over each interview with me soon after it occurred; the village women's cadres who located families with whom we could stay and who found women to cook for us; local transcribers, who patiently invented written renderings for oral dialect expressions, producing handwritten Chinese transcripts that often ran into the hundreds of pages. (Chinese word processing only became available several years into our project.) Written transcripts, however faithful, are not the same as oral narrations; they cannot convey subtleties of tone or pacing that are obvious in person and at least partly preserved on tape. Yet without these transcripts I would be far less sure that I had understood the four varieties of Shaanxi dialect we encountered in four different villages.

Interviewing in Shaanxi permanently rendered hilarious, at least for me, the idea that an outside researcher is ever a fly on the wall, or an omnicompetent investigator who can handle all aspects of the research herself. The stories retold in this book cannot be separated from the messy, complicating circumstances of their collection, or from the supporting apparatus that allowed me to learn what I did. Examining the features of my dependence and enmeshment, rather than trying to ignore them, has been a bracing and necessary exercise.[12]

The brouhaha that attended our arrival in each village never lasted long. Local officials had other matters to attend to, and none of them was interested in the protracted stories told by old women we had come to hear. Occasional eruptions of official activity punctuated our village stays. In Village T, a crew from the county television station swooped in one morning to film an interview, accompanied by several layers of officials, for a total of twenty-one people. But we were generally left alone. In Village Z, county officials couldn't have visited us even if they wanted to; the road from the county seat, forty-four kilometers away,[13] washed out in a rainstorm after our arrival. Villages are not the preferred place to linger for officials from what the local farmers refer to simply as "above." No one in an official position sat in on our interviews, directed us to particular interview subjects unless we asked, told older women what to say, or kept track of what they said. Our interlocutors were not shy in their willingness to be critical of state policies, past and present. Nor were they reluctant to provide long accounts of conflicts with family members, neighbors, and officials. We benefited from the oft-noted phenomenon that people choose to say things to an outsider they would not say to their next-door neighbor, because the outsider, a transient, will not reveal their secrets locally. Many people understood speaking "for the record" as an important activity. All of them gave every indication that they took these conversations seriously.

This book walks the methodological border between history and anthropology, posing various ethical and practical dilemmas for the author. Historians aim to reveal their sources and establish the unique circumstances of their subjects by fixing them in time and place. Many historians feel a particular obligation to restore the erasure of nonelite women from the historical record, although here the question of who "gives voice" to whom is a complicated one.[14] Anthropologists, in contrast, protect the anonymity of their sources and establish both the unique circumstances and the shared cultural assumptions of their subjects through ethnographic description rather than straightforward naming.[15] To this difference in disciplinary practices one must add the uncertainties of conducting fieldwork in rural China, where official approval at one moment (or by one level of authorities) can be succeeded by jittery accusations the next. To name women and their communities, or not to name? We were given permission by the women we interviewed to use their words and their names in print, but here is where an uncertainty comes in: could they know what they were consenting to? We were left trying to assess whether the publication and rapidly evolving circuits along which stories travel might boomerang in a way that could bring community distress, political trouble, or personal pain to them or to their relatives. We also wanted to honor their accounts of their own achievements. And we wanted to recognize the desire of communities with former labor heroines or activists to deploy the meager social capital that remained from those deeds, making a public claim for the value of their own lives.

After many years of discussion, we have decided to disguise the names of villages by using initials, and to use pseudonyms except in the case of women who were public figures, such as the labor models Cao Zhuxiang, Shan Xiuzhen, and Zhang Qiuxiang. Cao Zhuxiang was regionally famous and Zhang Qiuxiang nationally known; numerous published and archival documents, some cited in this book, attest to their fame, and their interviews supplement and enrich the written record in ways that should not prove problematic for them or their communities. Nevertheless, I have sometimes changed or avoided a name in one of their tales if

I thought the particular content of the story might bring distress to them or their relatives.

NARRATIVE AND MEMORY

Oral narratives are social as well as individual products. Information about us circulated incessantly through the villages in which we interviewed, earlier interviewees gave later ones free advice about what might interest us, later interviewees complained that they had been misrepresented by earlier ones, and so forth. Our interviews were influenced in specific ways by my obvious foreignness, as well as Gao Xiaoxian's status as an urban woman who works for a government-sponsored "mass" organization, and we paid a great deal of attention to interchanges where this was a factor. What was most important to many interviewees, however, was the chance to talk to someone interested in their long-neglected stories.[16]

Before we began our first interview trip, Gao Xiaoxian and I made lists, separately and together, of things we wanted to know. Because we wanted to understand what events each woman regarded as important, we did not provide many cues at the beginning of an interview.[17] We would explain our project briefly, ask each woman for an account of her own life, and follow up on whatever she said initially. Some women produced standard stories of pre-Liberation bitterness and post-Liberation happiness. Others rambled incoherently, and it was not always clear whether the problem was related to age, fatigue, nervousness about the interview, or our failure to explain ourselves adequately. In still other cases, a woman would sit down and launch into a detailed, passionate, and uninterruptible account of something that was bothering her, which might not have an obvious connection to the 1950s: bad treatment by an adult son, the death of a child several years previously, a Cultural Revolution–era humiliation, a 1980s business deal gone sour. Even when a woman's story about the 1950s was clear and concrete, she often punctuated it with an ongoing commentary about her life of hard work and suffering, producing a skein of statements linking the 1950s to subsequent periods and ultimately to present concerns. We usually followed the narrative wherever the teller wanted to take it, while also attempting to broaden our questions about the 1950s to elicit the richest account possible. On occasion we found ourselves wondering if by not imposing categories we were, in fact, imposing a very large categorical requirement: asking women to create a narrative structure out of their lives when they were not in the habit of doing so. Since Gao Xiaoxian is also an outsider, albeit of a different order, we have also both benefited from the triangulation of our different perspectives with the villages we visited. The questions we asked changed constantly as we talked and argued about what we were learning and how we were structuring conversations. This meant that no two interviews had the same structure, although they had many points of comparability. Where excerpts of the interviews are included in this book, I have been faithful to the original content, but have sometimes re-arranged or edited an excerpt in order to eliminate repetition and increase read-ability. I am aware that something of the recursive and emotion-laden nature of oral narratives, as well as the pacing, emphasis, and tonality of a story, are lost in the move to written form. Conveying the intensity and tenor of an interview, absent the somatic and dramatic presence of the teller, requires attention to how some-thing reads as well as how it once sounded.

Memory is not the repository of the "true"; as the French historian Jacques Le Goff suggests, it involves not just the establishment of traces but the rereading of those traces.[18] Memory appears to be created anew whenever it is called upon, as the teller actively creates new meanings. It entails constantly rearranging one's understanding of what one remembers in such a way that the coloring of the memory may shift.[19] Every telling enacts a loss, because as memory is restarted and resituated, it moves further away from the sensuous experience and the teller's earlier understanding of an event. But at the same time, every memory is also a creation—not necessarily a whole-cloth invention (although there are also those), but a product of the confluence of past events and present circumstances. As Alessandro Portelli writes, for histo-rians the helpfulness of oral narratives is "not so much in their ability to preserve the past, as in the very changes wrought by memory. These changes reveal the nar-rators' effort to make sense of the past and to give a form to their lives."[20] What people remember is the product of a continual process of reworking, recitation, invention, and sometimes carefully guarded silences that help shape what is said.[21]

Women may remember a particular aspect of self only in the process of answering our questions or of choosing what and what not to say to us. Conversely, they may neglect to include something central to their lives because we did not know enough to ask. Several days after a long informative interview with a woman in Village G about her divorce in the 1950s, we learned that she and many of her friends had been enthusiastic opera performers during the same period. When we called a group of them together and asked her why she had not mentioned opera to us ear-lier, she replied, *I didn't tell you anything you didn't ask me about.*[22] Deeply held as a speaker's interpretations might be, carefully crafted as they may be, they are still produced at a specific moment, for particular listeners.[23] Every time a woman re-sponded to our questions, or ignored them and instead told us something we didn't know enough to ask about, she was creating her story in response to us, but also si-multaneously with her family and neighbors, living and dead. It was often an oppor-tunity to exhume old grievances, rehearse new ones, conclude unfinished business, or salve injuries past and present.

Often enough in listening to rural women's stories, I have bemoaned the con-tamination of these tales, told as they are in the light of contemporary worries. Per-haps a historian can be forgiven for wanting a "pure" account of the past. As Jan Vansina bluntly reminds us, however, such purity "never occurs in any society, except perhaps among professional historians. All messages have some intent which has to do with the present, otherwise they would not be told in the present."[24] Maurice Halbwachs put it more poetically in the 1920s:

> We preserve memories of each epoch in our lives and these are continually reproduced; through them, as by a continual relationship, a sense of our identity is perpetuated. But precisely because these memories are repetitions, because they are successively engaged in very different systems of notions, at different periods in our lives, they have lost the form and the appearance they once had. They are not intact vertebra of fossil animals which would in themselves permit reconstruction of the entities of which they were once a part. One should rather compare them to those stones one finds fitted in certain Roman houses, which have been used as materials in very ancient buildings; their antiquity cannot be established by their form or their appearance but only by the fact that they still show the effaced vestiges of old characters.[25]

This book attends both to the "effaced vestiges" and to the new edifices they now support. It is shaped by tensions between narrative orderings of time and memory on the one hand, and habits of historical ordering on the other. Rather than despair at narrative inconsistencies in stories of the 1950s, it asks what we might learn from them.[26] Luise White reconfigures the question of narrative "mistakes" in describing the circulation of vampire stories in twentieth-century Africa: "The inaccuracies in these stories make them exceptionally reliable historical sources as well: they offer historians a way to see the world the way the storytellers did, as a world of vulnerability and unreasonable relationships."[27]

Oral narratives, then, are called forth under particular circumstances, unevenly recorded, selectively remembered, and artfully deployed by our village interlocutors as indirect commentary on a troubled present. Oral narratives told in the present about the past need to be valued as a history of the present precisely for the ways they slip older moorings of meaning and relodge to engage with new situations. The challenge is not to fix meaning and interpretation, but to keep track of what accounts for changing meanings and interpretations. And it is important to be aware of the ways oral narratives by old village women talk back to or talk past big state projects like rural socialism, while also managing to destabilize big feminist recuperation projects like the one in which I came of age as a historian: "making the invisible visible" by paying attention to the lives of women.

This book pays attention to oral narratives in the light of the written record, and vice versa. It reads narratives from one person in the light of another, narratives from one community in the light of another, and women's narratives in the light of those of the much smaller number of surviving men. Such a project presents more than the usual share of organizational conundrums. It requires keeping track of state and individual temporalities, without assuming that they are utterly discrete realms. It demands attention to opacity and lack of affect as well as to gripping tales, concern for lies and silences as well as for passionate truth claims. Above all, it compels respect for limits and dead ends—reluctant recognition that women's voices offer no direct line to hidden histories, that oral narratives are as contaminated as any other retrievable fragment of the past. It requires cultivating an interest in and respect for that contamination. And it extracts, finally, an admission of my own historical stakes as listener, writer, and teacher: I want these stories to matter, to stick with the reader, to make Big History look and feel different.

People who work with oral narratives sometimes distinguish between using them to get at specific information and using them to pay attention to narrative structure, elisions, silences, opacity, and lies—in essence, doing a close reading. This book does both. Mining these interviews for information, I look for common themes repeated by women who have never met one another. I am also caught up in individual moments of storytelling beauty and pain and clarity. The chapters that follow pay attention to confusion and discomfort (theirs and ours), and also to instances when a woman told us things we had not asked about and did not think we needed to know.

THE GENDER OF MEMORY

Does memory have a gender? If so, what does it look like and sound like? How do we know that the stories we heard, the judgment of what counts as an event and is worth remembering and telling, were inflected by the gender of the narrator rather than by rural residence, personal circumstance, or a host of other factors? What can memories tell us about gender as an axis of power, difference, attachment, grievance, and collectivity in 1950s rural China? Memory may not have a gender; such a formulation posits gender as immutable, rather than as a constantly shifting set of social and symbolic relationships. But memory is a social process, shaped by the social distinction of gender in ways impossible to ignore.[28]

In talking about the 1950s, women remembered a set of events that overlapped but did not duplicate those remembered by men. This is not surprising. State policies targeted women in specific ways. The ever-changing division of labor, affected by state initiatives as well as local expectations, continued to differentiate between tasks appropriate to men and those appropriate to women. The daily lives of girls and women did not look like those of boys and men, even within the same household. Without keeping gender constantly in view, we miss the ways women's labor, both acknowledged and invisible, shaped the course of socialist construction under Mao.

The stories we heard from women reflected a more distant relationship than that of men to the campaign time of the state. In women's accounts of their lives, recalled in interviews more than forty years later, campaign time was variously reproduced or altered, appropriated or overturned, ignored or amplified. Of course, not all women remembered in the same way; individual and community variations were important, as was their degree of political involvement. But where men would recite to us a series of political changes more or less in textbook order, women were far more likely to scramble calendar years and reorder or rename events. Such rearrangements should be understood not as errors, but rather as interpretations of the gendered past.

The most obvious temporal divide provided in state language was that of "before Liberation" (*jiefang qian*) and "after Liberation" (*jiefang hou*). Women were mobilized during the land reform of the late 1940s and early 1950s to "speak bitterness," narrating and interpreting the hardships they had experienced as children and young adults. They were also organized to participate in literacy classes and mutual aid teams. Through these novel practices they were encouraged to arrange their memories and personal narratives into categories of pre-Liberation suffering and post-Liberation opportunity. The use of the term "Liberation" for the change of state authority in 1949, which quickly became part of the daily vocabulary in rural China, itself encoded a particular understanding of events. Citing Liberation as a signpost in one's life meant organizing one's own memories into a personal and collective narrative of emancipatory progress.

Like all hegemonic vocabularies, however, this one was subject to being wrenched out of its intended context and deployed in ways that would mock the intentions of state officials, even if unintentionally. In official state terms, for instance, "the old society" refers to any time before the People's Republic was established in 1949, and Liberation signals the advent of "the new society."[29] Some women used the phrase "the old society" to refer to the 1940s, as per state language. But others said that the old society had lasted until the end of the Great Leap famine, in about 1963, encompassing the entire period we were trying to investigate. A Chinese researcher interviewing village women in another community found that some of them used the term "the old society" to refer not to the period before 1949, but rather to life prior to the economic reforms of the early 1980s.[30] In doing so they reworked a common official description of "speaking bitterness": "recalling the bitter [of the prerevolutionary past] while savoring the sweet [of the collective period]."[31] In contrast, women invoked "the old society" by lamenting the difficult circumstances of the collective years compared to the more abundant reform-era present.

This slippage is especially interesting because the meaning of the term "the old society" was firmly fixed for more than three decades before the reforms began. It is unlikely that interviewees simply forgot what the term commonly meant. Their recombination of chronology and event is a clue to their interpretation of their own past, couched in a twisting of official terminology. It encodes an unsubtle critique of the collective period, since the valence of the term "the old society" remains—as it was intended to be in official parlance—utterly negative. Here the language of the state is turned against the state by a "misremembering" of state temporality—one far more common among the women we interviewed than among the men.

In rural areas, campaign time centered on the reorganization of agricultural production into progressively larger collectives. The main signposts were land reform, mutual aid groups, unified purchase and sale of grain, lower producers' cooperatives, advanced producers' cooperatives, the Great Leap Forward, and the three years of catastrophe (not a campaign, but a recognizable event). These campaigns meant profound changes in daily life for both women and men, but whereas most men narrate their memories by campaign, and women labor models do so in part, ordinary women organize the stories of their past rather differently. They may recognize the names, but rearrange the order or rework the elements. This in itself often suggests what they remember as important.

For instance, all the women we interviewed understood the term "Great Leap Forward," but none of them used it in describing their own histories. They did not see the Great Leap as a unified national phenomenon; their version of local campaign time disaggregated it into constituent elements that had meaning for them. They talked about "the time when we smelted steel" or "the time when we ate in collective dining halls"—a policy measure in which people smashed their kitchen stoves, melted down their pots for steel, and ate in public dining halls, when a day's work was required for a day's food, and a few months of glorious eating were succeeded by several years of government-induced famine. The disaggregation suggests that although national policy had profound effects on rural life, what was remembered—or forgotten—was determined not by reference to national development goals, but by the changes wrought in domestic arrangements and the gendered apportioning of tasks.

Similarly, women in Village G referred in a locally specific way to the famine that followed the Great Leap. In national chronology, the famine is usually called "the three years of difficulty" or "the three years of disaster," but in Village G, people called it "the years of low standard when squash and vegetables were substituted." This was a version of a phrase in a November 1960 emergency government directive—gua cai dai, di biaozhun—calling on people to eat squash and other vegetables to deal with the shortage of staple grain, a clear regimen of deprivation. (In many areas of China, as one historian notes, the squash and vegetables were long gone by that time, and many people were eating leaves, bark, wild vegetables, and white clay.)[32] Here too, in their choice of language and matter-of-fact tone, women disaggregated the campaign and the famine into concrete elements that affected their daily lives. State language had given people a powerful new vocabulary with which to narrate their pasts. In each of these cases, women refashioned that vocabulary.

Gender does not explain all of these slippages and modes of rearrangement. (A common story told by youth "sent down" to rural locales during the Cultural Revolution is that when old peasants were organized to tell past stories of bitter suffering to the new arrivals, they horrified village leaders by talking about the Great Leap famine rather than the 1940s.) But the milestones of campaign time figure much more prominently in the stories of men than in those of women. Most of the

men we interviewed had once held positions of village responsibility, as accountants or bookkeepers or team heads. They code-switch more easily, speak of children less frequently, remember more completely the campaign time of political life—
perhaps because they participated in it more fully. The lives of most women have
intersected with state projects differently from those of men, and the women seem
to have absorbed state language less completely, appropriating and reworking it in
distinct ways. In a very literal sense, in their personal narratives rural women name
a different temporality from that of rural men.

A history of the 1950s written beyond the frame of campaign time will need to
take account of the terminology and the massive changes that campaign time
wrought. But it must also ask what rural women are practiced in remembering, and
what they have learned to forget. State temporality coexisted with other ways of understanding time. Marital temporality divided the lives of women between early
years in their natal village and life in a new community as a married-in bride.
Women recalled some major events by the months of the lunar calendar. Child rearing and the particular demands it entailed were also a major marker of memory.
Clearly campaign time helps to organize women's memories of the collective era, but
it does not encompass them entirely. In one community, as chapter 9 details, women
initially appeared to have forgotten the final two decades of collectivization—a pattern of memory I call "a wrinkle in time."[33] It is probably necessary, if uncomfortable to sequence-minded historians, to think in terms of multiple temporalities,
overlapping and jumbled, inflected in crosscutting ways by gender, marriage, level
of political activism, and age. Are silences, elisions of time, and eruptive memories
the aftermath of trauma? Of depoliticization? Are they the traces of exhaustion and
preoccupation with daily labor?

Women engaged in a memory practice that we did not hear from men: marking time
by the birth years of their children, ordered by the twelve-year cycle of the Chinese
zodiac (year of the rat, year of the ox, etc.). After a decade listening to women precisely name the animal of each child's birth year, while scrambling or forgetting the
events of collectivization, in 2006 we asked three women in Village B to organize
major events by chronology according to zodiac signs. We provided drawings of the
zodiac animals, with calendar years written on the side, and asked them once more
to describe events they had told us about over the years. Some events were national
in scope, such as the establishment of cooperatives. Some were local, such as the time
a jealous saboteur put salt in the bean curd he was selling and tried to discredit Cao
Zhuxiang by telling everyone that the inedible stuff was produced by her co-op. As
we called out the name of each event, each woman keyed the events to the births of
her own children. A series of "I can't remember when" replies was transformed into
assured chronology-making when we provided the zodiac animals.

There is nothing "natural" about this divergence in memory and language, this propensity to remember history according to children's birth years.[34] To begin with, we provided the drawings of zodiac animals. Gao Xiaoxian comments that as with so much else about our interviews, "if we had not asked about it, I am not sure if they would have used this method themselves. They would not have been able to talk clearly about their sense of time. We used that to help them fit their stories into various moments."[35] Still, we chose to provide the animals precisely because many prior years of interviewing had taught us that women spoke with great confidence when asked about the year of a child's birth, whereas inquiries about calendar years drew a blank response from all but the most active cadres. This divergence reflects the differential ways in which "male" and "female" were understood, and the uneven degree to which their normative tasks, including those associated with children, were addressed by state policy and local assumptions.

Women had specific ways of describing their past actions. Sometimes they drew on recent images of revolutionary heroism. Many told us stories of profound transformation in many aspects of village life. Encouraged by the Marriage Law campaigns of the early 1950s, some of them broke off parentally arranged engagements or ended marriages; others asserted their own preferences in choosing a husband. They learned to read in winter literacy classes, were trained as new-style midwives, or took on responsibility as women's cadres. All of them participated in the process of collectivization, the enthusiasms and hardships of the Great Leap Forward, and years of field labor with other women, in some cases becoming labor models. Their lives as young adults, in short, were marked in measurable daily ways by Party-state initiatives. They felt themselves to be different from and more fortunate than their mothers, and many of them contrasted their ability to move through public space in the 1950s with childhoods that were more spatially and materially constrained.

Nevertheless the dramatic rupture at the heart of "speak bitterness" stories is absent from the accounts of these women. Instead they spoke in perduring self-characterizations, in statements of stable identity that spanned the 1949 divide and the recent reform era as well: *I was never feudal; I was always capable; I worked for family harmony; I was a person of principle; I have always been kindhearted.*[36] Or, in a less optimistic register: *My life was bitter and pitiful in the collective period and the present as well as the pre-Liberation past.* The recurring themes in these stories draw on prerevolutionary notions of female virtue, reworked and intertwined with more recent categories of self provided by the revolution.[37] Several of the qualities the women emphasized—industriousness, competence, the ability to manage human relationships deftly—drew on culturally durable notions of "the good woman," even though the physical and social locations of these virtues were no longer confined to the household and might indeed be performed in the service of the collective.

The quality of being pitiful, although not virtuous in itself, was a recognized characteristic of the oppressed classes, and thus it can be said to ally one with revolutionary virtue. In these women's stories, however, being pitiful indicates something else as well: an oblique criticism of both the Party-state and the family for failing to recognize the virtuous sacrifices of the storytellers.

I cannot know whether interviews conducted in 1955 (or 1975 or 1930) would have turned up the same vocabulary of virtue among women. I cannot track what they might have said about themselves at other times and compare it to the vocabulary of newspapers or policy directives or the varying intensities of campaign language. Because rural women generally left no written records, and time travel is not in the historian's toolbox, I know much less than I would like about the temporality of the vocabulary in question, across the putative boundary of 1949 or even across the history of the People's Republic. Whether virtue has recently made a comeback under the trying circumstances of the reforms or has been there all along, and if so, with what variations of nuance, are all troubling and undecidable questions.

Perhaps women's narratives drifted so easily away from orthodox state usage because revolutionary language of the collective period, rich as it was on the topic of what women should be and do, had very little to say about crucial areas of women's daily lives. For all the years of the collective era, women were exhorted to go out and work in the fields, to contribute to socialist construction. Over time they found themselves compelled to do so in order to earn enough work points to feed their growing families. At home, they were told to promote harmonious family relations. But domestic work, except for the brief and disastrous dining hall experiment, was firmly located at home, mentioned only occasionally in state documents as a remnant destined to disappear in the indefinitely receding Communist future. Women may not remember the order of collectivization in the 1950s and beyond, but they recall very clearly staying up most of the night, working by faint lamplight in the years before electricity arrived in the early 1970s, to make the cloth and clothing and shoes their families needed. The state's success in lowering infant mortality, combined with its infrequent attention to birth planning before the 1970s, contributed to the rising number of children in those families and the general exhaustion of their mothers. The labor of clothing them happened on domestic time, which had no public language in rural revolutionary China.

When women recalled these activities, state vocabulary was of no help, and mere description of domestic tasks was inadequate to the new and challenging environment in which those tasks were now performed. Perhaps it is not surprising, then, that women reached for an older language of performance under duress, the language of womanly virtue available from several millennia of popular tales in local histories, operas, and stories from classical texts, circulating in village performances and (more recently) on television and video. Crafting narratives of the self in the collective era—what sorts of people they had been, how they had treated others, how others had treated them—they spoke often about what it meant to be a good woman and to deal properly with family members as a good daughter, daughter-in-law, wife, mother. The virtues they named most often—industriousness, attention to harmonious social relations, and competence—were compatible with behavior expected of a woman cadre or a labor model. But less politically active women incorporated these virtues into their self-descriptions as well. In reaching for a story, and a language in which to tell it, women defined themselves by narrating virtues quite distinct from those available to men. Such virtues were an undercurrent even in anecdotes in which women performed heroic revolutionary actions: fearlessly striding home late at night from a political meeting, jumping into a flooded field to save the crops, winnowing grain all night long. The paradox here is that a revolutionary state language that actively sought to remake women's behavior—the language of the model woman socialist citizen—yielded so completely in these stories to a more pliable, much older language of virtue.

Aging women narrate their childhood, youth, and middle years at a moment when their longevity, self-understanding, and economic vulnerability are all shaped by gender. Women born between the 1910s and the 1930s in central and southern Shaanxi have absorbed and sometimes benefited from more than one set of cataclysmic changes. Their stories highlight what they feel to be their enduring virtues, their important achievements, and their most deeply harbored grievances across decades of political transformation. They came of age in a time of serious chaos, and their stories of childhood are populated with the physical and sexual menace of bandits and soldiers (not always distinguishable) and punctuated with episodes of flight from famine or from human marauders. They lived a substantial part of their adult working lives in collectives of various sizes, and their accounts of that period encompass a range of story lines: individual accomplishment, periodic organizational chaos and community dissatisfaction, and the numbing domestic chores of feeding and clothing burgeoning families.

In the early twenty-first century, a quarter-century after the economic reforms began to dismantle collective agriculture, "collective memory" is formed in the recounting of a shared time, recalled through a set of shared conventions and further refined in interaction with others.[38] More literally, it is the memory of a life within a collective, a social formation that structured daily work, politics, and personal interactions. If recalling the collective past involves placing oneself within the perspective of the collective, then women must place themselves in relationship to a group that no longer exists, but that is nonetheless the group in which they spent their youth and much of their adult lives.

The women we interviewed must assimilate a complex political history. The Nationalist regime under which they spent their childhood was thoroughly repudiated by the founders of the People's Republic of China. The PRC regime, however, was not repudiated either by the post-Mao leadership or in popular discourse, even as its promises of development and equality through collectivization began to ring hollow, even as collectivization itself has lost popular support and been reversed in the name of "market socialism." Collectivization required both dramatic efforts and demanding daily work. Now those feats are being recalled two decades after collectivization was dismantled by women who are well aware that it never delivered on its promise of economic abundance.[39] They often recall those years as times of unremitting field work, domestic work, and childbearing. To complicate matters further, as the final chapter explores, older rural women understand themselves to have benefited from the subsequent economic reforms, yet simultaneously to have been disadvantaged by them.

Although they seldom express direct dissatisfaction with state policy, women describe themselves as virtuous and capable in meeting the demands of both state and family, while coping with lack of support and attention from both quarters. The construction of a remembered self in commonly understood terms of virtue, and the assertion that the speaker was constant in her virtue no matter what the circumstances, create a contrast with broader political change, which is variously implied to have been too quick, too thorough, not quick enough, or insufficiently thorough.

Although women characterize the present economic reform era as a time of far less privation and labor than the collective past, their stories of that past are also suffused with pride in their previous capabilities, now diminished, and resentment at sons and daughters-in-law who do not understand, value, or offer reciprocity for their past sacrifices. Present circumstances of uncertain support, emotional betrayal, and in some cases outright elder abuse invariably shape their memories and the telling of them to sympathetic outsiders. Their memories may be ephemeral, destined to disappear soon, resonating differently each time they are told in a present that no longer recognizes their salience. In the face of that massive indifference, the stories of aging rural women spoken in the present become a form of backtalk, a defiant assertion of gendered memory.

This returns us to the question of whether Chinese women, and rural women in particular, had a revolution. Yes, in the sense that space and time, as they lived and understood them, were profoundly reordered in the 1950s. The revolution they had, however, was shaped in particular ways by gender, understood not as an immutable property of humans, but as an ensemble of practices that were differentially addressed—and neglected—by revolutionary policies. This material requires attention to all its messages: all the ways that female virtue, performed in the service of the revolution, also provides a critique of that revolution and its progeny. Gendered memories are crucial to a good-enough story of the recent Chinese past.

2

No One Is Home

DEATH IN THE MOUNTAINS

When she was twelve years old, Xiuzhen's parents sent her to live with her future in-laws.[1] It was the mid-1920s, and Shaanxi Province was gripped by drought. Xiuzhen's parents feared that if her husband-to-be starved to death, she would become unmarriageable. Better, they thought, to have his family finish raising her. Later, if both young people survived, the two could formally wed.

Xiuzhen's future husband, an only child, lived thirty li *[about ten miles] from her parents' home in Beitun, Liquan County.[2] Most young women did not marry so far away from their parents, but both families were Christian.[3] Years earlier the betrothal had been brokered by matchmaker Li, who spoke of how wonderful the Dong family was. But shortly before Xiuzhen moved to the home of her in-laws, her older brother went to the mountains to trade for grain and came back angry. He said to Xiuzhen's mother, "You've made a bad match for the child, marrying her out to the Temple That Props Up Heaven [Dingtian si] in the northwest mountains!"*

When Xiuzhen's mother delivered her to her new home, she was filled with terrible regret. "How can I marry my daughter into these mountains? They don't even have a door, only a run-down cave dwelling, a fence to block the doorway at night, and an empty pot."[4] Nevertheless she left Xiuzhen there, as promised.

As the drought deepened into famine, tragedy visited both families. Xiuzhen's father died. Her brother was conscripted, and the second time he ran away from the Nationalist Army they shot him. His wife died shortly thereafter. Alone, Xiuzhen's mother left home to beg. By that time, more than half the county's population was dead or in flight. Streams and wells dried up. Crops withered or could not be planted. And still it did not rain.[5]

By 1929, the drought that led to Xiuzhen's early marriage had forced almost 800,000 people across central and south Shaanxi to leave home in search of food.[6] More than seven million residents of the province were affected in the famine's second year, and by its end three million people had died in central Shaanxi alone.[7] At the time, the Nationalist government had little effective presence in central Shaanxi. Warlords had already appropriated much of the farmers' grain reserves, and no local authority was well positioned to provide relief.[8] In 1929, a major newspaper reported the grisly case of a starving father eating his twelve-year-old daughter in Long County, on the border with Gansu Province, 160 *li* northwest of Xiuzhen's hometown. The following year, reports surfaced of Shaanxi people eating corpses found at the side of the road or digging up recently buried dead to eat them.[9] Riverbeds became so dry that horse-drawn carts could use them as roads, crops withered in the fields, and in Shaannan trees were stripped clean of their bark by ravenous villagers.[10] The famine had the most severe effects in the counties immediately north and west of Xi'an,[11] and Shan Xiuzhen was not the only young woman married off far from home in its wake.[12] Girls of marriageable age were more fortunate than younger ones, who were frequently sold, abandoned, or put to death.[13]

Meanwhile, in the mountains, Xiuzhen formally married at fifteen. Her husband, nine years older,[14] *left to find work. Her father-in-law lay terminally ill on the brick bed. He asked for a bowl of flour gruel, but there was no grain in the house. Almost seventy years after the event, recalling the moment still brings tears: "What could I do if he was dying? I had nothing. If you, the child, fled and left the parents unburied, how could Heaven bear it?" Xiuzhen borrowed a few copper cash from neighbors,*[15] *made a fifty-li round trip to a market village to buy a cup of wheat, ground it with a roller, sifted it in a bamboo sieve, and prepared the gruel. "I said, 'Dad, I've brought you the gruel. Eat a little. Dad. Dad.' He couldn't talk, but he knew in his heart what I had done. Tears rolled from his eyes. He didn't drink. He died that night." Her husband returned home only long enough to buy a coffin and bury him.*

The following year, Xiuzhen's mother-in-law fell ill while visiting relatives in the next valley. By the time Xiuzhen got the message and crossed the mountain, her mother-in-law was dead. Again Xiuzhen sent word to her husband to buy a set of boards and return home. "Then we carried the boards there. We put my mother-in-law in the coffin and came back and dug a grave and buried her. That was the right way to do it." Xiuzhen was seventeen, and the famine was entering its fifth year. She had discharged her obligation to care for her husband's parents and bury them properly.

Xiuzhen and her husband took to the road, going first to her natal home. Everyone who could flee had done so, and her family's house was abandoned. The couple moved on, begging as they went. No one was hiring. The Spring Festival came and went, but Liquan County was still deep in snow. Others warned them that they would

*die if they tried to cross the Qinling Mountains, but Xiuzhen knew that they would
starve if they stayed.*

The stories Shaanxi rural women tell about the years before 1949 are shaped by the
public practice of "speaking bitterness," organized and encouraged by Communist
cadres in the early 1950s. Speaking bitterness was most often elicited by Party-state
cadres from poor peasants and women in a public forum designed to break the
power of local elites and to build support for the new state. It was intended to mobilize the listeners, altering their sense of what was permissible and possible.[16] It
was meant to transform the speaker, through the act of narrating, from one who
accepted a bitter fate to one who moved beyond it into a happier future. Speak bitterness narratives, by definition, were denunciatory—of particular oppressors, and
more generally of "the old society" inhabited and controlled by those oppressors.[17]
Typically, speak bitterness stories culminated with the arrival of the Communists
in 1949, an event known as Liberation, which heralded an end to suffering and the
dawn of a new life, for rural people in general and women in particular.[18]

Speaking bitterness has outlasted this particular political moment. The practice
was revived periodically during the collective period, sometimes even performed
for foreign visitors in the last years of the Mao era. Its narrative conventions have
not disappeared from Chinese social life. They continue to exert a pull on the memories and self-conceptions of those who once spoke bitterness or heard it spoken.
Speaking bitterness has become the way that women of a certain age talk about their
early lives and their past selves.

This chapter begins with an account of the bitterness that can be spoken in stories told half a century after Liberation. The precariousness of rural Shaanxi life in
the 1930s and 1940s—marked by political rapaciousness, scarcity, and outright
war—had particular effects on women and girls. Women speak of flight from famine,
their labor in and beyond the family courtyard, the ordinary heartbreak of their
family losses, and the routine brutality of rampant banditry and militarism. Using
the narrative of Shan Xiuzhen as a touchstone, this account branches out to stories
told by women in four villages. It asks what we can learn about women's lives before 1949, and about what Liberation did and did not change in those lives, if we
take seriously these detailed accounts of women on the move.

At the heart of speak bitterness stories is a paradox. Women often emphasize
that they were confined to domestic space by feudal social norms, naming this
confinement as a root cause of their suffering. Nevertheless, movement across the
landscape fills their stories of the decades before Liberation: flight from famine, work
in the fields, trips to sell yarn and cloth at local markets, and panicked runs to fields
and caves where they could hide from marauders. The main story line of speak bitterness narratives, and the Party-state's claim that its revolution enabled women to

emerge from oppressed household confinement into free circulation, are undermined by the details of those stories. Nonetheless, speak bitterness narratives convey a larger truth about what women understand the revolution to have done for them. They place themselves, often in heroic and visually arresting scenes, at the center of large events whose full import they came to understand much later, in the context of a history the revolution gave them. In their stories, they become essential actors in that revolution.

THE BITTERNESS THAT CAN BE SPOKEN

Two words recur frequently in women's speak bitterness tales: "pitiful" and "feudal." "Pitiful" (Shaanxi dialect, *xihuang*) is a word women often use to characterize their childhood circumstances and those of their families—hungry, ill-clad and ill, sold, endangered, bereaved. The practice of speaking bitterness provides a matrix, not a script. The stories of loss are individual, detailed and, even at a half-century's remove, emotionally difficult to narrate and to hear. Naming one's past "pitiful" gives order to a childhood and young adulthood spent in a time of chaos and war. It provides a language for voicing what might otherwise have been unvoiceable traumas:[19] the death and disappearance of loved ones, loss and separation, cruel treatment at the hands of intimates and strangers, sexual violation, the danger that banditry or conscription or illness or accident could destroy a family in an hour, or that starvation might decimate it in a season.

"Pitiful" is invoked to describe the sufferings of women, men, and children, but "feudal" is almost always used to describe the situation of girls and women. They call feudal the norms decreeing that a woman should have her feet bound (usually by her mother), marry when and whom her parents chose, serve her husband and in-laws obediently, exert no control over household finances, and, above all, remain confined to the household. Women remember themselves as being shut away, out of sight. *In the old society women worked sitting upstairs,* says a woman in a village where in fact houses had no upstairs, only a low storage space. *They didn't come down. You didn't see them downstairs.*[20] They were constrained by violence as well as social convention: *When men got angry they beat women, and when women got angry, men also beat them.*[21] Older women were the gatekeepers. A mother kept her teenage daughters out of sight; a mother-in-law gave permission for her son's wife to return to her own family for a visit.[22] If the situation became intolerable, a woman's only recourse was to *eat a bit of opium and drink a bit of vinegar, and then die.*[23]

Women summarize this spatial confinement with an aphorism and an anecdote, both of them after-the-fact descriptions dating from the early post-1949 era. The aphorism is some variation of this: "No matter how good the woman, she will circle the kitchen stove; no matter how inferior the man, he will travel the world."[24] The anecdote recounts that whenever someone came to the door of a house asking if anyone was home, and only a woman was inside, she would answer, "No one is home." Village women did not tell this anecdote about themselves, but their daughters told it to summarize the benighted situation of their mothers before 1949, and Women's Federation cadres described it as a situation they encountered in 1949 and 1950, when they went door-to-door mobilizing women.[25] The teller always makes the moral clear: confinement to the home meant that a woman was not regarded as a person by herself or others. Women had no standing in the wider society.

Like "pitiful," the term "feudal" does not reside only in the pre-Liberation era; "feudal remnants" can be found in stories of post-Liberation society, particularly in the attitudes of older in-laws or backward husbands. Unlike "pitiful," however, "feudal" is always in the process of being superseded. After Liberation, the story goes, women were no longer confined at home. The revolution granted them a particular form of personhood: the ability to move safely in nondomestic space, to become economic contributors and political actors. Going out to meetings and classes, working in the fields, having a say in choosing one's own marriage partner, becoming a women's cadre or a labor model: all depended on the ability to move through, and sometimes beyond, village space.

Speak bitterness stories encode a powerful explanation and an end point for the terrible suffering of the early twentieth century. Taken as a genre, such stories have in common a clear narrative arc: "pitiful" is the problem, "feudalism" is the source of the problem, and "Liberation" is the solution. In spite of the power of this formulation, however, the details of these stories often deliver more complicated messages than the overall narrative arc would suggest. Powerful as the speak bitterness story line is, it gives little prominence to some of the important elements that made rural women "pitiful": the absence of able-bodied male kin and the presence of menacing male strangers; the presence of extractive state agents and the absence of any relief provided by the state; the requirement that women rely almost exclusively on their own labor to survive, as well as to feed and clothe their children. "Pitiful" does not always stay where the narrators say it belongs, in the pre-Liberation past. It appears as a powerful descriptor of some aspects of life under the collective, and women use it frequently in speaking of the reform-era present as well. The present chapter addresses the state of being "pitiful" in the 1920s, 1930s, and 1940s, but this is not the last word on the subject. Subsequent chapters discuss times when women understand their lives to have been "pitiful" after 1949.

"Feudal" and its story of perpetual confinement, meanwhile, are repeatedly contradicted by the particulars of the stories women tell. As Shan Xiuzhen's travels suggest, women often were not confined to domestic space during the 1930s and 1940s. They were out and about in a chaotic landscape in which physical mobility signified not emancipation but rather hardship, danger, exposure, and shame. Many women remember spending part of their childhood on the road as famine refugees. Some left home permanently, sold to families in marginally less perilous straits as "children to be raised as daughters-in-law." Bringing in a child to raise as a future bride was less expensive than paying the brideprice for a fully grown young woman.

Among those girls who were able to stay with their natal kin into adolescence, many recall the absence of able-bodied men. Their fathers and brothers died, sought work away from home, were forcibly conscripted into warlord or Nationalist armies, fled conscription and disappeared, or in some cases joined the Communist guerrillas. Left behind to fend for themselves, women and girls had to "go out" to farm, sell the products of their spinning and weaving, beg, or otherwise eke out a living. Girls and women made substantial contributions to the household economies of central and south Shaanxi, often becoming the sole support of such households. Some of their work, mainly textile production, was performed at home, but only women from economically stable households where men were present could afford to observe the norm of seclusion. Seclusion was a sign of privilege, one that poor women could not attain.

In the speak bitterness narrative, a bright line divides the state of being pitiful and feudal from the state of being human. It is called Liberation, the conventional term for the coming of the Communists to each locale, and more generally for the establishment of the People's Republic of China in 1949. Here too, the details complicate the plot. For most women, the appearance of Communist troops was at first indistinguishable from a dozen previous military incursions. Only later, when stability and social order were established, did the arrival of the Communists come to be remembered as Liberation.

FLIGHT

The Qinling Mountains were a mass of ice. So many slipped and fell. Step and slip, step and land on your rear end. I was young and strong. I was used to running around the mountains all day. My health was good. I had been hauling water since I was twelve. I didn't fall.

Crossing the Qinling, there were footholds in the side of the cliff. You didn't dare walk on it. There were no wide roads. We followed the path. There was no place to stay at night, no place at all.

It was close to the end of the first lunar month, and we were close to Tongshen Gorge. The snow was very deep. There was no moonlight that night, and the wind was very strong. We didn't dare go on. In the evening, we all stayed in a temple. I felt around and found a platform there. I swept the snow off it. I didn't know who else was staying there. It was dark. The next morning when I got up, I saw the old woman in the corner. Aiyao [cries]. My mother and I fell into each other's arms. Ai! I didn't dare to bring up the past. Only then were my mother and I able to meet. In my natal family only my mother and I were left, just the two of us.[26]

In the morning light, after the unexpected reunion with her mother, Xiuzhen got her first good look at their makeshift bed.

You know what it was? Someone had died and was in the coffin. The coffin had been stored there, waiting to be buried. The outside was sealed with some mud. We three living people had slept on a dead person for the night.

The next night we could not find a place to sleep. There was no temple on the south slope of the mountain. There was a tumbledown cave, used as a charcoal kiln. When it was dark and no one was there, my husband, my mother, and I stole over to the kiln cave and made our way inside for the night. We got up very early the next morning. There would have been a lot of trouble if others had seen us. People there were the most feudal. People in south Shaanxi believe deeply in gods and ghosts.

I have never in my life burned incense to the gods in a temple. Never. I don't believe in it. Where are the gods? Where are the ghosts? It is all about people. If people do good things, they are gods. If people do bad things, if they rob and steal, they are ghosts.

In retrospect, Xiuzhen vehemently rejects feudal attitudes about gods and ghosts. In the years when famine drove her to sleep in unorthodox places, her Christian beliefs—later denounced by the Communist Party as feudal—helped her maintain equanimity when she encountered coffins and haunted kilns. But in the telling, Xiuzhen telescopes several decades and proceeds directly from gods and ghosts through Jesus to Communism. She explains her Christianity as a family affair: *My mother believed, and my mother-in-law believed. Why didn't I ever burn incense for the temple gods? Basically, I didn't believe in them [laughs]. At that time I believed in Jesus. I believed in God. After I was married I followed my mother-in-law to go to worship.*

After Liberation, I had some doubts. I began to think that as long as it is a socialist country, society is a living heaven. Because of this, I joined the Chinese Communist Party.

I always think if there had not been the Communist Party, there wouldn't have been a new China.[27] *If there had not been a new China, there wouldn't have been me. In both my natal and marital families, it was considered a sign of longevity to be alive at sixty. I am in my eighties. This is the second life the Party has given me.*

What is important to Xiuzhen is that her own character did not change, even as her beliefs and her sense of what was "feudal" evolved. The transformation in her thinking, from Christian to Communist, did not require her to reject the person she had once been. *Even in the past, I was not feudal,* she says, explaining that she did not ask for earrings when she was married. *I tell you, it is said that people in the old society are feudal, but I was never feudal.* She narrates a life that has encompassed individual feats of derring-do, as well as unimaginable social changes—in her case, from famine refugee to labor model received by Chairman Mao. In that narration, the whole world changes. Women move from a world constrained by feudalism to one actively shaped by the Communist Party. Xiuzhen herself, however, remains constant of character.[28] As she tells it, long before the world acknowledged her, in a dramatic scene invoking cold, hunger, darkness, ghosts, and the redemptive power of kinship, she demonstrated her own fearlessness and her willingness to challenge accepted beliefs. It is as though the world caught up to her at Liberation, rather than Liberation transforming her. *I was never feudal.* The continuity afforded by that statement, and the sense of self it expresses, allow her to link her distant and more recent pasts, to embrace a speak bitterness story line without understanding herself as damaged by feudalism. Oppressed, yes. Damaged, no. It is an important distinction for a woman who identifies herself with the revolution—but it calls into question the iconic figure of the sequestered woman who was able to "stride outside the household door" only with the arrival of the Party.

In the early 1930s, however, Party membership was still many years in Xiuzhen's future. Youthful good health and her hardscrabble years as a daughter-in-law had made her tough enough to survive the trek through the mountains. Now she was responsible for keeping her mother alive as well. *We went to the south mountains together with my mother. My mother was too old to walk fast. My husband was a young man. He didn't pay attention [to me and my mother]. I had to support my mother by begging. I ate whatever greens I was able to beg. I cooked whatever flour I begged in a pot I set up by the side of the embankment, and fed it to my mother.* The three of them made their way to Zhashui, on the southern slopes of the Qinling range. After they had stayed for three months in an abandoned pigsty, a kindly woman at whose house they begged helped them find work in the household compound of a wealthy landlord named Yu.

Xiuzhen had never seen a household like this, headed by a man who collected rents in seven counties.[29] The women of his family wore bracelets and silver-topped shoes. Her mother watched the family's children, while Xiuzhen made the family's clothing and shoes, milled their grain, and went into the hills to gather grass for the pigs, in return for two meals of corn porridge a day.[30] She perfected her needlework skills to meet the Yu family's exacting standards, and was rewarded by hearing them say that her work was better than that of the girl she had replaced.

Starvation no longer loomed, and the Yu family never beat her, but Xiuzhen speaks of this time in her life as one of diminished personhood. *I pretended to be deaf, mute, and blind. You swear at me, I pretend I am deaf and don't hear it. When I saw unfairness, I wanted to say something, but I didn't dare. So I didn't speak. I pretended to be blind. When I saw something that I couldn't accept, I squeezed my eyes shut. In this way I was a slave in his house for three years.*

When Xiuzhen heard that the rains had returned to Liquan and Xianyang, she told Landlord Yu that she wanted to go home. By this time he had built two thatched rooms for Xiuzhen and her husband, arranging for Xiuzhen to work in the household of the township head, a man named Fang. She suspected that Yu wanted Fang, whose only son was mute, to adopt her husband as a son. She told her husband that if they did not leave soon, they might never be able to go home. *I thought, This is not right. I had my own home, the famine was ending, and I still had my parents, I still had my ancestors. I couldn't just stay there and lose my conscience.* Fang was reluctant to release the couple, but she convinced him that she just wanted to go home for a brief look.

When Xiuzhen and her family returned to her natal village in Liquan, they found only twenty people left in a settlement that had once held five hundred households. More than a hundred of the dwellings were gone too, pulled apart by people who had passed through as famine refugees or stayed, dying slowly. After a year in the virtually deserted village, in which frequent visits by bandits made their lives miserable, they took refuge in the mountain district of Shanghan, halfway between her natal home and her husband's mountain village. In 1936 Xiuzhen bore her first child; she would have four more by 1947, though none survived to adulthood.

Sometime in the mid-1930s, while she was staying in Shanghan after her return from the house of Landlord Yu, Xiuzhen saw a small contingent of soldiers from the Communist Eighth Route Army leading camels. They passed through quickly, leaving behind red and green signs pasted everywhere that said "Resist Japan, Save the Nation!" The soldiers did not stop or enter anyone's home, but Xiuzhen was afraid. She gathered in some of her grain and waited until they passed. This was her first encounter with the Communists.

By early 1938, Xiuzhen and her family had moved again, to Taiyao, in Tongguan County, at the eastern edge of Shaanxi. This was the ancestral home of her husband's family. His grandparents had lived there before his parents moved west to the Temple That Props Up Heaven, and in Taiyao Xiuzhen and her husband made contact with a network of relatives.[31] These connections made Tongguan a safer place for them to be than Xiuzhen's ravaged natal village. Nevertheless, Tongguan was among the most dangerous places in Shaanxi at that moment. Japanese forces, at the height of their advance across north China, were encamped just north across the Yellow River in neighboring Shanxi Province.[32] Two days after she arrived, the Japanese moved briefly across the river and bombed Tongguan train station and the road to Xi'an, hoping to establish a foothold in Shaanxi. Many people and livestock were killed.[33] In response, throughout 1938 Chinese Nationalist (Guomindang) troops massed on the Yellow River's southern bank, making frequent incursions across the Fengling Ford and repulsing Japanese attempts to cross.[34] The Japanese never did occupy Tongguan, but their proximity, and the presence of Guomindang troops with their own discipline problems and provisioning needs, made life difficult for civilians in the area.[35]

Xiuzhen's husband was soon conscripted to work as an orderly on the battlefield.

She and her aging mother settled down on land that belonged to her husband's family. (Only many years later, during the Cultural Revolution, would Xiuzhen learn about the tragic way that her family had come into possession of this land.) She rented some land as well. Her mother died soon thereafter. Xiuzhen's immediate problem was how to survive and support her five children. Her husband was seldom home during this period, and Xiuzhen became the sole farmer.

FOOTWORK AND FARMWORK

Shan Xiuzhen had been almost ten when her mother began to bind her feet, but her father kept up a steady flow of objections, and Xiuzhen finally unbound them when she was eleven. The following year, when she married into the mountains, she was grateful for her natural feet. *If I didn't have them, how would I have managed? People of my age have such small feet [she uses her hands to indicate about three inches]. My feet are big. People said, "Nobody wants you if you have big feet. Your marital family can't stand the sight of them." But when I went to my marital family, my father-in-law never objected, and my husband didn't either. I went barefoot. I worked in the field with bare feet. I worked on the mountain every day. I took the cattle out to the north mountain and cut firewood and carried it home. In those days I pulled the plow [li], the rake [pa], and the leveler [mo]. I used a rope to drag the millstone. My shoulder was always rubbed red or black and blue.*

Among women born in the first two decades of the century, small feet were still considered a sign of respectable upbringing and a desirable attribute in a potential daughter-in-law. Feet bound early and tight, what one woman called "real bound feet," were the prerogative of the rich, as the future labor model Cao Zhuxiang explains: *We talked about the little lotuses [bound feet] of girls from rich families. The [girls from] average village families who had no important people also bound their feet, but not that small. Rich families wanted their girls to have small feet and made embroidered shoes, the kind that were so small they could fit in a teacup.*[36] In these families, the women stayed secluded at home.

Footbinding began at a later age in poor families than in rich ones, if it happened at all. Poverty and family tragedy routinely trumped social norms. Another future labor model, Zhang Qiuxiang, born in about 1908,[37] never had her feet bound because, as she said, she *didn't have a mother, so no one concerned themselves with this.*[38] In the south of the province, Feng Sumei's mother, born at about the same time, came from a family *so poor that they didn't even have money for binding cloth.*[39] Cao Zhuxiang, born in 1918 in Weinan, never had her feet bound at all: *Usually footbinding started at the age of four or five, but my family had too many kids and they did not bind my feet. But they put cloth socks on my feet to restrain their growth, and I was not allowed to take the socks off when I was sleeping.*

Attitudes toward footbinding, even among young girls, were complicated. One woman born in 1912 tells of having her feet bound every day and secretly removing the bindings at night under the quilt, then being beaten for her actions. But another, born two decades later, recalls trying to bind her own feet secretly, after her mother refused to do so on the grounds that it was painful and made walking difficult.[40] By the 1920s, Christian families like Xiuzhen's were ceasing to bind feet. But many mothers, fearful about their daughters' marriageability, clung to the practice even when fathers were ready to abandon it.[41]

In the 1920s, local government campaigns against footbinding penalized poor families for practicing it. Xiuzhen was ahead of her time: she unbound her feet in about 1925, four years before a Natural Foot Society was established in Liquan and the practice was forbidden.[42] In Cao Zhuxiang's natal village, which was close to the county seat, she recalls that *the county magistrate often came to our village to check, bringing armed guards with him. They displayed the cloth for footbinding and small shoes, and denounced footbinding. If they caught a man binding his daughter's feet, they would cut his queue short. If they saw a woman with bound feet, they would stop her and take her bindings off. They would put the binding on top of their gun and leave in triumph. The villagers fled and adults kept kids home at the sight of the county guards.*[43] In Guanzhong and Shaannan women born before or during the early 1920s often had bound feet, but women born after that did not.[44]

Footbinding might have been a hindrance to field work, but it was never a bar, and its demise certainly made such participation easier. Women in poor farming families routinely went to the fields during the busy season, as attested by a local saying in Village T: "When the wheat and millet are ripe, the embroidering women get down off the bed."[45] (Women sat on brick platform beds, called *kang*, to spin and embroider; "get down off the bed" here means to go out to the fields.)

In Guanzhong, where dryland cultivation was the norm, winter wheat was planted in the fall and harvested in the early summer, followed by a crop of beans, maize, and cotton harvested in the fall. Many farmers also grew a fall opium crop.[46] Plowing, raking, and leveling were conventionally performed by men, who were also in charge of drilling holes for the seeds.[47] Girls and women hoed the wheat plants, and cut and tied them during the summer harvest season.[48] During the fall harvest in Guanzhong, women also harnessed the oxen, cut corn, picked beans, hauled home the crops in small wheeled carts, and separated the wheat from the chaff.[49] When the harvest was completed, the men of the village would move on to work as transient hired laborers (*maike*) in other villages farther east, presumably leaving the women to manage the corn and millet harvest.

Farther north in Village G, where poorer families planted their crops down the sides of a nearby gorge, girls and boys alike helped to terrace the fields.[50] Scarce water had to be drawn for daily use from very deep wells and carried one pail at a time to fields in the ravine. Firewood had to be hauled back out. A man raised by his widowed mother remembers: *My mother would take an axe and go to the old fields to cut wood. In the past, when women carried a hoe they didn't put it on their shoulders. They would pull the wood they cut in the gorge back home. As for drawing water, the well here used to be forty-eight* zhang *deep [about 524 feet]. My mother would draw the water and put it on the ledge there, and when someone she knew passed by, he would carry it back with a shoulder pole. That's how we got our drinking water and firewood.*[51]

In Shaannan, where rice was a staple crop harvested twice a year, girls and women routinely helped to transplant rice seedlings and weed the seedling beds.[52] In Feng Sumei's village in south Shaanxi, the saying went, "Never marry your daughter to Jiajiaba [a place name], because they irrigate with pots there." Sumei's mother drew water from a well and carried it to the rice fields, one bucket at a time. As soon as Sumei and her brother were old enough to carry their own small buckets, they joined her.[53] Girls in south Shaanxi also went to the hills with baskets strapped to their backs to find grass for the livestock, wood for cooking, and wild greens to supplement the family's meager stores of grain.[54] Many Guanzhong and Shaannan families grew small amounts of cotton, and it was the job of girls and women to pick the bolls, bring them home, lay them out in the courtyard to dry in the sun, and pick out the raw cotton in the evening.[55] In some families, women were completely responsible for thinning, hoeing, and topping the cotton plants.[56]

In the decades just before 1949, it was an accepted family strategy for men to seek work away from home as long-term laborers.[57] These families could rely on some amount of remitted income, but the field work was left to older men, women, and children. The same was true—minus the remittances—in the families of soldiers and for widows. In Shaanxi in the 1930s and 1940s, the presence of women and girls in the fields was not just a supplement to male labor at harvest time. Given the general absence of men, farming was becoming women's work.

Cao Zhuxiang, who married into a family with no adult men at home, initially relied on her brothers and nephew to help with farmwork.[58] Ma Li's mother, widowed with two small children, asked her brother to cultivate her land and gave him half the crop.[59] Often, however, girls and women stepped in to replace the absent men. Liu Guyu, a child daughter-in-law in Village G whose future husband had been conscripted, farmed side by side with her father-in-law, sowing with a soil drill, plowing, spreading fertilizer, and helping him operate the hay cutter to prepare feed for the donkey. Her mother-in-law, irked that Guyu was not performing the indoor tasks a girl was supposed to do, would yell at her, "I told you to spin today. You lazybones, just cutting grass for your dad." But Guyu was easily bored with spinning, which she was required to do after dark. She preferred to be out in the fields,[60] doing much of the labor her future husband would have done had he been at home.

Unmarried women in Guanzhong and Shaannan villages, as in many areas of rural China, were not supposed to be seen outside the household. Yet even as women who grew up poor reiterate the norm of female seclusion in their stories, their specific memories provide an insistent counterpoint. Cao Zhuxiang, born in 1918, recalls that in her youth, girls were not allowed out except at dusk, when they sometimes gathered in groups to discuss their dowries. She remembers spending most of her time in the family courtyard after she turned five, being taught to spin and weave. Yet she also recounts that she pushed her brother's delivery cart (he delivered flour to the county seat and beyond) and swept traces of flour from his empty sacks, cooking them for the family with wild vegetables she collected in the fields. She remembers working in the fields breaking up soil until she was eleven or twelve, and subsequently being kept in the house, yet she also describes getting her first menstrual period at age fourteen while she was out in the fields harvesting opium.[61] The social imperative that unmarried girls stay hidden was so strong that women remember themselves as shut away at home, but the details of their stories suggest otherwise.

Married women, too, were supposed to venture out only for visits to their natal families. Even when a woman watched village festivities from her doorway on the fifteenth of the first lunar month, she wore the long skirts that women were supposed to don over their other clothes when appearing in public.[62] Like footbinding, however, this stricture was more powerful in its hold on people's imaginations than on daily practice among the poor. Among married women whose husbands went out to work or were conscripted, the blurring of "inside" and "outside" activities had little resemblance to the division of labor encapsulated in the classical saying "Men till, women weave."

Shan Xiuzhen, for instance, became a farmer as soon as she stopped being a famine refugee. *I planted the land. Who else could you depend on? Men were not at home during the war against Japan. They went to carry wounded soldiers and dig trenches.* She grew wheat, a small patch of cotton, and watermelons to be sold for cash. In the fall she and her mother planted corn, millet, and beans. But farming by itself was not enough to make ends meet. The Tongguan County gazetteer reports that four of the years in which Xiuzhen farmed alone were marked by drought, although none was as serious as the one that had sent her over the Qinling Mountains.[63] Thirty bushels of the best grain Xiuzhen grew went to the landlord annually in rent. As she remembers it, a certain amount of wheat had to be turned in every month. Left without enough to eat, she would borrow grain, but the terms were ruinous. *If I ate one bushel [dou] of corn, I had to return one bushel of wheat. If I borrowed one bushel of wheat, I had to return two bushels of corn.*

Adding to the pressure on women like Xiuzhen was the awareness that any woman who went out to work in the fields was subject to abuse and shame. Lu Yulian's mother, a twenty-seven-year-old widow in south Shaanxi, tried to work the family's four *mu* (two-thirds of an acre) of rented paddy land with her bound feet. Able to handle the planting work herself, Yulian's mother was less successful at fending off local government demands for money and grain. *When I was about seven or eight, my mother was unable to meet the payments. They tied her to a persimmon tree, because they wanted money and she didn't have any. My uncle was related to the township director. Both my brother and I were just children. We went to beg this uncle to let my mother be set free. Later we let our uncle plant the land. As soon as my uncle planted the land, they did not charge him any money or grain. If we planted, we were charged high rates.* For Yulian's mother, a widow who had strong ideas about women's virtue and was determined not to remarry, this would have been a profoundly humiliating episode. Renting the land to her male relative in return for 40 percent of the rice harvest, she did not have enough grain to feed her family of three. Instead she and the children milled the rice and took it to the mountains to trade for corn, subsisting on the cheaper grain supplemented by soup made of wild greens.[64]

We were poor, Xiuzhen says. *We were ashamed when we worked in the field. In the old society, women from poor families often went to the fields to cut the wheat and to carry manure. Everyone knew that pitiful families didn't have men[65] to do the work. During the Anti-Japanese War, men were drafted for labor and to carry injured soldiers and were not at home. Who else would work in the fields if women didn't? You needed to eat. The Guomindang also wanted money. How could you manage if you didn't do it yourself?*

Women were also afraid to be in the fields on more immediate grounds: in an environment constantly traversed by bandits and soldiers, for a woman to be visible was dangerous. Several years after Xiuzhen settled in Tongguan, a fellow villager said to her husband, *"Look how dangerous it is for your wife to go outside." It was a danger zone, crossing the Weinan area. Everyone knew it.* Women who went to the fields were acutely aware of their poverty and vulnerability.

CLOTH MAKING

When Shan Xiuzhen turned eight, her mother set up a spinning wheel for her. Like many other young girls, she was then required to spin cotton daily, her mother's unceasing labor a model and a goad. *My natal mother was very strict with me. I was afraid of her. She did needlework at night. You couldn't stop spinning until she stopped working. I spun for others, not for myself. You were not allowed to run away.* Young girls were given quotas by their mothers, spinning two or three or five bobbins (*suizi*) a day, each one half an ounce to an ounce of thread. Only after they finished were they allowed out to play, although some remember playing whenever no one was around to supervise, sitting down to spin industriously as soon as an adult approached.[66] They also learned to fluff cotton with a bow in preparation for spinning.[67] They remember spinning as part of what made their mothers' lives and their own childhoods "pitiful": working at night, too poor to light an oil lamp, threading the spindle by the light of the glowing tip of an incense stick.[68] Yet the memory of spinning is also infused with cheery sociality: going to other people's houses to spin, pulling a dozen wheels into one big room to spin together.[69]

Village girls usually learned to weave when they became teenagers. An older relative or neighbor would teach them to tie the knots on the loom, then have them practice weaving without breaking the thread.[70] Women in central and south Shaanxi typically wove several thousand feet of cloth a year, using either homespun or purchased thread. Cloth was woven in long, narrow pieces. Coarse cloth, woven more quickly, was used for handkerchiefs and sacking material; seven or eight feet of fine cloth was required for a new set of clothing. If a family could afford it, they would keep the thicker cloth for themselves and sell the looser weave to others.[71] For the Spring Festival, women prepared new clothes for the children and as many adults as they could afford to clothe. Once a year, people pulled out the stuffing from their padded cotton jackets, washed the jacket itself, and then put the jackets back together again.[72] New cloth was dyed at home: pale colors for the lining, deep colors for the outer layer.[73] Women in the rice-growing areas used leaves and paddy mud to turn the cloth black.[74] In areas where no rice paddy mud was available, women used pomegranate leaves and skins boiled in water to produce black dye.[75]

Spinning, weaving, and needlework were the quintessential markers of women's skill, industry, and frugality. Women remember their early clumsiness and the scoldings they received. But in stories that otherwise have few moments of relief from hardship, and few evocations of emotions other than pity and fear, tales of spinning are different. Women recall the pleasure of their own growing mastery, the approval of mothers who normally had little energy or inclination to praise their children, and the scope for creativity in a generally forbidding environment:

> When I learned to spin I was almost ten. My mother smiled and said, "My big duck has gotten up on the frame." (Wang Xiqin 2006, b. 1932)
>
> Weaving was easy to learn. I would put on the belt, pump it with my feet, and slide the shuttle [suozi] back and forth. I wove flowers, plaids, squares. I wove whatever I thought looked good. (Zhang Chaofeng 2001, b. 1934)
>
> I wove very late. At the beginning, my mother thought the cloth I wove was not good. She wove better than I did. So she didn't permit me to use her loom. I started to weave in my early twenties. I saw her weaving and I knew how to do it. I knew how to set up the loom and the thread. I could weave even faster than she did. I spun faster than her too. Her thread was slippery. My thread was downy. So it was slow. But after I starched it, it went faster. Later she saw I could do it and then she let me do it. (Shan Xiuzhen 1997, b. 1913)

During the wartime years, when her husband was gone, Shan Xiuzhen planted almost a quarter of her rented land to cotton. She gathered in forty-five *jin* (almost fifty pounds) of raw cotton, bowed it, spun it, wove it, and sold it. Speed was important, because she needed the proceeds to repay the grain she had borrowed. In two days she could spin a *jin* (1.1 pounds) of thread, working far into the night.

This would buy her six *jin* of grain. In four days she could weave ten *zhang* (109 feet) of cloth. None of this was used to clothe the family; procuring enough food was the highest priority.

All the thread, clothing, and shoes worn by peasants in central and south Shaanxi (with the possible exception of red cloth for weddings)[76] was produced by local girls and women, although households sometimes specialized in one product and exchanged it for the others. Women's cloth production and needlework provided the only source of income for many families with dead, absent, or disabled husbands.[77] *Those with land had land,* says Cao Zhuxiang. *Those without land had to rely on their two hands.*[78] Yang Guishi, an only son whose father was conscripted by the Guomindang and did not return, never saw his mother sleep until he was twelve or thirteen. *My mother endured all kinds of hardships to raise me. She raised me by weaving and spinning. When I was very little, she lulled me to sleep when it got dark, and woke me up in the morning. So I never saw her sleeping. Sometimes they [the women in the village] would weave at night, and go to the market every day to sell what they had woven. In Lujing Town, she would sell cloth in the market and exchange the money for raw cotton to bow. There were quite a few women in the lane whose situation was similar to my mother's. They would go to Lujing Town together in order to sell the cloth and exchange it for raw cotton.*

Cloth making and needlework were important even in households that had income from farming or remittances from a man working outside the village. Wives, daughters, and daughters-in-law spun, wove, and made shoes for the market. They used the proceeds to clear debts, pay conscription taxes, and buy grain, oil, salt, raw cotton, thread (if they were weavers), cloth (if they were spinners), and sundries.[79] Sometimes a woman would take in weaving for neighbors, who provided the thread and paid her for her labor.[80] If men were living at home, sometimes they would take the cloth to market. More often, however, weaving brought women out of their homes to the periodic markets held on a rotating schedule in villages and nearby towns.[81]

Arriving at such a market in southern Shaanxi, a woman would find many other women selling and buying. *You held the bolts of cloth you had woven in your arms. Thread was sold by the bundle. There were two skeins twisted into each cluster, and eight clusters of thread, bundled up, were one* jin. *[You could sell it for] a bit more than one yuan. Sometimes we would trade it for raw cotton, a* jin *and a half or a bit less. One* jin *of raw cotton could make one* jin *of thread. It was all women who came to trade. There were no cloth dealers. It was sold to peasants. They all wore the cloth. At that time, people did not have things made outside. Those who didn't know how to weave bought cloth to wear.*[82] If a woman exchanged a *jin* of thread for 1.5 *jin* of raw cotton, the extra half a *jin* represented her profit, which could be sold directly, spun and sold, or exchanged for food.[83] Likewise a piece of cloth would garner a few dimes in profit over and above the cost of the raw material.[84]

Women also made and sold straw and cloth shoes and embroidered goods.[85] As a young married woman in the 1930s and 1940s, the future national labor model Zhang Qiuxiang took up a post at a nearby market held every five days, where she sold homemade shoes and bought materials for the next pair. She could make a pair in a day and a night, selling five pairs each market day for thirty or forty cents apiece.[86] Zheng Xiuhua and her brothers spent the late 1940s selling their hand-made grass shoes in the local market. During that time she also learned to embroider flowers on pillows and make door curtains that were bought by young women for their dowries. *Nobody on the street could embroider better than I did. Some sold pillows that were not well made for four or three and a half yuan. Mine were sold at five yuan.* Xiuhua turned this money over to her mother to buy grain, for her father was off fighting with Zhang Kui's band of Communist guerrillas, and to support the family her mother depended on her children's needlework and her own earnings from spinning, weaving, hauling firewood, and washing clothes.[87] Marketing textiles and shoes in a public place was a common part of life for poor girls and women, recounted matter-of-factly even by narrators who cited women's seclusion as the norm. Foraging, farming, spinning, weaving, sewing, and embroidering, women pieced together a livelihood in an environment marked by the absence of able-bodied men.

LOSS

Hunger, serious illness, forced separation, and death punctuate women's stories of life before 1949. Women talk of these events as individual catastrophes, but they often link them to recognizable historical events: the drought of 1928, the cholera epidemic of 1932, the Henan famine of 1942, the national spike in banditry, the conscription policies of the Nationalists. Events on this scale affected everyone, but they had particular effects on girls and young women, who were sent away to be live-in laborers, child daughters-in-law, and brides, or who found themselves heading households because their husbands were absent or dead. Many lost children to neonatal tetanus, measles, or diarrhea. These women were the lucky ones. Women who died in the famines or in childbirth, who did not survive the disappearance or death of their husbands, or who were sold as prostitutes have left no stories.

In between the dramatic episodes of famine, memories of ordinary hunger fill the stories of pre-1949 life. Many Guanzhong farmers grew wheat, but only the better-off among them could afford to eat it. Most sold their wheat and made flour from beans or less valuable grains. Steamed bread and thin gruel were spiced with dried peppers and wild vegetable leaves, with a bit of oil if it was available.[88] In the rice-growing regions of Shaannan, women talk of eating the smashed grains of rice that dealers could not sell, grains that are now used to feed chickens and pigs.[89] Girls like Zhang Chaofeng, sold as child daughters-in-law by desperate parents, thought it memorable that in their new homes there was enough to eat.[90]

Before the drought that sent Shan Xiuzhen over the mountains had fully abated, cholera swept Guanzhong. In Weinan County, it killed more than fifty thousand people between June and August 1932, leaving "village households desolate and bones of the dead everywhere."[91] Among the victims were Cao Zhuxiang's father, third sister, and brother-in-law. *People called the plague* "hulila." *Lots of people died. People died for nothing, without a clue. No one knew how many would be found dead the next morning. Sometimes the whole family died out. Of the two villages, north and south, only forty some households were left.*

In Shaannan's Nanzheng County a drought in 1941[92] came so early that local farmers, completely dependent on rainfall, could not even transplant the rice seedlings. Li Liujin's mother had already gone to the mountains, a hundred *li* (about thirty miles) away, doing needlework in exchange for wages paid in corn to support Liujin and her sick father. This makeshift arrangement, predicated on the mother's ability to work far from home, was apparently not enough to feed both father and daughter. After a few months, Liujin was given to another family as a "pawned daughter" (*yashen nü*), meant to ensure that subsequent children born to that family would survive. In fact, her daily life was that of a child laborer. *I was only eleven. I pushed the grinder at the mill from morning till night. I was with a red horse all the time. I pushed, grinding flour from four big bushels of wheat, 120 jin of flour. Except for eating and feeding the livestock, I never stopped, not even to comb my hair. In the afternoon, after the grinding was finished, I also went to cut the young grass growing in the field and brought it back to feed the livestock. At night, when you came back, they would give you some cotton and you would sit there and spin thread. My hair was matted and clumped. People said, "Aiyo, this girl's hair is a mess. It looks rusted." It was full of lots of lumps, and my ears were so itchy I couldn't stand it. When I touched one of the lumps, all at once I would pull out a clump of lice, crawling in every direction. That's because I had no time to comb my hair! Even at night I had to spin a skein of thread before I could sleep. When I got up in the morning, I had to grind again. I remember that one day they told me to cook. I boiled the rice into paste. It wasn't fully cooked. Aiya. They pushed me down and gave me a beating.* Fortunately for Liujin, her mother came back from working in the mountains after half a year, retrieved her daughter, and brought her home.[93]

The next year, drought struck neighboring Henan Province. Ruthless government extraction continued, leading rapidly to a famine. The price to purchase a woman in Henan fell to one-tenth of its usual level, and more than 100,000 refugees crossed into Shaanxi.[94] One man set off with his three daughters, ages fifteen, twelve, and ten, who took turns sitting on a three-wheeled cart. In Henan they had been eating boiled wheat straw, and their bodies had swelled. The family had decided that the only chance for survival was to take the three sisters to Heyang County in Shaanxi, where an aunt had relatives, and marry them off. When disaster struck a region, it was often the women in the community, who had married in from elsewhere and therefore had kin in other places, who provided life-saving connections.

It was snowing when the father and his three daughters reached the Henan city of Luoyang. After several miserable days huddling under a shared quilt, they abandoned the cart, got on a train for Heyang, and then walked to Leijiazhuang, not far from Village G. The father remained in Shaanxi just long enough to arrange three matches with the aid of his relative. He did not get to meet any of his future sons-in-law before he returned to Henan. The oldest sister was sold to a family whose son was away working as a carpenter. The second, Guyu, went to a family whose son had been conscripted. The youngest girl, Cunyu, was sold to a family with a retarded son. The family kept him hidden until the girls' father was safely gone.[95]

Guyu lived with her new family for five years before she was formally married. *When I came here my mother-in-law made a whole new set of clothes for me. She was afraid I was starved, and she was also afraid that I would eat too much and harm myself. She didn't allow me to eat as much as I wanted. Every day she only gave me two pieces of dry steamed bread.* Guyu's new family needed her labor; her mother-in-law was an opium addict who was too sick to cook regularly, and so Guyu was taught to make noodles and grind flour by her future father-in-law. *After I learned how to do it, my father-in-law never came into the kitchen again.*

Guyu was lucky. Her in-laws treated her well. Her future husband did not come home until she had been in the family four years, but his first words to her warmed her heart. *He said, "Look, you came from Henan. My dad is too poor to get me a wife. I've never seen you. You've never seen me. But we will be a family."* They married in a double ceremony with her husband's brother, who was also marrying a child daughter-in-law.[96]

Her sister Cunyu, two years younger, was not as fortunate. *My father left us here and went back. He didn't say anything. He just said, "It is good, you will have food to eat." He didn't say he was marrying me to someone* [maigei renjia]. *After he left, I saw someone, very ugly. I thought, I am afraid that is my husband* [nüxu]. *He was no good. He was ten years older than I was. He wasn't intelligent.* Her husband's mental disability was to affect her livelihood through the collective years and beyond.[97]

Mental illness, exacerbated by marital troubles and material hardship, afflicted many families. According to Zhou Guizhen of Village B, her father was driven to suicide by a series of misfortunes: his first wife's death, the haranguing of his second wife, the theft of his three cows, and the attempted theft of the grain given as a brideprice for Zhou's coming marriage. *When someone came and tried to steal the grain, they scared my father so badly that he developed a mental illness. He was treated for more than a year, but he wasn't cured. I went to my maternal uncle's house. When I came back, my father had jumped into the river, but he didn't die. At New Year's I went out, and my father hanged himself. Only my brothers and I were left at home, the three of us. Every night, if I didn't come back, my two brothers would be so worried they would move to the doorway, and not dare to enter the house. At night the three of us did not dare to sleep. We all sat on the kang in the dark. Really, in the old society I was bullied a lot by others. So after that, I always propagandized to others, saying that the old society bullied women and caused them great distress.*[98] Here Zhou Guizhen seamlessly links a series of vulnerabilities and misfortunes—emotional instability, repeated theft, abuse by those in authority—to something her story does *not* directly illustrate: the particular sufferings of women. In making this link, she gives meaning to her past, drawing on the political categories learned by village women in the years of speaking bitterness.

Death in childbirth or during the postpartum month of confinement was common. Zhou Guizhen was ten when she lost her mother to puerperal fever. *There was another child. When she realized she was not going to get better, she took the quilt and smothered the baby on the bed.* Shan Xiuzhen became pregnant almost every year from the late 1930s until 1946. She had one miscarriage and bore five children. The miscarriage happened three or four months into the pregnancy, as she went about the heavy work of farming in the summertime, right after the busy season. *I have to say, I must have been an idiot at that time. I carried a bag of wheat, five* dou *[150* jin *or 165 pounds] on my shoulders. You see how strong I was [laughs]. I was born strong. The miscarriage was not because of carrying things on my shoulders, but because of carrying them in front of me* [na xiaoyue bushi jian shi bao]. In the years when her husband was seldom at home, Xiuzhen carried her children to the fields. *I took a small basket and put the child in it down on the ground. I put it in front of me, so that the child was in front of me. I was afraid there were wild animals in back of me. Or I carried it on my back and picked corn. The corn leaves scratched my baby's face raw.* Her children all survived infancy, then succumbed one by one to measles, a serious threat to children and adults alike in Shaanxi in the 1930s and 1940s.[99] Measles also swept through Village G in 1944, when Qiao Yindi was twelve; during the seven days she lay ill her mother prepared a set of burial clothes for her. She remembers the week as a blur of sleep, pus-filled blisters, scabbing, and pockmarks. All of the adults who got measles in the village that year died.[100]

CONSCRIPTION AND THE ABSENCE OF MEN

Throughout the 1930s and 1940s, the men of poor families went to war. Across Shaanxi, 200,000 men had been conscripted by 1939, with quotas for each county.[101] Guomindang conscription regulations theoretically applied to all males, but the rich could always buy themselves out. Heyang, home of Village G, was one of the counties where recruits fetched the highest price, since it was near possible battle sites across the river in Shanxi.[102] Conscription was carried out through the local *baojia* system,[103] which divided the community into units for defense and taxation purposes. Powerful families headed the *baojia* units, and conscription patterns mirrored village relations of wealth and power.[104] The landlord who lived across from Cao Zhuxiang in Village B was not drafted; his father was in charge of the draft.[105]

Often daughters were the only resource a family could muster to save a father or son from conscription. Wang Xiqin was married into Village B as a child daughter-in-law in about 1944 so that her family could use the brideprice to ransom her father out of the army.[106] In the same village, a rich peasant paid Liu Fengqin's husband to take his place in the army in 1945 or 1946. Her family never saw the money. She does not know whether the rich man failed to pay up or whether her father-in-law gambled it away, but either way she had to support herself in her husband's absence, like so many other women, by spinning and weaving.[107] In Lu Guilan's family, *every time there was conscription, they came to our house, because we had no power and couldn't get out of it. When they should have been conscripting the younger brother of the head of the* baojia, *they conscripted my younger brother-in-law. When they came to get him, my mother-in-law tried to stop them and they pushed her down and broke her ribs. When she died, she was so light that you could pick her up in a dustpan.*[108]

Cao Zhuxiang, later a local leader and a regional labor model, was newly married when her husband was seized for the army in the 1930s, an event that she blames for his subsequent illness and death. *When he was young he was working in the field. The head of the* baojia *suddenly caught him from behind and took him away to the army. He was injured when he was captured. He was startled, and that was the root of his sickness. He was taken to Weinan. The neighbor saw him being taken away and quietly told me afterwards. Later my mother[-in-law] talked to an old relative whose son worked for an army office. Her son managed to place my husband in the telephone bureau, which was headed by my second sister's husband, to do communications work. But he became sick when he arrived at the bureau. For about two years he was unable to get rid of the sickness and was finally sent home.*

I had to borrow the money to treat his sicknesses one after another. Later a tumor developed near his chest, larger than a woman's breast. It stuck out from underneath his clothing. His whole body turned entirely yellow. He always complained that he was hungry. I have no idea what kind of cancer it was. It was incurable. The situation was hopeless.

I had to go to the county seat to get medicine and food. My older brother gave me some money. He himself did not dare to run around, because he too could be conscripted. I, the woman, had to go out and run around. . . . Once when I was in a medicine store, the alarm began to sound. The owner rushed me out of the store and locked the door. I ran to wherever I could, out of the south gate or the north gate, and hid my head in a pit that people used to brew bean sprouts.

It was the Guomindang's bombs. The Japanese bombs were a little earlier. . . . I don't know what year it was, but my husband died that year. The bombs leveled the ground. I jumped out of the hole when the alarm stopped and ran into the field when the alarm sounded. This happened several times before I got home. Everyone, in and out of the house, was crying out of fear and worry. I was worried about people in the house and was scared myself by the bomb in the field. In our area, when the airplanes came the sky became dark. Poor us, we all hid in the graveyard. In the past the rich all had big stone tombs covered with thick trees. People hid in there. Some climbed into the cypress trees so they would not be hurt by the exploding bombs on the ground. We were always fleeing this and that. At that time, I never imagined that I could live to today.

There were times when my husband wanted to eat lamb's blood. I went to the county seat to buy it for him. I had to hide from the bombs once on my way. When I got home he couldn't even speak. Inside the door my mother[-in-law] was crying, holding my baby. My second mother-in-law was also crying.[109] *My husband was dying. I tried to cook the lamb's blood at the bottom of the wok. We did not have a stove fire or anything else. I barely cooked a few pieces of lamb's blood. My husband saw me at home and his mind eased. He ate half a piece and closed his eyes. That was the last moment. The cancer had spread, and he was always vomiting blood. There was also blood in his urine. In the past we had no knowledge, and we did not have a doctor to look at him. How could I do otherwise?*

As a historical account, this story is confusing. The Guomindang bombed the Weinan train station on December 13, 1936, during the Xi'an incident, and Japanese forces also bombed the county seat in October 1938 and October 1939—later than the Guomindang bombing, not earlier, as Zhuxiang remembers.[110] She remembers seeking medicine for her dying husband during the bombing, and she remembers that he died that same year, in the late 1930s. Yet all available information suggests that her husband died in 1941, a year marked by a September eclipse—which she does not remember—but not by local bombing.[111] The Guomindang had no reason to bomb an area that they controlled, and the Japanese were overextended and bogged down far away from Weinan.

Although the larger events and Zhuxiang's personal history do not line up neatly, her story does illuminate how she and other women of her generation came to understand the link between their own lives and larger historical events. Zhuxiang quite likely did experience the bombings of the late 1930s. In 1936, when the Nationalists bombed Weinan, she was married and pregnant, doing most of the family's farmwork and errands while her husband worked away from home. In 1938 or 1939, during the Japanese bombing raids, she might have been out seeking medicine for her two-year-old daughter, who almost died of measles. In conflating a bombing with the last moments of her husband's life, even though the two events were separated by several years, Zhuxiang brings together a dramatic local episode of the war with her greatest personal loss, the one that came to define her subsequent career as a virtuous widow turned agricultural leader. Like Shan Xiuzhen, who fled a catastrophic famine, crossed the mountains, and slept on a tomb unaware that her lost mother was next to her, Zhuxiang tells a story rich with visual detail: the pit for fermenting bean sprouts, the shelter provided by rich men's graves, the dying stove fire over which she cooks lamb's blood. She places herself in this scene of terror, loss, and vivid memory fragments, frightened but resolute, determined to procure medicine and fulfill with honor her responsibility to her family. In her own telling, she is an unsung heroine, out and about in an era when women were supposed to be at home.

Cao Zhuxiang's story shows how conscription and war, as well as illness and death, decimated families and changed what was expected of women. Boys and men risked conscription every time they ventured out the door. Men press-ganged by the Weinan County government in October 1942 were tied up and left overnight in a local ironworks that caught fire, killing twenty-four men and seriously burning forty more. Eight months later more than eight hundred itinerant harvest laborers from the east of the province were seized in Weinan and turned over to meet the local conscription quota, although they were released once the provincial authorities discovered that they were not locals.[112] Zhuxiang herself remembers a neighbor chopping off two of his fingers with an axe so that he would be unable to fire a gun and therefore would not be conscriptable.[113]

The death of many men who entered the Guomindang Army, often from disease or hunger or execution for attempted desertion rather than from combat, left families permanently dependent on the labor and resourcefulness of women. Yet even with their husbands dead, conscription remained a threat. Cao Zhuxiang's son was six when his father died in the early 1940s, but he had to be counted for conscription purposes. *I had to pay a fee for my small son not to be drafted. I borrowed and prepared some cash in advance; even then, I was still short of money. It was my brother who gave the money to pay off the fee. But I could not ask for money from my brother all the time. So I harvested some cotton and made some clothes to sell for a few cash to pay the fees.*[114]

HIDING

Venturing outside put women at risk for abduction and rape, but seclusion at home did not offer much protection either. The distinction between bandits,[115] irregular forces, and regular soldiers was not always clear, nor was there much difference in their treatment of villagers. In households from which the men had fled or been carried off, older women fortified the doors, disguised girls and young women in their charge, or led them to hide in the fields and gorges. Feng Na, born in 1912, remembers the sexual threat of soldiers as linked to the absence of men. *I was fifteen or sixteen. When they came, they would take you away to be a wife. So scary! I was so scared that I hid. If you had men in your family, it would be better. If you had no men, you were in trouble.*[116] Small wonder that this memory is so vivid: in 1927 in Heyang County, where Feng Na lived, twenty-six thousand soldiers from at least seven different warlord forces were stationed.[117]

The establishment of a unified national government in Nanjing in 1928 did not stabilize the Shaanxi countryside. In 1932, a Henan man named Li Changyou led an army of five thousand men into southeast Shaanxi, staying in Village Z for a while and routing two militia units from the largest county township a few weeks later. Li's men occupied the township for half a year, conscripting the local men to perform corvée labor, raping the women, and generally terrorizing the population. His troops cut a hole in the right sleeve of each male conscript's coat and ran a rope through it, the better to identify them if they fled. One of his skirmishes with area militias resulted in the death of more than five hundred conscripts who were caught in the crossfire. Eventually Li's forces were shattered by the Nationalist troops of Yang Hucheng, and the remnants were pushed south into Sichuan, but not before they passed by Village Z one more time. Villagers were unable to harvest their crops during his six-month reign. A local history estimates that twenty thousand people in the area were burned out of their homes, more than twenty-seven hundred died (not counting those who succumbed to plague in the same year), two thousand women were raped, sixteen hundred young men were conscripted, and two thousand cattle were butchered.[118] Behind these aggregate numbers were innumerable small stories of catastrophe and escape. Yan Panwa, a fifteen-year-old boy at the time, saw his fifty-year-old father taken away by Li's forces. *He died and we never found his corpse.*[119] Liu Dongmei's mother fled into the mountains while pregnant with her, giving birth two months after her return. Her mother told her that Li's men killed everyone they saw.[120] Dong Guizhi, a teenager at the time, organizes her memories of those years around flight from Li's forces: *I got married when I was past twenty, after we had run away from Li Changyou. My whole family moved to a cave in the mountains for two or three years. If we saw that there were only one or two bandits [tufei] moving around the village, people would go down and clean them out. If there were more, we didn't dare. They burned down our whole village.*[121]

The region around Village Z remained plagued by bandits and soldiers. Li Duoduo and her five sisters spent much of the mid-1940s in hiding. *As soon as it was dark, my mother and father would put all the good things, such as silk and satin, on the bodies of us children. Then we wore very large clothes [on top of them] and it was difficult even to move. This was preparation in case the bandits came. Every day my father carried a basket on his back. We even put pots in the basket. We tied sheets and quilts up every day. If nothing happened today, my mother would cook. Whenever we heard any sound, we carried our things and ran away. Whenever the dogs barked, people fled, even if it was at midnight. If the dogs didn't bark, everybody was at home.*

When I was seven, I went with three girls to pick wild greens in the fields. When we came back there was no one in the village. There was a big platform on the plain, with a tree behind it. You could see as far as two li away. You could see people's shadows one or two li away. Then you knew something was wrong, and people here would run away. We four girls came back, but there was no one in the village. I knew where they had run to. We four girls, dragging each other and leaving our baskets behind, ran up to the gorge. The cliff surrounding the gorge was high, with tall grass in front.

When you sat there nobody could see you. I found my parents. Then I found my uncle carrying a big pig on his back. The pig weighed about a hundred jin, and it had a pot on its back. I remember he tied up the pig's snout so it wouldn't squeal.

Usually the young men ran out at night first. When we ran away, my father ran first and left us, because they mainly conscripted young men. They ran away and left us women and children behind.[122]

Most terrifying for the residents of Village Z were troops the villagers called Laomohai, soldiers from southern China who arrived in the 1940s, possibly under the command of the Guangxi militarist Bai Chongxi.[123] Li Duoduo, who was seven at the time, remembers that *Laomohai couldn't understand us when we talked. When we swore at them they couldn't understand. But we could understand them when they swore at us. Who knows where they were from? Nobody could understand what they said. I was young at that time and I didn't know what army it was. When they came they gathered chickens, sheep, and pigs together.*[124]

Xiao Gaiye, three years older than Li Duoduo, remembers something else about soldiers: sexual menace. *I still remember I was sleeping in the tunnel. My grandma said, "If they come, you cover your head tightly." But they came and wanted to pull off my quilt. My grandma said, "My girl is sick. Please don't uncover her. Please don't." They tore the quilt into pieces and used the pieces to make shoes. They were so frightening. If one of them came to your door for water, you didn't dare to move until he told you to move. When he took a drink he was afraid of being poisoned, so he would say, "You drink first." You drank a mouthful of water and then passed it to him. The Guomindang were not human beings. That I still remember.*[125] Flight remained a routine part of life into the late 1940s: *We would run and hide in ditches and sleep in the mountains at night. The Laomohai from Guangdong, Guangxi, if you had a daughter at home, they would break down your door. They conscripted the men and tattooed them. As for women, they would insult [rape] you. Now you need not be afraid no matter how many daughters you have. But in the old society, if you had even one daughter you would be scared to death. No matter who came, girls would have to run away.*[126]

WHERE LIBERATION LIES

The coming of the Communists was not a single event. In every village they arrived on the heels of a different local history. The term by which their appearance came to be known, "Liberation," would not yet have meant to villagers what it later came to mean: a promise, an end to the constant threat of starvation and marauders, a bright line between the past and the future. When Liberation arrived, its history had not yet been written, but that history now unavoidably inflects the telling.

For Shan Xiuzhen, the civil war between the Communists and the Nationalists that preceded Liberation was marked by a particularly terrifying day. *In 1947, the*

Communist Party was here on the east side, in Taiyao. The Guomindang troops were in four villages. The Nationalist troops also stayed inside the town of Shanchekou. Outside the town was the Eighth Route Army. They fought for ten days.

At that time, I was living in my old house. All the villagers had run away. I was the only one left in the house. Both my son and his father had run away. It was eleven or twelve o'clock, and the sun was shining. My Ninth Aunt and I were in the doorway. The airplanes flew very low, as low as the eaves of this house. I said, "This is terrible. Quick, let's go back." We ran back immediately. My aunt hadn't yet reached the house. There was a mill in the doorway. She burrowed under the mill. I had just gotten to the door and entered the courtyard gate when the airplane dropped two bombs next door. One was this thick and this high, pointed at the ends. It fell with no sound. It knocked all the branches off the pomegranate tree next door, but didn't explode. The other fell into the courtyard next door. It was round, a round lump, and it fell into the privy and blew the excrement into my courtyard, covering the whole yard. At that moment I had just entered the door and I choked in a cloud of smoke. I fell down and passed out. . . . It was lucky that the first one didn't explode. If it had, it would have been unthinkable. I lay face down in the yard, passed out, like a dead person. When the airplanes left, the Eighth Route Army came back.

In Xiuzhen's area, as in many other parts of Shaanxi, Liberation was preceded by a period of conflict in which control of an area moved back and forth between Nationalists and Communists.[127] Several days after the bombing, the Communist troops were gone, some moving east to attack Luoyang in Henan Province, others heading south to establish a base area in south Shaanxi.[128] Guomindang forces retook the area. *Oh, heavens! They came to the village and killed the cattle and ate them up, killed the pigs and ate every one, killed the chickens and ate them all. And then they told us, "I am here to fight for you. I am here to drive out thieves for you." I didn't say out loud, Who are the thieves? They would see something in your house and just take it.*

When Xiuzhen speaks of being bombed, she frames her story with an account of the military positions occupied by the Communist and Nationalist troops, details she could not have known at the time but learned later, when she became an activist and a Party member in 1950. Liberation tales invariably trace an arc from a menacing tumult of disorderly Nationalist troops to polite, quiet lines of Communist soldiers. Li Duoduo, for instance, born in 1940 in a settlement near Village Z, tells a story full of observant detail and specificity that would have occurred when she was nine years old: *Armies came and left, one after the other. Finally it was Liberation. When the New Fourth Army came, we peasants didn't know they were the New Fourth Army. I heard people call it something. It's been shown on TV. I can't remember now. Li Xiannian's troops and Xu Haidong's troops. We didn't know it was Xu Haidong's troops until Liberation. It took the Xu Haidong troops three days and nights to pass by. The soldiers marched three feet [chi] apart. They were all in gray uniforms and gray hats.* . . . *They passed by my mother's door to go up the mountain. They asked us whether we had any grain or not. I heard my mother say, "I have a bowl of rice." They said, "Aunt, please give me your rice. You have kids. I will give you some foreign flour." My mother said she couldn't accept it, no matter what they said. People were afraid that something bad would happen. They said, "Even if you don't accept it, I will give it to you." Finally they gave us a bag of peanuts and a bag of foreign flour.*

From then on, my mother started to send messages to my father, asking him to come back from the mountains. They asked all the young men to come back. When they came back, Liberation was declared. People knew everything after Liberation. We knew what the Xu Haidong troops were like.[129]

This story is reassuring in its material solidity: the gray coats, the peanuts, the mother's messages sent to the father hiding in the mountains. But it does not describe the events of 1949 near Village Z. Li Xiannian, who had led his troops into the region and established a nearby base area in the summer of 1946, had left the area by fall and returned to the North China Plain.[130] Xu Haidong and his Red 25th Army had passed through Village Z in late 1934, fifteen years before Liberation and six years before Li Duoduo was born. Separated from the main Communist forces making the Long March, nursing a head wound from a battle with Nationalist troops, Xu led his troops in several months of daring guerrilla warfare in the area, attempting to establish a base area, before moving on to Gansu and northern Shaanxi.[131] In 1940, the year that Li Duoduo was born, Xu Haidong began to spit up blood and collapsed while delivering a military report in central China; he spent most of the next two decades being treated for tuberculosis and convalescing at various locations in Anhui, Jiangsu, Shandong, Dalian, and Beijing.[132] At Liberation, he was nowhere near Shaanxi, although his reputation for military skill lingered. Both men were well-known war heroes, although Xu's health prevented him from enjoying the kind of illustrious career that Li Xiannian had in the PRC government. Years after Liberation, peasants in Village Z recalled with pride that both had been active in the vicinity.

Perhaps Li Duoduo's mother had seen Xu Haidong march through with his men, in neat rows three feet apart, and had told her daughter what the army looked like. But that seems unlikely, since every memoir of the war stresses the men's miserable conditions, the shortage of food, their worn-out straw sandals, and the quick-moving guerrilla combat of their sojourn in the area. Neither the neat marching formations nor the regulation uniforms seem plausible. Nevertheless Duoduo, born six years after the event, not only confidently provides these details but also places herself clearly in the scene: *They asked us whether we had any grain or not; I heard my mother say.* . . . *"You have kids."* . . . *They gave us a bag of peanuts.* The most revealing statement in her compelling tale of Liberation may be *It's been shown on TV.* Interviewed in 1999, a few years after the fiftieth anniversary of the Long March and on the fiftieth anniversary of Liberation, in a village with almost no indoor plumbing but at least one television set on every lane, Duoduo would have seen countless programs celebrating heroic Communist military exploits. When villagers talk about the particulars of Liberation, event, memory, and retrospective dramatization can no longer be disentangled. The solidity of this tale turns out to be illusory.

Compared to the vivid but unreliable tales of big troop movements, the accounts of family dilemmas are less cinematic but more unsettling. The civil war cut through Village Z in very personal ways, for Zhang Kui, leader of a nearby Communist guerilla band, was a local man born in 1917. It was said that Zhang Kui had first run off to the mountains in response to a passing insult: *Someone slapped him in the face. He got angry and ran away.* After his departure, *people bullied his brother, his sister-in-law and his wife every day.*[133] Zhang joined a group of local militarists who were opposed to the Guomindang, but did not ally with the Communists until the end of 1945.[134]

Once Zhang Kui was ensconced in the nearby mountains, others from the village went to join him, not always for explicitly political reasons, exposing their families to harassment and reprisal. He Gaizhen's brother passed through Zhang Kui's area on a trip to buy tobacco and never returned to Village Z. Later her brother was killed fighting the Guomindang. *My mother took my clothes to the riverbank, where there were no people, and cried all day long. I was still a little girl when my brother was a guerrilla. The* baojia *struggled against us. We could not even eat. They always called us "bandit's mother" or "bandit's sister." You couldn't eat what you cooked. They came over every day and ate the food. If you had nothing, they would drink. They knew my brother was a guerrilla.* Not until after 1949 did Gaizhen's family recover her brother's body, burying him in a graveyard set up for revolutionary martyrs in the hills above Village Z.[135]

Zheng Xiuhua's father joined the guerrillas in about 1945, when she was fifteen or sixteen.[136] Several years later, a Guomindang soldier demanded that Xiuhua marry him. *I dared not refuse. They would shoot you. . . . It was right before Liberation. The front lines were locked in a back-and-forth struggle. I was afraid they would beat my family. How pitiful I was. Who would take care of me? My father was not at home. The man wouldn't have dared if my father had been there.* Xiuhua reluctantly married the soldier and lived with him briefly, but by the time she gave birth to a child, the Communists had taken the area and her husband had been executed. The baby lived only a few months past birth. Soon after this, Xiuhua's father returned from the mountains, but within a few years he too was dead, his health ruined by his years with the guerrillas.[137]

Heyang County, on the west bank of the Yellow River, also became an area of back-and-forth fighting, described by the locals as "saw-pulling warfare." In December 1946, a security chief killed four Communist guerrilla fighters and sent their heads to the county seat, where they were displayed by the south gate of the city wall. By late 1947 Heyang had its own complement of guerrilla forces, and in spring

1948 People's Liberation Army (PLA) forces took control of the county seat twice, the last time for good.[138]

Qiao Yindi describes the panic that both Nationalist and Communist armies engendered. Like the stories of Shan Xiuzhen and Cao Zhuxiang, her tale puts her at the center of a visually arresting scene whose historical significance she only understood later. *I remember I was washing clothes in the irrigation pond* [laochi].[139] *I was sixteen or seventeen, already a young woman. I had a very long braid that hung down my back. My mother and some other family members were winnowing the grain. I saw nothing because I was doing the washing. My mother saw troops standing on both banks of the irrigation pond. She was terrified. She called me. I raised my head and as soon as I saw them I was so scared that I didn't know whether I should run or . . . I was carrying a lot of clothes and I was wearing a lot, and soaking some in the water. I couldn't do anything. We had never seen so many troops.*

My mother dragged me up to the edge of the irrigation pool in a hurry. I was so anxious that I fell several times and my legs were muddy and wet. Finally my mother and my aunt dragged me up to the winnowing ground. The troops surrounded it. At that time young women could never get away from them. My mother was so scared that she put a grain sieve on my head. My mother and my aunt dumped ten bushels of grain on my head. They got me into the house. When we got to the house, the soldiers knocked at the door. There was a cabinet to store grain and wheat when I was a girl. My family first put me in there in a hurry and then covered the top with a big basket. Only after that did they dare to open the gate. If the troops saw you, you could never escape.

After the back-and-forth fighting, there was no more fighting. I heard the grownups talking about Liberation, saying that the Central Army would not come back anymore.

In Village B, in Weinan County,[140] Guomindang troops were on the south bank of the Wei River, where the village was, and Communist troops were on the north bank. Cao Zhuxiang, who by this time had been a widow and the main farmer in her family for eight years, barricaded her family indoors and prepared for the worst. *I closed the door. I took my children, my mother, and even my brothers and my younger sister and we stayed in the back courtyard. People were very anxious. We would just grab something to eat and go to the fields. The children and my aunt-in-law would wait in the house.*

My own mother was anxious. When it got dark, the bandits came to get food and carry it away. They scared her so much that she threw up, and had diarrhea. I said to my mother, "I will stay in the date tree [zaoshu] *out back." The kids were underneath. "You keep a close eye on them, and if anything goes wrong, we will go over the wall and run away." We went on this way until the final evening—three days and three nights altogether. Then the fleeing army passed by that door over there. Everyone else all ran to the fields to hide. But my family and my aunt's family didn't have husbands* [wai qian ren]. *That day we felt every kind of fear there is.*

That night, we were terrified. I told my aunt, "It won't be good if we run away." Just outside the door was a well. We could jump into the well. Why fear death? At least we would not suffer that [rape].

I locked and barred the door and propped it closed with several pieces of wood. I crouched on the roof. I saw people with guns going by. They passed through. They were press-ganging people. It was the Guomindang. They were also looking for livestock. They chopped a crack in my door. It's been that way ever since. In the end, the GMD troops couldn't get the door open. The next day, they all fled. The Eighth Route Army came.[141]

Liberation, as Cao Zhuxiang recalls it, began with tentative interactions around providing food for the Communist soldiers: *They helped people out, and told us to make preserved vegetables [pao cai] for the army. They said the troops would be passing by right away. Everybody made several batches of preserved vegetables. The soldiers didn't stay here. They did the work they needed to—they taught, they talked, they left. Later we harvested the wheat.*

After the busy season, only then did things slowly normalize. Some of the men went to the county seat to look around. The county seat was all wrecked from fighting. After the busy season, I also went there to have a look. People all looked and cursed and talked. There were a lot of people there. They talked to the masses.

There were also people on the street selling cold noodles, gege [small unfilled flour dumplings], and other snacks. The Eighth Route Army bought them and ate them. They would pay on the spot, pay more than it cost. People were frightened and didn't want to take the money, but they had to. Afterwards, gradually, he gives the money, you take it. The GMD at that time had eaten people out of house and home, but who ever gave you money?[142]

After Weinan came under Communist control, PLA troops moved steadily toward Xiuzhen's area from the west. Guomindang forces fought fiercely from the city walls of the Tongguan County seat, but gave up on May 29. By the time the PLA covered the seven or so kilometers between the county seat and Xiuzhen's home of Shangmadian village in early June, all resistance had evaporated, and as she remembers it, no one fired a shot. Liberation, compared to the years of Japanese shelling and Guomindang bombing, was a quiet affair.[143] Her chief memory of the Communists is that they respectfully greeted all women, no matter what their age, as "Old Lady." Xiuzhen, who by that time had buried her mother and five children and farmed alone in Tongguan for more than a decade, was thirty-six years old.

NO ONE IS HOME

From the very first weeks of Communist government in central and south Shaanxi, official documents took note of women's mobility but chose to focus on the norm of seclusion as though it had been common practice. A report published within weeks of Liberation noted that women were hesitant about participating in farm-work, principally because they perceived it as men's work, shameful for women to do. In the very next paragraph, the report observed that women in Shaannan worked year-round in the fields, while in Guanzhong women did seasonal field work and spun and wove year-round. And yet the report's conclusion addressed only the first phenomenon, declaring that the main task for Party-state organizers was to change women's attitudes about labor being shameful.[144] This propaganda took the form of denouncing the feudal seclusion of women and celebrating their emergence into the fields and public life more generally, seeking community approval of a practice that was widespread but nonetheless denigrated.

Following in a line of reformers stretching back at least half a century to the late Qing, the Party-state named women's seclusion as the quintessential feature of an oppressive feudal order. It called upon organizers to roll back the forces of feudal-ism that had confined women to the inner chambers or the natal family courtyard. It deployed local cadres to convince fearful parents and in-laws that appearing be-fore non-kin men did not threaten a woman's virtue. It advocated prying newly mar-ried women free of the protective, disapproving, or punitive control of their moth-ers-in-law. As the next two chapters suggest, the conventional narrative of women's liberation by the CCP in the rural areas holds that the revolution made it possible for the first time for women to go out—to meetings, field work, literacy classes, and other households. Liberation for rural women, then, has been figured as movement through hitherto forbidden social space.

Defining liberation in these terms entailed forgetting that girls and women were already in public space, that they did not suddenly emerge as the result of regime change and new state efforts to draw them out. Formulas for speaking bitterness emphasized class-based suffering and exploitation, but did not highlight the absence of men and its close association with catastrophe, the labor women performed be-hind the courtyard gate, the fact that without women's spinning and weaving many households could not have paid their taxes, or the regularity with which women went out to farm, sell, work, beg, flee, hide, or be sold, in order to avoid starvation. The fact that Shaanxi women had all along been farm laborers and economic con-tributors was excluded from this powerful new state discourse, and eventually faded from public visibility, if not from individual memories.

In spite of its inadequacies, speaking bitterness was a transformative practice, one that women took up and made their own. The speak bitterness story names traumatic events that otherwise might be unspeakable. It assigns responsibility for these traumas to the distorted political and social relationships of the prerevolu-tionary decades. It takes them out of the realm of "fate." Then it places them firmly in the bitter past, encouraging women to see the present as shaped by their own ac-tions under the guidance, protection, and encouragement of a benevolent Party-state. When women narrate their pasts, half a century after the fact, their investment in these stories of bitterness is profound, and the theme of feudal seclusion remains a powerful explanation of oppression even for people who never experienced it. It is worth asking why.

In part, the speak bitterness story resolves an injury by misrecognizing it, substituting the bitterness of feudal confinement for the bitterness of being out and about in dangerous circumstances. When women say they were confined to the household by feudalism, they are naming a social norm for women—seclusion— to which they might once have aspired, but which poverty would not let them attain. By speaking bitterness, they reject a social norm that once, in a manner of speaking, rejected them. At the same time, when they assert that feudalism kept each of them secluded, they claim that the norm did once extend to them, that they did once qualify as the sort of respectable and virtuous women who should have been shielded from harm.[145]

Differences of place and generation mark these stories.[146] Women who were already married or widowed by 1949 were more likely than younger women to have taken on major farming tasks themselves. It is these women—Shan Xiuzhen, Cao Zhuxiang, and others—who speak most often of girls being confined to their homes, perhaps reflecting a norm that was already beginning to change a decade or two later. And it is these women, in their eighties by the time we interviewed them, who speak of the shame associated with women doing field work, although sometimes their shame seems to have been more about their farming technique than about their violation of feudal social norms. *I had to learn how to plow the soil and my mother worked with me,* comments Cao Zhuxiang about the period just after her husband died. *I was ashamed that the land that I plowed was not as good-looking as other people's plowed land, so I plowed my land at night.*[147] Women's presence in social space was common but unlauded, because of its associations with poverty and the potential for shame. This may be why women frequently assert that they were confined to the family courtyard before 1949, even as they describe a world in which seclusion was not possible for them.

Perhaps we might imagine a different background to the anecdote in which someone comes to the door and the woman inside calls out, "No one is home." In Chinese, the phrase most often used is *jiali mei ren,* literally "In the house there is no person." The story has been used to suggest that women did not regard themselves as people. When women talk about their own particular stories, however, the word *ren* is often meant to refer to men, and the phrase *mei ren,* "no one," is used most often to describe the absence of able-bodied male laborers from a household, both before and after 1949. Explaining why her natal family was better off than her marital family in the 1930s and 1940s, Cao Zhuxiang noted that her natal family had two brothers, whereas "here there was nobody [*zher shi mei ren*]," even though her marital family consisted of two adult women, her teenage husband, and several unmarried children.

Heard in this register, the statement "No one is home" is not a sign that a woman denigrates her own personhood. It merely suggests that she has been left to fend for herself. She might have called out "No one is home" while seated at the loom, her daughters or daughter-in-law spinning beside her, producing goods to exchange for grain to feed the family or pay the conscription fees for her son or buy back part of the harvest she had turned over to a landlord. Supporting the family was up to her. No one was home.

The speak bitterness story, for all its power, was far from an adequate narrative framework for women's lives. Its status as the only model of revolutionary self-narration has diverted attention from important questions about how the revolutionary process was understood at its inception, and how it has been remembered and reworked over the past half-century. Ironically, as women moved more safely around the village space and beyond, learning to reject the notions of respectability that they would have observed before 1949 if family circumstances had permitted, they also learned to misremember the story line of their past as one of confinement, rather than unprotected exposure. In doing so, they obliquely reinscribed the norm of confined virtue even as they denounced it.

After 1949, the Party-state made public space more secure, while valorizing, glorifying, and eventually requiring women's labor in that space. This was a considerable transformation, accompanied by an important silence. As subsequent chapters suggest, the labor performed inside domestic space during the collective period—and the early and largely unremarked exodus of men from farming that profoundly shaped women's working lives—were to remain as invisible in official post-Liberation narratives as they had been in stories of pre-Liberation bitterness.

3

Widow (or, the Virtue of Leadership)

In the summer of 1949, a few months after Liberation, Shan Xiuzhen received a summons. *The work team from outside, and the village head we had elected, were staying in the village school. The village head said, "The work team is calling you." I said, "You don't need to drag me." Even in the old society, I was basically not feudal. So I went.*

The primary school originally had been a Guan Gong temple. As I entered, I looked around. Why? I had been in that village for more than ten years and never been to this temple before. In the past, a woman who delivered food to teachers could only take it as far as the door. A woman who would enter a school belonging to others— what would such a woman be up to?

The new village leadership and Communist Party cadres did not take long to figure out that Xiuzhen had leadership potential. When the new state collected its first round of grain tax, her organizing skills enabled the village to turn in so much grain that the township government returned a portion of it to every household.[1] *From then on, they would call me every time they needed to do something. I said to them, "It would be more convenient to call a man to work with you." Dong Yuxiu said to me, "My good sister-in-law, what do you fear, working with us?" I said that I was not afraid. What she said was very pleasant to my ear. So I followed them, running around working.* By April of 1950, Xiuzhen had joined the Communist Party.[2]

This chapter explores how village women, supported and guided by cadres, helped to rearrange rural social space, introduce campaign time, and embody state initiatives in a localized, even personalized way. Later chapters take up the emergence of younger women activists (chapter 4), the mobilization of women as full-time field laborers (chapter 5), and the rise of rural women labor models to regional and national prominence (chapter 8). Each of these state-initiated projects targeted women as a distinct population to be mobilized, and women were crucial to the success of all of them. Participating in these projects, women changed their sense of who they were and what they might become. Sometimes they exulted in the transformation. Sometimes they expressed reluctance and anxiety. And sometimes they held stubbornly to older notions of virtuous conduct that turned out to be surprisingly compatible with what the new situation demanded of them.

Now, more than half a century later, the changes of the 1950s have been incorporated into local narratives and memories. One such local narrative is that of Cao Zhuxiang, who became a prominent regional labor model in central Shaanxi (Guanzhong). State initiatives worked through compromises with the local environment, gaining traction by appealing to locally understood norms and meanings. The presence of a local labor model, as well as her style of modelhood, meant that village involvement with new state projects also entailed the embrace of the familiar. Given the ferocity with which the Party-state denounced as "feudal" older requirements for proper womanly behavior, it is ironic that Zhuxiang's modelhood was enhanced by her personal circumstances as a virtuous widow who refused, even after Liberation, to remarry.

What the revolution did for rural women was to remove the stigma associated with "outside" labor, changing its context, structures of feeling, and rewards.[3] Such labor was no longer linked with family disaster, hardship, instability, and barely getting by. The People's Republic Party-state reorganized, valorized, and propagated a new gendered division of labor. Village social space was reconfigured. Schools and meeting grounds joined homes and private courtyards as places where women could appear, alone and in groups, and still remain respectable. Fields were first redistributed to women as well as men in a land reform campaign. Later, collectives included women in their membership. The fields rapidly became places where women were expected to labor with other women, rather than stealing out alone at night to furtively plow a crooked furrow, as Cao Zhuxiang had done.

Even as the new Party-state rearranged rural space, it also introduced a new temporality: campaign time. In the collective period, state temporality was not a remote property of national politics. Throughout the 1950s, formal state campaigns rearranged the daily groups in which farmers came together to labor in ever-larger collectives, providing a timetable for progressing from one to the next: labor exchange groups, mutual aid groups, lower and higher producers' cooperatives, and communes.[4] Campaigns were heralded by state slogans and intensive publicity, marked by the arrival of work teams and cadres from outside the village. In the weeks after a new campaign was introduced, local leaders and visiting cadres engaged farmers by means of discussion, persuasion, pressure, and mobilization, introducing changes in patterns of landownership, daily work patterns, taxation, and even marriage practices (discussed in the following chapter).[5]

A major feature of campaign time was the mobilization of women to participate regularly in field work. Women who had never worked in the fields, or had done so only when accompanied by male relatives at planting and harvest, began to go to the fields daily, usually in the company of other women. The gendered division of labor changed frequently, although gender itself always remained an important principle of organization. With the advent of higher producers' cooperatives in the mid-1950s, the workday was divided into distinct periods, each worth a defined number of work points, often followed by a required political meeting in the evening. The need to earn work points fundamentally altered how and with whom women spent their time, expanding women's networks and social influence.

Rearrangements of space and recalibrations of time were mandated in state pronouncements, but they were worked out through local relationships and practices, held in place by local understandings, and beset by local difficulties. From the inception of the People's Republic, state authorities at various levels made use of middle-aged women such as Zhuxiang, who were old hands at field work and willing to experiment with new agricultural techniques. By designating them as labor models, the Party-state introduced unfamiliar practices—from new fertilizers and seeds to mixed-gender work groups and countywide meetings—by encouraging villagers to associate them with locally known women and men.

Zhuxiang's story, as recounted by her and by many others in her village, requires a consideration of memory. Unlike most rural residents, labor models generated a paper trail, they were generally willing to be interviewed, and their communities welcomed inquiry into their accomplishments. Zhuxiang was the most eminent local face of the revolution in Village B, and villagers remember many of its changes through reference to her. People recall how she mobilized women to spin and weave in co-ops, and later to grow and harvest cotton in the collective. Collective labor in groups initiated, led, or supervised by Zhuxiang provided women an alternative social universe, a community of peers that helped them negotiate the difficult years after they married into the village. Much has been written about the role of architecture and of sacred sites as a repository for and stimulant to collective memory,[6] but little remains of such *lieux de memoire* in contemporary Chinese villages. And yet, memory is not only organized around inanimate monuments. A more transitory but still powerful spur to memory is the presence of locally prominent people. Labor models themselves, particularly if they are still alive, become "sites of memory" for their local communities, a sort of magnet for memory's filings, even at a distance of almost five decades. Zhuxiang, as labor model and as virtuous widow, was a central nexus in an unwritten web of relationships formed during the early years of the People's Republic, now accessible only through memory. Labor models embodied state goals but also often reconfigured them. Through their connections to other labor models, whom they met regularly at regional and national conferences during the collective period, they linked the village to a wider world of agricultural labor and social transformation. They were remembered as well by former government cadres who were assigned in the 1950s to work in villages, representing the wider nation to village women and vice versa. Although the social changes in which Zhuxiang played a prominent role have since been abandoned if not openly repudiated, in Village B and Weinan County her role in local history, her regional fame, and her connection with a larger political world remain a source of pride, a kind of cultural capital.

The Party-state provided the institutional context and public recognition that made Cao Zhuxiang an eminent local personage. Yet we miss much of what is important about this story if we think of "the state" as an abstract or external entity. Zhuxiang remained a resident of her marital village all her adult life, while becoming a Party member and a local official, a local embodiment of Party authority as well as an exemplar for women farmers. She enacted what Timothy Mitchell, speaking of a very different historical context, has called the "state effect."[7] By this he does not mean "an effect produced by the state," although the rural 1950s were rich in those. Rather he refers to the construction of a world that appears bifurcated between "individuals and their activities" on the one hand, and on the other "an inert 'structure' [the state] that somehow stands apart from individuals, precedes them, and contains and gives a framework to their lives." This binary, Mitchell continues, is created by daily practices: reorganizing space, establishing specific functions and hierarchies, supervising, and "the marking out of time into schedules and programs."[8]

Prior to 1949, the state was generally perceived as an external force bent on invasion and depredation of the local community. In the 1950s, perhaps for the first time, the creation of a Party-state order, and the social practices that gave shape to it, ran through rural communities and households in visible and memorable ways. A labor model's status as the embodiment of state virtue, even as she continued to reside in her rural community, made the production of a line between "state" and "society" a local project, extending even into domestic space. The state became a neighbor, perhaps even a member of the household. The state effect became of much greater concern to farmers than it had been under imperial rule or in the chaotic years of the Republic. The 1950s Party-state was different from the destructive yet weaker state formations that preceded it, in part because these practices—rearranging space, establishing hierarchies, organizing surveillance, recalibrating time—were located to an unprecedented extent in small rural villages, and carried out by local leaders such as Cao Zhuxiang. She inhabited, and in some respects embodied, the "diffuse and ambiguously defined zone" where the state effect was produced,[9] a sociocultural matrix of subjects and subjectifying practices.

Cao Zhuxiang was not the only person who produced a state effect in the households and work groups of Village B. Across central and south Shaanxi, male Party officials transferred down from the old liberated areas in the north, Women's Federation cadres recruited from cities and towns and deployed to villages, and local women activists developed by both these groups acted as agents of reorganization. This chapter interweaves the stories of Cao Zhuxiang and other rural women with the accounts of cadres assigned by the Women's Federation to do mobilization work in villages. These young women set out to transform women's place in village life through patient political work, one household at a time, convincing anxious or recalcitrant parents and in-laws that it was both respectable and advantageous to allow their young women to work away from the immediate supervision of kin. What they offered in return was the assurance that young women would work under the watchful eyes of respectable neighbors such as Cao Zhuxiang, returning with an income and with their virtue intact.

CAO ZHUXIANG AND THE CRUCIBLE OF BITTERNESS

Cao Zhuxiang has already appeared in the previous chapter, dodging bombs to procure medicine for her dying husband in the late 1930s and early 1940s, waiting out the final local battle of the civil war from a lookout perch in a date tree in her backyard. Her capsule biography is typical of those who came of age and married in the years of serious disruption by crop pests, disease, bandits, militarists, and invaders. Born into a farming family in 1918, Zhuxiang was betrothed and married into Village B in Weinan County at seventeen,[10] shortly after her father died in the cholera epidemic of 1932. The brideprice was twenty-four silver yuan. With her father's death, her family fortunes had become precarious enough that her meager dowry was paid for entirely with funds she had earned as a young teenager harvesting opium. Her marital family was scarcely more secure. Her husband had lost his father in a construction accident and his uncle in the cholera epidemic. Their widows, whom she called Mother (*Ma*) and Second Mother (*Erma*), lived with their children in a household with no adult men. Zhuxiang's new husband was three years younger than his bride. *In the past feudal society, my build was tall and nice. I was much taller than he was. We did not match each other. At that time, it did not matter whether or not you liked him.*[11]

As soon as she married, Zhuxiang began to do farmwork with her Second Mother. *That's why I was never really a daughter-in-law. For a daughter-in-law, there were many restrictions in better-off families. She was not allowed to go out of the door easily. But in my situation, I went to work in the field right away.* Her natal family was nearby, and her older brother and older sister's son often showed up to help. As chapter 2 recounted, her husband was snatched from the fields by a conscription patrol almost as soon as he was old enough to provide adult labor power, released after much family intervention, and assigned to a job in the county seat for two years. Then he returned home ill with tuberculosis and a tumor and died in 1941. His death left Zhuxiang a twenty-four-year-old widow with a three-year-old daughter, a six-month-old son, and a sizable medical debt. At that point she decided that she had to learn to farm on her own. She asked her brother to teach her the complete range of farming skills, including those not usually performed by women: plowing, raking, and leveling the land. After some years of practice she became an experienced farmer, growing wheat, melons, beans, cotton, and oil plants. She cleared the debts from her husband's illness and burial.

Aside from calling on her brother for help, Zhuxiang made a point of working alone in the fields so that no one could accuse her of improper conduct. *I didn't call in anyone, and didn't hire anyone. I was afraid that others would make idle talk. My neighbors said that my family had never before had such a capable person. In the fields I quietly threw myself into the work* [maitou kugan]. *I didn't gossip or waste time. So they had no basis for idle talk.*[12]

CLOTHING THE REVOLUTION

In spite of the bitterness of her formative years, Zhuxiang did not step forward spontaneously to take a role in the revolution. A month after the Communists arrived in her village in May 1949, a propaganda team assembled the villagers to elect a village head and a women's chair. Most adult men had fled the area, so the villagers who voted were the old, the young, the sick, and some women. *At the end they elected me. I was scared to death. The Guomindang, the Japanese, they had all elected cadres. It amounted to an attack on you.*[13] *You would just wait to see how they would punish you. So I took the children, locked the door, and went to my mother's house.* Eventually a cadre from the old Communist base area in north Shaanxi, the village head, and a woman friend persuaded Zhuxiang to return to Village B to take up the job of women's chair, over the objections of her brother.[14]

Zhuxiang's poverty and family circumstances, which had marked her as a dangerously exposed and vulnerable person in the old society, now made her available as a skilled leader of women—mustering them, at first, to do things they had always done, but for new purposes and in new work arrangements. Zhuxiang began her work as women's chair, under the direction of the Women's Federation,[15] by organizing village women to make shoes for the People's Liberation Army troops passing through during the summer and early autumn—one pair per household per day. As women finished the shoes she piled them in two empty rooms in a nearby village, and then borrowed a cart to move them to the riverbank where someone could receive them for the army.[16] Across Guanzhong, cooking, washing, and sewing—all domestic tasks performed by women—now became a priority of the new Party-state. In Heyang County, where Village G was located, the cadres mobilized women to provision 135,000 troops, a massive project requiring 600,000 *jin* of fresh bean sprouts, one hundred pigs, 426,000 *jin* of flour, almost four million kilograms of boiled water, and twenty-five welcome meetings, in addition to miscellaneous flowers, eggs, handkerchiefs, and letters asking after the soldiers' welfare.[17] Women in

Dali County lined up for a mile on both banks of the Zhi River one afternoon, washing and repairing thousands of items of clothing for the soldiers, and also worked with men to repair the roads over which the soldiers would pass.[18]

Women's troop support in Guanzhong was not without its glitches. Some cadres grew impatient with talking women into performing the work, and just levied contributions on them. Some women were unwilling to wash clothes for the soldiers, complaining that they had enough work to do in their own households.[19] Many of the goods given to the troops were recorded as "loans" from the masses,[20] and one can surmise that these requisitions were not always greeted joyously. The disciplined and courteous provisioning practices of the PLA troops, however, distinguished them from the numerous militarist and Guomindang troops that had terrorized the population before them.[21]

The events that led to Cao Zhuxiang's recognition as a labor model began in the spring of 1950, when more than two million people in Guanzhong were hard-pressed by a grain shortage.[22] The Party secretary of the district committee asked Zhuxiang what could be done in her village,[23] and she proposed organizing women to spin and weave for money, using cotton she had stored in her own house. The secretary offered her an interest-free loan of eighty yuan to invest in additional raw materials, and promised that the new supply and marketing co-op (*gongxiao she*) would sell any cloth the women could produce.

By the time Zhuxiang returned from her meeting with the Party secretary it was 11 o'clock at night, but she hurriedly summoned seven women she knew to a midnight meeting. Like Zhuxiang, they were all from households in which there were no adult male laborers or the men who remained were inadequate in some way. The first was a widow ten years older than Zhuxiang. The second had a mentally ill mother-in-law who was kept locked in a back room, a father-in-law who gambled compulsively and had given away his daughter to settle a gambling debt, and an absent husband who had been paid by a rich farmer during the Guomindang years to take his place in the army and had not yet returned home. She provided some of the household income by spending much of each day weaving in Zhuxiang's home.[24] The third, Zhuxiang's relative by marriage, had a husband in intermittent trouble with the law for petty thievery, card playing, and opium smoking. The husband of the fourth had been conscripted before 1949, and after he returned home he proved not very competent; he later jumped into a well and died. The crude and bad-tempered husband of the fifth woman was known for beating his own mother, although he did manage to do the farmwork. The opium-smoking husband of the sixth woman had sold the family's land. The seventh woman lived with her disabled husband, five of her twelve children, and the young wife of a nephew who was working in the county seat.[25] All these women knew how to spin and weave, and many had done so for the market.

The following morning Zhuxiang set out at first light to collect the promised eighty-yuan loan from the government. Then the women went to a market south of the village and purchased some thread. *We wouldn't even stop to eat. We set up three looms. I would light the coal oil lamp, climb up on the loom, and get the weaving done in three days. The village leaders all joked, "We are afraid you didn't sleep all night. Don't tire everyone out." An old man who lived nearby tied up two carts' worth and pushed it to the co-op. He calculated very clearly. Then we would cross the river and go to the small markets. There were many people selling thread at these small markets, so we would collect thread. The first time we sold cloth, we made several tens of yuan. I sent those eighty yuan over to the Party secretary. Secretary Liang said that we should put the money back into production, and solve the problem of people's livelihood. When I had time I would work in the fields, and when it was dark we would add an extra shift and make cloth.*[26] When they sold cloth, they set aside money to purchase more thread, then divided up the rest among households. If one member of the group was in particular need, they would advance her an extra share of the profits and pay her a bit less the next time, a procedure facilitated by their longstanding familiarity with each other's household situations.[27] The group not only made enough to support all of its members, but within a month had earned enough money to purchase eight *dou* of wheat.[28] As more and more women came to them and asked for advice, Zhuxiang returned to the Party secretary and secured additional start-up loans of two hundred yuan.[29]

By the time of the 1950 summer harvest, Zhuxiang's spinning and weaving group of seven had enlarged to twenty-one and transformed itself into a short-term agricultural mutual aid group, harvesting the wheat from eighty-nine *mu* of land. This freed up six men to work outside the village as hired harvest hands. It also, says one of the labor model documents, "broke the old habit of believing that women could not do farm work," although that belief was already mostly honored in the breach.[30] Then the group, designed to meet short-term needs, disbanded.

Organizing women's textile production co-ops was a promising strategy early in the new order,[31] building on skills that women had long used to help their households survive. Home textile production was not, however, of lasting interest to the Party-state, and collectivizing it never became a priority. Officials soon focused their attention on agriculture. As early as spring 1950, even before land reform, the national Women's Federation instructed its local branches to mobilize women for field work in labor exchange groups.[32] Spinning, weaving, and shoemaking once again became domestic affairs, hidden away at home and invisible for purposes of generating income or assessing women's actual labor burden.

DUNDIAN

While Cao Zhuxiang was moving into a position of leadership, novice women cadres from the world beyond the village were learning how to mobilize women like her across Shaanxi. Unlike the Guomindang regime that preceded it, the Communist Party-state established itself as a daily presence in rural areas, in part by billeting cadres from various organizations in farming households. This practice, which ranged in duration from a few months to a year, was called *dundian*, literally "to squat in a spot." Some male *dundian* cadres were sent down from the old base areas in the north to work in Guanzhong and Shaannan villages as agricultural technicians and Party political guides.[33] Creating networks and language for women, however, as well as the daily work of mobilizing them, was largely women's work. It was performed by a younger, less experienced group of cadres: women often barely out of high school (if they had gone to high school), trained and organized by the Women's Federation, and assigned to rural Shaanxi villages to live and work.[34]

One such young woman, Xu Nini, recalls, *How enthusiastic I was in those years. During the movement to lower rents and oppose tyrants, in south Shaanxi, I didn't sleep for three days and nights, mobilizing the masses. When leadership orders would come down, we would set out at two in the morning, five or six of us. I was the only woman. We carried backpacks and trekked for several tens of* li. *From Xixiang to Shahe was eighty* li *[twenty-seven miles]. We covered it in one day. On the second day we covered eighty* li *to Chenggu. On the third day we went to Hanzhong. I had my period, and my legs were rubbed raw from the paper. When we were on the road and got our periods, paper was issued for us to bring with us. Rural women used cloth, then washed and reused it.*

In each place we stayed one night, setting out again before dawn. We didn't know the road. There was one household in each valley. I went to all of them. I was determined. The mountains were high, but to join the revolution we had to overcome difficulties. Li Chengyuan was a big local bandit [tufei] *who had fled at Liberation. We were hoping to catch him. Now, when I think about it, I was very immature. I didn't even know what he looked like. At the time I thought that if I were murdered, it would be glorious. I didn't care how filthy it was, how dirty the people or the bedding was.*[35]

Dundian cadres were instructed to go to the fields to work with local women, eat and sleep in their homes (paying them a modest fee), mediate family conflicts, encourage them to take nighttime literacy classes, organize daycare for them, and talk to them about the importance of whatever political task was at hand.[36] They were to identify potential women leaders, convince them to take up leadership roles, train them in the necessary skills, support them if they met opposition, and recommend them for state recognition. Once a village woman was selected as a women's chair, she too entered the cadre training system, attending classes organized by the county and district Women's Federation branches.[37]

Women's Federation *dundian* cadres came from diverse backgrounds, but generally not from great privilege. Some had been revolutionaries for years, and had spent time in the north Shaanxi base area training as teachers or propaganda workers.[38] Others came from the areas of Shaanxi formerly controlled by the Guomindang. Some had been teachers or middle school students; others had struggled to receive a rudimentary education in an era when schooling for girls was still rare.[39] One cadre had briefly been the concubine of a Guomindang official before Liberation.[40] Another had worked the foot pedals at her uncle's flour milling shop, where she took refuge when her father tried to marry her to clear a banking debt. Cadre training offered her a way not to return home to a marriage she opposed.[41] In the rush to build a cadre presence in the countryside, many women who had received minimal education were recruited; those with a middle school diploma were regarded as intellectuals.[42] What all these new women cadres had in common was a commitment to liberating women. To them, this meant reducing women's dependence on men by bringing them out to work in the fields and raising their economic and social status.[43] After a brief training class devoted to the rudiments of Marxism-Leninism, the work of Mao, the history of Chinese women, and the history of the development of societies,[44] women were assigned to a rural post.

Life as a woman *dundian* cadre was not easy. In late 1949 and early 1950, the process of clearing bandits and rogue militarists from the countryside was not yet complete. It was dangerous for women cadres to go out alone. One bandit's last act before his execution was to stare at Zhao Feng'e, who was dressed like a boy, and threaten her.[45] Even after the countryside became more secure, the daily work routine was grueling. Material support was scant. Although the Women's Federation usually worked on specific projects under the direction of the provincial or prefectural Party Committee,[46] it was less prestigious and well-funded than many other official organizations. As one former Federation cadre, Li Xiuwa, wryly observed, *There was a saying that the labor union has power, the Youth League has money, but the Women's Federation has neither.*[47] There were no days off, and some women cadres hesitated even to take the customary rural noon nap for fear that the peasants would criticize them when they went on to call meetings late into the night.[48] Everything they did and said was scrutinized by villagers. A 1950 Women's Federation report expressed worry that the casual social behavior of some *dundian* cadres was creating a backlash among the locals: "Some women cadres engaged in horseplay or got on intimate terms with men cadres. This made a very bad impression on ordinary people, who were unwilling to let their daughters and daughters-in-law be close with women cadres. Women cadres should examine their behavior at all times, because this will not only affect the individual's work, but also affect women members of the masses who may not be able to go out to participate in work."[49]

The Party-state assigned *dundian* cadres to one campaign after another: land reform, decreasing rent and opposing local despots, resisting U.S. aggression and aiding Korea, eliminating illiteracy, propagandizing and implementing the Marriage Law, and establishing mutual aid groups and cooperatives.[50] Each of these national campaigns targeted the entire community, but the specific task of the Women's Federation cadres was to mobilize women to participate. In the very earliest projects undertaken by the new state—eliminating bandits and winning political loyalty from former soldiers in the Guomindang Army—Federation cadres made use of gendered differences in political loyalty, encouraging women to win over the men in their households. Liu Zhaofeng explains that *dundian* cadres like herself *mobilized women to explain things to their family: ask their husbands and sons to leave secrecy behind, come clean, confess the bad things they'd done to the government, and hand in their guns. We mobilized women to disclose whose families had guns.*[51] Promoting controversial policies by deploying women as political workers inside their own households soon became standard state procedure.

Dundian cadres had to develop new skills of their own, even as they encouraged peasant women to do the same. Liu Zhaofeng recounts a humiliating memory: *As a nineteen-year-old woman in 1950, joining the land reform was part of my learning process. I was asked to call women to attend a meeting and make speeches to propagandize the policies. I was on the stage talking to the women. I talked and talked and suddenly forgot what to say in the middle of my speech. I was so angry with myself that I burst into tears. How stupid my brain was! I memorized carefully but forgot what to say when I made the speech.*[52]

Cao Zhuxiang was not the only woman to have a horrified reaction when she was elected women's chair. Village women were generally reluctant to be elected as women's representatives, and their families were dubious about the effect on their reputations and time spent away from domestic work. The women themselves had no local leadership models other than the men who had been pressed into service and often abused as local unit heads under the Guomindang regime.[53] *Dundian* cadres spent hours sitting on the *kang* with village women, talking, listening, cajoling, persuading, and encouraging. As Wang Guihua put it, the young cadres were *looking for daughters-in-law, not daughters,*[54] because they wanted to recruit local cadres who were not going to leave the community upon marriage. Zhao Feng'e describes the process: *We women cadres could go to people's homes, take off our shoes, climb up on the* kang, *and stretch out our feet on the side of the warm* kang *of the mother-in-law or the daughter-in-law. Men couldn't do this. Heart-to-heart talks, mobilizing one household at a time—men didn't have the conditions to do this work. Every day I had a big task, making the rounds of quite a few households. I couldn't use direct propaganda down at the grassroots. On the one hand, in our villages, feudal power was a very serious problem. . . . On the other hand, previous anti-Communist propaganda had said that the CCP would permit divorce and take women away. . . . When I went into people's houses, I would talk about daily life. Is your daughter-in-law filial? How about your son? How is the health of the elders? Are your grandsons well-behaved? Where did your daughter marry out to? It was ordinary conversation. The main thing was to establish a close relationship. Some old ladies wanted to make me their goddaughter. That's how good our relationship was. I didn't do it, for fear of being criticized for establishing private relationships. . . . I would help around the house, even emptying the chamber pots for the old ladies. I would act as a sister to the young wives. I called the older people "mama" and "grandma," and the young wives "elder sister-in-law."*[55]

Even as they established family-style relationships with village women, cadres felt continual anxiety about their own families. One remembers interviewing model women cotton cultivators while she was eight months pregnant, balancing her notebook on her belly as she wrote.[56] Another attended a county meeting for cadres on the new grain policy only twenty-eight days after giving birth for the first time. *I was having my month of postpartum confinement [zuo yuezi], but I had to set an example. I thought, They have put me in charge of a township. How can I go down to the countryside and lead others if I don't understand the policy? I am a person of rather strong character. I don't want to show weakness. When the meeting was over, I went down [to the countryside] immediately. It was a dozen* li *[four miles] from where I lived. I found a pull cart and brought a temporary wet nurse and my child and my mother along with me. At that time my enthusiasm for work was very high. As soon as I got them settled in the afternoon, I shuttled back and forth between the township and the district. I left the child behind with the temporary wet nurse. She was a woman with a child who had a lot of milk and a fat baby. But at night she had no milk. My child kicked up a terrible fuss, but I didn't know. I had gone to the township to make arrangements.*

The next day, my mother arranged for someone to bring me a message that the baby had almost cried herself to death because she hadn't gotten anything to eat. I didn't know anyone and wasn't familiar with the place. Every time I met someone, I asked about a wet nurse, and I heard about someone who said she still had a bit of milk. I quickly brought my child over to her one-room house. She lived in the back half and I lived in the front half. I bought some meat for her, to make her milk come down. I also brought my mother over. I got things arranged for them, and I went to work.[57]

However harrowing this search for a wet nurse, bringing one's mother and child to a *dundian* site was an unusual measure to begin with, and was generally not permitted. After their fifty-six days of maternity leave, women cadres would leave their babies with a wet nurse or a relative.[58] Liu Zhaofeng recalls, *One month after I gave birth, I was riding a bicycle all day, looking everywhere for a nursemaid. I had three children, in 1954, 1956, and 1958. Two girls and a boy. We sent them to the home of the wet nurse for a year, and then brought them back for my mother-in-law to take care of. The oldest child stayed with her for one year. Then she came back and one of my relatives took care of her until she went to nursery school at three. The second child stayed with my mother-in-law for six years, and came back when she started school. The third child was taken care of by a former nursery school worker from the Women's Federation until he was three and went to nursery school.*[59] Discontinuous relationships with children were taken as a matter of course. As the Federation cadre Li Xiuwa observes, *When the women cadres came back, they could not recognize their chil-*

dren and their children could not recognize them. Sometimes you had to change wet nurses several times for one child. But women cadres overcame such difficult conditions without any complaint—first, because people were carrying out revolution wholeheartedly; second, because we could see that the lives of these women masses were so pitiful. If we women cadres didn't go to liberate them, who else would?[60]

LAND REFORM

Plans for land reform in Weinan were announced in spring 1950. The county Peasant Association was founded in May, and the first land reform cadre training class of five hundred was held in June. Women's Federation propaganda called on women to join in the land reform for the sake of their own liberation: "Only after the liberation of the working people as a whole can we women be liberated from feudal oppression. For example, buy-and-sell marriage was based on the feudal economic system. It does not exist in the Soviet Union because the working people became the masters of the country and do not treat women like oxen and horses. Thus, we have to make clear the relationship between the land reform movement and our women's liberation."[61]

By the time the campaign finally got under way in late 1950,[62] Weinan County's farmers were deep in another crisis. After the summer wheat harvest, it did not rain for more than two months. When the rain finally came in autumn, it caused spot flooding along the Wei River. By the spring of 1951, many villages were reporting food shortages, borrowing grain from each other, digging up their seed crops to eat, and even, in one township, asking the government to issue begging permits. In April 1951, reports of deaths from starvation and the sale of children came in from Fuping County, not far to the northwest of Weinan.[63]

This immediate crisis forced a tactical shift. Instead of seizing the assets of its wealthiest residents through land reform, the Weinan County government encouraged wealthy families to loan grain to poorer families at interest, assuring them that they would not receive an unfavorable class label as a result. The government also organized moneymaking sidelines; loaned wheat to the poorest farmers; distributed relief grain to the families of revolutionary martyrs, soldiers, and refugees; and advanced payment in foodstuffs to farmers against their future cotton crop.[64]

Land reform in central Shaanxi, which ran from October 1950 to the end of May 1951, was carried out entirely in this unpromising context.[65] Across Guanzhong, an estimated twelve thousand cadres were assigned to the land reform; in Weinan County alone, 1,439 cadres were deployed.[66] Work teams from outside the village took the lead, guiding local investigations and meetings to determine the class status of each village resident.[67] They had to distinguish between small numbers of absentee "despotic" landlords—for instance, Guomindang Army officers who resided elsewhere but owned large tracts of land in their home villages—and "native" landlords, often hardworking former famine refugees who had acquired enough land to hire farmhands and seasonal laborers.[68] Below the landlords were rich peasants. This group included small land rentiers who had a nonagricultural business and rented their land to others, and small land managers who lived on a portion of rent proceeds, but mainly were people who personally joined in the farm-work but also relied substantially on the labor of long-term hired farmhands. Be-low those were middle peasants, who usually owned an ox and several dozen *mu* of land and could basically support themselves. Poor peasants, too, had some land, and their lives depended on their own labor. Farmhands had neither land nor tools, and worked for others to support themselves.[69]

Village women, particularly those from poorer households, soon became an im-portant element in the political rituals of land reform meetings. At these meetings women first learned to "speak bitterness," the practice that did so much to shape the narratives on which this book draws.[70] As Feng Gaixia, a young activist, re-members it, *All the women sat together. Before the official meeting, people would talk about what they would say when it was their turn. We mobilized them. It was a slow process. After that they understood that the land reform meant overthrowing the land-lords who exploited the peasants. That is, we poor people wanted to be our own mas-ters. From now on, we will not be oppressed anymore, so we will not suffer bitterness or hardship as long-term hired hands* [changgong] *for the landlord, or* mangeda, *that is local dialect, meaning "maidservant." We were all mobilized by someone else to be-gin with.*[71]

Women had to be instructed in how to understand and narrate what had hap-pened to them in the past, and cadres had to be taught how to instruct them. A 1950 Women's Federation bulletin offered pointers gleaned from experience in neighboring Henan Province. Women must learn that it was not their fate to be poor; to think that way was superstitious. Old women, and husbands of all ages, needed to be convinced that young wives would benefit from attending meetings. Wives had to be taught not to obstruct husbands who were active in the land re-form. It was not enough that women had suffered: their understanding of that suf-fering had to be channeled and shaped. "Take the special bitterness that women have suffered and raise it so that it is understood in terms of class [*tigao dao jieji-shang lai renshi*]," cadres were told.[72] In this way, their bitterness could become pro-ductive and meaningful. Women reportedly could not be expected to have the same level of consciousness as that of men, but the land reform campaign could help iden-tify women from landless or land-poor families who could lead and participate in Women's Federation branches at the township level. Such women, elected as local women's chairs, remained in their homes and worked full time at farm and domestic labor. But from 1950 on, they could also be found at meetings of elected represen-tatives at the county level and above.[73]

Sometimes mobilization meant improvisation. Feng Gaixia comments, *The land reform was a new type of work and nobody knew how to do it. I remember among our group of women, some of them acted the part of landlords, and others practiced how to struggle landlords. It was cold, winter. In the evening, we struggled the land-lords. Aiya, how tall was I? The older man who headed the people's militia put his jacket on me and it was so long it reached down to here. I remember that they taught us songs to struggle the landlord: "You have land, you have fields, where are your crops? If the poor didn't labor and you had to depend on the crops alone, you'd have only dog farts to eat." Also, "The men in your family don't work, the women in your family don't weave, where does your money come from? Today you have to tell me."*[74]

Cadres like Wang Guihua found that mobilizing women to speak bitterness was relatively easy, because they were less entangled than men in local power relation-ships. *Men were more complicated, hard to mobilize. They were more educated and experienced, had seen more.*[75] Bringing women out into public activity, cadres found that women were less cautious than men about upsetting a nexus of obligations and power in which they had not been central participants, and also less suspicious of Party-state initiatives. A Women's Federation document urged organizers to build on women's strengths: "Because women remember their exploitation better and are rather single-minded, they do better in telling their sufferings at struggle meetings."[76] Women's Federation cadres like Xu Nini noticed that men and women articulated their grievances differently. *Women in struggle meetings cried on stage. Men didn't. In confiscation and distribution, we mobilized women to participate. It was very im-portant to choose the right ones, to find women who had been very oppressed. They were very good speakers who spoke very concretely. They were usually in their twen-ties, newly married, not unmarried. We also had some middle-aged and older women. Married women were more mature and had been more oppressed.*[77] Women who had been brought into families as child daughters-in-law (*tongyangxi*) were often par-ticularly willing to speak out against the landlords,[78] as were middle-aged women in their forties and fifties who had been maids or laborers. Liu Zhaofeng remem-bers, *They cried and the audience cried too. Some former child daughters-in-law of landlords talked about having no clothes to wear in the winter time, how they ground the landlords' wheat and looked after their children and worked overtime in their homes.*[79] Inexperienced *dundian* cadres sometimes found that they had to restrain older women in speak bitterness meetings from becoming so agitated that they wanted to physically harm the landlords.[80]

The class labels assigned through the land reform did not always correlate neatly with the situations of village women, and the Women's Federation reminded local cadres that marriage could complicate a woman's class status. Poor peasant girls who had been sold to the rich as child brides, concubines, or servants should not be treated as landlords or rich peasants unless they had "lived the same lives as their husbands for three years. If they have worked hard and lived hard lives, they should still be considered as having the class status of their original families." Landlord daughters who had been married off to poor people after Liberation "should be considered working people."[81] Such instruction left ample room for local understandings of an individual woman's suffering, and local norms of virtue, to affect assignment of class labels.

Cao Zhuxiang's participation in land reform went well beyond speaking bitterness. Under the guidance of *dundian* cadres, she and other activists raided the home of a local leader of the religious group Yi Guan Dao, denounced by the new Party-state as a reactionary and potentially subversive organization.[82] *There was a double wall in the house, and they hid the head of the Yi Guan Dao behind the wall. A hole this big next to the stove was covered with a reed mat. After dark they would have activities, and during the day he would stay in the house. We did not know where they were hiding him. That night a few of us women backbone cadres secretly slipped off to a big persimmon tree at the entrance to Qiao Village. As soon as the whistle blew, we all climbed out of the tree and rushed in. We started to search the house. There were lots of things in that room. Gold, silver, money, and valuables. They were involved in counterrevolutionary activities.*[83]

For Zhuxiang, an abstract class label took on visceral meanings when she entered the home of a landlord and compared the humble food provided to her by the land reform work team with what the landlord ate. *The team head sent food to the house: steamed bread made of black flour, a plate of turnips, and a plate of hot peppers. I ate over here, and the landlord's family ate over there. The whole family was sitting on the* kang, *eating wheat cakes [*guokui*] this thick and this big. I asked them, "When did you move your stuff [i.e., wealth] out?" The younger brother snorted through his blocked-up nose and said, "I don't have it anymore." He tried to go out, but Old Xu saw him coming and fastened and locked the door. These people and their children were all very fierce. They could have defeated us. The landlord's children started to fight with me, and only after a few militia were called did they go down one by one.*[84]

Raiding a landlord's house, engaging in political cooperation with some men and openly confronting others, all were unprecedented experiences for Cao Zhuxiang. In retrospect, however, she does not speak about these activities as particularly important transitions. Perhaps that is because for all its political importance, the land reform did not effect a massive transfer of resources in central and south Shaanxi, where even the landlords were relatively poor. Zhuxiang comments, *When we had a big meeting to decide on people's status, some landlords got the news early and transferred their property. We were left with just the tattered [*polan*] landlords, like the one who opened a flower shop in the county seat two years before Liberation. But then he came back and became a tattered landlord. He had nothing in his house. He was struggled against several times. We couldn't get hold of the real landlords. People like him didn't own much, but they got the label of landlord.*[85] In Village Z as well, activists failed to find a class enemy whose property could help ease shortages for the poor. One landlord *didn't even have a collar on his shirt. His shoes were also pieced* *together. That kind of landlord was really pitiful. They just ate sweet potato leaves every day. They were labeled landlords because they had bought a lot of hill land in various places. But they had no crops near their houses. Such a pitiful landlord was called a landlord, while a rich landlord was also called landlord. Those rich landlords, oh my mother, they hired employees. There were no such well-off landlords here.*[86]

At the beginning of the land reform campaign, landlords and rich peasants together owned only 13 percent of Guanzhong land. In all, only 12 percent of all farmland was redistributed, with the poorest third of the population receiving about one additional *mu* (.15 acres) of land apiece.[87] In Cao Zhuxiang's village, one household out of forty-two in her immediate neighborhood (east and west village) received the landlord label. The larger administrative village of which it was a part had only four landlords, mainly of the "tattered" variety. In all, four or five households received land. Zhuxiang was classified as a lower-middle peasant, receiving farm tools but no land. At the campaign's end, the average per capita landholding in Village B was three to four *mu*.[88]

The significance of assigning class labels, however, did not lie solely in resource distribution. The label of "poor peasant" now catapulted a family to the top of the social order, even if it did not make them substantially richer. Still, the valence of the word "poor" did not change overnight. In Village Z, Liu Dongmei's in-laws refused the label of "poor peasant," fearing that others would laugh at them, and asked to be assigned the status of "lower-middle peasant" instead.[89] Likewise Yang Guishi's mother in Village G, a proud widow with an iron will, was horrified when her teenage son came home with two sacks of confiscated grain that the work team had distributed to him as "fruits of victory." She promptly hit him and ordered him to return them. Eventually the chair of the peasant's association gave the family an iron shovel instead.[90] Politically active peasants like Shan Xiuzhen had other reasons for rejecting the label "poor." Given the opportunity to self-report class status, the new Party members in her village declared themselves middle peasants, even though no one had enough land to qualify, because they did not want to be allocated land that should go to those still poorer than they.[91]

When land deeds were issued, other conflicts emerged.[92] Although land was assigned to every man, woman, and child in a household,[93] land deeds were issued to the family. Party-state policy stipulated that the names of all adult men and women should appear on these deeds, but in many villages across Shaanxi, only the names of the men appeared. In Village Z, this set off conflict between Women's Federation cadres and local Party authorities. Recalling a long-ago argument, He Gaizhen invokes the revolutionary concept of *fanshen*, literally "turn over the body," which has the extended meaning of casting off economic and political oppression and assuming full citizenship: *What is our fanshen after all? When people were signed onto the land deeds, men were signed on. Women should also have been signed on. We women had no rights to the land. Only men had those rights. That would have been equality, equality of men and women. But the district secretary never allowed women to be signed on. The district secretary shouted and shouted.*

According to Chair Zhao, the Women's Federation district cadre, that's why she cried and fought with the district secretary. She cried so hard that later her eyes were all swollen. Afterwards she told me about it. Later I said to the district secretary, "What Chair Zhao said is correct. If you are raising women's consciousness, what are you going to raise it with? You say that women have consciousness, that women have fan-shened and hold up half the sky.[94] *But we still haven't fanshened. The land deed is all about men's rights. Women have no rights there. She quarreled with you to make you see this. Her eyes are swollen from crying. For what? This is to fight for women's half of the sky, for women's political rights."*[95] In late 1952, the provincial Women's Federation told its local branches to suggest that local leaders follow provincial guidelines and write women's names on the deeds issued to the household.[96] The language of the directive—suggesting that local male leaders follow state policy—hints at the frustrations of representing the interests of women within a state apparatus that was not always paying attention.[97]

Ironically, land reform obscured the crucial role played by women's spinning and weaving in the survival of Shaanxi households. At a 1950 meeting of Women's Federation cadres from around the region, for instance, participants mentioned that when class labels were given out, some women weavers had been counted as "the main labor power of the family." This violated Party-state regulations, it was explained; "main labor" was supposed to refer to agricultural production. Women who spun and wove as their main economic activity could be classified as laborers, but only women who farmed for four full months in a year could be counted as agricultural laborers. Perhaps this rule protected some poor spinning and weaving households from a richer class label. At the same time, however, it directed attention away from the contribution of women's nonfarm labor to household income, beginning a long process in which women's home cloth production would not be counted as remunerable labor.[98]

Women were crucial to the political confrontations that inaugurated land reform, but the reform itself had paradoxical effects on women. It counted them in land allotments, but did not always name them on land deeds. Women were called upon to speak bitterness to the landlords about general exploitation as well as gender-specific abuse, but their gender-specific labor as textile producers was rendered invisible. In one respect, however, land reform changed women's lives in a direct and unambiguous way: it began to provide them with new ways of thinking about themselves and their capabilities. *Dundian* cadres like Liu Zhaofeng, propelled by revolutionary enthusiasm, learned to make village space their own, day or night. *When the meeting ended at one or two in the morning, we were not afraid at all, and walked the five or six* li *back home alone, with only a stick in our hands. When I recall this I feel I was bold then, that now I would feel afraid. The revolutionary spirit at that time was so strong.*[99] For peasant women the change was equally profound. Shan Xiuzhen, who had been fearless well before the revolution touched her community, now had an expanded vocabulary to explain her actions and her virtues: *I was the chair of the township peasant association. I ran around outside the home from morning till night. The landlord said I was a mad person. He didn't understand liberation, what "standing up" was.*[100] *Before this, could you know you were a human being? If three or five men were standing there and you walked by, you had to go around them, because if we women passed in front of them, we brought bad luck to them.*

I was afraid of nothing. There were wild animals in the mountains, but I never saw them. I didn't go by car at night when I went back to Tongguan from meetings in Xi'an. I walked directly to Tongguan, into my cotton field. I walked the last forty li [thirteen miles] by myself, starting at two o'clock in the morning. When I got here, the sun was just coming up. I walked by myself on the road. There were no wild animals.[101]

MUTUAL AID GROUPS
AND THE HAZARDS OF LEADERSHIP

From late 1950 to the end of 1953, Cao Zhuxiang's village experimented with mutual aid groups, in which farming households kept their land but pooled their labor in an organized way.[102] Although establishing mutual aid groups in rural areas was a top priority of the Party-state, this was a rocky process of false starts and quarrels. Zhuxiang was the head of most of the groups and a central figure in the painstaking work of devising arrangements, analyzing their failures, and trying again. In the spring of 1951, many of the villagers organized a labor exchange team, with men in one team and women in another. The team went from one plot of land to another, working one family's holdings at a time. Men hauled fertilizer to the fields, and women hoed. But the group had no way to reward people differentially according to how hard they worked, and so before long the process was abandoned and only her core group of seven women continued to work together. Toward the end of 1951 Zhuxiang tried again, with six small groups of men and six of women. Again there were problems. Some households did not want women working for them, fearing that they would do the job inadequately.[103] When women went to hoe the land, men would also show up to hoe it, and then arguments would break out over who had completed the job and who should get credit for it. Conflicts within families proliferated. In an attempt to overcome these gender wars, Zhuxiang reorganized the seventy-three men and women from thirty-eight households into an "associated group" divided into eight smaller units. Households joined as a group, and men and women worked together. But labor power and livestock were distributed unevenly among the groups, leading to delays in production. It took until the end of 1952 to put together a stable mutual aid group of thirty-six households, with Zhuxiang as its head.[104]

In spite of these difficulties, the experiments yielded impressive results in the production of wheat, cotton, and millet, as well as in collecting fertilizer, digging wells, and caring for livestock. Zhuxiang's group was also lauded for social and political achievements: helping to plow the fields of army dependents, writing letters to support and encourage troops in Korea, taking the lead in selling grain to the state, collecting garbage, vaccinating members, sending all school-age children to school, ending the arrangement of marriages and the ill-treatment of daughters and daughters-in-law, and hanging up portraits of Chairman Mao in each household. (One man was quoted as commenting that a picture of Mao—and presumably the practices associated with him—did more to improve a family's fortunes than a picture of the God of Wealth.)[105]

The township government invested in the success of Zhuxiang's team, lending its members 4,750 *jin* of wheat during the 1952 spring grain shortage.[106] This sort of support paid off, because successful groups such as hers then became an asset to the Party-state, which was working to draw suspicious peasants in other villages into mutual aid groups.[107] Zhuxiang's success also aided the Women's Federation project of drawing more women into the fields to hoe crops, plant trees, select cotton seeds, carry fertilizer, and join in the summer harvest and winnowing.[108] The Women's Federation publicized the lessons that should be drawn from Zhuxiang's group: "After Liberation, under the leadership of the party, she came to understand why she had suffered before, because of Guomindang reactionary control and oppression by the landlord class. She also understood that to *fanshen* one must go out and labor and become the master. Therefore she joined every movement actively and led women in it."[109] The work of attracting peasants into such groups, and involving women in production, continued across Guanzhong well into 1953.[110] By that time Zhuxiang's mutual aid group had an elaborate governing structure and was divided into subgroups, each with a head and vice head and regular procedures for meetings, production planning, labor contests, work-point distribution, collective newspaper reading, childcare by older people, and criticism/self-criticism.[111]

When Cao Zhuxiang and other rural women ascended to local leadership positions, they entered an unfamiliar, hazardous zone where local village tensions intersected with the fraught and volatile politics of the Party-state. In the early 1950s, the ensemble of class labels, mutual aid groups, grain purchase, *dundian* cadres, and local women's leadership extended the blurry boundaries of the state into village households. Any action a woman leader took could make a local enemy; any local tension could be incorporated by outside cadres, whether unwittingly or with malice, into a higher-level conflict. Women's entry into public space, conventionally portrayed as an emergence from darkness into revolution's sunshine, cast its own shadows.

Stories of political recrimination are painful for women to tell. Quarrels and scheming inside a community, and their links to a wider polity full of conflict, are difficult to reconstruct. Years have passed; many of the local participants have died;

work teams sent from outside the community have long since departed and dissolved. Accounts of conflict, even more than other kinds of accounts, are full of confusing and contradictory detail. The likelihood is high of getting it wrong, mistak-
ing a partial story for the whole, becoming an unwitting participant in ongoing
tensions. Painful stories told by women leaders remind us that some aspects of the
past exert continued emotional force in the present, although what might once have
been talked about as a class struggle is now retold in the language of virtue. Such
tales compel attention for both the residual sense of injury they express and the powerful claims to vindication they make.

Cao Zhuxiang had not been a leader for very long when she faced her first set
of accusations. During the 1952 experiments with mutual aid groups, a work team
was sent to Village B to supervise. Zhuxiang had enemies by this time, who quickly
moved to establish an alliance with the newly arrived outsiders. The official account
of agricultural collectivization in Weinan, published in 1993, includes a brief, sanitized account of this episode. It reads in full: "Just at this time, a minority of backward members of the masses spread rumors, stirring up trouble, spreading this piece
of doggerel around the village group: 'Boxiao's pen, Wenxiu's mouth, Zhuxiang's labor modelhood, and the leg of Chuanwa's mother.' It mocked them for 'showing off
and seeking the limelight,' and almost caused the dissolution of the united group.
But with the concern and assistance of every level of Party committee, first they restored the mutual aid group, and subsequently carried out reorganization."[112]

The official story implies that the conflict is simply one of "backward" village
members, perhaps jealous of Zhuxiang and her leadership cohort, causing trouble
on purely personal grounds. Behind their satirical jingle about legs, mouths, pens,
and labor models, however, was a broader ripple of resistance to the incipient state
project of collectivization. Across the Guanzhong region, where Village B was located, the attempt to establish year-round mutual aid groups, begun in late 1950,
was slow to catch on. A year later, Weinan County had only sixty-three households
in fourteen year-round groups, although the number of harvest-season groups exceeded three thousand.[113] By late 1952, almost half of the peasants in eleven Guanzhong counties were in mutual aid groups, but fewer than a fifth of the groups were
year-round.[114] Throughout 1953, the Party leadership of Weinan Prefecture was still
issuing directives on how to run the groups, as well as running training classes for
leaders. Party documents mentioned that some peasants had tried to dissolve the
mutual aid groups. They referred obliquely to "the spontaneous power of the small
peasant economy" and the need to "educate people on the memories and comparisons of production, life, and popular control before and after Liberation, and con-
solidate faith in the mutual aid groups road."[115] Apparently some peasants, having
acquired their own land, wanted nothing more than to farm it with members of their
own households.

When a complex, unevenly executed state initiative such as this one met local village relationships, political resentment took on personal, even intimate, dimensions. Zhuxiang's account of the "pen, mouth, labor model, legs" incident, which is considerably racier than the official version, depicts political rivalry entangled with sexual betrayal. Wuliu, the chair of the Peasant Association and Zhuxiang's ally, was apparently so distressed by attacks on him that he successfully took his own life by jumping in a well. But in Zhuxiang's telling, the root cause of the accusations and of Wuliu's suicide was the adultery of his wife, whose paramour dreamed up the accusations. Wuliu's suicide triggered an investigation, and Zhuxiang's name was cleared.

Zhuxiang does not say explicitly what she learned from this episode, but the way that she frames it is instructive. As a woman in authority, she was assumed to derive her power from someone else—"Boxiao's pen" or "Wenxiu's mouth." And on any side of a political conflict, power could always be undermined by a woman's unvirtuous acts. Wuliu had been driven to suicide by a convergence of specious political innuendo and his wife's sexual disloyalty. The practice of virtue, Zhuxiang might well have concluded, was a necessary minimum to protect one's reputation and political efficacy.

Cao Zhuxiang's organizing efforts were most successful when they visibly improved the lives of her group members. Zhuang Xiaoxia, whose mother-in-law was one of the seven in the original co-op, recalls, *My mother[-in-law] followed Secretary Cao. They would have meetings every day until the middle of the night. When they worked, no one brought up the state* [gongjia]. *We just wanted to improve our own position.*[116] Zhuxiang's mutual aid group decided to make bean curd to sell, an activity that led to a much-recounted local conflict with farmer Dang Yingjie and his wife. As Zhuxiang remembers it, *That woman sabotaged things. She would go out and talk nonsense, singing a tune to rival ours* [gen za chang duitai xi]. *Dang Yingjie sold his bean curd privately, while we sold it as a group. Our bean curd was good, and we didn't mix the dregs in with it. He made rotten bean curd and said it was mine. People bought that bean curd, and he said that Cao Zhuxiang made it.*

Dang Yingjie was a bare-stick commander [a general without soldiers]. Nonsense came out of his mouth all day long. He committed a few petty thefts, but he didn't do any serious harm. In the end, everybody knew that my bean curd was firm. A work group came in. They investigated and discovered that he was sabotaging a mutual aid group. They locked him up for a few days. His family had parents and children in need of support, so they just educated him for a bit. Later he didn't dare to do it again. He tried to make fools of us, but he couldn't stop us.[117]

Dang Yingjie and his wife are no longer present to explain what motivated them to engage in this act of culinary and commercial sabotage. Speaking more than half a century later, a man in Zhuxiang's village refers to a "class enemy" sabotaging the bean curd production,[118] but Dang had been labeled a poor peasant, not a class enemy. Perhaps he feared competition from a more competent group of bean curd producers. Perhaps he worried that their collective organization would give them a market advantage—a worry that might not have been rooted in political hostility to collectivization per se. Perhaps irritations of a purely personal nature were at play. But Zhou Guizhen, one of the young woman village activists mentored by Cao Zhuxiang, believes that the root of the problem was Dang's resentment of the emergence of a local woman with resources and authority. Guizhen's account returns to the theme of "No one is there": *They were grinding the bean curd and putting salt in. As soon as you put salt in, the bean curd won't set. The message [about Zhuxiang's bean curd operation] was, "You're a woman, you have to take the responsibility." They were trying to harm you, to ruin you, to make it so you couldn't do something successfully. In the end, the old lady still did it successfully.*

Gao Xiaoxian: Why did they want to ruin her?

Zhou Guizhen: Well, you're a woman, without anyone [meaning, without a man] at home.[119]

In 2006, we assembled three of Cao Zhuxiang's younger colleagues to make a timeline of major events of the 1950s, with the Chinese zodiac signs for the birth years of their children as memory aids. We began by asking them to name major events between Liberation and the advent of economic reforms in the early 1980s. They named the bean curd sabotage caper right alongside major national initiatives such as land reform and mutual aid teams. Therein, perhaps, lies a clue to change in the 1950s. State initiatives took on meaning, and are retained in memory, when they collided with idiosyncratic local circumstances and personal relationships. At the same time, Dang Yingjie provided the required local resistance and obstructionism necessary to a really satisfactory narrative of Zhuxiang's determination and integrity. Whether he was a class enemy, a feudal-minded male chauvinist, or simply an aggrieved and cranky local entrepreneur, the history of mutual aid groups in Village B is never recounted without him. In the process, the bean curd, like Cao Zhuxiang, has taken on an iconic quality: a substance in which hard work, honesty, and high-quality cooperative production assumed material form.

WOMEN AND THE HOUSEHOLD STATE EFFECT

In October 1953, the Central Committee of the CCP issued a resolution that proved deeply unpopular with farmers. "Unified purchase and marketing" (*tonggou tongxiao*) of grain, later expanded to include cotton and vegetable oil, was intended to stabilize prices and supplies by restricting nonstate markets in agricultural commodities.[120] Rather than storing good harvests against future need, peasants were permitted to keep just enough grain for their own consumption, delivering the remainder to the state at a fixed purchase price.[121] Often grain purchased from farmers after the harvest was sold back to them the following spring.[122]

In Shaanxi as elsewhere, farmers were reluctant to hand over their grain, and local cadres were unwilling to cooperate.[123] Echoing peasant anxieties, cadres in the Baoji area of south Shaanxi asked, "If the peasants sell their grain, what will they eat in the future?" Compounding the difficulty, purchasing stations were understaffed and storage space was limited. Local government and Party organizations found themselves renting extra rooms from peasant households to store the grain.[124]

Rural cadres at every level were assigned the task of finding out how much people were actually producing and how much they had available for sale. Then they were responsible for convincing, encouraging, pressuring, and cajoling peasants, one household at a time, to sell their grain.[125] But not every household could meet its sales quota; some did not farm well, some consumed everything they grew, and surpluses, where they existed, were small. One village activist commented that she much preferred going to other people's villages to do this work, because convincing one's own neighbors was particularly difficult. *Imagine that: take out your grain and sell it to the state. That was not easy. We worked all winter on snowy and rainy days.*[126] With hunger a very recent memory, villagers' resistance was determined, albeit covert. He Gaizhen asks, *Who was willing to take out their own grain? Everyone said he had no grain. Later some grain was discovered and some was not. In a team, if someone had grain, people persuaded him to speak out. If he spoke out, the state could buy his grain and then distribute it to those who had none.*[127]

Rural women often controlled the household grain supply. Whether they were more recalcitrant than the men or more willing to cooperate, they became an important target of mobilization in their own right. *Dundian* cadre Xu Nini remembers doing this work: *The woman herself was in charge of the household. She had some ways of thinking that were more difficult to deal with than the men. She was familiar with her household, as the housewife in charge of food grain. She always wanted to have more, so sometimes her husband would want to sell, but she couldn't accept it.*

First we got to the bottom of things. If you had it, you had to sell it. If you didn't have it, we wouldn't ask for it. So the masses supported us. There was one man who came and hung on to my leg, but I was confident that justice was on my side, because the people had already understood what his situation was. He had a surplus. When he hung onto my leg, it was to show that he would not sell the grain, and also to threaten you, and to try to influence others, showing them who was fierce, who was in the right. If he made such a fuss, maybe the others wouldn't sell. That's what he was trying to accomplish. But the others didn't follow him. In that family, the woman was a bit better. She was one of our activists. It was the man who was unreasonable.[128] Whenever a woman could be convinced that state goals and the well-being of her family were not in conflict, the policy had a better chance of succeeding without coercion, house-to-house searches, or divisive finger-pointing among households who were also being exhorted to work together in co-ops. When a woman supported unified purchase and sales, the state effect could extend to the level of the household.

MODELING LABOR, MODELING VIRTUE

One day in 1950, just after Cao Zhuxiang had founded the spinning and weaving group, a county cadre came to her house. He praised her neat rows of crops and the meticulous way she cared for her livestock. *"Your livestock, the way you cut grass and dump dirt for them: I've gone to many houses, and the work is not done this carefully. The dirt clods are all very small." He said, "Even your mule leads a good life." I joked with him and said that I washed the dirt and spread it under the livestock. He said, "You meet the requirements for a labor model. You even exceed them."*[129]

In 1951, Zhuxiang was selected as a labor model by the Northwest Region organization of the Women's Federation. Shan Xiuzhen had been similarly honored a few months earlier.[130] At a county labor model meeting, Zhuxiang was presented with a pickaxe, a shovel, a hoe, and a mug. She turned the farm tools over to her mutual aid group, but kept the mug for her own use.[131] In 1952, she became the second Party member in the entire township.[132] Her mutual aid group, and a similar group led by Xiuzhen in Tongguan, were mentioned by the provincial Women's Federation as models.[133] As collectivization proceeded, Zhuxiang became chair of a co-op and a Party secretary.[134] She continued to be selected as a labor model, and later became known as one of the "Five Silver Flowers," provincial heroines of cotton production. In official accounts Zhuxiang's initial reluctance to become a leader, her flight from the village to avoid becoming the women's chair, disappears. Instead we are told, "[Her] hardworking and upstanding style was discovered by the people's government, she became head of the village women, she *fanshen*ed, was deeply moved, enthusiastic and active about every kind of work, protected every policy of the Party and government, respected the laws of the government, and took the lead in responding to every government call."[135]

But by her own account, it was not easy for Zhuxiang to learn to be a public figure. Encountering strangers, particularly male strangers, at her first countywide meeting for land reform activists in 1951, she felt very much adrift. *They asked me to join the meeting. It scared me. I said, "I won't go. I am a woman." There were still very few women cadres. No matter what they said, I wouldn't go. But they insisted that I go. You don't know how embarrassed I was to be at that meeting. This was the first time I had left the village.* (This is unlikely, given her forays to buy medicine for her husband before 1949. But it underscores how unprecedented this experience was for her.) *At the meeting, I did not dare to sit in front of people. I carried a small bench and sat on the side. Dangting, the Women's Federation chair in charge of our township, didn't leave me. She was afraid I would secretly run back home. I took a look and saw that there were very few women. It was not like the countryside.*

I was very feudal. When they called us to eat, I took a piece of steamed bread and went back and sat in the room to eat. I didn't dare go in among those people. Bureau Director Li said that wouldn't do, that I was feudal. No matter what he said, I wouldn't go there. He got me a piece of stuffed steamed bread, a bowl, and a few vegetables. I took it and sat in my place.[136]

Zhuxiang gradually learned to talk to others, particularly after she was chosen as a district labor model and began attending meetings in Xi'an and elsewhere. At every stage, the support and advice and sheer presence of *dundian* cadres, from the Women's Federation and other Party-state organizations, were crucial. Behind these cadres, directing and funding them, was a central leadership determined to establish its presence in local communities, in part by supporting the development of women leaders.[137]

In official materials, models were typically lauded for their hardscrabble origins and suffering in early life, allegiance to the Party after 1949, technical skill, political awareness, and contribution to current campaigns. Cao Zhuxiang, the records tell us, consistently made connections between the local production process and the national political situation, whether that meant preparing care packages for the soldiers in Korea or selling cotton to the state.[138] She worked to develop Party and Youth League members and to mediate disputes. A handwritten piece on Zhuxiang, probably written in 1954, has her leading the villagers to repair wells, inspiring laggards by invoking China's international role: "Some people said that the weather was too cold. . . . At that time, Cao Zhuxiang said bravely, 'The Volunteer Army beat the American devils in a world of ice and snow, without any fear of death. They protected our good life. Now Chairman Mao has called us to dig wells and prevent drought in order to increase output. How can we be afraid of cold weather? We must overcome difficulties and struggle against the weather in order to complete the wells.' With her encouragement, people expressed the opinion that, 'We won't lower our head because of difficulties. We should increase our production in order to support the Volunteer Army.'"[139] The document describes how Zhuxiang organized a village "patriotic pact" to complete the summer wheat harvest, and then learned and applied advanced techniques of seed selection, planting, hoeing, and pest prevention. It concludes with an account of her concern about "current affairs, political study, and productive knowledge," which led her to organize group newspaper readings and encourage her group members to attend winter literacy classes.[140]

Perhaps most important for the Party-state's rural goals, labor model stories put a local face on the determination to collectivize. A 1953 report on Zhuxiang's mutual aid group gave a very detailed account of its achievements, and then mentioned that the members of the group were in debt to the team and still extremely poor. One member commented plaintively, "I know that the co-op has a future and many benefits. I also hear what Chairman Mao has to say. It is just that when I go home there is nothing to eat."[141] As a labor model, Zhuxiang was meant to embody the daily practices and new forms of organization that might enable her neighbors to leave poverty behind.

Farming skill was not enough to make a woman an effective leader. She had to be beyond gossip and above reproach, a woman who could command the respect of her neighbors.[142] Cao Zhuxiang's status as a revolutionary labor model would not have been possible without a much older figure of model womanly behavior: the virtuous widow. Marriage in rural China has been and is generally still exogamous and patrilocal; women marry into the villages of their husbands, and in the 1950s co-resided with their parents-in-law. The virtuous widow is a powerful figure in Chinese popular ethics, local history, and fiction, refusing to remarry after her husband's death in order to bring up her children properly and care for the parents of her dead husband.[143] Dating back at least to Mencius (fourth–third century B.C.E.), who features his own widowed mother in his writings as an exemplar, the virtuous widow was a stock figure in Qing- and Republican-era gazetteers, with local examples listed as a source of pride.[144] The virtuous widow had a doppelganger in prerevolutionary popular culture: the lascivious widow, whose dubious conduct was expressed in the old saying "Gossip hangs around a widow's door." In the 1950s, when the objective was to pull women out of the domestic sphere and into collective agricultural production, a move that jostled uneasily against village notions of respectability, the labor model doing the persuading also had to be a model of probity. Here Zhuxiang was exemplary.

Initially, when her husband died in 1941, Zhuxiang's brother had persuaded her not to remarry because she had two young children and a mother-in-law to care for. Zhuxiang did not say whether she and her brother were aware of the more than 1,350 virtuous widows in late imperial Weinan County who had been honored by having their names published in the 1892 gazetteer, some with brief accounts of their heroic efforts to care for their families. Nor does she mention ever having seen the memorial arches to widows that dotted the county's landscape, at least twelve of which were listed in that same work.[145] But her brother was quite clear on her duty to raise her son to adulthood, no matter what—and, he added, the members of her husband's lineage would not push her out precisely because she had a son. Bringing a new husband into her dead husband's family ("calling in a son-in-law") seemed to her impossible; she had watched another family in the village try to do so, and they had faced considerable social embarrassment and opposition. Nor was her decision merely a function of family and village opinion. She felt strongly that she wanted to watch out for her own children and that she did not want people gossiping about her. For Zhuxiang, this reasoning remained unchanged by the advent of a new regime or the new leadership roles in which she found herself. Here is how she explained it to us, when questioned by Gao Xiaoxian:

Gao Xiaoxian: Just after Liberation, you were so young. You became the women's chair and studied the Marriage Law. At the time, did you think about trying to fight for your marriage rights, and find another [husband]?

Cao Zhuxiang: I had no intention of doing that.

Gao Xiaoxian: If you met someone appropriate in the course of your work, why not look for another at that time?

Cao Zhuxiang: My shortcoming is that I am stubborn and that I never give up. Chair Sun of the Women's Federation talked about just this matter, and I got so angry that I said a few things. In the end I felt that this leader meant well, but I could not do that.

Gao Xiaoxian: Why couldn't you do that?

Cao Zhuxiang: One thing was that I didn't want to create that [situation] for my son. The child was older. [I thought,] Now I have already escaped from the kang and the knife edge [i.e., passed the most difficult time]. No one ever said a single gossipy word about me. This struggle for honor, I wanted to struggle to the end, just like I had already vowed to do. I would not bring shame to the name of Cao, or to the name of Wang [her husband's surname]. I would do what needed to be done. I was dead-set on this. That was my fate.

Gao Xiaoxian: When you became chair, and team leader, did you look for a husband? You had a right to a happy marriage. Why not just let other people talk as they pleased?

Cao Zhuxiang: Chair Sun propagandized the Marriage Law to me, and found a bureau chief in Xi'an for me. The mother-in-law was dead. I said, "Even if you find me a Party secretary, there is absolutely no way. What would I do with my children? I cannot throw my children over there with you." I explained the reasons to her. "If you want me to work, I will work. As for that matter, don't speak of it again. I will help the neighbors and the people in the village get things done, I am willing to do anything."

Gao Xiaoxian: And you didn't think about it [anymore]?

Cao Zhuxiang: Anyone who tried to talk about it in front of me found there was no way. I didn't care if it was a man or a woman.

Gao Xiaoxian: First of all, you were caring for children by yourself, it wasn't easy, and you had both administrative work and field work. You didn't even think about it? When you had difficulties in your work, to have a companion who understood you, someone who could help you with field work, who could help you take care of the children . . .

Cao Zhuxiang [interrupting]: Hardship. That was my fate. Farmers are not afraid to eat bitterness. People have two hands. Whether it was needle-work, heavy labor, light labor, you couldn't deter me. I could do it all. I didn't ask for anything from anyone. There was also my

> *mother's family, and also my older brother. If there were any*
> *difficulties, he could always help me. I never believed in spirits,*
> *I didn't believe in devils, I didn't have my fortune told. I told my*
> *own fortune. I didn't need other people to tell it for me.*
>
> Gao Xiaoxian: *You can really eat bitterness!*
>
> Cao Zhuxiang: *People come into this world. No one laughs at you for eating*
> *bitterness or wearing tattered clothes. Even when I was young,*
> *I didn't have anything good to wear. I won't dress myself to look*
> *younger. I hadn't even ever worn a striped shirt of plain cloth.*
>
> Gao Xiaoxian: *My way of thinking is this. I feel that if you can find someone to*
> *care for you, it is much better than living alone. At the time, why*
> *didn't you . . .*
>
> Cao Zhuxiang [interrupting]: *I didn't depend on him. I don't live badly now. My*
> *children are all grown now. When you think about all this, it is*
> *not that hard to understand [why I did it].*[146]

This interchange gives one pause. Gao Xiaoxian, a Women's Federation cadre born in 1948, argues gently for companionate marriage. This is certainly not an idea imported recently from abroad—it has circulated in its current form in urban China for close to a century—but it finds no acceptance here. One can speculate that marriage had not offered much to Zhuxiang: a husband who had not yet reached puberty when she married, was away from home for the few years in which he was a healthy adult, and returned home to die at the age of twenty-one, leaving her with dependents of several generations. Almost a decade later, at Liberation, Zhuxiang was thirty-two, a mature woman and an experienced farmer. Her mother-in-law had died, and her children were no longer toddlers and could help with farmwork. Reluctance to begin another marriage at that stage in her life is certainly understandable, especially because notions that might encourage remarriage—such as the expectation that marriage would be a source of sexual or emotional companionship—were nowhere operative in her social world. Rather than seeking the new marriage freedoms promised by the state, Zhuxiang argues for correct behavior, the honor of her natal and marital families, and her duty to her children, particularly her son.

Zhuxiang's unassailable virtue, her lack of complicating personal or sexual involvements, and no doubt her stubbornness as well, were all compatible with—in fact, necessary to—her success as a local leader and a labor model. The state line on virtuous widowhood was that it was a remnant of older "feudal" thinking, to be repudiated in favor of a new revolutionary morality. And yet none of the women who were chosen as early rural labor models in Shaanxi had personal histories that might expose them to criticism. Zhuxiang's reputation as a faithful widow meant that she had the local prestige to be effective as a model. As Li Xiuwa, a former *dundian* cadre, explained, *Cao Zhuxiang was widowed very young, and was restrained by the remnants of feudalism. She could not remarry, because she had a son. She had to remain as a widow in that family. From the time she was in her twenties, she devoted her youth to that family. Cao Zhuxiang could carry loads on a shoulder pole, push a cart, plow, and urge a draft animal on with shouts. She had all the skills of plowing, sowing, raking, milling, and winnowing. Cao Zhuxiang was extremely capable, and so she had prestige in the village. Not prestige in our current sense, but rather prestige given to her by feudal remnants. They said, "This woman is capable, honest, can eat bitterness, and on this basis we [the provincial Women's Federation] can spread a new prestige, not only by having her join in production, but by having her join in political movements. She will not only lead her own small family, but will also lead the bigger [collective] family."*[147] Zhuxiang's feudal virtues made her more available for work and more acceptable to villagers. Local authorities were quick to come to her defense when her personal conduct was questioned. Zhuxiang herself recounts that just after the land reform, when a man made the passing comment "She is only a young woman with no husband," the township head *grabbed him right away and told him off. He gave him such a talking-to that he was very embarrassed. After that, no one had any other idle things to say.* State authorities had a stake in her virtuous conduct, which was incorporated seamlessly into her emergence as a labor model—not by a faraway anonymous state apparatus, but by the fellow villagers who wrote up her life as a model for outside consumption.[148]

The story of Zhuxiang's virtuous widowhood has another layer whose significance I did not fully understand until 2006, a decade after our first interview, when she and her son and a neighbor all retold us a story we had not absorbed in our earlier conversations. In the 1930s, Zhuxiang married and moved in with her widowed mother-in-law and Erma, the widow of her husband's uncle. At that time, the male clansmen of the two deceased men were in the midst of an effort to send Erma back to her natal family and repossess her twenty *mu* of land. Erma fought back with a lawsuit, but the case dragged on for years. She and her late husband had adopted a son, but when she tried to take him to the ancestral graveyard to pay his respects, establishing him as a legitimate heir to the land, the clansmen had her beaten.

Zhuxiang was thus well aware that widowed women were vulnerable to dispossession. Zhuxiang, her son, and one of the women activists she had mentored gave us more than a few indications that the clansmen had ambitions to do the same to her after her own husband died.[149] Ultimately they found it difficult to do so because, as she put it, *Luckily I had this son, and so no one in the village would dare take advantage of me. I had given birth to my own baby boy on the* kang *of the Wang family.* Her determination to remain a widow and to bring up her children, particularly her son, was a claim both to honor and to property rights, held in trust for her son. After 1949, when the Women's Federation cadres, full of their citified notions of companionate marriage and women's equality, broached the possibility of remarriage, she greeted their suggestion with deep suspicion. It sounded to her as though they were picking up where the greedy clansmen had left off.[150]

And yet Cao Zhuxiang, in her fierce declaration of independence and pride, exceeded the portrait of a widow determined at all costs to uphold the patriline. She rejected fortune telling, but accepted her fate—embraced it, in fact—in the terms of plain living and eating bitterness that revolutionary language provided her. She drew on a locally understood conception of virtue—one that *she* did not call feudal, even if we or the Women's Federation cadre might do so. She understood her desire to raise her son, to "struggle for honor," to do every kind of work, to depend on no one, as a seamless web of selfless activities, all of which made her available to act for the collective. She incorporated the feudal virtue of chaste widowhood into her own personal narrative of revolutionary determination, drawing upon the common requirement of hard work for virtuous widows and labor models alike.

Cao Zhuxiang's refusal to consider proposals that she remarry even after 1949 kept her domestic life uncontroversial, unencumbered by wifely duties, and available for collective projects.[151] As the new state propagated its notions of an ideal new woman for a new society, it built upon some of the same behaviors it was explicitly criticizing as "feudal virtue." A revolution that explicitly set itself in opposition to widow chastity and arranged marriage worked quite differently at the grassroots—in part because of what rural people admired and would tolerate. Farmers enacted a state effect in a way that could be locally understood, at least in part because it commingled with preexisting norms. At the edge of the state's presence, revolutionary agendas depended on deeply held notions of personal honor, as well as individual stubbornness. The state effect in Shaanxi villages was rich in heterogeneous elements of cultural memory, recombined in ways never specified or anticipated by central state planners.

4

Activist

When Feng Gaixia speaks of her youthful career as a marriage freedom activist, she connects her tale to the national story by breaking into song. *Here are the lyrics of the Women's Freedom Song. I might not be able to sing it so well now because it's been many decades:*

> *The old society is like a dark and bitter well, ten thousand* zhang[1] *deep*
> *The bottom of the well pressing down on us common folk*
> *Women on the bottom layer*
> *Unable to see the sunshine, unable to see the sky*
> *Countless days and months, countless years*
> *Endless work as beasts of burden, suffering endless bitterness*
> *Who will come to save us*
> *The Communist Party and Mao Zedong will come to save us*
> *He led our whole China striding toward the light*
> *The women of the past could not overturn the King of Hell's throne*
> *Today we break the iron chains*
> *Women have all become free people*
> *We can also take part in the nation's great events*
> *Let the reactionaries suffer a tragic death*
> *Everyone work together on the front lines and in the rear*
> *Produce industriously, don't slack off*
> *And we will build a new China for ourselves that will last a hundred million years.*[2]

Gaixia remembers herself as noncompliant from the moment in 1949 when she was betrothed by her parents at the age of fourteen. *My mother cut out a paper pattern for a pair of red cloth shoes for me to wear when I got on the wedding sedan chair.*

She left it there for me for several days, but I wouldn't make the shoes. I felt, I hadn't even seen him and I didn't know what he was like. Once I said to my mother, "I'd rather die than accept him. If you marry me off when I am so young, I am not going to leave even if I have to die." So I threw it back at her and didn't make the shoes. The old lady matchmaker came to us and I would curse her and tell her to get out.

After Liberation Gaixia became a land reform activist, and by the time she was eighteen she was the head of the township Women's Federation. What she heard about the Party-state's marriage policy from the land reform team emboldened her to break off her own engagement. *In the past, there was nothing to give you backbone, right? After listening to the work team, you came to understand these things. [These ideas] were like a mirror held up to you, and you looked and compared.* When she returned home in between meetings, she worked on persuading her family. *The thinking of the parents was that the daughter is already a member of someone else's family. If you call off the engagement, they are going to lose face. They were doing things for the benefit of their children. They would say that that family is rich and has a better situation.* Fortunately for Gaixia, her grandfather sided with her and helped to bring her father around. *So my mother was the only one left. There was nothing she could do now.*

Still, her intended husband was unwilling to give up the match. Gaixia decided to confront him directly. *One day that matchmaker, that blind old lady, called me to their house. At that time, people liked to write down the eight characters of the year in which you were born. There is a coin and you have a red string tied to it. And then you tell the fortune teller your age, your birth date, and the year you were born and also the [animal zodiac] sign that you have. All these are tied up to that coin, and that is the ceremony for the engagement. I wanted her to take that coin back for me. I went to her house and she also called the man over.*

This was the first time Gaixia had met her intended husband. *Aiya, it really felt extremely awkward. The man was asking, "Why do you want to call off the marriage?" I said, "Because it is arranged. I've never seen you before today. This is just like 'buying a cat in the bag.' We are strangers to each other, right? We do not communicate with each other."*

In the end, he even threatened me. But I was not afraid because I was already the director of the Women's Federation. So I educated him. I told him that now I understand the Marriage Law. Now women are free, and I myself am going to choose the one I love, someone that I can communicate with, share my life with, have a common language with. And in the end, I was successful. We returned all the things that he had given me: a long piece of red cloth, two pairs of socks, a big bottle of facial cream, a bar of soap. Anyway, we were kids. I didn't care much about this. But he kept the eight characters of my birth for more than a year.

Sometimes, when I had meetings in Zhoujiaping, I bumped into him. He was always there as if deliberately, wanting to make things difficult for me. He was really narrow-

minded. Well, if you don't like it, you don't like it. You can't force me. I had already made up my mind. That kind of person, how could I marry him? We had already called off the marriage. So what are you doing here? Acting like a hoodlum? I didn't want to speak to him. I just glared at him and then I left. And I didn't tell my mother. Otherwise she would say, "Look what shame you have brought us."

Young women activists were profoundly marked by the state initiatives of the early People's Republic. Half a generation younger than Shan Xiuzhen and Cao Zhuxiang, newly married or of marriageable age in the early 1950s, these women entered social networks formed in literacy classes, songfests, opera troupes, and dance performances, as well as production groups. There they acquired language to explain their activities and decisions to themselves and their often skeptical kin and neighbors. Many were recruited to join the Communist Youth League or the Communist Party; some served as women's chairs in their home villages; and a small number went on to careers as full-time cadres. For young women, reading, singing, dancing, and working provided revolutionary praxis in the 1950s and mnemonic devices half a century later. This chapter begins with their memories of these new activities. Their actions and emotional investments helped to bring state initiatives into village households and local social interactions.

The remainder of the chapter reexamines the Party-state campaign for marriage reform initiated by the 1950 Marriage Law, putting women's memories rather than state policy at the center of the inquiry. Marriage reform had the potential to transform the transition of these young women into adulthood and alter the course of their subsequent lives. In some respects, the early Party-state campaigns for land reform and marriage reform worked at cross-purposes. Land reform distributed resources to the peasant household, helping to make good on the revolution's implicit promise for many poor peasant men: that it would improve their situations so that they could afford to bring in a bride.[3] Marriage reform, in contrast, posed a potential threat to the acquisition of brides and the stability of conjugal unions. More broadly, it disturbed the unity of the multigenerational household. But this formulation of dueling policy narratives is inadequate to explain changes in young women's lives, for the Marriage Law and the possibilities it introduced were worked out in complex articulations with local village practices.

Discussion of this Marriage Law has been dominated by two powerful political narratives. The first, a Party-state narrative, claims that the revolution successfully brought many aspects of women's emancipation to the Chinese countryside, and that the Marriage Law promised to usher women into personhood, free-choice marriage, and political participation in building a new society.[4] It also maintains that this promise was not immediately fulfilled because of "feudal remnants," in the form of bad attitudes and violence from husbands, mothers-in-law, and some cadres.

The second narrative comes from the world of scholarship. In Anglophone writing on China and much Chinese-language scholarship as well, the May Fourth movement of 1919, and the New Culture movement that preceded and framed it, is associated with women's emancipation, the overthrow of feudalism and tradition, and a move away from family-controlled marriages to ones based on companion-ate free choice.[5] This story line holds that when the May Fourth agenda, borne into rural areas by Communist Party cadres, encountered rural Chinese conservatism, the Party blinked, softened its stance, backpedaled on its goals, and sold out women's interests in the process. Overwhelmed with collectivization and a host of other controversial policies, cadres made the disruptive policy of marriage reform a low priority. This is also a story about feudal remnants, but ultimately it faults the Party for having an inadequate notion of the measures required to emancipate women.[6]

Understanding marriage reform in rural China requires a fuller look at what appealed to young rural women about activism. Peasant resistance, including resistance by older women, certainly limited and shaped rural marriage reform. But a story that centers on peasant benightedness or bad faith on the part of the state risks making women, particularly younger women, invisible. And a story that foregrounds the heroic young woman speaking out against oppression, however politically seductive, understates the complexity of the situations in which women developed their sense of possible and appropriate behavior. An inquiry centered on rural women, not just at the "speak bitterness" moment but over a period of years, suggests that the Marriage Law was understood and used in ways unforeseen and not endorsed by its Party-state authors, and produced more long-term effects than its feminist critics realized. Women's decisions to divorce or to remain in a marriage entailed wrenching negotiations with themselves, their families, and local cadres. In those interactions lie clues to the variable, locally articulated shapes of the state effect.

BEYOND FEUDALISM

When Feng Gaixia first became a land reform activist, her distraught mother showed her disapproval by withholding food. *We could be out of the house for the whole day, and when I came back she wouldn't keep anything for me to eat.* Nevertheless Gaixia continued her activities: *As soon as she wasn't looking, I would run out. It's like the lock of your heart is opened with a key. I felt, There is nothing that I should be afraid of. If you want to curse me, then curse me. I am going to do what I like. I have to go outside of the house and I have to work. I am not doing anything shameful.*

Remembering their early years of activism, women talk about home as a place controlled by fearful parents and anxious in-laws, worried that their young women would come to harm or slip out of their control. If a young married woman appeared to have activist potential, *dundian* cadres would try to address her mother-in-law's fear that untrammeled movement around the village would inexorably lead her to engage in sexual misconduct or demand a divorce. Having recently paid considerable sums to acquire a daughter-in-law to carry on the family line, the elders were afraid of losing their investment. Coming home from nighttime meetings, a young wife often found a father-in-law who had locked the door, a scolding mother-in-law who had not saved food for her, or a husband who withdrew into sullen silence or exploded in verbal or physical abuse.[7] Many of these women quote their elders uttering some variation of the aphorism "There are only men governors, no women county heads. Women can only move around the kitchen stove." The ubiquity of this statement marks it as likely to have been circulated by Party-state cadres. Whether or not it ever actually issued from the mouth of an older person, it encapsulates everything about the domestic as a space of confinement that these young women were learning to reject.

Women quickly learned to name these domestic conflicts in the language of feudalism and feudal remnants. Prior to the revolution, "feudalism" had been a standard piece of Party vocabulary, deployed by Mao Zedong in the phrase "semifeudal, semicolonial." In Mao's usage, "semifeudal" referred to the entire set of power relations centered on landholding, patriarchal clans, and state authority, and "semicolonial" referred to China's political and economic status in relation to expansive foreign powers. How and when "feudal" came to refer to family practices is not clear. But in stories told by women about the 1950s, "feudalism" described gendered experience centered on the domestic realm, both before and after Liberation. Cao Zhuxiang used the term, for instance, to refer to pre-1949 practices of confining girls to the home, buying child brides, mistreating daughters-in-law, and footbinding. Describing events that occurred after 1949, she used "feudalism" to talk about a family that tried to prevent the daughter-in-law from attending literacy classes.[8] Feudalism was the term applied to marriage customs that kept women concealed or subordinated. A popular song denouncing arranged marriage and the fact that young people did not see each other before their wedding day opened with the lyric, "Feudal marriage is really blind / who can see a cat if it's in a bag when you buy it?" Feng Gaixia called the practice whereby a bride covered her shoe soles with paper to avoid taking the dust (and symbolically the wealth) of her natal family onto the sedan chair and into her new home "feudal remnant thinking," and labeled domestic ceremonies on the wedding day "feudal family rituals."[9] In the realm of work and political activity, a woman who found it difficult to step forward and take a public role might also be called feudal. As we saw in chapter 3, Cao Zhuxiang used this term to describe her embarrassed behavior at a county meeting where she was one of very few women. Zhou Guizhen, a young activist trained by Zhuxiang in the 1950s, describes a local woman as "having feudal remnants in her head" because she thought it was shameful to have the family's name mentioned on the radio.[10] Of the ten older men we interviewed, six did not mention feudalism at all. The other four used the term as women did: to refer to footbinding, women's seclusion, women's low literacy rate, and marriage practices. Apparently men, too, were encouraged to imagine modernity as a liberation from particular gender practices. The domestic context was one crucial dimension in defining "feudalism" and marking off feudal time from the revolutionary present.

WINTER SCHOOL

Shaanxi village girls rarely received any schooling before 1949.[11] Those few girls who briefly attended school felt uncomfortable surrounded by boy students, and seldom stayed long.[12] After 1949, in addition to requiring families to send both boys and girls to school, cadres set about encouraging illiterate adults, the majority of them women, to learn to read.[13] The Women's Federation cadre Wang Meihua saw this as a way to begin to mobilize women: *Why did we start with literacy? At that time, families would only let a woman go out of the house if she was going to learn how to read. When women enjoyed more contact with the outside world by attending literacy classes, their thinking became more liberated little by little.*[14]

For the younger married women of Shaanxi villages, literacy was an important component in the expansion of their social worlds. As a mutual aid group leader in 1951, Zhou Guizhen's duties included mobilizing women to attend school at night and in the slack season. She threw herself into the task of becoming literate, working through three elementary school textbooks, learning to write the name of everyone in the village so that she could record their work points, and pasting up copies of the *Northwest Women's Pictorial (Xibei funü huabao)* all over the walls of her house.[15] Guizhen joined the Party in 1955 and describes herself as happiest at that time, comfortable with her growing responsibilities as a cadre, sure that she could do anything.[16]

Winter school, organized during the cold months of hiatus from farmwork, was conceptualized as a place where women could be taught literacy and apprised of current events, state policies, common knowledge about hygiene and production, and the deeds of women labor models.[17] Women cadres were instructed to ask permission from husbands and mothers-in-law to let younger women attend winter school.[18] Liu Zhaofeng would say to the family, *In the old society, you didn't have the chance to go to school. It's a pity that you don't know how to read. Now people know how to read, so they can join the revolution and work.*[19] Cadres stressed that a literate woman was less likely to be tricked in economic transactions, better at handling everyday life, more filial, and more compatible with her husband.[20]

Local literate people, as well as *dundian* cadres, were recruited to teach at the winter schools. Instructors taught their students a few characters at each session, mostly having to do with agricultural production or with women's daily life.[21] Some winter schools taught basic arithmetic as well. Women were encouraged to hang the written characters for daily objects on their spinning wheels, looms, and

doors.[22] By 1953, a province-wide literacy campaign required that every rural family have a small blackboard on which women could write.[23] Shan Xiuzhen, already
a cadre by this time, taught herself to read by asking people who sat next to her at
meetings to teach her, and learned to write by drawing characters on her chest with
her fingers.[24]

And yet, literacy was difficult to acquire and sustain for rural women who were
juggling their regular duties in the fields and at home, evening political meetings,
and school.[25] Cao Zhuxiang, who had increasing responsibilities for local governance, soon found that she had no time for night school. She felt constrained by
her lack of literacy throughout her later career, relying on assistants who could
read.[26] For women in their childbearing years, the burden of domestic chores and
children made consistent attendance difficult. Yang Anxiu, who later became a midwife, recalls a night school that lasted only two weeks: *The teacher was willing to
teach, but everyone was afraid of staying up at night and having to work the next day.
At that time, we made all our own clothes and shoes. Women put forward the request
that they not go, because they had to work in the daytime and do needlework at night.
What's more, people had more children at that time, at least three or four. People my
age did not want to go. They said, "What good is this to us? If we learn, it is like the
old saying, 'By the time the temple was built, the lord was old.' We need to take care
of this and that and have no time to study."* So people just stopped doing it. Many
women never went to night classes. Others lost the ability to read over time, because the daily round of tasks did not allow them to continue learning.[27] A renewed
campaign for literacy began in 1956, and during the Great Leap Forward classes
were proposed under the slogan "Socialism is heaven, but illiterate people cannot
reach it."[28] These efforts left no discernible memories among the younger women
we interviewed, who were then in their peak childbearing years. Winter school provided an early means to draw women out of a "feudal" domestic context, but widespread literacy among adult women remained an elusive and fleeting goal.

PERFORMANCES: SONG, DANCE, OPERA, MEETINGS

Singing—which women remember as a gendered practice performed mainly by
women[29]—was one of the means by which women were integrated into public space.
The point here is not that 1950s China resembled the set of a giant socialist realist
musical, full of happy singing peasants. Songs provided a personal connection to
state initiatives such as land reform, the literacy drive, and the Marriage Law, linking the formal messages imparted in political meetings to the work of daily life.[30]
As that work was reconfigured and women were drawn out in groups to work in
the fields, the songs lightened the heavy load of work and helped explain to them
the significance of what they were doing.

For Cao Zhuxiang, music marked the difference in emotional tenor between field work before the revolution and after. Her work organizing co-ops in the early 1950s was still purposeful, but no longer grim. *We were happy and sang as we worked all day. As soon as it got dark we would go to school, and make up songs, and under these circumstances a day was very lively. We never stopped being busy, even at home. Time would pass without our noticing it—now you would need to go to the fields, now it would be time to go home. . . . We were always humming away as we went about our business.*[31] He Gaizhen, then a young activist, recalls, *We sang every day, even when we were in bed at night. In the morning, my mother said, "Gaizhen, you still haven't gotten up? Are you still singing in bed?" I said, "Okay, I am getting up."*[32]

As new forms of performance were introduced, old ones were resignified. The *yangge* (sprout song), a north Shaanxi line dance in which a dozen or more people moved to a drumbeat, became popular on public occasions.[33] In Village Z, He Gaizhen first saw the *yangge* performed by soldiers of the People's Liberation Army in the days immediately after Liberation, and later she and other young women were taught to dance by the Party secretary of the district. One of her early tasks as an activist was organizing musicians and women *yangge* dancers to perform on holidays.[34] In Village G, an area with a long-standing tradition of opera performances, young women and men were organized to sing opera in the 1950s, giving them new opportunities to meet.[35] A male teacher was in charge of the village troupe of about forty people, five or six of them women.[36] They trained from script books during the winter slack season, rehearsing during the day in a large village square under the teacher's direction.[37] Even with women in the troupe, some men continued the traditional practice of singing women's roles, and some women played male characters. They performed during the Spring Festival, accompanied by cymbals, drums, wooden clappers, and several kinds of stringed instruments. Their repertoire included old favorites, such as the story of Wang Baochuan and Xue Pinggui, and the Tang Dynasty tale of an immortal white snake who turned herself into a beautiful woman and married a mortal. Both were open to reinterpretation in support of free-choice marriage.[38] By about 1956, new-style operas such as *You Cannot Take That Road*, a paean to the glories of mechanization, became popular.[39]

The pleasure that the women of Village G took in singing opera, and the confidence that it gave them, was evident even half a century later. As Lei Caiwa put it, *The first time I performed on stage, I was so frightened that my hands shook. I was very scared. I didn't dare to go out in front of the curtain. After I sang for a while, I got bolder. As soon as I began to sing, I would get more optimistic, happier. Sometimes when I had an argument with my mother-in-law or my husband, I would come back from singing and it wouldn't be important anymore. I would feel much better.*[40] When Zhang Qiurong's mother opposed her learning opera, reflecting the widespread attitude that opera singers were low-class, a neighbor who was a Party member told her, *This is propaganda. Let the child sing it.* After her marriage, Qiurong continued to sing over the objections of her mother-in-law. *She said what she wanted to say, and I sang what I wanted to sing.*[41] Musical performances legitimized women's presence at public occasions, bringing the vocabulary and gestures of state campaigns into music, motion, family relationships, even the way a woman carried herself.[42]

Political meetings, too, lent a performative quality to the state effect. Sallying forth to do battle with the landlords in the early 1950s, women imagined themselves as successors to the revolutionary heroines who risked their lives before 1949. *People told us about how Liu Hulan sacrificed her life for the revolution, how she was not afraid even when her head was put under the knife of the enemy.*[43] *Chairman Mao used this phrase to describe her: "She lived in greatness and died gloriously." In this spirit, we mobilized women one after another. Later on, we established a women's militia regiment. We reasoned with the landlords. We struggled them. We took our spears with red tassels, just like the one you've seen in the film* The Sparkling Red Star. *We guarded the landlords in front and in back.*[44] Memories of the land reform have taken on a cinematic aura, inflected by films that women have seen subsequently as well as by their own actions at the time.

Meetings also enlarged the social worlds of young village women who worked actively on land reform, marriage reform, or literacy. Their enhanced access to public space expanded their notions of who they might be and what they could accomplish. Recommended for Communist Youth League membership, they attended countywide gatherings of ten days or more, where they learned about new state policies and how to communicate them in their home villages.[45] Promoted to positions of responsibility as women's chairs or propaganda secretaries, they found the work easy—or so it seems from the vantage point of a more troubled present. Lu Yulian comments, *During Liberation, people all saw things the same way. No one was a troublemaker. No one asked for any compensation to attend meetings, even when they lasted for eight or ten days. . . . After Liberation, peasants' thinking—because there was a change in epoch—everyone's consciousness was raised. Everyone was very active.*[46] The proliferation of meetings led to the popular saying "The Guomindang had many taxes, the Communists have many meetings," but without the sense of grievance that later became attached to it.

Just as parents and in-laws had feared, one result of all these meetings was unsupervised youthful socializing. Feng Gaixia, who had already broken off her engagement, joined the Communist Youth League. *Every day my cousin and her friends would go to Youth League meetings with me. My cousin had a good understanding of women's freedom and freedom of marriage, and so she wanted freedom for herself. Young people often came together for meetings at the township. At that time, a young man took a liking to her, and she also took a liking to him. Parents thought this was unacceptable. People would laugh at you if you even walked together. They would say, "Oh, that girl is really like a wild horse." In today's terms, it means that she doesn't know how to behave. When we had men comrades and women comrades coming together talking and singing, having meetings and making speeches together, some of the older people were not used to seeing this. But slowly they got used to it.*[47] Gradually rural people came to accept the ubiquitous meetings of the collective period as a respectable place for women to spend their time.

As the 1950s wore on, the reconfiguration of space was soon taken for granted, and the pleasure many women expressed about their expanded social world when they spoke of that time evaporated in their accounts of subsequent decades. They remember songs, dances, and opera performances from the first years after Liberation, not from the later collective years. In their stories of the collective period as a whole, women generally associated labor in collective space and attendance at public meetings with fatigue, resentment, and the constraints of growing families and continued poverty. In one community, as chapter 9 details, they forgot several decades altogether. Given that intervening history, it is all the more striking that they recall the early 1950s with such specificity, as a time when certain types of youthful defiance were supported and praised, and when much seemed possible.

MARRIAGE

No Party-state initiative aimed for more profound domestic change than the Marriage Law of 1950, which announced the abolition of "the arbitrary and compulsory feudal marriage system." The Law forbade compulsion and third-party interference in partner choice, outlawed child betrothals and concubinage, banned interference with widow remarriage, set the minimum age for marriage at twenty for men and eighteen for women, and required couples to register their marriage with local governments. It also established the rights of husband and wife to manage and inherit family property and protected children born out of wedlock. Finally, it introduced procedures for divorce, mediation, property settlements, and child support.[48]

This was an ambitious attempt to alter daily social practice and to raise the status of women, particularly in rural areas where "feudal" ideas had been less often challenged than in the cities of pre-1949 China.[49] The Marriage Law attempted to insert state regulation into what had been an economic and social transaction between families. It introduced the possibility of giving young people control over their own marriages, a previously unimaginable practice in Shaanxi villages. And it was accompanied by a campaign to alter rural betrothal and wedding practices, some of the most important rituals of village life.[50]

In pre-Liberation Shaanxi, marriage had provided women a chance to move into a wealthier family or community, while allowing men to expand their network of affinal kin and fulfill their obligation to continue the family line. A transfer of resources from the groom's family to that of the bride was customary at engagement, in recognition that the natal family had incurred expenses in raising a girl, only to lose her labor as she reached maturity.[51] Some of that wealth was then used to prepare a dowry of household goods and clothing for the bride. Money from marrying out a daughter often allowed a family to bring in a wife for a son, who would be responsible for supporting his parents until they died and attending to their ancestral tablets thereafter. For a poor man's family, acquiring a bride required years of saving for the bridewealth and the wedding ceremony itself. For less income, a girl's family could send her to another family as a child daughter-in-law, as Xiuzhen's family had done during the drought, saving on the expense of raising her to adulthood. Among the poor, it was common to find child daughters-in-law, brothers sharing wives, and men unable to marry at all.[52]

Parents turned to matchmakers, usually women, in deciding on marriages for their children. Because most women had grown up in one village and married into another, their social networks spanned several communities. Older sisters, sisters-in-law, and more distant women relatives were often involved in finding an appropriate family and proposing a match to the woman's parents.[53] Engagements could be arranged when a child was very young, sometimes to the offspring of friends or relatives.[54] Most women married no more than a few miles from their natal homes. Families without sons sometimes brought in a husband for their daughter, or married her to a family in the same village so that she could continue to help them out.[55]

Strictly speaking, a couple was not supposed to see one another until their wedding day, but by the 1940s this stricture had been relaxed. Yang Anxiu got a glimpse of her fiancé *outside the window of my sister-in-law's house. My sister-in-law said, "Come and have a look." He wasn't dressed well. The black jacket he wore was borrowed and too old to tell the color, like a pair of summer shoes. He wore a melon-shaped cap like my brother and father. But theirs were made of black satin, good material. His was of cotton cloth and did not match. "What a disappointment. Oh, my goodness. To live my life in that household?" But you dared not say that.*

Then they came to my house. You were embarrassed to look at his face, but he could look at you. My mother-in-law took my hand and held my arm up to check whether I had body odor. It could be passed on from your generation to the younger generation. It could not be cured. So people were afraid of that. She took my hands and had a look and felt my fingernails. She was satisfied and said she agreed. This counted as meeting the person. After a dinner in the afternoon, they all left. It was just a short visit.

In the end, my father agreed to the marriage. "Do you agree?" I said yes. At that time my father agreed. How would I dare to say I didn't agree?[56]

Engagement rituals followed. After the eight characters specifying the woman's birth date and time were sent to the man's home, his parents and the matchmaker sent gifts of pork, cake, cloth, shoes, socks, jewelry, and cosmetics for the bride in the *chahua* (sticking the flower) or *daihua* (wearing the flower) ceremony.[57] Even in the poorest families, it was customary for the man's family to give the bride at least one set of clothes, including the padded pants and jacket worn during the cold winter months. With the *song xi tie* (sending the wedding invitation) ceremony, when the matchmaker delivered an announcement of the year, month, and day on which the wedding ceremony would take place, the engagement rituals were complete.[58]

In the several months between the *daihua* ceremony and the wedding, the natal family would invite a tailor or mobilize the family's women to fashion the gift cloth into pants, jackets, a long gown, pillowcases, pillows, quilts, sheets, door curtains, and other goods for the dowry. The natal family might also provide chests and a table, a wine pot, a copper pot for boiling water, teacups and a teapot, a water pipe, and shoes, socks, and a hat for the groom. The future bride busied herself embroidering: decorations for cases, cabinets, and tables; socks with embroidered soles for the mother-in-law; shoes, handkerchiefs, and pillow covers; and presents for the children. In Village G, with its strong tradition of weaving, the grandmother or mother of the bride spent years preparing several hundred handwoven handkerchiefs to be given out to wedding guests.[59]

Regardless of when a girl became engaged or was given as a "child raised to be a bride," formal wedding ceremonies took place sometime after menarche. On the wedding day, the groom's family sent women relatives in small sedan chairs to the bride's house, bringing a larger sedan chair, decorated with inlaid glass and red tassels and carried by men or livestock, to transport her to her new home. The escort party had a meal at the bride's house. Then the bride, wearing a red satin jacket, blue satin trousers, an embroidered skirt, shoes embroidered with lotuses and hung with bells, a cluster of flowers, a hat adorned with phoenixes, a veil on her head, and a handkerchief in her hand, entered the sedan chair. Several women from her own family (never including her own mother) came with her, in other sedan chairs. The curtain was lowered and the procession set off, accompanied by musicians.[60]

Because women usually did not marry into distant villages, the bride's journey was often very short, but the rituals surrounding it emphasized the break with her natal family and her entry into a new network of kin.[61] She was carried to the sedan chair so that she would not bring the soil of her natal family to her new home.[62] On the wedding night, guests were invited to tease the new couple, demanding candies, tangerines, and nuts, asking the bride to sing, and making jokes at the couple's expense. Some hid a piece of charcoal under the bedding. Men were the major participants in the teasing. The crowd could get raucous, with bystanders carrying on until sunrise, sometimes even hitting the bride with a clothing brush.[63]

The transition from natal to marital family has been portrayed as a traumatic moment in the life of a woman. Leaving those she knew, she entered a household of strangers, having seen her husband only briefly, if at all, prior to the wedding. In rural Shaanxi, young men were often working away from home for long periods of time, leaving the new bride to develop relationships with her mother-in-law, her husband's unmarried sisters, and the wives of his brothers. Yuan Xi of Village G, born in 1922 and married in the late 1930s, recalls, *At my mother-in-law's house, I couldn't go out of the gate. When I sent off people who came to see me from my mother's family, I could only stand at the gate to send them off. I missed my mother so much it was pitiful. At that time, I cooked and did needlework. I would ask the grownups* [dang-jia ren] *what they wanted to eat. Whatever they said they wanted, I would make.*[64] Prudence dictated that a new daughter-in-law should be obedient and work hard, but it is easy to imagine a period of loneliness and meager emotional satisfaction.[65]

Still, women's accounts of early married life often stress the kindness of mothers-in-law and the sociability of sisters-in-law.[66] A wife's adjustment to her new home was eased by the common practice of frequent or extended visits to her natal family. Several days after her wedding, it was customary for the bride to return to her mother's house without her husband for a visit of several days, escorted by her relatives. In Village Z, in the eastern part of Shaannan, and Village G, in the northern area of Guanzhong, young married women made extended visits to their natal families that amounted to virtual coresidence up until the birth of a first child. *After you were married, for four days you would go back to your mother's house for a visit. You would stay there for four days, then come back to your mother-in-law's house for four days. After that there were no rules* [bu guan le]. *Someone would come from your mother's house to get you. "Half a year as a daughter-in-law, half a year as a guest [in your mother's house; bannian xizi, bannian ke]." You would stay in your mother-in-law's house less than ten days, then stay in your mother's house for two or three months. The first year you were a stranger* [sheng]. *By the second year you would gradually start going back to your mother's house less. After you had a child, you went less.*[67] When a couple married young, it was often several years before they began to have sexual relations. A husband working away from home could cause a similar delay. In her husband's absence, the wife often went to live with her own family, returning to her new home when field work required her assistance or for important ritual occasions such as the Spring Festival. Women also returned to their mothers' homes if they were not getting along with their husbands.[68] The domestic lives of "confined" village women, encompassing periodic residence in at least two villages, were in some respects more mobile than those of village men.

MARRIAGE LAW

Preoccupied with the land reform, the provincial Party-state apparatus and the nascent Women's Federation branches at the county level had little spare energy to devote to implementing the 1950 Marriage Law.[69] A flurry of directives from the central and provincial governments in 1950 and 1951 showed serious concern with how the law was being received, as well as frustration when lower levels did not respond promptly.[70] Local reports about the Marriage Law give glimpses of a state apparatus scrambling to assemble itself, and provide a daunting account of opposition to the law and the new sources of instability it introduced. Many rural families reportedly feared that the law would mean the loss both of wives and property, and they could not understand why a Party that was supposed to represent the interests of the poor was permitting this to happen. Men feared that if the free choice of partners was instituted, only smart and rich men would be able to marry. Cadres were not doing enough to dispel such fears, one report averred—adding that the fears were not ungrounded.[71] Success stories punctuated a much larger catalogue of violence: armed mobs of men reclaiming divorced wives by force; ex-husbands carrying concealed knives and attempting murder, in one case in the courtroom itself; a husband who pushed his wife off a cliff rather than agreeing to a divorce; another who raped and strangled his wife, plunged a stick into her vagina, and left the body in the hills; a man who put shackles on his wife's ankles after she requested a divorce, which she wore for six weeks before other people discovered the situation, meanwhile continuing to cut firewood and grass, carry loads of water, and dig for taro in the hills; a wife who poisoned her husband and another who attempted to stab herself when the courts incorrectly refused to grant them divorces; a court that tried four mediations rather than approving a divorce, until the husband finally chopped off two of his wife's fingers one night.[72] Such cases were not the norm, but they indexed resistance to marriage reform as well as the limits of state presence in the villages. The Women's Federation issued a gloomy report at the end of 1950, counting 195 instances of death related to marriage cases, and commenting that the actual number was probably higher.[73]

These problems were exacerbated by ambivalence or outright hostility on the part of male rural cadres, who were often at loggerheads with Women's Federation workers over the Marriage Law. Some cadres expressed the fear that the law's support of free-choice marriage would "throw all under Heaven into turmoil" and deprive the poor of wives, unintentionally benefiting the rich and powerful.[74] Other cadres, newly powerful themselves, used the law to jettison their own rural wives as they moved on to urban careers.[75] A report in late 1950 from the old Communist base area, supposedly the most ideologically advanced place in the province, struck a despairing note: "Cadres with conservative views and backward feudal ideas are unwilling and fear to educate the masses about the new Marriage Law. They do not understand that women should rise, and are rising, against feudalistic oppression, and that we should take the position of women's liberation."[76]

Not far from Village B, an attempt in 1951 at mass education about the law ended in a public relations debacle when the Xi'an City Women's Federation took up the case of a woman from the rural suburbs who was seeking a divorce from her abusive husband. Federation cadres arranged for the divorce decree to be announced in the city stadium in front of a large crowd, but they were unprepared for what happened next, recalls Liu Zhaofeng: *The people in the audience were not sufficiently mobilized. They were not prepared to accept divorce in the first place. When the divorce was announced at the meeting, the people in the audience all stood up suddenly, throwing stones and scolding. After the judges finished reading the judgment, people wrecked their car.*[77] The wife had to be smuggled out of the stadium, with a crowd threatening to beat her to death.[78] *That's how feudal it was,* Zhaofeng comments. *The city Women's Federation had fouled it up that time! Not so good. We began to carry out this [campaign] before the masses had accepted divorce.*[79]

Chastened by the hostile response, Women's Federation organizers turned to long-term education, but change in marriage practices was slow. In a township just northeast of Village B, a Marriage Problems Work Team sent by the provincial government in 1952 found a host of unsanctioned practices: buy-and-sell marriages, underage marriages, polygamy, children raised as daughters-in-law, and marriages in which a second husband was brought into a household to support the parents and children of the (presumably incapacitated) first husband.[80] The team collected local sayings commenting on normative marriage practices. "The rich make friends with the rich, the poor marry the poor" (*furen jiao fuyou, qiongren jie qiongqin*) described the constraints on possible marriage partners. The possibilities of hypergamy were suggested by the saying "Marry an official, be a lady; marry a pig butcher, turn over intestines" (*genshang zuo guande, zuo niangzi, genshang sha zhude, fan changzi*). "When husbands are angry they beat their wives; when wives are angry their husbands beat them" (*nanren shengle qi da poniang, poniang sheng le qi nanren da*) summarized conjugal relations. On the emotional distance between mothers-in-law and daughters-in-law: "Daughter is heart and son is root; even the best daughter-in-law is of a different surname" (*nü shi xin, er shi gen, za hao de xifu wai xing ren*). On the mother-in-law's domestic tyranny: "The home of even the nicest mother-in-law has its law of the land" (*zai hao de a jia you wang fa*, literally, king's rules). On the behavior expected of a proper daughter-in-law: "No fighting back when beaten, no answering back when cursed" (*da buhuan shou, ma buhuan kou*).

In spite of the discontent implied by these sayings, the investigation group found that villagers and local cadres misunderstood and disliked the Marriage Law. Parents worried that their shy and honest sons, not to mention those who were poor, blind, lame, or stupid, would be incapable of finding wives for themselves. Here, too, popular attitudes were conveyed in an aphorism: "In the skies there is no rain without clouds; in the world there is no marriage without matchmakers" (*tianshang wuyun bu xiayu, shishang wumei bu chengqin*). In this village and others, cadres could be found arranging marriages for their underage children, interfering in the marriages of their own sisters, and looking the other way when villagers ignored the provisions of the law.

Undaunted, the Marriage Problems team established a cultural work group and an information station, keeping meticulous records of their work. They organized cadres and villagers to study the law, and then administered a fourteen-question exam, forcing cadres to study so that they wouldn't be outdone by ordinary villagers.[81] In the process they unearthed a certain amount of policy conflation among villagers. When asked why children born out of wedlock had to be protected, one hapless man answered that the new society protected children born to girls and widows because of the Resist America Aid Korea campaign and because the nation was underpopulated—two unrelated reasons that have the virtue of rhyming in Chinese (*kang Mei yuan Chao, guojia ren shao*).

After twenty-three days the team could point to modest accomplishments,[82] but they expressed uncertainty about whether local cadres would continue the work. This reflected a widespread dilemma: central and provincial Party-state authorities could not count on local cooperation in enforcing the most basic provisions of the Marriage Law.[83] The national Party-state began to plan for a month of concentrated Marriage Law implementation work in 1953, to begin on March 8, International Women's Day, and run until April 12.[84]

In early 1953 Gan Yifei, the head of the Shaanxi Provincial Propaganda Department, addressed a meeting of women's representatives preparing for the campaign. His speech demonstrates how thoroughly free-choice marriage had become articulated with state goals for family stability and nation-building:

> The feudal marriage system is an evil system. It shackles women and men. . . . Because they didn't marry out of love, they didn't have sexual intercourse, fought with each other, quarreled, broke bowls and pots, or lay on the *kang* without moving. Many women and men had no way out and jumped in wells or hanged themselves. . . . Because people were not satisfied with their marriages and didn't have sexual relations, they committed adultery. Sometimes one man had a couple of women. Sometimes one woman had a couple of men. Adultery causes murders and affects social security. . . . According to Shaanxi statistics for the first half of 1952, 196 women and 90 men killed themselves or were killed because of marriage problems. This means implementing the Marriage Law is not purely an issue of liberating women. It is also an issue of liberating men . . . Abolishing the feudal marriage system is most beneficial to women. So women, young women in particular, are most eager to abolish it and the most devoted [to the cause]. This is also an issue for men . . . How well marriage problems are solved determines whether people will live a happy life or a bitter one, whether the family will be harmonious or not. So, this is not only an issue about husband and wife, about family, but also about liberating social productivity, democracy and solidarity, the unity of nationalities, the campaign Resist America Aid Korea, and production and construction. We shouldn't take it as just women's business, the Women's Federation business, the court's business, or the district and township cadres' business. This is the responsibility of all men and women, of all revolutionary comrades.[85]

Gan directly addressed the problems of cadre collusion and ineptitude:

> But some cadres are conservative, refusing marriage reform, and are against marriage freedom for men and women and against divorce . . . A couple somewhere in Chang'an county couldn't get along. A cadre asked the wife to make a patriotic pledge

that she should take off her trousers when they slept.[86] But the pledge was not carried out. So the township head stood outside and asked the woman to throw her trousers out the window. After she threw them out, the couple fought on the *kang*. Finally the township head had to throw the trousers back. People who couldn't get along like this couple should get divorced . . . Some comrades don't understand this. They blame either men or women for their disharmony. We say it's not the mistake of either men or women. It is the mistake of the feudal marriage system of the old society.

Gan also put forward an argument for coalition-building:

> It shouldn't be only a few young women and a few Women's Federation cadres who implement the new Marriage Law. If anyone thinks the new Marriage Law is a law to oppose men and parents-in-law, she will be isolated. She won't be able to liberate women even if she wants to. Probably more women will be killed. Just think, in such a situation, how can we gain success if we oppose the men—half of the population— and old women and some middle-aged and young women—half of the women? . . . So, if we want to liberate women, we must gain their support.

Gan advised activists not to disrupt village relationships except when absolutely necessary. At speak bitterness meetings, he said, women should be guided to talk about the old society's marriage system, rather than denouncing their in-laws and husbands: "Class struggle is not suitable to solve this problem. So, we should be very careful in implementation. Any carelessness may lead to death. We want to save women, but carelessness may hurt them. We want to eliminate women's bitterness, but carelessness may add to it." Adultery cases should be dealt with cautiously:

> Each adulterer has uncles, grandparents, brothers and sisters. If adulterers are publicly struggled, it seems that only two people are struggled, but in fact all their relatives are shamed . . . If a village struggles two or three such couples, there will surely be chaos in the whole village. Probably some people will be driven to death. We implement the Marriage Law for the purpose of liberating women, not for driving people to death. If more people are driven to death, what's the advantage of implementing the Marriage Law?[87]

During the Marriage Law Month of 1953, Women's Federation cadres took the coalition-building injunction to heart. Unlike the situation during the land reform, the stated objective of mobilizing women was to bring an end to conflict, not to incite it. The Federation cadre Li Xiuwa observed, *If you only called for free marriage or for rejecting the orders of the parents and the word of the matchmaker, the peasantry could not accept it. This Marriage Law was very comprehensive, including respecting the older people and caring for the young, mutual respect between couples, and educating young children, so the Women's Federation focused on carrying it out thoroughly. In this way, even old ladies would support us.* Cadres saw themselves as protecting all women and girls by keeping the focus on family harmony.[88]

In the Village T area, Feng Gaixia and her fellow activists sought to involve the entire community in the month's activities. *Under the Moon Tower gate on Xieyue Street, we held a rally that drew ten thousand people. We climbed up that tower, put up the megaphone, and talked about the damage done by arranged marriage in the old society.*[89] Gaixia combined her enthusiasm for the Marriage Law with her love of public singing. Her favorite was "Lan Huahua" (Dark Blue Flower), a folk song from north Shaanxi. Sung in a young woman's voice, it blended a denunciation of arranged marriage to a "monkey-faced old man" with romantic longing for a handsome young one.[90] Gaixia and her fellow activists also performed several full-length operas, including one based on the story of Liang Meiye, a woman from nearby Hua County, who had broken off an arranged engagement and married a man of her choice in 1952, just as Gaixia herself had done.[91]

The easiest issues to address in the campaign were those that did not directly challenge parental authority: requiring couples to register their marriages with local authorities,[92] sending child daughters-in-law who had not yet borne children back to their natal families, and dismantling concubinage in favor of "one husband, one wife." Even before the Marriage Law Month, during the land reform campaign, whenever possible child daughters-in-law were assigned land in their natal families and sent back to live with them.[93] Former child daughters-in-law who had already married stayed with their husband, particularly if they already had children.[94] The few men who had been able to afford a wife and a concubine before 1949 were told to pick one of the women and divorce the other. This may have done little for women's marriage freedom, but it did have the effect of further circumscribing the power of local elites, already truncated in the land reform, by making their marriage status subject to state control. Divorce in this situation did not always alter the living arrangements, however. In Cao Zhuxiang's village, one man divorced his wife in favor of his concubine. The principal wife remained in the same courtyard as her ex-husband and his wife, with whom she got along. Until collectivization rendered the question moot, her ex-husband cultivated her land. Some years later she remarried, to a man introduced to her by Zhuxiang.[95] Although on-the-ground relationships were worked out with a great deal of practicality, there was apparently no compromise on the question of "one husband, one wife." Even the former Communist guerrilla leader Zhang Kui in Village Z had to divorce one of his two wives.[96]

Cadres did not denounce betrothal presents, as long as they did not appear to set up a "buy-and-sell marriage."[97] But young activists like Gaixia made it a point of pride not to demand goods from the family of the groom. When she married a fellow activist of her own choosing in 1952, *I didn't ask anything from him. I thought that since we have equality between men and women, self-reliance, women should have self-respect, so I didn't even ask for a single piece of thread from him. When we became engaged, his family bought four knots of cloth for the engagement, but when we got married we didn't even ask for half a length of thread.*[98] Gaixia decided to make her own wedding procession a model of what a new-style ceremony should be, without a sedan chair. *My mother lay on her bed and cried for several days. When I called her, she ignored me. When I brought food to her, she wouldn't eat. Her thinking was that this daughter is going to be married off without a sedan chair, and people will laugh at us. Other families all had elaborate weddings. When you see this, you feel happy to have raised this daughter. My mother believed if you don't sit in the wedding sedan, it looks as though you have married your daughter off to a poor family. She simply couldn't persuade herself. I tried to work on her and say, "We are both work-ing. You don't have to worry about this. We are going to have a good life in the future. We are going to build our home with our own hands." After several days of working on her, my grandfather said, "I support you." Also, my father is an open-minded man. After a bit of an argument, he didn't have much trouble with this.*

The young people and teachers arranged things for me. When everything was ready, they went to my home. My family made tea for them and served candy. They danced the yangge *dance. I held hands with my husband* [airen, *literally "lover," popularized by the new Party-state as a term for "spouse"] and joined the* yangge *dance troupe. Hand in hand, men and women all together, with red ropes tied around our waists, off we went. We danced the* yangge *dance all the way to his home.*

Among the villagers, there was no trouble with the young people. The elderly were not used to it. "This girl has cheap bones. She jumps over the meat platter and eats the bean curd dregs. The man they found for her originally was so good, but she is go-ing with someone else, who is poor and doesn't have parents. There is nobody to take care of things for them." They said that I didn't want the good life that was given to me. "When she got married, she went on foot." This was what the elderly said.

Later on, nobody had a wedding sedan chair, and all the weddings were like this. I was the first one to do so. Since I was the party secretary in the township, when-ever there was a wedding, I would be invited to be the witness. Because I was work-ing to promote the Marriage Law in the township, I was also someone who had a say. So they all invited me to preside at marriage ceremonies. Since I hadn't ridden on a wedding sedan chair, how could they take one? From then on, that tradition was changed.[99]

New wedding garb was actively promoted by the Party-state as the sign of an egalitarian marriage that reaffirmed the value of physical labor. Grooms no longer wore the long robes of a scholar, and brides gave up the customary long pink gowns (*qipao*) and red satin head coverings decorated with embroidered phoenixes.[100] In the early 1950s, both men and women wore black or blue jackets and matching pants. Flashes of color were provided by the bride's pink blouse, and later by the new custom of single larger flowers described by Gaixia, *one for the bride to put on the groom, one for the groom to put on the bride.*[101] Abandoning the elaborate coif-fures that went with the phoenix hat, brides wore their hair in two long braids. The painful ritual of using threads to remove facial hair was abandoned, and young women who continued to pluck their eyebrows were teased when they went to meetings in the county.[102] In subsequent years, the *yangge* dance as a means of trans-porting the bride was supplanted in turn by bicycles, tractors, and (more recently) automobiles, each successive change linking rural weddings to the changing content of socialist modernity.

Activism was important to Gaixia as she ended an arranged betrothal, climbed up on the Moon Tower to sing about the Marriage Law, and made her free-choice marriage a joyous public demonstration of how to marry without a sedan chair. For many other young women activists, however, the new world opened up to them by campaign time could not trump family need. Feng Sumei grew up near Village T and became a land reform activist, guarding the landlord, going to meetings, danc-ing the *yangge*, and joining the Communist Youth League, all with her parents' approval. When she turned eighteen in 1953, however, her parents made a "trading relatives" (*huanqin*) match for her. *My elder brother married Old Yi's younger sister, and I married Old Yi. Why? Because his family was too poor to find a wife for him. My family was also poor, but our house was better than theirs after the land reform. But my brother was blind in one eye. The medical conditions were not so good when we were young. So both families had no other way.*

I saw some other girls married into better families, literate and with better condi-tions. But my mother-in-law's family was so poor and illiterate. They lived on the yel-low mud slope. People described that mud as "like glue when it rains, like a knife when it doesn't." Life was so hard that if you had one meal, you would not have the next. My mother-in-law was a small-foot, and my father-in-law never worked. They de-pended on the bamboo rain-caps Old Yi made. He would sell them, and that way they could buy some corn and oil. They searched for firewood in the mountains. They had no money for that.

I did not agree to the engagement. Their family was too poor, without even a piece of tile on their house. They were given a one-room place in the new society after the land reform. That was only a room for sleeping, with a wall inside for separation. Al-together there were four people including the parents, but only one room. They had no place to put me. I could not figure out how they lived before my marriage. There was a dirt loft, with a ladder to go up. It is really shameful to say that his younger sis-ter still slept in the same bed with her parents at the age of marriage. He himself slept in the bed in the loft.

Sumei knew that trading relatives was illegal, and she didn't want the marriage. But her father's desire to marry his daughter into a secure family was trumped by the need to bring in a bride for his disabled son. He threatened her: if she did not comply, he would no longer recognize her as his daughter. Her family urged her to resign herself to the marriage. *My mother asked my brother-in-law and other rela-tives to persuade me. They said, "Well, girls' fate is like seeds. If they are planted in a thin field, then that is their fate; if they are planted in a rich field, then that is also their fate." Disagreement was useless. Trading relatives was decided by parents. I knew that arranged marriages were not permitted. I was a Communist Youth League member then. But people were still conservative. You had no say about your own business. And parents would no longer regard you as their daughter. I was really afraid of that.*

The two families had to have the wedding on the same day. They were afraid that we might break the agreement. They didn't even have a quilt—no bed, no table, no box, not even a fire basin for the winter. Nothing. My family gave me a basin, a shelf, a pillow, a teapot, cups, a quilt, and a sheet. His family separated the original sleeping room into two, and we slept in the back one. They had nothing in the room. Even the bed was borrowed. They borrowed a table, a wooden box to hold clothes, and a quilt. Old Yi had no winter jacket. It was snowing. He borrowed a winter jacket, and a pair of trousers. He had no trousers, and no shoes. All these things were borrowed. After the wedding he returned everything. We were supposed to visit others when the New Year came. I just sewed a new jacket and trousers for him using the cloth my family gave me, because my family was happy about the wedding and gave me six suits and some cloth. My family also gave me a quilt. We also used a mat in summer. It was too cold to sleep on a mat in winter. I asked for one more quilt from my mother to make a cotton-padded mattress.

Aware of the Marriage Law and dissatisfied with her personal situation, Sumei was unable to connect the two. Her objections were less about free choice or Old Yi than about the very difficult material conditions to which her family was consigning her, conditions that the revolution had not begun to touch. No *dundian* cadre or revolutionary nostrum could resolve her dilemma, which pitted her relationship with her parents against her own desires. She remembers this conflict with a blend of resentment, resignation, and an activist's determination to improve what she could not escape: *No matter whether it's a mound or a cliff, you have to jump. His family was poor when I married. But I could work hard to make it better.*[103]

CONSIDERING DIVORCE

The question of divorce was at the heart of village suspicions about marriage reform. Even at the height of the Marriage Law campaign, divorce in Shaanxi villages was rare. It was socially and financially complicated to break an engagement, as Feng Gaixia had done. It could be challenging to send child daughters-in-law back to their natal families, given the privation that had caused such matches to be made in the first place. But it was far more difficult—and less acceptable to the members of rural communities—to obtain a divorce.[104] Across central and south Shaanxi, the numbers of divorces recorded by county authorities remained small (see Table 2).[105] Village Z had five or six cases of divorce in the early 1950s, and local residents felt that to be a lot. Decades after the campaign, Village G considered itself unusual because there had been several dozen divorces in the 1950s.[106]

Women's loyalties, sense of personal virtue, affective investments, community

TABLE 2 Divorce in Shaanxi Province and selected counties, 1954–56

Date	Total Number of Divorces	Reasons for Divorce				Mediated and Not Divorced	Unsuccessful Court Mediation; Transferred Up
		Alienation of Affection	Abuse	Bigamy	Other		
Shaanxi							
1954	14,184	12,570	642	353	619	4,233	5,485
1955	9,075	6,493	366	225	362	3,113	3,161
1956	8,838	7,660	533	258	387	3,865	3,188
1956 January– June only	4,776	4,043	317	167	249	2,074	1,703
Weinan County							
1954	98	85	7	2	4	6	14
1955	No report	No report	No report	No report	No report	No report	No report
January–June 1956	82	54	10	4	14	51	35
Heyang County							
1954	246	224	14	5	3	24	63
1955	179	158	14	3 .	4	56	88
January–June 1956	85	77	5	1	2	33	38
Danfeng County							
1954	64	60	0	1	3	7	21
October 2– December 31, 1955	13	12	0	0	1	0	5
January–June 1956	94	68	26	0	0	63	37
Nanzheng County							
1954	310	217	10	8	13	100	95
July 1– September 30, 1955	9	9	0	0	0	19	9
January–June 1956	106	72	14	9	11	70	80

SOURCES: 1954: MZT 198–417, Shaanxi Provincial Archives; 1955: MZT 198–458, Shaanxi Provincial Archives; 1956: MZT 198–527, Shaanxi Provincial Archives.

ties, and political activism all came into play when they contemplated leaving a marriage. Li Liujin was the only person in her village to initiate a divorce in the early 1950s.[107] Married at fourteen, she had never much liked her husband or her in-laws. Father and son played cards or *majiang* all the time and were often in debt. *That old man was quite a piece of work* [na dongxi]. *The old mother-in-law was also not very smart* [mei sha shuiping]. *My husband was not very accomplished* [mei ming-tang] *either.* Nevertheless she was young and obedient. She bore a daughter at seventeen and a son two years later, who died of measles just before his first birthday. After Liberation, called to a work meeting because she knew how to transplant rice seedlings, she returned to find the door barred by her father-in-law. *When I came back, they hadn't left any food for me! Next door to me lived the women's chair. I said, "What's the problem here? Someone tells me to go to a meeting and when I come back there's nothing for me to eat! What kind of reasoning is this?" They all didn't open their mouths. They didn't speak. I went and found [the women's chair] to go tell them that this was not right. It was like this in that family, quarrelling all the time, from 1949 to 1953.*

Only after the Marriage Law arrived did I get a divorce. I hadn't considered divorce before that. At last came the propaganda. I thought, I have no choice. I simply proposed a divorce! The cadres mediated, but there was no way to settle it. The way I saw it, at the time I was only twenty-two. I said, "How can I spend year after year in this family, for the rest of my life? I am not even allowed to participate in activities in society. They keep such tight control over me."

Throughout the divorce proceedings, Liujin feared violent reprisal from her husband. Each time she walked to court in Balipu, which was many hours from her village, she worried. *They summoned him to court, but he wouldn't agree to a divorce. After I went to court, that year, it happened that someone on their way [to court] to get a divorce got halfway there and was murdered, beaten to death. There were quite a few cases of murder. Those judges, those people who asked questions, asked my husband to stay and talked to him, and told me to leave quickly. I came out and made several turns [taking a circuitous route to avoid being intercepted].*

Women who divorced were entitled to a share of household property, but county-level directives for cadres instructed them to urge women to give up any property claims, particularly if they had remarried.[108] Liujin was given the right to the grain from the six *fen* of paddy land that had been her land reform allotment. Because it was too awkward to collect the rice directly from her ex-husband, she asked another family to cultivate it for her and collected rice for two years, until collectivization ended private ownership.

Although Liujin had been given custody of her six-year-old daughter, as was customary in divorces at that time, people in the township government soon began to lobby her to leave the child with her ex-husband. *They said, "You are still young. After your divorce, it is impossible that you will stay at home [and not remarry]. If you go out [remarry], you will have children. If you leave her here, he can take her home with him, and later he can find her a mother-in-law and have a relative." So I thought about it. If I take her with me and go, he'll come to harass me. I also thought this way: I am in my twenties, I'll have children later. So I left my daughter to him.* In subsequent years, Liujin saw her daughter infrequently, but the connection survived.

If we had gone to see my daughter, they wouldn't have let me, so I didn't go. Some-times I ran into her on the road. She knew I went to see her [maternal] aunt and her family. She found excuses, to get grass for pigs and things like that, and went to the side of the road to see me. When I saw her, I would give her a bit of money.

Soon after her divorce, an acquaintance offered to introduce Liujin to a poten-tial second husband. Liujin had two initial conditions: the man should not be too old or suffer from hereditary underarm odor (*huchoubing*). The prospective groom, a teacher, met these two conditions, but still she hesitated: *In the end they took me there to have a look. Ai. He was not so great* [bu zenyang]. *You haven't met my hus-band; he's not very good-looking. I thought about it again. He had a tiled house with several rooms. He seemed to be intelligent. He had a son from a previous marriage. His wife had died. At the time I thought, You might meet a good family, but not en-counter a good person. I also thought, His son will be like my son. I will regard him as my own. So I agreed.*

Then I said, "The problem with my last marriage was that the man did not want me running around and being socially active. If anyone tries again to keep tight con-trol of me, it won't work." After I told him these conditions, he didn't oppose them. I got married in 1953. For nine years after I remarried I did not have a child. I said that if I don't give birth to a child here, I won't have a single person close to me here. I also thought that if I didn't have another child, I would make a scene with my ex-husband [shua laipi] *and get my daughter. The daughter is mine! I would sue him in court to get my daughter. Later I gave birth to another child. So I gave up and didn't think about it anymore.* In her second marriage, Liujin had four children. She went on to be a people's representative, a township director of the Women's Federation, and later a township vice head and then head.[109]

Liujin's divorce seems rather straightforward. A woman marries young, dislikes the gambling and conservatism of her marital family, becomes an activist, and de-velops the will and the means to leave, overcoming fear and tolerating the loss of her child in order to fashion a life she finds livable. But even among activists, the question of divorce was seldom so easily resolved. One of the great paradoxes of the early 1950s is that rural women leaders and labor models were not well-positioned, and often were not personally inclined, to be social pioneers in challenging local standards of virtuous behavior. Many activists made deliberate and conscious de-cisions to hew to older normative roles for women. One woman, who was recruited as a women's activist and village official in 1949, encountered opposition from her husband, a former hired laborer, when she tried to go out to meetings. Ten years older than his wife, he was convinced by local gossip that she would run off with one of the male cadres who were training her as a local leader. One night in 1950 he became violent. *My husband got mad and yelled at me that I ran around the whole day. He cursed, "If you are going to run around like this, just get out of here. Let's go to the township seat. We can't live like this. Let's divorce." I said, "I won't go with you.*

So shameful. I don't want to lose face. I never thought of divorcing you. I want to live with you. I never wanted to leave you." He was so angry that he pulled my arm and I hurt my head. I struggled not to go with him. I didn't want to bother the [officials at the] township seat. I didn't want to lose face. You were the head of women! Look, your husband treated you like this. I also had feudal thoughts back then. I just refused to go. He pulled me and I hurt my head on the doorsill and my face swelled this big. But when cadres from the Women's Federation and other government organizations wanted to criticize her husband, she made a canny political assessment of how this would affect her work. *I was afraid the old people around there wouldn't accept it. They would say, "Look at her. She has just been a director of the women's committee for a few days and she pulled her husband to a meeting to struggle him." It would definitely be harmful to mobilizing women.* Instead she chose to explain over and over to her husband that she would not divorce him, that she and he were *bitter melons on the same vine.*[110]

Finally the work team head of the administrative village got so mad. . . . He said, "I won't bother to care about you even if you are killed. You are so sympathetic to feudal thinking." But feudal thoughts had been there for thousands of years. It's impossible to make old people and young people accept things all at once. You have to be an example so that you can liberate other women. In order to liberate the whole country, the Communists climbed snowy mountains and went through grasslands. So many of our forebears died. Compared to that, my contribution and my hard work were nothing.

So I set myself as an example to others. I was very kind to my parents-in-law. I never quarreled with my sister-in-law all these years. I just wouldn't divorce my husband. . . . This made it much easier for me to mobilize other women. For the sake of liberating women, the bitterness I ate was nothing. During the Marriage Law Movement Month [in 1953] men and women accused each other of sexual misconduct [zuofeng wenti]. I set myself as an example to others. There was no gossip about me on this issue, although I worked together with men.[111] Here she negotiates the complicated intersection of virtue, revolution, and political efficacy. Although she refers to herself as having been "feudal" in her thinking, she clearly communicates her sense that she did the right thing, both politically and ethically. As a faithful wife and dutiful daughter-in-law, she sacrifices herself for the collective liberation of women, a sacrifice that is itself a virtue consciously modeled on the Long Marchers, even though the behavior in question entails refusing to divorce a violent husband.

This little homily should not be mistaken for a happy ending. This woman had a continually stormy relationship with her husband.[112] One Women's Federation official who spent a great deal of time in her home as a *dundian* cadre recalls her chasing her husband around the household millstone with a stick, threatening to beat him. Another, who held a top position in the provincial Women's Federation, recalls that it was actually the woman herself who wanted a divorce, and that it was the Federation cadres who cautioned her to weigh the benefits of staying married. If she divorced, they said, even though her husband was beating her, village opinion would not let her stay in the village, and she would lose her activist position. If she had made the Marriage Law her own personal cause, it would have ended her budding cadre career.

The disposition of child daughter-in-law marriages was also more complicated than a reading of the law suggests. In most Party-state accounts, the child daughter-in-law is little more than a chattel laborer, abused by a cruel mother-in-law and the rest of the family until she is old enough to be formally married and bear children, preferably sons, for the patriline of her husband. But women who had been sent to the families of their husbands as child daughters-in-law often had profound affection for members of their marital families, even if the marriage itself was disastrous. The mother-in-law of such a woman was also, in effect, her mother.

Consider the story of Zhang Chaofeng, the child who burned the banknotes, born in 1934. She was eight when her mother sent her away. *It was winter. My mother called me home. I was wearing a tattered set of clothes. She coaxed me. She told me, "You'll have white steamed bread to eat there, and flowered clothes. Go. Go, and in a couple of days Mother will come to see you." That's what she told me. I was very young, a dumb kid.*

Chaofeng was not to marry for another five years. In the interim, she was raised by her mother-in-law. *My mother-in-law was good to me, and also loved me,* she says, using language she does not use about her own mother. When Chaofeng's parents asked her to return home for a visit, she refused. In her new home, she had enough to eat. Chaofeng may have known at the time, and certainly understood later, that her new family was waiting to see whether she was healthy enough for their son to marry, and it was not in their interest to mistreat her. *This family, they were always feeding me and watching me. If I really didn't work out, they planned to sell me and arrange another wife for their son.* Coming from a family where food and maternal attention were both in short supply, Chaofeng preferred her new family, where she had access to both. She speaks of love and kind treatment, and does not dwell on the possibility that she could have been resold if she had not fattened up satisfactorily.

Chaofeng did not know her husband well. For the first few years in her new home, he was working away from home as a carpenter, returning only to help with the harvest. When they married formally in 1947, she was thirteen and he was twenty-seven. Still barely an adolescent, she learned about sex in the same way as many other young rural brides: *I was young and didn't understand. But the man was older, and sexually mature; he understood. If he came after you, you couldn't refuse. There was no way. You just had to submit. You might dislike it or think it was strange, but you were young, so you felt embarrassed to talk about it.* When we asked her if she and her husband fought about sex she responded, *We didn't quarrel, but I was not too satisfied.* But her husband was seldom at home. The relationship with the most important person in her daily life—her mother-in-law—remained good.

The larger political drama unfolding around Chaofeng left her almost untouched at first. Liberation, an event of supreme significance in national narratives, does not figure in her stories. But she remembers learning to read in a three-month intensive class for women. An older, more experienced women's activist convinced her mother-in-law to let her go to meetings. By 1951 or 1952, Chaofeng had been elected as a local women's leader (*funü xiaodui zhang*). Over the next few years her political responsibility steadily increased, from small-group leader to women's team leader to women's brigade leader and Women's Federation representative. She joined the Party in 1955, becoming one of seven people in the local branch.

As a cadre, Chaofeng studied the Marriage Law, and she knew that her marriage did not conform to its requirements. Initially, however, she did not think about applying the law to herself: *I had been a child daughter-in-law. I just got married when they said to get married. They talked about people having control over their own marriage. But I was born in the old society, and I couldn't do anything about it.* She was grateful to her mother-in-law, and her household was well-regarded in the village partly because the two had an exemplary relationship: *When I got a bit older I understood things. I returned her kindness. I worked hard at everything. When she would give me money, I didn't want to spend it. When I went out to meetings, I would buy the old folks something to eat and bring it back. My family was famous in the village for "respecting the mother-in-law and loving the daughter-in-law* [zunpo aixi].*"

Like the story of the child daughter-in-law as abused chattel laborer, by the mid-1950s this too was a well-understood revolutionary story: a young woman activist devotes her energy to mobilizing village women for collective production, while skillfully maintaining family harmony. But as the 1950s drew to a close, Chaofeng's marriage moved from silent incompatibility to open conflict, and her thoughts turned back to the Marriage Law she had studied earlier in the decade. *The feeling between the two of us was no good. He was fourteen or fifteen years older than I was. I carried this burden with me. I had studied about how to implement the Marriage Law. I felt in order to liberate others, I had to liberate myself first. Just at that time, the two of us started fighting, and things fell apart.*

The immediate cause of the argument was that the couple had not conceived a child. Chaofeng's husband, who continued to work elsewhere and came back to the village only twice a year for the wheat sowing and harvest, wanted to adopt. Chaofeng, convinced that she could bear children, refused. Others said that she was healthy, suggesting that the fertility problem was his. One of her husband's testes was bigger than the other, a condition known in Chinese medicine by the starkly descriptive term "one-sided droop" (*pianzhui*).[113] She wondered if this might be the problem, and wanted them both to go to Xi'an for a medical examination. He objected that the city was far away and the roads were no good. Her mother-in-law silently supported her, never reproaching her for the lack of children. Chaofeng's arguments with her husband grew more frequent and heated. She told him that he was free to bring in someone else's child, but she would not care for it. She proposed that they separate. He picked up a stool and threw it at her, gashing her head and leaving a permanent scar.

Chaofeng remembers 1959 and 1960 as the most difficult time of her life. She does not mention the hunger that was then beginning to spread as the Great Leap Forward of 1958–59 devolved into famine. Her memories of this juncture concern her own ambivalence about her marriage, what she calls *a struggle in my own thinking*. She considered the years of kindness from her mother-in-law, weighing the possibility of waiting until her in-laws were older before acting. After her husband threw the stool at her, however, she decided to take action.

Because Chaofeng had already cohabited with her husband, her legal status was no longer that of a child daughter-in-law who could simply return to her family of origin. Her case required a divorce proceeding. When only one party desired a divorce, the Marriage Law required mediation first by the local government, then by the district court. In the prevalent Party story of the march to marriage freedom, the child daughter-in-law is always a sympathetic character, and local Party officials emerge to support battered wives and uphold the law. But when Chaofeng began to talk openly of divorce, those from whom she might have expected to draw support were cool or dismayed. An official of the commune Women's Federation made it clear that she regarded this as a personal issue, not a matter of politics. *It's your problem,* she said. *You decide. If you feel that it's not working, think of a way to solve the problem.* The local Party secretary reminded her that her aging mother-in-law had treated her well. A divorce, he told Chaofeng, would be a blow to the old woman and have a bad influence on society. Perhaps he was concerned that other women would be encouraged to follow Chaofeng's example. He might also have worried that she would lose her stature as an essential political activist whose personal life was above reproach, damaging the Party's prestige. He went to her family twice to mediate, a process that seems to have consisted mainly of trying to persuade her to go on as before.

Meanwhile, perhaps just as the Party secretary had feared, gossip began to circulate in the village about Chaofeng's motivations. Her neighbors were divided in their opinions: *The main comment was that we had a good relationship between mother-in-law and daughter-in-law, but that since I had become a village cadre I had gotten grand ideas, that I looked down on farmers and wanted to find a cadre for myself. That was one comment. Another was that I had no conscience, that I was casting my mother-in-law aside and leaving, that my mother-in-law had raised me from the age of eight until now, that I had grown up and my wings had hardened.* Forty years later, Chaofeng comes close to tears when she repeats the accusation that she was abandoning the older woman.

Chaofeng had already had a painful conversation with her mother-in-law. *All that she could say to me was, "My good child, look at how good I have been to you. How can you abandon your mother?" She tried to persuade me. I said, "This is not about you. I have been thinking of you all along. If not for your sake, I would not have stayed until now." I said to her, "I cannot die at the same time you do. You cannot be with me for my whole life. Life is passing me by!" My mother-in-law was an intelligent woman. She stopped trying to persuade me and did not intervene. "Do as you wish."*

Eventually Chaofeng filed for divorce. Rather than live with her mother-in-law during the proceedings, she stayed with her parents. It had been eighteen years since she had left home as a child daughter-in-law. A few months later a man from the court appeared at her parents' house and summoned her back to her husband's village, where her divorce petition was granted. She left immediately afterwards, still fearing violence. *I didn't take away anything that the court had awarded to me. I left with empty hands. I was somewhat frightened when I walked to the road. I borrowed a bike from my sworn sister in the village and rode it to the road.*[114] *I was afraid that he would chase me and kill me. I was so scared. I got to the road and went back to my natal family.*

A year later she remarried, to a man from her ex-husband's village, although the new couple did not return there to live. In November 1962 she gave birth to a son, the first of four children in six years. Many of the people who had criticized her began to rethink their opinions. Clearly, they said to one another, her long period of childlessness had not been her fault. Perhaps she was fated to be a member of her new husband's family. Her ex-husband, however, was still angry and violent. He assaulted her new husband on several occasions and even brought a lawsuit alleging that the new husband had been the cause of her decision to divorce. Since she was never summoned to court, she does not know if or how the case was decided. But in 1963, her ex-husband married a widow in the village and subsequently had two children. She laughs when she tells us this. *He also made a good marriage,* she says.

In the early 1960s, Chaofeng followed her second husband to his new job in Baoji, a city more than three hundred kilometers and a world away from Village G. She never worked as a women's cadre again. She had exercised her right to divorce as specified in the revolutionary Marriage Law, albeit with little support from the local agents of the revolution. In the process she had lost the community where she had been an activist, forfeiting the status and sense of self provided by that work. She did not return to the village for almost forty years. Her memories of rural life as a women's leader in the collective era end in the early 1960s, when her life as a mother began.

For one moment in the early 1960s, however, those two phases of life overlapped. The moment reminds us that the narratives provided by the revolution, powerful as they were, fall far short of explaining the tangled relationships in which people lived. The story is simple: after her first child was born in 1962, just before she moved away to Baoji, her former mother-in-law appeared suddenly at the home Chaofeng shared with her new husband. *You're doing well,* she said to Chaofeng. *You were married for more than ten years and didn't have a child, and here you've had a child, a son, in your second year here.* She gave Chaofeng a gift: diapers for the new baby. Then she left.[115]

HARMONICS: DOMESTICATING THE STATE EFFECT

If Zhang Chaofeng had remained in the countryside after her divorce, her domestic history would likely have disqualified her from becoming a labor model. Labor models were expected to be models of stability in their domestic lives, using their prestige to advocate family harmony in the homes of their younger neighbors. Such work included remonstrating with in-laws to allow young women greater freedom,[116] but also persuading young wives to remain in difficult marriages. In Village B, for instance, many of the young women mentored by Cao Zhuxiang had complicated families: mothers who died in childbirth, suicidal fathers, fathers-in-law who smoked opium, disabled fathers-in-law, delusional mothers-in-law, husbands who engaged in gambling and petty thievery, suicidal husbands, hoodlum husbands, husbands who beat their own mothers. In this unpromising environment, Zhuxiang made domestic harmony her theme.

Zhuang Xiaoxia, newly married in the 1950s, looks back on Zhuxiang's interventions with an approving eye, even though the personal cost to her was high. Xiaoxia's grandfather had arranged for her to marry a second cousin from a large and poor family. Her parents had reservations about the marriage but deferred to their elders. Xiaoxia herself was aware that the Marriage Law discouraged, although it did not absolutely prohibit, marriage between close cousins.[117] But she decided not to exercise her rights under the law: *[I was afraid] that it would make my grandfather die of anger. As it was, he died three months after I got married. Why? My mother and my grandfather had a terrible quarrel. I was already gone, and my mother said to my grandfather, "The responsibility for sending her to their kang is on your shoulders." She made my grandfather so angry that he lowered his head and didn't talk. Three months later he died. I have always felt that it was me and my mother who caused my grandfather to die of anger.*

The marriage did not go well. Xiaoxia considered divorce, but Zhuxiang dissuaded her. *Sometimes he swore at me and hit me. I went to Secretary Cao's place and said to her: "He has a bad temper. I really can't live with him." Secretary Cao asked me what I wanted. At the time I was young and couldn't express myself. Secretary Cao encouraged me, saying, "If a person is poor, he can become rich, if he works. Later, life will gradually get better." That's how she encouraged me.*

Later, as time went by, he no longer hit me. My mother-in-law was always scold-

ing him, "We have to get along. You should be good to her. If you are not good to her, how can you face your great-uncle? He saw that our family was pitiful, and gave this child to us. Her parents don't come to visit us because they don't like it that you hit their child." That's how my mother-in-law worked on him so that he wouldn't lose his temper. And that's how we got to where we are today.[118]

Xiaoxia consigns her negative feelings about the marriage to the past. Like Cao Zhuxiang, who later introduced her into the Communist Party, she stakes a claim to superior virtue on her ability to maintain harmony in the family. A disquisition on her own sense of virtue segues into a tirade about young women in the 1990s: *They can't match me. They have not suffered bitterness. All they know is having money to spend, but they don't know where the money came from. They throw away their clothing before it is worn out. If the food doesn't taste good, they dump it. They know nothing about frugality. In a difficult struggle, they would be no match for me. Younger people nowadays, most don't have harmonious households. They also cannot match me in respecting the old.*

As the stories of Chaofeng and Xiaoxia suggest, in the early 1950s many young women village activists found themselves caught in personal situations that did not match the world promised to them by Party-state initiatives. Family need and opinion had far more influence on their fates—and, it appears, far more traction in their psyches—than the rhetoric of gender equality and free-choice marriage. Aware of the Marriage Law and conscious that their own marriages did not conform to its provisions, they were reluctant to take actions that would alienate their families. Local officials and *dundian* cadres were not always supportive of women who sought to exercise their rights under the Marriage Law. Women who stayed in unhappy situations, and even some, like Chaofeng, who left, described their own actions as exemplary: they remained considerate of their elders, concerned about harmonious relations with their in-laws, hardworking in the face of indolent spouses, and generally above reproach. In all these respects they embodied prerevolutionary standards of virtue. As with Cao Zhuxiang, their choices may have enhanced their capacity to become village leaders, respected for their industry, their skilled handling of relationships, and their progressive thinking, even when they remained in marriages that could easily be seen as "feudal."

BEYOND CAMPAIGN TIME

By the mid-1950s, Marriage Law work had become routinized. Each year after the 1953 campaign, as International Women's Day (celebrated on March 8) approached, provincial authorities would declare a month of activities to publicize the law with an eye to family harmony.[119] Activities at the county level followed a clear formula: five days to locate typical local cases and write propaganda about them; eleven days for publicity via wall newspapers, broadcasts, clapper talks, and cross talks, and for meetings; six days to sum up.[120] Beyond the annual month of activities, the central government concentrated its efforts on ensuring that couples registered their marriages, inserting the state into domains of rural life where it had not previously been involved.[121] County authorities recorded the total number of marriages approved and the ones disallowed because the marriage was arranged, the applicants were too young, or it fell into the catchall of "other." Quarterly statistics across the province indicated that most divorce suits involved alienation of affection, with smaller numbers of plaintiffs citing abuse, bigamy, and other reasons. As elsewhere in China, authorities shifted emphasis to promote mediation rather than divorce. Large numbers of cases were either successfully mediated at the local level, meaning that no divorce was granted, or were referred to higher courts (see Table 2).[122]

Gradually, conforming to a slower temporality than that of campaign time, rural marriage practices changed in Shaanxi.[123] Families no longer brought in young girls to raise as future brides. Concubinage, never affordable for the rural poor, came to an end. People began to register their marriages and generally to observe the mandated minimum marriage age: eighteen for women and twenty for men. And the Marriage Law campaigns, brief and limited though they were, did have a certain penumbra effect. Young women who had no specific memories of the campaigns nevertheless picked up the ambient notion that they should have some say in partner choice.

Throughout the collective period, parents continued to be deeply involved in choosing partners for their children. In what were colloquially called "half-free, half-arranged" matches, couples were introduced by a matchmaker with parental approval. They then had the opportunity to meet and agree to, or reject, the match—a limited right to speak and decide, within parentally set limits. It remained locally acceptable for parents to engage their children at seven or ten years of age, without any interaction between the future spouses.[124] Matchmakers were still essential to sealing a marriage transaction, even when the partners had found each other without assistance. Sedan chairs and phoenix hats disappeared, but the exchange of goods at marriage, if not outright brideprice, remained a central part of the process.[125] Young women remained unwilling to marry into families or villages poorer than their own.[126] Mothers continued to prefer that their daughters marry nearby, for both emotional and material reasons.[127] Change in marriage practices occurred, not in response to a single state intervention, but over a longer, more gradual and less easily traceable shift in social interactions and mores.

Women who learned to sing and read and taught others to do the same, women who made daring marriage choices or reconciled themselves to difficult home situations, now recall the early 1950s as the moment that most captured their imagination. They remember their activist years as the era of new songs, new sociality, and new possibilities. Some of these women later saw their activist careers cut short or interrupted—Gaixia's by illness, many others by subsequent political criticism, geographic moves, or the relentless demands of parenting. The 1950s remain the moment against which aging village women measure all subsequent moments, as well as the behavior of subsequent generations, and find them both wanting. Decisions about whom to love, whether to argue, and when to take solace from being filial or patriotic or industrious or determined—each of these has become a narrative element in a carefully fashioned melodrama of the self. The actual parameters of social change outlined in the Marriage Law, and how much the law did or did not deliver in women's individual lives, are only a small amount of what captivates them in memory. The memories of their own individual actions and emotions loom much larger.[128]

The May Fourth story about companionate marriage and the backwardness of Chinese village women contains, constrains, and sometimes misrepresents rural women, and it endures up until the present moment in state discourses about the "quality" (*suzhi*) of peasants in general and rural women in particular. It could even be argued that Party-state authorities need to regard the rural woman as needing rescue and uplift in order to justify continued interventions in rural life. Cadres and local leaders then assume the position of uplifting agents, if not always adequately performing the work. May Fourth thinking, and the failure of "backward" peasants to measure up to the challenge of modernizing marriage, is not the most helpful way to look at how marriage changed during China's collective past. What requires more attention are women's own stakes—affective, practical, and political— in maintaining or leaving a marriage. Their actions helped to constitute them as virtuous women, worthy of approbation and legible to their own communities. At the center of this inquiry should be the question of how rural women understood their own relationships, communities, and choices, and how they remember those choices as they look at the very different contemporary arrangements surrounding them now.

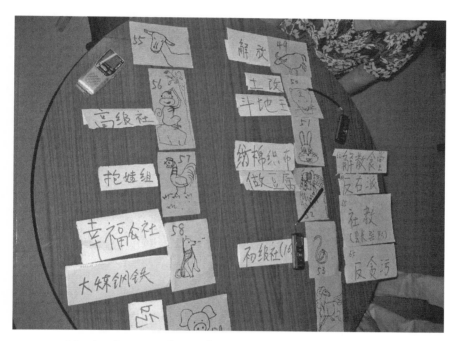

FIGURE 1. Mapping time, 2006. Signs refer to major political events in the history of Village B (photo by the author)

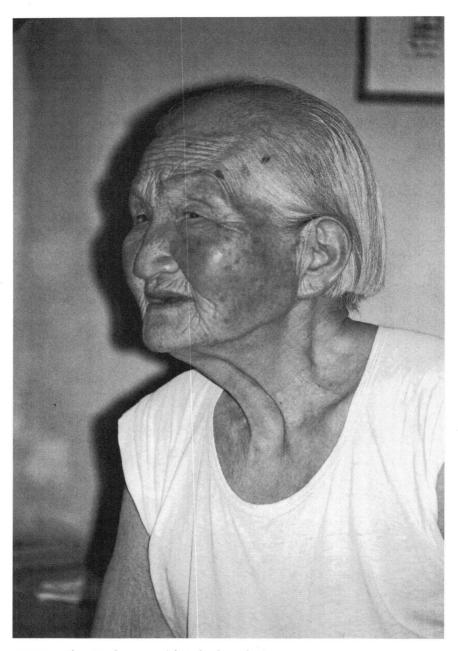

FIGURE 2. Shan Xiuzhen, 1997 (photo by the author)

FIGURE 3. Cao Zhuxiang growing cotton, 1950s (photo courtesy of Cao Zhuxiang)

FIGURE 4. Cao Zhuxiang as a labor model in the 1950s or 1960s (photo courtesy of Cao Zhuxiang)

FIGURE 5. Cao Zhuxiang, 1996 (photo by the author)

FIGURE 6. Zhang Qiuxiang (center), Cao Zhuxiang (far right), and others, date unknown (photo courtesy of Cao Zhuxiang)

FIGURE 7. Zhang Qiuxiang, 1996 (photo by the author)

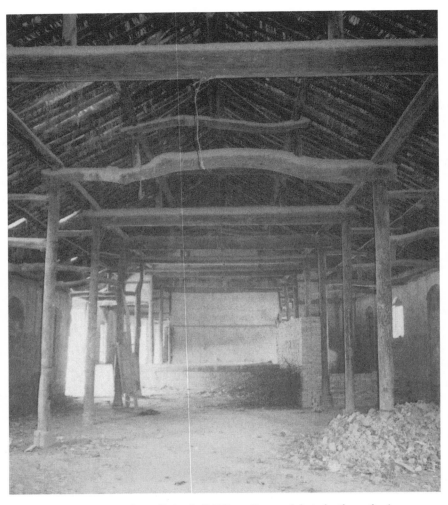

FIGURE 8. Former Great Leap dining hall, Village G, 2001 (photo by the author)

5

Farmer

Until 1954 Qiao Yindi had never left Village G. But at the age of twenty-two she joined her husband in Xinjiang, where he had been assigned to do statistical work for the Health Bureau. The journey with her toddler daughter in the back of a truck was long and difficult, the three years spent among strangers lonely and disorienting. Yindi never stopped longing for Village G during her years in Xinjiang. The village, a dry brown place crisscrossed by deep gorges, emerges in her telling as a kind of green oasis. After three years away she told her husband that it was time to go home.

When she returned to Village G in 1957 with her husband and two daughters, the place Yindi had known and longed for had been transformed. Village land had been collectivized, a process she had heard about only through infrequent letters from home.[1] As collectivization proceeded, the daily round of tasks in which women spent their days changed profoundly. Before her departure for Xinjiang, Yindi had gone to the fields during the busy season each year to weed beans and help cut wheat. Most of her time, however, had been spent on household chores and on spinning and weaving, both for her family's use and for the local market. Now the women of Village G were farmers. They hoed the fields together. Men no longer cut wheat, although they bundled it up and hauled it away. Women continued to spin and weave at home, but did not sell their cloth at market anymore. Field work was their main activity. Daily life, the gendered division of labor, and the networks of community relationships all had been altered in the process of collectivization.

The participation and support of women, mobilized by women cadres, helped make rural collectivization possible. Across Shaanxi, women became an important part of the farming workforce—at some points, even its mainstay. If collectives relied on women, however, women were dependent on the collectives as well. Co-ops paid their farmers in work points, and women, like men, needed to work in order to support their families and keep them out of debt to the collective. Women earned a consistently lower work-point rate than men, even as the range of tasks thought appropriate for women was continually expanded. Activists regarded themselves as the political equals of men, but a division of labor (and a pay gap) predicated on gender difference was widely taken for granted in the fields and at home. By the mid-1950s, men in many farming communities were beginning to leave the fields, either for collective sidelines or for paid employment beyond the village. Agriculture gradually became the major content of women's work.[2]

THE RISE OF CO-OPS

The transformation that appeared so thoroughgoing to Qiao Yindi on her return from Xinjiang was an uneven and difficult process. In the mutual aid groups that followed land reform, people from several households had planted and harvested one another's land in sequence, while households kept their own crops. The groups were intended to improve peasant welfare while accomplishing the even more important task of bolstering the national economy. The Party-state leadership—which farmers refer to vaguely, yet with precision, as "the above"—understood mutual aid groups as a transitional form. The future was to be one of "collective and socialist farming."[3]

In late 1953, local Party organizations were still trying to iron out the problems with mutual aid groups when a directive came from the Central Committee in Beijing mandating another change: agricultural producers' cooperatives.[4] Later, when they were superseded by more fully collectivized units known as "higher producers' cooperatives," these early co-ops were retrospectively renamed "lower producers' cooperatives." Lower co-ops were larger than the mutual aid groups, sometimes comprising a whole neighborhood or village with several dozen households.[5] In a lower co-op, farmers kept ownership of their land, livestock, and tools, while pooling their labor.[6] They farmed their combined landholdings and sometimes engaged in sidelines as a unit. A management committee, led by a chair and vice chair, coordinated the work and authorized expenditures, which were recorded by a bookkeeper and disbursed by a cashier.[7] After the harvest, the chair and accountant paid the agricultural taxes and put aside some reserve funds for future expenditures. Then they distributed the bulk of the crop to households based on how much land, tools, and livestock they had contributed and how many work points they had earned. Co-op members determined the percentage of crop distribution based on a household's land and equipment, and the percentage based on its labor. The most common split nationally was 70 percent to land and 30 percent to labor. Membership was to be voluntary.[8]

Putting together this kind of organization and convincing farmers to join it was a difficult task for local authorities. The co-ops were announced just as local cadres were being asked to implement the widely disliked unified purchase and sale of grain.[9] Casting about for how to begin, the Weinan County leadership turned to Cao Zhuxiang's village, which already had a large mutual aid group under competent leadership. In its first year of operation, Zhuxiang's group had paid people 80 percent of their income based on their land and 20 percent based on their labor. In the second year, the group had reversed the percentages.[10] In effect, Zhuxiang's mutual aid group was already operating as a producers' cooperative. By the end of 1953 it had become one of four lower co-ops in the county, with Zhuxiang as its chair.[11]

Shan Xiuzhen, too, got an early start on co-op building. In her account we see the process at its most ideal and idealized. Xiuzhen heard at a 1953 meeting that a co-op had been established by Li Shunda across the Yellow River in Shanxi. With her characteristic verve and energy, she stopped at the Tongguan County seat on her way back home and proposed to found one herself. *Shanxi did it. Only the Yellow River separates us. Why couldn't we in Shaanxi do it? I was very excited. Seven or eight people from the county committee came to stay in Shangmadian, my village, and held a meeting at night for the people of the connected mutual aid groups, studying the process of organizing agricultural producers' co-ops. One way to do it was with land at eighty percent and labor at twenty percent. I discussed this with the three Party members in the group and said I didn't want to do this land eight and labor two, but land and labor, half and half, or at most land four and labor six. They said this would work. It would motivate labor enthusiasm. It wasn't only the Party members—many of the masses were advanced too, especially the poor peasants. Poor peasants had less land and all of them were willing.*

Xiuzhen set off with several other people and three mules for the county seat forty *li* away to obtain the best wheat seed, Bima No. 1.[12] With the help of the improved seeds, *in 1953, the agricultural producers' co-op had a very good wheat harvest, a bumper harvest. Everybody was very happy. People were allocated more than they had been when working individually. The masses watched the Shan Xiuzhen co-op. . . . After the bumper harvest, Tongguan County organized many agricultural producers' co-ops.*[13]

Across Guanzhong and Shaannan in 1954 and 1955 cadres did the painstaking work required to build lower co-ops and train people to run them.[14] But most people were far less enthusiastic about the co-ops than Shan Xiuzhen and her neighbors. Co-op membership was supposed to be voluntary, but the pressure to organize new co-ops was considerable. Some cadres were said to be lowering standards or using coercive methods so that they could exceed their quota of newly established co-ops. One government document reported thirty-two co-op-related suicides in Weinan Prefecture alone. Peasants were reported to be cutting down their trees, selling their livestock, and squandering collective resources in protest at the prospect of joining. In the county just west of Heyang, peasants pulled more than one-quarter of the total livestock out of the co-ops, and in several cases the co-ops dissolved altogether.[15]

As they had when mutual aid groups were formed, cadres recognized the importance of winning over rural women to the new initiative. Like men, women were reluctant to give up their land and tools, and they worried that more people in a co-op meant more trouble. Older women were not eager to take care of their grandchildren while their daughters-in-law worked the land.[16] Women's Federation cadres set out to remind women of the vulnerability of family farming, talking up the material benefits of the lower co-ops. Drawing vivid contrasts between the material insecurity of life before 1949 and the improvements made by mutual aid groups, cadres described the co-ops as the next point in an arc of steady improvement.

Evident in Women's Federation work reports and directives were two assumptions: that women needed to be mobilized by appealing to their gender-specific interests, and that their ability to influence the men in their households was a valuable asset. Gone was the earlier portrayal of women as powerless victims of patriarchal authority. Only under socialism, cadres argued, would women become equal to men. In a co-op, short-term childcare could be arranged during the busy season, and women could take turns cooking while earning equal pay for equal work in the fields.[17] By mid-1954 Women's Federation workers reported that the numbers of women participating in co-ops, taking on leadership positions, and participating in labor were all on the rise.[18] A detailed organizational blueprint for lower co-ops, adopted by the National People's Congress in early 1956, guaranteed that women had the same rights as men to join cooperatives. It stipulated that some percentage of leadership positions should be reserved for women, required the co-ops to help women overcome difficulties that prevented them from participating in agriculture, required protection of postpartum women, and called for the establishment of daycare facilities for the busy season.[19] Nationally the Women's Federation instructed each of its branches to make sure that local cadres and peasants understood these provisions, taught women new farming skills, paid them work points under their own names and not those of the household heads, and guaranteed equal pay for equal work.[20] Each of these measures suggested that women were crucial to the success of collectivizing agriculture.

Zhuxiang's co-op was singled out as a model by the prefecture in early 1955. Perhaps, the leadership reasoned, if co-op heads from less successful sites saw how Zhuxiang was running her co-op, they could improve their own.[21] This success story could be used to convince women who feared that if they joined a co-op, they would once again not have enough to eat.[22] Even in Zhuxiang's co-op, however, it took all her leadership skill, as well as support from other men and women activists, to convince the members that this new form of organization was worthwhile. Her younger neighbor Zhuang Xiaoxia observes, *There were people who entered the collective, but their thinking hadn't caught up with them. They felt that after they entered they weren't as free as before. There was one person who created a lot of conflicts. He saw that now it was planting time, and the work was very intense. Yet he still went elsewhere, speculating, and collected some money. He put it in his pocket. His land was being planted by us women. Afterwards he still wanted to have grain distributed to him. That was the contradiction. He went out speculating, and came home in the evening. We held meetings for him, educated him, and called him back. There were meetings almost every night. If we hadn't had meetings, there would have been more and more contradictions. Whenever there was a problem, as soon as it got dark we would hold a meeting to discuss it.*[23]

Managing a co-op required not only shrewd judgments of people, but also close attention to accounting. Returning home from a three-week meeting, Zhuxiang found that her vice-chair, in cahoots with another man, had sold vegetables belonging to the co-op and pocketed the money. *At that time, the co-op members were all in an uproar talking about it. I didn't publicize it, I just called my accountant— that one was reliable—and I had him bring the work records. I asked the leadership to look at them. In all, the vice-chair embezzled more than sixty yuan. After that, he stepped down.*[24]

Learning to run a complex organization with one's untrustworthy neighbors had its challenges, but the lower co-ops also brought some benefits. Members no longer had to worry about their individual crops and livestock, wondering whether the crops would fail and there would be nothing to eat.[25] People no longer had to shuttle back and forth between scattered plots of household land; instead the collective members moved systematically through the entire group's holdings.[26] Gathering wormwood in the mountains to be soaked and used as green fertilizer was done more efficiently in groups, allowing farmers to enact the local saying, "If you want to see a wheat pile, see the fertilizer pile first."[27] The state also provided the co-ops with fertilizer and improved seed strains, much of it distributed through technical extension stations. As Xiuzhen's experience suggests, crop yields from the lower co-op lands improved accordingly.[28] Negative incentives also came into play: in Village T, a household that did not join the lower co-op found that the collective would not let water into its irrigation ditches, or loan it the collective's cattle for plowing. Soon enough, everyone in the area joined.[29]

HIGHER CO-OPS

Many in the Party-state leadership had envisioned socialist collectivization taking more than a decade, but Mao Zedong wanted to speed up the process.[30] Mao's favored form became known as the higher co-op, in which farmers were remunerated in cash and kind strictly on the basis of their labor, measured in work points. By the summer of 1955 he was complaining to a conference of Party secretaries, using the standard gendered trope of feudal backwardness: "An upsurge in the new, socialist mass movement is imminent throughout the countryside. But some of our comrades, tottering along like a woman with bound feet, are complaining all the time, 'You're going too fast, much too fast.' Too much carping, unwarranted complaints, boundless anxiety and countless taboos—all this they take as the right policy to guide the socialist mass movement in the rural areas."[31] Meanwhile some actually existing rural women—unlike the caricature of backwardness offered in Mao's comment—were among the more active proponents of collectivization. In September 1955, the Weinan prefectural Party secretary personally led a work group of cadres from the prefecture to "an experimental site in Baiyang Township"—more than likely Cao Zhuxiang's village—to publicize Mao's report "On Problems in Agricultural Collectivization."[32] Spurred on by the pressure and prestige of Mao, collectivization moved forward far more rapidly than Shaanxi planners had anticipated. By the end of 1956, most rural households were members of higher producers' cooperatives.[33]

Higher co-ops were larger than their precursors.[34] In Village Z, for instance, the north village and south village lower co-ops were combined.[35] In Xiuzhen's county, five villages comprising more than 840 people in about 270 households joined the higher co-op. Some land and livestock were transferred from one village to another.[36] These adjustments would have been unthinkable in the lower co-ops, but now private landownership was abolished, and livestock and tools were pooled. Households retained only modest vegetable garden plots and small farm tools.[37] The co-op was to decide what and how much to produce in coordination with higher-level state plans. Fields were squared, and in some areas machine cultivation was introduced.[38] For daily work assignments and accounting, peasants interacted most frequently with the former lower co-ops, now known as production brigades. Sometimes brigades were further subdivided into temporary production groups.[39]

Peasants earned work points for their labor in higher co-ops. At the end of each year, part of a collective's grain was sold to the state and income from sideline production was tallied. Then the co-op figured its net income, after deducting production expenses and money set aside for the reserve and welfare funds.[40] In Shaanxi, the government decreed that between 60 and 70 percent of the co-op's income should be distributed to its members.[41] If the net annual income of the co-op was ten thousand yuan, and the total number of work points earned by everyone in the village was ten thousand, then each work point would have been worth one yuan. (Work points in the early 1950s were usually worth a third or less of this.) But work points were not the only factor in determining a household's income. A certain amount of "eating grain" (*kouliang*) was distributed to households each year according to the number of people in the household. This was not free grain. If a household with many members received five hundred *jin* of grain, and the price of grain was set at one yuan per *jin,* then the household owed the collective five hundred yuan. This amount was deducted from the work point–based cash distribution to households. A household that owed five hundred yuan in grain costs, but had earned only three hundred yuan of work points, would owe money to the collective. Households short on work points had to come up with cash, go into debt to the collective, or borrow food grain from families with a surplus.[42]

Like land reform, the higher co-op campaign in Shaanxi took place in a period of inclement weather. The area around Village B suffered drought in 1955 and flash floods the following year.[43] A major drought in Village T in 1955 was followed by a catastrophic September rainstorm that washed away more than seven hundred homes. The next two years were no better: in 1956, 1,617 stranded peasants had to be evacuated by boat, and in July 1957, flooding caused significant damage to fields, irrigation systems, and homes.[44] Village Z, at the eastern end of Shaannan, was similarly afflicted that month: twenty-nine people died when the waters rose after two explosive rainstorms.[45] Village G had no rainfall at all in the summer and fall of 1957.[46]

Exacerbating the unforgiving weather conditions were problems of organization and economic interest. Many farmers felt that the higher co-ops were too big, and disliked the fact that land and livestock could be transferred out of their home area to another team in the co-op.[47] Peasants who had more land and labor power did not want to give up the return to land they had enjoyed in the lower co-ops, or pool their labor power with peasants who had less. Even many cadres and activists shared this reluctance.[48] The speed of the transition, and the complexity of the new organizations, presented problems for *dundian* cadres and local leaders alike. Xu Nini, who was first a Women's Federation cadre and later a district head, recalls, *At the beginning, the activism of the peasants was high. The mutual aid groups were the best. The lower producers' cooperatives were okay, but before they were finished, there was a call for the higher producers' cooperatives, and before they were finished, a call for the communes. The twists and turns in peasant thinking, including the turns in my own thinking, hadn't rounded the bend yet. Our work was really very hard to do. Most people could go along with the tide, because they had faith in the Party members. But the concrete problems—people's thinking, management work, the techniques involved in running a large collective—none of those could keep up. The ones who wanted this in their hearts were not the majority.*[49]

At the time, however, the speed of the transition and the political and management problems it caused were not issues that could be raised directly, given Mao's enthusiasm for higher co-ops.[50] Newly minted leaders such as Cao Zhuxiang expressed their hesitation in purely local terms. When asked to become chair of a particularly large amalgamated higher co-op formed in 1957, she first demurred. *I said, "Secretary Feng, I cannot take this on. This is too big, the people involved are very complicated." He said, "Big, small, it's all the same. With more people, we'll give you people under you. It will be very sturdy." I said, "If there is trouble, it will make prob-*

lems for you. Just call on someone else to become the leader." He said, "I cannot agree with you." We didn't agree for a while. I said, "What's so good about being a leader? It involves lots of worries, lots of talking, lots of travel. I am still a woman. One has to go in and out of a lot of places. It is not convenient for me to get things done." I said to him, "Suppose I don't manage things well. I don't like people talking about me. Why don't you ask Chair Qiao to do it?"[51] Ultimately Zhuxiang acquiesced, becoming chair of the higher co-op, but her hesitation, expressed as "I am a woman and leadership is difficult," can also be heard as an oblique commentary on the size of the unit and the local opposition it was engendering.

Even in model co-ops with strong leadership, conflicts erupted among members. In Tongguan County, two of Shan Xiuzhen's production groups underreported how much grain they had harvested, distributing a portion of it privately. In her view, they stole grain from the group, kept double books, and denied wrongdoing. Only after an eight-month investigation, in which an outside team of twenty people came to the village and key players were summoned to the county court, was the truth of the matter cleared up and the group leaders removed from their positions. Xiuzhen found this period very difficult because many of the investigators initially doubted her word. As a woman, she said, she was assumed to be less credible. She felt that her lack of vigilance had permitted the theft to happen in the first place.[52] Yet this incident, like that of Cao Zhuxiang's reluctance to lead, can also be understood as a reflection of local tensions—in this case, between farmers and the state over the continually unpopular unified purchase and marketing of grain.[53]

MOBILIZING WOMEN

In early 1956, the Central Committee sponsored a national three-volume collection of reports celebrating "the high tide of socialism in China's villages," organized by province.[54] Shaanxi's provincial Party committee followed suit with a collection of its own in the fall.[55] Although the Shaanxi volume highlighted success stories, on the way to the inevitable happy denouement it gave accounts of many problems. Peasants enumerated their worries about giving up their land, wondering aloud how widows and other vulnerable households could survive depending solely on income from labor. The collection offered examples of cooperatives that had assigned lighter work or offered material support to women in households without able-bodied men.[56] The editors waxed eloquent on the contributions women could make—if only men could be convinced that women were useful: "Outstanding achievements and vivid examples of women participating in labor in the agricultural collective illustrate the usefulness of the women masses on the production front, which is so amazing! In the co-ops, if there remains someone who still says that women are 'useless,' even to the point where he does not want to provide women with a fair and rational reward for their labor, you can use this essay to demolish his argument, and cause him to feel his lack of logic." The key to success, the editors continued, was for cadres to put time and ingenuity into mobilizing women.[57] As in previous campaigns, this task fell mainly to the Women's Federation.

On International Women's Day in 1956, women farmers across Shaanxi Province were called upon to work for the co-op 150 rather than the usual 100 or so days per year. (In cotton-growing regions of Guanzhong and in the Shaannan mountains, the estimated average was already 150 to 200 days.) The Federation organized labor contests to see which teams could field the most woman laborers or produce the highest yield of a particular crop.[58] Federation cadres also gave more attention to training "women backbone cadres" to staff the co-ops.[59] Women team leaders were crucial in getting women into the fields, as the former activist Liu Dongmei explains: *If you did not go, if you as the train engine did not go, the caboose would not go either. You had to work diligently.*[60] The provincial Federation convened periodic meetings for hundreds of "rural women socialist construction activists" to report on their experiences, receive awards, and set goals.[61]

In spite of the indefatigable efforts of *dundian* cadres from the Women's Federation, women's participation in co-op activities remained uneven. A 1956 report on four Shaannan counties, including Village T's Nanzheng County, found some areas where women were not showing up even though their labor was needed, and other areas where co-ops had not found enough tasks to keep women busy. Women were reported to have made comments such as "How does socialism bring happiness? Humans are changed into cattle"; "We turn over clods of earth every day. Is this called women's 'turning over' [*fanshen*]?"; and even "If women have to work so hard, why do they marry men?" The report also mentioned that two women had miscarried because of overwork, while two others gave birth in fields in the hills, and that women's health required more attention from leaders than it was receiving.[62]

Women's attitude toward field work in the collective period is difficult to disentangle from the more generalized discontent people now express about that period—an attitude encouraged and supported by current Party-state policies favoring household cultivation and a more mobile labor force. The burden of women's domestic labor—for which no work points were paid—also affected women's availability, energy, and enthusiasm. Several things can be said about women's memories of field work in the 1950s. First, for both married and unmarried women, the ability to work in the fields side by side with other women their own age was a pleasurable expansion of their social world.[63] The need for work points overrode earlier opposition by mothers, mothers-in-law, and husbands to women "going out."[64] The requirement that women labor collectively gave young women, who ten years earlier would have been isolated in the homes of their in-laws, a sanctioned occasion to see one another. In the words of one activist, *Working together, there were a lot of people and it was lively. Alone in the house, working by yourself, you felt nervous. I felt more comfortable working with a lot of people.*[65] Like field work, the numerous evening meetings of the co-op period provided an opportunity to see other young people. Zhang Chaofeng, the child bride turned women's leader, recalled, *Every day after dark they would ring the bell to call a meeting and would say, "Tomorrow at such-and-such a time, we will work at such-and-such." They would arrange it all. The next day, as soon as the team leader finished eating, he rang the bell, and everyone grabbed their farm tools and went to the fields together. We talked, worked, and laughed. It was fun.*[66]

Second, the collectives profoundly changed the rhythm of rural life and the place of women's work within it. After the transition to higher co-ops, a farming household's entire income was calculated in work points, and women's daily routine quickly became organized around the need to earn them. The work-point system was set up to ensure maximum participation in farming labor. People were expected to report to the fields promptly at the ringing of a bell, and those who arrived late would have their work points docked.[67] A day was divided into three work periods. An early-morning shift began at dawn, with an hour's break for breakfast at about 9:30. The midday shift ran from 10:30 until about 1, followed by a rest period. The afternoon shift ran for about four hours from midafternoon until early evening.[68] Work points were recorded separately for each shift. In Village G, women received three work points for the morning shift, two for midday, and three for the afternoon.[69] In Village Z, men were expected to work twenty-eight days out of the month, and women were given quotas as well. If a woman could not finish her work for the day, her husband's work points were deducted from his pay and used to supplement hers. These reductions could result in a household grain shortfall at the end of the year.[70] Members of the collective were guaranteed a basic food grain ration (*kouliang*), but if they did not show up to labor, the team made deductions from it.[71] One disgruntled woman farmer comments, *If you didn't work, they would not give you work points, and you couldn't eat. If you worked more, you got more, and only then would they distribute grain to you. Labor more, get more; labor less, get less. When you labored you had to be there early. If you went late or missed a time period, they would dock your work points. They wouldn't be able to record a whole day for you.*[72] In women's stories, the cheerful musical sociality of the first years after the revolution quickly gave way to a more practical imperative: women's labor in the fields was absolutely necessary to keep their families from going into debt to the collective.

Third, the advent of the higher co-ops meant a marked decline in women's individual handicraft production for the market. Immediately after 1949, markets had revived and even increased, flush with the results of new handicraft production.[73] Now women no longer went regularly to rural markets to buy or sell thread and cloth. They made cloth and clothing for their own families, but spent their daylight hours shuttling back and forth between unpaid domestic chores and field work remunerated in work points.[74] Cloth making, formerly a source of household income, was now politically suspect and disappeared into the shadow barter economy or stopped altogether. Home handicraft production of other goods declined, although some co-ops organized women to make baskets and bamboo curtains, paying in work points and selling the products to augment the co-op's cash reserves.[75] Higher levels of the Party-state—"the above"—directed co-ops to focus their sideline production on agriculture. In Cao Zhuxiang's collective, sidelines did so by servicing plows and tractors.[76] Village Z ran a castor-oil mill using seeds grown by the higher co-op and grew walnuts to sell. Local sidelines remained small in number and scale.[77] The narrowing of legitimate sideline production limited the means by which women could add to household income. Work points earned in the fields became the only legitimate measure of their economic contribution.

Fourth, the constant pressure to appear in the fields or be penalized overrode measures that were meant to take account of women's reproductive health and domestic labor. In Village Z, women with heavy menstrual periods were allowed to rest for three days, but would earn no work points if they did, so few took advantage of the provision.[78] In Village T, women were not supposed to work in the paddies during their menses, but as one commented, *How could you not go since you had so many kids who needed food? I dared not rest. I also went when I was pregnant. I rested when it rained sometimes and nobody worked. If you rested at home, you would be short of money when they counted at the end of the year, since you didn't work much. Then how could we find money to make up the grain shortage?*[79]

Looking back, many blame the aches and pains of old age on the unrelenting work they did in those years,[80] and the memory of exhaustion fuels their retrospective discontent with the collective. *We were all there working on the corn. We went to the field to dig. It was so far. We were so pitiful. We were so tired after we came back. When people who went to dig came back, their faces were pale. Even their eyes and lips were white. I said, "Hurry up and wash it off." They said, "What is there to wash?" You looked at me and laughed, I looked at you and laughed. We saw our own faces.*[81]

WORK POINTS: A USEFUL CATEGORY OF GENDER ANALYSIS

The worth of a day's labor in work points was determined, not by the length of the day or by the task performed, but according to what sort of person was performing the labor.[82] The co-op members, under the direction of the group leader, made periodic evaluations to decide how many points each person would receive,[83] a process fraught with debate and full of local variation. Nevertheless, the pattern across regions has been well documented: a man doing field labor typically earned ten points per day, whereas a woman earned between six and eight.[84] In spite of the attention to equal pay for equal work in co-op regulations, and the explicit dictum that co-ops should not discriminate against women members, it was extremely rare for a woman to be paid the same number of work points per day as a man.[85]

When women were brought into farm labor, they were supposed to be assigned gender-appropriate jobs,[86] but the notion of what counted as appropriate work for women shifted continually across the collective period. Before 1949, for instance, the wheat across central Shaanxi had been harvested by migrant male laborers known as *maike*. After 1949, women cut the wheat.[87] As women's field work became routine in Village Z, an elaborate gendered division of labor emerged. Men plowed, dug holes for the corn crop, and carried loads of manure on shoulder poles to fertilize the corn. Boys tended cattle. Women never performed these tasks. The work performed by women, however, was often just as physically demanding as that performed by men. While men led the cattle to plow the wheat field, women dug up by hand the four corners of the field where the plow could not reach. Like men, women carried manure, albeit in lighter sacks rather than with shoulder poles. Women planted the corn seeds in the holes dug by men. They hoed and harvested and hauled the wheat and the corn, planted green beans and soybeans, and worked side by side with men in the rice paddies transplanting seedlings. Any work that women could do in Village Z, no matter how heavy, was called "hand work." There was no generic name, however, for work done only by men.[88]

The Women's Federation worked to address two attitudes held by co-op leaders: that women were incapable of performing any labor of value, and that they could be assigned to any task without regard to gender-specific needs.[89] The two attitudes, seemingly contradictory, were sometimes linked. One co-op leader reportedly refused to assign tasks to women, telling them, "Just go home and sit on your *kang*," but when they insisted on assignments he sent them to haul manure without any help, sneering to one man, "Just let them do it, since they are so capable." Regardless of what women did in his co-op, they earned about half the daily work points of men. The district Federation decided to circulate their report of this situation across the province as an example of how not to treat women co-op members. The report concluded that the co-op and others like it needed to "seriously implement equal pay for equal work. Equal pay for equal work means, no matter whether it is women, seniors, or half-laborers, as long as they do the same amount and the same quality as men, they should get the same points. Equal pay for equal work is important to women's enthusiasm and a powerful weapon to fight against the thought that men are superior to women." The district Women's Federation appended a note directly addressing the gendered division of labor: "Even if the tasks are different, if women's work requires skill and meticulousness, they should get the same work points."[90]

In taking on the entangled issues of equal pay and accommodation of gendered difference, Women's Federation cadres were anticipating debates about equality, difference, and discrimination that emerged two decades later in the United States.[91] "Equal pay for equal work," guaranteed "to men and women alike without exception" in co-op regulations,[92] was subject to interpretation. Did it mean equal pay for identical work, or equal pay for work of equivalent value? How should equivalent value be calculated? "Women are different from men in physiology," stated a Women's Federation summary of its work in 1955. "They have the difficulties of weakness, menstruation, pregnancy, childcare, and housework. We should assign women tasks following women's traits . . . Women who are physically strong, who have no children, who have natural feet and less housework, were assigned to work in fields far away or on slopes. Women who were physically weak and have many children and more housework were assigned to fields nearby."[93] When women were given work different from that assigned to men, should this be understood as resulting from long-term physiological difference ("weakness"), temporary indisposition (menstruation, pregnancy), or a widely accepted social division of labor based on gender difference (housework)? How, precisely, should differences among women in age, strength, physical dexterity, and skill be factored in? What is striking in the Women's Federation writings of this period is the determination to define and advocate for women's interests, in the face of indifferent local leadership and inconsistent state support.

Several decades after the event, when Western feminist scholars in the 1980s began to write about women's status in rural China, they posed skeptical questions about the ubiquitous gendered disparity in daily work-point earnings, but their queries were generally met with puzzlement. Cadres and farmers, both male and female, typically explained such disparity as a consequence of the need for physical strength in farm labor.[94] They proffered this explanation even in situations where the tasks in question required no brute force (e.g., picking tea, where women's "natural dexterity" was said to give them an advantage), where men were paid ten points for technical tasks such as flipping a switch while women performed physical labor for fewer points,[95] or where women's production was bringing in more income to the collective than that of men. Margery Wolf, interviewing farm women about this situation in the early 1980s, detected an undercurrent of resentment about the disparity, but it was only an undercurrent.

The interviews that inform the present book were conducted many years after the demise of the work-point system, when presumably there was no political risk in denouncing it. Yet even then the disparity in daily earnings occasioned little commentary, and the few comments there were divided clearly along generational lines. The older generation of Cao Zhuxiang and Shan Xiuzhen, women who were in their thirties when collectivization began, were matter-of-fact about the pay system. They regarded it as natural, even though they themselves had long since broken the gender barrier where farmwork was concerned and were visibly engaged in building model cooperatives that achieved regional, even national, recognition. Zhuxiang's explanation was brief: *There were men to do the heavy work, so of course men earned more work points. Women's labor power was weaker, so they got fewer work points.*[96] Xiuzhen had made equal pay for equal work one of the key conditions in setting up her higher producers' cooperative, and even in retrospect she sees it as crucial in fostering women's participation. *The top promoted equal pay for equal work. So our branch and our brigade implemented it. If women didn't work, whom could you depend upon to plant crops? You had to bring women's enthusiasm into play. You shouldn't hurt their enthusiasm.* And yet to Xiuzhen, the persistent disparity in what men and women actually earned was unremarkable. Men earned more, she said, because they did the heavier work: cutting wormwood in the mountains, delivering fertilizer to the fields in heavy baskets, plowing and raking. True, some women also did all of these tasks, she said, and took on much else besides: hoeing the wheat in spring and cutting it in the summer, tending the cotton at every stage, sowing beans and corn in the fall planting. But the standard of value remained the heaviest tasks, and even when women could match men trip for trip in hauling goods, they usually could not shoulder a load of fully compacted manure baskets, transport fertilizer up to fields in mountainous areas, or carry as much wormwood down from the hills as men did.[97] *Among the men, the highest was twelve points, eleven, ten. Women were eight points or seven. The highest for women was nine. We didn't dare to set a woman's points too high in case she couldn't take the work. The women didn't want it too high. If it was high you had to work about the same as the men who got ten points. Men did the heavy work. Women who earned nine points did more or less the same as men who earned ten points, but still they could not catch up with men.* Xiuzhen held herself to a higher standard of productivity, going to the mountains alongside the men for days at a stretch to cut wormwood with a sickle. When she did the same work as a man, she earned the same number of work points. As far as she was concerned, this exhausted the complexities of equal pay for equal work.[98]

For the younger generation of women cadres and activists who came of age during the 1950s, in contrast, proving one's capability often meant a conscious struggle for both equal productivity and equal remuneration. In Village Z, for instance, a youth team made up of more than thirty men and women experimented with close cropping of sweet potatoes and corn.[99] The leader of the team's women, He Gaizhen, remembers that men received ten work points and women six, and it was always men who were sent to the county seat to receive technical training.[100] Against this assumption of women's lesser value, young women strove to prove their worth. Ma Li, one of the team members, recalls her enthusiasm: *They said I was something of a dummy [ergan]. Whenever I was asked to work, I went, even if it was windy or raining. We were capable at that time. We did the same as men. There was an old man on the east side, Yan Panwa, who was the secretary of the higher co-op. He was in charge of money in the brigade. He said, "How could it be possible that women are as capable as men?" I was working in the field. A young man said to me, "Try hard to-*

*day to show him." I transplanted seedlings faster than the men. Later he stood aside
and looked quietly. Women were really as capable as men.* He said, "Women should
get the same work points as men now." But the brigade didn't agree. Even after she
stopped working on the youth team, Ma Li and three of her strongest women comrades signed up for the most difficult tasks, such as carrying heavy loads of green
bean stalks over long distances. At one point they each managed to earn twelve work
points for carrying one hundred *jin* of corn, the same rate earned by men. Still, men
continued to complain about the substandard quality of women's field work. *The
team leader said, "All day long we talk about how men and women are equal. But the
field that the women dug was so bad." A man called Biegaizi up over there could turn
over a clod of hard soil this big. When Feng Zhimei, Liu Xinye, and I were digging, he
pulled our hair and said, "Look how small a lump you dug. The lumps are too small,
even though you are digging hard." He said, "Men and women are equal. But why can't
you dig as well as I can?"*[101]

In Village T, men could earn as much as five hundred *gong* per year—one *gong*
was ten work points, the equivalent of a standard workday for men—because certain
tasks conventionally done by men, such as cutting grass, paid the very high rate of
several dozen points a day. Women, in contrast, were not assigned these tasks and
never reached four hundred *gong* per year.[102] Li Liujin, one of the women who had
braved a threatening husband to obtain a divorce, describes a struggle for equal work
points that lasted for several years: *We had to fight on behalf of women for equality
between men and women, equal pay for equal work. We had done the same work as
you, so we should get the same compensation. That's why those people called me "Cock-
fighting Old Eight [zheng jizi lao ba]". I said, "I am not fighting for my own benefit.
All of our women should get this treatment. You see, some are doing the same job, but
are compensated differently. Men get ten points, and women are given eight. This is not
something unchangeable. When transplanting seedlings, you transplant one row, I
transplant one row. At the end of the day, I should get paid as much as you do. If you
get ten points, I want ten points, too." We achieved this during the higher co-ops. When
carrying urine for fertilizer, you got a strip of paper for each trip telling how much
work you had done. At the end of the day, your trips would be counted. For example,
if one trip carrying urine was half a point, ten trips would be five points. Twenty trips
would be ten points. If a man carried it, that's how much it was. If I, a woman, carried
it, that's also how much it was. . . . If you kept up with the number of rows when digging seedlings, at the end of the day, you got paid the same. This lasted straight through
until the land was distributed to households in 1982.*[103] But the piecework arrangement described by Liujin remained a rarity in the collective era. Far more common
was the allocation of fixed points per person regardless of the task being performed,
with gender as a salient category.[104]

A small number of women were able to improve their daily earnings by taking
on responsibility as local cadres. Rural grassroots cadres were by and large not "sep-

arated from production" or paid a salary by the collectives. Rather their work, including the work of attending meetings, was compensated in work points, just like the work of members of the collective who farmed full time. Juggling the duties of farmer and cadre—the latter including fighting for women's equal pay—enabled Li Liujin to earn more money than other women and some men. *When I did cadre work in the village, at the end of the year when we had evaluations, the village would give me some work points as recorded here. I earned slightly more points than men did, about four or five hundred, maybe five or six hundred, because no day went unrecorded. That's why people made up this kind of saying about you: "You don't shift the carrying pole from shoulder to shoulder or the hoe from hand to hand, but every day you get work points [qiandan bu huan jian, chuba bu huan shou, gongfen tiantian you]." But you were running around every day outside, doing cadre work [gongzuo]—what could you do? After we ran around we would come back and join in labor. I would come back, and as soon as I ate I would hurry there. . . . If I had a meeting at the brigade, if I made a trip there, they recorded the work as a business trip [chuqin tian]. So at the end, counted together, it was quite a lot. As much as a strong laborer.*[105]

Other women who became low-level cadres recall, however, that the work brought additional responsibilities without increased income. Feng Sumei, a women's chair for many years, found that attending meetings worked to her economic disadvantage. *About being a cadre. It is supposed to be to serve the people. But it could also make one angry sometimes. The meetings of the production team were not held in the daytime like those in cities, but at night, usually till twelve o'clock. It was dark, but the team could not afford a flashlight. It was usually held at Gaotoulang. You had to manage to come back no matter whether it was dark or raining. No shoes, only bare feet. You would get work points as you labored. So if you asked them to record that you had been at a meeting all day, the bookkeeper might not be there or might forget about it, and might not get around to it later. In fact, peasants, those who were not leaders and only worked, could earn more work points. If you attended the meeting for a whole day, it was eight work points. People who cut grass would earn more than ten work points. Meetings at night were not counted as work points. They were considered a duty. Busy in the daytime and many meetings at night.*[106]

Across rural Shaanxi, Women's Federation reports continued to mention that women routinely were paid less than men even when they did the same task with the same high-quality results.[107] Yet women do not appear to have fastened on the lower pay rate as a consistent source of serious discontent, and many maintain that they were regarded as equal even when they were assigned several fewer points than men for a day's labor. In part this is because equality was generally understood as a feature of a public, political domain, not an economic domain. The state proclaimed as an established fact that men and women were equal, meaning that they enjoyed equal political status. The official Party-state analysis held that political equality had been achieved the moment the state stepped forward to guarantee it, and that women's ability to enjoy this equal political status was limited only by feudal remnants located in the household, not by state-endorsed work-point practices.[108]

In the public economic domain of the rural co-op, in contrast, the operative assumption was not gender equality, but gender difference. As the disparities in daily work assignments suggest, most commonly this meant physical difference, justified by reference to a popular understanding of women's relative weakness and encoded in the work-point system.[109] Difference was also the operative assumption at home: women were understood to be naturally responsible for domestic tasks, an expectation that in turn shaped their participation in public economic activity. What is interesting and puzzling here is that no one articulated difference as a problem, either in state documents or in individual reminiscences, except when the issue was neglect of women's health. Difference was so much a part of the taken-for-granted, commonsense arrangements that it merited virtually no comment, even as its consequences ramified throughout the stories told to us by rural women.

This foundational assumption that difference was immutable, and had nothing to do with equality, may help to explain why women often did not object (at least not consistently and vociferously) to the work-point gap, which marked them as less valuable than men in the only recognized coin of the socialist realm: public labor. Women and men alike understood women's participation in collective work to be less than that of men, not because women were physically frail, but because their time was divided between public and domestic labor. Married women with heavy domestic burdens did not always work a full day in the fields, because their farmwork was interspersed with household chores that proliferated as the number of their children grew.[110]

FEMINIZING FARMWORK

From the time of the higher co-ops, women were expected to be in the fields year-round. In Village T, in the rice-growing region, Feng Sumei described the women's annual round of farming tasks, beginning shortly after the Spring Festival marking the lunar New Year: *The first thing in spring, we turned the soil in the potato field, and then planted potatoes. Then we cut green fertilizer, leveled the slopes, and collected fertilizer. Men mainly did heavy work such as building terraced fields and reservoirs. Women usually collected fertilizer. When that was done we made rice seedling beds, and broke clods in the wheat field and then fertilized them. Winter wheat was planted in broad rows, so after we dug in the spring there were large clods. We broke the large clods into small ones, using wooden hammers. These tasks were all done in the first, second, and third months. In the fourth month we gathered in the vegetables, and from the fifth month to the sixth month we gathered in the wheat. We transplanted rice seedlings while we were gathering wheat. It depended on the season. Transplant-*

ing rice seedlings started from the beginning of summer [lixia, around May 5] *to the summer solstice* [xiazhi, June 21]. *It took more than a month to finish it. The work was unending. After the transplanting came digging seedlings, weeding, and hoeing the rice. We would dig and then, in case there was a drought, we would also spread a layer of mud on it. It was done in the sixth and seventh months, until it was impossible for a person to get into the paddy. In the seventh month, we also started to plant Chinese cabbage* [youcai] *seedlings. When that was finished it was time to gather in the early corn. We usually cut the early corn in the middle of the seventh lunar month. After harvesting the early corn, it was time to harvest the late corn. Then it was time to plow the field and plant vegetable seeds. The work came, one task after another. Cutting the late corn started from late in the seventh month and continued until early in the ninth month. Planting vegetables had to happen in the winter months. Then we would sow the wheat. In the twelfth month, we had to fertilize the wheat field once. Then the work let up a bit, and it was time to prepare for the lunar New Year. We fertilized the field once more after the New Year.*[111] In this unceasing round of farming tasks, women increasingly took the lead. *Men were digging channels and building reservoirs at that time. Women carried fertilizer, planted potatoes, fertilized wheat, hoed vegetables—all these were done by women. Women suffered more and worked more than men when gathering in wheat. Men worked mainly outside. Women not only had to work outside, but also take care of children, feed the pigs, wash, starch, sew, mend.*[112]

In Village Z, even the work of flood control fell to women. They carried heavy stones to build embankments along the Dan River, which flowed level with the embankment and was prone to frequent flooding. With the aid of two *dundian* cadres from the district government, they constructed dikes to replace the patchwork of sandbags and thorns with which the community had fended off floods before Liberation. *How stable it is,* comments Liu Dongmei, looking at the dikes she helped to build almost half a century ago. *It has lasted for many years. If one part was washed away, we mended it. . . . I had no children when I started to work. What was there not to like? I liked it. I got money. I got work points. I earned according to my labor. All were women. Very few young men.*[113]

A world of obscured history inheres in that last sentence, recalling Xiuzhen's earlier comment about equal pay for equal work: *If women didn't work, whom could you depend upon to plant crops?*[114] Where were the men? According to official materials about the "high tide," the entry of women into the regular agricultural workforce had freed up men for other sorts of co-op labor. In one western Guanzhong co-op, women had taken over hoeing, seed sorting, cutting and threshing wheat, and watering the corn crop during a drought. Because women were doing these tasks, the co-op had been able to transfer twenty-four men to build a new village wall, apply more fertilizer, and engage in income-producing sidelines for the collective. Women's work in the fields had also saved the co-op the expense of hiring short-term laborers from outside.[115] Near Xi'an, the deployment of women to hoe weeds freed men for the putatively more skilled labor of tending melons and engaging in other sidelines. The co-op leadership exhorted women to perform their household chores and needlework on rainy days and during the slack season, lest these important unpaid tasks be neglected.[116] In Village Z, all sorts of heavy labor were considered appropriate for women, but anything involving machinery was the province of men. Women milled flour for their individual families by hauling the grain to a collectively owned millstone, then leading the collective's donkey around the millstone themselves. When the Village Z co-op was finally able to purchase a water-powered mill, it became a brigade sideline, with men operating the machinery in return for work points.[117] From the time of the lower co-ops on, men tended to be assigned to collective sidelines such as small-scale food-processing plants (including bean curd making), or tile and brick factories.[118] The limited sidelines staffed by women tended to pay less than those performed by men.[119]

Most work that involved being on the road, even short term, was assigned to men. In Village Z, the co-op sent men out to do transport work and to sell eggs in the Danfeng County seat as a collective sideline. The men handed their cash over to the team and were issued work points.[120] Men were sent to perform miscellaneous errands for the co-op such as buying agricultural tools and sending for carpenters.[121] Many men in Guanzhong and Shaannan, like Qiao Yindi's husband, who was sent to Xinjiang in the early 1950s, continued the pre-Liberation practice of working outside the village.[122] In 1956 thirteen thousand peasants from Guanzhong were working on temporary construction crews in the city of Xi'an.[123] Some men worked part time or full time for new rural institutions such as village credit stations, which made loans to individuals, and township credit unions, which made loans to the collective.[124] If a man took a full-time administrative job in the nearest township, he usually earned a salary, not work points, affording his family some portion of income that was not tied to the year's harvest.[125] Men were also more likely to be sent by the co-op to work on reservoirs outside the village. A day of work on the Qiangjiawan reservoir near Village T, for instance, could bring in more than twenty work points.[126]

Beginning in the mid-1950s and accelerating with the Great Leap Forward, women became the heart of the ordinary farming workforce. Men involved in sidelines or contract work came back to the fields only during the busy seasons of plowing and harvesting. As Shan Xiuzhen observed, *People said, "If women weren't sent out, there was no one in the fields." That means they [the men] all went to town. Also, more men went out to do sideline work and make money. They fired the kiln, made cement, drove mules, worked as carpenters, as blacksmiths and as bamboo craftsmen. Farming was mainly done by women.*[127] By 1956, a Women's Federation report from

Danfeng County claimed, women were doing almost 90 percent of the wheat hoeing, as well as applying pesticides, rescuing the wheat harvest from rotting in the fields after untimely rains, and collecting fertilizer.[128]

In Village B and other central Shaanxi communities, women took over every stage of cotton cultivation. Planting took place in the early spring, followed by hoeing, thinning the seedlings, pruning the plants, weeding, applying insecticide, hoeing again, and picking the cotton. The work required women's presence in the field in each of the three periods of the workday.[129] Before collectivization, household cotton yields had been seventy or eighty *jin* per *mu*; in the collective, the yield for Cao Zhuxiang's group exceeded two hundred *jin* per *mu*.[130] A few villages away Zhang Qiuxiang, soon to be a national cotton-growing champion, learned to grow cotton from *dundian* agricultural technicians in 1956, during the lower co-op stage. By the following year she was experimenting with a small one-*mu* high-yield plot that produced 230 *jin* of cotton.[131] Women's experimental fields became showcases for new seeds and techniques, and the Women's Federation used the opportunity to identify model groups, praise activists at meetings and in print, and hang up signs saying "This field is cultivated by women."[132]

Women's labor contributed to the farming achievements of the collective period, including substantial increases in yields of wheat, cotton, and corn. Across Shaanxi, both the area sown to wheat and the output per hectare rose steadily throughout the 1950s, enabled by better seeds and crop care, more manure, and improved irrigation.[133] Nevertheless overall yields in the 1950s remained low, partly because chemical fertilizers were not widely available or affordable.[134] The main form of fertilizer was human waste, produced in households but jealously measured and collected by the co-ops. Feng Sumei explained, *Every family [in Village T] had a fertilizer pit. The team used a fertilizer-measuring tool to see how thick the fertilizer was. The tool was a glass tube with a weight hanging under it. When the tool was put into the fertilizer pit, it showed the degree of the thickness of the fertilizer. Families took turns carrying fertilizer till it was empty. Individuals were not allowed to carry fertilizer here [for their own use on garden plots], because we had more land and fewer people, and fertilizer was in demand. We sometimes went to Hanzhong city to buy fertilizer, or to collect manure. Some people even sent students to Hanzhong city to steal manure, and the students were caught and beaten. Public toilets in Hanzhong were all under the charge of the teams nearby. If you went to steal and were caught, you would surely be beaten by them. Fertilizer was turned in to the team for money. It depended on the degree of its thickness. Less money if it was not thick. People who carried fertilizer were given work points per two-basket load [tiao]. The weight of the two baskets of fertilizer was recorded on the wall. Then at the end, all the marks were counted together to see how many baskets you had carried and how many work points you had earned and how much it was worth.*[135]

Ma Li, a former activist on the youth team in Village Z, remembers, *The collec-*

tive had no money at all. It couldn't afford fertilizer. We used fertilizer we ourselves produced, light fertilizer from toilets to fertilize the land. There was nothing in the fertilizer. So there was not enough grain. Here the explicit point of comparison is the recent years of economic reform and family farming. *It was said that [during the collective] the whole team harvested more than six hundred* jin *of wheat in Yaogou. Now even a single family can harvest more than one thousand* jin *of wheat. The family that did it used a bag of urea, two bags of diamine, and a bag of stinky fertilizer in their field.*[136] Given the lack of inputs and the partial exodus of men, the increase in crop yields, some of it achieved by women working with rudimentary equipment, is all the more impressive.

NO ONE IS HOME, REDUX

When a man left the village during the collective period to seek long-term work elsewhere, the results were not always salutary for the woman he left behind. Such was the case with Feng Sumei, the woman whose father had traded her to a much poorer family so that her one-eyed brother could get a wife. Sumei encouraged her husband to leave Village T in 1955 and go to work building the Baocheng railroad, because she believed that hard work outside the village could improve their lot. She borrowed a quilt and some money for him from her mother, and made clothes for him to wear as he went off to become a worker. *When Old Yi left, there were only my father-in-law, my mother-in-law, and my son, altogether four people. Just imagine, the two old ones in my family never worked—they all depended on me. . . . If I had left at that time, they could not have survived . . . they could not have gotten enough food from the team. My father-in-law enjoyed eating but never worked. My mother-in-law was a small-foot, and therefore could only work at home and take care of the child. My son could not walk yet. My mother-in-law could be helpful. She had a nickname, "Erbobo," meaning sometimes clever while sometimes stupid. I never requested too much. Only to take good care of my child and the family was enough.*

For three years, Sumei heard nothing from her husband. Unbeknown to her, he had been transferred to work in Shanxi Province. She received no remittances. *My husband never sent a letter or one cent to me till my eldest son was five.* Eventually she discovered that her father-in-law was keeping letters and money from her. *Every letter he sent was kept by my father-in-law, and he did not mention it to me sometimes. . . . Someone said to me, "Yi Faming sent more than three hundred yuan to your father-in-law, but not a cent to you." I said I did not know that. At last, my father-in-law told me. I said the cotton trousers I had made for the wedding had already worn out and I wanted a new pair. He would not give me money. Finally he gave me two yuan. I remember that I bought six* chi *of cloth for 2.40 yuan—I borrowed four* jiao. *I asked him for the amount of money I had borrowed, but he only gave me two* jiao. *I even had a quarrel with him about this.*

All the others said that he kept the money and bought cigarettes and wine every day without giving me one cent. Usually my in-laws did not cook, but it was my mother-in-law who was in charge of cooking when there was meat to cook, and my father-in-law always sat in front of the cooker. When the meat was ready, you took one piece, he took one piece, it would soon disappear. You could only have a few pieces, then there was nothing left. If there was some meat left, you would never see it later. You could do nothing. They never cooked when you were at home. They only had soup. But as soon as you were out, they would slice the meat and steam the bread. When you got home, again there was nothing left. Everyone said, "You, the daughter-in-law, are too honest." Others said, "Money was sent back and your father-in-law was smoking the golden-leaf cigarettes from Sichuan instead of the native soaked-leaf ones." They all said, "You should go to talk to him, since he is wasting money."

Desperate to support her son, Sumei took up sideline work at night: *One jin of palm fiber rope was worth four jiao. I usually made palm fiber rope at night because I had no time during the daytime. It was cold, so I just sat in the room and made the rope without light. I could make one jin of rope in about three or four nights. That was just pocket money, or in case my child was ill.* Eventually she went to track down her husband in Shanxi, taking her son with her. She remained with him for about eight months, then returned home to tend to her in-laws. After that, her husband sent small amounts of money so that she could buy grain from the collective to make up the shortfall in her work-point earnings.

Still, life remained very difficult. *I suffered a lot. I went to search for firewood in the rocky valley no matter whether it was summer or winter. I went out together with the men before dawn. They usually carried the firewood on their shoulders. I only took a cold rice ball because I had no flour to make steamed bread. I did not know how to tie the firewood up and had to ask others for help. I just followed them, carrying the firewood on my back. My mother-in-law wasted a lot of firewood—one bunch of firewood could only last two or three days. Then I had to go out again. I searched for the thin leaves in winter and one day cut firewood and the next day searched for grass. Then my second son was born. I was the only one in the house who could earn work points in the collective. We had less labor power, so we got less firewood and less grain. Families with more labor power had surplus grain. Our household was short of grain. We got less at the beginning, and in the end they would supplement it with corn, but it wasn't properly dried out. So we had no food to eat in the second year and had to borrow others' stored grain.* Sumei took on the heaviest tasks she could handle, the ones that paid the most work points: cutting and carrying a hundred *jin* of grass, carrying manure, working on construction at two area reservoirs. *[Luckily] school fees were cheap at that time and I made all the clothes and shoes. I never bought any. I worked during the daytime and sewed and made ropes at night.*

Sumei attributes some of her difficulties to ungenerous and shifty in-laws, but her memories are also tinged with bitterness about the collective leadership, although she remained a Party member and a local activist. In her telling, the burdens that the collective left unaddressed changed little for three decades. *I was quite pessimistic at that time. At every Party member meeting, some people who had no wives and children would criticize me. Like Zhu Peihua in the second team. He said, "You are too selfish." Just this sentence, which I still remember now. "You, Feng Sumei, are so selfish that only death could change it." [After my father-in-law's death] I had an old person [her mother-in-law], four children, and me. There was nothing left of my husband's thirty or so yuan after he covered his food expenses. He never even gave me five yuan when he came back home to visit. There were three children in school. You could not see the children and the old starve to death. My third child once said, "Mom, the porridge we eat is so thin that we can see the reflection of bamboo leaves." I was sad whenever I recalled this [cries]. I would just grind a bowl of rice into paste, then add some water. The five of us just drank this. I cried at home and put on a smiling face when I went out for meetings, and then would be worried again when I came back home. This was in the 1970s. Life was really hard at that time. . . . No matter how good the labor in your family was, one person alone could not make it no matter how hard she worked. One workday was only worth 0.20 yuan. It was so cheap. Sometimes it was even less than 0.20, only several cents. The highest was about 0.30 or 0.40. The yearly average was 0.20. If I were literate, I would write a history about that. You could open and read it now. . . . All of this would make a good novel.*[137]

Sumei's tale contains many other subplots. She waged a determined and ultimately successful campaign to clear her husband's name when he was accused of misdeeds in his factory late in the Cultural Revolution, making the rounds of officials to persuade each one to lend support. By raising pigs, saving, and borrowing from her brother, she managed to buy a house for her family in the 1960s and to build a new house when her son married in the 1970s. In 1984 she left her position as women's chair in Village T and began a reform-era career as a peddler in Baoji city, eventually providing work for several of her children there as well. When we met her in 1997, she had just returned to the village and was caring for a grandchild while his parents continued to earn money in the city.

Sumei draws on her memories of her own conduct during the collective period to bolster her sense of worth. Her capable hard work, she says, has brought her the respect of her children and of the wider community: *My contribution [to the family] was greater [than that of my husband]. My children always speak gently in my presence. They are always smiling. My daughters-in-law are also nice. Just like the old saying, "If you are filial to the old, your children will be filial to you." I have that very experience. . . . If I had not supported the family, his family would already have collapsed long ago. People in Old Yi's factory all know that my prestige is high. People in Village T, in B commune, all trusted me.*[138]

Sumei is able to look back with satisfaction from a comfortable old age, for which she herself accumulated most of the resources. She is surrounded by grown sons who treat her well and daughters-in-law who mostly seem to stay out of conflicts with her. She has not forgotten old injuries, but her manner of talking about them indicates that they, like their perpetrators, belong to the past. When she mentions her capable performance, it does not have the force of a contemporary accusation. Nevertheless, she invokes a past spent in virtuous hard work in order to support a claim on the present, a claim for attention, economic support, and above all recognition. Central to this claim is her situation as a woman left alone, the only source of work-point income in a household of aging in-laws and young children.

DISAFFECTION

As the collective period wore on, whatever positive sentiments women felt about daily participation in collective farmwork dissipated. The discontent that emerged among both men and women during the collective years began with the unified purchase and marketing of grain, then extended to modes of pay under the collective, taking the form of grumbling about cadre privilege, malingering on the job, and concealing grain from the state. A Women's Federation cadre who spent many *dundian* years in the countryside recalls the waning of enthusiasm: *Even if you dawdled* [moyang gong], *you would earn the same. Activism suffered. When work was decided according to ability, activism was high. . . . Some dragged their feet at work. They weren't satisfied, to the extent that a few tried to pull out of the collective. . . . In the past we had laid a basis for the mutual aid groups by doing thought education among the women. But now they would show up but not put out any effort, because it was of no benefit to them. Their income was distributed according to work points. It was men ten points, women eight. Women still couldn't completely attain equality.*[139]

Li Liujin, who fought for a piecework system and equal pay for women, characterizes the discontent somewhat differently. For her the issue was one of absolute poverty. *Starting from the higher co-ops, people didn't want to put themselves into the work. They wanted to avoid doing anything. There were people who just killed time* [huntou] *all the time. And at that time there was no chemical fertilizer. We only had farmyard manure, but not enough. I have to laugh when I remember the time I raised a female pig. That was in the 1950s. It had some piglets. They didn't even have hair. One look and I could see they were no good. I raised those pigs until New Year, then slaughtered them and got fifty-plus jin of meat. I didn't have much to feed them. The whole production team only slaughtered two pigs for New Year. When there was nothing to feed them, what choice was there? We didn't have enough to eat ourselves. How could we have food for the pigs? Ai. All those years, that was all because of the collective.*[140]

Work slowdowns were punctuated by sarcastic commentary directed at cadres. Feng Sumei, accustomed to hard work and local responsibility, found it frustrating that the work-point system required attendance but could not elicit individual effort.

Anyhow you had to be there [in the fields] no matter whether you were dawdling or just standing there. If you worked fast, you would be mocked as an "activist" or "pseudo-activist." Bad people influenced good people. There used to be an ironic saying: "Whether it is eating porridge or boiling broad beans, the activists lead the way." So you could not head forward. You could not talk to them. You had to dawdle together with them. For instance, digging seedlings, honest people dug one by one, but the dishonest did not even stir the water when they dug. So in the time of the collective, grass appeared again right after you hoed. You could tell how dishonest they were—they never used their energy but only shook their hoes. Their thinking was not so advanced, and you could do nothing. The honest suffered from losses while the dishonest took advantage of them. I was never assigned light work that earned a lot of work points. All that kind of work was assigned to families with more labor power and families who were close to the leaders.[141] In memory, it is often unclear whether such patterns dated from before or after the Great Leap Forward. Although the Leap stands out and specific stories are attached to it, the practice of slowdowns seems to have begun earlier and become pervasive later.

Still, comments Wang Zhaoru, a male production team leader in Village G for more than twenty years, there were gendered differences in how farmers regarded the collective, and women were more industrious and tractable than men. *When I was a team leader, the women were easier to mobilize than the men. The men were very lazy. No one believed in the collective. This attitude took shape gradually. People's consciousness changed. People discovered that they had been stupid, that there was no point in working this hard.*[142] By the end, another male former cadre comments, *people were no longer of one mind. The team leader could talk himself hoarse and rack his brains, but he couldn't persuade the masses. The quality of labor was lower every year.*[143] Amid the generalized disaffection, however, women's laboring lives had changed substantially. Farming was no longer feasible without them, and the livelihood of their families was no longer sustainable without their continuous work in the fields.

6

Midwife

In 1947, after a day spent hauling in the corn harvest, Yang Anxiu miscarried at five months. She was seventeen. *My husband was away from home, hiding from military conscription. My mother-in-law slept on the other side of the house, and I shared a room with my elder sister-in-law. There was no light at night. I was bleeding. I said, "What is happening?" Finally, I struggled to climb to the edge of the bed. By the second half of the night, I could not endure the contractions. I moaned and knelt on the ground.*

In the morning, my sister-in-law said, "I heard you moan once, and then you made no sound. What happened last night?" I said, "Sister-in-law, come look, what is this flowing out in front?" It was winter and there was no light. I said it looked like blood and it seemed that something had dropped. And there was also a cord. She looked and said, "Aiya, you have miscarried." The head was already this big and the body was this long. She used fire tongs to put it on a board, and told my mother-in-law.

My mother-in-law said nothing. Later she said, "It is nothing serious. A miscarriage at several months is nothing." My sister-in-law said, "We should make some food for her. Her face is too yellow." I put my old trousers on and lay down. Finally my mother-in-law said, "What are you afraid of? Go ahead and eat something! Back in my day we didn't do anything special even if we miscarried in the seventh month."

I stayed home for only three days. Then it was time to sow the wheat, and I went to the fields. I cried often, whenever I had a free moment. I thought, What's going on here? I have been married into such a poor family. They don't take care of you even when you have a miscarriage.

Three years later, pregnant again, Anxiu went into labor one morning in spring 1950. The revolution had not altered the dynamics in her family, nor yet touched the local methods and dangers of childbirth. *I felt the pain, but I did not say anything. My mother-in-law was hot-tempered. "Are you really in labor?" If you said something, she would say, "How can you tell that to others? Aren't you ashamed? Having a child is just a natural phenomenon." So I dared not say anything. I just walked back and forth. At noon, I said I would go make some noodles, but I couldn't do it. I served one bowl of boiled bread to my mother-in-law. I just had the soup and could not eat anything.*

In the afternoon, I heard the old people say it would be better to walk around. I felt the pain in my back, like a blunt saw sawing you. It was terrible. I leaned on this and that. Then it got dark. My aunt's sister came and asked, "Does your back hurt a lot?" She said to call a midwife. The going rate of pay for a midwife was a chicken, a three-foot piece of red cloth, a pair of shoes, one bushel of wheat, and money.[1] *I said no. I had seen the midwife deliver a baby next door and I was scared to death. She put her whole hand in the vagina. Just like digging seedlings in the field. The woman's eyes were rolled back in her head. So I said no. Also, we were poor. Even food was a problem. How could you call in a midwife?*

It had been a whole day. It pushed me to the edge, it almost killed me. Finally I put my hand here and pushed, leaning on the edge of the bed. I sat on a small chair supporting myself with my two hands. What should I do? My husband was not at home. Again I wanted to go to the toilet. My aunt's sister squatted and held a piece of cloth in her hands. The umbilical cord was too short, only about five inches. Finally she had it in her hands. She did not know to separate the perineum. It was so painful that the flesh was jumping. By late night, it was so painful that everything was swollen.

I gave birth on May 18. It was very hot. I just lay on one side like this on the bed all day long. They brought me food. Finally, on the fourth day, my husband came back. He said, "You're just sleeping on your side like this?" I said yes. He went out to the kitchen. My mother-in-law was very feudal. She said, "You entered the room?" "Yes. Why not?" "Anxiu just had the baby. You came back at night and just entered the room?" She meant that he should walk around for a while outside first, otherwise he might bring something unlucky into the room. He said to me, "Why didn't you tell me you had the baby? You just talked about sleeping and lying down." I said, "What is there to say about it? It's been several days."

Then I said, "My bottom is terribly painful. Get some hot water for me to wash." He boiled the water. After washing, he said, "No wonder you can't endure it. It was festering." I could not put my two legs together. When I lay down, I had to prop them up. Later my husband said to his mother, "Ma, her lower body has a festering sore. It is in terrible shape." She said there were some Chinese honey locust thorns in the back, that he should cut some to lance it. He lanced it several times but could not break it. Then he used a porcelain tile to break it and let the pus out. It was unbelievably painful. I cried for the whole evening. I said it was so terrible and I never wanted to have another child. I could not endure it.

The next day, my sister-in-law said to go to Nanguan in Hanzhong to Doctor Li Shen for some medicine. I went there and they gave me some red ginseng [hong shen-

dan] *to put on. It was very painful, as though someone were taking your flesh and twisting it. By the second half of the night, I could no longer endure it. I said to boil some water to wash it off. The medicine had soaked into the flesh. When it was put on for the second time, it was not painful again. But for forty days after that, until after the month of confinement, I could only walk by leaning against the wall. Now there is still a scar here like a wheat stalk. So I cannot sit for a long time even now.*[2]

Miscarriage, painful and protracted labor, an unskilled birth attendant, post-partum infection, a sharp-tongued mother-in-law, and a well-meaning but hapless husband had combined to make Anxiu miserable. She never became pregnant again after the first child, although she later adopted two children. When she was selected for midwife training in 1954 she was determined to make childbirth easier for others. Leaving her young son and her one-year-old adopted daughter for several weeks to take the training course, she returned to the village and successfully delivered her first baby the next day. *So when I did midwifery, they all said that I was careful. Because I myself had experienced it. I said, "I suffered a lot and will not let you suffer like that." I delivered babies for three generations. I delivered most of the people here in Village T, except for some who went to the hospital.*[3]

Yang Anxiu became a midwife as part of a state initiative for childbirth reform, one of the first issues through which rural Chinese women encountered their new government. Women's health was articulated as a state priority, and good midwifery practices were central to achieving it, as expressed in the national slogan "One pregnancy, one live birth; one live birth, one healthy child."[4] Continuing the language and policies begun by its Nationalist predecessor, the new Party-state was committed to a far more extensive presence in rural areas. State agents envisioned a straight-forward process: they would bring scientific knowledge and practice to the countryside, dislodging the old-style midwives they held responsible for the death of many infants and their mothers.[5]

In print, state authorities castigated these practitioners for their ignorance. Then, in a nod to the limitation on state resources and the practicalities of rural childbirth, they proceeded to retrain and use them, supplementing their presence in the village with newly trained personnel such as Yang Anxiu. Encounters between state officials and midwives presented a sharp contrast to the confrontational tactics of land reform. In spite of some sharply worded national propaganda, in practice old-style midwives were not caricatured, attacked, or discarded. Their techniques were investigated and reported in full. The women themselves were offered additional training and treated as an important resource. Some midwives active before Liberation even participated in training the new, post-Liberation generation of midwives. This continuity in the practices and personnel of childbirth showed flexibility and pragmatism, a willingness to incorporate rather than denounce skilled old-style midwives, to build on their skills while improving the quality of health care they delivered.

In some respects, the campaign for new-style midwifery, which featured sterilization of delivery instruments and having the woman in labor lie down rather than sit, was an early success for the new Party-state. Throughout the 1950s China saw a substantial decrease in infant mortality; from a high of around three hundred per thousand, it may have been cut in half.[6] By 1959, the number of midwives had increased from 15,700 to 35,290. Far greater was the number of "assistant midwives," old-style midwives who were retrained and women who took a short midwifery course, whose ranks grew from 44,000 to 774,983.[7]

In spite of these dramatic statistics, the state was not consistent in its attention to women's reproductive health. Preoccupied with increasing farm output to fund industrialization, planners put far more resources into mobilizing women's productive labor (*laodong*) than into changing the conditions of their reproductive labor and childbirth (*shengchan*). The limited change in childbirth practices, particularly in poor areas, can be understood as part of the inconsistent attention to the health needs of rural women and farmers more generally. In Shaanxi, new-style childbirth did not become common until the 1970s, well after the push for collectivization in the 1950s. A short-lived attempt to create rural birthing centers during the Great Leap Forward soon foundered. Most rural Shaanxi women gave birth at home, attended by old-style midwives who had undergone minimal retraining. The heralded revolution in reproduction proceeded on a much slower timeline than the revolution in production.[8]

This chapter begins with an account of old-style childbirth and midwifery as they were understood in the early years of the People's Republic, placing Party-state attempts to modernize midwifery in the context of a half-century-long reform agenda begun by the Nationalists. It describes village midwifery and practices in the early 1950s, as well as the ambitious, if short-lived, attempt to collectivize birthing along with farming. It draws on interviews with midwives and stories told by childbearing women, both of which offer indirect commentary on changing family relationships. The chapter concludes by exploring the layering of temporalities around the act of childbirth itself, where progressive, scientific, sterile health care delivery time jostled against birthing stories peopled by ghosts and punctuated by mysterious midwife deaths. Change in rural childbirth practices was not fully captured by campaign language and temporality. In the realm of childbirth, even more than in marriage practices, the outer limit of revolution's scope becomes apparent.

RURAL PRACTICES AND OLD-STYLE MIDWIVES

In the body culture of rural Shaanxi, women's reproductive functions were regarded as polluting and unmentionable. Menarche often took young women by surprise. *I was thirteen. My grandma asked me to pick some peppers and she cooked them for lunch. At night, I had a bad bellyache. I called for my grandma, saying, "My stomach hurts a lot."* She blamed me. *"Who asked you to eat so many peppers at lunch? You ate too much, and now you have fire"* [a pathogenic term in Chinese medicine]. *When I got up in the morning, I saw there was red on the quilt and sheet. I didn't understand. Finally I told my grandma. My grandma looked and said, "Chop your head off* [kan naoke]. *You got your period yesterday. Look how dirty you made the sheets!" She took out the quilting and washed the quilt cover.*[9] Only after they began to menstruate did their mothers (or mothers-in-law) instruct them in the use of rags fashioned into pads, which had to be kept out of sight. Cao Zhuxiang recalls, *We did not dare to expose the washed pads in front of the house. Instead we put them on the firewood in the backyard where other people would not see. We put our washed pants there too.*[10] Everyone detested this chore. *We young kids hated washing them because they were so dirty, and we would secretly throw some of them in the ditch. We washed some and threw some away.*[11] Women's Federation reports in the early 1950s found that many rural women, lacking hygienic knowledge, not only hid the rags, but used them over and over again without washing them at all.[12]

Sexual relations were treated with similar reticence, and marriage between teenagers was often not consummated until several years after the nuptial ceremony. Cao Zhuxiang describes her lack of sexual knowledge before she was married: *My mother and sisters never told me anything about sex. When we got married he was only fourteen years old. We both did not understand anything about sex between men and women. For quite a long period of time we did not have sex. I felt embarrassed, and he also did not know how. Adults did not discuss this kind of thing. Young men got together, trying to give my husband some ideas, and teased him. In the past people were naive. They were even embarrassed when they had babies. Because of that, we had a baby only after several years of marriage.*[13]

Childbirth itself was regarded in Chinese medical and ritual writings as a polluting and dangerous occasion.[14] A saying popular in Nanzheng County summarized the peril: "As the child rushes toward birth, the mother rushes toward death."[15] In difficult births, the survival of mother and child depended on the skill of the local midwife. Old-style midwives who were interviewed by government agencies in 1950 provided a catalogue of complicated births and draconian methods of dealing with them. In "well-circle labor" (*jingquansheng*), when the birth canal was too narrow for the baby to descend, a midwife might push down on the woman's belly to push the baby out, use her legs to support the woman's back and pull her backward, or (more ominously) "chop the well rope with an axe or use an axe to hit the mouth of the well three times." If the child still did not emerge, the midwife would ask the older generation in the family which one they wanted to save, the mother or the child. If they chose the mother, she would fashion a hook from a nail or use a firewood-trimming knife to pull the baby out, or sometimes dismember it in utero with a knife or sickle.[16] In horizontal labor (*e'laosheng*), if a hand or foot presented first and the midwife could not put it back in, she might prick it with a needle, cut it off with a knife, or sprinkle salt on it. (Villagers believed that if a pregnant woman went outside the door with salt in her hand, during labor the baby would reach out its hand to ask for salt.)[17] In "watermelon labor" (*xiguasheng*), the baby emerged still encased in the amniotic sac, and a midwife who did not know enough to break the sac might mistakenly bury the baby alive. An experienced midwife, however, would tear the sac with her hand and pull the baby out. If the baby did not cry, she would tear a piece off the paper on the window and burn it in front of the child's chest to help it breathe.[18] In protracted labor (*mansheng*), which might go on for several days, the midwife might forcibly separate the two parts of the pubic bone by breaking the symphysis pubis (*gufeng*), which would leave the mother permanently disabled. Then two assistants would pull the woman's legs as wide as possible while the midwife put some oil on her hand and tried to extract the baby. If the baby's buttocks presented first (*lianhuasheng*), the midwife would force them back in and try to pull out the legs instead. If the head began to protrude before the water broke (*dingbaosheng*), she would break the water manually, then push the baby downward with her hands until it descended completely.[19] In the case of a retained placenta, old-style midwives tried to deliver it manually and then stanch the bleeding by having the woman drink a decoction of yellow wormwood water, ink, and children's urine to cool down her blood.[20]

Such descriptions underscore the skill and knowledge of experienced midwives, as well as the brutal methods to which they sometimes resorted. Death during childbirth was a common occurrence in Shaanxi villages before 1949. Shi Cuiyu lost her mother and two aunts to childbirth within a hundred days, a catastrophe that left thirteen children motherless. Later, when she began to study midwifery in Village G, she understood that what she had witnessed with one of her aunts was complications from a retained placenta. *After the baby came down, the placenta adhered. Finally, it was so pitiful, they tied her hair and hung her from the roof. The old-style midwife couldn't get the placenta out. Nobody sent for a doctor. At that time medical science was not advanced. People didn't go to doctors. So she pulled it down and tore it out roughly. Oh, the blood. In the end my aunt died of a massive hemorrhage. When I studied the new method of midwifery, the more I learned, the more I thought of how pitiful my aunt was. Now if the placenta doesn't come out, they have methods to handle it. So pitiful, she died and left five children. Some were given to others. Nobody took care of them.*[21]

Danger for both mother and child extended past the moment of childbirth into the first postpartum month.[22] It was (and remains) the custom for women to rest for at least a month after childbirth, when a woman's body was considered unclean.[23] This interlude was known as "sitting the month" (*zuo yuezi*). Insofar as possible, a woman was not to get down from the *kang*, let alone leave the house, and could not come into contact with cold water or perform any work. Compendia of local customs give a fulsome account of the goods and attention lavished on mother and baby. On the third day after childbirth, the young woman's mother could visit, bringing presents: chickens, sugar, pigs' feet, and eggs, known in the Village T area as the four-happiness presents (*si xi li*). It was considered auspicious for the postpartum woman to eat food from her mother's family during this month, because this was said to cement the newborn's ties with his mother's family.[24] Chicken, eggs, dried steamed bread, flatbread, noodles, and a decoction of boiled dates and walnuts, sometimes with loquats and brown sugar, were favored foods for new mothers,[25] giving them unusual priority access to nutritious food as they recovered and began to nurse. After ten or twenty days, members of the mother's natal family would visit for a baby-viewing (*kanwa*) ceremony, bringing stacks of bedding and clothing and diapers for the baby to add to those that the mother-in-law had made, and staying for a ceremonial meal. In Village G, the mother-in-law's family would also bring *huamo*, intricately sculpted and brilliantly dyed figurines of flowers, crabs, phoenixes, fish, cats, and other creatures made out of dried steamed bread and decorated with walnuts, dates, and eggs.[26]

The actual practice of "sitting the month," however, could be considerably less cheery. A frequent problem threatening the infant was "four-six wind" (*siliufeng*), the colloquial term for tetanus neonatorum, or umbilical tetanus. Much criticism of old-style midwifery centered on unsanitary means of cutting the umbilical cord, which could cause tetanus neonatorum in the baby and puerperal fever in the mother.[27] If a woman gave birth in summertime, the old-style midwife might cut the cord with fire, in the belief that a baby's belly in summer was cold and that using fire would prevent future belly pain. In winter the belly was thought to be hot, so the cord was cut with scissors about eight inches away from the belly. The midwife then squeezed out the blood and flesh in the cord, tied it in a knot, passed it through a piece of oilpaper, covered it with a layer of cotton, and wrapped it in a cloth.[28] If the scissors were not sterile and the cut became infected, the disease would come on a few days after birth (hence the name "four-six wind") with crying, vomiting (*yongkou*), inability to nurse, and convulsions. Some old-style midwives said that if a pregnant woman became frightened or angry when pregnant, particularly if her anger was not expressed, then tetanus neonatorum would result.[29] Common midwife remedies to prevent tetanus included applying "mouth-opening pellets" (*kaikouxian*) to the baby's mouth at birth, burning incense on either side of the baby's mouth and cheeks, treating the umbilicus or the inside of the mouth with cure-all tablets (*wanyingding*) and pills to alleviate internal heat (*qingxinwan*), or applying a concoction of rat's testes dried in red orpiment powder to the inside of the mouth.[30] In Liquan, a 1950 health survey reported, midwives would use a pottery shard to scratch the chest of a one-day-old. Then they would burn Chinese mugwort leaves (*aiye*) on a coin and bring the coin close to the infant's eyes, ears, mouth, and nose, raising bean-size blisters.[31] If the baby developed tetanus neonatorum anyway, there were two locally accepted cures: to catch a live pigeon, tear the skin from its chest, and apply its still-warm skin to the umbilicus, or to feed the baby a dried rat fetus.[32]

Government reports attributed women's postpartum health problems to poor care. In some areas, women were forbidden to sleep for a day and a night, or longer, for fear of bleeding; they were required to sit upright on the *kang*. *When you got up on the* kang *they made you sit, not lie down. They put a sack stuffed with dirt and ash underneath me. I had to sit for two days. I didn't sleep much. Only when I stopped bleeding heavily did they take it away. Then could I put on pants and lie down and sleep. It wore me out.*[33] No fresh air was allowed in the room. Investigators after 1949 found that most women were given only porridge or vegetable broth for the first few days after birth, followed by noodles or dried pieces of steamed bread. They were not supposed to eat meat or eggs. In mountainous areas, nothing except corn was available, leading to weakness in women and their babies.[34]

MODERNIZING MIDWIFERY

In promoting the scientific modernization of childbirth, the Party-state was continuing an effort to train and register midwives begun by the Nationalists during the Nanjing decade (1927–37).[35] In Republican China, the division between new- and old-style midwives was profound. New-style midwives tended to be from middle- or upper-class families and to work in urban areas. Old-style midwives, who far outnumbered them, were primarily rural.[36] Nationalist policy recognized that old-style midwives would be important for many years to come, but their practices were sharply criticized by public health specialists.[37] Cataloguing problems including generalized poverty, rural ignorance of germ theory, and superstitions about childbirth, reformers from the 1920s on pointed to village midwives as the embodiment of rural backwardness. One commentator wrote of the disastrous consequences of using cow dung to dress the umbilical cord in Fujian. Another "lamented that because of their lack of education many older midwives failed to grasp the basic concepts of modern medicine, reverting to traditional methods soon after graduating from the course."[38] Marion Yang illustrated a 1928 article about midwifery training with a photo of a woman sitting in a basket, with the male basket carrier standing next to her. The caption was chilling: "Old type Chinese midwife (sitting in basket). Can only walk about on hands and knees. Has been seen to get up from this posture, wipe her hands on her clothes and put her fingers into the vagina without any further cleansing."[39] Old-style midwives were the oft-maligned other against which modern medical practice was defined; they were, however, the only resource available in most rural areas.[40] And, as Li Ting'an noted in a 1935 study of rural health care, most villagers had little faith in new-style midwifery.[41] Like many other Nationalist initiatives, government regulations on midwifery had limited effect, especially in the countryside.[42]

The 1937 Japanese invasion and the move of the Nationalist government from Nanjing to Sichuan did not enhance efforts to train new-style midwives in rural areas, nor did the subsequent civil war. As late as 1948, a study by the International Children's Emergency Fund (Guoji ertong jinji jijin hui) commented that the entire nation had only about ten thousand licensed midwives, most of them in urban areas. The report estimated that 80 percent of deliveries were done by old-style midwives, linking this to the assertion that 80 percent of all infant deaths were caused by umbilical tetanus.[43] According to the Shaanxi Health Department, only twenty-four midwives had been officially registered in the province between 1939 and 1945. Outside of Xi'an city, the report said, with one new-style midwife assigned to each rural county, "it [was] very difficult for new-style midwifery to enter deeply into the villages."[44]

Soon after Liberation, the Communist Party-state took up the effort to retrain old-style midwives and train new-style midwives.[45] The main difference between the Nationalists and the Communist Party here was not ideological, but practical: the Communist Party had a far more extensive and effective rural presence, and the scope of its efforts to reform rural midwifery accordingly affected many more people.[46]

In June 1950, for instance, young Women's Federation workers visited West Weiqu village, just south of Xi'an, accompanied by two new-style midwives from the Chang'an County seat.[47] Their purpose was to survey health work among village women and children—a striking rural state-building priority so early, before land reform had even begun.[48] Their initial experiences were not encouraging. Villagers were busy with the wheat harvest and a dam building project. Most women were out in the fields and unavailable for meetings. Because the surveyors were asking about children and who had delivered them, some villagers feared that the team intended to seize the children or punish the midwives. Encountering puzzled or suspicious silence, the team had to move their work from West to East Weiqu, where the district women's chair lived. Accompanied and legitimized by her, they went to the homes of the production group leaders (every one of them male) to explain the survey to the wives and sisters-in-law of the household. In this manner, they located the six old-style midwives in the village and interviewed them one by one.[49]

Initially frightened that the government would outlaw their work, these women gradually warmed up when the visitors explained that they themselves had no knowledge of midwifery and were there to learn. The midwives described a fully elaborated set of techniques for assisting at difficult births, as well as a pharmacopoeia for the prevention and treatment of umbilical tetanus or tetanus neonatorum. Some of these methods—crude episiotomies, instructions on how to dismember a fetus if birthing it would kill the mother—were graphic reminders of the dangers of childbirth and the limitations of village facilities. Other problems, such as the ubiquity of tetanus neonatorum, which in this area accounted for almost half of all infant deaths, were clearly a consequence of unsterile procedures.[50] In East Weiqu, the total infant mortality rate was 38 percent (195 deaths), apparently comparable to villages in other areas of China.[51] Two Shaanxi folk sayings summed up this situation: "We only see the bride, not the new mother" and "We only see the mother hold her child, but not the child walking."[52]

Even as they provided graphic descriptions of difficult and dangerous births, unsterile procedures, and poverty, early government reports were also forthright about the skills of many old-style midwives. A report from Huayin County mentioned the midwife Hao née Chen, who at age seventy had been delivering children for more than forty years and was known across several counties for her skill with difficult births. Investigators noted that Hao had one of the dreaded S-shaped hooks, more than one foot (*chi*) long, but that no one had ever seen her resort to using it. Instead she used the method of rotating the baby (*huizhuan fa*) or cranium puncture (*toulu chuanci fa*). "The only shortcoming," the report concluded, "is that she does not know about sterilization [*xiao du*], and so women and infants are often at risk of illness."[53]

In East Weiqu, investigators learned that all but eight of the village's 522 children had been birthed using these old-style methods.[54] Of the three women who had given birth new-style, some more than once, one was the sister of a new-style midwife.[55] The others, whose mothers-in-law were "very old" and therefore presumably unable to take charge, had learned about new-style birth from the local women's representative.[56] These eight children were all alive and healthy, the report noted, and so villagers admired the new method. But they were also suspicious of it.

The Women's Federation made the reform of old-style midwives a priority as early as mid-1950, when the Ministry of Health hosted a national conference of maternity and child health workers, launching a campaign to eliminate puerperal fever and tetanus neonatorum.[57] Nationally, much written propaganda framed childbirth as a political issue, characterizing old-style midwifery as "one of the feudal shackles on the cultural life of laboring women, including the fact that most people regard pregnant women who are about to give birth as scandalous, dirty, and criminal."[58] Articles from the national publication *Women of New China (Xin Zhongguo funü)*, continuing the criticisms expressed by their Nationalist predecessors, referred to rural midwifery as "feudal, superstitious, backward," and characterized old-style midwives as "feudal-minded, conceited and not interested in studying."[59] A short story titled "Childbirth" ("Yang Wawa"), published in 1950 in Shanghai, offered an extreme contrast between skilled modern doctors whose powers verged on the magical, and muddle-headed midwives with filthy hands. The story centers on a young woman named Fenglian who has already lost two babies, one to a miscarriage and the second to umbilical tetanus. As Fenglian's mother-in-law becomes convinced that Fenglian is unable to produce a healthy baby, family relations deteriorate. When Fenglian's third baby reaches term, the mother-in-law sends for the village midwife, a woman who (improbably) believes that one needs dirty hands to deliver a healthy fair-skinned baby. The midwife forces Fenglian to run and perform gymnastic maneuvers to hasten delivery, and when Fenglian collapses, tries to convince the mother-in-law that since Fenglian is going to die anyway, she might as well cut her open and save the baby. Fortunately Fenglian's husband consults the village Party secretary, who convinces the family to bring in a woman doctor. The doctor administers two (unspecified but clearly scientific) injections to Fenglian, sits down and eats a meal, and lectures the midwife on the need for better hygienic practices. While the doctor and family are discussing hygiene in an adjoining room, Fenglian revives and gives birth to a healthy baby with no further medical assistance, although the doctor does go into the room when the baby cries to tie off the cord in a sterile fashion. The midwife is observed to have a cleaner face and hands thereafter, but nothing is said about retraining her.[60]

This sharply worded propaganda, which caricatured and criticized old-style midwives as embodiments of feudalism, diverged sharply from the way government policy dealt with old-style midwives in practice. *Dundian* cadres in villages were far more likely to train midwives than to target them, and the retraining was coordinated nationally by the Ministry of Health and the Women's Federation.[61] By 1951, the slogan guiding women's health work in the Northwest Region was "Promote new-style midwifery, reform old midwives, train new midwives."[62] In November, the Shaanxi Women's Federation declared its intention to work with public health departments to retrain thirty-three hundred old-style midwives by the end of the year.[63] They planned to begin with mass meetings, and then to create the usual publicity: illustrations, bamboo-clapper storytelling, street theater, handbills, and wall and blackboard newspapers.[64] They would "give the typical cases of the deaths from tetanus and puerperal fever caused by old midwifery in order to show the harm of old midwifery and explain the advantages of new midwifery," and "use various posters to show sanitation and the new midwifery: midwifery implements, the pregnancy examination, preparation before delivery (how to sterilize), infant deformities, and so on." The key to getting people's attention, the Federation reported, was to locate cases familiar to local people: "For example, the medical station can use an example in their county where the old midwives cut open the belly to get the baby, causing the death of the mother and child. People want to listen to these, and can accept this easily."[65]

In talking so openly about childbirth, propaganda workers were engaging in public speech about matters usually left undiscussed. A technical handbook aimed at midwives said that because of feudal superstition, even a woman who was obviously pregnant could not bring herself to say so directly, resorting to euphemisms. At one public meeting about health attended by more than a hundred women, all of them blushed, giggled, and left when the subject was broached, except for those who were too shy to move. When a second meeting was called, not one person came. In a telling comparison with the Communist economic program, the author concluded, "We know that this movement for women's and children's health is extremely difficult, many times more difficult than reducing rent and interest."[66]

Midwife retraining itself was practical and conciliatory. Local cadres were careful not to treat old-style midwives as political enemies. In the course of a three-week investigative trip, one team taught ten old-style midwives to wash their hands in boiled water and sterilize their scissors. "One experience of this group," press reports commented, "is that the attitude toward old-style midwives should be unifying, educating, and gradually reforming them; one cannot mock, make fun of, or attack them."[67] Of a 1951 retraining class, cadres reported:

> They may have some worry when they first come [to study] and show uneasiness. In some places, people have spread rumors that the purpose of the class is to liquidate and struggle and settle accounts with those who delivered dead infants. Some of them were afraid of being blamed, some of them worried about their children and housework. Addressing these worries, the cadres of the Women's Federation gave them thought education, dispelled the rumors, and imparted general knowledge about health and the harm of old-style midwifery, which caused babies to contract tetanus and mothers to suffer puerperal fever and death. By using actual examples, group discussion, and other methods, we helped them feel more emotionally settled.[68]

Stories of model retrained midwives emphasized the importance of treating them respectfully, building on the positive feelings they had for the government as a result of land reform, and relentlessly encouraging them to accept retraining.[69]

After the political and affective questions were settled, the Shaanxi instructors turned to birthing procedures. Their methods were similar to those outlined in a Shandong government pamphlet, which described how old-style midwives should be retrained in courses lasting about ten days. Topics included "where children come from" (including an introduction to the anatomy of female sexual organs), what to pay attention to during pregnancy, the advantages of new-style midwifery, predelivery preparations, delivery, the management of difficult births, the postpartum month, and a final section on children's diseases, vaccinations, the propagation of new-style midwifery, and the preparation of work reports.[70] An appendix on "rules for midwives" was divided into six do's and six don'ts. Do have the woman deliver lying down, clip fingernails and wash hands with soap or alcohol, boil the scissors, use mouth-to-mouth resuscitation if the baby is not breathing, apply eye drops, and vaccinate. Do not have the woman sit on a *kang*, squat, stand, or sit to give birth; cut the cord with sorghum stalks or tile shards or teeth; bathe the baby in a dirty basin; pull on the cord or placenta; put one's hand into the vagina or tear the vaginal opening; or act rashly (*luan dong shou*) in the case of a difficult birth.[71] The Shaanxi classes were accompanied by a practicum, in which new-style midwives taught old-style midwives how to conduct prenatal examinations, sterilize equipment before delivery, and take emergency measures when the newborn did not breathe on its own. Reports offered redemptive scenes in which old-style midwives reflected critically on their former methods: "Liu Jing from Ansai says, 'In the past, if the child wasn't coming out, we would push the waist, which pressed the child to death.' Shi Xiuying says, 'I used to deliver children. Only three or four out of ten would live. We used anything at hand, and cut an umbilical cord without sterilizing.' They promised that from now on they will work following scientific methods, creating happiness for working women and the next generation."[72] Old-style midwives who had completed retraining were sent out to assist new-style midwives in deliveries, then were organized into study groups that were supposed to meet once a week and stay in contact with health workers and Women's Federation cadres on a monthly basis.[73]

One 1954 pamphlet went beyond redemption in its discussion of reformed midwives, hewing to a narrative formula honed to perfection in inspirational labor model stories. It portrayed a midwife publicizing new-style midwifery at the temple fair, ignoring the jeers of neighbors who mocked her for disgracing her ancestors by hauling around pictures of naked women. Unable to move around easily because of her bound feet, this same model midwife braved a violent rainstorm, slid down into a shallow ravine, and then clambered up to the other side to reach a woman in labor. When she received an award in January 1953 at the Northwest Region meeting for health work models, the account quotes her as saying, "I was so happy that I shed tears. If it were not for Chairman Mao and the Communist Party, how would I be where I am today? I will not forget this honor for the rest of my life."[74] Here the specifics of childbirth recede into the broader theme of enthusiastic model women working for the collective good, overcoming local suspicion and physical hardship under the leadership of the Party. Gone are the graphic details of earlier government reports on midwifery practices.

National plans for midwifery remained ambitious throughout the early 1950s, suggesting that a complete transformation of rural childbirth practices was imminent. By August 1951, it was reported, 100,000 old-style midwives nationwide had undergone retraining, and more than ten thousand sites had constructed midwifery stations. A Ministry of Health plan issued by the central government announced the goal of one station for every five villages in 1952.[75] And in 1953, the Federation declared June to be "women and children hygiene campaign month."[76] State planners imagined that midwifery, like agriculture, would be reshaped through a combination of socialist planning and campaign-time initiatives.

VILLAGE PRACTICE

Experienced old-style midwives, minimally retrained after Liberation, remained central to the project of reforming village childbirth. The most skilled among them often had been trained by their own mothers. The Village B midwife Wu Shuxian had a reputation based on her skill and the fact that she had given birth to twelve children. Like other old-style midwives, she preferred that a woman give birth in a squatting position, to aid her in pushing forcefully. She knew how to brew a bit of gold in water and give it to a pregnant woman to ward off premature labor, but she also knew how to sterilize scissors. Her customary payment before Liberation was modest: a towel, a handkerchief, or a pair of shoes.[77] She took a training class in the township in the 1950s, learning to sing a midwife's song that summed up the basic procedures of new-style birth, and enjoyed a local reputation for dedication and skill. As her daughter-in-law tells it, *Sometimes she would go in a big snowstorm or a rainstorm. She would use a walking stick, throw something on, and go. Sometimes there were posterior births. Even then my mother delivered them all. She never lost anyone in delivering babies. Sometimes when a doctor was doing a delivery and the baby wouldn't come down, they would call her and she would bring it down.*[78] Wu Shuxian continued work as a midwife well into the 1970s, delivering more than a hundred babies in the course of her career.[79]

Local officials hoped eventually to supplant old-style midwives with women who had undergone a complete course of scientific, modern midwife training. The new-style midwife, agent of a new state, was to symbolize and deliver the benefits of modernity to rural women.[80] Her training, however, could be quite brief. Yang Anxiu, whose unhappy birth experiences opened this chapter, completed a two-week course in 1954. *I was very nervous when I was studying. I saw all the others were literate. I could not write. To tell the truth, I was timid about taking this on. They used a doll with a placenta and umbilical cord to tell us how to deliver babies. They would have a woman lie on the desk, put the doll on her belly, and then tell us how to deliver and sterilize.* Anxiu learned how to manage breech births, transverse presentation, and other difficult cases.[81] *After we studied, they said to go practice twice with a teacher. But I was still afraid. I thought, this was such an important thing, how could I dare to do it?* The very first baby Anxiu delivered was breech. *I learned it one day, and then the next day I delivered two breech babies. I thought, it was good that I learned that. If I hadn't gone to study, how could I have dealt with two breech births? But the teacher told us how to deal with it, to give mouth-to-mouth resuscitation. Most breech births have their legs come out first. They cannot cry. You clean out their mouths, suck the amniotic fluid out, and breathe into their mouths. Then they can come to life.* In the early years of her practice Anxiu returned to the district twice a year for a week of further training.[82] Later, after the Great Leap Forward, the commune held study sessions for midwives on the fifteenth of each month.[83] Anxiu went on to forty years of successful midwife practice, presiding over so many breech births that she began refusing requests from grateful parents to become a godmother (*ganniang*), because she would have acquired too many godchildren.

If the newly trained midwives encountered an unusually difficult birth, they were instructed to send the woman to the hospital without delay.[84] Yet well into the reform period, Anxiu told us, even women undergoing terribly difficult labor would insist that she deliver their child at home. *They say, "To be in hospital is not like here, where people take care of us very well." If she is uncomfortable somewhere, we will massage her. If it is hot like today, we will fan her. We will chat with her. We will wipe her brow. In the hospital, you are just put in bed and left alone, because they do things according to plan. They only show up when you are ready to deliver the baby. So people say, "It is not as good as having a child at home. And it costs so much money."*[85]

Some new-style midwives completed a more comprehensive year-long course, including a three-month practicum.[86] They studied obstetrics and gynecology, internal medicine, surgery, and pediatrics, learning about breech and transverse presentations and how to teach a woman to crouch to turn the fetus around. They studied the symptoms of molar pregnancies and other medical problems. Shi Cuiyu, a Village G midwife, attended classes in 1958 with students from all over Heyang County, each supported by her production brigade. The practicum began at the county hospital and included stints at some of the health stations run by the commune. But even with the extended training, a midwife's first delivery was nerve-wracking. *The teacher asked students to practice in turn, one by one. It was a normal birth [pingchan]. After the baby came down, I used one hand to press and the other to protect the perineum. My hand felt the baby, hot and soft. I was so scared that my hand had no strength and my heart beat fast. My teacher caught my hand immediately and said to me in a low voice, "Don't be afraid. This is how it is." Aiya, I was still scared. Sweat dripped from my forehead. I felt the same way at my second delivery. Later I became stronger. By the time I came back to the village, I had delivered five or six and I was not nervous at all.*[87] Cuiyu's return to the village marked the beginning of the end of the career of the village's old-style midwives. Still in her twenties at the time, she addressed them respectfully as "Aunt" or "Mama" and often called on them to assist her at deliveries, but once she began to practice, she estimates, 95 percent of the deliveries in Village G were no longer done by the older women.[88]

In addition to emphasizing hand washing and sterilization, new-style childbirth in 1950s China ideally entailed prenatal checkups,[89] instructing the woman to lie down while in labor, and helping her to expel the umbilical cord and placenta without pulling or causing excessive blood loss. The newborn was to be washed thoroughly to remove the vernix, rather than just having its mouth wiped out with dirty raw cotton. Fresh air was to be allowed into the room, and the postpartum woman was to be provided with soft hot food such as eggs.[90] Each of these instructions was favorably compared to old-style practices.[91] Trained as a midwife after 1949, Ma Li recalls that with old-style delivery *people did not dare to pick up the baby and just put it on the ground until the amniotic sac came down and the placenta came out. Now people pick up the baby first and then use forceps to take out the woman's placenta.*[92] Aside from sterilization, the most noted change was having the woman lie down rather than sit or squat. He Gaizhen, who gave birth to children both before and after Liberation, explained that lying down was believed to be better for the mother: *In the old society, midwives told people to sit on the ground. They were afraid that it would get the kang dirty. . . . Sitting down, people would get dizzy. They said that it was blood enchanting the heart [xue mi xin]. Watching the fresh blood flowing out, several basins' worth. That was the old society, sitting on the ground, watching the fresh blood and getting dizzy. Ai, after all lying down is more comfortable. When I had the baby, she had me lie down, and after a while he was born. That way I didn't hurt from head to foot.*[93]

Not all women were delighted with the new method, as Shi Cuiyu discovered in her first delivery back at the village. *She wouldn't lie down. She was suffering. I told her to lie down flat and hold up her bottom. She bled a lot. She said, "Ai, is this your new method? Ai, let me get up. I'm suffering so much." I said, "You can't get up. Lying down is keeping you from bleeding." Let me tell you, the new method is so different from the old. Nobody knows how many women had gynecological diseases or uterine prolapse because of the old method. I remember two people who had prolapse. I brought them medicine. One couldn't walk. If it is serious, it can be as big as an eggplant. Women are so pitiful. That was the result of childbirth.*[94]

The spread of new-style midwifery practices in the Chinese countryside was uneven. Exposure to the new methods did not mean that women would continue to use them for subsequent births. A 1953 report estimated that nationally only 5 to 10 percent of women were using new-style midwifery methods in the countryside and mentioned that some midwives had reverted to the old methods.[95] Kang Xingfen, who had five children between 1963 and 1973, delivered her first child in the Village Z health station but her subsequent four (including one breech birth) at home with only her husband's assistance. Her encounter with new-style midwifery did not affect her own approach to disinfection, as she told us:

Gao Xiaoxian: *When you gave birth, cutting the cord, did you know about it? What did you cut it with?*

Kang Xingfen: *A scissors.*

Gao Xiaoxian: *Did you disinfect the scissors?*

Kang Xingfen: *Disinfect the scissors? Who gave a damn about that? You would just cut and tie it.*

Gao Xiaoxian: *You didn't wrap up the spot where the belly button was?*

Kang Xingfen: *No.*[96]

Even Ma Li, who had been trained as a midwife herself, was unable to prevent the death of her second child from umbilical tetanus. *It was too fast. My mother was there. At night I felt uncomfortable. I asked her to set up the fire. Before the water even boiled, my baby nearly came out. After it was delivered I knew it was a boy. My brother picked up the baby and wrapped him. I said, "It's fine for you just to wrap him up."*

Only the scissors were not sterilized. I had learned midwifery. I said they were not sterilized. He said, "Aiya, how many people were not sterilized in the old society! Don't worry."[97] It was not until the Great Leap Forward and later that new-style midwifery became more commonplace and women began to ask new-style midwives to attend their births, most of which still took place at home.[98] Infant deaths from umbilical tetanus remained common well into the 1970s.[99]

The hours a midwife worked were by nature unpredictable, sometimes lasting all night.[100] No matter how skilled a woman became, midwifery was a difficult, taxing job. Shi Cuiyu said, *The more I practiced, the more skilled I became. But medical science is different from doing administration. The longer you do it, the more difficult it becomes. People usually say, "Three years of learning makes a good doctor, ten years of learning destroys a doctor." Why? The more you learn, the more difficult it is, the more complicated things you come across. I remember I had such a case after I came back. I can't remember if it was in 1959 or 1960. It was a vesicular mole. I was so scared. It was a difficult labor. A vesicular mole has no fetus. It was very soft. This big. The amniotic sac was broken and fluid flew everywhere. It was white when it came down. After all the fluid was gone, so scary, there was nothing. I have never seen such a thing again in all the many years since.*[101]

Nevertheless, like Yang Anxiu, Shi Cuiyu was unequivocal about the importance and satisfaction of this work. *A good midwife should work hard for babies and women giving birth. You should be kind to them. You shouldn't distance yourself from them or be hard on them. You shouldn't mind dirt and fatigue. It was said at that time that "there is no dirty work, only dirty thinking." You are working with excrement, urine, and blood. I didn't mind. The teachers told you clearly, "If you think it is dirty and tiring, you can never be a good midwife."*

Because of the work I did, I am close to other women in the village. The woman who came by just now, the woman cooking in that house—her children were all delivered by me. I was there chatting and laughing just now. My thinking is different from others, more open. There is nothing to be afraid of. You say whatever you should, do whatever you should. Some people said about me, "She is good at talking," because I would speak to them at meetings, on topics such as the advantages of midwifery. Even in front of men, it didn't matter. That was my job, right? Women hold up half the sky. How can you laugh at those who labor and deliver? Without them, there would be no society.[102]

Gradually, as midwife skills were standardized, the death rate of women in childbirth began to fall. For members of Cao Zhuxiang's generation, the contrast with pre-1949 circumstances was striking: *The biggest change compared with before Liberation was that there was no suffering, death, or injury in women's childbirth.*[103] For women born a decade and a half later, such deaths became a matter of received knowledge about the past rather than daily experience. *When I was young,* comments a Village G woman born in 1934, *I heard the adults talking about women dying in childbirth. I never heard of a case after I grew up.*[104]

COLLECTIVIZING BIRTH

As collectivization proceeded, women's health was discussed less in the context of dispelling feudal superstition, and more as part of the project to mobilize women for collective labor. Collectivization altered the institutional supervision of childbirth, as co-ops, communes, and subsequently production brigades became responsible for childbirth services and keeping track of maternity leave.[105] Beginning in 1951, local health departments, with assistance from the Women's Federation, took primary responsibility for establishing midwifery stations (*jiesheng zhan*) in many townships. These stations were often a supervisory and training facility rather than a place where women gave birth, sending representatives down to the co-op level to inspect the work of local midwives and offer support for their work.[106] When co-ops were established, midwives were paid in work points, and postpartum women got fifty days' rest at half the average work points they had earned in the three months before giving birth.[107] Becoming a new-style midwife brought a woman some financial advantages. Shi Cuiyu noted, *During the collective period, delivering babies helped my household economically. I got six points or eight points a day and they [more highly paid men] got ten or twelve. But they got nothing for rainy days or festivals. I got mine all year long.*[108] In the early years of the collective, Yang Anxiu delivered more than a hundred babies per year. At first she earned 180 *gong* per year, and later 240 *gong*, which was comparable to the work points of the highest-earning women in the village.[109]

By late 1956, Weinan County had applied the principles of central planning to midwifery, collecting statistics on the percentage of new-style births in each township and then setting higher target quotas for the coming year. That year several townships were already reporting that 95 percent of all births were new-style, though many others had not yet reached 50 percent.[110] When lower co-ops were amalgamated into the larger higher co-ops, however, it became unclear who was supposed to run the midwifery stations. In the name of frugality, one co-op eliminated work points for midwives, who were paid nothing for a year; they were forced to spend their own money on medical supplies.[111] In response to such problems, in 1957 officials from the county offices for women's and children's health spent time in each station, attempting to standardize work rules and evaluate the work of midwives. What they found was sobering: "Because we organized and trained too many midwives in 1956, and because the training time was too short, these midwives are not very qualified. Umbilical tetanus happened in all areas. Some are dishonest and corrupt." The solution, officials decided, was more training, based on midwifery textbooks and local examples.[112] In 1957 government documents reflected awareness that in the final year of the First Five Year Plan, women's and children's health work needed to show achievements commensurate with those in production.[113]

The practice of measuring women's reproductive health by the temporality of production campaigns intensified during the Great Leap Forward. In August 1958, the Women's Federation convened a province-wide health worker meeting in Jingyang to plan the establishment of birth stations (*chan yuan*) throughout the countryside.[114] Li Qiming, vice governor of the province, designated rural birth stations as the centerpiece of the Party-state's health work in the countryside. With 2,626 birth stations and 524 rural hospitals already established, he noted, Shaanxi was poised to "promote a Great Leap Forward in health work." He pointed out that an eleven-day stay at the birth station for a mother and baby in one county cost only six yuan, and during that same period the husband was free to amass more than thirty yuan worth of work points. He added, "Based on the number of 451 women in birth stations in 1957 in the county, if each woman was in the hospital for ten days, it would save 4,510 work days otherwise spent taking care of them, allowing people to participate in agricultural production." Socializing childbirth and postpartum care would benefit both household income and the collective economy.

The provincial Party committee initially proposed to establish a hospital in every township and a birth station in every commune within four months, operating under the Great Leap slogan "One day is equal to twenty years." But in the flush of early Great Leap enthusiasm, the conference organizers proposed an even more ambitious timetable: within forty days, every township should have a hospital and a birth station, and every commune should have a health worker, a childcare worker, and a midwife, as well as a midwifery station, a small clinic, and a childcare center.[115] At the Jingyang meeting, the district in which Village T was located was singled out for praise. Within a two-week period, it was reported, health workers there had already established birth stations in every township.[116] The station where Yang Anxiu worked, near Village T, had three rooms. In two of the rooms, a woman could deliver her baby and then spend three days in bed, bringing her own rice to be cooked by the staff. The third room was a daycare center, where Anxiu helped a teacher care for children when no one was in labor.[117] Key to this ambitious birth station project, said the conference organizers, was mobilizing the population. But birth stations were an unfunded mandate in communities with little to spare. Although the conference document paid tribute to the wisdom of the masses in many paragraphs of overheated prose, the specific means of involving the population often consisted of exhorting each commune member to donate a small amount to fund the birth stations. By 1959, as the Great Leap Forward began to unravel, visitors from the Women's Federation reported troubling shortages and poor sanitary conditions in some of the province's birth stations:

> The biggest difficulty of birth stations is that they have no quilts. Because most families have only one quilt, if the woman takes the quilt with her the whole family has nothing to cover themselves. When the two stations were set up, ordinary women collected money to make one public quilt for each station. If there are two women giving birth in the hospital, one of them has to use the midwife's quilt.

The hygiene of the station in the first brigade is very bad. The walls are dirty and the dirt is thick. Midwifery tools are everywhere. There are no medical dressings or string for tying off umbilical cords. There is not enough medicine, either. The pot for sterilization was under the bed and had been forgotten for a long time. Another salient problem of the hospital is the lack of money for more medicine and dressings. They have no money for lamp oil. They don't charge laboring women for being in the hospital. Under such circumstances, the two midwives make money to subsidize this station by washing clothes and doing needlework for road workers nearby or picking herbs in the mountains. They suggested charging each woman who gives birth 1.5 yuan for midwifery tools and medicine. But in fact this is difficult to implement.[118]

It is not surprising that many of these stations were dismantled when collective dining halls were disbanded and ceased providing grain to the stations. Right before the stations closed, some saw increased attendance; in Village G women came to the birth station during the three hard years because they could get better food than at home. Although no eggs were available at that time, the station was given a ration of flour and brown sugar for postpartum women.[119] In Village T, the birth station closed in 1961: *It lasted only two years. You couldn't do anything without support from the top. You needed firewood to boil the water, and you yourself needed to survive, to eat. So it was closed.*[120]

In the system that eventually emerged in the 1960s and 1970s, every production brigade had a medical station with a midwife attached to it; she would most commonly go to a woman's home during labor and childbirth. Families paid the station a set amount per birth (0.5 yuan in the Village T area).[121] The brigade, in turn, paid the midwives in work points. When no women were giving birth, the brigade assigned the midwives to deliver soup and medicine, work on publicity about women's health, assist the agrarian science team, feed the collective's pigs, or help out with daycare. In some villages midwives went regularly to pregnant women's homes for prenatal examinations, since the idea of going to a hospital or even a village clinic still seemed strange to many women.[122] But the attempt to centralize childbirth in one accessible, convenient facility did not begin to take hold until after the end of the collective era.

In addition to offering midwifery services, the collectives were supposed to protect the reproductive health of women farmers. Co-op regulations stipulated that nursing mothers should be assigned to work in nearby fields and allowed time to feed their babies. Women more than seven months pregnant should be assigned to lighter work, and not permitted to carry heavy loads on shoulder poles. County-level Women's Federations publicized cases in which assigning women to carry sand and perform other heavy labor resulted in miscarriages, cautioning against such practices.[123] The Women's Federation promoted a policy known as the "three transfers and three nontransfers": "During menstruation, women should be transferred to dry places, not wet ones; during pregnancy, women should be transferred to posts with light labor requirements, not to those with heavy ones; during lactation, women should be transferred to near places, not to far places."[124] Strong women with natural feet, no children, and lighter housework burdens were to be assigned to fields farther away or in the hills. Weaker women, and those with many children or heavy housework responsibilities, were to be assigned to work nearby and given lighter tasks.[125] The woman's team leader in each co-op was responsible for arranging lighter work assignments for menstruating or pregnant team members. In the Village T area, each woman of childbearing age had a card with her name on it hanging in the team headquarters, and women who had their periods would turn over the cards themselves if they wished to request a lighter assignment.[126] The need for work points often took precedence over the desire to make such requests. But the very process of hanging up a card for each woman established that a woman's reproductive status was a matter of collective interest, a norm that would become the source of conflict several decades later with the advent of stringent state-mandated birth planning.[127]

From 1958 on, women were entitled to a month of rest in late pregnancy and a month for postpartum recovery. But as the previous chapter suggested, many women could not afford to claim these benefits: *We were so poor that we dared not take such long leaves. We could only try to find some light work to do and ask others to do the heavy work, because you ate according to your work points.*[128] The imperative to labor in the fields sometimes impinged directly on the labor of childbirth.[129] Yang Anxiu told of one young woman who raced to dig a few more rows of potatoes as her contractions increased in frequency. Anxiu's point was that women farmers in the collective era were tough and capable, and that young women today, who take to their beds in advance of labor, cannot compare to the women of her own generation. Nevertheless pervasive anxiety about work points seeps out around the edges of the story: *I said to stop digging and to go back. "Aiya, Aunt, after I have a child, I cannot work for a month. What should I do? The pain is not so serious." I said, "Shuping, if you try to dig up one or two rows, you might not be able to finish." I saw her go to the toilet frequently. She went five or six times during the length of time we have been talking here. Finally I said, "Shuping, stop digging. Just finish this row and pick these up. This is not the time to earn work points." She said, "It is not so serious. I can dig at least two or three more rows. I think it is not time yet." Finally, her water broke in the field ditch. There was nothing to be done about it. I supported her as we went back. I did not even have time to wash my hands when her child's head crowned.* Another woman in the same work team was afraid to stop work before the morning shift was over: *When she was in second-stage labor, she said to me, "Great-aunt, I can't go back until noon." I said, "Go back. My daughter-in-law is recording work points. We will keep working and record a whole morning's work until noon for you." She said, "No, I can't do that. If people carrying corn come back and do not see me, and you record a whole morning for me, they will report it to the top. Then you will be in trouble."* I said, *"It doesn't matter."* I asked her to go back immediately, and she did. *How tough she was! She carried two buckets of water by herself, boiled it and washed her hair. By the time she dried her hair, the baby's head had already crowned.*[130] Postpartum confinement and recuperation were affected by the work-point imperative as well, with women returning to field work much sooner than the customary hundred days. A common complaint in the stories of many women is that arthritis and other ailments contracted from not resting properly after childbirth have flared up to torment them in their old age.[131]

One area of reproductive health that received a mixed reception in rural areas was contraception. In 1956, decades before the advent of the one-child family policy, the Chinese state made its first foray into publicizing contraception in rural areas.[132] The provincial Health Bureau and the Women's Federation took the lead in this work. Cadres attended county and township meetings where they learned about condoms and diaphragms. Then they returned home and publicized the benefits of birth planning to local women, telling them that bearing more children meant a more exhausting burden for them.[133] Health Bureau officials reminded organizers to direct their efforts to men as well, "to achieve cooperation between the two parties."[134] County women's and children's clinics and hospitals were also urged to sell contraceptive devices and medicines, although in 1956 such activities were still in the experimental stage.[135] As late as 1958, when the advent of the Great Leap Forward halted their efforts, the Women's Federation was calling on its cadres to learn birth control policies, set an example by making personal birth plans, and offer contraceptive guidance to village women.[136]

Although cadres showed samples of birth control devices, they did not hand them out. Work reports from the Health Bureau suggested that many villagers saw contracepting as immoral behavior, believing that the number of children one had was predestined. The Bureau appended a warning that birth control propagandists should avoid "degenerating into vulgar erroneous tendencies." The tendencies were not specified, but the discomfort with explicit talk about sexual relations was obvious.[137] The Health Bureau also proposed that each clinic collect the name, age, and profession of each woman who requested birth control, as well as those of her husband; her childbirth and contraception history; her reasons for wanting birth control; and the effectiveness of any method prescribed to her. This ambitious early attempt at registration and statistical data collection was not widely implemented.[138] But Zhang Chaofeng, who was working as a women's cadre in Village G, reports that the initial response to contraception propaganda was negative. *The masses were not used to this. They said, "You are meddling in everything, even having children. If I have one, you won't be raising it, so what business is it of yours?"*[139] Soon enough, however, this attitude would change. The improved health care situation succeeded in reducing the infant mortality rate. In the overall context of collectivization, the increasing number of children put a growing economic strain on families and an overwhelming domestic burden on women.

BEYOND CAMPAIGN TIME: BIRTHING STORIES

Most rural Shaanxi babies continued to be delivered at home, sometimes by mid-wives but more frequently by mothers-in-law or with no assistance at all. Well into the co-op period, some families felt that they could not afford or did not need the services of a midwife, and not every village had one within easy access. Many women tell of catching the baby themselves, cutting the cord and wrapping the child, while neighbors worked out of earshot in the collective fields or husbands hurried to summon a midwife who did not arrive in time.[140] In Village G, Liu Guyu gave birth to her fifth child just after she put bread in the steamer for the midday meal; the child was born before the bread had finished cooking.[141]

Some women were reluctant to have any outsider present when they gave birth, even a midwife. One day Ma Li, a young midwife-in-training, received an urgent message that her cousin's wife, who had lost a baby the previous year, was in the middle of a difficult labor. Ma Li ran to the house of her teacher, the veteran mid-wife Liu Xihan, and the two women hurried to the cousin's house. Although her mother-in-law had summoned the midwives, Ma Li's cousin was not happy to see them. In between contractions she berated the two midwives: *"I'm suffering. You come to see me in labor. Do you think you are watching a game?" She wouldn't let you be close. . . . We sat there for several hours but they didn't let us examine her. [Liu Xihan] said, "I'm here for your own good. We are all women. What are we looking at?"* By the time the woman consented to let the midwives examine her, it was too late. *One of the baby's arms was hanging there. The midwife [Liu Xihan] put the arm back. Then it came out again. Again she put it back. Liu Xihan said the baby would die. The baby's arm came out and its head was inside. Finally we took it out. But it died after it came out.*[142]

In addition to its obvious potential for pain and danger, childbirth was a major turning point in the integration of young brides into the household of their in-laws. After marriage, as we have seen, many women in central and south Shaanxi made the transition to their marital homes gradually, returning to their natal homes often and sometimes staying there for weeks. But it was taboo to give birth in the house of one's natal family.[143] If a mother thought that her visiting daughter might go into labor, she would hurry to send her back to her mother-in-law's house.[144] A mother who called in a midwife for her own daughter would be criticized by the husband's family, even held responsible if something went wrong.[145] Local belief held that *alive or dead, your own mother does not see it. . . . If it was dead, she didn't see the pesti-lent energy. If it was alive she didn't see it either.* The taboo against having a mother attend her daughter in labor and childbirth extended to women in uxorilocal marriages who lived with their mothers. Thus He Gaizhen was left to deliver her own child, because her mother was not permitted to help and a relative who had been brought in to assist did not want to risk pollution from contact with childbirth, since she needed to cook for the Spring Festival: *The baby was so slippery that I dropped her in the basin when I tried to catch her and she swallowed a mouthful of water. Her nose was not in good condition for more than a hundred days.*[146]

For both ritual and practical reasons, a woman's first childbirth usually brought to an end the stage of life when she could visit her own mother's house frequently. It was also a moment, sometimes the first moment, when a mother-in-law was fully in charge of a young wife's well-being. Mothers-in-law feature prominently in women's childbirth stories from before and after 1949, and their portrayal is not always positive. Many women blame miscarriages on physical and emotional conflicts with their mothers-in-law or other senior women in their husbands' families.[147] Some recall the birth of their first child not only as painful and frightening, but also as a moment that highlighted feelings of alienation from their mothers-in-law, their husbands, or both. Li Liujin, one of the activists whose divorce was described in chapter 4, had been embroiled in a simmering conflict with her husband's family for several years because of her political activities. Her two childbirth experiences, one in the late 1940s and the other just after Liberation, underscored her unhappiness with her husband and his family. *I was seventeen when I gave birth to my first baby. The day I went into labor, it was dark, and [my husband and I] were sleeping in the same bed. Nobody said anything. Before he went to cut wood, I got up to cook for him. . . . When I crouched by the pot, stirring, it was hurting so badly. At last I pushed myself to drain the rice quickly and started cooking it. When he got up to eat, I didn't say anything. He didn't know I was going into labor, and I didn't say anything either.*

Then he left. I was in labor. I was walking around and around the room and my stomach was hurting so badly. I was only seventeen! So I was turning around and around, walking to and fro. When it was time to eat breakfast, I began to give birth. My stomach was hurting unbelievably, but something was wrong and the baby wouldn't come down.

I sat on a short stool and pressed my rear end against it. . . . I couldn't sleep. What could I do? Heavens. It was unbearable to sit down. Finally, I walked in and out of the house. It hurt so badly . . . straight through to the afternoon. When I was a girl, I heard someone say that when you are giving birth to a baby, after you move around, you should sleep. Others said that you shouldn't sleep or it would crawl onto your heart. I thought it over and said, Whatever happens, dead or alive, I am going to sleep. I struggled to crawl onto my bed and stretched out to sleep. When I was lying on the bed, all at once I felt pressure two times. I pushed twice, and the baby rushed forward. Dingding guangguang, two pushes and the baby rolled down. After it came down,

*the old woman [mother-in-law] got some water in a wooden basin and put it down
beside my bed. She gave me a pair of scissors. I cut the baby's umbilical cord myself
and made a knot. I put a piece of old cotton on the top. I had prepared some pieces of
cloth and bags ahead of time. After I washed the baby, I wrapped it in some cloth from
a pair of pants. The placenta came out by itself. That's it.*

*[My husband] had gone to cut firewood and had not come back yet. . . . Nowadays
a husband and wife, if they feel something, they will talk about it. That's how the feeling between a husband and wife should be. But I didn't say anything and he didn't
know. That's how it was when I gave birth to my first baby.*

*When I had my second baby, it was crop-watching season. We set up a bed, watch-
ing over the crops. . . . My stomach began to hurt again, so I crawled out of bed. It was
just like what happened before: when my water broke [the baby] moved back. I went
to the bedroom, swept the floor, and stretched out on the floor. I lay there until the
baby dropped, and only then got up. Think about it! It was just like that: I lay on the
floor, and the baby dropped onto the floor. Then I pulled myself up to pick up the baby
and wrap it up on the bed. That's how it was then.*[148]

Government documents and the birthing stories of individual women cannot
tell us how widespread this sort of isolating family dynamic was, or when it
changed. Some young women activists in the 1950s learned about new-style midwifery in the course of their organizing work. They had the confidence, and perhaps the outside support, to request that midwives attend them at childbirth.[149]
When women of Li Liujin's generation describe the more recent childbirth experiences of their own daughters-in-law, they speak of hospitals, high fees, and women
who lead much softer work lives than they did, and thus sometimes have much
harder first labors. The midwives among them talk as well of recent complicated
births that they have attended. In their villages, women no longer give birth alone,
and a bride often does not live in the same household with her mother-in-law, much
less under her authority. Still, it is difficult to imagine that these sorts of family relationships changed as quickly as midwifery practices. Childbirth was shaped not
only by state campaigns, but by the entire matrix of social relationships in which
midwives and laboring women were enmeshed.[150] And as one final story about the
midwife Liu Xihan suggests, these relationships extended beyond the visible connections of village society into the realm of the unseen spirit world.

LIU XIHAN AND THE GHOSTS
OF CHILDBIRTH'S DANGER

The midwife Liu Xihan was born in about 1906 in Xiguan village, into a family later
classified as "half-landlord." At seven she began to help her mother with household
tasks and midwifery. She married at fourteen into what later became a middle peasant family and moved to Village Z, where she worked at home as a weaver and be-

gan to practice midwifery sometime before 1949. After Liberation she became an activist, a group leader in the Peasant Association, and a member of the Women's Federation. She received additional training in midwifery, and in February 1952 became head of the Village Z midwifery station run by the Women's Federation, one of thirteen stations being established around the county. Within three years she had eight people working under her direction. Of the forty-one children she had delivered by 1955, none developed tetanus neonatorum, nor did their mothers suffer from postpartum diseases.[151] Her prestige among villagers was high. He Gaizhen blames the 1953 death of her newborn son from sepsis on the fact that Liu Xihan was unable to attend the birth. Her next son, born the following year, was delivered by Liu Xihan and survived. Liu Xihan charged nothing for her services, although the town government paid for her instruments.[152]

Liu Xihan was a vocal advocate for new-style midwifery, even singing songs that explained its advantages.[153] She was a model citizen in other respects as well, persuading her husband and neighbors to sell surplus grain to the state in 1954. A neighbor cursed her for promoting the unpopular unified purchase and marketing of grain, saying, "Liu Xihan, you are taking my pot and my quilt away. I'll hang myself in your doorway." Nevertheless, a report of her model activities says, she continued her patient persuasion, reminding the old woman about food shortages in the old society until she relented and sold her surplus. In every respect, Liu Xihan seemed exemplary of the kind of new rural woman citizen cultivated by the Party-state.[154]

And yet, when village women remember Liu Xihan, who died in the late 1950s or early 1960s, their memories are more complex than the straightforward march toward safer childbirth (and unified grain purchase) featured in government publications and internal documents. Even as village women laud her skills of new-style midwifery, they also place her in a genealogy of midwives put at risk by powerful, dangerous forces present when a child was born. Childbirth, in their telling, was risky not only for the woman in labor, but for those who attended her, and new-style midwifery did not remove the danger.

Villagers believed that the pollution of childbirth could affect the midwife or those who came in contact with her. Ma Li recalls that after she assisted Liu Xihan at a birth and brought some cucumbers home, no one would eat them: [They said,] "She is too dirty. Didn't you see what she went to do?" . . . Later, everybody laughed at me and nobody ate the things I had touched. Then I started to hate midwife work.[155] Another woman recalls that Liu Xihan's predecessor had also been a skilled old-style midwife, but frequent contact with the blood of childbirth had made her go blind. That was why the woman refused to learn midwifery herself when Liu Xihan offered to teach her: No, my eyes are not good. I don't want to learn it. If I learn it, the blood will ruin my eyes. I won't learn.[156]

Even after Liberation, after the midwife station was founded and Liu Xihan be-

came its head, as sterile practices became more commonplace and tetanus neonatorum became less common, the perils of delivering children did not recede. Ultimately, people said, Liu Xihan had "died of midwifery" (*jiesheng gei sile, ba ming
gei songle*). Called to attend a birth, she found herself delivering something mal-
formed and odorous.[157] *When she delivered it, she didn't know whether it was a baby
or not. She was so scared that she got a fever that night. On the second day people sent
a message to her son. The son went there and carried her back. It was in the afternoon. . . . By four in the afternoon, she breathed her last breath and died. Oh, that old
woman, she was such a good midwife. As soon as someone called her, she would respond. She would say, "That person is suffering." As soon as she was called she would
say, "I am going."*[158]

This was not the whole story behind Liu Xihan's death. One day several months
before her death, she had confided a troubling episode to one of the village women,
swearing her to secrecy. The listener remembers the story this way: *That year, she
came and said to me—I never dared tell anyone else—"Gaizhen, I dare not say it. Please
don't tell others. Otherwise the government will struggle against me." One night, a
young man called her outside her window, "Aunt, come to deliver a baby for me." Just
these words. She said, "Okay, I am coming." She put on her clothes and carried the
medicine box on her back.*

*She said the young man carried the medicine box for her. They went to the east
slope. When she came back, she forgot to bring her box. It had a cross on it. Her husband said the next day, "Ya, where is your box?" She said that she had asked the young
man to bring her some water to wash her hands. The young man said, "Aunt, we have
no water. And I have nothing to cook some food for you." "I don't want to eat. Just give
me some water and let me wash my hands. I won't eat anything of yours. Let me wash
my hands." The man said there was no water. So she wiped her hands on a stone and
then went back home.*

*Her husband went to look for her box. It was on a tomb of a family. She had wiped
the blood from her hands on the tomb. She only told me about it. She dared not tell
others. If she told others, the state would struggle against her. She was so scared and
dared not say so. This was superstitious. She delivered a baby for dead people. The old
woman died not long after that.*[159]

In this story, the new-style midwife, full of the spirit of service shared by many
midwives of her generation and venerated in state publications, goes off to deliver
a baby. Afterwards she is afraid. But there is the matter of the lost medical kit with
its red cross on the lid, and the place where her husband discovers it confirms that
something is terribly wrong. She has unknowingly put her medical skill at the service of a spectral otherworld, has delivered a ghost baby—a frightening boundary
violation. Although she experiences this as an individual fear, it draws upon a powerful collective fear of much longer standing, expressed in numerous Chinese stories of the supernatural with almost exactly this plot line.[160]

Liu Xihan fears something else as well: she fears that her fear will get her criticized for lingering superstition, she who has embraced science and propagated it so enthusiastically in the village. Here the world of science brushes up against an older set of beliefs in the person of the midwife, in an environment where only science can be spoken if one is to be progressive, useful, and above reproach. So she keeps silent, or almost silent. And then, like a recurring nightmare, another monstrous birth comes her way, and this time it kills her.

The question here is not whether contact with ghosts and monsters killed Liu Xihan, or even whether recurring trauma hastened her death.[161] Whether she herself connected the two traumatic births cannot be known to us. What we do know is that women who remember her for her skill, her commitment to new-style childbirth, and her compassion also remember her death as caused by midwifery. As our interviewee, herself an enthusiastic 1950s activist, put it, Liu Xihan "died of midwifery."

For women in the early years of the People's Republic, the liminal and dangerous nature of childbirth was as real in the 1950s, and in the 1990s remained as real in their memories, as the need to sterilize medical instruments.[162] These women certainly live partly by state temporality; they recount with feeling how campaigns changed their lives. But state temporality coexisted, perhaps even defined itself against, other temporalities that did not disappear with the advent of a new state regime.

The normative stories state authorities told about the transformation of childbirth, tales peopled by investigative teams, ambitious planners, and model midwives, do not exhaust the subject. This is in part because state attention to reproductive health was inconsistent, distracted and often overwhelmed by competing demands. Childbirth, embedded in household dynamics, recurrent and episodic rather than linear, was not easily addressed on campaign time, using available categories of production quotas and leaps toward modernity. But the account offered in normative stories is also inadequate because knowledge, belief, and practice circulated in complex ways not captured by the model of the state as conveyor of scientific knowledge. And this in turn suggests that a fully historicized understanding of rural childbirth and midwifery, and of the 1950s in rural China more generally, while it surely must include a full accounting of state campaigns, must entail as well an investigation of the memories women are willing and able to narrate.

7

Mother

The year before we interviewed Liu Dongmei, a high fever left her blind in one eye. Before her illness, she had been known in Village Z for the skill and artistry of her embroidery. Families bought her fine pillows to decorate the marriage beds of their daughters, and her navel-protecting baby bibs were popular with new mothers. Dongmei's tales were full of intelligence and energy. Born in 1932, she had been a Protestant since the age of seven, when her mother converted in the hope, later twice fulfilled, that the Christian god would give her a son. Helping her mother sell silk cocoons at market, eight-year-old Dongmei was observant enough to recognize a man who had purchased cocoons the previous day, and bold enough to remind him that he owed her money. Impressed, he picked her as a bride for his grandson, whom she married years later. As a young cadre in the 1950s, Dongmei hauled rocks to build levees along the Dan River and was, her sister-in-law says, *strong enough to carry a film projector for twenty* li. In 1995 she produced some of the most beautiful squares in a gigantic quilt displayed in Huairou at the UN Fourth World Conference on Women. Liu Dongmei told these stories with happiness and pride. But when she talked about being a mother during the collective era, what she remembered was fatigue and too many children. Those memories were full of anger.[1]

With the end of incessant warfare and the successful retraining of village midwives, many families in rural 1950s Shaanxi found themselves with four, five, or even more surviving children. The burden of supporting and caring for them fell most heavily on women, who were also responding to the state's new demands for their labor in the fields. The result was utter exhaustion. Recounting their lives during the collective era, women routinely scramble the chronology of mutual aid groups and higher cooperatives, move the old society forward a few decades, and reorder the names of campaigns. And yet, the years in which their children were born, marked off by the lunar calendar and the zodiac cycle of twelve animals (year of the rat, year of the ox, etc.), remain their most reliable way of organizing time in memory.

This chapter follows those memories. It turns from campaign time to domestic time, in which women performed the work of feeding, clothing, and caring for growing numbers of children. Financial and political necessity required that women show up each day to engage in collective field work, even as their domestic responsibilities remained constant, unnamed, and unremunerated.[2] Their days in the field were shorter and their work points fewer than those of men, yet their workdays were far longer. The Women's Federation made attempts to organize rural childcare groups for the harvest season, and a few of our interviewees worked briefly in sewing groups organized by the collective. But the socialization of domestic tasks was not pursued consistently by national or local leadership. Zhang Chaofeng observes, *In the 1950s, on the status front, now we had status, but the workload was heavier than before.*[3]

Ubiquitous in women's stories, domestic labor figured very little in the written record of the 1950s. In women's narratives of the collective era, needlework is the activity that most epitomizes the incessant, ephemeral, and occasionally creative temporality of domestic life. Memories of collective field work are interwoven with accounts of late nights spent sewing on the *kang* (an old image of women's industriousness) and in brigade meetings (a newer one). Analysis of the collective period—its accomplishments, shortcomings, gendered division of labor, and transformation of women's lives—must acknowledge that rural socialism made much of women's actual labor invisible. It should also take account of the material products of that labor—not only products for workaday use such as shoe soles and clothing, but also the individually designed handwoven sheets and kerchiefs, embroidered shoe liners and pillow facings, and meticulously sculpted and painted dough ornaments (*huamo*) that expressed the creative and playful corners of lives in which leisure and even sleep were in chronically short supply.

This chapter begins with the new invisibility of women's rural domestic labor, which arguably garnered more attention from imperial rulers and early twentieth-century reformers than it did from the post-1949 state. The chapter explores the work necessary to feed and clothe families, and the unexpected strain that growing families put on three-generation households in the collectives. It looks at the powerful recurrent image of needlework performed by lamplight, an enduring symbol of women's industrious virtue that found new expression in the collective era. The chapter concludes with a return to the question of children: the frustrating inconsistency of childcare, the particularities of maternal attachment, and the effect of child-rearing fatigue on this generation's attitudes toward the state birth planning policy of the later reform era.

MAKING THE VISIBLE INVISIBLE

At the heart of imperial political thought was the precept that values inculcated in the family, usually by women, were the very foundation of social order and state function. The domestic, in this sense, was not at all private. Late imperial statecraft writers ceaselessly promoted women's handicraft labor as crucial to the health of the agrarian economy and hence the stability of the state itself.[4] Imperial state officials regarded the domestic realm both as the foundation of their power and as an appropriate subject for their encomia.[5]

Early twentieth-century activists reversed the positive valence that late imperial thinkers had assigned to the family as the foundation of the state. Instead they argued that men learned deferential behavior in the family and carried these bad habits into the public realm, making them into slavish citizens and China into a slavish nation.[6] The "traditional" women described by these reformers were no longer praised as moral exemplars and tireless household producers. Instead they were described as foot-bound, confined to the inner quarters, denied the most rudimentary education, economically unproductive, and crushed under the weight of an oppressive feudal tradition centered on the family. The self-proclaimed task of reformers and revolutionaries was to remove this weight and liberate the potential of women as educated citizens, as laborers, and as human beings.[7] Empirically accurate in some respects (or about some women) and distorted in others, this representation shifted attention to the domestic as the source of public ills rather than the foundation of public order.

Twentieth-century writings on the family also reversed the values assigned to the urban and the rural. Earlier, agriculture had been regarded as more essential and more virtuous than trade, and farming families embodied society's core values. By the twentieth century, however, many reformers saw the cities as the place where a Chinese modernity would be fashioned. The domestic realm was identified as a key node for the installation of modern practices, epitomized by the "small household" of a free-choice urban conjugal couple.[8] Rural families were understood to be mired in feudal thinking, unable to rise to the level of urban civilized practice. In 1927, early in his revolutionary career, Mao Zedong echoed these themes in what became a famous statement on women's burdens: "A man in China is usually subjected to the domination of three systems of authority: (1) the state system (political authority) . . . (2) the clan system (clan authority) . . . and (3) the supernatural system (religious authority). . . . As for women, in addition to being dominated by these three systems of authority, they are also dominated by the men (the authority of the husband)."[9]

In the early stages of the revolution, Mao was as eloquent as any imperial statecraft writer in detailing just how much household economic activity was performed by women. Writing from southeastern Jiangxi in 1930, he noted:

Strictly speaking, in terms of farming, women's duties are much heavier than those of men . . . Women assist men in carrying the muck and grain, transplanting rice seedlings, weeding fields, uprooting the weeds in the paths between the fields and on the edges of the fields, turning over the soil, and cutting the grain. But although men help out, women are chiefly responsible for hulling grain, polishing grain, watering gardens, transplanting vegetables, cutting wood, mowing grass, making tea, cooking meals, raising pigs and other domestic animals, washing and ironing clothes, mending clothes, making shoes, sweeping floors, and doing dishes. Besides these tasks, raising children is also a woman's duty; thus, the toil of women is harder than that of men. Women's tasks come one after another, and their work never ends.[10]

For Mao, political authority vested in the landlord class was the primary source of oppression for Chinese peasants, and its overthrow would weaken the other three forms of authority, liberating women as an almost incidental byproduct of a wider revolutionary process.[11] As the Communist Party shifted its main venue of revolutionary activity to the countryside after 1927, it experimented with marriage and family reform but came to focus its primary efforts on strengthening the military, increasing economic production, and guiding local governance.

This emphasis on what came to be constituted as the new public realm continued after the establishment of the People's Republic. Activity in rural areas in the 1950s focused primarily on establishing Party and mass organizations, collectivizing, and incorporating women more fully into farm production. Aside from the Marriage Law campaign, the reconfiguration of family relations was a far less prominent policy goal.[12] What was new in this period was the vastly enhanced importance of the public realm: it was to be the locus of social change, the designated sphere of valued activity, the place where citizens would naturally invest their loyalty and love.

This was not a state silence about women. Women were everywhere visible— as state subjects, and as labor models, cadres, and agricultural workers moving happily through public space. Women's labor was praised, encouraged, and publicized, but it was the labor of agricultural production, narrowly defined as that which increased crop output. The socialist state did not recognize the domestic realm as the foundation of the state (as imperial thinkers had done) or as a key cause of social and political backwardness (as early twentieth-century revolutionaries had done). This was a silence about the productive and affective activity taking place in the domestic realm, an important sphere of gendered relations.

The domestic realm is not a self-evident, easily delineated physical space, but rather a cultural and ideological domain. State policy pronouncements after 1949, while attending intermittently to questions of marriage reform and family harmony, most often described the domestic realm as the place where feudal remnants lurked, hindering the socialist project. But feudal remnants were expected to disappear, and domestic work was slated for eventual socialization, although the details remained unclear. No one in China in the 1950s predicted that the household would wither away, although the Great Leap Forward in 1958 grandly promised to socialize some of its functions with the slogan (unmellifluous in English) "Eating will be dining-hall-ized, labor will be militarized, and wearing clothes will be sewing-machine-ized" (*chifan shitang hua, laodong junshihua, chuanyi fengren hua*). The prospect of socialized domestic labor soon dimmed with the Leap's collapse. No longer a major source of political order, nor a serious impediment to modernity, the domestic was regarded as a residual, reactive realm of human activity.

Even while de-emphasizing the domestic realm, this same socialist state transformed it in ways more thoroughgoing and profound than any previous regime, through its policies on production and its mobilization of women as state subjects.[13] But women's ongoing domestic responsibilities, which utterly saturated their daily routines, could not be voiced, much less addressed as a labor problem, in the terms provided by the revolution. The chief form of household economic activity performed by women—spinning and weaving for the market—had been eliminated in the early years of the revolution.[14] With the regulation and restriction of markets, other sidelines run by women (livestock raising, handicrafts) also assumed a much less important role in generating household income.[15] After that, in revolutionary parlance, there was no such thing as domestic labor (*laodong*). "Labor" was usually reserved for field work and collective sideline production, just as the term "work" (*gongzuo*) referred only to salaried labor.[16] What went on in the home was not labor, but domestic tasks (*jiawu huo*).

HOME LIFE

For most of the socialist period, farmers continued to prepare and consume food and produce and wash clothing at home, while raising large numbers of children. Domestic tasks were unending, and no one in the rural environment—cadres, men, or the women themselves—questioned the division of labor that consigned most of them to women.[17] Even when a man helped haul firewood or water, stoked the kitchen fire, watched a child, swept the yard, or cooked the occasional meal while his wife was off at a meeting or delivering a baby, the main responsibility for domestic labor and household management fell to the able-bodied women of the household.[18] In Shan Xiuzhen's village, people put it this way: *A man is a rake. A woman is a box. If the rake is missing a tine it doesn't matter, but you need to worry if the box has no bottom. Look at the family. Women should be good at arranging family issues.*[19] And yet, in Village Z, some men continued to make light of domestic work in order to make fun of the idea that a woman could do a man's job in the fields. Ma Li recounts their banter: *The man would say, "Men and women are equal. You go carry fertilizer. I will stay at home and take care of the kids." [Or] they would say, "Now you are liberated, men and women are equal. You go be team leaders and do the field work. I'll sit at home." I would laugh, "Men and women are equal. You work. I also have to work: raising pigs, sewing. Can you do this?" Men did nothing during the meetings [while women sewed].*

Gao Xiaoxian: Did you say that men should also do housework like women did when you propagandized that men and women are equal?

       Ma Li: Who did housework for you? They just sat there.

Gao Xiaoxian: Did men help women with housework in those years?

       Ma Li: Men who helped in those years are still helping now. Men who didn't help in those years are still doing nothing. Good men helped.[20]

Childbearing, child rearing, food preparation, laundry, and needlework bracketed the working day defined by work points, creeping into all of its interstices as well: *I fed the pig first before I went to the field. On my way back, I collected some grass for the pig. I nursed my kid first after I came back home. Then I cooked immediately.*[21] Kitchens were dark, with small windows. "Because they burned wood and grass," notes one local history journal from the Village T area, "the kitchen was smoky, black and unhygienic."[22] In Village G, where water supply was a problem, women went daily to the well at the end of their street to draw water from two hundred meters below ground. Three to five people were required to operate the pulley, and each bucket of water took fifteen minutes to draw. Women asked men to help them carry the full buckets home if they were too heavy.[23]

Most newly married couples lived with the husband's parents during the early 1950s. The cooking and childcare performed by the elders helped make it possible for younger married women to earn work points in the fields. *My mother[-in-law] boiled the rice and took care of the kids for me. When I came back home, I was very respectful to them. When you sat down at the table, you would go to the door and say, "Ma, come quickly and let's eat." The old folks worked very hard too.*[24]

Even with women earning work points from field work, many families had to go into debt to the collective. Liu Dongmei, the embroiderer, had ten children, eight of whom lived to adulthood: *We had too many people. We were really short of money. In a year we would come up fifty yuan short. After we saved forty or fifty yuan, we returned it. Women could not earn much. Before it was seven points for women. How much could you earn in a year? In the mountains, even ghosts did not have much work to do. My husband, if he worked twenty or thirty workdays [gong] a month bowing cotton in the brigade, the work points he earned came to several dozen yuan a month. What money could he earn? He barely got by.*[25] From the 1960s on, women were once again permitted to raise pigs for sale and to produce handicrafts. The money they earned enabled their families to clear their debts to the collective.[26] Only as children grew older and began to bring in work points did the situations of these families begin to ease.

Men had the authority to approve or disapprove daily household expenditures, but women exerted considerable control, as Xiao Gaiye recounts: *My husband was in a higher position. What I wanted to do, I said to him ahead of time. I consulted him. If he agreed, I would do it. If he didn't agree, I didn't do it. If I really had to do it, I would say it to him first. If he agreed, I did it. If he disagreed, I did it anyway.*[27] When a family undertook a major expenditure, such as expanding an old house or building a new one, it was frequently the wife who borrowed money from neighbors,[28] repaying them with funds she earned from whatever sidelines were permitted. Ma Li recalls the extended effort entailed in such transactions: *The tile I used for building the house was worth 120 yuan. I needed to save money for two years. I borrowed some money for tile from a person who was earning money in the brigade. He said, "You give me some every year when you sell your pig." I raised the pig for a year and got only forty-eight yuan in the end. I said, "Look, I am short two yuan. I will give you this much now." He was good and said, "It is fine if you only give me twenty yuan. Take the money back and make clothes for your children for the spring festival." I said, "If I don't give it to you now, I can't give you any money until next year." He said, "It's fine if you can pay your debt in full in four or five years." And I did.*[29]

Sending children to school did not cost much in fees, but the money required for their clothing and books often made it impossible to keep them in school. Liu Dongmei regrets her children's illiteracy: *We supported two of them through junior high school. All the others cannot read. The fifth finished junior high school. And also the tenth. All the others never went to school. It was not so expensive, but you had no money. You worked hard but what you had was not enough to pay for their clothing. The money would not come to my hand. You could not get money from digging in the field.*[30]

Divorce was rare in these financially strapped households, but arguments were common. *When I got angry, I would mutter at home for a long time. Then [my husband] would leave. He had a hot temper, and I was fierce. Whenever something happened, I carried on and on. My kids would say, "Mom, what are you going on about? Dad has already left."*[31] A wife might curse her husband when the children needed something and there was no money to buy it, and the husband would curse or beat her in response. Couples also fought about the size and gender composition of their proliferating families. Preference for at least one son remained strong during the collective period, among men and women alike. Liu Dongmei, whose mother had converted to Christianity in hopes of bearing a son, remembers a quarrel with her own husband after their third daughter was born: *He cursed me because I only had daughters. I was also angry. I cursed him, "You have a bad fate. You make me only have daughters. You have a bad fate. And you still want more." When I had the fourth daughter, he did not give her to others. Just kept on having them. And having daughters made you angry. After I had a son I was happy.*[32]

In multigenerational households, the relationship between a woman and her husband's parents could also be complicated. Feng Sumei, left with her children and in-laws while her husband worked away from home, links her filial behavior toward her mother-in-law with her desire as a cadre to set a good example in her community. *My mother-in-law was a small-foot. If she helped with the housework you should say nothing, and if she didn't, you should also say nothing. I never said anything about her eating eggs every day. So my relatives, my husband, and many others all say that I was a filial daughter-in-law. My mother-in-law did not work in the fields. She did not even know when the beans in the garden were overripe, or where our family plot was. She only knew how to say "I have no vegetables," not how to pick some in the field, or even how to send a child to pick some. If you left home for several days on business, she would eat up all the pickled and salted vegetables that I had made, and did not know how to make any more.*

She often suffered from stomachaches and cried. I would immediately take her to doctors of Chinese and Western medicine, and then give her injections. My husband was not at home, and the children were still young. I did not expect her to do anything for me after her recovery. I sewed and washed clothes for her, and took her as my own mother. I thought of myself as her daughter, not her daughter-in-law.

All of this was in order to bring the others along with me. If some mothers- or daughters-in-law did not behave well, we would speak at the meeting without pointing out who it was, and say in general that you cannot oppress your daughter-in-law now like you could in the old society, when the mother-in-law was to enjoy while the daughter-in-law was to serve. Instead the old should love the young and the young should love the old. It looks like work on this issue was done pretty well. Just like in my family. People say, "Villages look at other villages and families look at other families, while the masses look at the cadres."[33]

In making this connection between domestic filiality, proper cadre behavior, and public harmony, Sumei was linking imperial notions of womanly virtue with fealty to a newer revolutionary project. When elite women in late imperial China wrote about family relationships, they never celebrated their relationships with their children. Rather they talked about what they did for their mothers-in-law, how filial and responsible (and sometimes affectionate and admiring) they were.[34] In the 1950s women from every background, including poor rural women, were being asked to direct similar sentiments—loyalty, responsibility, admiration—toward the revolutionary process, rather than their mothers-in-law. But if revolutionary virtue required filial behavior, then the mother-in-law might never feel the difference.

As the collective period wore on and families grew, many parents-in-law, exhausted by the economic and logistical demands of grandchildren, moved to separate their living arrangements from those of their married sons.[35] In a multigenerational household, often the daughters-in-law who had children did not go to the fields, on the grounds that the children were small and the domestic burden heavy. A family with many young children sometimes did not earn enough work points to cover the grain they needed for food. It was usually possible to borrow from the production team, but if grandparents were still able to work in the fields and were part of the same household as their grandchildren, their labor subsidized their sons and daughters-in-law. Dividing the household was an oblique way for aging parents to protect themselves and push the younger generation to work harder, although it was also common practice for grandparents to feed their grandchildren if the parents were not doing well economically.[36] For the generation of our interviewees, household separation from parents-in-law meant increased economic stress, as Kang Xingfen observes: *When our child was two, the in-laws asked to separate households. They saw that there were a lot of children, that we couldn't get ahead, and had to depend on others. The children didn't eat well or wear good clothing, and couldn't get grain to eat. Aiya, at the end of the year when we brought the grain back in the collective, I don't know if it is that the land wasn't well cultivated or what, but we were not distributed much grain. I am telling it like it was. Every year during the collective, we were short forty or fifty yuan. Sometimes sixty or seventy yuan.*[37] During the hard years of the early 1960s, Qiao Yindi recalls, household separations accelerated: *My father-in-law said that we should eat separately, that everyone should eat with their own families. Grain was short. There were too many people and they couldn't take care of all of them. It was a burden to the old folks.*[38] Gradually, across rural China in the collective period, it became the practice for adult children to separate out after having their first child.[39]

Household separation was an accounting rather than a spatial decision. The house, grain, and other possessions were divided up, but often nobody moved; the separated households merely stopped pooling their budgets and set up two stoves rather than one. When Qiao Yindi's in-laws initiated a separation, *we didn't divide up the living space. We lived as before. We didn't move. We ate the grain we harvested. We got grain according to the number of people. You ate this. Then you got whatever you harvested later. The elders weren't responsible for that any longer. The parents took care of their own kids. Then the old folks didn't need to bother about it. Otherwise, parents didn't take the responsibility and relied on the older generation. Later, the old folks only took care of their own cooking and food.*[40] For aging parents, separating households meant giving up the vaunted ideal of a multigenerational household and the firm guarantee of old-age support in exchange for an immediate lightening of their domestic burden. But childcare and other daily tasks were also affected, and household separation further increased the workload of women with young children.[41]

Official concern about disturbing maltreatment of the elderly was present as well by 1957, in ominous anticipation of a contemporary problem. As a Women's Federation report put it, "Some elderly people cannot earn work points, and need to feed themselves, so the phenomenon of abusing and abandoning elderly people has become more serious than before. This makes many old people worry about old age, and they lose their confidence in the socialist way." To deal with this problem, local cadres were instructed to explain that "supporting parents is a natural senti-ment among family members, the responsibility of daughters-in-law, the traditional virtue of our nation, the moral standard of the new society, and an obligation writ-ten in the Marriage Law. This is because the elders contribute a lot to raising the next generation for the nation. Because they work hard for their whole lives to make good fortune for family and nation, we have to make sure that they have a happy life in their old age. . . . Explain that abusing and abandoning old people is not only intolerable in terms of human morality, but also against the law."[42] Woman-work in the countryside reinforced the importance of family harmony, even while making unprecedented demands upon families. Women of both generations—mothers-in-law and daughters-in-law—bore the brunt of these new pressures.

NEEDLEWORK AT NIGHT

In rural women's tales of self, the mother bent over her needlework is a pervasive figure.[43] Throughout the collective period, women remained responsible for cloth-ing their ever-larger families through their own labor in a region where machine-made cloth was scarce and rationed. (Zhou Guizhen recalls a big event in the early years of her marriage: a trip to the county seat with her sister-in-law to view a bolt of machine-woven cloth.)[44] Brigade sewing teams charged fees that growing fam-ilies often could not afford,[45] and ready-made clothes and shoes were slow to arrive. In countless stories from imperial China, the figure of the mother busy at needle-work had embodied industriousness, loving sacrifice, and suffering. The suffering mother bent over her sewing in the 1950s differed from the classical version, how-ever, in that she had additional obligations to meet. She went each day to the col-lective fields to earn work points her family could not do without, and she often ventured out again in the evenings to attend political meetings.

Needlework in women's stories of home holds the place that singing does in the field work stories: it encapsulates the memories of an entire epoch. In the years im-mediately after 1949, women continued to spin and weave at home, rising before dawn or staying up late to make cotton thread and cloth for home use, even after they stopped producing for the market.[46] *At night we spun by moonlight,* says Shan Xiuzhen. *We lit the lamps and wove. In the moonlight we made shoe soles, twisted thread, and treated the nighttime like day.*[47] In Village G, Yuan Xi provided all the cloth for her own family's clothing and that of her natal family as well, a total of twelve people.[48] In the hard years after the Great Leap Forward, as we will see, fam-ilies traded this handwoven cloth for grain grown in mountain villages, providing a hedge against starvation. In the later years of the collective period, some grew cot-ton on the small private plots allocated to them by the collective and wove it into cloth, dying it black by boiling it in a pot.[49]

The main nighttime chore was sewing, done by the light of an oil lamp with a cotton wick that produced stinging smoke along with light.[50] In Village G, which had no electricity until 1972, Wang Youna remembers, *We had an oil lamp for sewing at night. When it was cold, I put my legs under the covers. I put a bench on the covers and placed the lamp on the bench. I was afraid the oil would splash on the covers when my kids turned. When I felt sleepy, I lay down and slept. It is not true that it is difficult to do needlework nowadays. There are lights now. Lights are so bright.*[51]

Xiao Gaiye recalls the cumulative exhaustion. *When [the children's] father was alive, I never slept at night. When there was no electricity, I lit a lamp and did needlework. When my sons woke up, I held them up to pee and then put them down. I worked past midnight making clothes for my sons. I worked in the collective during the day. I never slept. I was so pitiful. When I made winter clothes, if I had some time during the day I would spread the material out and get it ready to sew. At night, I sewed it and sewed buttons on it. I was so pitiful. I had so many sons. I was so tired.*[52] Shi Ranwa waited until her children were asleep at night to *spread the cotton cloth out on their bodies and make clothing for them.*[53] Spinning at night epitomized maternal sacrifice for Jiang Qiuwa: *When I spun, I saw my child urinating. It was wet. I changed the cloth for the child and I slept on the wet side and left the warm place for my child. That's how I brought up my children.*[54]

Needlework followed women everywhere, as Ma Li observes: *We sewed while we were walking and carrying things. We also sewed in the fields. A young man said, "Look at that woman. She took her sewing with her even when she went to the toilet." We had no other way. Whenever we had some time we sewed. Otherwise, what could the kids wear?*[55] Liu Fengqin distinguishes between the paid labor of field work and the unpaid labor of needlework by using distinct terms lost in translation: *I would go to the fields with a book bag on my back, taking my needlework along. When people were resting, I would sit and do needlework. As soon as they said, "Time to get to work [shang gong]," I would put the work [huo] aside.*[56]

Piles of sewing, along with children, accompanied women to brigade meetings. Wang Youna remembers, *We had meetings every two days or so. Doing needlework at meetings was allowed at first. Later, it wasn't. I took needlework, such as the kids' shoe soles, to the meetings. I did some while we were waiting for others to come. I hid it as soon as the meeting started. I took the younger kids to the meetings.*[57] Not everyone could juggle the sewing and the children. Feng Sumei, ever attentive to women's domestic burdens, noticed that *women who took children did not take sewing. Women who did not take children took sewing, because they were usually busy and had no time for sewing. It wouldn't have been good to ask them not to sew at meetings. Only at formal brigade meetings was it not permitted. Everyone did some sewing while they waited for others before the meetings began.*[58]

Providing shoes for growing children was a special challenge. Soles were made of cotton and padding, stitched in intricate patterns to hold the multiple layers together. A single layer of cotton was fashioned into a shoe upper for fall and spring, and a double layer was stuffed with batting for winter. But children often exceeded this quota, going through a pair of shoes every two or three months.[59] He Gaizhen observes that no mother was exempt from this labor: *You had to do it whether you were a cadre or not. There was no one selling shoes here at that time. We all made shoes by ourselves. I never let my kids wear broken shoes when they were in school. Other kids all wore broken shoes. My kids' shoes had white bottoms. For each kid, one pair of padded cotton shoes in the winter, one pair of thin shoes in the spring, one in the summer, one more pair in the fall. Four pairs a year. If I didn't do it, who would have made them?*[60] Zhuang Xiaoxia recalls, *Once I made a pair of shoes in a night. The child was waiting to wear them the next day, leaving home to do something, so when it was dark, in one evening, I didn't sleep and made a pair for him.*[61] Qian Tao-hua, a mother of six, marvels at how this staple of domestic work has disappeared: *Nobody nowadays has seen these things. They all wear ready-made things. After 1966 there were shoes sold. Nobody made shoes. We had to take care of the kids. We ruined our eyes.*[62] Women cadres took their bundles of partially assembled shoe soles to meetings in the county seat because there, unlike in the villages, they could work by electric lamplight at night.[63]

After the Great Leap Forward, in the 1960s, sideline production became more permissible. This meant different nighttime tasks for women in each village. Ma Li made ropes for pocket money: *I worked outside in the daytime and made ropes and straw shoes at night. If I made five pairs of straw shoes tonight, I could sell them for 0.50 yuan. That's how I could buy some salt.*[64] He Gaizhen, Liu Dongmei, and Zheng Xiuhua in Village Z added embroidery to the nightly round of needlework.[65] The pillows they produced, long bolsters of satin and velvet with intricate embroidered flowers and fruit on each end, were part of each new bride's dowry. It was the custom for the natal family to stuff grain in the pillows—each one could hold a bushel—for the bride to bring to her new household.[66] He Gaizhen also made embroidered door curtains, with silk she hand-reeled from cocoons and dyed herself. *My family had money at that time. People said I was leading a life with enough firewood and flour. But I wanted to work. With money, nobody is afraid it will hurt the hand. I wanted to do it. It was not interesting just to sit there. You had to do something when you sat there. I took the money to the mountains and the fields. I traded for grain and I sold for money. I took the grain back to eat and I took the money back to use. I didn't want to waste time.*

Gaizhen's pleasure in the creativity of needlework emerges in the details of the telling. *When I got pregnant, I saw people sewing clothes for their kids every day. I learned. When I was in the month of confinement my mother was very busy in the family restaurant and had no time to take care of me. My mother said, "What to do? My Gaizhen gave birth to a girl but she has no clothes for her. It's already been a month but she can't take the baby out of the room." I had already made the clothes earlier, but she didn't know. I didn't let her see. I used two legs of my husband's trousers to make a small jacket and a pair of small black trousers. The jacket had no collar. I also made her a pair of shoes, using red silk fabric. I made her a hat like a monk's in the old days. I made a flower and pasted it to the hat. It was a double-layered flower. It looked like a bud.*

On the day I went to cut wheat, I dressed my baby beautifully. "Oh, the clothes fit. Who made them? Who sewed them?" I said, "I made them. I sewed them." It was the fashion to have a flower hat like a dog's head. One flower on this side, one on the other side, and a little velvet on the top. That's how she wore it. To be a woman, you should know how to make these. Later I made a door curtain for my daughter with a lion on it. I used a piece of black silk for the lion's eyebrows and pasted it to the curtain. It was very beautiful.[67]

Embroidery brought the pleasures of discretionary income and aesthetic design. But for Zheng Xiuhua, whose designs were among the most famous in the area and who taught other village women to embroider, the work was also an absolute necessity: *The children disturbed you so that you could not work. It took me a very long time to finish. I embroidered a piece each day, working fast, because I wanted money. I drew the flowers myself. It was for a bowl of food. I was pitiful and had no other choices. Nobody taught me. I could remember the designs of others if I saw them. Then I drew them from memory. If you did not embroider, you had no way [to get by]. You needed money even if you wanted to buy some matches. I spent the money I earned from embroidery to buy food. The pocket money in my family mainly depended on my embroidery.*[68] Liu Dongmei, who embroidered up to twenty pairs of pillows each year, puts it more bluntly. *In the evenings I would come back from the fields and immediately pick up the needle and start to embroider pillows. A pair of pillows could trade for twenty* jin *of grain. It could last for a period of time. Then I made another pair for twenty* jin *of grain to last for another period of time. At the beginning, I would make a pair of pillows and then the child could have something to wear. I have been embroidering pillows for my whole life. All my life I have depended on my fingers to eat. I suffered my whole life.* In an oblique commentary on the financial burden of getting a son established in life, she continues, *Just a couple of days ago I was saying that my whole life I worked all day long to earn money to build houses for others. I am the most pitiful one. What's the good of having so many children? Now, if they are filial, you will be fine. If they are not filial, you will die of pitifulness [ba ni keliansile].*[69]

In some Guanzhong villages women have continued to spin occasionally into the twenty-first century.[70] In Village G, women weave sheets, quilts, handkerchiefs, baby socks, diapers, and dishcloths in checkered patterns of their own design, putting them away for daughters, future daughters-in-law, and grandchildren.[71] Some also weave their own funeral clothing.[72] But although women talk now about how they might make their hand-produced goods attractive to the global market, they no longer stay up far into the night doing needlework.

When women talk about the years dominated by the endless round of domestic tasks, they refer to their lives as "bitter." They do not connect their domestic burden to the state requirement that women earn work points in the fields, or to the question of what counted as remunerated labor. During the collective period, only the Women's Federation seems to have argued—occasionally—for the classification of housework as labor. A 1953 article in the national Federation journal, *Xin Zhongguo funü* (Women of New China), stated the problem succinctly, using the term *laodong* for domestic labor:

> We have investigated several households and have come to understand that women also perform a great deal of labor [*laodong*] in the household. Aside from taking care of the children, a housewife must cook three meals a day, make three pairs of shoes for each person, as well as one unlined and one padded jacket apiece, do the washing and the mending, and keep the house and its environs clean. Although this labor does not directly create production value for agriculture, it serves peasant livelihood and production, and without it, livelihood and production will all suffer great losses.[73]

In December 1956 Cao Guanqun, a former provincial Federation leader, updated this analysis for the era of expanded collectives:

> If in the past housework served individual peasants . . . today it assists the agricultural production of the co-op. It serves collective peasants and co-op members. It has new meanings. It is still needed for production, indispensable in peasant life. Housework cannot be socialized very soon, not even in the next few five-year plans. Housework is necessary and serves socialist production. Women are better suited for housework than men. It's glorious for women to take over this kind of labor [*laodong*]. Co-ops should take this into consideration when requiring women's attendance. Aside from workdays, time must be reserved for women themselves to allocate to housework and sideline production. Reasonable division of housework should also be advocated.[74]

But when local Women's Federation branches tried to address the housework question, they did not propose not to collectivize, compensate, or address the question of who did what. Perhaps, they suggested, housework (*jiawu huo*) should be performed during the slack season. Or perhaps production teams should set aside a designated period of the workday during which everyone (meaning, all the women) would carry out household tasks in a unified fashion. Although the Federation named one co-op that had used this method to "solve the contradiction between farmwork and housework,"[75] domestic tasks were generally not addressed as labor. Women themselves, however, sometimes used the language of compulsory, regular, disciplined labor to talk about their needlework; they spoke, for instance, of "adding a night shift working for the children."[76]

CHILDCARE

The childcare crisis garnered more attention in the official record than housework, perhaps because childcare could not be deferred to the midnight hour. Not every household had a mother-in-law available to watch the children.[77] Early in the 1950s, when mutual aid groups were first being established, the provincial Women's Federation named organized childcare as the key to bringing women out to work in the fields.[78] *Before that, when women worked, the older child would look after the younger one. If there was no one to take care of the baby, people would tether it to the bedside. This would cause serious problems, and there were some accidents. That's why organizing day nurseries and kindergartens could greatly affect the liberation of women.*[79] Many of the *dundian* cadres most active in organizing childcare were women such as those described in chapter 3, who had left their own young children with wet nurses to go to the countryside. Working with the Health Bureau, the Women's Federation trained childcare workers, produced how-to pamphlets for the public, and publicized success stories in the press. Internal work reports discussed women's reluctance to place their children with non-family members, lack of confidence on the part of older women that they could adequately care for children, how to pay childcare workers (work points, labor exchange, cash, and gifts were all mentioned), and how much to pay for the care of various age groups (children under the age of two cost more).

The publicity emphasized that childcare groups should be self-reliant, with minor assistance from local government when necessary. Ideally the masses could be mobilized to provide a building, beds, mats, toys, and other expenses. In how-to publications, most difficulties were quickly resolved through propaganda and mobilization. More attention was devoted to organization and funding than to the actual methods of caring for children, although some publications did talk about disease prevention, the need for warm-hearted caregivers, and the best ways to fashion inexpensive toys out of local materials.[80] Annual reports from county-level Women's Federations triumphantly counted the number of childcare groups founded, the number of children attending, the number of women now able to participate in production, and the amount of farmland they were able to cultivate as a result.[81]

Most childcare groups (*baowa zu*) were seasonal, organized on the basis of existing mutual aid groups, which meant that children were put in the care of neighbors who were already familiar to them. Bigger daycare centers (*tuoer suo*) aimed to accommodate from several dozen to seventy or eighty children, serving several mutual aid groups, a co-op, or a township.[82] At first they were based on the principle of work exchange: *If you earned ten work points every day, and some old lady took care of three or five children for you, you would give her one or two work points. If there were no laborers in her family, it was a situation of "I take care of your children and you help me harvest wheat from the fields, and bring grain home for me."*[83]

But some mothers found themselves paying out much of what they earned; at two points per day per child, Zheng Xiuhua could keep only two of the six daily work points she made.[84]

Later the lower cooperatives began to pay daycare workers in work points.[85] In 1956, with a national campaign under way to raise the number of days women spent in the fields, the Shaanxi Women's Federation called for each of its local branches to found at least one year-round daycare center or nursery school and for counties to train eleven thousand childcare workers in a two-week period.[86] In Weinan, the county Federation signaled the importance of this work by publicizing the county Party Committee's support and using the term "backbone" (*gugan*) to refer to child-care workers. A team of trainers—two from the Party Committee, four from the Women's Federation, two from the Health Department, and one from the district police—held day-and-a-half training sessions across the county. They lectured to 955 trainees, two of whom were men; the report noted that "one collective even sent a man to participate in the training, in case women couldn't remember what they had learned." More than 70 percent of the trainees were young or middle-aged people, a signal that the work was too important to be left exclusively to the old, even though younger women were not always enthusiastic about it. Trainers addressed this directly, reporting one result of the sessions: "People's socialist consciousness was greatly improved. Some people thought childcare work not glorious, not im-portant. Some women cadres showed no confidence in childcare work. They thought it had been raised several times in the past but never lasted long. They thought it was just lip service. The training corrected their thinking. The fact that many chil-dren fell in the river and drowned while their mothers were participating in pro-duction, and nobody took care of them, educated trainees. They realized the im-portance of childcare work and determined to work hard on it."[87]

The task of organizing childcare groups fell to the township level of the Women's Federation and, at the village level, the women's representative and the women team leaders.[88] In spite of the rosy picture of a staff of young, highly trained childcare workers, often people who were no longer capable of field work were assigned to watch the children. Zhou Guizhen describes the situation in Village B: *There were two old ladies. One had a bad leg. The other old lady, her eyes were no good. When she worked in the fields she couldn't see the crops, and she hoed them all under. That wouldn't do. But she still had to do something to eat. They weren't so old, so I arranged for them to take care of three children each, and paid them seven work points a day.*[89] Establishment of daycare centers was articulated as a key political task during the Great Leap, but the effort soon foundered. As late as the 1970s, Village Z women left their small children sitting in the square in front of the school while they hauled baskets of fertilizer down to the fields, coming back to check on them between loads.[90] One women's team leader in Village T lost an eight-year-old son in 1976 when he fell into the urine vat under the privy while everyone else was out harvesting the rice. The vat held the year's accumulation of urine, which was being stored for use on the next year's rice crop. She found him when she stirred the privy looking for him, and his foot floated up.[91]

MATERNAL ATTACHMENT

Embedded in a woman's stories about motherhood was often a trace of satisfaction—that she had acquitted herself honorably, fulfilling her duty to provide material security, care, and moral guidance. Women did not talk much about affection, love, longing, ambivalence, anxiety, and other emotions closely associated with mothering in contemporary China.[92] These are themes of recent provenance; in the imperial era, for instance, women's written representations of self centered on filial devotion and wifely loyalty rather than maternal attachment. In spoken memories of the collective period, accounts of the emotional valences of motherhood are fragmentary but intriguing: the powerful gratitude sons feel toward their widowed mothers, the grief mothers express over their dead children, and the understated, matter-of-fact manner in which women activists and cadres discuss their own child rearing.

Widowed Mother, Filial Son

Sons born in the 1930s and 1940s stayed in the same household with their mothers well into adult life, while daughters married out. So perhaps it is not surprising that of all the stories interviewees told about their mothers, the one in which the mother emerges most clearly as a character in her own right, not just as a vessel for pre-Liberation suffering, is told by an adult son. In Chinese popular lore, the virtuous widow is notable not only for her chastity, but for her dedication to bringing up her children, particularly sons, with a combination of self-denial, steely will, and uncompromising strictness, enforced when necessary by corporal punishment. Her dedication is repaid by the undying gratitude and filial behavior of her adult son.[93] This cultural icon apparently walked the land in fleshly form well into the years of the People's Republic. Yang Guishi, born in 1938 in Village G, lost his father when he was an infant. He speaks of his mother's lifetime of service to him and eventually to his children: *My mother always said that my ancestors were very good people, that when she married here it was like falling into a storehouse of happiness. My father joined the army before I was one year old, fighting for the GMD at Zhongtiao Mountain, and never came back, and so there is only me. My mother was resolute about not leaving [remarrying], that she must bring me up. She was twenty when my father passed away. My mother supported herself and me by weaving. Until I was twelve or thirteen I never saw her sleep much. When I was very little, she lulled me to sleep when it got dark, and woke me up in the morning. So I never saw her sleeping. There were quite a few women in the lane whose situation was similar to my mother's.*

They would weave at night, and go to the Lujin town market every day to sell what they had woven and exchange it for raw cotton.

When I was little, I was very naughty. My mother only had me. She was afraid that I would get into trouble at home, so she sent me to school. [To Zhuqing, one of the women in the village:] I was taught by your father. I was very naughty, and your father pinched me so my leg was black and blue. At that time, people didn't beat; they pinched. When she found out, my mother beat me. She didn't spare me. Even though she only had me, an only child, when it came to education she didn't neglect it at all. When he pinched me, my leg swelled up this big, but she wasn't upset about it. When it came to my studies, she didn't do a half-hearted job. I couldn't get away with things.

I studied carpentry with an old carpenter in our alley. As I just said, I was very naughty when I was young. After ten days or so he beat me and sent me back home. My mother cried, and so did I. My mother said, "You are really impossible, and you can't be educated. So what are you going to do when you grow up? If you don't learn a skill, what will you do?" I never resisted what my mother said, so the next day I went back there with her. When I was there, I was really restless. I worked for fifteen days and came back again. My mother yelled at me. She was unwilling to beat me, so she could only cry. Both mother and son cried for the whole evening. The next day I went back again.

From 1958 to 1962, I worked at the Xi'an Sanqiao automobile factory. My wife was in the village earning work points. It was very hard for the family. I gave all the money I earned each month to my family. When I came back I gave it to my mother. My thinking was very feudal. I only considered my mother. You see I had a wife, but I didn't take that into account. When I came back, everything was decided by my mother, and I concentrated on her.

In 1962, supporting the front line of agriculture was brought up. So I applied to come back, because at that time my mother was having a difficult time. I talked to the group leader. "Why are you coming back? What a moment!" Before he had been fat, but the rations had made him very thin. "Good child, this is the situation: if you can flee, then just flee from here." That sentence made me mad. This would mean giving up on my mother, who had raised me with huge difficulties. If I listened to him, I would let my mother starve to death. I was determined to go back.

She took care of me until I was in my forties, straight through. I have five children. She took care of the youngest until he was five, and then she passed away, in 1976. My mother had no daughters. At the end, I was the one who took care of her in the hospital. As soon as it was dark I would borrow five linked chairs and sleep there beside my mother. Day and night, I was the only one there. I said, "Ma, if you feel that something is wrong with you, pull on my ears and shake me." That's how I took care of her, and after just thirty days, she passed away. My mother sacrificed a lot. Even after more than twenty years, whenever I bring up my mother, my eyes still fill with tears. She never had it easy, but she was truly kindhearted.[94]

The practice in which a son recites the virtues of his mother, familiar to any member of the late imperial elite, remains powerful in this early twenty-first century village. Here the sanctioned cultural figure of the widowed mother combines with the equally valorized filiality of a son who was separated from his mother only by her death—not by his marriage, as a woman would have been—to create a statement of enduring attachment. Nothing about the story, with the exception of its passing description of hunger during the Great Leap famine, suggests the changes in women's work and mothering that collectivization brought about.

Childhood Illness, Death, Grief

Infant mortality from umbilical tetanus or childbirth trauma, as we have seen, declined substantially in the 1950s. It became less common for women to have childbirth histories like one of our interviewees, born in the early 1920s, who had fourteen pregnancies and three surviving children. (She terminated three pregnancies, drowned one daughter at birth, and lost seven children to illness.) But young children continued to die of measles, meningitis, and illnesses of unknown etiology well into the 1960s. At least twelve of the sixty village women we interviewed (not including *dundian* cadres) lost one child or more to illness after 1949. Mothers note the death of children at birth or in infancy matter-of-factly, but say more about the deaths of children who lived long enough for the women to have strong individual memories of them. Embedded in some of these stories are indirect complaints about parental workload and inept medical care, as well as the particular grief and problems entailed in the loss of a son, regardless of age.

For one Women's Federation activist, provincial labor model, and co-op cadre, her son's birth in 1954 helped to mollify her husband, who was very dissatisfied with her frequent absences from home to attend meetings. The child suffered from meningitis and its aftereffects; she blames his illness on the fact that she had sent him out to a wet nurse with inferior milk. Two years later, she gave birth to a daughter, who was given to a wet nurse after six days and stayed with her until she was in middle school. In 1958, the activist went to Beijing for three months of meetings; two weeks after her departure her son's illness flared up and he died. She was not told of his death. When she returned to the province she went first to Xi'an, where she was hospitalized with a stomach inflammation. At the time she was pregnant and wanted an abortion, and was mystified by the refusal of the hospital authorities to give her one. Eventually one of the Women's Federation cadres told her that her son had died. Returning home to her village, she pushed through a waiting crowd of sympathetic villagers, went directly to her house, covered her head with a quilt, and cried for a long time. When she gave birth to another daughter several months later, her husband, still almost deranged with grief, reproached her for cutting off his patriline. *A daughter doesn't support the mother's house; you can't use ashes to build a wall. Ten daughters in flowered clothes are not worth one crippled son. You were such an activist that you snuffed [literally, "cut short"] the incense on my grave.*[95]

For Zheng Xiuhua, grief at the loss of three sons in quick succession between 1958 and 1960 is intensified by bitterness about poor medical care and the poverty that would have made the children a burden had they lived. One of these children, born in 1950, died at ten: *He was sick for a month, was not treated properly, and died.* A second, born in 1953, died of measles at seven. The third, born in 1955, died at three of unclear causes. *There was no clinic at that time. They had built a row of buildings, but nobody was there. I had three children and spent more than eighty yuan for them to see a doctor. But none of them was cured. More than eighty yuan was a big sum of money, and I borrowed from many places. The economy was in difficulty at that time. . . . I could not have afforded their marriages [if they had lived]. I would have had to find wives for them. Four sons need four wives. I only had to find one wife for my son.*[96]

The fiercest grief was expressed by mothers who had successfully raised sons to adulthood, only to see the men succumb to cancer, epilepsy, hepatitis, and other diseases. These were recent deaths at the time of our interviews. We stayed on two occasions in Village G in an elaborate house that the local Party secretary had built for his son, who died before he could marry and take up residence. Other young men left widows and children, and the loss expressed by their mothers was mixed with anxiety about the future and their own old age. Ma Li had lost her youngest son the previous year after he left the village to work as a miner: *My son died at the age of twenty-seven last March. Some young men went to work in Tianshui. Later, when he came back he was sick. Nobody could tell what his disease was. Then he died. What do you expect me to say? I can't explain it. It was my fourth child.*

On the third day after he came back from Tianshui, I said, "Son, are you sick?" He said yes. I said, "Why didn't you come back earlier if you were sick?" He said, "I couldn't come back. I had no money in the coal mine." He had been there more than a year. I asked doctors to give him some injections first and then I asked Xiao Xu to take him to the county hospital. A young man in the brigade said, "Aunt, I'm afraid he won't last long. You'd better go with us." I had been cooking for the post office for more than twenty years. Shuomin, in the post office, said, "This is going to cost money. I can find a thousand yuan for you now." I gave the money to the young man and asked him to take my son to Shangnan hospital. He underwent emergency treatment for three days. On the third day they called and said to take him back immediately, because he wouldn't last long. He died as soon as he was taken back home. Three months after her son's death, Ma Li's husband was paralyzed by a stroke. *You ask me to talk about it, but I can't. In the past I could remember everything. I lost my son. My heart is uneasy. I am in my sixties. My life is pitiful. If I don't make money, I have not a cent to get along. I spent thousands of yuan to try to cure my youngest son's disease. Now I have no money. My first son is working in Shu. We have lived separately for more than ten years. My two daughters have both married. They have their own lives. I shouldn't have lost my son. He was already twenty-seven years old.*

I have the daughter-in-law. My grandson is already over one year old. I was afraid she would take my grandson away if she remarried. I have called in someone for my daughter-in-law to marry. Otherwise, what can you do? If I tell her to marry again, she will take my grandson away. If I don't let her go, it is not okay. But if I let her go and then I take care of my grandson, how can I bring up my grandson in a few days? And if my grandson follows his mother, I will worry about him. If he is in my home, there is no question of whether he is treated equally. As peasants say, "If you are not blood relatives, your hearts can't be connected." You can't help worrying.

I have a big piece of land behind my house. I buried my son there. I have never gone there in the past year. I don't want to go there. My son was already so old. If it weren't for my grandson, I would have taken my life. "You left me such a young son. Now I am so pitiful." How much can others help you even if they are willing to help you? The most pitiful thing is how poor we are. If my son were at my side, if we had known what illness it was, he could have gotten treatment earlier. I am always thinking about how pitiful my son's death was.[97] In this tale and others like it, a mother saw her security evaporate with the death of an adult son—a dilemma unaddressed either by collectivization or by the era of household farming that has succeeded it.

Cadres, Loyalty, Understatement

The grief attached to these stories of death has a searing clarity. More puzzling is the emotional valence of the workaday tales cadres and activists tell about reconciling motherhood with their public activities. Cao Zhuxiang, virtuous widow, co-op leader, and regional labor model, married off her daughter in 1958. The ceremony was hastily arranged because the groom had to return to his job at the Yumen oil field in Gansu. Zhuxiang approved of the match, but did not attend the simple ceremony; her schedule was already full. *I told her, I won't come to your wedding that day. I have to go to the county for the meeting. You can order several dishes. But don't be too extravagant.* She asked other relatives to represent her there. On the second day, when local practice required that Zhuxiang send a meal to the newly-weds, she was still attending the meeting. On the third day, when the daughter returned to her natal home for the customary visit, Zhuxiang was still at the meeting. At that point her daughter called her back so that she could present the couple with a piece of steamed bread and a few eggs. *They went back [to the husband's family] after the meal. I was very busy. I had to go back to the meeting. That was how my daughter got married.*[98]

As one of Zhuxiang's younger activist protégées sums it up: *In order to do a good job with the collective, we all neglected our households. Secretary Cao had a son and a daughter at home. Her daughter was young, and had no father. She also neglected her household. We wanted to do a good job with the farming. If we did a good job, everyone would get more, and we would make a bigger contribution to the collective. Spurred on by Secretary Cao, we were always first in our brigade and in the commune.*[99]

What made Cao Zhuxiang go off to the county seat for an endless meeting (one of many) during the week her daughter was marrying? And why did she tell us this story with no apparent affect? We know that Zhuxiang took on the complete burden of supporting a household from the moment she married, and was always in danger of being stigmatized because she did farmwork. Later, as a widow, she worked vigorously to keep herself above reproach. The new society gave her a way to excel by doing what she had always done—farmwork—and also giving her opportunities to organize. It made labor glorious, rewarding her publicly for it, and gave her local political authority as well. Perhaps it is not surprising that the Party-state that gave her all this commanded her absolute loyalty and work, that it came first, whereas a private matter such as a daughter's wedding was a distant second.

But how to understand the flatness with which she told this story, a flatness that affected many of her tales of post-1949 life? Should we understand her matter-of-fact, uninterested tone as a sign of indifference to a prerevolutionary maternal role that had once been required but was now coded as "traditional"? But in telling us other stories about her daughter, Zhuxiang had expressed self-reproach at her inability to provide for her daughter because she was the only adult at home. In the early 1950s, Zhuxiang told us, at age eleven, her daughter was able to go to school, an opportunity Zhuxiang herself never had: *Later she went to school north of the river for half a year. She suffered a lot that year. She had nothing. Nobody delivered clothes to her. It was very cold that winter. My daughter's legs were frozen. I was so sad. At that time someone was living in my home. She said, "Aiya, why don't you deliver winter clothes to your daughter early?" I said, "Who can go there? The river is rising. There is nobody [that is, no man] here."* Zhuxiang's demands on herself in the realm of motherhood, as in co-op leadership and personal comportment, were strict. Yet they apparently did not extend to supervising her daughter's wedding at a time of intense political activity. Could it be that the flatness in her tale of the wedding expressed the shape of her commitment to the revolution—which involved, and still involves in memory, putting the meeting first over the wedding, and not feeling or giving voice to regrets? Gao Xiaoxian and I spent many evenings trying to decide: Why was Zhuxiang's sense of her own life so opaque to both of us, even though each of us brought different personal histories and current questions to the listening?

What is the structure of feeling, the organization of memory, that gives some of the telling of these stories affect and color, while leaving others to a cooler recounting? We know that for some activists, long years of reciting "speak bitterness" stories may have honed to perfection the story of their bitter past. Every detail of suffering is perfectly crafted in the telling. Life as a labor model, on the other hand, though endlessly busy, did not have much of a dramatic structure, and has not been repeatedly narrativized with a particular required affect. Yet Zhuxiang spent very little time on the "speak bitterness" circuit. And while life in post-1949 meetings, and perhaps the domestic life of a labor model, cannot match the dramatic content of her pre-1949 adventures—going out to look for medicine for a dying husband while the county seat was being bombed, or barricading the house to keep marauding soldiers out right before Liberation—it does have its moments: overcoming terror at speaking in front of a crowd, figuring out how to handle a recalcitrant villager who puts salt in the co-op's bean curd to try to sabotage operations. So, again, why the flatness? Is it an ex post facto repudiation of socialism, an assessment that nothing from that time period constitutes a usable past, a history of the present? This seems unlikely, given the skill of Zhuxiang and other rural women at salvaging a sense of optimism from their memories of the past. Zhuxiang's cool opacity raises larger questions about what we used to think was an uncomplicated source, a source we all yearned for: the face-to-face interview with a subaltern who speaks.[100]

The official record about labor models such as Cao Zhuxiang, eloquent on the subjects of cotton cultivation, battles with nature, and the perfidy of political enemies, is curiously silent about children. Although works published in the 1950s discuss how to organize childcare facilities for the busy agricultural season, no labor heroine is ever described as being in need of such assistance in order to perform her historical role. Without subscribing to an essentialist notion of a sacred mother-child bond, or assuming a transhistorical norm of concern about childcare, one still might be tempted to see that silence as a failure by the state, even a cynical attempt to promote women as models without ever acknowledging the material and emotional costs of their modelhood. The silence could be read, in short, as one step in the Long March of bad faith by which the state touted women as equal to men, and as equally available for heroic labor, by simply pretending that their circumstances were the same as those of men.[101] But such condemnation, no matter how briefly satisfying, is both politically foolish and historically untenable. It ignores the zeal with which labor heroines took on (and still recall without apparent ambivalence) their model status and the honors it brought them, as well as the daily work it entailed.

The lives of Women's Federation *dundian* cadres who spent years living in rural areas while their children were brought up by relatives point to a similar set of circumstances. As chapter 3 suggested, some recall feeling harried by the need to scramble and piece together wet nurse and childcare arrangements so that they could return to work. But such sporadic contact with their own children was taken for granted as a feature of working life. *Cadres' children didn't know their mothers,* said one former cadre who had left each of her three daughters behind in the 1950s to go organize childcare for rural women so that they could participate in agricultural production. Later, during the 1960s, when she was transferred to another area, the children were left with her husband and a housekeeper. During the Cultural Revolution, the housekeeper left. The children, home alone, squabbled on the bed, pushing the bedding onto the stove, where it caught fire. Miraculously, no one was injured, but when her husband returned home, he sat down and cried, saying, "This is what the revolution has brought us." But her children, the cadre assured us, have grown up fine. Then, speaking to us in 1997, she delivered a heartfelt denunciation of family values in the 1990s: that people were getting divorced too easily and no one cared about providing a home for their children.[102] She did not share the perception of ironies that might occur to a listener. Nor was her account suffused with regrets, although she expressed exasperation with how difficult things had been. This moment in the revolution, even as it required women cadres to set aside their own children so completely, felt right to them.[103]

One of those cadres, now long retired, explains that having many children could expose one to political ridicule, as well as logistical difficulties. *During the Anti-Rightist movement [of 1957–59] someone stuck up a big character poster, with a cartoon of me surrounded by children, and with a big stomach besides. I didn't see it, but my husband told me about it later. There was no birth planning then. If there had been, I definitely would not have had four children. Two at the most. My mother took charge of all of them. I would give birth to one and give it to my mother. I thought, if I take charge of the children, my work will suffer. Besides, my mother was then in her sixties, and could still take charge of them. One should take charge of one's children, but I didn't personally educate my children. I would go down to the countryside for ten days or two weeks. When I came back, my mother was very good at discovering if there was a problem, and she would tell me about it and I would educate them. I had strict standards. My lowest standard was that they should not be a hindrance to society. That was my most basic standard. Now my four daughters all listen to me, and besides that they all work hard at their jobs. The leadership trusts them. I achieved my goal.[104]*

For many women cadres in the 1950s, the commitment to work and to the revolution opened up a profound sense of possibility and a desire to excel. When they encountered loss and difficulty, they turned to revolutionary models for solace. Zhao Feng'e, a *dundian* cadre in various Guanzhong counties during the 1950s, lost her first two babies, twins, when they were born prematurely at a rudimentary county hospital. She compared her loss to what she knew about senior women revolutionaries. *We have a tradition. During the revolutionary war period, when the enemy occupied North Shaanxi, Hai Tao [later head of the Shaanxi Women's Federation] gave her oldest child to a peasant, and only found the child after Liberation. Elder Sister Deng [the wife of Premier Zhou Enlai] had no children. For the sake of the revolutionary enterprise, for a long time she did not want children. We learned from the generation that went before us. At the time, I wasn't like people these days, who get so sad. I didn't let it get to me. . . . After those two premature births, when I was resting, Hai Tao came down to the countryside to Huayin, and found me. . . . And Chen Muhua [a longtime revolutionary, later a vice premier of the State Council and holder of many other high offices], didn't she just find her daughter recently? I saw it in the paper, or on TV, not long ago. . . . I thought about the women workers before Liberation, how pitiful they were. They gave birth to their children in the factory workshops, and would sneak out to breastfeed them. There were some who couldn't feed their children even once a day. Our models were the older generation and our predecessors; our point of comparison was the life of workers before Liberation. So we overcame difficulties without complaint, under whatever circumstances.*[105]

MATERNAL AMBIVALENCE

Whatever the complexities of maternal attachment in China in the 1950s, there is no doubt that many women felt they had too many children. *There was no family planning at that time,* comments a woman who raised six children. *People had so many kids. Women's bodies were so tired.*[106] When a mother of three in Village B miscarried in the early 1970s after hauling down a heavy sack of grain from attic storage, she reports her major response as relief: *The old woman across the way said, "When people miscarry they are all unhappy. And here you are so happy!" I said that I was very happy. I felt relieved about that miscarriage, that I would no longer be exhausted. I feel that birth planning is great. If we had had birth planning before, I would have been relieved. Later [in 1976], when we had birth planning, I aborted [gua le] the pregnancy after my youngest daughter. I haven't been pregnant since then. I have an IUD. Everyone else has had theirs removed, but until now I haven't removed mine.*[107]

Criticisms of the state are generally muted or oblique in rural women's stories. But on the question of birth control, the state does not escape their ire. Unlike the size of collectives or the mandatory sale of grain, this was a realm in which many wanted more state intervention than they got. Liu Dongmei told us, *When we were working in the collective, the state was in charge of everything. They took charge of telling us to grow the grain properly, harvest more, and eat more. But they didn't take charge of births [zhua wa]. They did not control childbirth.*

To have more children means to suffer more, to be worn out. I have eight children and you might think it's too funny, two sons and six daughters. I had lots of children, I starved, I endured extreme bitterness [zhuasile, esile, kusile]. After Liberation, I had so many children that I got angry. Why didn't they control it and tell people not to have more children? It was pitiful.

Gao Xiaoxian: *You had many children at that time. Did you ever think of having fewer children or birth planning back then?*

Liu Dongmei: *What birth planning? Finally when I had the tenth, birth planning started. Who ever talked to us about birth planning?*

Gao Xiaoian: *Were there any popular methods among the people for having fewer children?*

Liu Dongmei: *People said to take a certain kind of medicine and to go to the*
              doctor. But the doctor said, "Why did you come to me—it was
              immoral [sangde] and sinful [zaonie]." So people were really piti-
              ful. Later I heard that birth planning came. I rushed to the hospital
              to get an IUD. Otherwise, I would have had one or two more. It
              would have been unbelievable. Can you imagine there was some-
              one who had thirteen births? When we worked in the field, women
              talked freely. "Everything is controlled. Why not control people
              having children?"[108]

Other women did terminate pregnancies, even in the years before birth planning was a high state priority. In 1963, Zhuang Xiaoxia was an activist with three
children, ages five to twelve. Pregnant again and exhausted, she attended a meeting in the Weinan County seat. Her roommate at the meeting, a woman from a
neighboring county, introduced her to the concept of birth planning and offered to
arrange for her to have a D and C (the available method of abortion at that time)
and an IUD inserted at a nearby hospital. Xiaoxia took her up on the offer, telling
no one in her family until fourteen years later, when serious birth planning began
in her village: *The district hospital came to the village, and they wanted me to take*
the lead in getting an IUD. I secretly told the person that I already had one. They wanted
me to propagandize the advantages of having one, so I called all the women together
for a meeting and talked to them. That was when my mother-in-law [the midwife Wu
Shuxian] found out. She smiled and scolded me: "You are audacious [dan da]. You are
a thief [zei wa dan]." I said, "I didn't have any more children. They didn't tire you out
and they didn't tire me out, and we didn't need to give them grain from the land."[109]
By the late 1960s, D and C procedures were well known to village women.[110] In the
decades of post–Great Leap collective agriculture, whose specifics often blur in
memory, more than one woman mentioned one year with great emphasis: 1971,
the year that tubal ligations became available in some villages.[111] Many of the women
actively sought them out.[112]

The state's later draconian attempt to limit births to one child per family (soon
modified in the countryside to two children if the first was a daughter) has rendered Liu Dongmei's complaint about state neglect of family planning of historical
interest only. But it provides an important reminder that women's desires and state
policies both shifted over time. As birth planning work intensified in rural areas
after 1979, women who had borne many children in the 1950s and 1960s became
its strongest supporters, many of them serving as local birth planning cadres.[113]
Their personal experience had led them to feel, passionately, that it was difficult to
support and care for many children properly. The older women had clear notions
that the Party had liberated them from feudal women's subordination, but also that
their lives were dominated by endless domestic work and child rearing, as well as

the need to earn work points to make ends meet in conditions of poverty.[114] When women who were of childbearing age during the collective years tried to communicate with younger women in the 1980s and 1990s about the burden of too many children and the need to limit births, they were speaking to a generation who had not shared their experience of privation and exhaustion. In the early 1980s, their heartfelt expressions about the value of small families, backed up by relentless local persuasion and sometimes coercion, fell on the ears of younger women at a very different moment, when children were once again coming to be associated with prosperity, and were still necessary for old-age security. Community responses to the older women doing family planning work were often hostile, as the former women's team leader Feng Sumei remembers: *The work of family planning took a lot of thought and energy. You could not persuade them by talking once or twice. It usually happened that they closed their doors and paid no attention to you. You could not be angry at that. They would not call the dog off for you or offer you a seat. Then you knocked at the door and called out. They would be a bit embarrassed and only then would they open the door. If you came across a woman unexpectedly sometimes, when you talked to her, she would not pay any attention to you. You went to them every day. Gradually she would be persuaded.*[115]

A former woman cadre acknowledged the need for one son, but not more: *At that time, people all said that women who do family planning are sword-wielding killers. Even so, I thought, this is the Party's policy. I would explain the reasoning to her clearly. I would say to her, "There are so many people in your generation. What is going to happen if you don't do this? It's not going to work. Generally speaking, there should be one to carry on the family line. Later, when you die at a ripe old age, there will be someone to bury you. That is the way it should be. Why do you want so much suffering for yourself? It is not advisable to have too many sons. One is as good as ten as long as you can have one."*[116]

Many stories of birth planning work in the late 1970s and early 1980s suggest that although no one liked the new policy, men resisted the state's new campaign more vociferously than women did. Perhaps in the early years of the reform era, women ten years younger than the 1950s generation either shared or understood the experience of bearing too many children when there were too few resources to raise them. *I shed a lot of tears when I was a cadre,* says Feng Sumei. *Some people came to my door to curse me. They cursed me while jumping up and down. There was a man, who already had five children and would not go to [have his wife] get an IUD, who said, "Why don't you go? Why just ask my wife to go?" In most families, women agreed with the family planning, but men did not. Some women came to you stealthily, "Give me a D and C," while telling a lie about going to town. How heavy the housework and sewing burden is for women if they have too many children! So the woman agreed, but her husband cursed me. During the period when I was women's team leader,*

more than ten years, there were some men who cursed me, but no women—their think-
ing could all be straightened out.[117]

These generational and gender differences remind us that the successes and failures and human cost of the birth planning campaign that began in 1979, like other state initiatives, only make sense if we consider the diverse understandings of the various people involved. It is not enough to posit an abstract state on the one hand and a reified family on the other, with hapless family planning workers shuttling back and forth between the two, suffering violence. The legacy of mothering in the collective years—its losses, its fleeting pleasures, its place among other commitments, above all its endless round of unrecognized labor—continues to shape the desires and conflicts of the present.

8

Model

To become an agricultural labor model or a village leader, a man had to be good, even innovative, at what had always been man's work. A woman labor model, in contrast, had to do something completely different from what women had conventionally been recognized as doing, even while continuing to do most of what she had done before. Women labor models pioneered shifts in the gendered division of labor that affected men as well as women, easing the transfer of men out of agriculture into dam construction, rural industry, and technical supervisory positions. Rural development cannot be understood without reference to women labor models, who blurred the boundary between state and society even while embodying the effect of state initiatives.

Hundreds of *dundian* cadres fanned out across central and southern Shaanxi villages in the 1950s. They identified exceptional women as labor models: skilled farmers, dedicated midwives, astute livestock handlers, and tenacious cotton-growing heroines. Labor models were called into being by state officials and coached by local cadres, who produced a voluminous contemporary and retrospective written record of their existence. Publicity about them was meant to encourage other women to emulate their activities, and the official record provides an account of the qualities that Party-state officials—whose reiterated statements were heard as the voice of the state—desired of women. As repositories of community virtue and achievement, labor models were landmarks connecting the space of individual villages to imagined regional, national, and even international spaces. They inhabited the diffuse and ambiguous zone where the state effect was produced.

This chapter investigates the collective creation of women labor models from the early 1950s through the early 1960s, focusing on the blurry boundaries between state activity, community stories, and individual lives. Drawing on labor model reports and publicity created by local cadres and news reporters in the 1950s, it also relies upon the retrospective self-narrations of former labor models and former cadres collected in the 1990s and early 2000s.[1] The story centers on three Shaanxi women labor models who grew high-yield cotton: Zhang Qiuxiang of Weinan, who became a national labor model and member of the Chinese People's Political Consultative Conference and the provincial People's Congress;[2] Shan Xiuzhen of Tongguan, the heroine of chapter 2, selected as a national labor model in 1962;[3] and Cao Zhuxiang of Weinan, the virtuous leader of chapter 3.[4] It also draws on the experiences of the cooperative leader Lu Guilan, who became a provincial labor model in 1951 and a national model in 1957.[5]

Labor models are among the few rural women who appear by name in written records. But the reader looking to labor model literature for a coherent account of a specific life, or even a dense account of rural collectivization featuring actual people, will be disappointed. This is not biography in the common sense of the term: a story of a person moving through time. Rather labor model stories compel attention to the social production of a woman's life for particular purposes, and to its circulation, transformation, and recollection as the product of many different people and interactions.

One of the major state projects for which women labor models were deployed throughout central Shaanxi in the 1950s was cotton cultivation. The idea that women should grow cotton was publicized at provincial meetings, in press accounts of experimental plots tended by enterprising women models, and through contests to apply and improve the best techniques developed by women farmers. This chapter traces the discovery that women were uniquely suited to cotton cultivation, the removal of men to other economic activities, and the distinct roles played by married and unmarried women in labor contests.

Finally, the chapter considers the revelations contemporary readers have come to expect from biography, particularly knowledge of a person's inner thoughts and emotions as revealed by the full range of sources and memories. Labor model stories call into question the existence, or at least the presumed shape, of interiority. The chapter concludes with some thoughts about whether biography is possible or desirable in the wake of a major state project such as collectivization, and whether we should perhaps be asking other kinds of questions about the lives of rural women in this period.

LINEAGES OF VIRTUE

Stories of rural women labor models in the 1950s echoed many themes of older tales about virtuous women: industriousness, suffering, attention to the welfare of others, self-sacrifice (albeit for the collective rather than the patriline), and absence of sexual controversy.[6] Like the virtuous widows and devoted mothers in late imperial stories, labor models were active and determined. In the imperial era, publication of the biographies of virtuous women had brought glory to their families and communities, even as it promoted models of good behavior for the wider reading and listening public. Something similar can be said of the labor models designated by the Communist Party in the Shaanganning Border Region in the late 1930s and early 1940s. Mao Zedong and other Party leaders saw labor models as a bridge between the masses and the leaders, taking opinions and directions to the people and bringing suggestions and demands back to the leadership.[7] They were, in short, the linchpin of the Communist Party's mass line.[8]

In 1950, these labor model practices from the "old districts" of the wartime Communist base areas became the template for the "new districts" of Shaanxi, mainly in the center and south of the province, which had not been part of the original liberated zone. Ten agricultural labor models from the province were selected to attend a national meeting in October 1950, and by December of that year, peasant representatives from around Shaanxi had been mobilized to locate and train labor models.[9] By 1954, fostering and nominating women labor models were standard tasks for the Women's Federation.[10]

As the story of Cao Zhuxiang in chapter 3 suggests, a village or production team that produced a famous labor model often saw its achievements publicized across the province or even the nation. Labor models, like virtuous women in an older regime, became sources of community social capital. At the same time, they embodied and furthered the aims of the state. Like the imperial officials who encouraged the production of gazetteers, Party-state officials hoped to promote emulation of labor models by promulgating the record of their heroic activity.

Of course, the differences between older tales of virtue and their 1950s counterparts were substantial. Virtuous women in early China were often lauded for their sage and sometimes audacious advice to rulers,[11] but paragons from the late imperial era were more commonly praised for their activities in the domestic realm. Labor model stories from the 1950s recombined and transformed elements from both of these eras. Like the women in early Chinese texts, the 1950s labor model was typically involved in a political project: building socialism. Unlike the early Chinese heroines, she did not pursue this project by catching the ear of a powerful man, although encounters with powerful men became part of the story for the labor models who met Zhou Enlai and Mao Zedong. Rather, like the late imperial paragons, the 1950s labor model achieved political goals through the careful performance of quotidian labor, performed in this instance outside rather than within the domestic realm.

Virtuous women in classical texts and gazetteers were typically aged or dead by the time their stories surfaced. In fact, many of those stories required a death, dramatic or otherwise, to complete the story of a life virtuously lived. In contrast, the careers of most rural women labor models in the 1950s and 1960s involved their ongoing participation. A woman such as Zhang Qiuxiang, who became famous for growing cotton, was expected to continue to innovate in cotton production, report on her achievements at provincial meetings, attend national ceremonies where labor models were honored, and generally signify, publicly and continuously, that state initiatives were producing salutary local changes. Dead labor models were of limited utility.[12] To be effective, a labor model had to be alive, actively meeting new challenges in accordance with changing Party-state goals.

SEARCHING

Records from the Yuan Dynasty suggest that virtuous women of that period were identified when their neighbors informed local officials, who in turn recommended them to the emperor.[13] One can well imagine that the process was not quite so spontaneous or linear, that many family and community interests were entailed in securing the rewards and prestige associated with a chaste widow or a faithful maiden. Nevertheless the identification appears to have proceeded upward from local society to officialdom, in response to parameters laid out by the court.

In the early years of the People's Republic in Shaanxi, however, virtuous women were not merely called forth by the state and named by their neighbors. They had to be created. As a 1951 set of instructions from the Civil Administration Bureau to local officials put it, labor models were to be both "trained and discovered."[14] Party or government cadres were the implied agents in the creation of labor models. *Dundian* cadres identified potential leaders, cajoled them to take up leadership roles, trained them in the necessary skills, supported them if they met opposition, and recommended them for state recognition.

For outsiders to a community, the assiduous effort involved in identifying labor models could easily go wrong. Undiscerning cadres, a 1951 report pointed out, had made mistakes, selecting former unruly soldiers, Guomindang administrators, landlords, and even a bandit as labor models. Included in this catalogue of inappropriate choices was one situation in which several seventeen- and eighteen-year-old girls had been named labor models.[15] The document did not specify why this was an error; it was assumed that the reader would know, just as she would know why a bandit was not an appropriate choice. It may be that young unmarried women, or for that matter young married women, were not regarded as possessing the experience or the local respect that would make them effective labor models. Additionally, one former Women's Federation cadre suggests, slightly older women (those in their thirties and forties at Liberation) had suffered firsthand the problems of the old society. Some had been famine refugees; others had married into difficult family situations. They had a clear sense of gratitude toward the Party, a sentiment that was easy for cadres to tap in mobilizing them for field work: *At that time, middle-*

aged women were the first to stride out the household door. One of the characteristics of these model workers was that they were enterprising women, which meant that whatever they did, they wanted it be perfect. They always said, "What could we do in the old society? Now women are liberated. The Party cultivates us, so we should win honor for the Party." The second characteristic was that these [model workers] were very hardworking and sincere.[16]

Young Women's Federation cadres, working as part of a larger *dundian* work team, most frequently did the work of identifying potential women leaders and developing them into full-fledged labor models. In villages with no experienced women farmers, the cadres identified potential models, typically young married women, and organized classes to teach them farming skills.[17] By 1952 they were announcing award ceremonies at which model women, sometimes as individuals and sometimes in groups, were presented with embroidered flags of honor and useful farming implements: sprayers, walking plows, small hoes, and towels. The achievements of such models were announced at countywide meetings.[18] For women who were to become models beyond the local level, however, whenever new national priorities required embodied and lively exemplars, a further process of training and grooming was required: the production of an articulate speaking subject.

SPEAKING

By the mid-1950s, increasing cotton production was a national priority. Sown in April and harvested in October, cotton had been central Shaanxi's chief economic crop since the 1930s, with a hiatus during the war.[19] By 1952 acreage sown to cotton in the province was back to prewar levels.[20] In the clear before-and-after story told in Party-state publications, cotton production was low before 1949, averaging only twenty-six *jin* per *mu* in 1949.[21] It was said, "Seven lumps, eight lumps, if a *mu* can produce three bundles of raw cotton [thirty *jin* of ginned cotton], the peasants laugh with joy." By 1954 production had risen to forty-two *jin* per *mu*, and some peasants reportedly thought it could go no higher.[22]

Textile exports were central to the purchase of Soviet equipment and to capital accumulation, and improving cotton cultivation was an important part of this effort.[23] Central Shaanxi was regarded as a key location to provide cotton to the northwestern region and North China's industrial cotton mills. Prior to the 1950s, women had picked and processed cotton grown in Guanzhong, but after the establishment of the lower co-ops state authorities began to promote women farmers as the primary cultivators of cotton.[24] Cotton growing was suddenly discovered by the Party-state to be suitable work for women, who were thought to have the required dexterous fingers and to pay meticulous attention to detail.[25] This involved an adjustment in the gendered division of labor, as men gradually moved out of cotton farming and into sideline production.[26]

Dundian cadres from the Agriculture Bureau worked with local leaders to improve cotton cultivation. When they went to mobilize women for cotton production, cadres turned first to older women from extremely poor families who had been forced by circumstance to learn how to farm. Cao Zhuxiang remembers, *We were growing cotton all along. In 1952 the technical station said that we weren't cultivating enough land in cotton. Chair Qi came over to tell me this. I said, "People say the cotton won't grow, but if you stamp on it, it won't die either." [That is, it was taking up land but not yielding a good crop.] Chair Qi said, "This is the old way of talking about things. It will grow." Old Qiao and Old Niu from the technical station came to help me cultivate the cotton and take care of it.* Under the guidance of agrotechnicians, Cao Zhuxiang learned about crop diseases. Instead of using cooking ashes to kill insects, she began to use chemical fertilizers and pesticides: *From 1952 I grew cotton, and of the cotton I sowed, none of it died.*[27]

Not far from Cao Zhuxiang, in Balidian village, Shuangwang Township, another woman excelled at cotton cultivation. Her name was Zhang Qiuxiang, and her skill had already come to light at the first provincial cotton meeting, held in Weinan in April 1954. Beginning with a one-*mu* plot of land and then expanding, she had managed to produce almost two hundred *jin* per *mu* and then to raise the output each year, mainly by careful application of fertilizer.[28] By 1955 Qiuxiang's village was said to have effected a "miracle": a field that produced 1,250 *jin* of unginned cotton per *mu*.[29] Women's Federation cadres thought that Qiuxiang would be a promising model, and set out to get her cooperation.[30] Looking for ways to publicize her experience and to make her an easily understood model for other village women, cadres from different government departments arrived in her village.[31]

Born in Shandong in 1908, Zhang Qiuxiang was an experienced farmer from an extremely poor family, who had experienced life as a refugee, farming and selling handmade shoes at market before 1949. At some point she married and bore two children. As was common in many Guanzhong households, her husband worked away from home most of the time in the 1940s and 1950s. In the land reform after 1949 she was given a piece of temple land, full of bricks and roof tiles that had to be cleared before the land could be cultivated. In the next few years she joined the effort to organize co-ops. By the mid-1950s, she had already served as village head (*They picked me because at that time no one wanted to be a cadre. They were afraid of offending people*), had led several mutual aid groups, and would go on to head the lower and higher co-ops and the commune.[32] Her revolutionary loyalties were profound, and her farming skills were exemplary. In 1956 she was named a county and provincial labor model, and by 1957 she was a national labor model.[33] For her to be an effective model, however, more was required: she had to learn to speak in public, explain policies, hold people's attention, and fire their enthusiasm.[34] Regardless of her cotton-growing skill, Qiuxiang was inarticulate: *Zhang Qiuxiang had a hard time expressing herself. She wasn't educated. One time, she was invited to the provincial capital to attend a meeting, probably the March Eighth Women's Day meeting. During the meeting, the old lady was eager to introduce her experience but couldn't do it.*[35] Undaunted, a group of *dundian* Women's Federation cadres set to work. They followed her around the fields, patiently interviewing her and transforming what she said into maxims, then teaching her to recite them until she became a fluent speaker. They were responsible for composing her most famous jingle, which sounds felicitous in Chinese if not in English:

> Use dialectics   *Yunyong bianzheng fa*
> look at the sky, look at the ground   *kantian kandi*
> grow the cotton.   *wu mianhua.*[36]

When cadres talk about how they composed a jingle for Zhang Qiuxiang, we may be tempted to compose our own story of state intervention: an articulate labor model is created out of unlikely raw material. Apparently Qiuxiang was not found in the cotton fields reciting jingles about dialectics to herself. Perhaps we feel a small "aha": the state, like the man behind the curtain in *Wizard of Oz*, is caught in the act of producing and packaging an apparently authentic, grassroots labor heroine.

The danger in rushing to this interpretation is that it confirms what we are already prepared to know. In the wake of years of revelations from China about Mao Zedong's secret sex life, internecine Party struggle, Great Leap Forward starvation, and Cultural Revolution violence, we take these earlier tales as measures of our outgrown naiveté. Today, with equal assurance, we know a different truth about Chinese socialism: that underneath a thin veneer of state pronouncements was a broader, often coercive layer of state manipulation (where jingles were composed and labor models circulated), and under that was an inchoate "real China" where long-suffering peasants resided under socialism, by turns pliant and resistant, but always distinct from something called "the state."

This dismissive commonsense knowledge of Chinese socialism, like earlier waves of revolutionary sympathy, is too simple. The jingle anecdote and others like it offer glimpses of the arduous process by which labor heroines were produced through the painstaking daily work of Women's Federation and other cadres. They hoped to make the vocabulary of dialectics, as well as new cultivation techniques, more familiar by having a rural labor model demonstrate them. At the same time, village women themselves made considerable efforts to learn new skills and overcome personal terrors. Commented one former cadre, *It is not that the Party and the Women's Federation supported them and they succeeded. Not that easy. Zhang Qiuxiang could not read or make a speech, could not sum up her own experience. When we asked about her cotton-growing experience, she just said, "You plant, hoe regularly, top the cotton plants well." It was our comrades from the Women's Federation who picked up important content from her words and drew out the important points. After this she experienced a lot and got to know the world, and found her wings. This shows that our Women's Federation put out considerable labor and hard work to cultivate these models, and carefully helped them, hand in hand.*[37] With Women's Federation cadres helping to write some of her speeches, Qiuxiang's tales began to include comments about how capable women were: *When we started to cultivate the high-yield cotton fields in 1955, some of the men in the co-op made fun of us, saying, "Women are only capable of embroidering flowers on shoes. How can they boast that they are going to grow high-yield cotton!" We paid no attention to these sarcastic remarks. We encouraged each other with the fact that women had* fanshen*ed, and put our hearts into keeping on with what we were doing.*[38] As Qiuxiang's fame grew, *dundian* cadres remained in her village and acted as her secretarial staff. They helped the illiterate cotton-growing champion welcome visitors and reply to the dozens of letters that arrived daily from all over China, asking for cotton seeds, advice, and encouragement.[39]

Qiuxiang's achievements were publicized at the first provincial cotton meeting for women cotton growers, held in Weinan in April 1956.[40] Under the tutelage of *dundian* cadres, she learned how to present her farming experiences in vivid anecdotes, a skill still evident when we interviewed her forty years later: *In 1956, the crops were very good. The cotton was good, and so was the corn. Then the water came and flooded the place. I was the co-op head and the village head. I mobilized the masses to go to the plains. At the time, young people were all capable. The corn was ripe. I jumped into the river and called people to all jump in. We moved several dozen* mu *of corn to higher ground. When we got it to the yard, we sunned it dry, spreading the stalks on the ground.*[41] When a labor model spoke well, the quotidian tasks of farming became opportunities for personal and collective heroism.

In 1956, Qiuxiang was officially named a labor model and sent to Beijing for a national meeting. Her account of being selected follows the conventions of labor model self-presentation: unassuming modesty, surprise, and continued determination to excel. *They told me that I was going to Beijing for a meeting. I didn't know yet that I was a labor model. The township sent me to the province [i.e., Xi'an], and then to Beijing. Of course it put me in a happy mood. But to be a labor model, you must put in bitter effort [dei xia ku]. I had always done that. It wasn't in order to become a labor model. If I didn't do something well, it disturbed me.*[42]

Once the credentials and prestige of a labor model had been established, the woman's main task in speaking publicly was no longer to testify to her past, but rather to mobilize efforts for the next task at hand. Thus we find Shan Xiuzhen in a 1961 speech to Weinan County commune members, reporting on a recent meeting of cotton producers and reminding everyone of the importance of pest control ("The bugs are just like enemies who attack us fiercely"), weeding, flood prevention, and manure application.[43] By this point in her career, overt evocation of her background was no longer necessary. Her life story was public property, framing the way her exhortations to labor were to be understood and heeded.

LABORING

In a 2005 essay on model women cotton farmers, Gao Xiaoxian points out that the work of increasing cotton yields in the mid-1950s often involved long-term village residence ("squatting"), not only by Women's Federation cadres, but also by highly skilled agrotechnicians from provincial offices, agricultural universities, and even departments of the Central Committee. These technicians were responsible for many of the innovations in seed selection, planting, weeding, and harvesting. Rather than publicizing these innovations directly, they used the stories of labor heroines to communicate specialized information about cotton-growing techniques. Stories centered on hard work, group cooperation, and sacrifice had a solidity that, as Gao puts it, "could be seen, touched, and studied," and thus made accessible to farmers across the cotton belt. Labor models were the medium for a technical message.[44]

They had another important function as well: to model the political behavior required of an active citizen committed to collectivization in the countryside and, beyond that, to the general line of the Party. Technical expertise was necessary, but not sufficient. Concern with national and even international affairs was also required. Most rural women labor models were lauded, not only for high cotton yields or waterworks repair, but for preparing care packages for faraway soldiers, in line with the Party-state's Resist America Aid Korea campaign. International solidarity with Korea took a very familiar form: the vernacular practice of needlework, by which women stitched themselves into the international situation. The packages contained patches, sewing kits, items for daily use, and small handmade gifts. Reports on labor model achievements counted the number of care packages, wallets, and gloves produced by groups of women, just as they counted the tons of cotton sold to the state. Here gendered rural labor was performed by people who never left home, but who understood themselves to be in a relationship with faraway places they would never see. Women also organized groups to do the plowing for army dependents whose menfolk were in Korea, and used their newfound literacy to write letters for the troops. (Whether women actually spent substantial amounts of time on such activity is not the point; what was important was the scope of model activity.) One required characteristic of a labor model was to take the lead in such work, making connections between the local production process, the national political situation, and international political solidarity. Instigated by outside cadres, but developed and given local shape by local models, awareness of the national and the international were introduced simultaneously.[45]

When the Party-state tightened its control over rural grain markets, labor models were reliably found taking the lead in selling and even donating grain to the state.[46] Cotton-growing labor models were expected to set an example by turning over the best cotton, in rising quantities, to the supply and marketing organizations rather than hoarding it.[47] As cooperatives enlarged from mutual aid groups to lower cooperatives and then to advanced cooperatives, enthusiastic labor models were key to persuading recalcitrant peasants to participate.[48]

Labor models were intended to stimulate active emulation, often in the form of labor competitions.[49] In Shaanxi, the most famous and longest-running labor competition was the Silver Flowers Contest, run by the provincial Women's Federation in the cotton-producing districts of Guanzhong from 1956 until the early 1980s.[50] The Silver Flowers Contest was aimed at encouraging women to take up cotton field management and achieve bumper cotton harvests. It was inaugurated in April 1956, at a meeting of women cotton growers called by the Women's Federation under the direction of the Shaanxi Party Committee. At a time when many Shaanxi women still did not engage in regular field work for the collective, coming into the fields only during the busy season, the Party-state's aim was to increase the production of cotton, a labor-intensive crop, by mobilizing underutilized women's labor to tend it. At the meeting, attended by 674 women, the experience of women cultivators was showcased alongside technical discussions of seed varieties and growing techniques. With Zhang Qiuxiang as their leading representative, all those present signed a pledge to lead women in taking charge of most cotton-growing tasks, bring women into the fields at least 140 labor days each year, and organize labor contests between collective units.

In the course of these contests, the Women's Federation dubbed Zhang Qiuxiang, Cao Zhuxiang, Shan Xiuzhen, and two other locally famous women cotton growers the "Five Silver Flowers," after a popular movie titled *Five Golden Flowers*.[51] Each woman led a cotton-growing group that contracted to take responsibility for cultivation and was paid according to output. Women learned techniques from one another and took responsibility for clearly specified tasks.[52] In Village B Zhuxiang counseled the young women in her group that they should "study from and catch up to Shuangwang," where Qiuxiang's team was located, but that under cover of this modest slogan they should try to try to surpass the output of Qiuxiang's team.[53] In Shan Xiuzhen's county, a vice secretary of the Party Committee challenged her: *He said, "Zhang Qiuxiang planted high-yield cotton in 1956. Can you do it too?" I said, "Why not? I can." Then I went to Big Sister Zhang in Weinan to get some experience. In the first year, the cotton grew very well. But we still lacked experience. There was too much water and fertilizer. The cotton grew too tall. The masses said, "You have to climb a tree to pick this cotton." This was not so good. We got an average of 210 jin of ginned cotton. Failure is the mother of success. We summed up our lessons.*[54]

For several decades, groups led by these women and other, less well-known models publicized new techniques of cotton production, as well as a finely honed division of labor based on group contracts and individual quotas.[55] The Party-state supported these efforts, not only with its agrotechnicians and Women's Federation cadres, but also by offering material support. Once a labor model was selected, a number of interests converged on having her project succeed, and resource streams helped to assure that outcome. The Chinese People's Bank, for instance, worked with the credit cooperative of Qiuxiang's township to make sure that her co-op received timely loans. By 1958, the bank had made twenty-seven loans to Qiuxiang's group, totaling 3,889 yuan. This concrete help, as a bank report frankly noted, helped overcome peasant reservations that it was impossible to raise cotton output to more than a thousand *jin* per *mu*. In the second year of Qiuxiang's experiment, the bank delayed a loan for purchasing pesticide, and Qiuxiang had to make do with a bottle of insecticide provided by the technical station. Directed by higher leadership not to let this happen again, the bank subsequently made six fertilizer loans and four insecticide loans to the co-op in quick succession. As Qiuxiang herself was quoted as saying in the bank report, "Without the leadership of the Party and your [the bank's] support for me, even if my ability was greater than it is, it would have been absolutely impossible to make the thousand *jin* per *mu* of cotton a reality."[56]

By the time of the Great Leap Forward, women had become the mainstay of the cotton-growing workforce, in spite of some objections from men who had been displaced and who feared that their work-point income would suffer.[57] In one story publicized about a Guanzhong cotton-growing collective, a man was unhappy that women picking cotton were earning more than he could earn plowing. He asked to be transferred to the cotton-picking detail, only to find that he could not keep up with the women. Slinking away, he reportedly was heard to say to other men, "It is right that men and women should get equal pay for equal work. Don't just look at the fact that the women are doing light tasks. We can't do what they do."[58] Male opposition dissipated when men were encouraged to take up sideline occupations that paid better or were regarded as requiring more technical skill—part of the movement of men out of basic agriculture that is traced in other chapters of this book.[59]

As an important crop both for the defense industry and for the agricultural products market, cotton brought in relatively good returns to the communes that grew it. More than half of the province's cotton crop was produced in the Weinan area, and women were now regarded as fully equal to the exacting technical demands of growing it.[60] As one Women's Federation official put it, *Women are mentally alert and have skillful hands which are very suitable for cotton planting. Women took care of every detail of cotton planting from the beginning to the end.*[61] Shan Xiuzhen, too, found women uniquely suited to the work: *Men couldn't do it. You had to be very careful in planting cotton. Have you heard people say, "Planting cotton is like embroidering flowers: you can't miss a single stitch"? You couldn't cheat even a little bit. One plant at a time: you had to be not only fast, but also careful.*[62] If needlework prepared women to manage cotton fields, however, another Great Leap saying made it clear that they would have to give it up in order to take up this new task: "Quit your needles, put aside your thread, try to be the champion on the cotton-growing frontline" (*tingxia zhen, fangxia xian, wu mian zhanxian zheng zhuangyuan*).[63] In Qiuxiang's home brigade, the assignment of women to cotton cultivation was formalized in the early 1960s; the vice head of the brigade was responsible for the grain and vegetable crops, but the women's brigade leader was responsible for cotton.[64] More than 90 percent of the cotton fields under cultivation in the commune system were reportedly assigned to women to cultivate, as were about half of the wheat and corn fields.[65] In Xiuzhen's production team, four different cotton-growing groups with seven or eight women in each emerged. Xiuzhen was blunt in expressing her preference for unmarried women in her groups: *They all wanted to come. Those with a heavy family burden and two children, I didn't want. You had to be more careful about planting cotton than taking care of kids. Girls had no encumbrances. They could come whenever you called them.*[66]

As labor models took on additional leadership responsibilities, attendance at meetings supplanted the tasks for which they had been named models in the first place. Already in 1951, a Civil Administration Bureau report complained, "The burden of labor models is so heavy that in some places, . . . no matter whether the matter is big or small, people ask them to lead. . . . Various levels of government ask them to attend so many meetings. There are also the Department of Agriculture and Forestry, the Bureau of Agriculture and Forestry, Special Regions, county and district, while the journalists from newspapers often want to interview them. All this has wasted a lot of their time that should be spent on production. They are nearly as busy as [full-time] cadres who are not engaged in production."[67] Several years later, when Qiuxiang made a speech to a national congress of women activists during the Great Leap Forward, she recalled that members of her commune had been unhappy that meetings took her away from home. *There are still weeds in our field. You can't just take care of others,* they told her, complaining that other communes were threatening to surpass them.

But for Qiuxiang, this was a teachable moment. As she told the audience, the aim of socialist competition was to increase the yield not of one or two plots, but of all cotton fields. Socialist construction could be advanced only if cotton production could be improved nationwide. To reinforce the point, she stopped off for a week on her way home from a meeting to help Xue Junxiu, one of her Silver Flowers competitors, to rescue her cotton crop from cutworms, even though Qiuxiang's son was sick at home. Later Qiuxiang congratulated Junxiu when her group's output exceeded Qiuxiang's own.[68] Subsequently the two women, whose collective fields adjoined each other, signed a joint pledge in March 1959 to produce an average of 7,500 *jin* of unginned cotton per *mu*, and challenged all the cotton growers in Weinan County to compete with them. They publicized their challenge, which was endorsed by the vice chair of Shaanxi Province, at a meeting of more than four hundred women heads of "Qiuxiang groups."[69] Well into the autumn of 1959, the newspapers continued to publicize their working relationship and friendship, sometimes in feature stories rich with dramatic recreated dialogue.[70] "In competition," as a news report put it in 1960, "they were both rivals and allies."[71]

WRITING

Labor models were made, not born, and in the paper trail their careers left behind we can discern the process of their creation. From the early years of the People's Republic, local cadres were instructed to write accounts of labor model achievements in the dry mode of bureaucratic data collection. A 1951 Shaanxi provincial government directive specified that such accounts should first clarify what sort of model the person was: "The basic types can be divided into pest-control model, flood-fighting model, manure accumulation model, intensive cultivation model, disaster relief and famine-fighting model, production model, . . . ordinary model, and other kinds of model mutual aid groups, model villages, and so on." Second, the writer should include concrete experiences: How much manure had the model applied to the soil? How deep was the plowing? How often were crops rotated, irrigated, fumigated? What was the average output? By how much did it surpass the average output in the area? Third, what was the makeup of the village, its method of organizing labor and keeping accounts, its output, its penchant for production competitions? Fourth, what were the patriotic activities and improvements in political consciousness fostered by the labor models? Finally, the writers were exhorted, "Try your best to be comprehensive, material, and detailed."[72] Material about women labor models, who were being mobilized for tasks that they had not routinely performed before, was a subset of this larger bureaucratically defined genre.[73]

By 1956, when advanced producers from across Shaanxi Province gathered for a meeting, the documentation of labor model exploits had grown more elaborate, refined, and dramatic. Archival records of the meeting contain stories with a visual specificity missing in the earlier reports, although the virtues of the labor models were similar. Zhang Qiuxiang was praised for her compassion as a village head, helping to obtain relief grain for families who ran out of food in 1953 and feeding her own children beans after the family ran out of grain, rather than taking them to the county seat where her husband was working. She also drew notice for her patient work to convince several other women to join her in hoeing the winter wheat fields, a task that was not yet a part of the village routine. Predictably the result was an outstanding harvest, resulting in the adoption of winter hoeing by the entire village—and an implicit message that drawing women into the fields would increase the intensity of cultivation and improve the results.[74]

Shan Xiuzhen's 1956 file described three heroic moments in her work as co-op head. In the first, an upper-middle peasant who wanted to withdraw from the collective in 1955 tried to embarrass her by kneeling to her in public and demanding money the collective owed him. Drawing on her Party education, Xiuzhen defused the situation with gentle words and patient explanations. In the second incident, the collective decided in 1954 to send fifteen laborers into hilly territory to cut green fertilizer for the cotton crop. The men doing the cutting needed to have steamed bread and noodles delivered to them each day, but women were reluctant to take on the task for fear of being gossiped about. (Sexual misconduct in the hills was the implied content of the gossip they feared.) Keeping her eye on production targets and her hands on the cooking pot, Chair Shan personally prepared and delivered the food, leading to record output in crop production. In the third anecdote she noticed that one of the draft animals was sick, got speedy attention for the animal from the veterinarian, meticulously boiled water and hand-fed medicine to the animal, and thus saved the life of a collective resource valued at three hundred yuan.[75] Together these three incidents showcased the virtues of a woman labor model: gentle and patient but firm in her Communist commitments to the collective; unafraid of hard work and immune to sexual gossip, in part because her conduct was irreproachable; meticulous and tender in caring for collective livestock, on which she lavished maternal levels of attention.[76] The virtues required of a good wife, wise mother, and thrifty homemaker were here applied to the project of collectivization. Lu Guilan, another woman head of a higher-co-op, described in a 1956 speech how she had declined to use co-op funds to renovate the office, opting instead to invest in livestock and repair tools rather than buying new ones. Through diligence and frugality, she taught her co-op members that "managing a co-op is like managing a household; you have to budget well."[77]

Material on labor models for a wider audience emphasized the completion of specified technical tasks. In a 1956 publication of reports by labor models to a province-wide meeting on cotton field management, Zhang Qiuxiang, assisted by a Women's Federation cadre who served as her scribe and editor, presented tasks in cotton cultivation as a series of handy maxims about carefully preparing the soil, spreading fertilizer, selecting and preparing the seeds, planting early, thinning, weeding, irrigating at the right moments, topping the plants, battling pests, and using improved techniques to harvest the bolls.[78] The tone in such publications was practical, detailed, and matter-of-fact, with labor models providing an embodied demonstration of agricultural extension work.[79]

By early 1958 exhortation and competition became dominant features of labor model stories, as the name Zhang Qiuxiang became a shorthand way of talking about high-yield cotton production.[80] At a March meeting of 101 cotton growers from across Shaanxi, official reports noted that Qiuxiang was producing more than eight times the average yield of cotton per *mu*, and called for organizing groups of cadres, youth, and women to work on experimental plots and try to duplicate her achievement.[81] Later that month, the provincial Party Committee issued a directive calling Qiuxiang's approach "a relatively complete, scientific combination of advanced cotton-growing techniques and peasants' experience." The proximate goal, said the Party Committee, was to create 5,386 Zhang Qiuxiangs, fifty-one Qiuxiang teams, and seven thousand-*jin* communes across central Shaanxi.[82] In April, just prior to the formal launch of the Great Leap Forward, the Women's Federation publicized the slogan "Study Qiuxiang, catch up with Qiuxiang."[83] Innovations such as Qiuxiang fields[84] (experimental cotton plots), Qiuxiang cotton-growing groups of a dozen or so women, learn-from-Qiuxiang labor contests, and, in 1959, "Go all out, catch up with Qiuxiang again" events soon followed.[85] Pamphlets introduced by Women's Federation cadres and published by the Shaanxi Provincial Press, bearing titles like *"Silly Girls" Launch a "Cotton Satellite"* and *We Caught Up with Zhang Qiuxiang,* encouraged the spread of Qiuxiang fields across the cotton belt.[86] Qiuxiang herself was lauded in a national Women's Federation publication as "the first woman researcher of peasant origin" (*diyige nongmin chushen de nüyanjiuyuan*).[87] Speeches in which she claimed steadily rising cotton yields and explained in great detail how to achieve them were published in the provincial newspaper and other venues.[88] She was photographed inspecting cotton fields and lecturing to teachers and students at a state farm.[89] She became a delegate to the National People's Congress.[90]

Shortly after Zhang Qiuxiang was named a woman researcher of peasant origin, the *Shaanxi ribao* reported that the vice chair of the National Women's Federation, Kang Keqing, paid her a courtesy call, sloshing through a rainstorm to visit the storied experimental cotton plot.[91] She was followed four months later, the same newspaper reported, by a Soviet expert stationed in Xi'an, also braving a drizzle. The Soviet visitor reportedly told Qiuxiang that the Chinese Great Leap Forward was unprecedented anywhere, past or present, and that the Soviet people were extremely happy at the achievements attained by the Chinese people. When he asked her how her high level of output had been attained, she modestly smiled and replied, "It is mainly the result of the Party's leadership and everyone's Communist mode of daring to think, daring to speak, and daring to act, along with learning from the Soviet elder brother." The emissary, astonished, is said to have replied, "Your experience is very rich, and the Soviet people should learn from you and from all Chinese agricultural experts. When I return to the Soviet Union, I will tell the Soviet people in detail about the miracles you have created. The Soviet people are very concerned with the construction of China." And with that, Zhang Qiuxiang presented him with a five- or six-*jin* turnip and a cotton stalk with more than fifty bolls as a memento of his trip.[92]

This sort of political fantasia became more stylized as the Great Leap wore on and began to founder. By early 1959 Qiuxiang was quoted speaking in verse about the connection between politics and cotton:

The General Line is a beacon   *Zong luxian shi dengta*
It illuminates the people's hearts   *Zhaode renxin kaile hua*
  and they flower
In recent years since the General Line   *Jinnian youle zong luxian*
The cotton has bloomed bigger than   *Yao mianhua kaifang bi yun da.*[93]
  the clouds.

The connection between cotton cultivation, labor model heroism, and national political goals endured in the difficult years that followed. Qiuxiang was a featured speaker at the tenth-anniversary celebration of the founding of the People's Republic in 1959, as famine loomed. Her remarks drew a stark contrast between pre-Liberation suffering and post-Liberation happiness, touted increased cotton yields, and lauded her commune's water-control work for bringing an end to frequent flooding. In spite of the serious drought of 1959, she said, the commune was still able to irrigate and achieve a bumper harvest. Her remarks were subsequently "reworked, supplemented, and verified" by the Weinan County Department of Agriculture, Forestry, Fisheries and Livestock, which sharpened the language and clarified the point of each story so that the talk became a paean to the benefits of people's communes.[94] As a national labor model, Qiuxiang was no longer just a living, breathing means of agricultural extension, an embodiment of the state effect. She was a spokesperson for the viability of collectivization.[95]

In the aftermath of the Great Leap, the Shaanxi Women's Federation continually referred to the prestige and achievements of Zhang Qiuxiang, citing cotton production as one area that had continued to improve. (Whether or not the claims of increased cotton production were accurate—and given Shaanxi's relatively stable situation, they are not necessarily fabrications of the Great Leap Forward's "exaggeration wind"—requires further investigation.)[96] Accounts of Qiuxiang's ongoing success served as a means of salvaging the wreckage left by the Leap. One such report made a canny appeal to peasants' material interests by explaining how much Qiuxiang's brigade and each member in it were going to earn in cash and grain supplements. This would have been a powerful argument in a province facing food shortages.[97] The report ended with a newly composed "folk song" linking Qiuxiang contests to the people's communes:

The People's Communes, a spray of blooms   *Renmin gongshe yizhi hua*
The sweet smell fills ten thousand rooms   *Huakai shili xiang wanjia*
In each place women strive and vie   *Funü daochu nao jingsai*
Qiuxiang's red flag everywhere flies.[98]   *Qiuxiang hongqi biandi cha.*

Labor models, exhibiting thrift and industry, were to lead the way to economic recovery without sacrificing political fealty.[99]

By March 1961, the central Shaanxi cotton-growing economy was feeling the full effects of bad weather and the multiple failures of the Great Leap Forward, although most of the problems were not openly articulated. The day before International Women's Day, and a month before cotton planting, the *Weinan Daily* featured articles attributed to each of the Five Silver Flowers, by now all well-known cotton growers. Zhang Qiuxiang focused on drought resistance, Xue Junxiu on seed selection, Shan Xiuzhen on attention to local conditions, Gao Zhenxian on plowing, and Cao Zhuxiang on the need to balance cotton and grain cultivation.[100] The five women then toured the county together, holding forums on cotton cultivation. They discussed drought and a livestock shortage that made it necessary to share animals across production teams—indirect references to increasingly difficult conditions.[101]

Muted references to crisis continued in the summer of 1961, when the Agriculture Bureau and the Women's Federation jointly sponsored a meeting of cotton growers. Gone were the ambitious production goals of 1958, replaced by sober discussions of shrinking plots seeded during a drought, then buffeted by summer flooding. The report of the meeting noted that 15 percent of the cotton fields were now interplanted with grain. Because some counties left interplanting outside the state purchase quotas, potentially increasing the amount of grain available to eat, peasants were said to be lavishing attention on the interplanted grain while neglecting the cotton crop. The cotton growers announced that they did not support this practice, but they also stated that grain production needed to be improved in cotton areas and that the food supply should be secured before the state started purchasing grain. Unspecified, but clearly on everyone's mind, were pervasive shortages. The conferees acknowledged that the Qiuxiang model was now difficult to spread, because many felt that it would not work without high inputs of fertilizer and labor. The meeting reaffirmed that the essence of the Qiuxiang model was not expensive inputs, but rather the grasp of "objective laws" of scientific cultivation: *Look at the sky, look at the ground, grow the cotton.* But it retreated from the intense efforts to mobilize women for farmwork that had characterized the Great Leap Forward (discussed in the next chapter). The report raised doubts about whether women could so easily give up their needlework and rush headlong into the cotton fields. Women had their own physical characteristics, the report said (a reference to menstruation, pregnancy, and reproductive health), as well as the burden of household chores. It was necessary for labor management to take account of these circumstances.[102]

Nevertheless the linkage of women cotton-growing labor models and broad Party-state political goals continued through to the end of the three hard years. A 1960 feature in the *Weinan Daily* explained how Xue Junxiu and Cao Zhuxiang had benefited from studying the works of Mao Zedong, a theme that had not been broached so explicitly in the labor model literature heretofore. The article made an argument for increased literacy among women farmers while simultaneously attesting to the power of Mao's prose.[103] In late 1961, Zhang Qiuxiang gave a front-page interview to the *Shaanxi Daily* emphasizing that peasants should sell their cotton to the state—a clear indication that the tug-of-war between peasants and purchasing authorities had sharpened further under conditions of shortage.[104] A 1962 pamphlet about Shan Xiuzhen published by the Women's Federation as a study guide for grassroots women's cadres took political virtue, not agriculture, as its organizing matrix. Titled *Shan Xiuzhen, Glorious Proletarian Fighter,* this thirteen-page work was divided by subheads that distilled the essence of her achievement in ethical terms, such as "High Aspirations, Great Zeal" and "Consider the Big Picture, Advance in the Face of Difficulties."[105] Xiuzhen reinforced the point in other publications. "I am a peasant woman," she said in a newspaper piece a few months later. "From childhood I suffered bitterness and begged. I did not understand anything. As soon as there was leadership from the Party, then I *fanshen*ed and saw the sun, understanding that communism was the happiest, most ideal society for humankind."[106]

By 1964, as limited assessments of Great Leap failures entered public conversation, labor models were praised for precisely the qualities that would have earned them criticism five years earlier. A front-page newspaper feature about Xiuzhen, for instance, praised her refusal in 1959 and 1960 to set unrealistic production goals or report inflated yields. As the nation entered its post-Leap recovery, she and other labor models were once again made to embody the qualities most valued at that moment. These included honesty, practical knowledge (she devoted part of one 1963 interview to a discussion of the superior qualities of goat dung as fertilizer), consistency in speech and deed, modesty (continuing to address Qiuxiang as "Teacher" even after her cotton yield surpassed Qiuxiang's), and Party loyalty.[107]

Written accounts about labor models did one of two things. Some presented technical material in relatively colorful, sprightly form by using labor models and their cotton-growing apprentices as an organizing device. Others, in a manner similar to Liu Xiang's Han Dynasty *Biographies of Exemplary Women (Lienü zhuan),* presented exemplary figures and their moral behavior. Like the *Biographies* and later exemplar texts,[108] they often signaled the most relevant virtue of the labor model in the title. As the content of these stories became more explicitly entwined with dedication to communism, the specificity of the women became less important than their status as vessels for revolutionary virtues.[109]

Accounts devoted to women labor models usually did not make more than passing reference to the gender of the model.[110] Cao Zhuxiang, for instance, was not a model because she did an exceptional job of juggling childcare and field work, or because she explicitly addressed the problems of drawing women into production outside the domestic space. She neither articulated nor overcame the gendered differences in daily responsibilities and social expectations that stubbornly endured beneath the Party's proclamations of equality between men and women. Or if she did so, it was not the job of labor model stories to report it. Their purpose was to publicize local successes in cotton production, group organization, and political fealty. Even as the movement of women into collective production fundamentally altered their position within a particular social division of labor, the labor heroine literature—and quite possibly the labor heroine subject position itself—underplayed that massive change.

REMEMBERING

As we have seen, when the 1950s crescendoed into the Great Leap Forward, written accounts of labor model lives became simultaneously more colorful and more flat, full of heroic exploits and retrospectively imagined politicized dialogue, but increasingly devoid of surprise or depth. The historian in search of biographical insight is tempted to look elsewhere, in the liveliness of in-person interviews, but the results are mixed: by turns animated and reflective, or affectless and opaque. Cao Zhuxiang, for instance, conveyed a vivid sense of how she experienced her new circuit of public activity as a labor model, also providing a glimpse into how her activities affected her young son and how poor the new rural models were: *That winter [of 1951] there were several meetings in the county, followed by a meeting in the district. The meeting included land reform activists, but there were also cadres and labor models. I didn't go back home between the two meetings. I was gone for several weeks, a month. It scared my younger child. Everybody came here to scare my child: "Your mom has gone away. Your mom won't come back." They sent me off to the county seat to participate in a forum. Early the next day we took a bus to Xi'an. Everybody lived in a hotel. There were lots of cadres from the countryside, working groups. We met for almost ten days. People from north Shaanxi and Luonan. The people from the countryside were very pitiful. Even the unlined clothes we had to borrow from each other. Later they mobilized the people in the city of Xi'an to give us support. The courtyard of the hotel was filled up with quilts, some cotton-filled, some unlined, some lined, some of thick wool. At least they wanted people who came to the meetings to have something warm to wear. At that time, when I went to meetings, I carried my own quilt.*

When Zhuxiang returned home, her son was astonished and relieved. The next time she went to a meeting, this one for labor models, she brought her son along. *That was also a big hotel. That time I brought my son and he didn't leave my side. No matter what, he had to go with me. Later people said, "Just bring him with you." My son was just this tall. I didn't let him go out. He stayed in the room all day while I went to meetings.*[111]

Zhuxiang's son, Wang Jiji, remembers being taken to Xi'an by his mother when he was about ten, and the memory has a magical quality in the telling. *In 1950, when they had a big meeting for labor models in Xi'an, she took me. I got the name I have now at that time. I was called Wang Jiwa [literally "machine child" or "child of the organization," which could have been a shorthand way of referring either to modern farm machinery or to the Party]. Someone gave each of us children ten yuan. At that time, ten yuan could buy a fountain pen, which was really great. My mother bought me and my sister each a Huaqing fountain pen. She was afraid I would lose it, so she asked someone to engrave my name on it. The person asked what my name was. I said I was called Wang Jiji [Activist Wang], so he carved my name as "Wang Jiji," and from that time on I was called Wang Jiji.*[112]

Taken as a whole, however, when labor models reminisced about their lives in the collective period, their accounts quickly devolved into a series of meetings they had attended, with very little of the concrete freshness that characterized their pre-1949 stories. Accounts of village people and events, not to mention problems and conflicts, disappeared almost completely. Zhang Qiuxiang, for instance, puzzled us when we interviewed her. She had a particular story to tell, one that began with an account of her thirteen meetings with Premier Zhou Enlai and her nine meetings with Mao. To her, the essence of those meetings was the personal concern that Zhou in particular had shown her. She remembered, *[During the Great Leap Forward] I was called to the central government for a meeting, and I went by train. I saw Chairman Mao and Premier Zhou. They called me to the meeting room to talk. Zhou received me in the State Council and asked whether the life of the masses was good or not. Premier Zhou asked, "When you were smelting steel, were the masses' pots smashed? We asked that you be brought here so that we can understand what is happening." They prepared white rice and a big table of food. The leaders were really good. Here I was, a village woman. I ate and shed tears.*

After the meeting was over, everyone asked him to write something in our notebooks. I also asked him to write something. After this I came back and showed everyone my book. When I came back, I went everywhere talking to people about it. . . . Every year I went to the cotton meeting. That year it was in Huairen Tang. Everyone was sitting properly, but the leaders hadn't come yet. Premier Zhou came, but he didn't go up on the stage. He stood at the table, took out his book, and said to me, "Qiuxiang, you are here." Later some people said, "He only spoke to her, he didn't speak to me." Premier Zhou cared a lot about the masses.[113]

When it came to other topics, however, Qiuxiang's recitation was punctuated with long silences, and her account was devoid of engagement or warmth, except when she spoke of Premier Zhou. She was uninterested in discussing the specific daily practices of her labor model career, whether from age, fatigue, or irritation at our persistent questioning about difficulties in organizing other villagers. We were left wondering if perhaps she was so close to death that she went in and out of understanding what she was being asked, or whether she had so completely come to inhabit her identity as a labor model that she could not think outside its boundaries. She grew more disaffected every time Gao Xiaoxian asked her about difficulties she had encountered in her work, until finally she refused to speak at all.[114] The abrupt end to the interview was particularly surprising to us because stories of overcoming difficulties were the standard fare of labor model narratives; there was nothing controversial or intrusive about posing such questions.

Her reticence may have reflected the painful memories stimulated by our questions. Like many eminent labor models and leaders at all levels, she was attacked in the mid-1960s, during the Cultural Revolution: *I was labeled a counterrevolutionary. They objected to my being in meetings all the time. There were three or four people in the village [who felt this way].*

Gao Xiaoxian: *Were these three or four people cadres?*

Zhang Qiuxiang: *No. They were fiercer than cadres.*

Gao Xiaoxian: *What was their basis for saying you were a counter-revolutionary?*

Zhang Qiuxiang: *That I wasn't engaging in production, and was running around from place to place* [hu pao] *all day.*

Labeled a "fake labor model" in a criticism and struggle meeting, she was denied permission to attend a meeting in Beijing. In her absence, as she tells it, Zhou Enlai personally interceded on her behalf. *Premier Zhou said, "Is anyone here from Xi'an?" The people from Xi'an all stood up. Premier Zhou then said, "The students have all arrived. Why hasn't the teacher come?" The person in front said I hadn't yet been liberated [from the political accusations against her]. Premier Zhou said, "Not liberated yet? Growing cotton, engaging in production, what is counterrevolutionary about that?" In the afternoon the meeting concluded, and that night they telephoned the county and told them to send me. I said, "I don't even have any money." The county committee called a driver to take me in a car to the train station. They gave me the money. I took the train, a sleeper car, to Beijing. On the train I got sick, and I was running a fever. I got to the guest house and stayed in their office. I also saw Premier Zhou. After I came back from that meeting, the province sent a work group to live in the village. They arrested that person [who had accused her] and took him away, and talked to me. At night they had a mass meeting. . . . From that time on I was liberated.*[115]

Qiuxiang was subsequently rehabilitated, but she spent the post-Mao years in straitened circumstances. The central and regional leaders who had lauded her achievements either died too soon to help her in her old age, or were unconcerned about how she was living when she was not providing window dressing on the dais in Beijing. The rundown house in which we interviewed her—much poorer than others in neighboring villages—had been built only after the Women's Federation interceded to get her some retirement pay as a former national labor model. Any number of remembered injuries too painful to recount to strangers could have accounted for her sudden withdrawal in the conversation with us—or not. This was a silence we could not read.

Perhaps more or different conversations would have helped. Looking back across the twelve-year span of our joint research at our 1996 conversation with Zhang Qiuxiang, Gao Xiaoxian reflected in 2008: *We were insufficiently prepared. I feel that I didn't have a clear understanding of her circumstances at that time. Also, we spent a very short time with her. . . . We had not had previous contact with her. Add to that the fact that a foreigner was present and that several local Women's Federation cadres were accompanying us. To suddenly appear at an interview and ask about a lot of internal* [neibu] *circumstances, I feel that it was not necessarily possible to get answers* [buyiding neng wenchulai]. *But if we had been able to continue on, stayed there, and done preparatory work with her, or if we had gone through the process of becoming familiar to her, like we did with Cao Zhuxiang when we lived in her village, I feel that maybe the interaction would have been different.*

I didn't completely understand Zhang Qiuxiang or her current life circumstances. I didn't understand her personality. And maybe the way we entered her door, maybe it wasn't the right time, or the right environment. Because at the time, her living circumstances were really bad. It was a striking contrast with her circumstances and psychology when she was a labor model. So at that time, when she considered her present circumstances, she might think, "How come at that time I was so glorious [huihuang] *and now I am so wretched* [qican]?" *This might have been a blow to her. I wasn't sensitive to this, and didn't handle it properly.*

These past few years, as I have been working in rural areas, I have realized that in doing interviews, there is nothing that cannot be asked. If there is something that you cannot ask, it means that your interviewing is too clumsy, that you don't understand the person you are interviewing. That's how I feel about our interviewing the first year. So when I looked at the early interviews for pieces I was writing in 2003 and 2004, my face kept turning red, because some of the questions I asked were so immature.

So I can only say that research is like art [yishu]. *Artists often look back and say that there was something they regret not doing well. But that process cannot be repeated. It's the same with research. Whenever you start a new project, you will always encounter similar problems. Because if you knew everything about it, there would be no reason to do research. The reason you want to do research about it is because you don't know about it [laughs]!*[116] Perhaps more, or different, or differently asked questions would have yielded a different sense of Zhang Qiuxiang. But interviews are not an infinitely flexible occasion under the best of circumstances, and they cannot always be revisited.[117]

A cautionary tale for the historian presents itself here, about the silences that surround our Holy Grail, "the historical record." In all our interviewing, what silences structured answers, what fears went unspoken, what uncertainties flattened affect? This question does not refer to the basic circumstances in which we interviewed. We moved freely and unaccompanied through our interviews; Gao Xiaoxian was a familiar and trusted figure; people demonstrably poured out their hearts to us on certain questions, often to the evident discomfort of their children or their neighbors. These were not Potemkin villages or narratives carefully groomed for a foreigner. But memory-work is not conducted in easily mappable terrain. The piece of Qiuxiang's story that trails off into silence does not have the cinematic appeal of her exploits as a labor heroine; it does not even have a plot line. It may be about unresolved political grievances, or a memory of conflict with kin or neighbors, or something we do not know enough to guess at and were too inexperienced to ask in the opening year of this project. There is something here worth tracking, if only to puzzle over its indeterminacy.[118]

Ironically, it was precisely when the labor models grew most animated that the puzzle of how to understand their relationship to modelhood and the state seemed most unsolvable. Although after four decades these women confused details from some of the movements in which they played such leading roles, they were unswerving in their eloquence—delivered still in an idiom that would have been familiar to a 1950s audience—about the life the revolution gave them. As Lu Guilan put it, *Although my parents gave birth to me, it was the Party that brought me up: Mao and the Women's Federation. . . . In July 1949, the district sent a cadre to my house. I was at the loom weaving. He pulled me off the loom to go to a meeting. They wanted to select someone who had suffered, who was capable. At the time I had no formal name* [guanming]; *my childhood name was Rongrong. My name, Lu Guilan, was given to me that day. . . . I didn't worry about death or life. My mother said to me, "Child! Aren't you afraid that the GMD will murder you? Liu Hulan had her head cut off." I said I wasn't afraid. I joined the Party and took an oath, and said it clearly. I don't fear a mountain of swords or a sea of flame. My death will be weightier than Mount Tai."*[119] *From that time, every level of the Women's Federation came looking for me. . . . Every level of the Party and government consciously trained and educated* [peiyang] *me. They spent more on me than what it costs to train a university student. From the roots to the shoot* [qigen fa miao] *I was trained by the Women's Federation. I can labor and eat bitterness.*[120]

Far from a source of transgressive, disgruntled, or even reflective stories, memory seems to have become the place where labor model discourse from the collective era, subsequently discarded by a reform-era world with scant regard for these women, survived most intact. Consider two such memories of meeting Chairman Mao.

For Lu Guilan, the chance to be a delegate to a meeting in Beijing offered community and, away from home, a giddy sociality with other women from similar backgrounds. She mocked her own country bumpkin naiveté amid Beijing grandeur: *Oh, my goodness. The food, the lodging! It was the Beijing Hotel. Look, when you walk in, the door turns. People go into the empty space and it turns automatically. I didn't understand it. There was even a joke. Shan Xiuzhen went to the Beijing Hotel. Here's a mirror, there's a mirror in the room. She entered and said, "Oops! How come here's me and there's me too?" We were very close when we went to meetings at the province. Zhang Qiuxiang, Shan Xiuzhen, Cao Zhuxiang. . . . At night we sang opera [and accompanied ourselves] with dishes, bowls and chopsticks. We sewed shoe soles. . . . We chatted all day long. . . . They called me the director of the chat office. . . . It was so much fun. I still miss those big sisters now.*[121]

The pinnacle of attendance at any national meeting was proximity to the Party-state's top leadership, an experience that produced intense emotions in the retelling. Here the informal hilarity of a women-only opera party in a Beijing hotel room was replaced by the solemn joy of drawing close to the Party's acknowledged heart. As a delegate to the second meeting of the First National Women's Congress, Shan Xiu-zhen saw Chairman Mao in March 1953: *No one slept the first night. The second day, I don't remember where we stayed, we were happy all evening. We took baths and washed our clothes and everything was clean and tidy. . . . In Huairen Hall, everything was in order. . . . The Shaanxi representatives were in the middle and I was in the front. After the representatives were seated, Chairman Mao, the premier [Zhou Enlai], Chairman Liu [Shaoqi], the chief commander, and other leaders of the central government came in, over fifty people. . . . When Chairman Mao came, the correct thing for you to do was to welcome him. We weren't to move, because if we moved there would be chaos. People would say that women had no consciousness and didn't follow the rules. We didn't dare to tug on Chairman Mao to shake hands. We were supposed to love and protect Chairman Mao. "All you people, if Chairman Mao shook hands with all of you, wouldn't you be worried about Chairman Mao?" They talked to us in advance. I was sitting there properly. Chairman Mao came. There were many people and we sat in a circle. Chairman Mao was smiling and took off his cap. The only thing I did was clap. [Chairman Mao] walked around twice. If he didn't walk around twice, the women on this side would have been able to see him, but those on that side would not. People were so happy that they were crying.*

This was the first time, in Beijing, I had my picture taken with Chairman Mao. It was a pity that among the Shaanxi representatives, only Director Yan and I were from the countryside. The picture was seven feet long and five feet wide, and it cost seventeen yuan and was unaffordable. I didn't have money and didn't have a copy printed. When the meeting was over, I came back. . . .

What I regret is this. At the third women's representative meeting in 1957, Chairman Mao received us and took pictures with us. [Zhang] Qiuxiang and [Cao] Zhu-xiang were in the picture. Each of us got a copy. But the pity is that it was taken away and lost in the Cultural Revolution in 1966. This is the thing I regret the most.[122]

Meetings—occasions for workaday reporting and listening, for occasional out-of-town camaraderie and hilarity—were also the place at which labor models were most thoroughly interpellated as political subjects. Even at a distance of almost half a century, even given the personal and political effects of unhappy intervening events, the moment of sighting Chairman Mao seems untarnished, a celebrity sighting that reshaped the meaning of their daily labor. In their personal stories, even more than in the writings meant to publicize their achievements and laud their political consciousness, these women emerge most completely as full participants in the political moment that produced them.

BIOGRAPHY AND INTERIORITY

Labor model stories were a form of biography-in-process intimately connected to the social, intended to communicate, inspire, and mobilize in their own time, the period of early socialism in China. The question is how we might make use of such stories as historical material, how they might function in historical time.

In spite of the prominence of rural China in state initiatives and propaganda, the changes wrought by socialism in the everyday existence and consciousness of peasants remain frustratingly opaque. Rural labor models, as some of the few women who have names and trajectories in that paper trail, offer one way to explore these questions. And yet, in spite of the heft of the sources and the possibility of interviews with women who recall those years, the prospects for historically illuminating biography are complicated—perhaps no less complicated than they are for the virtuous women of Liu Xiang's *Biographies of Exemplary Women* or the chaste widows in Ming-Qing gazetteers.

Interviews suggest that emergence as a labor model, with its accompanying public activities, profoundly shaped these women's sense of who they were and their memories of that time. As revealing as oral narratives can be about struggles and compromises invisible in the written sources, women recalling their past as labor models did so in language provided by the historical process they are recalling. Their stories sometimes called that past to account, sometimes used it to call the present and its insufficiencies to account, sometimes narrated their virtue and value to a world that was currently neglecting them. What they never did was stand apart from that past and reject the subject positions that collectivization offered them, even though those positions have long since ceased to exist. Their intense relationship to their labor modelhood was as evident in their memories of singing in a Beijing hotel room or meeting Chairman Mao as it was in their accounts of their heroic exploits in the cotton fields. Their memories, in short, were neither in opposition to, nor even separated from, the project of state-building or the language of official history.

Many of these women came to inhabit the position of labor model to such a degree that their subjectivity cannot be apprehended independent of it. As they approach the end of their lives, they continue to draw on language once provided by the state (and since abandoned by it) to express their sense of who they were and what they accomplished. Certain aspects of labor model lives—sexuality, some political conflicts, obscure sources of retrospective bitterness—remain inaccessible, unaddressed or incompletely addressed in print, and unasked or unanswered (although not always absent) in interviews. In spite of Gao Xiaoxian's unfulfilled desire (which I share) to go back and try again and again, their stories call into question the idea—already under fire in many disciplines, but generally sacrosanct in historical research—that if we could just dig deep enough, the authentic person with an interior persona distinct from the public model would be waiting to reveal herself.

An imagined pure interiority, tales of nonnormative personal change, life apart from or in resistance to state discourse, the truth of the self or selves, cannot be recovered through research on the 1950s. Indeed the 1950s materials, and memories of the 1950s as recounted more recently, suggest that the whole project of a search for the real selves of a real past is chimerical. What the 1950s offer us is the possibility of constructing an account of how new women were brought into being, not by state fiat, but by the labor of cadres, the women themselves, their village communities, and regional or national reading and listening publics. These life stories direct our attention, not to hidden inner truths or the sort of life writing engaged in by contemporary biographers and historians, but to shared world-making projects. They suggest that the interior self is itself a historically situated and peculiar idea, and that our attachment to it as historians deserves a gaze as skeptical as any we turn on our source materials. Labor models do not necessarily tell us what we want to know, but perhaps they offer us lessons we need to hear.

9

Laborer

Gao Xiaoxian: *In your view, what is equality between men and women?*

Liu Dongmei: *Equality between men and women? Whatever you men can do, I can too. You can carry water, so can I. You can carry earth, so can I. You can carry stones, so can I.*

Gao Xiaoxian: *What else?*

Liu Dongmei: *What else can there be?*

Campaign time and domestic time collided with unprecedented intensity during the Great Leap Forward, briefly and memorably upending every aspect of rural life. The Great Leap, launched in May 1958, was a massive national campaign aimed at overtaking the industrial output of Great Britain and catching up with the United States through intensive production campaigns.[1] The Great Leap played out differently in each community. The ultimate outcome in rural areas, however, was catastrophic: institutional collapse, hunger, and, in many places, famine.

This chapter begins with a brief summary of national Party-state policy on the Great Leap and the effect of steel smelting and public works projects on the gendered division of labor. Then it traces Shaanxi women's memories of their mass move to the fields, and of the changes in domestic work and home life encapsulated in the phrase "the time when we ate in the dining halls."[2] The promise of plenty soon evaporated, and the chapter explores the onset of famine in 1959–61, later labeled "the three years of difficulty" or "the three years of disaster." The survival strategies of Shaanxi farming families during those years depended in part on women's skill at foraging and on their ability to produce woven goods that could be traded for food.

In the wake of the Great Leap Forward, local chronologies lost even a tenuous linkage to a national story of progress and diverged, sometimes permanently, from official accounts. Many women used the phrase "the old society," the state term for the era before 1949, to mean any time prior to the recovery from the Great Leap famine in about 1963. Some even expanded "the old society" to encompass the entire span of history before the economic reforms of the 1980s. They regarded much of the collective period as a time of hardship, eventually superseded by a radically different, if not always more secure, reform period. Their adaptation of official language bespeaks an interpretation of state categories. Why were some events remembered with great specificity—if not always accuracy—while others were reworked and forgotten? The unevenness with which events were absorbed and retold from one village locale to another, and the distinctive ways that women remember some aspects of the Leap, help us to explore what collectivization meant to those it affected most.

In addition to hardship, disillusionment, and the slippage of state language, the Great Leap left another legacy: the definitive emergence of women as a mainstay of the agricultural labor force. A gendered division of labor remained central to the Great Leap Forward, even as the tasks deemed appropriate for women continued to change and expand. As men moved first into Great Leap construction projects, then into management, technical work, and small-scale collective enterprises, women replaced them in the fields. A central argument of this chapter is that the expanded mobilization of women during the Great Leap Forward, which was much discussed in Party-state documents, consolidated a trend toward a long-term feminization of agriculture, which was virtually unheralded. A gendered analysis of the Great Leap Forward and its aftermath suggests that this feminization of agriculture undergirded the rural economic development of the Mao years, supporting the central accumulation strategy of the Party-state.

GREAT LEAP LABOR: THE DEPARTURE OF MEN (AND SOME WOMEN)

In the early 1950s, the end to years of warfare and the redistribution of land had enabled an increase in farm production. The new state sought a steady improvement in rural living standards, but it also needed to extract a rural surplus sufficient to fund industrialization, acquired through taxation and state grain purchases. Collectivization eliminated private ownership of land and created the possibility of further increases in productivity. By the late 1950s, with advanced producer cooperatives spreading across rural China, Mao decided to catapult China into the ranks of industrialized nations by deploying the only resource in ample supply: rural labor.[3]

In March 1958 a Communist Party work conference devised the central slogan of the Great Leap Forward: "Go all-out, aim high, and achieve more, faster, better, and more economical results." Advanced producer cooperatives, already too large in the opinion of many farmers, were to be combined into even larger communes, which would coordinate agricultural production, build irrigation canals and roads, and take on the duties of the former township governments.[4] In May 1958, the second session of the Eighth Party Congress formalized the Party-state's commitment to the Leap and approved ambitious production targets.[5] In August, another conference dubbed the Great Leap Forward "active preparation for the transition to Communism."[6]

By summertime, the formation of people's communes was well under way.[7] In Weinan Prefecture, 4,200 higher co-ops were combined into 280 communes.[8] Communes were subdivided into management districts (*guanli qu*), then into brigades (*shengchan dadui*) and teams (*shengchan dui*).[9] Cao Zhuxiang's Red Star cooperative combined with a similar unit to become the seventh battalion of the Happiness People's Commune.[10] These enlarged production units were intended to provide economies of scale, freeing some farm laborers to undertake large infrastructural projects such as reservoir and railroad construction. Suddenly an acute labor shortage gripped Shaanxi villages. As men were sent off to work on collective construction, often far from home, or to smelt steel in small-scale ("backyard") furnaces, cadres redoubled their efforts to mobilize women to go into the fields.

Initially village women were enthusiastic about the promise of the Leap,[11] less because it would propel them into communism than because it offered the promise of plenty to rural populations that had never known any such thing. The expansive Party-state vision of modernity promised industrial production everywhere. It provided language for unimaginable wonders: "Electric lights and telephones upstairs and downstairs, pushing the grindstone without cattle, lighting without oil, walking without using one's legs, eating without using one's mouth" (*diandeng dianhua, loushang louxia, tuimo buyao niu, zhaoliang buyao you, zoulu bu yong tui, chifan bu yong zui*). (The last two phrases were a jocular peasant commentary, quite possibly added later, on the farfetched nature of the first few.)[12] A policy initiative known as the Five Changes (*wuhua*) included, for the first time, the socialization and mechanization of domestic tasks. Even as their daily labor burden grew with the addition of farming tasks, night shifts, and new projects, women were encouraged to work toward a future in which the burden of grueling daily domestic labor would abate.[13] This possibility contributed in no small part to the excitement with which women responded to the Leap.

In October 1958, the national *People's Daily* urged producers throughout China to inaugurate a mass steel-smelting drive to augment the production of the nation's established steel-producing centers.[14] In Shaanxi, men in every commune were mobilized to operate the steel furnaces, which at the height of the fall 1958 campaign often ran day and night. Teams of men left home for forty or fifty days at a time to tend smelters, often located in mountain districts or distant counties.[15] The *dundian* cadre Liu Zhaofeng recalls, *They took all the male labor to the front line of steel making. People took iron cooking pans and iron basins from home. The iron cross-pieces on doors were also taken to make steel.*[16] The need for labor seemed inexhaustible, and sometimes women as well as men were mobilized to travel to smelting facilities far from their own backyard. A five-day conference of women activists in October 1958 called on women to serve the steel industry through "women's furnaces," "women's factories," and women's mining and steel transport teams.[17]

The deployment of women to smelt steel was a precarious and chaotic affair. Li Liujin, who lived near Village T, was first called on to lead women in shouldering loads of husked rice to feed men at a smelting center several days' walk away. Soon she was assigned to travel with a group of twenty-four women to a coal mine two counties north. *Aiya, they kept saying that they needed people. All the men had already gone, but they still kept needing people. There was no choice. The night we arrived, there was a mobilization meeting. They told us that it would be three to five years before we could go back. At home they had said that we would stay for ten days or so. Some of the women had sent their children to their natal families. Aiya, that night, everybody in the building was crying their eyes out. I tried to comfort them. But afterwards, I buried my head in my quilt and cried for a while.*

Why was I crying? Because we had lost one woman on the way. She was a bit slow in the head. She was only this tall. Her man, who was also a bit slow, had gone to Beiba to smelt steel, and we only brought her along in order to make up our quota. We were supposed to get off the train at Donghedian. Everybody got off the train except her, and the train left. What were we supposed to do? There would be big trouble if she was lost.

The next day, after I had arranged things for the women and told them what I was doing, I went to find that woman. Some people said, "Take the train." I said, "How can I look for her from inside a train?" I put on my clothes, a sweater, and my gloves, and I left. I walked, asking everywhere I went. I followed the railroad line. When there was a school, I would leave a letter at the school. I would look for their leaders and ask them to tell the students, so that if they ran into her—someone not very tall, carrying a bedroll on her back—they should pass a message to us at thus-and-such a place in Feng County. Ai, on my way I ran into a man leading a donkey pulling a cart. He had a towel around his head. I said, "Did you see a woman on this road, carrying a bedroll on her back?" He said, "Aiya, that women stayed in our dining hall last night. This morning, she said she was going to smelt iron, to an old factory in Hongshanliang. She followed two other workers there to smelt steel." He said, "Our dining hall is just ahead." Good. I also went to their dining hall. It was getting dark. A cadre was living in the dining hall. His last name was Wang, and he had a radish-flower scar by one of his eyes. I recognized this person. He had worked in our area before. I told him what had happened. He said, "Yes. That person came here. She left this morning." Later that night, he went to stay at someone else's home overnight, and gave me his bed in the dining hall. I stayed overnight there.

The second day, I climbed over the snow-filled Qinling Mountains, asking every-where I went and walking ten or twenty li before I found the old factory. I asked around. They said that she had come there, and was washing clothes for everybody. People said, "She is here, she is here." Everybody recognized her. We were all from the same town-ship. I found that woman. It would have been a mess if I hadn't found her.

I was given some lighter work, carrying dried charcoal [majiao gan tan, literally, horse foot dried charcoal]. In the mine, the dried charcoal was burned in pieces this long. You split the piece into two and carried it on your shoulder. Then they told me to go to where they were piling ore on top of the mountain and to sit there issuing tick-ets. If you hauled more, I would issue you a red ticket. If you hauled less, I would is-sue you a white ticket. Still less, no ticket. At twelve midnight, I was still on the moun-tain. Heavens, I was so freezing cold that my lips were swollen. When I smiled, my lips would crack and bleed. Imagine that. I stayed there for ten days.

Liujin's group left the mountain far earlier than the authorities had told them they could. *They ran away. Both men and women, as well as the director of the credit co-op and the people who worked for the credit co-op. They ran away together. The people over there ran away from there, and those of us over here came down the moun-tain, and we all came back home. We stayed ten days altogether. That's the story, that's it. That's what we accomplished that year. It was as left as left could be. Too left.*[18]

Work assignments were determined by the brigade leadership during the Great Leap Forward, and refusal was not an option.[19] And yet the confusion and uncer-tainty entailed in moving large numbers of men and women around the landscape meant that irregularities, absences, and even group resistance—in this case, people from an entire township voting with their feet—were not impossible. At the same time, the deployment of women on large projects meant that women too young to have known the famines and flight endured by Shan Xiuzhen's generation found themselves, often for the first time, moving beyond the circuit of natal and marital families.[20]

Li Liujin's picaresque adventure was not unique, but a more common way for women to contribute to the steel campaign was by dredging and panning sand from a nearby river bottom to extract bits of iron ore. *In order to smelt steel you need iron,* recalls Liu Zhenxi of Village B, *so we sent people to the river to dredge black sand, and then we set up stoves, and the workers smelted the black sand into raw iron bars to give the state for construction. At that time, smelting steel, that was all men. Women dredged.*[21]

Work on water control and supply in central and south Shaanxi, as well as on the Longhai railroad, drew men and women out of their home villages during the Great Leap Forward.[22] Labor models took the lead in organizing women to work on water-control projects near their own villages. Shan Xiuzhen, now head of a brigade and vice chair of a commune, organized several hundred women and men to build and repair dikes and reservoirs.[23]

From 1956 to 1962 many men from Village B went to work on a reservoir project, possibly on the You River, living there year-round and earning work points as well as extra grain allotments.[24] From Village T in Shaannan, both men and women went to the Hongsi embankment reservoir site for several months, and later worked on the Qingjiawan reservoir. Workers stayed there for several weeks at a time, earning higher work points than they could at home. Women pushed carts, hauled baskets of dirt on shoulder poles, and worked on earth-ramming crews. Some were drawn to do this work because of the higher pay rates, but in families where no man was at home the woman in the family was required to go, regardless of the childcare difficulties such an assignment presented.[25] In Village G, women went for a month at a time to work on the Cheyang River reservoir and dig out and repair irrigation ponds. They ate collectively and billeted with local families.[26]

In Village Z, women spent much of the winter building stone dikes along the river, leaving home before dawn and coming back after dark. The work began before the Great Leap and continued into the 1970s.[27] He Gaizhen, a cadre before and during the Great Leap, laughs when asked if women took part in the construction. *How could it be built without women? Oh, mother* [ma ya]. *We carried sand and stones with back baskets and shoulder poles. All women were required to carry stones with shoulder poles. After the big stones were laid, women poured small stones in and filled it. We built the embankment and picked up the stones on the ground and threw them up on the embankment. Then the land was level.*[28] Liu Dongmei adds that at the height of Great Leap activity, women were required to work night shifts. *Everyone went to the dikes at night, blindly feeling their way in the dark. What could you do in the dark? We did not want to do that. We would rather get up early in the morning and work early. And yet we could not sleep. It was the same policy all over the country.*[29]

In the village, men were in the minority, comments Zhou Guizhen of the period from the mid-1950s to the mid-1990s. *They all went outside to work.*[30] Some women smelted steel and built reservoirs and worked on the railroad alongside men, but once everyone had gone off to work on these large-scale projects, says Li Liujin, *the only people left at home were women.*[31] With male leaders working away from the villages, women moved into leadership positions, assuming positions of authority over the men who remained.[32]

These new leadership responsibilities required dealing with disruptions caused by state policies. In about 1960, eighty families displaced by reservoir construction along the You River were resettled in the commune to which Village B belonged.[33] Zhou Guizhen, the woman activist who had been mentored by Cao Zhuxiang, had become a Village B team leader when her predecessor went off to the reservoir with most of the other local men. Guizhen made resettlement arrangements for the twenty families assigned to her production team, but in subsequent years a series of conflicts erupted between the newcomers and the locals. A man from the migrant group accused Guizhen of discrimination, cursing her as "even fiercer than a man." Guizhen also suffered criticism from villagers unhappy that outsiders had settled in the area, affecting the size of everyone's grain allotment. Conflicts between the resettled people and the local population continued during and after the Cultural Revolution.[34]

GREAT LEAP FARMING AND
THE FEMINIZATION OF AGRICULTURE

In the autumn of 1958, the bumper crops of cotton and cornstalks in Village B began to fall over in the fields, and it became the women's job to harvest them before they rotted.[35] Cao Zhuxiang describes the rainy autumn as a time of frenetic activity. *Men were smelting steel and women were looking for iron in the river. Everybody was busy. During the day, the doors were all locked. There were only several people left cooking in the dining hall. When it was time to eat, they would bring food to the riverbank. . . . We rushed around harvesting, picking corn with no time to shuck it and leaving it in the field. The cart was busy sending things here and there and couldn't come back. That year, no matter where you threw the crops, in the field or on the ground, nobody took them. When could we shuck the corn? Still, we harvested it all and didn't leave it to rot.*[36] The "we" in question were the women of Village B, who went out in the dark to rescue the crops after a full day of work at the riverbank.[37] They soon found themselves responsible for the winter wheat planting and harvest as well.[38]

At first, women did farmwork in the interstices of Great Leap activities. They panned for iron during the day and shucked the corn at night, or panned for iron when the crops did not require their immediate attention.[39] Or when men and women without domestic burdens went off to work on construction projects, the "half-labor powers"—women with children at home, and older women—did the farmwork.[40] But with the Leap in full swing, Party-state emphasis shifted from encouraging diligence and thrift in women to mobilizing them as the main farm labor force.[41] Over time, farming became a task not just for "half-labor powers," but for all women, including those with young children who had not been caught up in earlier waves of field work mobilization. Cao Zhuxiang, drawing on the farming skills she had learned of necessity as a young married woman and later a widow, taught Guizhen and the other women of Village B what they needed to know. *All the men were in the south building the railroad. Secretary Cao led these women to study how to plow, rake, harness a draft animal to a cart and urge it on with shouts, remove manure from the pigsty, and chop hay with a hay cutter. In the fields I hitched up the reins and plowed with an ox. Women were all over the place doing this sort of activity. In our village there were no men. It was all women. At that time there was no one in the village, and women did all of that labor in the fields.*[42] Guizhen spent her days *hoeing, digging embankments, hauling manure, applying fertilizer, stamping down the cornstalks and collecting manure. At that time, water for irrigation was not electrically powered like it is now. It was all pushed in on water carts. In the fields, four people pushed a water cart to irrigate the wheat.*[43] Women were exhorted to plant trees and raise pigs, silkworms, and chickens.[44]

It was during the Great Leap Forward that Zhang Qiuxiang and the other cotton-growing heroines discussed in chapter 8 received sustained national publicity for pioneering new techniques of intensive cultivation and exhibiting determination, zeal for production, and political enthusiasm. Locally prominent models at the county level were likewise portrayed as Great Leap consciousness incarnate. The range of models expanded beyond experienced farmers such as Zhang Qiuxiang and Cao Zhuxiang to include very young women and collective groups of women. In Danfeng County, for instance, an eighteen-year-old named Zhang Chunfang became an all-purpose labor model for Great Leap initiatives. She reportedly organized women to smelt steel side by side with men; mobilized women in her mountainous area to farm; supervised the construction of two large aqueducts and four small irrigation canals; led young women in her commune to disassemble and wash quilts and clothing, paint walls, kill sparrows and rats, and fill in rat holes; taught herself to read and write; and overcame local superstitions to dig up and move her grandfather's remains in order to make room for new fields. But her primary accomplishment was persuading more than forty other women to join the local militia. Military training was described as a means by which women could overcome the limitations of their gender: "She often complained that she should not be a woman, so when 'everybody is a soldier' was implemented in the rural areas, she was so happy that she said, 'Now women and men are equal, we finally get the chance to protect the motherland and annihilate the enemy.'"[45]

In Danfeng County, the 130 women of the May First co-op were collectively named a model for "putting politics in command," "attending to ideology first and practice second" (*xian wu xu hou wu shi*), and "letting ideology lead practice" (*yi xu dai shi*). In what must be read in hindsight as an ominous instance of Great Leap magical thinking, the women convinced themselves—based on studying the cotton-growing experiences of Zhang Qiuxiang—that they could increase the output of an experimental sorghum field from one thousand *jin* per *mu* to thirty thousand *jin*. One woman was reported as saying, "Like Zhang Qiuxiang, we are all women. She can do this, why can't we? I think this all depends on whether you have confidence." They also designed agricultural tools and machines to chop vegetables, mill grain, thresh rice, and dust crops, thus demonstrating women's technical expertise and "refuting some people's thinking that women were clumsy, closed-minded, confused, and incapable of achievement." The report continued that the co-op's Party Committee chair and some other cadres, faced with the facts, were compelled to praise the women's accomplishments, calling them "heroes among women," and convening meetings to publicize their experience.[46]

The Women's Federation seized on this intensified mobilization of women to argue that the move of women into farming offered possibilities for gender equality, as one report proclaimed: "It is good for increasing production, while also eliminating women's superstitious inferiority complex, establishing women's self-confidence, and changing the mistaken viewpoint in society of discriminating against women."[47] But many farming women saw their participation in more prosaic terms: they had to work in order to eat in the collective dining halls, and failure to show up to work would draw public criticism.[48] Liu Dongmei of Village Z recalls, *If you did not work in the field, you would be fined. There was a woman here whose husband was a worker. She had a child. Only mother and child were at home. She was twenty-eight years old. That was her first child. She could not work. They deducted her share and the child's share. An adult got a full share [shi cheng]. A child got 70 percent of that. They had no grain to eat. It was all deducted, not only the adult's share, but also the child's. It was very strict.*[49] No farmwork task was considered too skilled, too heavy, or too shameful for women. No longer controversial, women's constant presence in the fields was required, because the men were gone. The feminization of agriculture had begun.[50]

GO ALL-OUT, AIM HIGH

The Party-state wanted more of women than maintaining the agricultural home front. Women were expected to raise crop output to unprecedented levels by means of deep plowing and dense planting on experimental high-yield fields. In the Village T area, Li Liujin and other women on her production team applied intensive methods to the wheat crop, with disastrous results. *We did deep plowing that year, over one meter deep. Like that—you push the spade in, and push in again deep with all your strength. Then throw it up on top to dig deep. Whenever it rained, we did deep plowing. It makes me laugh. The higher levels [shangtou] said to do it that way. It required so much strength to turn over the sublayer of yellow mud. We sowed more than fifty jin of wheat seeds on nine fen of land, instead of the usual thirty-plus jin. At first the wheat grew very well. The higher levels came to visit, and so did women from the district. But then the wheat all fell over. The stalks were so thin that we had to put up frames [to support them]. Even with frames we did not harvest much. The ears of wheat [suizi] were very small, and the stalks were very thin.*

If you sow too densely, that's what happens. We didn't master the technology. We weren't thinking about how to grow crops scientifically. We thought if we did what the higher levels said, we couldn't go wrong [zuobude cuo]. If the higher levels said that plowing deep would yield high output, ai, if that's what they said, then we plowed deep. I doubted that deep plowing would bring high output. Some women plowed and plowed and got angry. But what was the point of being angry? You had already plowed the land. "Women's experimental field." You had the sign stuck right there.[51]

In 1959, a Women's Federation delegation found similar problems in another Shaannan village. Women had lavished 150 *jin* of wheat seeds and twelve thousand *jin* of fertilizer on each *mu* of field. *They also added grass ash once. Now it looks nice. But when you separate the wheat, you'll find that the roots have become yellow and some have fallen off. It's obvious that the seedlings are too dense. They need to thin out some seedlings, but they don't know how much they should thin out, how much they should keep, and how to thin. They have no technical guidance.* This inspection group saw the problem as one of technical ignorance.[52] But setting a sky-high goal and attempting to meet it using untested methods was not just a statement of technical naiveté. It was a response to political pressures whose ultimate source lay far outside rural communities.

Cadres at every level felt compelled to contribute to the Leap's production goals. Slogans such as "However big people's courage is, that is how much the land will produce" and "Stamp on the earth, hand grasps heaven, one *mu* of land can produce several tens of thousands of *jin*" linked production to political and moral will.[53] Across rural China, the desire of local officials to win glory and avoid disgrace for themselves and their communities led to what later became known as the "exaggeration wind" (*fukua feng*).[54] In 1958, communities overreported their crop output, sometimes egregiously.[55] He Gaizhen reports, *[Cadres] would claim that the yield per* mu *was several thousand* jin, *writing it on signs and sticking them in the ground. There was no such yield, even from the experimental fields. There was no fertilizer except what came from public toilets. What could grow?*[56] A tragic cycle ensued. Delighted that the hoped-for agricultural surplus was materializing to fund industrialization, state authorities raised the quotas of grain to be delivered to the state, contributing directly to famine conditions in many districts by late 1958.[57]

Reluctance to exaggerate had political costs, but it quite likely saved lives, and in retrospect it is remembered as a virtue. Toward the end of her life, Cao Zhuxiang described herself as one who *didn't chase after the high tide. I am a stubborn* [jiang] *person. To chase after the high tide you had to beat that drum. . . . Whether you were of one heart or not, you beat the gongs. I didn't beat the gongs and drums.*[58] Zhou Guizhen recalls the pressures Zhuxiang felt as a labor model to make inflated claims about her cotton yields. *That year when they were doing the exaggerating, the old lady was incapable of that. She always reported accurately, and people wanted her to inflate the reports, but she reported them low. At that time there were some people in the county, if you didn't do things according to their plan, you wouldn't rise higher, and people did things in order to rise. But the old lady was very honest. "If I produce that much, that's how much it is. If I make a report with no basis, what will happen later?" In the end, when we went to the county to attend that cotton meeting with several hundred people, we were the ones whose cotton yield was the highest, 120* jin. *The people in Shuangwang [Zhang Qiuxiang's home community] only had 110* jin. *She wasn't afraid that Zhang Quixiang and others would move up beyond her.*[59] Resisting the pressures to exaggerate seems uncomplicated half a century later. During the time that Zhang Qiuxiang and the other models were rising to prominence, however, it seemed both necessary and desirable to set high goals and strive to reach them, and not only for self-serving reasons. Remaining a labor model brought benefits to one's village: extra fertilizer, access to rural credit, and technical assistance. Coaxing more than a thousand *jin* of crop per *mu* from experimental fields, in a tribute to the Soviet *Sputnik* program of space exploration, was referred to as "launching a satellite."[60] In an era when the collective imagination encompassed electric lights, multistory dwellings, and socialized food preparation, mere factual reporting of crop output could be construed by the Party-state, and by one's neighbors, as a failure to strive for a future everyone wanted, a future in which even a peasant woman could be in the scientific vanguard of building socialism.

THE FIVE CHANGES

The promise of a profoundly different everyday future was most evident in discussions of the Five Changes (*wuhua*), aimed at reassigning domestic tasks to the production brigades. Eating was to take place in dining halls, clothing was to be made by sewing machines, babies were to be born in birthing stations, children were to be cared for in daycare centers, and flour was to be milled by machine.[61] Many of these tasks—cooking, sewing, delivering newborns, and caring for children—were still to be performed by women, but now in a socialized setting rather than in individual households.

The official purpose of the Five Changes was to liberate women's labor power for participation in collective agriculture.[62] Shan Xiuzhen reminded women activists in October 1958 that with the time they were no longer spending on household tasks, they could cultivate high-yield plots, deep-plow the wheat fields, improve agricultural tools, and collect or manufacture fertilizer, including bacterial (*xijun*) fertilizer.[63] In 1958, she established in her commune seven daycare centers, seven nursery schools, nine dining halls, and nine sewing factories. With several other women, she even devised a machine that could cut twenty-eight pieces of steamed bread at a time.[64]

By publicizing Xiuzhen's achievements in this realm, the Party-state provided belated public recognition that the burden of domestic labor fell on women, and that no previous state policy had addressed that burden adequately. Now that women were needed in the fields, not to mention at the smelters, reservoirs, and bacterial fertilizer factories, Party-state organizations named some of the main tasks that took hours of women's effort every day. The proposed method for liberating women's labor for field work, however, was to be strictly do-it-yourself, "relying on the masses" to build and fund new local institutions to perform domestic tasks. This approach reflected practical limitations: the Party-state had neither money nor personnel to contribute to implementing the Five Changes. But an equally important factor was the generalized Great Leap reliance on mobilizing the masses, rather than waiting for science or experts to solve local problems.

The members of the model May First Co-op in Danfeng County organized themselves in May 1958 to socialize housework. After five days of hard labor, they reportedly established "three collective dining halls, one daycare center and three daycare groups, one nursery school, one birth station, two sewing groups, and three laundry groups." It took this many facilities to serve a co-op of 716 people, indirectly suggesting the amount of unpaid, invisible labor normally undertaken by women at home.[65] The result: "Women's labor power was thoroughly liberated, and the rate of women's field work participation throughout the commune reached 100%.... Because women broke free from the burden of domestic tasks [baituo le jiawu tuolei], they joined in production wholeheartedly.... This summer, 55 women went down in the paddies to plant . . . rice. Twelve women studied and became skilled at plowing, raking, pushing the dirt truck, and making ridge-bordered fields, the whole range of agricultural skills."[66] As one sanguine report from 1958 commented, "Because of the implementation of the Changes in childcare, dining halls, and sewing, women say happily, 'In the past our bodies were in the field but our minds were home, worrying about the children, piglets, cooking, and sewing waiting for us there. But now children get care and education, dining halls manage the cooking, and sewing machines take care of sewing. So we can cheerfully take on the tasks of production.'"[67]

In spite of these highly publicized achievements, socializing domestic labor was an uneven process. Machine milling of flour has left virtually no written traces. The establishment of birth stations for childbirth, already explored in chapter 6, was brief and more decentralized than the term "stations" would suggest. At the same time, women's reproductive health was imperiled by the intensive work demands of the Great Leap. Women cadres and midwives reported an increased incidence of uterine prolapse.[68] In Village G, the midwife Shi Cuiyu treated cases of prolapse (like an eggplant) with manipulation and medicine, but to no avail.[69] Lu Yulian, a woman cadre in Shaannan, was sent to a neighboring district on an investigative team, where she found nine women with prolapse in three villages. She attributed their condition to a lack of rest time after childbirth; as soon as the month of confinement was over, they had returned immediately to heavy labor. It was in the last half of 1960. How pitiful these women were. It [the uterus] was like a light bulb. It was hard to breathe. It even made it impossible to rest properly at night. In this district, women were offered free treatment and release from field work, but it is not clear how widely available such treatment was.[70]

As for the never-ending task of making clothes, collective sewing groups played only a minor role. Cao Zhuxiang, as Party secretary of her production brigade,[71] organized a sewing group staffed by women who were paid in work points. The group charged a few *jiao* to make an item of clothing. For those who had no cash on hand, the debt was recorded and deducted at the end of the year from the work points they had earned. For families with a bit of money to spend, this lightened the burden of making clothing and shoes by hand, but families in economic difficulty continued to rely on the labor of their own women.[72] By 1959, Women's Federation reports were commenting on serious problems in the sewing groups: lack of machines, irregular participation by seamstresses ("some participated in other jobs and some were sick at home, doing nothing"), patchy regulations, inconsistent leadership, and sloppy recordkeeping, all leading to complaints among commune members.[73]

Another of the Five Changes, childcare centers, received more attention in Women's Federation writings.[74] Daycare became "one of the key problems in consolidating the people's communes, and a major political task." Nationally the establishment of adequate childcare facilities was described as "gradually transferring the main task of educating children from the household to society." Youth League and Party members were encouraged to take up daycare work.[75] In Shaanxi, the deputy Federation director Li Jinzhao presented a spirited case for the importance of childcare. Of the three million women laborers in the province, she said, about 60 percent had young children, and 30 percent of these could not find anyone to care for them. Childcare had freed up women to grow cotton, build dams, and conserve water and soil, thanks to the establishment of 7,631 kindergartens and 36,294 childcare groups, taking care of 651,330 children ages one to six. Still, she continued, a further push was required to broaden availability and raise quality. Li proposed that collectives subsidize childcare costs to raise women's enthusiasm for sending their children to the centers.[76] The Women's Federation provided textbooks to train childcare workers and established model nursery schools. Reinforcing the fact that childcare was women's work, Federation work reports advocated "paying attention to solving the problem of women's children."[77]

Feng Xiaoqin, a mother of three (she would later have three more), worked in the Village Z childcare center (*tuoer suo*) before and during the Great Leap: *It had two small rooms. People would bring the children in the morning. Their parents would come get them after dark. The children were all ages three to seven. For the two-year-olds, families arranged for old people to take care of them. The ones who came here could all walk. I taught them to sing, gave them a few toys to play with, and taught them to read characters if they wanted to learn them. If they didn't, I didn't push it. In Dongguan there was also a nursery school [youeryuan]. Mine was the only center in this village. The better-off [villages] ran nursery schools. The worse ones didn't.*[78]

By the end of 1958, the Federation was calling for the establishment of at least one twenty-four-hour center in each county within three weeks. But the plan was as notable for its litany of problems as for its grand ambitions and unrealistic timetable. Existing centers, it noted, were inadequately staffed by caregivers of "impure status": "Some are too old. Some have infectious diseases. Generally they lack knowledge of childcare. They think their job is to stop children from crying. . . . Many childcare centers and kindergartens have no regular and suitable rooms and necessary tools and toys. The hygienic conditions are bad, which causes children's illnesses. . . . In winter, because of the lack of heating equipment, fewer and fewer children come to childcare centers and kindergartens." Not surprisingly, many mothers were unwilling to send their children to the centers, while local political leaders regarded these problems as "a trivial thing, women's business or a kid's matter." The Federation proposed few alternatives other than returning to these same skeptical parents and local cadres to build up the centers: "There should be tables and chairs, quilts and toys. In winter, heating problems should receive serious attention. To solve these problems, communes may spend some welfare money on necessary equipment. But the more important thing is to depend on the masses. Mobilize the masses to provide better rooms for children. Mobilize parents to bring quilts, utensils, and toys for their own children. Communes may subsidize some really poor families. Mobilize the masses to build heated brick beds [*kang*] and seal windows for the children so that they can play on a warm bed in winter."[79]

Across Shaanxi, the establishment, duration, and quality of these centers were uneven. Even during the Great Leap, many parents carried their children to the fields rather than take them to a distant childcare center.[80] When the Leap foundered, most daycare centers closed.[81] As chapter 7 suggested, childcare during the collective period remained a matter of short-lived local groups, patched-together supervision by grandparents and older siblings, or the risky business of leaving children alone.[82] Some women in Village T would carry three or four children in baskets at the end of shoulder poles down to the paddies to work;[83] others left them at home. *I put them in their bedding,* Kang Ruqing remembers, *and one would rock the cradle, and the littlest one would cry. In the past, raising children was really pitiful. The ones who were a bit older would come to the paddy embankment with me, and stand on the embankment and play.*[84] To the north, in Village G, Liu Guyu tied her children to the window: *My older sister-in-law and my third aunt said to me, "As for taking care of children, God* [lao tianye] *does half and you do the other half." I couldn't take care of my children. I went to work in the fields and left the children on the* kang. *I only dressed them in tops and left their bottoms naked. I tied them with a rope to the window frame. When I came back, their poop was all in a line. I cleaned everything up all at once.*[85]

Women recalled the difficulties of intensified field work during the Great Leap Forward partly in terms of the childcare hardships it engendered.[86] Liu Dongmei comments, *Children were left at home for the old folks to take care of. If the children cried, just let them cry. No choice. You dared not stay at home. If you stayed at home, your work points would be reduced.*[87] The oral narratives of village women are punctuated with tales of children injured, frightened by animals, left tied to the *kang*, drowned, or dead of diseases not treated in time. Yang Anxiu, the midwife who prided herself on delivering children safely, had far less control over the well-being of her own toddler. *My husband left for steel and iron making in 1958. Nobody else was at home. I was a cadre at that time. As a cadre, I usually didn't get home until after dark. This scared my child. One day, I came back at night from deep-digging the field in Wufeng. When I went to the back of my house, I heard my child crying. He was just two years old. I asked why he was crying. He had pooped in the living room and was shaking the bolt on the door. I was so angry I cried. I said, "What are you doing here? What made you so scared?" "Mommy, Mommy, hurry up. There was a rat coming from the window to bite me. I hit it with my fist and it ran away."*[88] A 1961 Shaanxi Federation report offered the grim statistic that 30 percent of all children ages one to five had no one to care for them at home, adding that during the summer harvest season more than a hundred children across the province had been bitten by wolves or drowned.[89]

The Party-state's recognition that domestic labor was time-consuming emerged only in a context in which women were needed in the fields. As the high-stakes attempt to propel the countryside toward communism began to fail, the analysis of domestic burdens, and the attempt to ameliorate them, faded as well. Nowhere is this pattern more obvious than in the most widely implemented and vividly remembered of the Five Changes: the dining halls.

EATING ON DINING HALL TIME

Of all the transformations the Great Leap Forward wrought in the countryside, the most fundamental change in daily domestic patterns was the advent of collective dining halls. In the summer and autumn of 1958 households turned over to the collective whatever grain and vegetables they had on hand.[90] Many also turned in their pots to be melted down for steel smelting, and in some villages they smashed their household stoves and pots. He Gaizhen remembers the situation in Village Z: *In order to have the dining hall, the team leader broke your pots so that no family had its own pots. Once your pots were broken, you couldn't eat at home.*[91] Other Village Z women corroborate her story: *There were no pots in the houses. People had taken all the pots. There were just the circles where the pots had been [set into the stove].*[92] People of laboring age were promised that they could eat their fill in the collective dining halls in return for a day's labor. The elderly and children were to have their food provided as well, and women in the last stage of pregnancy were to be fed at the birthing stations.[93]

Communes were left to work out the details of dining hall operation on their own. In Village B, the brigade controlled the grain mill, stored foodstuffs in warehouses, and distributed them to dining halls run by each production team.[94] Smaller canteens were sometimes set up on a makeshift basis in someone's house.[95]

In Village G, four teams combined to open a dining hall that served more than a thousand people each day, but it was soon divided into smaller units, each serving a single team, or about forty households.[96] As with any political initiative, individual persuasion by local cadres was important. In Village Z, the cadre Lu Yulian argued for efficiency: *We would tell them that dining halls would save labor power and firewood. It saved the effort of people who cooked, and it saved grain.*[97] For women in particular, dining halls offered relief from a time-consuming daily task. Qiao Yindi in Village G said, *I thought it was good. You didn't have to rush home exhausted and do the cooking.*[98] Her fellow villager Ouyang Xiu agreed: *When we first started to eat in the dining halls, women were very happy about it, because they didn't have to cook. But that was a very short time.*[99]

Collective eating made it possible to feed the large numbers of people working away from home on reservoirs, smelting, and other projects. Cao Zhuxiang was responsible for sending food to the smelting center at the riverbank near Village B. *I was running around at night. Who knew what sleep was? At night, there were two flour grinders in the brigade, and we ground flour and the people from the dining hall came over to get it. I didn't sleep the whole night. Every day we sent flour for more than one hundred people who were smelting steel.*[100] If the dining halls enabled collective labor, however, they also disrupted many of the practices of village life. When someone married or died, families had no grain or other foodstuffs at home to provide the customary hospitality. On Li Duoduo's wedding day, only her brother and sister-in-law accompanied her to her new home, and they left without eating the traditional wedding banquet. *Nobody else came. In the dining hall, if a person came, they had to register for their meal. Otherwise you couldn't get anything to eat.* The dining hall prepared rice that day—a special treat—but only because the wedding was held on the eighth of the final lunar month, a day customarily observed with a special meal.[101] When young married women went to visit their natal families, they were permitted to have the dining hall staff weigh out three or four days' worth of grain to take with them, at four ounces per meal and two meals per day, totaling eight ounces (*liang*) for each day of their absence. But as Duoduo observes, *You couldn't stay very long at your natal family. We didn't earn work points during that time. There wasn't enough grain. We had no money for food and no money paid for our work. If you worked today, you could eat today. If you didn't work today, you had nothing to eat.*[102] Local socializing decreased, because people could no longer drop in on a neighbor to share a meal. As Zhou Guizhen put it, *During the dining hall period there were no more relatives.*[103] Until the Great Leap, one benefit of socialism had been that poor peasants could now afford to engage in social reciprocity, hosting wedding banquets and first-month rituals, exchanging gifts and extending hospitality.[104] Now such practices disappeared.

Very quickly, the "day's food for a day's work" rule devolved into a crude form of labor control. In Village Z, Shi Ranwa found that *if you didn't go to work this morn-*

ing, at mealtime when you came to get your food, they would ask, "What did you do this morning?" I would say, "This morning I didn't go, this morning I did such and such." Then the person would dump the ladle of food back into the pot and not give it to you to eat.[105] In Village T, Qian Taohua reports, *If someone didn't work, the team wouldn't give him work points and he couldn't eat. Someone would say, "My foot was hurt. I carried the hoe, how can you not give me food?"*[106] At the height of the smelting projects, Yang Anxiu's dining hall in Village T set another requirement for a day's food: a contribution of metal from each household. *Every time you went to eat, they would collect iron, copper, or silver from you. If you had nothing, you could not eat. I have to laugh about the candlestick that I had for my wedding. It was made of copper, three levels, as tall as this. The bottom of the stick was this large. There was a tray in the middle with a doll on it. That day, I really had no other choice. They said they would not let me eat. Okay. I took the candlestick and turned it in. After a while, they said they were collecting silver. At that time, it was the fashion to celebrate the completion of a month after having a baby. For the full-month celebration, someone bought a hat for my child. There was a silver bell on it. I turned it in for food. My granddaughter said this year, "Grandma, where is your silver? All the others have silver. Where is your silver chain? Where is the silver coin for the full-month celebration from my great-grandma?" I said they were all traded for food. If you did not give it to them, the dining hall would not give you food. The upper levels asked for it. I don't know what for. If you really had nothing, it was also okay. You could also get food. But they were trying to control you.*[107]

Operating a dining hall posed formidable challenges. Cao Zhuxiang likened the skills required by the dining halls to the demands of raising a family. *You took charge of the team just like you would take charge of a family. Every month you had to keep close track of the grain. In assigning people to the dining hall, you had to assign people who were not extravagant and wasteful. Eating out of one big pot, you had to assign a good leader. . . . I was not in charge of our grain. The storehouse keeper kept count. Often the cadres underneath kept close track. . . . If the big beam is not straight, the beams underneath are crooked.*[108] The dining halls, like the public works projects and agriculture, had a pronounced gendered division of labor. Men became managers, accountants, and storehouse keepers; women chopped vegetables, cooked, and fed the pigs.[109]

Cooks in the dining halls were required to produce a precise number of steamed bread rolls from each *jin* of flour.[110] Grain was allocated on a strict per person basis, and dining hall staff doled out portions accordingly. In Village T, this task fell to Li Liujin: *Every day, I had to allocate the grain. Each person had only four ounces [liang], two per meal. At that time, the wheat was washed and milled together with bran and wheat flour. We would cook for everyone. When it was cooked, we would use bowls to ladle it. It was just like gruel [huhu]. I would count how many people were eating together and weigh it accordingly. When it was cooked, it was according to the ladleful. According to the average number of people, we would ladle so many iron spoonfuls.*[111]

The spread of dining halls across the rural landscape was marked by new tensions. People disliked having to stand in line, as Zhao Chaofeng comments about Village G: *So many people ate in the dining hall, eighty or a hundred. You had to wait for a long time for noodles and steamed bread. The masses were dissatisfied. They said it delayed production. But the Party secretary said, "Don't even think about eating from your own pot. Don't think about doing it even until the time of your grandson."*[112] People had varying opinions about what was good to eat, as Lu Yulian observes: *Some preferred sweet, some preferred salty.*[113] They could be self-serving, as He Gaizhen ruefully remembers: *I ate with a group of men. There was only me, one woman. They were fierce. They would ladle up the fat and let me drink the soup.*[114]

Women's Federation cadres who were "squatting" in villages remember that the demand to create such complex organizations virtually overnight led to popular resistance and a daunting array of logistical challenges. Just as with the steel-smelting campaign, however, these experienced cadres understood that open criticism was not possible. Liu Zhaofeng, one such cadre, recalls, *At that time, we were still fluttering with fear. Zhang and I were studying and discussing the advantages of eating in the dining halls. We talked in private: Were there any advantages? It was just moving people around. There was no foundation among the masses, no economic base either. Alas! We dared not say such words. From the present perspective, the move to organize dining halls was premature. [Nevertheless] we thought that whatever the whole Party was mobilizing for, our Women's Federation should cooperate to do it enthusiastically, and should mobilize women to participate in the campaign. We had no other thoughts.*[115] As one squatting cadre commented, *Women went along with the tide. Most didn't dare to oppose the dining halls openly, because of Party prestige.*[116] Likewise, local women cadres such as Zhou Guizhen—the activists painstakingly mentored by the Women's Federation cadres—felt obliged to remain silent about their reservations. *We propagandized to people and said that the dining hall was good. We didn't dare to say that it was not good. I myself was a cadre. If you were a cadre, when you propagandized to people you had to say this was good. If you said it was no good, others would say, "You cadres all say it's no good, yet you are scolding others."*[117]

But Shan Xiuzhen took a dim view of the dining halls, and she made her objections known. *There was only one point I was not convinced about: taking people's things and their household goods out and sharing them. To eat in the dining hall and take out things from every household was egalitarianism [pingjun zhuyi]. I said that it would dampen the people's socialist enthusiasm. We were supposed to be promoting the enthusiasm of the masses for socialism. There was a lot of this sort of extreme action [gao lihai] in Henan, but our Shaanxi was stable.*[118]

First a reflection of Great Leap Forward euphoria, then a barometer of its local grievances, the dining halls soon became a site of its collapse. In 1959, when the dining halls ran short of food, the promised release from domestic labor became a burden of a different kind: hunger. In some accounts, famine began in 1958, the same year as the Great Leap Forward.[119] A good grain harvest was undermined by problems with food storage, distribution, and extraction. Then came the 1959 harvest, uniformly characterized as a bad one.[120] Nationally, Defense Minister Peng Dehuai reported that food shortages began early in 1959. By 1960, grain production had fallen 26.4 percent from 1957 levels, and in 1960 and 1961 large areas of rural China suffered from famine.[121] Mao mentioned Shandong, Henan, and Gansu as seriously affected areas; Anhui was also hard-hit.[122] Absolute output was not the only issue. Provinces such as Shanxi, with relatively low average grain output, had relatively few deaths. Yet in grain-abundant areas such as Sichuan and Hunan, and in parts of Henan, people starved to death although storehouses were full.[123]

Later the Party-state would formulate an official explanation for the failure of the Great Leap: bad weather, mistakes in the work, and the need to repay the debt to the Soviet Union, with whom relations were at the breaking point. But in spite of a run of truly bad weather—in Shaanxi, encompassing both serious drought and widespread flooding[124]—it is clear that the famine of 1959–61 was not a "natural" disaster, but a human-made one.[125]

The grain harvest of 1958 was reported as the largest ever, 375 million tons—twice that of the previous year—partly because of the "exaggeration wind."[126] The top leadership accepted these estimates and made several fateful decisions. They ordered certain provinces (Sichuan, Yunnan, Gansu) to export grain to other regions of China. They permitted 10 percent less acreage to be planted to grain in 1959. A convergence of these and other factors led to famine. D. Gale Johnson lists "excessive procurement, the protection of urban consumers from the worst effects of the food shortages, the continued export of grain while people starved, the output declines in 1959, 1960, and 1961, and waste of food in communal dining halls." Carl Riskin broadens the list to include "output collapse, irrational methods of cultivation, destruction of work incentives, wasteful consumption of available food grain, ignorance of the planning authorities, over-procurement of grain by the government, increased exports in the midst of the crisis, failure to initiate imports in time, bad weather, etc."[127] Serious disagreements at the highest level of the Party-state exacerbated these problems. When reports of shortages first surfaced in 1959, the government briefly moderated its policies, but after Mao reacted violently to a challenge of Great Leap policies by Peng Dehuai at the Lushan Plenum in July 1959, major adjustments were not made until 1961.[128]

Viewed from the village level, the heart of the problem was that much of the grain harvest was leaving the village in the form of state procurement.[129] The "exaggeration wind" gave higher-level state authorities misleading signals and encouraged intensified state extraction from the rural areas. Asked why there was not enough to eat, Zhuang Xiaoxia replies, *It was all given to the state. Secretary Cao [Zhuxiang] said, "The state has difficulties, and we all have to help shoulder some of them." We sent more grain. Furthermore that year the harvest was also not good. This went on for two years, 1961 and 1962. By 1963, it was a bit better.*[130] At the same time, and probably also related to hunger, some women remember that their neighbors quickly lost their enthusiasm for round-the-clock projects, that they became "passive" (*xiaoji*) about field work and "did a sloppy job," leading to a drop in the harvest.[131] Xiaoxia observes, *People's thinking was not unified, and although they said they were working, those who discussed were discussing, those who made shoe soles were making shoe soles, everyone sat there waiting, and when the bell rang they came back. Or they were loafing around, not working hard. Grain was short, money was short. Grain was short not just in one person's family, but everywhere.*[132]

The shortage was felt immediately in the dining halls, Xiaoxia remembers: *The first year we didn't have rationing and people were satisfied. By the second year, they said that the state had to repay debts to the Soviet Union, and they gave us rations. A few ounces a day, very pitiful.*[133] In Village B, the plan to feed the elderly and sick in a "Good Fortune Kitchen" (*xingfu zao*) ran into trouble when many people claimed to be sick in order to get access to the food.[134] Soon plans to feed the elderly and children special food, never elaborate to begin with, were abandoned.[135] As they had done in pre-Liberation times of shortage, women limited their own food consumption in order to give more to the men and children in their families.[136] Parents took cornmeal gruel for themselves, because it could be thinned out with water, and saved the steamed bread for their children.[137] Zheng Xiuhua tried to protect her brother: *I worked and planted overtime at night. I could get a bowl of cornmeal gruel. I wouldn't eat it. I would take it to my brother and let him eat. He was in school. I would not have anything at night. I would go to work the next morning. We had no choice at that time. Everyone was like this, not only me.*[138]

As the food crisis worsened, the quality of the dining hall food degenerated further. Steamed bread disappeared from the menu. Cornmeal gruel with a few leaves mixed in became the staple offering. Noodles were served occasionally, but there were usually not enough to go around.[139] In Village Z, Shi Ranwa observes, *For those who needed to eat a lot, a gourdful of food was not enough.*[140] *In the morning we ate sweet potato gruel. . . . At noon we ate milled coarse grain, with a bit of sweet potato in it. There was no steamed bread, flat cakes, or* guokui mo *[a thick flatbread]. Our life here was bitter.*[141] Daily rations dipped to dangerously low levels. In Village G, the assistant village accountant Gao Yuzhong remembers, *The winter of 1960 was the most difficult time. The grain ration was "three low, two ordinary, three high." The "three low" was from October to December, the "two ordinary" January to February, and the "three high" March, April, May. "Low" went down to fifteen* jin *[of grain per month], ordinary to eighteen* jin, *high to twenty* jin.[142] Even the highest of these was a starvation ration; fifteen *jin* of wheat flour per month would provide fewer than a thousand calories per day.[143] Shan Xiuzhen estimated that people working full time in the fields needed two *jin* per day, or three times the "high" ration.[144]

By 1959, an inspection team visiting dining halls in a central Shaannan commune found that several of them had no grain supplies whatsoever. *They picked some bean residue from the city and mixed the residue with radish leaves for the two meals per day.* The locals explained the shortage by saying that in the first heady days of the dining halls, they had eaten a whopping *jin* of grain per person per meal, wasting grain through bad cooking practices as well. The inspectors had only ineffectual recommendations to offer: persuade peasants to sell hoarded personal stores of grain to the commune, organize commune members to collect wild vegetables and plant early-ripening vegetables, and develop grain-saving ways of preparing food.[145]

In November 1960, during the worst year of the famine in Shaanxi, the Central Committee put out a directive on food substitutes with the slogan "Squash and vegetables should substitute [for grain], lower the standards [for food allotments]" (*gua cai dai, di biaozhun*). (In fact, the squash and vegetables were long gone by that time, and many people were eating leaves, bark, wild vegetables, and white clay.)[146] In the local parlance of Village G, "the time when we ate in the dining halls" soon became "the time of low allotments and food substitutes." Gao Yuzhong recalls, *You couldn't eat your fill. Squash and vegetables were substituted [for grain] [gua cai dai], for example turnip leaves, cabbage stalks, and sweet potato leaves.*[147] Wang Fugui, a man who earlier had been the village head, comments, *That was when we used sweet potatoes as a staple because there wasn't enough flour. We didn't eat well. Sweet potato steamed bread, sweet potato flour. There was very little grain.*[148] People began to eat steamed buns made from milled cornstalks mixed into a paste.

Squatting cadres such as Liu Zhaofeng suffered along with the farmers. *We were starving after eating in the dining hall but had nothing else to eat. Before I washed the cooking pot every night, I scraped off all the crust sticking to it and added hot pepper and vinegar to it. I took the crust back, and those men comrades were so starving that they heated it on the stove and ate it. People were all swollen.*[149] Even under these conditions some cadres continued to feel that open criticism was unimaginable. For Xu Nini, *What I did and what I thought were two different things. . . . In 1961, there were hard times in the commune. We had thin gruel and ate carrots, two meals a day. Also carrot tops. Everyone's excrement was red. People asked me, "Are carrot tops good to eat?" I said, yes, yes. I pretended. Of course carrot tops were no good to eat.*[150]

Violent accusations and quarrels began to punctuate meals in the dining halls. In Village Z, He Gaizhen watched as favoritism and suspicion poisoned daily encounters: *There was a person who ladled the sweet potato porridge for others. If he had a close relationship with a person, he would ladle from the bottom for that person, where it was full of sweet potatoes. Then you could have enough food. If he wasn't close to you, he ladled thin porridge for you. Then you couldn't get enough food.*[151]

Ouyang Xiu found similar practices in Village G: *The people who managed things, and the cooks, ate a bit more. When it was the masses' turn, there wasn't much left.*[152] Comments Zheng Xiuhua of Village Z: *I was not a cadre, how could I eat freely?*[153]

Many disputes concerned the food supply for children. Yang Anxiu recounts one such story: *One day, they hid some food when they were cooking the rice. I was very angry. I said to the storehouse keeper [baoguan], "Now, all the food is gone. Look at the child who's crying. You sent him to the field to get food. You are hungry enough to cry. I am also hungry enough to cry." Finally a woman who was tending the fire said that there was some food hidden in the bucket. I took some out and heated it, and each of us had a bowl. I had a quarrel with the storekeeper. I said, "How could you do that? You yourself have children. How could you let a child cry like that? How can the adults have peace of mind while they are working in the field? Mothers cry and children cry. It's a mess." From then on, every time, they would leave some food for the schoolchildren.*[154] When Xiao Gaiye brought half a bowl of rice home for her sick infant son in 1958, she was accused of stealing food from the collective and her entire family was subjected to a large criticism meeting. *My son's bottom was burned. He was lying at home, just over one year old. I took a half bowl of food for my son, and asked my mother-in-law to take it back to feed him, because I was work-ing. They stopped my mother-in-law and grabbed the bowl away. They told my mother-in-law, my husband, and me to announce over the loudspeaker that I stole the food. I was struggled against in the dining hall.* Furious, Xiao and her husband managed to move their household registration to Xiao's natal village, taking the children and Xiao's mother-in-law there to live until 1964.[155] Stealing did become endemic in the final days of the dining halls. The Shaannan cadre Xu Nini, who spent time in sev-eral villages, remembers, *We saw things but couldn't talk about them. At the end there was so much stealing there was nothing left to eat. In Jiangjiahe, one person died of hunger. When it was investigated, they found that the people were drinking soup. The commune members were in bad shape. Only after we reported it did the government give them grain. But the grain never made it into the hands of those who needed it. . . . The managers stole too. There was corruption among the village cadres.*[156]

Of the early 1960s, Xu Nini concludes, *People let out a long sigh of relief when Mao disbanded the dining halls.*[157] But villagers recall that the most difficult times began after that.[158] In Village T, the production brigade distributed the meager remaining stores of food, mostly coarse grains, to households. State grain that had been collected from farmers and sold back to the rural areas was also allotted to the brigade.[159] Zheng Xiuhua remembers, *Then every family [in Village Z] built their own kitchen stove again. . . . Even though the grain was distributed to families, you did not dare to eat more. If you ate more, you would have nothing left later.*[160] *How could it be enough?* asks He Gaizhen. *They gave you so little unified sales grain [that is, grain the state had purchased]. When the women cooked, they would put in more vegetables and less grain, so the grain could last longer.*[161]

The famine depressed fertility and birth rates, even as infant mortality and overall death rates rose. Irregular menses, infertility, and infant mortality became common as the hunger deepened.[162] Nationally the decline in mortality achieved since
1949 was reversed, rising in 1960 to forty-five deaths per thousand.[163] Judith Banister estimates that nationally, from 1958 to 1961, thirty million people died in excess of what would have been expected from a normal trend in death rates.[164]

The famine's severity varied by region.[165] Although several provinces bordering
it were in particularly dire straits, Shaanxi was not among the most affected areas;
from 1958 to 1962, it ranked eighteenth out of twenty-one provinces for "abnormal" deaths. These were estimated at 187,000 across the province, slightly more than
1 percent of the predisaster population. Nevertheless almost one-third of the province's 101 counties were retrospectively designated disaster areas, including the
home counties of Village T and Village Z, both in Shaannan, where abnormal deaths
accounted for 3.6 percent of the predisaster population.[166] In Village Z, many fell
ill, and a later investigation confirmed that at least seventy-two people had suffered
from edema. Most were cured after free treatment from the brigade, but some older
people died.[167] The situation was similar in Village G, at the poorer northern end
of Guanzhong.[168] In Village B, a richer community in the heart of Guanzhong, no
one died, but many went hungry.[169] Weinan Prefecture reported an increase in cases
of child exchange marriage and abandonment of the elderly.[170]

SURVIVAL STRATEGIES

In the famine years most families did not take to the road as refugees, as Shan Xiuzhen had done in earlier times.[171] Conditions in Shaanxi were better than those in
surrounding provinces,[172] and the state system of unified purchase and sales, work
points, residence registration, and marketing restrictions—the whole collective apparatus assembled during the 1950s—meant that opportunities for work and begging elsewhere were drastically curtailed. Instead farmers devised survival strategies closer to home.

As reports of agricultural success diverged from what the peasants saw every
day, and the food crisis worsened, people discontinued the breakneck pace of field
work. Liu Liujin remembers, *People [in Village Z] showed up to work but they didn't
put in any effort* [chu gong bu chu li]. *People killed a lot of time* [mo]. *So for the whole
year, you didn't work hard. You killed time by gossiping, biabiabia, and didn't put in
any effort. So we had little income from production.*[173] Zhou Guizhen observes, *People
[in Village B] went to the fields. They would sleep in the fields in order to get those
two work points. When they went home they would have nothing to eat.*[174]

Peasants devoted their spare time and energy to scavenging for food. Zhou
Guizhen observes, *Those few years [in Village B] were very troubling. We would take
the bark and leaves of the elm tree* [yushu] *and grind them into flour to eat.*[175] In Vil-

lage T, Li Liujin *had to figure out what to do if there wasn't enough to eat. Each day we had four ounces* [liang] *of grain. From the dining hall, we took some rice porridge back. My mother was frugal at home. We grew some vegetables in the garden. She would pick some vegetables. You couldn't fry them, because there was no oil. She would add a little salt and boil them until they were soft, get the porridge ready, and put the vegetables in and stir them. That way it was a bit drier and there was a bit more of it, and she would give it to her grandson and granddaughter to eat.*[176] In Village G, Xiang Jinwa fought with her husband about feeding their married daughter: *We had no food. We picked chive flowers by hand and mixed it with a little bit of flour. I married my child out. When I made something good, I called her back to eat with us. My husband was very stubborn and uneducated. He just remembered that her grain ration was no longer in our household, so he didn't let her eat here. I quarreled with my husband fiercely at home. I said, "I won't eat. Let me starve to death. I want my child to live."*[177] Small acts of generosity across village households were worthy of note, says Li Fenglian: *At that time, someone in my lane gave birth to a child in the middle of the night, and was very hungry. My mother gave her a piece of steamed bread from our house to eat. I still remember that.*[178]

With the onset of shortages, women's weaving again became a source of income that kept starvation at bay, as it had been for many households before 1949. Before the famine, women had stopped selling their homespun thread and cloth at local markets. Private production for the market was frowned upon, and the ongoing demands of Great Leap construction, field work, and domestic labor left little time for such activity. Now men from Guanzhong settlements took cloth woven by their wives north to the mountains to trade. Mountain settlements were poorer than the plains villages, and because they grew no cotton they were chronically short of clothing. But their scattered residences had made it impractical to organize dining halls or eliminate all private crop cultivation, so in this period of famine they had corn and sweet potatoes to sell—not as prized as wheat flour, but an improvement over the seeds and ground-up locust tree leaves that were available at home.[179]

He Gaizhen describes how women in Village Z took their local specialty of embroidered goods into the neighboring mountains, engaging in a trade that was nowhere acknowledged in official accounts of women's work. *People like our sister-in-law, who knew how to get along, made colorful thread and shoes and took them to the mountains to sell. Those who didn't know how to get along didn't have enough to eat. Only women did it. Able women went to the mountains to trade grain. Lazy women did not have enough food. Straw shoes could be traded for grain. In those days people in the mountains wore them to climb slopes. People dug up the garlic from the Zhouhe team to trade for grain. Straw shoes, garlic, colorful thread, children's shoes. Even the red silk fabric I am wearing could be traded for grain. Women did the trading. If you succeeded in trading for grain, you kept records by drawing strokes on the wall of the family you traded with. You kept the record and then your husband went to pick up the grain.*[180]

Aside from gathering wild vegetables and trading homespun cloth for grain, a third important source of sustenance was remittances from men who were working away from home. Zhou Guizhen's husband, a schoolteacher in a township near Village B, saved a bit of his wages to buy grain tickets, which could be redeemed for flour when he came home on periodic visits.[181] In the villages, those who worked in cooperative-run handicrafts and were paid a salary did not suffer as much privation as their neighbors. The money earned by He Gaizhen's husband, a mat maker in the Village Z co-op, allowed her to buy supplementary biscuits in the cooperative to feed her children.[182] Nonagricultural income from men who had left the fields remained, as it had been before 1949, a crucial resource for family survival.

In the wake of the Leap's failure, some of its most ambitious experiments were dismantled.[183] Communes remained the highest unit of rural organization, but many were subdivided. The market town of Village Z, for instance, was divided into six smaller units by 1962. Brigades and later their subunit teams became the basic accounting unit according to which grain quotas were figured and work points were distributed.[184] Villagers were permitted to cultivate small family plots to grow turnips, cabbage, garlic, corn, and wheat for their own consumption.[185] By about 1963, people remember, life began to get better, although nationally malnutrition, rickets, and other problems were still being reported.[186]

In Village Z, production gradually returned to normal. As before the Leap, normalcy was shaped by the constraints of more people than land and low returns from the crops. Each year, grain was sold to the state and cash was distributed to the villagers according to the number of work points they had earned. In years of bumper harvest, a day's labor was worth less than 0.5 yuan, and in years of bad harvests the amount sank to 0.2 yuan. The brigade developed a few small-scale sidelines—grain milling, medicinal herbs—to augment the collective income. Experiments with cotton cultivation were ended, and cloth was brought in from Guanzhong, because the local land was needed for grain. An adult's annual grain needs were calculated at one *jin* per day, further indication that the fifteen to twenty *jin* per month allocated during the three hard years had been drastically inadequate.

CAMPAIGN TEMPORALITY
AND THE WRINKLE IN TIME

When women, particularly those who were not village activists, talk about the hardships of the famine that followed the Great Leap, they seldom offer direct commentary on state policy. Instead they recount their loss of enthusiasm for Great Leap–style agriculture, the difficulties of feeding family members, and their concern about children. Unlike *dundian* and local cadres, ordinary village women remembered the dining hall years not as a disastrous error in national policy, but as a local event. A fragment of conversation between a Village Z woman and Gao Xiao-xian captures this framework for memory:

Gao Xiaoxian: *How many meals a day did you eat in the dining halls?*

Shi Ranwa: *Two meals. In homes here, all the stoves had been smashed. You weren't permitted to cook at home. The grain and everything else was stored in the dining halls. It was very common to eat in the dining halls.*

Gao Xiaoxian: *Yes, it was common. The whole nation was eating in dining halls.*

Shi Ranwa: *Everyone was?*[187]

This woman's genuine surprise suggests that in spite of an unprecedented Party-state attempt to link local efforts to national progress, parts of the rural population understood the dining halls as a local affliction, not as the springboard for a nationwide leap into communism. Nor has the rural Shaanxi population been touched by the late twentieth-century discussion among Chinese intellectuals about the causes of the Great Leap disaster and the role of the dining halls in exacerbating food shortages. For village women, the time of the dining halls remains, as it was in the late 1950s, a deeply personal and painful story. It marked the end of women's enthusiasm for collectivization, and no further stories of transformation are told about the remaining years of the collective.

How women understand the Great Leap and the famine must be sought both in the events they chose to narrate and those that they have confused, rearranged, or forgotten outright. In Village B, in the penumbra of a labor model such as Cao Zhu-xiang, all the women we interviewed could recite the categories of campaign time without much deviation. But we cannot assume uniformity of memory across locales. When we interviewed in Village Z, in the mountains of southeastern Shaanxi near the provincial border, we found a memoryscape marked by forgetting.[188]

Memory in the mountains is not less vivid than that in the flatlands. As we have seen, people talk of pre-Liberation bandits, of songs from the Marriage Law campaigns, of spinning and weaving and childbearing and the dining halls. Yet in Village Z, which was neither a labor model's home like Village B nor an "advanced" site like Village T, one woman after another recited to us a curiously foreshortened story. Liberation, they said, was followed by collectivization, then by the dining halls. Subsequently, as one woman put it, *because the dining halls didn't work out so well, after a year or two the land was redistributed to households, and things have been getting better ever since.*

This startled us the first time we heard it, because the dining halls were closed in 1959 or 1960, but land was not contracted out to households until the early 1980s. Subsequently, several other women told us a version of this story unprompted, corroborated by passers-by or other household members. Some said that land went to the households immediately after the dining halls disbanded; others said it happened four or five years later; still others fixed the date at 1971. In this narration, as many as two decades had gone missing, taking with them the entire Cultural Revolution and most of the history of collective agriculture. We were witnessing, to borrow a phrase from the children's author Madeleine L'Engle, a wrinkle in time.[189]

How were we to understand this? Perhaps, we thought, the women of Village Z were simply reporting a factual change in production arrangements. Because of the disastrous failure of Great Leap policies, Dali Yang has found that household contracting of agricultural production "was widely adopted throughout the country without central approval in the early 1960s" and persisted into the middle of the decade in spite of central opposition.[190] It is certainly possible that Village Z land was contracted out to households for a period in the wake of the Great Leap. The village is in a remote area near the mountains, where the road from the county seat—the link to higher political authority—washes out after every rainstorm. Given the location of this village, we wondered, maybe the villagers just never got around to recollectivizing, and no one ever noticed? As more people told us this story of household distribution of land,[191] we searched frantically through the scant surviving village records to see whether Village Z had in fact begun the economic reforms two decades earlier than the rest of China. But the village has no records of what happened to local land arrangements in the early 1960s.[192] The men who might have presided over such a measure are dead, and the women's memories are ambiguous. If land was returned to the households for a few years, why does no one mention any struggle attendant upon the return of control to the collective? Why, instead, do they narrate the major events of their lives as though land never returned to the collective at all?

Eventually, on our nightly walks as far up and down the mountain roads as we could get before dark, Gao Xiaoxian told me that she thought we were making a mistake. In an attempt to discern the categories through which these women understood their own experience, we had been trying to say as little as possible about the signal events of campaign time. Instead we had asked people in Village Z to tell us about their lives without providing any categories at all. In addition to the wrinkle in time, this had produced a number of confusing and comical results. Our first interview that year, with our village landlady, mainly elicited a story of how she had been cheated by an acquaintance twelve years earlier, in the mid-1980s. Her account of the 1950s featured a hopelessly scrambled sequencing of events. Another interview, with a man who had formerly been the brigade accountant, sounded like a text about the correct and glorious leadership of the Communist Party. His oration was delivered at a (slow) speed more appropriate for a language laboratory tape than an interview; my one consolation was that I could understand each and every word. Our experiment with completely open-ended interviews, we concluded, was a spectacular and informative failure. Faced with inchoate rambling, extended complaints about events far more recent than the 1950s, and now disappearing decades, we admitted to ourselves that by not imposing categories we were asking the women of Village Z to create a chronologically ordered narrative structure of their lives when they were not in the habit of doing so.

Over the next few days we began to ask tentative questions about the Cultural Revolution and the national campaign in which all agricultural units were exhorted to learn from the model Dazhai farming brigade—that is, about the 1960s and 1970s. In short order, it became apparent that people were still being paid work points for work in collective fields in the 1970s. Collectivization had lasted into the 1980s, and people remembered, when asked, many details of its operation. Prompted by our questions about specific policies and social arrangements, the vanished decades reappeared.

Yet troubling questions remain about the persistent absence of these decades from individual and shared narratives of village history. This wrinkle in time, like the one in L'Engle's story, was a telescoping of chronology and event. What counts as an event? Did these women remember only events like the advent of dining halls that rearranged their domestic space? Perhaps individual and shared memory highlighted events that had a profound personal effect: receiving land twice, in the 1950s and sometime later. Were people reading the longer-lasting transformations of the reform era back into the earlier past, providing a genealogy for household cultivation, which has once again become the taken-for-granted organization of rural life? Were the years of collective agriculture after the Great Leap so uneventful that they did not merit unsolicited mention? Would women rather forget the years of past poverty? Or was the collective period too crammed with childbearing, field work, and unpaid, invisible reproductive labor of all sorts to linger in memory as more than an exhausting blur of indeterminate length? Forgetting and misremembering, as some of the best oral history scholars have noted, are themselves an interpretation.[193] Our task, still ongoing, is to make that interpretation explicit, and then to raise questions about its ambiguities, some of which we cannot answer.

In the three other villages where we did extended interviewing, women did not telescope entire decades of collective life in such a dramatic fashion.[194] But in Village G, the ways that women used the terms "old society" and "new society" bear mentioning. "Liberation," in the widely used parlance introduced by the Party-state, referred to 1949. Anything before that was conventionally denoted as the "old society"; anything later was the "new society." In the stories of Village G women, however, the "new society" began after the dining halls disbanded, the worst of the food shortages passed, and family plots were permitted. It followed the "time of low allotments and food substitutes." *When we got to the new society, only then did life get better* is a statement perfectly compatible with the logics of campaign time—but not when it is explained as beginning in the 1970s rather than 1949, as in *The new society started from the time when we were learning from Dazhai and recording work points.* And when a woman sings us a song extolling the virtues of free-choice marriage and marriage licenses from the county government, and then describes it as a song of the "old society," it only reinforces the point that all of the signposts of campaign time are movable in memory's terrain.[195]

Disruptive and disturbing as the Great Leap was, terrible as the years of low allotment and hunger were, for Shaanxi villagers they have not left the classic marks of trauma, which may remain unvoiced because of the unbearable psychic cost entailed.[196] The years before the 1949 Liberation, with their accumulated losses and desperate dilemmas, might once have been experienced as trauma. But one important aspect of the state effect is that through many years of public approbation for speaking bitterness, the trauma of prerevolutionary life has been articulated repeatedly and shaped by available language. Then it has been consigned to the past, set up as a touchstone against which all subsequent events are to be measured. This, in turn, may have had the effect of demoting subsequent events, such as the Great Leap famine, which might otherwise have attained the status of trauma. For many years, the Great Leap and its aftermath were forbidden subjects, and they remain politically sensitive nationally. In Shaanxi villages, however, far from being unarticulable, the Great Leap is talked about, remembered sharply, and moved around so as to rearrange the remembered chronology of the revolution. Speaking bitterness was a state-sponsored practice firmly intended to be directed at the prerevolutionary past, and the Leap is often talked about as though it were part of that past— the "old society." Women do not directly blame the Party-state for the years of low allotments and food substitution, but they surely have not forgotten those years.

What fades in memory is not the Great Leap or the famine, but the heft and length of the years that follow. Although village women do not say so, these are precisely the years in which their daily participation in agriculture went from a short-term crisis management measure to an unremarkable and arduous feature of daily life. The years after the Great Leap were also the most intensive years of child rearing for many of the women we interviewed. On the agricultural front, they were years of relative stability but not per capita growth, years unleavened by visionary promises of poverty's end. Perhaps it is not surprising that a brief and disastrous utopian moment has left sharper traces than the long period of stasis that followed. It is across that gulf, now almost half a century long, that women regard their youth from the vantage point of old age in the reform economy.

HIDDEN ACCUMULATION

One important change not articulated in any state slogan, but nonetheless central to the state's economic strategy since about 1960, is the feminization of agriculture in Shaanxi.[197] Usually described as a feature of the post-Mao reforms, it began in

Shaanxi almost three decades earlier.[198] Unlike steel smelting, collective dining halls, and the "exaggeration wind," the widespread mobilization of women into farming outlasted the Leap and the subsequent famine. Some men took up supervisory or technical positions in the fields. Others did not leave the villages, but worked in small-scale collective industry.[199] Still others lived mostly in the cities from the 1970s on, as temporary contract workers. Increasingly, farming was done by women— during the day. Nights were spent on domestic work.

Referring to the 1970s slogan that farmers should learn from the model agricultural brigade Dazhai, one sardonic saying in Shaanxi ran: *The young [male] laborers are looking for extra money, [while] women and children are learning from Dazhai.* A former Women's Federation official put it wryly: *Women did not hold up half the sky; in agricultural production, they held up more than half: 70 to 80 percent of the sky. They were the main force in agricultural production.*[200] Women's move into the fields was much-heralded, but the departure of men and the overall feminization of agriculture were not.

Women's move into agriculture, with no diminution in the burden of domestic labor and an increase in the number of surviving children, may account for some of the wrinkles in memory and blurring of detail with which they narrate the post-famine years. After the three hard years, the gendered landscape of memory is largely featureless until the early 1980s. But in addition to the clues this provides about the course of socialist construction and its differentiated effects, the feminization of agriculture is important for another reason, one of national importance. Agriculture was the main sector that the Maoist economy depended on to generate a surplus to fund industrialization, a process that the PRC scholar Wen Tiejun has dubbed "State Capitalist Primitive Accumulation."[201] The gendered division of labor that underwrote this accumulation, by assigning field work to women in addition to domestic tasks, is notably absent from discussions of the collective period across the political spectrum. Women's labor in the fields freed men, not only to work on the short-lived and often ill-fated projects of the Great Leap, but also to develop small-scale rural industries in the years that followed. Women were also a significant component of what economists call "human capital"—uncompensated at home, undercompensated in the fields, and crucial to economic development in both domains. Given the conditions in rural Shaanxi, perhaps it is time to explore the possibility that rural women were the linchpin of Chinese economic development under Mao, in turn laying the groundwork for the post-Mao economic boom that has so dominated contemporary news coverage of China. Some significant portion of "State Capitalist Primitive Accumulation" was hidden accumulation, carried out in the years when basic farming and the tending of crucial state-required crops such as cotton became in large part women's work. Hidden too was the domestic labor performed by these industrious accumulators, though the traces remain in memories of sleep deprivation and needlework at night.

Suggesting that women's role in agriculture be placed front and center is not a claim for a single new key explanatory factor for development during the collective era; there is no single key.[202] Perhaps, however, we should ask not only "Did Chinese women have a revolution?" but also "Would China's revolution have been possible without the visible and invisible labor of Chinese women?" What happens to our story of turning points in Chinese history, and history more generally, if we no longer approach gender as an enlivening supplement, but instead put it at the heart of the story?

Narrator

I always taught my two grandsons and granddaughter, "Your grandma was the most pitiful one. . . . At that time, I even hated to throw away a small amount of leftover and burned rice. I would soak it in hot water or boil it with some vegetables and eat it. Now you kids, even with the food left from breakfast, such as white rice, will say, 'Grandma, throw it away. I can't eat it.' If it is left over from last night or the day before, maybe you can't eat it. But this is only from breakfast. 'How can people eat this? Grandma, you will be sick after you eat this.'" They have a point. But we people from the 1950s lived such an awful life. My husband always criticizes me: "You son of a turtle, you must have died from hunger in a former life. You hate to waste even a kernel of grain."[1]

Aging women narrate their childhood, youth, and middle years from the vantage point of the present. Their longevity, self-understanding, and economic vulnerability are shaped by gender, just as their laboring lives were during the collective period. They highlight what they feel to be their enduring virtues, their important achievements, and their most deeply harbored grievances. Each story is an interpretation, encoded not just in what is remembered, forgotten, and rearranged, but also in pacing, emphasis, and tonality, none of which survives the conversion to textual form intact. Deeply held and carefully crafted, these interpretations are produced at a specific moment for particular listeners. They are shaped by who the interviewers are, by the particular clarity of the women's memories of youth, by what we ask and are prepared to hear, by how the aging narrator may be feeling that day, and by the family and community she imagines as listeners.

The moment when those stories can still be heard is almost over. Zhang Qiuxiang died in 2000, Shan Xiuzhen in 2006,[2] Cao Zhuxiang in 2008. Qiao Yindi, whose story of riding by truck to Xinjiang in the 1950s opens chapter 5, suffered a stroke and could barely speak when I returned to Village G to interview her again in 2004. Women in several villages were weaving their funeral clothes or preparing their coffins. But still, for the moment, they talk.

Their stories of youth are intertwined with memories of revolution. Even those who misremember the stages of collectivization, or rename major government campaigns, often have vivid memories of moments in the early 1950s when they sang about free-choice marriage, performed in a local opera, or went door-to-door during the fall harvest mobilizing their neighbors to work a night shift at the winnowing ground. They recall the initial revolutionary moment as a setting for stories of their own enthusiasm and possibility.

That moment is succeeded, all too often, by a blurred memory of decades in which political changes were overshadowed by the demands of burgeoning families, and in which revolution, though never repudiated, could no longer be associated with expanded possibilities. Here they remember their continued state of being "pitiful" and worn down by domestic work and poverty, their ability to maintain family harmony even when their patience was tried by lazy parents-in-law, and their capacity for hard work and competent management of scarce family resources. These are memories of personal virtue, often accompanied by the observation that their children and grandchildren neither appreciate their accomplishments nor would be capable of equaling them if called upon to do so.

Village women's memories are markedly gendered, but not all in the same way. Labor models recall their contributions to building socialism, particularly their leadership in women's cotton cultivation. Former women's chairs remember the difficult process of mobilizing women for field work, and later the bitter task of explaining and implementing an unpopular birth planning policy. Ordinary village women narrate their own pasts with the household at the center. In their stories, the domestic work so scandalously absent from most official documents of the collective period is given its due.

Finally, in talking about the present, these elderly (often widowed) women point to the ironies and contradictions of the post-Mao economic reforms, which have once again transformed the countryside. Announcing that they had made a mistake in extending public ownership too far too fast in the countryside, from the early 1980s state officials have presided over a return to family farming, based on long-term inheritable leases rather than private ownership, and the dismantling of most features of the collective. The results are mixed and complex: improvement in rural living standards, large-scale migration of young rural people to the cities, encroachment of industry on rural lands, and emerging inequalities among regions and households and between the urban and rural sectors.

These rural women have entered old age in an era marked by increases in both prosperity and insecurity. In some respects, their stories are striking for their optimism. They applaud many aspects of the economic reforms that have reshaped rural areas since 1982,[3] explaining in very concrete terms that life is materially much better now than it was in the 1950s. They do not regret the passing of the collectives. And yet they do not repudiate them, either. When women recall collective labor, they are looking back over the more than twenty years since collectivization ended. The experiment's failures, the dissatisfactions many felt with its long years of flat living standards and numerous aggravations, are muted now. People are not settling accounts with the collective period anymore, and often the details of how the program worked are no longer important to them, if they ever were. Many women tell a story in which life got better twice, once in the 1950s and again in the 1980s. In this story, collectivization and decollectivization do not contradict each other; both count as progress. Even as the events they recount suggest the massive discontinuities and disruptions in official activity since 1949, these women tell a story marked by generalized material improvement.

Nevertheless the demise of the collective and the social changes intensified by the reforms have marked the old age of rural women in disturbing ways. They speak to us, and through us also address others, in the face of massive indifference.

The Chinese Constitution mandates that children support their aging parents and forbids maltreatment of old people.[4] The economic pressures of the current reform era, however, as well as decades of cumulative change in household arrangements, have undermined the position of aging parents. As their children have married, formed new households, struggled and not always succeeded in an increasingly competitive market, some of these older women have suffered from elder neglect, even elder abuse, that would probably—we cannot be certain—have been unacceptable in the collective era.

The linchpin in rural elder care has long been the filial daughter-in-law. Women who married in the 1950s and 1960s by and large continued to fulfill that role. When they speak of those years, the care they provided for in-laws remains central to their narrations of a virtuous self. But now that it is their turn to enjoy the perquisites of the mother-in-law—respect and material support—social expectations have changed. Their daughters-in-law and sons prefer conjugal intimacy and a prosperous "small household" to one constrained by the demands of elder care. Many elderly women are widows, and the number "eating alone"—that is, responsible for their own household budget—is striking. In many cases material support from sons, especially those in economic trouble, is intermittent, insufficient, or nonexistent. Even when the sons and their families are living in the same compound, the elderly parent may have to fend for herself. Elderly widows and widowers who seek to establish a new household by remarrying may find their matches opposed by grown children who fear loss of family property. Even as they approve the relative abundance of material goods in the present, many old women see their own access to such goods limited by local poverty and changing family values.

Without pathos or much self-pity about the infirmities of old age,[5] their stories about the 1950s remonstrate with family members and a wider society that depended on, expected, yet generally failed to recognize much of their labor, and that now increasingly regards them as a burden. These stories remind us that rural socialist construction relied on women's heroic work in the cotton fields and their systematically occluded domestic labor as well. They suggest that just as socialism was profoundly gendered, so is the memory of its layered transformations, difficulties, and meanings.

This chapter explores the shared progress narrative of aging rural women, wherein they fashion a heroic and virtuous past to redeem a diminished present. It also traces the new visibility of the domestic realm in the reform era. The domestic realm is no longer a site of unremunerated labor. In one of the reform's less salutary changes, it has become a realm of marginalization for many elderly women. Recounting stories women tell about the recent past, this final chapter highlights the ongoing practices by which they continue to claim space for themselves.

PROGRESS

As women tell it, the revolution brought new possibilities. Not by changing the work women did every day, for women had always worked. Not even by attacking old customs: maintaining her widowhood brought an emergent leader like Cao Zhuxiang nothing but respect. Rather the revolution changed the environment in which rural women worked. It removed some of the worst threats to safety and livelihood: conscripting armies and marauding soldiers. It cushioned the effects of chronic shortage, providing seed grain and short-term loans in the slack season. In the 1950s, women joined in an ambitious attempt to construct a socialist modernity. Many new practices emerged to create the state effect, the production and reproduction of a blurry zone of difference between state and society that reordered village space and time and the lives of rural women in unprecedented ways. A closer look at this optimistic narrative of progress, however, suggests that its cheery presentation encompasses other themes, each of them critical, ambivalent, and inflected by gender.

The first theme concerns state policies about land tenure. "Life got better twice" is not an unending story of progress but a story of progress with two nodes, remarkably similar in their effect on farmers: the distribution of land to households in the early 1950s land reform, and the contracting of land to households in the early 1980s reforms. In both cases, households are the primary production unit. This version of progress writes out collectivization.

The two moments of land distribution (1950s and 1980s) are not identical, even in memory. The women's stories make it clear that the first moment was one of great material instability. And they do talk about the formation of mutual aid groups and lower producers' cooperatives with approval, if not affection, as arrangements that improved their daily lives. But the benefits that collectivization wrought in its early moments are not enough to redeem the Great Leap Forward, the years of disruption, and the material stagnation that followed. Those years are not featured in the optimistic narrative of progress recounted by these rural women.

Instead, when they sum up the most important moments of change, the two conjunctures when they received land stand out. The first distribution marks an end to political chaos (a shared memory) and family vulnerability (an individual and often painful memory). It brings to a close a stage of life (childhood or young adulthood, depending on their age) and opens up a horizon of optimistic development. In narrating the land reform, women look both backward and forward. In describing the second distribution, they look only forward. Our interviewees do not talk about the post-Mao reforms as bringing a bad interlude to an end.[6] Rather they mark the reforms as a moment when access to material goods became much easier. They make this change concrete, for example, by comparing the number of clothing items and household goods they received at marriage with those received by their daughters, daughters-in-law, or granddaughters. When she married in the late 1940s, Village B resident Wang Xiqin recalls, *My natal family made a quilt for me. My husband's family also made a quilt. My children's father took a quilt with him when he went out to work, leaving only one quilt at home. Now their father and I have five or six quilts. My daughter-in-law has more than ten quilts. How can the early days compare with this?*[7] Wang Xiqin understands these material improvements to be inseparable from a rise in the status of women. *I can bring money home and use it now. In the early days when someone brought money home, you didn't dare to spend it as you pleased. I am in charge of the household in my family. Before, it was not your turn. . . . Now my words count in the family. Even giving gifts to relatives, we give them whatever I decide. Did you dare to do so in the early days? When someone in my natal family had a birthday, I steamed several pieces of bread. My father-in-law threw them away and didn't allow me to go out the door.*[8] Such descriptions reflect the fact that women's authority in the family increased as they bore children and aged, but the more general rise in the status of daughters-in-law is important here as well.[9]

A second theme in the progress narrative involves features of the 1950s not directly linked to land tenure that women understand as beneficial to them: the Marriage Law, literacy classes, an end to marauders, the ability to go to meetings and sing opera and socialize with people other than close kin. For many of them, the early 1950s broadened their social worlds in ways that reverberated through the succeeding decades, motivating them to shoulder positions of responsibility long after the revolution's luster had faded. For some, the availability of tubal ligations in the early 1970s and the increased access to education for their children in the

1960s and 1970s are important points in a story of personal relief, accomplishment, or satisfaction. Their story is inflected by gender, in that these measures of progress are less dramatic or salient for men.

This narrative of unending progress also contains old injuries. In his beautifully crafted 1996 ethnography of the Kongs of Dachuan, *The Temple of Memories,* Jun Jing reminds us that the national politics of remembrance in post-Mao China involves tragic memories of the Great Leap Forward and the Cultural Revolution that cannot be completely acknowledged. "At the local level," he writes, "memories of past suffering are often repressed lest they open old wounds and threaten the existing order of social relations."[10] Although the village women whose stories are told here did not suffer the worst of the Great Leap famine, it was a time associated with significant hardship. The Cultural Revolution had a more sustained impact in urban areas than in the countryside, but in central and south Shaanxi many villages were touched directly by political struggle, attacks on local cadres, and violence.[11] Women cadres and labor models were not exempt. In Cao Zhuxiang's village, the Cultural Revolution saw clashes between locals and refugees who had been resettled there when they were displaced by reservoir construction. Zhou Guizhen, Zhuxiang's protégée and a village cadre, once again came under attack by the reservoir migrants. Zhuxiang herself was confronted with allegations, eventually disproved, that she had driven a man in the village to suicide: *They wanted to say that the old lady forced him to jump in the well. She got so angry that she spat blood on the spot.*[12] It was during this time that Zhang Qiuxiang was detained as a counterrevolutionary until, in her telling, Zhou Enlai personally intervened to free her.[13]

Although intense Cultural Revolution activity was brief in rural areas, it affected how women understood the early years of socialism that preceded it. The Cultural Revolution strengthened their attachment to the achievements and recognition they had enjoyed in the 1950s. They retold stories of the 1950s to deflect the accusations hurled at them during the Cultural Revolution, and have continued to tell them in the reform era, in response to those (often long gone) who once attacked them. In Village T, Li Liujin remembers her sense of injury and outrage: *I had been working so hard for more than ten years. I didn't have anything to be ashamed of. What did they say about me? They said some bad things, damn them. They said that I held my kid and said, "The car runs dududu, inside sits a big fat pig"* [qiche zoule dududu, wu (na) litou zuode dafeizhu]. *Hnh. That I was insulting the people in the car. They made this up about you. So I couldn't accept this kind of thing. I remember it was weeding season, July. We went to the field to pull weeds and I was called back. They made a pointed hat for me. Hnh, it was very tall, more than one meter, and they put it on my head. Aiya! I was very unhappy. I sat on the bank of Northern Ditch. I said, I'll just bury my head in the water and die. But my second thought was that I had two kids, one born in 1962, the other in 1964. If I died, the two children would be done for, too. I said, As long as I have my life I'll live on, one step at a time. So I didn't say anything,*

*but I was crying. I did not say, For all those years since the 1950s, I have been work-
ing very hard day and night. Any task arranged by the higher levels, at the lower levels I resolutely completed it. Even after the meetings at night, I would pass along the
messages to everyone, one at a time. I always worked so hard, and when they gave me
this pointed hat to wear, I couldn't accept it. I could only cry. I didn't say anything.*

*They paraded us all the way to Xiajia'an and then to Zhoujiaping. My nephew was
in a store. He came out and took a look. "Aiya, what is my aunt doing there?" He went
right back into the store, crying. Straight until I got home, I didn't open my mouth. As
soon as I took off the pointed hat, I lay on the bed and cried. I said to myself, Is this
my reward for working so hard for so many years? In the end, my title as women's
chair was even revoked. At the time, I made up my mind: not only will I not do anything for the Communist Party anymore, but my son and my grandson won't either.
Nothing good comes of it. It was like this from 1966 to 1967. It let up for the three years
1967 to 1969.*

*In 1969 came the policy of "Put down your burden, start the machine" [fangxia
baofu, kaidong jiqi]. If you had been wronged, they called it "Put down your burden." They wanted you to complain about any injustice or bitterness you had suffered.
So I talked about my bitterness, crying and talking for a whole morning. I talked about
it from beginning to end, how I had been wrongly accused, how I had worked as a
cadre, how hard I had worked, what I had done. After I spoke I felt a bit better. After
the movement ended, they wanted me to be the women's chair. "I won't do it." They
brought it up again and I wouldn't do it. In the end, they opened my file, filled out
the forms for me according to the information in my file, and reported to the higher
levels that I was appointed as women's chair. They spent time persuading me. They
cleared my name, saying that this incident had never happened. From 1969, I was a
women's chair again until 1973. In 1973, people came down from the county to reorganize. After the reorganization, I was selected as deputy Party secretary, and I was
in that position until 1984.*

*That was the right thing to do. You cannot just take the individual into account.
Individuality should be subordinated to the Party. It wouldn't work if you asked the
Party to subordinate itself to you as an individual. The most important thing should
be the major national issues. So in the end, I went back to working hard for them.*[14]

In the case of the renowned labor model Shan Xiuzhen, her Cultural Revolution
travails pushed her to uncover a hidden piece of family history that had not been
spoken of during the land reform of the early 1950s. One day in 1966 she found
that the class label she had been assigned during the land reform—lower-middle
peasant—had been called into question. Suddenly her entire history as a revolutionary woman leader was open to repudiation: *Even we women were bullied. Women
were so pitiful. At night in the last month of the year, women holding babies in their
arms had to write big-character posters or they couldn't get out of the school. It was
snowing. I felt that these sisters were too pitiful.*

Along the road you passed to come here, there were posters pasted everywhere, from the road to my door. The only place they didn't paste them was on my body. They said I was a person in power who was taking the capitalist road. I was not allowed to enter the gate of the brigade from 1966 to 1967. I was not allowed to go to some places. I was asked to work in the fields all day long. "Your history is unclear, you are a capitalist person in power"—that is what the big-character posters said about me. They said, "You are a counterrevolutionary. Your history is not clear. You were an escaped landlord."

In one day, so many big-character posters about my husband's family background came out. One big-character poster said Americans had been to my house in the old society. "Ai," I said, "in the old society, I was not President Jiang Jieshi, why would Americans come to my house?" But the big-character poster said it. I felt that this was no good. I had to find out the history of my husband's family.

I asked an old man in his nineties, who was called Old Wansheng. I said, "Uncle, where did my husband's father come from? Who else was in the Dong family? The big-character posters say I am a landlord who slipped through the net in Liquan and fled here." I said, "I have worked for a landlord, but I am not a landlord." I said to Uncle Wansheng, "I am not against the big-character posters. That is Marxism. Those are Marxist big-character posters." I said, "Don't be afraid. You tell me. I won't go to the teachers in the school."

Uncle Wansheng asked me, "Child, why do you ask about these things?" I said, "Because I don't know about it. When we first came back here [in the 1930s, after crossing the Qinling Mountain as famine refugees], we didn't even have chopsticks and a bowl here. Where did our eight and a half mu of land come from? The land is first-class land. My mother-in-law's natal family was farming the land when we got here."

He said, "That eight and a half mu of land is the price for the life of your husband's grandpa. Your grandpa worked in the Liu family. At the Spring Festival, they owed your grandpa two strings of copper cash. He went to ask for the money. They didn't give him the money; instead they beat him. Your grandpa got angry and went up to the old house and got some opium. He drank it and died."

Aiya, at that moment it was as though a knife had pierced my heart. I thought about how pitiful people of earlier generations in my family were. [Cries.] How the old society stole their lives away one at a time! Aiya, my heart hurt so much. Uncle Wansheng said, "That's the price for your grandpa's life. There were village regulations in the old society. 'He worked for you till the Spring Festival. He had a wife and children. You didn't give him money. You beat him and caused his death, tormented him.'" As soon as my grandfather was buried, the land was given to the family in payment for his life.

That is how I became clear about the history of the earlier generations. I bought several big white sheets of paper. I stole off quietly to the school at night to ask Teacher Song to write for me. I wanted the broad masses, the poor and lower-middle peasants, to know me, to know what kind of person I was. Whether I was a landlord who had slipped through the net, or one whose ancestors had had their lives cut short in the old society. Nobody said anything after the big-character poster came out. Nobody opposed it.[15]

Even before Shan Xiuzhen was fully cleared, she found herself once again leading women to bring in the harvest while the men went off to make cultural revolution. *The two main cadres were overthrown at that time. Only the accountant and I were left. We two consulted. All the men in the team ran off to Tongguan to "beat, smash, and loot"* [dazaqiang].[16] *I held a meeting for the women. I said, "We shouldn't go with them. There are more than a thousand people here, old people and kids. If we don't gather in the crops, we will have nothing to eat." The women were great. Everyone harvested the wheat, hoed the field, and planted cotton. I said, "Let's try to make a good showing. Let's plant the crops well." As a result, in 1966 and 1967 our brigade had bumper harvests, and we got more food grain.*[17]

Such tales remind us that everything we learn about the 1950s from oral narratives is marked not only by the passage of time, but by subsequent events that shape how women look back on their early years as leaders. Li Liujin and Shan Xiuzhen, scorned and then rehabilitated, resumed leadership responsibilities, buoyed in part by a sense of self formed in the activist years of the 1950s. Perhaps they also understood that there was no other place to stand: their relationships and interests lay with their communities even when some community members turned on them.

The unified story line of "forward march" narrated by rural women is itself full of elisions, which reappear in the details of the stories. Yet the plot does march forward. It may be that the most discernible trace of the Maoist state in Chinese villages today is found in the pervasiveness of the motif of progress.[18] Villagers counted both collectivization and the economic reforms as achievements of the Party-state, even as they included details of personal disappointment, unfulfilled longings, and contemporary pain. Those among our interviewees who once served as cadres continued to concern themselves with the question of national progress. They worried about the decrease in local Party activity and a lack of attention to woman-work.[19] Shan Xiuzhen fretted about a decline in social order and public security, as well as a growing drug problem that had come to Tongguan County along with prosperity from a recently discovered gold mine.[20] Long after the Party-state ceased to require their services, they continued to describe the state effect in their own villages, although the production of a state-society line no longer passed through them or the organizations (Women's Federation, production team) to which they had devoted their adult political lives.

Although the vision of a socialist modernity now has been abandoned in all but name, its traces remain in the memories of individual labor heroines, and in the stories farmers tell, the expectations they now take for granted, about how life is supposed to be. It is precisely those expectations—that life will get better materially, that opportunities will continue to broaden—that have fueled enthusiasm and support for the reforms. Those expectations may also contribute to the fury animating recent peasant protests in places where the reforms have stalled, gone awry, or produced corruption and local tyranny.[21]

ERUPTION OF THE DOMESTIC
AND EXCLUSION OF THE AGED

The new visions of modernity endorsed by higher levels of the Party-state in the 1980s accelerated a change in rural households that had begun during the collective period. When collectivization abrogated land inheritance rights in the 1950s, it began to erode the previous practice in which aging parents lived with their married sons in a multigenerational household. It became customary for young married couples to reside with the husband's parents only until they had their first few children, after which they separated out.[22] As chapter 7 suggested, many grandparents were just as happy not to be living under the same roof with large broods of grandchildren needing care and economic support.

At the end of the twentieth century, political activism was by and large a thing of the past in Shaanxi villages. Able-bodied young women of the 1950s generation had joined struggle meetings against landlords, danced the *yangge,* and led women's production groups. Half a century later, their daughters and granddaughters decamped to seek employment in Xi'an, coastal towns and cities, and in some cases foreign lands.[23] A woman's participation in choosing her husband was no longer controversial. Child brides, arranged marriages, and long years of subservience to a tyrannical mother-in-law were no longer accepted as the norm. Couples who remained in the villages normally formed their own households at marriage or soon thereafter. The improved supply of consumer goods and generally rising incomes obviated the need for needlework or grain winnowing at night.

With the reforms, the nuclear family household emerged into public discussion as one sign of a modernity that socialism was now thought to have delayed. Once neglected, the domestic space became everywhere celebrated. It appeared in state writings, emergent social science, and popular discourse as the location of consumption and the repository of affect. It also became a sanctioned location for economic production and the creation of wealth, as evidenced in the state's periodic campaigns to publicize newly rich households. The household became one of the places where Party-state leaders vocalized fantasies of increasing prosperity for all. If the domestic was celebrated as a private realm, it was nevertheless essential to public dreams.[24]

Although "the domestic" was now considered private, "the private" was not located only within the physical confines of household space.[25] "The private" has taken on new meanings in the reform era, from state endorsements of private enterprise to celebrations of intimate and affective life in a newly flourishing popular culture. In cities, new forms of public intimacy, including but not limited to call-in hotlines and karaoke bars, are redefining the contours of private life, and the proliferation of rural dance halls and entertainment venues in boomtown county seats suggests that similar redefinitions may become more pervasive in the countryside as well. Much writing about contemporary China links the private and the domestic as the return of two repressed "natural" desires: for capitalism on the one hand and a haven in a heartless world on the other.[26]

In one of the revolution's bitter ironies, however, the domestic realm has been reconfigured in a form that excludes and penalizes the older women who kept it running in the years of its public invisibility. Some are in dire circumstances. Having taken dutiful care of their husbands' parents, they now find themselves, as they age, discarded by their own grown and married children, who are caught up in the attractions of a new definition of modernity centered on the acquisitive, ambitious, and consuming family unit. These adult children are responding as well to unprecedented economic pressures, confronting the possibility that the ambient prosperity will never be accessible to them.

Some elderly women complain of sons denying them support or refusing to speak to them, sons whose wives won't let them give their mothers grain, sons who curse and beat their parents, sons they occasionally take to court to sue for support. They address these contemporary situations of pain and hardship in various ways. They recount their exemplary conduct and compare themselves favorably to succeeding generations of women, as Li Liujin does in Village T: *Aiya, in the 1950s women lived difficult lives and knew the value of salt and rice. These women nowadays, I sometimes laugh, those in their twenties and thirties, they are in the honey pot. Those who were born in the 1970s don't know how good they have it. They didn't experience the difficult days. They are full of desires, but they cannot take hardship.*[27] In Village B, Zhuang Xiaoxia decries the clothing and conduct of younger women: *Now, what they eat, the clothes they wear, the way they spend money, everything they do is different from me. I'm not used to it. They wear skirts, sandals, leather shoes. They curl their hair. They are very unrestrained. Married or not, they are all like that. Nothing is the same as it was.*[28] They are particularly distressed by the sexual behavior of younger women. *I can't get used to some of them running around. Their husbands are good but they casually divorce them and take up with someone older who has money, wanting to marry him. I can't get used to that.*[29]

In spite of such blanket denunciations directed at younger women, they do not complain about their own daughters. Daughters, who customarily marry out and are not expected by their parents to provide old-age support, appear to be generous with their material resources and to have less fraught relationships with their mothers, confounding the generations-old preference for sons.[30] Kang Ruqing says with pleasure, *My older daughter gives me spending money, and gives me clothes to wear, winter and summer. She always takes care of me.*[31] Qian Taohua muses, *If I did not have daughters, I would have only grain. When my daughters come, they buy me meat, nutritious food, nonstaple food, and thread. If it were not for my daughters, I would have very little money. They know you are still suffering* [ni hai shou le xie zui]. *They buy me everything I wear.*[32] Women marvel at and take some pride in the improved living conditions of their daughters, all the while referring back to their own youth, as when Kang Ruqing explains, *You see in the past, we suffered so many hardships. We all lived in thatch houses. The children had nothing to wear. If someone said they were going away, you would rush to wash something, and if it rained, you would rush to dry it by the fire. There was no money to have clothing made, so when we had to make clothing we would rush to weave a basket and carry it off and sell it, and rush to have clothing made for the children. We had nothing. My older daughter lives in a multistoried house, with lots of room. She has rugs spread on the floor, a brick floor. It's like a small store in her house.*[33]

Some women express pride in both their daughters and their sons, whose adult conduct validates their own parenting skills. Li Liujin observes, *My daughters all learned from me. They are all very capable. Especially the daughter who works in the cigarette factory, she gets along with everyone at home and outside. She goes to a lot of trouble, and knows how to arrange things. Everyone she used to teach and every school she went to, all the teachers and students loved her. She taught the students well and was very conscientious. . . . My sons and daughters have all grown up capable, because of the way they were brought up* [guanjiao]. *No matter whose house I go to, they are all like that. When I go to the homes of my children's in-laws, which of them doesn't treat me with respect?*[34]

In speaking of their current status as members of the senior generation, women highlight their pride in treating their daughters-in-law well. *When my daughter-in-law came into the family,* says He Gaizhen, *I didn't give her any test. I swept the ground outside and inside every morning. I also swept the floor in her room. Then I boiled water and put it on her table. I cooked the breakfast and called her out to eat. Daughter-in-law and daughter should be the same.* They also recall training their own daughters to become good daughters-in-law: *As soon as my daughter went to that family, I taught her, "Never make the older generation angry. You eat whatever they cook."*[35]

Among these happier stories, however, are other tales full of resentment at sons and daughters-in-law who do not understand, value, or offer reciprocity for a woman's past sacrifices. Wedding costs have risen steadily in rural China. Women whose children married in the 1980s or later sometimes went into debt to provide the cloth, linens, clothing, and other household goods required to bring in a daughter-in-law. Expensive weddings are not new; the 1950s, with their simple ceremonies, were anomalous in that respect. But the other half of the unspoken social contract, wherein parents brought in wives for their sons and the young couple then supported them in their old age, has attenuated, particularly in families that have not flourished economically under the reforms. The daughter-in-law is often cast as the source of friction, if not the villain, in these situations.

Asked to compare her own experience as a daughter-in-law with that of her sons' wives, Xiao Gaiye appropriates and twists an older language of political liberation, introducing the notion of "too much *fanshen,*" a phrase that would have had no meaning in the term's original context: *Now people have* fanshen*ed. People hadn't* fanshen*ed in my time. . . . We were shy and dared not make the old people angry. Now wives are in charge of the household and young men are only assistants. In my time, we respected our husband so much and even the older generation [in-laws] were a layer of sky. I didn't care how you [in-laws] treated me; regardless, I came to your house and called you father and mother. No matter whether you treated me badly or well, I was your daughter-in-law. You were older. Now it is scary. People have* fanshen*ed too much. They* fanshen*ed so much that they don't support old people.*

People in big places are not like this. I have been to many places: across the Yellow River to Shanxi, and to Xi'an and Chengdu. People in big places are nice. Only in the mountains here, women have fanshen*ed too much. . . . His wife doesn't let him support the older generation. My son does not dare to be stubborn. I don't want to make it difficult for them to get along. If they give me food, I eat. If they don't give it to me, I just let it go. What's the point of making them fight because of me, an old person?*

Why say, "Don't let out the family ugliness," if it is the truth? I say what is on my mind. Some people never talk about their families. I am in my sixties. I am frank, so I told you.[36]

"Too much *fanshen*" is the antithesis of joining a revolutionary collective; it means to act as a selfish individual, concerned only about one's immediate family circle, from which aging in-laws are excluded. Here again, as when they narrate the collective period, women speak of their difficulties in a domestic idiom. Just as they do not hold the state directly accountable for women's double burden during the collective years, and do not name it directly in descriptions of post–Great Leap Forward hunger, so in speaking about reform-era hardships they do not say much about how the minimal guarantees offered by the collective have been dismantled, putting rural families under increased economic pressure. Instead they fashion a narrative skein in which their past suffering correlates with the ability to "eat bitterness," work competently, and behave ethically. This narrative draws some of its power from the "speak bitterness" practices of the revolutionary era, as well as from the much older cultural trope of the suffering mother. In contrast, the current generation of younger adults emerges as sated, spoiled, even cruel. As Ma Li comments, *We respected the old when we were daughters-in-law. Now do they respect anyone? They are more fierce than the mothers-in-law. When we came back [from the fields] we fed the pigs, washed dishes, cooked, and made shoes for all members of the family, old and young. Now daughters-in-law are so busy that they go out to play right after meals. They come back to make some food and then go out to play again, taking the kids out with them at night.*[37]

One such story told by Kang Ruqing took the form of a single unstoppable speech that looped from the present (1997) back to the Great Leap famine. *Here, in our village, with these [township and village] enterprises, most people have built their houses. They have sofas and refrigerators. In the past, who had ever seen such things? Who had seen what a refrigerator was? What a sofa was? Who had seen one? In 1961 I bought a radish and some greens, two* mao *[dimes] per* jin. *We were doing sidelines. It was raining outside, and in the collective, inside and out, in the fields and on the embankments, there was no work to do. I plaited a few rain hats, the bamboo hats you wear when it rains. One rain hat could buy one* jin *of radishes. In those days a whole family ate one* jin *of unhusked millet [guzi] per day. One* jin *of unhusked millet was only half a* jin *of husked millet, and it was rotten besides. You ate this. Today, who lives like that? Sweet potato leaves we ate, potato leaves we ate, broad bean leaves we ate, broad bean stalks we ate, and those sweet potato stalks we also milled, along with turnips, and crushed them into flour, and ate them as a paste. It wasn't as good as the feed we give the pigs nowadays. A boiled paste, and when we ate it neither adults nor children could defecate [la bu xia lai].*

That's what life was like in the 1960s. Society now—white rice, refined flour—and still they say this kind doesn't taste good, that kind doesn't taste good. These people are all living in unbelievably good conditions. They have never seen anything like the way we lived then.

Widowed in 1964 at age thirty-four, Ruqing raised her four children alone, steadfastly refusing to remarry. Her son had reassured her that he and his brother would care for her in her old age, but relations between Ruqing and her sons' wives were not good. *My younger daughter-in-law said, "Why are we supporting her?" She was talking about me. My younger son said, "She does a lot of work for us. She does the housework at home, she raises pigs and chickens." She said, "Each family should support her for a year." That's what my younger daughter-in-law wanted and proposed, each family one year. I should live with my oldest son one year. In the end, my daughter and my natal mother said, "You should live separately and have them give you grain," so in the end I lived separately, beginning in 1981.* Her sons gave her so little support that she left the village in 1984 to work for a decade as a cook and maid, returning only when her health began to decline.

In 1997, when Ruqing invoked a lifetime of capable hard work, her account shuttled back and forth between the collective years and the present, taking the form of a tirade addressed alternately to her sons and their wives, none of whom was present. *This birth planning is all very good. My oldest son says, "If you had raised only me, I would give you everything you needed to eat and to wear. You raised us all, my sisters and brothers, and now everyone is afraid of taking a loss" [chi le kui le]. He can't give it to you. If you burn a bit of wood, he is not willing. He says he is tak-*

ing a loss, that they have to divide everything equally. If the son gives you something, the daughter-in-law won't let him. If she won't let him, I don't want it, either. I am a good-natured person.

In the past, whenever there was water in the paddy fields, it was all the women who went to work. In 1958, we would work all day in the paddies, come back, and get food ladled out to us in the dining halls. If they were doing it right, they would ladle you out some of the thicker stuff. If they weren't doing it right, they would give you the thin stuff, and you would go home and get some wild vegetables, mix them in the pot, heat it and eat it. That is why our oldest child didn't continue to study. They were hungry, but there was nothing to eat. What was the use of studying? You were so hungry it was terrible. That's how we were in the past, little to eat and nothing to wear, not enough to wear.

When the oldest daughter-in-law married in, we couldn't entertain guests. We threw some dishes together. Now she still raises objections about that. She says that when she married here, we didn't give her a banquet, it was just ordinary, there was nothing to eat. But no one's family was prosperous. In the collective they distributed grain. You only got something to eat when someone distributed it to you. If they didn't distribute it to you, you didn't have anything to eat.

Someone scolds me, saying "No ability." Your mother[-in-law] counts as someone with ability. In the whole brigade, she counts as someone with ability. The old man got sick in 1958, so I also had to support a sick person and raise these young sons and daughters. Is this someone with "no ability"? Working all day long, working all day outside, doing sidelines in the evening to make a bit of money for salt, is this "no ability"? Is it "no ability" to live in a thatched house that you dug, and every year to raise a few pigs, you slaughter them and you can eat some meat, you sell them and you can build a tiled house? After a tiled house is in your hands then you can build a multistoried house, and I help you out, I work for you. This counts as having ability.

It is enough that a member of the weaker sex managed to bring up all these small children, and also got wives for you, got my daughters started in life, and these grandsons, I raised them for you. This person is someone with ability. "No ability." You try doing this. You still have your husbands, who labor for you. A family with one woman, for so many years, raising the children. That counts as having ability.

Nowadays the daughter-in-law has turned things upside down. The mother-in-law is the daughter-in-law, and the daughter-in-law is the mother-in-law. You work for her. These days daughters-in-law don't work. She won't even wash an item of clothing for you. If you have time, you wash clothes for her kids and for her, but she can't wash one item for you. As for me, I don't say anything, I don't do anything about it. If you have work and you ask me to do it for you, I just do it, I don't say much about it. In recent years I have been gone most of the time. As long as you have a bowl of rice for me to eat, it's all right. I don't fight over things. If you give me something, I just take it, and if you don't give it to me, I don't ask you for anything.[38]

Even when the son emerges as the negligent party, communities regard the daughter-in-law as the potential solution to a case of elder neglect. When we first met Liu Fengqin, in 1996, her husband was still alive. Her four sons had each married and separated out their households. She had raised three grandsons for them. She and her husband were farming a small plot of land, growing enough to eat. Her sons did not help with the farming, although her daughter and son-in-law sometimes lent a hand. She and her husband had already prepared their coffins and placed them in the house. She told us that if she had it to do over again, she would have preferred to have one daughter and one son—a son because he does not marry out and is always in the same village.[39]

When we saw her ten years later, in 2006, she was eighty, almost blind from cataracts the doctors said were inoperable. Her husband had recently died. She spent her days at home on a disorderly bed while her divorced third son was at work, feeling her way to the outhouse when necessary and sometimes sitting in her doorway to chat with passers-by. This son brought her some steamed bread in the morning and occasionally cooked at night. Her daughters, married into other villages and with children and obligations of their own, came by with food every few days, straightened up the place, and washed clothes. But her other three sons, two of whom lived a block away, contributed nothing to her care. *So I am left alone. No one takes care of me. No one takes care at all.*[40]

When we asked her neighbors what could be done, they agreed that it was a terrible situation, but professed helplessness. In Village B, they explained to us, the custom was for an aged parent to live with one child (if any) and become the responsibility solely of that child, without any obligation from the rest. The first son was a widower—that is, there was no daughter-in-law—and thus was not regarded as capable of providing care. The second son was married to a women's cadre, and the neighbors thought that someone could talk to her about the situation. The third son, with whom she lived, was divorced and thus had no wife who could care for Fengqin. The fourth son's wife was not on speaking terms with her at all, possibly because of a property dispute. In short, the villagers understood the source of the problem as a shortage of responsible daughters-in-law to provide hands-on care, rather than a shortage of sons. Arrangements for the care of the elderly had clearly not caught up with the new practice of separating out households at marriage.[41]

In recounting their current troubles, rural women call upon the past. They retell the collective era as a background set of demanding circumstances that called forth individual sacrifice and suffering from them. They speak proudly of their attributes: capacity for hard work, activist enthusiasm, ability to manage difficult people, fair-mindedness. Then they move on to address a troubled present in which their physical ability has diminished, but they have been denied their just rewards by those they have cared for most. Noting the fact of improved material abundance in reform-era China, women link it to personal and ethical failures on the part of the younger generation. Their stories alternate, sometimes awkwardly, between the progress narrative and a narrative of personal injury (we are capable and virtuous but often misunderstood; we have been attacked; our children enjoy the fruits of our lifetime labor but don't understand what it cost us; our children neglect us). The progress narrative gives social significance to their virtue and hard work. The injury narrative, full of particularity and detail but seldom mentioned when these women make summary statements about their lives, offers only the scant comfort of being virtuous but unappreciated. These are accounts in which the domestic erupts as a site of new conflict, not intimacy and consumption.

Marriage has changed profoundly in many of the ways longed for and antici-pated by the young *yangge*-dancing activists of the 1950s. But it still has major im-plications for family property—all the more so now that the reforms have made the household a prime location of economic activity. In a sad irony, it is sometimes the former activists, now grown old, who are pushed aside by grown children looking out for their own independent households—the long-term results of marriage re-form these same activists had worked for in their youth.

He Gaizhen found herself in this situation in the 1980s. Soon after she was wid-owed in 1982, when the reforms made it possible for farmers to leave their home villages, Gaizhen's grown son decided to go to Xinjiang as a contract laborer. He left behind Gaizhen, his wife, and his two children. With the family's main labor power gone, Gaizhen scrambled for money to start a microbusiness, borrowing at her son's behest from her deceased husband's relatives in Henan. She was deeply hurt when she found that her son was mailing remittances from Xinjiang to his wife to augment their savings, rather than helping her clear the family debt. Gaizhen rued the fact that she was literate—the rare girl who had had four years of school-ing before 1949—and could understand what her son had written. *I mean, if I couldn't read, if I didn't read his letters, I wouldn't have known. I wouldn't have been through all that. As soon as I read the letters, I said, "What is going on with my son?"* In 1999, many years after the event, she was still in a one-sided dialogue with her son: *"What were you doing? You sent money to your wife. You told your wife to count it properly and spend it, and to save what was left over. You saw me there enduring the situation, with no money. You tell me, if you were old, would this make you sad or not? You knew I had no money even when you were at home. You asked me to go to Henan to borrow two hundred yuan. But you mailed money to your wife."... When I think about that time, I say, "You, my son, are blind in your heart."*

Staying under the same roof with a sullen daughter-in-law who was hoarding remittances from an unfilial son seemed to Gaizhen to be an untenable situation. She accepted a marriage proposal from a widower, only to find out after she moved in with him and his grown children that his sons were violently opposed to the match. *They were not willing and so it was very awkward. It was pitiful. At every meal he explained to his children. He would talk. That was how we came back [to live in her new husband's home], explaining and explaining. Later, it was so strange. My teeth ached very badly, as if they were on fire. All night I didn't sleep. I didn't want to eat during the day. At some meals, I only had half a bowl of rice. Sometimes I didn't eat at all. Thus I couldn't do anything. I was not in good health.*

Gaizhen decided that she could not return to the home of her daughter-in-law, even though the house was legally hers. She moved out to stay with a relative. Her new husband, who stayed in his own house, was unable to cope with being berated by his own children. *I was living here, in this house on the market street. My old man* [renjia lao hanr] *came by and said, "At home there is always too much talk"* [wuli zongshi zuicui lali]. *The old man was shaking when he was here. . . . He never stopped shaking. He took off his shoes and lay there on the kang. Then the old man said the following: "The old ox plowed the field and died at knifepoint"* [lao niu li di dao jian si]. *. . . We all said, "What does this mean, and why is he talking this way?" . . . "The old ox" meant that he, the old man, brought up his children all his life. Now the ox was old. So the point of the knife butchered you, because they no longer needed you. The old ox plowed the field and died at knifepoint. The meat could be eaten. The bones could be sold for money. . . . The group of us didn't understand what he was saying. . . . He left and didn't come back. [He went to] the cooperative clinic. They had built a shack where sick people could come and be treated. They also cooked there. But just then, no one was there. He got into the room and hanged himself.*

Why? It was because his sons weren't willing. They were always quarreling and arguing at home. I had been sleeping over here at this house on the market street and I didn't know. . . . From the time I [married] there until my husband died, until the day he was buried, it was only one hundred days.

He Gaizhen eventually returned home to live with her daughter-in-law and her son, now back from Xinjiang. She felt entitled to do so because this was her natal village; her first husband had been called in as a son-in-law, and she had built the house herself. Nevertheless it took a court order to persuade her son and daughter-in-law to take her back. *I went to the commune first. The commune mediated and asked me to wait for a while and they called my son there. He saw me sitting there and he scrambled off and ran away. Later we went to court and sat at the table. The judge put on his robes and his hat.* (Here she may be embellishing the scene with details from a TV historical drama; local rural judges did not wear robes and hats in the early 1980s.) *He said, "Dalin, you go and sit beside your mother." The judge blamed him. He said that if Dalin didn't accept me, didn't acknowledge me as his flesh and blood, he would punish him to set an example for other sons, for other young men, who were not supporting the older generation financially. He said, "If you take your mother back this afternoon, I will say nothing. If you don't support your mother financially, you will see what happens [zai shuo]." Then he got up and left. I followed him. My daughter-in-law was secretly listening outside the door. She stood there with her daughter in her arms. I went home.*

My daughter-in-law lay in bed for six days. I cooked all day. She has never been close to the pots. I cooked for six days, but she didn't eat. I went to the store to buy dried fruit for her to eat. This showed that I was not angry. From then on things got better. It blew over and she got better. . . . My neighbor—a few days ago her son beat her with a stick. My son never beat me. My son never cursed me. Only now that I am old, he doesn't like it when I talk. I never talk when I am at home. I don't talk much to him. What is there to say? I don't talk if I have nothing to say. Why make him angry?[42]

Beyond the painful particulars of this case is a wider story of aging women, particularly in mountainous areas where reform-era prosperity has been slow to arrive. Gaizhen and her neighbors have children who are themselves already at middle age, older than the young laborers who have been able to head for the coast or the inland cities to look for work. Under economic pressure, grown sons grow surly toward their (mostly) widowed mothers, while daughters-in-law try to preserve resources for their own nuclear families. He Gaizhen, because her first marriage was uxorilocal and the house was her natal family property, was unusual in her willingness to claim the right to live there. Her difficulty with her son and daughter-in-law did not make her nostalgic for older marriage practices, or doubtful about the worth of her youthful activism. On the contrary, her years of activism—bolstered by the fact that the house had always belonged to her family, not to her son's patriline—helped provide her with the sense of entitlement and indignation that sent her to court. But she made it clear that many decades after the Marriage Law guaranteed free choice of marriage partners, long after Cao Zhuxiang chose virtuous widowhood over a new match, the remarriage of older people remained controversial.[43]

Gao Xiaoxian: *Your son and your daughter-in-law were a free love match. Then why, when older people remarry, do most sons oppose it?*

He Gaizhen: *They are against it. It was only much later that there was propaganda, saying that old people can find a partner. In the old days it was not done this way. My son made a big fuss about it.*

Gao Xiaoxian: *So, you didn't think of looking for another husband again?*

He Gaizhen: *No, I didn't. I stopped thinking about that. I came back to my home. I had no such ideas any more. I put my whole heart into taking care of my grandson and my granddaughter.*[44]

In the years when the revolution promised equality to women, they were not well served by the disappearance of the domestic realm from revolutionary visions. Now, in the revolution's wake and their own old age, they are equally unlikely to be rescued by the return of the domestic realm as a modern place of intimacy. He Gaizhen speaks for many older village women in her terse assessment of the present and future, in which "pitiful" is once again predominant. *I make straw shoes.*

The year before last, I earned a lot by making dried persimmons. If I had got 0.30 yuan more, I would have made one hundred yuan. I spend the money on my laundry powder, my toothpaste. I pay if I take the corn to grind. I pay if I go to have noodles made at the noodle machine. I eat together with my son and daughter-in-law. I have never asked him for money. He buys the oil, salt, and vinegar. When I earn more money from selling straw shoes, I also buy some. I made two pairs a day, from the unraveled fibers of plastic bags. I buy them. I keep the bags under my bed. I washed them in the river with washing powder. You should make them beautiful. If you make them dirty, who will want to buy them? I washed them very white. I sell the shoes for five yuan a pair. You tell me, what else can we do? Our sons are peasants. They can't make money. How can you stretch out your hand and ask for money from them?

When people get old, they are pitiful. You can't make money. You just hang on this way. I also smoke. I have to buy cigarettes. All with money I have earned myself. I am capable. If I didn't do it, what would my whole family do? I'll be in trouble when I can't get around anymore.[45]

Sadly, even as rural economic life has once again shifted dramatically, as the 1950s generation has moved beyond childbearing age, as the years of nighttime farm tasks and needlework recede, "pitiful" remains a durable term used by older rural women in assessing their lives. The causes they cite have changed. They spent their youth in a society of raw privation and danger. They gave their adult working lives, willingly or not, to a set of social arrangements that extracted endless work and effort from them, and that has now been repudiated. Many among them do not enjoy the security of the old family practice of support by their children. He Gaizhen also found it impossible to claim, late in life, the freedom of marriage she had sung about in the 1950s; the children of her new husband, as well as a chorus of disapproving villagers, prevented it. "Pitiful" no longer describes a state of reactive suffering from remote, abstract societal forces. Now women use it to describe the troubles of their old age in an environment in which the rules of filiality have changed.

Speaking bitterness remains a familiar mode for village women, and every account we heard bore some traces of it. But the speaking bitterness trajectory from oppression to liberation does not begin to exhaust the varieties of problems, or the elusiveness of revolutionary promises, presented in these narratives. At the same time, the devolutionary story "We practiced virtue but our successors do not," while prominent in many narratives, usually coexists with an assessment that women today have material goods and possibilities our older speakers could not have imagined for themselves. Even a combination of the two stories ("The world is much better for women, but individual women are less worthy than we were") suggests that gender arrangements are not on a linear march from a feudal past to a longed-for postsocialist future.

We are left, then, with a more modest sense of gender as a contingent set of practices and understandings embedded in a changing context. At extraordinary moments, such as the moment of the revolution, some of the meanings of gender have been stripped away. More often, they accrete and shift slowly. Many of the elements in these tales would be recognizable to the grandmothers of these storytellers. Certainly the pride in one's own industriousness, in the deft handling of a household and a family, as well as the well-developed sense of grievance animating the statement "I was pitiful," echo venerable elements of female virtue. But the world in which those stories are played out has added new venues for the performance of gendered virtue, while discrediting and eliminating some of the practices that once formed its core. Maintaining one's chastity is no longer the central feature of these stories, although loyalty to the marital family still looms large. But the ability to perform well as a cadre, or to lead heroic efforts in collective labor, has been added to a repertoire of remembered virtuous practices.

Scholarship on women in China's twentieth-century revolution has moved beyond its initial focus on whether Party-state policies were good or bad for women.[46] Freed from that important but insufficient question, we can begin to look at all of the ways the revolution was gendered, within and beyond articulated policy: in its reconfiguration of space, its relationship to nonrevolutionary temporalities, its production of an embodied state effect, even in its strategies for socialist accumulation.

Such a reconsideration may force us to revise a few of our commonsense assumptions about the Chinese revolution. The Party-state's claim that it freed women to move from "inner" to "outer" domains, where "outer" was privileged as the domain of paid work, political visibility, and liberation, bears rethinking. When labor in the "inner" realm became inarticulable in the state-provided language of liberation— residual, uninteresting, slated to wither away at some undefined future moment— large parts of women's daily existence went missing, unavailable to be addressed, even by themselves, except in the language of late-night virtue at their needlework. Nevertheless the contents of domestic time shifted dramatically across the collective period, affected by the disappearance of sidelines, the appearance and survival of children, the slow disaggregation of extended families. The entanglements of domestic time with campaign time in the lives of women suggest that the official story of political change, as it was lived by half the rural population, is radically incomplete.

The Chinese revolution is illegible without attention to gender. Nevertheless no single person, let alone a collectivity, is completely explicable by reference to gender. It needs to be understood as one in an array of powerful relationships. The deep generational markers in the tales of all these women, the mixed unease and approbation with which they regard their successors, remind us that gender is not the only useful category of analysis and that its intersection with other categories necessarily fractures it. The category "woman" or even "rural woman" is marked deeply by variations in age and locale, each with its own array of subordinations, norms, and transgressions, all circulating simultaneously in contemporary China. These gendered accounts of a personal past are themselves shifting, making a claim on the contemporary moment in which they are uttered.

For historians, these tales provide a fuller account of critical years of transformation in rural China, one that enriches and disrupts, providing sensuous detail and emotional coloration as well as new themes and arguments. The stories suggest that socialist construction in the Mao years, as well as the foundations of unparalleled economic growth in the recent reform period, were dependent to an important degree upon the unacknowledged labor of rural women. When they assert the stability of their virtuous remembered selves across time, aging women create continuity in the face of state inconstancy and familial neglect. They narrate a world full of hardship, indexing stubborn inequities that have yet to be recognized or addressed. In crafting a remembered self, they scour the past for usable stories, speaking powerfully to present injuries and dilemmas.

Women's stories tell us about what socialism was, locally, in places far from its central apparatus, for people whose situation was never fully apprehended or valued by Party-state planners or dreamers. The world that gave rise to these stories has disappeared, and the capacity to hear what the narrators have to say may well be diminishing. It is unclear whether aging rural women, their stories and their memories, will become part of a resilient collective memory.[47] The memories recounted by rural women expand a listener's sense of a vanished past. They should be central as well to the ethics and politics of fashioning a livable present.

APPENDIX

Interviews

Name	Name as Written in Chinese	Notes	Place	Date of interview
Weinan, August 1996				
Wang Xiqin	王西芹	Pseudonym	Village B	8/6/96
Cao Zhuxiang	曹竹香	Actual name	Village B	8/2/96–8/4/96
Zhou Guizhen	周桂珍	Pseudonym	Village B	8/4/96
Zhang Xiuyu, Li Xiuwa, Ma Ruyun, Wang Meihua	张秀玉, 李秀娃, 马如云, 王梅花	Pseudonyms	Weinan city	8/9/96
Liu Fengqin	刘凤琴	Pseudonym	Village B	8/8/96
Ma Ruhua	马茹花	Pseudonym	Village B	8/5/96
Zhang Qiuxiang	张秋香	Actual name	Village B	8/7/96
Zhuang Xiaoxia	庄小霞	Pseudonym	Village B	8/5/96
Zheng Caigui	郑彩桂	Pseudonym	Xi'an	8/14/96
Lu Guilan	鲁桂兰	Actual name	Xianyang	8/15/96
Zhao Feng'e	赵凤娥	Pseudonym	Xi'an	8/12/96
Liu Zhaofeng	刘招凤	Pseudonym	Xi'an	8/13/96
Tongguan/Huayin, June 1997				
Shan Xiuzhen	山秀珍	Actual name	Tongguan	6/28/97 and 6/29/97
Gao Zhenxian	高贞贤	Actual name	Huayin	6/29/97
Nanzheng, July 1997				
Wang Guihua	王桂花	Pseudonym	Hanzhong	7/2/97
Xu Nini	徐妮妮	Pseudonym	Hanzhong	7/3/97
Li Xiulan	李秀兰	Pseudonym	Village T	7/6/97
Yang Anxiu	杨安秀	Pseudonym	Village T	7/7/97

Name	Name as Written in Chinese	Notes	Place	Date of interview
Feng Gaixia	冯改霞	Pseudonym	Village T	7/7/97
Qian Taohua	钱桃花	Pseudonym	Village T	7/5/97
Kang Ruqing	康汝清	Pseudonym	Village T	7/5/97
Sun Jixiu	孙吉秀	Pseudonym	Village T	7/5/97
Wang Fangfang	王芳芳	Pseudonym	Village T	7/6/97
Li Liujin	李六斤	Pseudonym	Village T	7/6/97
Feng Sumei	冯素梅	Pseudonym	Village T	7/4/97 and 7/7/97
Yuan Xiaoli	袁小丽	Pseudonym	Village T	7/4/97
Li Xiaomei	李小梅	Pseudonym	Village T	7/4/97
Song Yufen	宋玉芬	Pseudonym	Village T	7/5/97
Zhang Xiuli	张秀丽	Pseudonym	Village T	7/4/97
Wang Youna	王友娜	Pseudonym	Village T	7/6/97

Danfeng, July–August 1999

Name	Name as Written in Chinese	Notes	Place	Date of interview
He Gaizhen	何改珍	Pseudonym	Village Z	7/28/99
Lu Yulian	鲁玉莲	Pseudonym	Village Z	7/27/99
Zheng Xiuhua	郑秀花	Pseudonym	Village Z	7/30/99
Wang Caizhen	王彩珍	Pseudonym	Village Z	8/2/99
Dong Guizhi	董桂枝	Pseudonym	Village Z	8/3/99
He Shuangyan	何双燕	Pseudonym	Village Z	7/28/99
Li Duoduo	李朵朵	Pseudonym	Village Z	8/1/99
Ma Fangxian	马芳贤	Pseudonym	Village Z	7/27/99
Zhang Zizhen	张自珍	Pseudonym	Village Z	7/27/99
Shi Ranwa	石冉娃	Pseudonym	Village Z	7/31/99
Kang Xingfen	康杏芬	Pseudonym	Village Z	7/29/99
Hu Layue	胡腊月	Pseudonym	Village Z	8/1/99
Xiao Gaiye	肖改叶	Pseudonym	Village Z	7/30/99
Liu Dongmei	刘冬梅	Pseudonym	Village Z	7/26/99 and 7/29/99
Li Xiumei	李秀梅	Pseudonym	Village Z	7/31/99
Yan Panwa	颜盼娃	Pseudonym	Village Z	7/26/99
Feng Xiaoqin	冯小芹	Pseudonym	Village Z	8/1/99
Ma Li	马丽	Pseudonym	Village Z	7/28/99 and 7/31/99
Qu Guiyue	屈桂月	Pseudonym	Village Z	7/26/99
Liu Dongmei and He Gaizhen	刘冬梅, 何改珍	Pseudonym	Village Z	7/31/99

Heyang, March 2001

Name	Name as Written in Chinese	Notes	Place	Date of interview
Yuan Xi	袁茜	Pseudonym	Village G	3/25/01
Jiang Qiuwa	蒋秋桂	Pseudonym	Village G	3/26/01
Qiao Yindi	乔引娣	Pseudonym	Village G	3/26/01
Feng Na	冯娜	Pseudonym	Village G	3/31/01
Yu Xiaoli	于小莉	Pseudonym	Village G	3/25/01
Feng Zaicai and Wang Fugui	冯在财/王福贵	Pseudonym	Village G	3/31/01

Name	Name as Written in Chinese	Notes	Place	Date of interview
Xiang Jinwa	向金桂	Pseudonym	Village G	3/29/01
Zhang Meihua	张梅花	Pseudonym	Village G	3/29/01
Lei Caiwa	雷彩娃	Pseudonym	Village G	3/27/01
Lei Caiwa, Li Fenglian, Zhang Qiurong, Liu Xifeng, and Zhang Meihua	雷彩娃, 李凤莲, 张秋绒, 刘西凤, 张 梅花	Pseudonym	Village G	3/29/01
Yang Hui'e	扬惠娥	Pseudonym	Village G	3/24/01
Zhang Chaofeng	张朝凤	Pseudonym	Village G	3/24/01
Liu Cunyu	刘存雨	Pseudonym	Village G	3/28/01
Liu Guyu	刘谷雨	Pseudonym	Village G	3/28/01
Shi Cuiyu	石翠玉	Pseudonym	Village G	3/27/01

Heyang, June 2004

Name	Name as Written in Chinese	Notes	Place	Date of interview
Zhang Qiurong	张秋绒	Pseudonym	Village G	6/27/04
Li Fenglian	李凤莲	Pseudonym	Village G	6/27/04
Liu Guyu	刘谷雨	Pseudonym	Village G	6/27/04
Ouyang Xiu	欧阳秀	Pseudonym	Village G	6/28/04
Zhang Chaofeng	张朝凤	Pseudonym	Village G	6/28/04
Shi Cuiyu	石翠玉	Pseudonym	Village G	6/28/04
Peng Guimin	彭贵民	Pseudonym	Village G	6/28/04
Gao Yuzhong	高育忠	Pseudonym	Village G	6/28/04
Wang Zhaoru	王兆如	Pseudonym	Village G	6/29/04
Yang Guishi	杨贵石	Pseudonym	Village G	6/29/04
Qiao Yindi	乔引娣	Pseudonym	Village G	6/29/04
Liu Xiuzhen	刘秀珍	Pseudonym	Village G	6/30/04

Weinan, August–September 2006

Name	Name as Written in Chinese	Notes	Place	Date of interview
Cao Zhuxiang	曹竹香	Actual name	Village B	8/29/06
Wang Jiji	王积极	Actual name	Village B	8/29/06
Zhou Guizhen	周桂珍	Pseudonym	Village B	8/29/06
Wang Xiqin	王西芹	Pseudonym	Village B	8/30/06
Wang Xiqin and Zhuang Xiaoxia	王西芹, 庄小霞	Pseudonym	Village B	8/30/06
Chen Chunhua	陈春华	Pseudonym	Village B	8/30/06
Zhuang Xiaoxia	庄小霞	Pseudonym	Village B	8/30/06
Liu Zhenxi	刘真西	Pseudonym	Village B	8/31/06
Wang Nilan	王妮兰	Pseudonym	Village B	8/31/06
Zhou Guizhen, Wang Xiqin, and Zhuang Xiaoxia	周桂珍, 王西芹, 庄小霞	Pseudonym	Village B	8/31/06
Liu Fengqin	刘凤琴	Pseudonym	Village B	8/30/06

Xi'an, September 2006

Name	Name as Written in Chinese	Notes	Place	Date of interview
Li Jingzhao	李晋昭	Actual name	Xi'an	9/1/06

NOTES

INTRODUCTION

1. Interview with Zhang Chaofeng 2001. She was born in 1934 and would have been five years old by Chinese reckoning, in which a child was considered a year old at birth.

2. Many scholars eschew the term "Liberation" because it assumes a thoroughgoing positive transformation. I use it in this book because it remains part of the language in which Chinese villagers recall and interpret their own past.

3. Images of blue bills in circulation at the time can be found at http://aes.iupui.edu/ rwise/banknotes/china/chio79_f.jpg; http://aes.iupui.edu/rwise/banknotes/china/China P73-10Yuan-1934-donated_f.jpg; http://aes.iupui.edu/rwise/banknotes/china/ChinaP218d -10Yuan-1936_f.jpg; and http://aes.iupui.edu/rwise/banknotes/china/ChinaP460-50Cents -1936_f.jpg.

4. In the mid-1930s women could earn about nine yuan a month in a Xi'an textile factory, perhaps about the same as full-time rural home weavers in the province, but no one seems to have recorded rates of pay for wet nurses (Vermeer 1988: 344–45, 335).

5. A 1941 survey of average rural household living expenses in twenty-four Guanzhong counties by the Northwest Agricultural College in Xi'an suggests that wartime inflation increased household expenditures between 1936 and 1941; food grain expenditures increased more than eightfold, and fuel expenditure almost sixfold. The survey tallied average living expenses in 1936 at 321.9 yuan per year; by 1941 the figure had risen to 2,139.5 yuan. For a detailed breakdown and discussion, see Vermeer 1988: 410–11.

6. A *jin* is half a kilogram.

7. A "good-enough story" invokes a whimsical but not entirely random parallel with the concept of the "good-enough mother," developed by the psychoanalyst Donald Winnicott in the mid-twentieth century. In Winnicott's theory, a good-enough mother is not always perfectly attuned to her child's needs, but her mothering is sufficient to permit the child's healthy development—unlike that of an overattentive mother who, in taking care of every

detail, leaves her child no psychic room to individuate. (One brief explanation is Abram and Hjulmand 2007: 220–21. My thanks to Sheila Namir for this reference.) Similarly, a good-enough story leaves enough space for the development of open-ended interpretations and ambiguity, rather than presenting a seamless, finished narrative that merely reinforces what the listener already understands herself to know. This book is not in any way a Winnicottian work, but in considering the life of stories, I have found Winnicott's concept productive—that is, "good enough" to think with.

8. On statist and other political uses of space and time, see Boyarin 1994b; Rutz 1992; and Verdery 1992. Tyrene White (2006: 7–8) offers a vivid description of how a campaign worked.

9. Nevertheless, extremely helpful works on the rural 1950s and early 1960s exist, including Myrdal 1967; Schurmann 1968; Yang 1969; Shue 1980, 1990; Friedman et al. 1991; Hinton 1997; Thaxton 2008; and Chan, Madsen, and Unger 2009.

10. Vogel (1971), Lieberthal (1980), and Solinger (1984) discuss various aspects of local politics and community in the 1950s. More recent works drawing on interviews conducted in urban China include Ho 2004 and 2006.

11. Readers in the China field will be aware that the choice of the term "farmer" or "peasant" is not an innocent one. For a brief summary of the issues, see Cohen 2005: 60–74, 312–14. In this book I sometimes use the term "peasant" to refer to those engaged in agriculture in post-1949 China, when the Chinese term to which it corresponds—*nongmin*, denoting agriculturalists as a collective political subject—came into general popular use.

12. Space does not permit a thorough and nuanced exposition of these arguments. Some of the most important English-language sources that discuss rural women in the 1950s are Andors 1983; Croll 1980; Davin 1976; Diamond 1975; Johnson 1983; and Stacey 1983. For an assessment of the entire period of collective agriculture with respect to gender equality, see Wolf 1985.

13. Hershatter 1986, 1997; Honig and Hershatter 1988.

14. Kelly 1984.

15. See the appendix for a full list of interviewees. Each of us has a set of interview tapes and transcripts; we plan to make them available to researchers after we both finish the writing projects that draw on them.

16. The underground Communist presence was another matter; see, for instance, Weinan diqu difang zhi bianji weiyuan hui 1996: 101–6, 108–9, 114–16; Nanzheng xian difang zhi bianji weiyuan hui 1990: 13–16. Parts of Nanzheng County near but not including Village T founded Soviet governments in early 1935 (13) as part of a briefly successful attempt to build a base area on the Shaanxi-Sichuan border between late 1932 and mid-1935. For the history of that base area, which for a time was second in size only to the central base area in Jiangxi, see Lin 1982; *Chuan Shaan geming genjudi shiliao xuanji* 1986; and Wen 1987.

17. On the gendered division of labor, see Wolf 1985; Jacka 1997.

18. Mitchell 1991, 1999.

19. Jonathan Boyarin (1994a: ix) describes the state as "a highly contingent artifact of groups contending for legitimacy vis-à-vis their own sense of 'insiderhood,' their control of positions within hierarchies, and their control of geographic territories." For works in the China field that complicate notions of a simple state-society boundary, see Shue 1988; Fried-

man et al. 1991; Friedman et al. 2005; Diamant 2000; Diamant, Lubman, and O'Brien 2005; Perry 1994; and Dutton 2005.

20. The reference here is to a foundational work in Chinese feminist literary criticism: Meng Yue and Dai Jinhua's *Voices Emerging into the Foreground of History* (1989; sometimes translated as *Emerging from the Horizon of History*).

21. Highlights of this literature are surveyed in the notes to chapter 9.

22. Yan Hairong (2003) refers to the state of these villages as the "spectralization of the rural." The classic discussions are Nora 1996, 1997, 1998, 2001.

23. As Honig (1997: 140) comments, "Any particular rendition of a life history is a product of the personal present."

1. FRAMES

1. Village T briefing 1997.

2. Shaanxi sheng Danfeng xian jiaotong ju 1990: 7; Village Z briefing 1999.

3. Village G in 2001 had twenty-seven hundred people in six hundred households. The village is in the Jinshui River catchment area of the Yellow River system, under the Wuluo Mountains. As of 2001, the village had 7,705 *mu* of flat land under cultivation, as well as 2,000 *mu* of sloping land in the nearby gorge and 200 *mu* of land along the river (Village G briefing 2001). A *mu* is one-sixth of an acre. For a concise description of the difference between Guanzhong's irrigated plain areas (including Village B) and its dry upland areas (including Village G), see Vermeer 1981: 227–28. On Heyang in the late 1910s, see Teichman 1921: 80. On the importance of cotton growing in the 1930s, see Gu Zhizhong 1932: 195. At that time the county had close economic relations with neighboring Shanxi Province, and its main exports were cotton and medicinal herbs (201). On major Party initiatives in the county after 1949, see Zhonggong Heyang xianwei zuzhi bu 2000. For summary accounts of material life (clothing, food, dwellings, transport, festivals) in Weinan Prefecture, home of Villages B and G, from the 1940s to the 1990s, see Weinan diqu difang zhi bianji weiyuan hui 1996: 769–78.

4. For a sampling of recent spirited discussions about archives and "the archive," some of it inspired or incited by Derrida's 1995 *Archive Fever,* see Bradley 1999; Osborne 1999; and Steedman 1998 and 2002.

5. The Shaanxi Provincial Archives houses documents from all the major departments of the provincial government. Archival documents have been hand-sewn into books sorted by government agency (Civil Administration [Minzheng ting], Agriculture [Nongye ting], Public Health [Weisheng ting], and Women's Federation [Fulian]), or occasionally by policy initiative (Marriage Law), and within each agency by time period. Some of these books are designated to be kept perpetually (*yongjiu*) and others merely long term (*changqi*). Why a document landed in one book or another is no longer clear, but the division means that documents about a particular subject—campaigns to implement the Marriage Law, for example—are spread across numerous files.

Directives emanated from the supervising ministry in Beijing, and reports were transmitted downward from the province to the county and city levels asking for information, hectoring when reports were not forthcoming, transmitting directives from higher levels, generating directions to the counties about how to proceed. Reports flowed upward as well. Horizontal transmissions occurred when several government departments concerned with the same issue (the Marriage Law, for instance) either issued joint pronouncements or kept copies of one another's documents.

6. In the earliest years of the People's Republic, Shaanxi was part of the regional Northwest Bureau.

7. Starting in 1959, the central government sent urgent demands to the provincial government that it survey the extent of disaster in every district, including the acreage affected, the type of disaster, the number of people and livestock dead, and a host of other indices. The provincial Civil Administration Bureau asked every district for reports. Hanzhong District sent a telegram in code, duly translated on the original, saying that much of the district was under water. Other counties sent in estimates of thousands of people without enough grain or padded cotton clothing to survive the winter.

8. Amin (1995: 4) offers a useful warning here: "The desire to discover in oral history an entirely different source from the archival offers a faint promise. But for me it was not a question of counterposing local remembrance against authorized accounts: the process by which historians gain access to pasts is richly problematic, as is the relationship between memory and record, and the possibilities of arriving at a more nuanced narrative, a thicker description, seem enhanced by putting the problems on display."

9. Village T briefing 1997.

10. I was unable to satisfy another request, delivered repeatedly by village officials with varying degrees of obliqueness, that I help to procure investment capital for assorted local ventures. By 1999, when foreign-funded development projects had begun to dot the Chinese countryside and local expectations of foreigners had expanded, it was not just officials who were doing the asking. Gao Xiaoxian and I, who were staying as usual in a farmer's home, were approached by our landlady, who hoped that we could buy some medical machinery for the local hospital, fund a large pig-raising operation in her front courtyard, and finance a bathhouse business she wanted to open. Each year my inability to come up with enterprise funding, or to make my lack of connections comprehensible to villagers, discomfited me more and more, even though I understood it as indicative of shifts in the local environment that had little to do with me.

11. Interview with Qiao Yindi 2001.

12. Anthropologists and historians have generated a thoughtful literature on related dilemmas; for examples, see Feuchtwang 1998; Kopijn 1998; Visweswaran 1994. For a discussion of the dynamics of a joint research project involving a similar partnership between a Chinese and a non-Chinese researcher, see Jaschok and Shui 2000.

13. The distance is from Shaanxi sheng Danfeng xian jiaotong ju 1990: 7. The road was built along the route of a footpath in 1966, after the main events described in this book.

14. Hershatter 1997, chapter 1.

15. Dudley (1998) offers a thoughtful discussion of the differing practices of oral history and ethnography.

16. Three works that have collected oral histories of Chinese women are Du Fangqin 1998; Li Xiaojiang 2003; Zhang Shao 1997.

17. Oakley (1981) discusses interviewing women as a feminist practice.

18. Le Goff 1992: 52.

19. As one team of cognitive psychologists has written, recitation itself shapes memory: "The act of rehearsing the event through language can influence the way the event is organized in memory and, perhaps, recalled in the future" (Pennebaker and Banasik 1997: 7–8).

20. Portelli 1991: 52.

21. The vast literatures on memory and on oral narratives generated by psychologists, historians, sociologists, literary scholars, anthropologists, and others cannot be summarized here. Sources useful to the present study include Bloch 1996; Vansina 1965, 1985; Pennebaker and Banasik 1997; Portelli 1991, 1997, 1998, 2003; Amin 1995; Bohannon and Symons 1992; Brown and Kulik 2000; Connerton 1989; Conway 1997; Cruikshank et al. 1990; Feuchtwang 2000; Grele 1991; Haaken 1998; Heehs 2000; Hodgkin and Radstone 2003; Huyssen 1995; Kovács 1992; Lambek 1996, 2003; Larsen 1992; Neisser 1988, 2000a, 2000b; Neisser and Harsch 1992; Neisser and Libby 2000; Passerini 1987; Perelli 1994; Pillemer 1998, 2000; Radstone and Hodgkin 2003; Schwarz 2003; Singer 1997; Thaxton 1997; Tonkin 1992; Wertsch 2002; White, Miescher, and Cohen 2001; White 1998. On silences in particular, see Visweswaran 1994; White 2000a, 2000b; Passerini 2003; Pohlandt-McCormick 2000.

22. Interview with Lei Caiwa 2001. Vansina (1985: 62–63) writes, "Researchers should also realize that what one does and asks is often of great interest to the whole community or society in which they work. People will talk about them, form opinions, develop rumors about them, and sometimes even discuss what to say if asked this or that. Even if interviews are kept private, which is not possible in many cultures anyway, the interviewee is of course eagerly asked what this meeting was all about. Just as the researcher reports to other scholars, the interviewee reports to his friends."

23. For extended, eloquent, and daunting discussions of these issues, see Portelli 1991, 1997, 1998.

24. Vansina 1985: 91–92. See also Huyssen 1995: 3.

25. Halbwachs 1992: 47.

26. As Portelli (1991: 256, 199) reminds us, "Oral historians consider hearsay, opinion, beliefs, value judgments, and even errors as part of the peculiar usefulness of oral sources. . . . Contradictions and the verbal strategies used to keep them under control reveal a great deal about cultural attitudes and power relationships." He continues, "That is why it is more correct to speak of 'narrative' and 'narrators,' rather than 'testimony' and 'informants.' . . . 'Narrative' implies an awareness of the role of verbal organization and the inherent ambiguity and connotative aura of language, which can be rendered less ambiguous only at the price of heavy loss of information. 'Narrator,' on the other hand, spotlights the speaker's subjective presence" (256).

27. White 2000a: 5. For a treatment of ghost stories that does not use the term "inaccuracies"—perhaps because anthropologists are less haunted by the accuracy question than are historians—see Mueggler 2007.

28. For salient discussions of gender and memory, memory of gender, gender in memory, and related topics in other places, see Passerini 1987; Hamilton 2003; Leydesdorff, Passerini, and Thompson 1996; Brücker 1996; Piscitelli 1996; White 2004; Tai 2001b.

29. The terms "old society" and "new society" were not inaugurated by the Communist Party-state, although their usage was popularized after 1949. They can be seen as well in a

Guomindang textbook aimed at young people in 1947, in which a lesson on raising the status of women begins, "In the old society, the status of men and women was not equal, and therefore they were also unequal before the law. In the new society, women can join in social activities, enjoy equal rights with men, and have the same duties" (*Qingnian chengren yong guomin changshi keben [xia]* 1947: 3).

30. Wang Guohong 1993.

31. On this practice in an urban setting, see Ho 2004.

32. Gao Hua 2005: 162–63.

33. The term is from L'Engle 1975; see chapter 9 for further discussion.

34. For a discussion of related issues, see Gupta 1994.

35. Gao Xiaoxian, personal communication, Nov. 6, 2008.

36. On how interviewees represent themselves as having fixed identities, see Passerini 1987: 4, 17, 21, 27–28.

37. Their accounts of their own virtue are not centered on chastity (although they sometimes mention it). In this they depart from accounts of virtuous chaste women in the late Imperial and Republican periods, ubiquitous in local gazetteers and biographies.

38. Halbwachs (1992: 38) explains, "One is rather astonished when reading psychological treatises that deal with memory to find that people are considered there as isolated beings. . . . Yet it is in society that people normally acquire their memories. It is also in society that they recall, recognize, and localize their memories. . . . Most frequently, we appeal to our memory only in order to answer questions which others have asked us, or that we suppose they could have asked us. . . . Most of the time, when I remember, it is others who spur me on; their memory comes to the aid of mine and mine relies on theirs. . . . It is in this sense that there exists a collective memory and social frameworks for memory; it is to the degree that our individual thought places itself in these frameworks and participates in this memory that it is capable of the act of recollection." On collective memory, see also Boyarin 1994b: 26; Crane 1997; Confino 1997; Pennebaker 1997; Wertsch 2002.

39. For postsocialist memories drawn from other locales, see Malysheva and Bertaux 1996; Skultans 1998; Tai 2001a; Kaneff 2004; Wertsch 2002.

2. NO ONE IS HOME

1. Official materials give Shan Xiuzhen's birth year as 1913. See Weinan diqu nongye hezuo shi bianwei hui bian 1993: 512; Zhongguo renmin zhengzhi xieshang huiyi Shaanxi sheng Tongguan xian weiyuan hui wenshi ziliao weiyuan hui 1999: frontispiece, 3; Zhang et al. 1992: 13. Except where otherwise noted, all information about Shan Xiuzhen comes from our interviews with her in 1997.

2. Zhang et al. 1992: 14.

3. Two Swedish Protestant missionaries were sent by the American Christian Association (Meiguo jidu jiao xietong hui) to Liquan County in 1911, founding two churches, one in the county seat and one in Xiuzhen's home township of Beitun. Even in the late 1940s, however, the entire county had only about 400 Protestants and 650 Catholics (Liquan xian difang zhi bianzuan weihui 1999: 888–89).

4. Beitun, now a township, is on the eastern border of Liquan County, about thirty-five

miles northwest of Xi'an. A topographical map of the county does indeed show mountains rising sharply just north of the township. Today the entire area is under the jurisdiction of the Xianyang municipality (*Shaanxi sheng ditu ce* 1991: 5–6, 101; Liquan xian difang zhi 1999: frontispiece map).

5. At the beginning of 1925, in Liquan County, little rain fell and the summer harvest was scant. The worst drought, however, began in 1928. The county gazetteer reports that in 1929 there was no summer wheat harvest or fall harvest: "Starving people perished daily, accumulating in the hundreds and mounting into the thousands, turning vast expanses into wasteland, and people sold their sons and daughters, scattering to the four directions to flee the disaster." Of the county's 129,000 inhabitants, 66,000 died or fled. The drought continued into 1930, compounded in 1931 by a cholera outbreak that killed more than five thousand people. In 1932 and 1933 drought continued (Liquan xian difang zhi bianzuan weihui 1999: 148, 293). From 1928 to 1933 relief agencies distributed grain, seeds, flour, clothing, and relief payments, but much of it is said to have been appropriated by government officials and merchants (753).

6. Xia 2000: 90. Shaanxi had 1,233 recorded disasters of various magnitudes between 1912 and 1948, including floods, drought, insects, windstorms, hail, freezes, earthquakes, epidemics, and "other" (including everything from blizzards to mine disasters and collapsing mountains). Of these incidents, 569 were droughts and 346 were floods (34). A 1936 survey of why peasants in all provinces left home between 1931 and 1933 found that for Shaanxi, the two major causes were natural disasters (34.6 percent) and "bandits," which included local warfare (28.5 percent; 101). In Guanzhong, writes Vermeer (1988: 30–31), agriculture was almost exclusively dependent on rainfall, and drought was the major cause of the famine. It extended even to Shaannan areas generally more prone to flooding (Shaanxi sheng Danfeng xian shuili zhi bianzuan zu 1990: 70). On the North China drought and famine of 1876–79 and its effects in Shaanxi, especially Guanzhong, see He 1980. On the great drought and famine of 1898–1901 in Shaanxi, in which an estimated two million people died, see Nichols 1902: 228–41. For a capsule history of droughts, flooding, and hail in Weinan Prefecture from earliest times to 1989, see Weinan diqu difang zhi bianji weiyuan hui 1996: 743–51. For contemporary reports of 1930s disasters in Shaanxi, see *Xibei xiangdao* 1936: 9 (June 21), 32; and 15 (Aug. 21), 221–26.

7. Xia 2000: 90; Cao 2005: 23. The drought extended across Shaanxi, Gansu, Suiyuan, Shanxi, Hebei, Chahar, Rehe, and Henan, and in 1929 the Sino-Western Relief Association reported six million deaths (Van de Ven 2003: 131). In 1932, a member of the local elite in Tongguan mused to a visitor that so many people were selling women and girls out of Shaanxi as a result of the drought that it was likely to affect the province's gender ratio (and, by implication, the marriage prospects for men; Guo 1932: 52).

8. For a stark discussion of this situation, see Vermeer 1988: 28–38, 45–46.

9. Xia 2000: 410. These stories were originally reported in the *Dagong bao*.

10. Nanzheng xian difang zhi bianji weiyuan hui 1990: 141.

11. Vermeer 1988: 34, 408. Vermeer also cites a 1938 investigation of Guanzhong that finds the northern and western areas of the province lagging behind the eastern and central areas on many indicators: footbinding rates, the male:female ratio, and death rates remained higher in the north and west, and education rates were lower (though minuscule for women

in both regions: 2.9 percent in the east and 0.1 percent in the west). See Jiang Jie, "An Investigation of the Rural Population of Guanzhong," *Xibei nonglin* 3 (July 1938): 53–54, 102, 126, 156, cited in Vermeer 1988: 408, 518n74.

12. Yang Hui'e, born a decade later than Xiuzhen in the same county of Liquan, was sold at the age of seven to a family in Heyang County, almost two hundred *li* away. The future national labor model Zhang Qiuxiang was brought east from Jingyang County by her parents and married off in Weinan in 1929. Lu Guilan, a future regional labor model, was carried from Xingping by her father in a basket tied to a shoulder pole, eventually becoming a child daughter-in-law in Xianyang at the age of eight. Her new sister-in-law was also a famine refugee, picked up by her husband's family from the side of the road (interviews with Yang Hui'e 2001; Zhang Qiuxiang 1996; Lu Guilan 1996).

13. Surveys conducted in Guanzhong in 1936, after the famine was over, found that the male:female ratio had reached 118.5:100 in some districts, and as high as 129:100 for the age groups born during the famine. Vermeer (1988: 32–33) summarizes the results of the two surveys.

14. Zhang et al. 1992: 14.

15. Ibid., 15.

16. Hinton 1997; Anagnost 1997: 28–44; McLaren 2000; Guo and Sun 2002.

17. Speak bitterness stories have important links to a number of prerevolutionary genres. McLaren (2000) compares them to bridal laments; one might also trace their derivation from practices of public complaint and expressions of anger by women, such as "reviling the street" (Smith 1894: 220–21). My thanks to Susan Mann for suggesting the latter similarity.

18. The classic fictional account of the pre-Liberation period in central Shaanxi, and its effects on one particular family, is Liu Qing 1996: 1–18, translated into English as Liu Ching 1977: 1–19. See also Chen 1993.

19. Felman and Laub (1992), recounting psychoanalytic work with Holocaust survivors, describe the difficulties of narrating traumatic events that hitherto have not been voiceable, because they have been experienced as "overwhelming shock" (57) rather than as a known event. Laub describes the survivors' fear that narrating these events may cause them to be relived in an unendurable manner. Although there are obvious historical differences between the Holocaust and the sufferings of pre-1949 Chinese peasants, there is at least one important parallel: the ability to narrate unbearable losses presents the possibility of "repossession" (91) of the experience of separation and loss. For this reason, speaking bitterness should be taken seriously as a profoundly transformative practice, not a routinized piece of political theater.

20. Interview with He Gaizhen 1999.

21. Interview with Zhuang Xiaoxia 1996.

22. Interviews with He Gaizhen 1999; Zhang Qiuxiang 1996.

23. Interview with Zhuang Xiaoxia 1996. Lu Guilan (interview 1996) also mentions suicide by opium.

24. Versions of this aphorism were uttered in interviews with Cao Zhuxiang 1996, Zhuang Xiaoxia 1996, Wang Meihua 1996, Wang Nilan 2006, He Gaizhen 1999, and Liu Zhenxi (a man) 2006. The idea that women belong in domestic space is also encoded in some of the terms for women and men. Women are often referred to as *wuli ren*, "person in the room,"

a phrase also well known in standard Chinese. But in Guanzhong, specifically Weinan and Heyang Counties, glossaries of local dialect terms also refer to men as *waiqian ren* or *waitian ren*, "the person out in front" or "the person outside" (Heyang xianzhi bianzuan weiyuan hui 1996: 805; Weinan xianzhi bianji weiyuan hui 1987: 794). Weinan diqu difang zhi bianji weiyuan hui (1996: 913) glosses *waiqian ren* as "husband." These terms were often used by the women we interviewed.

25. Versions of this anecdote were uttered by Wang Meihua (interview 1996), Liu Zhaofeng (interview 1996), and Wang Nilan (interview 2006).

26. In an interview written up by a group of Chinese officials five years earlier, Xiuzhen is recorded as saying that she reunited with her mother in a temple in Chunhua, before crossing the mountains (Zhang et al. 1992: 15).

27. This was a popular slogan in the Mao era, as well as the title of a song.

28. For similar modes of self-narration as a rebel in autobiographies of women from more elite Chinese families, see Croll 1996. In her work on Turin factory workers, Luisa Passerini (1987: 61) finds that that fixed identity "can be considered a specific feature of self-representations in oral narration." Alessandro Portelli (1991: 53, 61, 118–30), in his interviews with workers, likewise finds narrators sometimes distinguishing between a past and a present self, sometimes providing a "thread of stability and permanence" (126) in statements such as "I have always had a fighting spirit" (127). Speak bitterness narratives would seem to lend themselves to the recounting of dramatic characterological changes, but in fact fixed identity statements were much more common in our interviews.

29. According to statistics collected at the time of the land reform, in 1949 of 180,000 people in Xiuzhen's home county of Liquan, only about three thousand people (or 240 households) were classified as landlords, while four thousand people (300 households) were classified as rich peasants. Landlord landholdings amounted to about thirteen *mu* per capita, while poor and lower-middle peasant landholdings (more than ninety thousand people in more than twenty thousand households) averaged a bit more than two *mu* per person. Middle peasants, comprising more than ten thousand households and seventy-eight thousand people, cultivated more than 50 percent of the arable land. Landlords and rich peasants together were only 4 percent of the population, although they occupied about 30 percent of the arable land (Liquan xian difang zhi 1999: 294). Nevertheless, with such small numbers, it is not likely that Xiuzhen had much contact with landlord households.

30. A printed interview with her reports that she cooked and did needlework for the household's concubine, while her husband did farming for the family and her mother did errands for the concubine's sister-in-law (Zhang et al. 1992: 16).

31. Tongguan County had also been hard-hit by the drought, and many peasants had fled. But by mid-1933, a traveler through the county found, most had returned (Gu and Lu 1937). In 1938, partly because of population movements occasioned by the Japanese invasion of neighboring Shanxi, the county's population had swelled to 60,877 people, up almost 57 percent from the population at the beginning of the Republican period (*Tongguan juan* 1997: 37).

32. *Tongguan juan* 1997: 15.

33. Xiuzhen gives dates with great specificity, but she moves back and forth between lunar and solar calendars and does not always clarify which one she is using. She says that she

arrived on the twenty-ninth of the first month and that the bombing took place on the first day of the second month. The local gazetteer gives the date of the bombing as February 28 (Tongguan xianzhi bianzuan weiyuan hui 1992: 18).

34. *Tongguan juan* 1997: 15–16. More details of these skirmishes are given in Tongguan xianzhi bianzuan weiyuan hui 1992: 18; Guo 1992: 266–67.

35. Population density in Tongguan reached its pre-1949 high in 1938, with 136.8 people per square kilometer. Because of the county's position as the gateway to Shaanxi from both Henan and Shanxi Provinces, one local history notes that people were incessantly on the move, particularly during wartime, with soldiers defending the passes, and refugees, political officials, and merchants moving in and out (*Tongguan juan* 1997: 53, 54). Other counties where we interviewed substantial numbers of women—Weinan, Nanzheng, Danfeng, and Heyang—were not directly attacked by the Japanese.

36. Interview with Cao Zhuxiang 1996.

37. Zhang Qiuxiang's year of birth is given as 1908 in Weinan diqu nongye hezuo shi bianwei hui bian 1993: 511, and as 1903 in Weinan xianzhi bianji weiyuan hui 1987: 617. A file on her as she was first emerging as a cotton-growing champion in 1956 gives her age as forty-seven, which would put her birth date in 1909 or 1910 (FL 178–161–074).

38. Interview with Zhang Qiuxiang 1996.

39. Interview with Feng Sumei 1997.

40. Interviews with Feng Na 2001; Li Xiaomei 1997. This account, based on four main locations, may not capture all local variations. In Xingping County, west of Xi'an, one former Women's Federation cadre reports that women born in the mid-1930s almost all had their feet bound and that inducing families to unbind their daughters' feet required a major campaign at the time of the land reform in the early 1950s (interview with Liu Zhaofeng 1996).

41. Interview with Zhang Zizhen 1999. On the ubiquity of footbinding in late Qing Shaanxi and its absolute necessity for marriage, see Nichols 1902: 134–35. For footbinding as practice and representation, see Ko 2005.

42. Liquan xian difang zhi 1999: 28. On earlier Natural Foot Society activities in Weinan Prefecture, see Weinan diqu difang zhi bianji weiyuan hui 1996: 270.

43. Interview with Cao Zhuxiang 1996.

44. Interviews with Song Yufen 1997; Feng Sumei 1997; Liu Fengqin 1996; Qiao Yindi 2001; Zhou Guizhen 1996.

45. Interview with Wang Zhaoru 2004.

46. Interview with Qiao Yindi 2001. Kaplan Murray (1985: 234) describes this cropping pattern for the eighteenth century, minus the opium. She says that maize became a major food crop toward the end of the nineteenth century, in tandem with the rise of cotton cultivation (296–311). Buck's (1964 [1937]: 58) Republican-era survey comments that in the late 1920s and early 1930s corn was mainly a spring crop but was sown in the summer in a few areas. Vermeer (1988: 256) says that maize production expanded rapidly beginning in the 1950s. For a discussion of soils, fertilizers, draft animals, seed varieties, and cropping patterns ranging from the 1930s to the 1980s, see Vermeer 1988: 222–89, 324–82. British consular official Eric Teichman (1921: 84) described the Wei River plain as one of "the great cotton-growing areas of Central Shensi." Cotton was a staple crop that in the late 1910s was

also being exported to Japan. In the late nineteenth century, some land was also devoted to commercially produced opium, a fall crop harvested in the third lunar month (Kaplan Murray 1985: 73–74). In 1920, Teichman (1921: vi) wrote that opium had been briefly suppressed in 1916–17, but by 1920 was again being cultivated and taxed by local officials. By the late 1920s, it was widely grown in the Wei Valley. Buck found that opium in Weinan County took up 7.7 percent of the cropping area, and was cultivated on 64 percent of the farms (Buck 1982: 178, 184, cited in Kaplan Murray 1985: 79). The national government attempted opium suppression in the province after the Japanese invasion, in an attempt to divert farmland to wheat and cotton (Shen 1977: 172–73).

47. The farm tools used for each of these tasks had not changed for several thousand years: the plow was drawn by an ox, and the other operations relied on human labor power (Liquan xian difang zhi bianzuan weihui 1999: 293; interview with Cao Zhuxiang 1996).

48. Interviews with Zhou Guizhen 1996; Zhang Qiuxiang 1996; Cao Zhuxiang 1996; Qiao Yindi 2001; Zhang Chaofeng 2001. A traveler through Shaanxi in the late Qing noted, "The care of the cotton-crop is the especial province of the women. They pick the raw cotton, spin it into thread, weave and dye the cloth, and make the clothes of the entire family" (Nichols 1902: 129).

49. Interviews with Cao Zhuxiang 1996; Liu Fengqin 1996.

50. Interview with Lei Caiwa 2001.

51. Interview with Yang Guishi 2004. For a description of similar water hauling by women in Heyang County in the early 1990s, see Holm 2003: 866. He writes, "The time-consuming nature of the task has given rise to an informal women's network, a well-side sorority, that is a characteristic feature of village life in Heyang."

52. Interviews with Qian Taohua 1997; Feng Sumei 1997; Li Liujin 1997.

53. Interview with Feng Sumei 1997.

54. Interviews with Qian Taohua 1997; Wang Youna 1997; Li Xiulan 1997; Zhang Xiuli 1997; Lu Yulian 1999.

55. Interviews with Zhou Guizhen 1996; Liu Zhenxi 2006; Qian Taohua 1997; Zhang Chaofeng 2001.

56. Interview with Cao Zhuxiang 1996.

57. Interview with Liu Zhenxi 2006. Wang Xiqin (interview 1996) had a husband from Village B who began working at a shop in Weinan at the age of fourteen. Li Xiulan's (interview 1997) father, who lived in the Village T area, worked away from home as a carpenter in the 1930s. Feng Na's (interview 2001) future husband, who lived in Village G, did the same in the 1920s and 1930s. See also the many stories of child daughters-in-law in this chapter whose future husbands were not at home when the girls entered the household.

58. Interview with Cao Zhuxiang 1996.

59. Interview with Ma Li 1999.

60. Interview with Liu Guyu 2001.

61. A traveler in Shaanxi in 1902 noted, "But if there is no liquor-slavery in Shensi [Shaanxi], the opium-curse more than takes its place. Begging by the road-side, sleeping under the shadow of the houses, or moping idly on the benches of the tea-houses, are found the victims of the blight on the land. They are always distinguished by their sallowness and their rags" (Nichols 1902: 132). According to Vermeer (1988: 4), the long-running campaign

to eradicate opium was not successful until 1939–40, when the Japanese invasion forced many GMD officials to relocate to western China. For further details, see 325–29.

62. Interviews with Liu Zhenxi 2006; He Gaizhen 1999.

63. The Tongguan gazetteer reports a summer drought in 1942, a spring and summer drought in 1944, a drought and below-normal grain harvest for the entire year in 1947, and a summer drought in 1948 (Tongguan xianzhi bianzuan weiyuan hui 1992: 89).

64. Interview with Lu Yulian 1999.

65. Xiuzhen uses the term *ren,* which can be translated as "people" but which in Guanzhong dialect means "men." See the discussion at the end of this chapter.

66. Interviews with Qian Taohua 1997; Wang Youna 1997; Feng Na 2001; Zhou Guizhen 2006; Zhang Chaofeng 2001; Feng Sumei 1997; Lei Caiwa 2001.

67. Interview with Liu Guyu 2004.

68. Interviews with Yang Anxiu 1997; Feng Sumei 1997.

69. Interviews with Ouyang Xiu 2004; Zhang Chaofeng 2001; Lei Caiwa 2001.

70. Interviews with Ouyang Xiu 2004; Zhou Guizhen 2006; Liu Fengqin 2006.

71. Interviews with Cao Zhuxiang 1996, 2006; Qiao Yindi 2001.

72. Interview with Zhou Guizhen 2006.

73. Ibid.

74. Interviews with Li Liujin 1997; Feng Sumei 1997.

75. Interview with Zhang Chaofeng 2001.

76. Interview with Liu Guyu 2001.

77. Interviews with Zhang Chaofeng 2001; Gao Zhenxian 1997; Wang Xiqin 2006; Li Liujin 1997; Wang Youna 1997; Feng Na 2001; Yu Xiaoli 2001; Wang Zhaoru 2004. Enumerating households one by one from memory in 2006, Liu Zhenxi estimated that twelve of forty-two households in Village B, the poorest in the village, had women producing cloth for sale.

78. Interview with Cao Zhuxiang 2006.

79. Interviews with Zhuang Xiaoxia 1996; Shan Xiuzhen 1997; Cao Zhuxiang 1996; Yang Anxiu 1997; Qian Taohua 1997; Liu Dongmei 1999; Qiao Yindi 2001; Lei Caiwa 2001; Ma Li 1999.

80. Interviews with Qian Taohua 1997; Wang Youna 1997; Li Xiulan 1997; Li Liujin 1997; Ma Fangxian 1999.

81. Interviews with Zhang Chaofeng 2001; Liu Cunyu 2001; Liu Zhenxi 2006; Zhuang Xiaoxia 1996; Wang Xiqin 2006; Cao Zhuxiang 2006.

82. Interview with Li Liujin 1997. On women in the market, see also interview with Li Xiulan 1997.

83. Interview with Yang Anxiu 1997.

84. Markets varied from one region to another. In Village T they were frequented mostly by local people, and women did not take their cloth into the surrounding mountains to sell. In Village B, in Guanzhong, cloth merchants came from outside the area, joining local consumers to buy the coarse and fine cloth woven by local women. In Village Z it was common for women and their male relatives to take cloth to the mountain areas to trade for grain (interviews with Li Liujin 1997; Cao Zhuxiang 2006; Ma Li 1999).

85. Interview with Ma Li 1999.

86. Interview with Zhang Qiuxiang 1996.

87. Interview with Zheng Xiuhua 1999.
88. Interview with Zhang Chaofeng 2001.
89. Interviews with Yang Anxiu 1997; Lu Yulian 1999.
90. Interview with Zhang Chaofeng 2001.
91. Weinan xianzhi bianji weiyuan hui 1987: 17. In Heyang County 2,129 people died (Heyang xianzhi bianzuan weiyuan hui 1996: 13). Cholera was also reported in Danfeng (Danfeng xianzhi bianji weiyuan hui 1994: 20).
92. Nanzheng xian difang zhi bianji weiyuan hui 1990: 141.
93. Interview with Li Liujin 1997.
94. Service 1974: 17, 11. The "normal" price of a woman is given here as three thousand yuan.
95. The brideprice reflected the age of each girl. Guyu is not sure how much wheat her father received, but she thinks that her own brideprice was four thousand yuan. Her older sister fetched a price of seven thousand yuan, ten-year-old Cunyu much less (interview with Liu Guyu 2001).
96. Guyu liked the other bride well enough, but she could not bring herself to address her as "elder sister-in-law" (*saozi*), since she was three years younger. The two got along well, dividing the household labor. From 1949 to 1968, Guyu bore five sons and two daughters. The oldest went deaf after being dosed with bezoar for convulsions when he was three, but all of the children survived to adulthood (interviews with Liu Guyu 2001, 2004).
97. Interview with Liu Cunyu 2001. *Maigei renjia* in Shaanxi dialect means to be married to someone, not to be sold to them.
98. Interview with Zhou Guizhen 1996.
99. After the age of thirty-two, Xiuzhen never again became pregnant: *I didn't plan [i.e., use birth control]. I didn't give birth anymore. I didn't want more. Babies couldn't survive after they were born.* Before her milk from the last baby had dried up, however, she adopted a two-month-old boy whose mother had just died. This son survived a childhood bout with measles and was caring for Xiuzhen, then in her eighties, at the time of our interview. *He was raised on my milk. I had milk at that time. He ate his fill on my milk. This son was very obedient. He is very nice to me. He had two sons and two daughters. He was never stubborn with me. He is very obedient. My son, my daughter-in-law, and my grandchildren have never been stubborn with me* (interview with Shan Xiuzhen 1997).
100. The other major threat to young children was diarrhea, which would strike without warning. Qiao Yindi lost several younger siblings in the 1940s, when they were toddlers. She ascribes their illness to too much watermelon, but whatever the cause, the lack of medical care in Village G made any diarrhea potentially fatal (interview 2001). A 1949 survey cited by Vermeer (1981: 223) found that one-third of all children born between 1939 and 1948 in Guanzhong had died, most commonly of tetanus, measles, pneumonia, dysentery, and diphtheria.
101. The regulations issued in 1937 made men ages eighteen to twenty-five liable for three years of active service, while men ages twenty-six to forty-five could be called up as citizen soldiers (*guomin bing*). Widespread abuse of the published regulations, which provided procedures for drawing lots and exemptions for only sons and were supposed to be applied across income levels, was reported. The conscription quota for Shang County (later Danfeng

County, where Village Z is located) was raised to more than five thousand men during the War of Resistance against Japan, leading to several rounds of conscription each year, often at gunpoint, and the frequent flight of young men from the county. Abolished in 1945, conscription was reinstituted when civil war broke out in 1946 (Danfeng xianzhi bianji weiyuan hui 1994: 475). In Heyang County, where Village G is located, the quota in 1939 was 1,428 men; in 1940 it was 1,848 men. By 1942 there were no more lots to draw, but the quota had grown to 3,900 people, with exemptions being sold at spiraling prices and layers of officials pocketing portions of the payments (Heyang xianzhi bianzuan weiyuan hui 1996: 574). Vermeer (1988: 409–10), who gives the provincial figure of 200,000 conscripts and comments on the high prices in Heyang, writes that by 1939 "trading in recruits was widespread, and prices for recruits rose fast." For annual quotas and actual conscription numbers in Weinan County from 1937 to 1948, ranging as high as 7,049 men in 1940, with a total of 34,321 men conscripted over the eleven-year period, see Weinan xianzhi bianji weiyuan hui 1987: 503. On conscription in Nanzheng County (home of Village T), see Nanzheng xian difang zhi bianji weiyuan hui 1990: 474. For further discussion of national conscription regulations and their attendant corruption and abuse, see Van de Ven 2003: 145–46, 253–58.

102. *Xibei nongbao* 1, no. 3 (1946): 110–15, cited in Vermeer 1988: 410, 519n80. This report notes that a recruit cost between two hundred and one thousand yuan in Guanzhong. Presumably a man's family had to pay this much to have a man from a poorer family take his place.

103. In the late 1920s and early 1930s, the Nanjing government reinstituted a *baojia* system that bore some relationship to a similar system used in imperial times. All households were to register; ten households formed a *jia*; ten *jia* formed a *bao*. Men ages nineteen to forty registered under this system were supposed to be trained as local militia for "assistance with local disaster relief, road building, protection against banditry, and the construction of blockhouses and stockades" (Van de Ven 2003: 144). For the 1933 reinstatement of the *baojia* system in Shaanxi, its intensification during the war years, and detailed charts on the numbers of *bao* and *jia* in each county, see Shaanxi sheng minzheng ting 1940. On *baojia* data for Weinan and Heyang Counties, see Weinan diqu difang zhi bianji weiyuan hui 1996: 19–21.

104. On Guomindang conscription and conscription abuse in a Sichuan village, see Ruf 1998: 24–28. On rich households buying exemptions in Weinan County and the seizing of passers-by and itinerant farm laborers and the poor, see Weinan xianzhi bianji weiyuan hui 1987: 503.

105. Interview with Cao Zhuxiang 1996.

106. Interview with Wang Xiqin 1996.

107. Interview with Liu Fengqin 1996. In 1947, exemptions were publicly traded at the rate of more than one hundred *jin* of wheat per soldier (Weinan xianzhi bianji weiyuan hui 1987: 503).

108. Interview with Lu Guilan 1996.

109. Her second mother-in-law was the widow of her father-in-law's brother, who lived with them. See chapter 3.

110. Weinan xianzhi bianji weiyuan hui 1987: 17, 18.

111. Cao Zhuxiang was born in September 1918 (Weinan xianzhi bianji weiyuan hui 1987: 617; in our interview with her in 1996 she gave her birth date not by calendar year but

as the year of the horse, which is 1918). She was betrothed and married at seventeen by Chinese reckoning, which adds a year to one's age at birth and again at each lunar new year. Following this logic and information she gave us about when her children were born, she was married in 1934, had her daughter in 1937, and had her son toward the end of 1940. Only after her son's birth did her husband die. Documents about Zhuxiang assembled in the early 1950s, when she first became a local agricultural leader, all give the date of her husband's death as 1941. See interview with Cao Zhuxiang 1996; FL 178-27-025 (1952); FL 178-209-009 (1953). On September 21, 1941, a total eclipse of the sun darkened the sky at noon: "The stars appeared, birds and sparrows flew about chaotically, and chickens and dogs rushed around confused" (Weinan xianzhi bianji weiyuan hui 1987: 19).

112. The men were from Shang County, later Danfeng County, home of Village Z. Weinan xianzhi bianji weiyuan hui 1987: 19, 503.

113. Interview with Cao Zhuxiang 1996.

114. Ibid.

115. Teichman (1921: 74–76) provides a vivid description of Shaanxi bandits and their interchangeability with regular soldiers in the 1910s. The warlord period (1916–28) was probably the high point for banditry, but because the Guomindang was slow to extend its effective control over the province, banditry continued into the 1930s. Billingsley (1988: 30) writes, "Under warlordism Shaanxi became the domain of men of violence of every hue from genuine peasant rebels to warlord-backed bandit armies and landlord-sponsored militias. . . . Apart from the north of the province, birthplace of many peasant rebellions in the past, and the south, famine-prone and always troubled by bandits, during the Republican period even sections of the fertile Wei River valley were host to strong and long-lived gangs. Although accurate figures are hard to come by, Shaanxi's mid-1920's bandit population undoubtedly numbered several tens of thousands. With borders facing Gansu, Ningxia, Suiyuan, Shanxi, Henan, Hubei, and Sichuan, Shaanxi was also constantly prone to incursions by outside gangs." On bandits in early Republican Shaanxi, see Ran 1995: 9, 19, 80, 111–14, 136–37, 187–90, 208–10. On the 1930s, see Li and Yuan 2006, especially 454–57. They estimate the number of Shaanxi bandits in the mid-1930s at more than 100,000 (454).

116. Interview with Feng Na 2001.

117. This was during the period of the national Northern Expedition. In the winter of 1927, Village G was one of four villages whose peasant associations united to launch an attack on local militarist forces, capturing one commander and killing another. Only with the arrival of the National Army in July 1928 did this particular episode of turmoil come to an end (Heyang xianzhi bianzuan weiyuan hui 1996: 12).

118. Danfeng xianzhi bianji weiyuan hui 1994: 485. Yan Panwa (interview 1999) says that Li Changyou occupied Village Z for forty-one days and returned again in the ninth month of the lunar calendar, which is consistent with the written account.

119. Interview with Yan Panwa 1999.

120. Interview with Liu Dongmei 1999.

121. Interview with Dong Guizhi 1999.

122. Interview with Li Duoduo 1999.

123. The term "Laomohai" was used by several women in Village Z. Bai Chongxi was alternately an ally and an adversary of Jiang Jieshi from the 1920s until the Guomindang was

driven from the mainland in 1949. During the War of Resistance against Japan, Bai was a major strategist and deputy chief of the General Staff. In November 1941 he stayed in Longjusai, the largest township (and later the county seat). In June 1943, the commander of the Guomindang Fifth War District, Li Zongren, another member of the "Guangxi clique," and at this point or soon thereafter director of Jiang Jieshi's headquarters (and later still, very briefly, acting president of the Republic of China), came to inspect defenses and also passed through Longjusai. Finally, in November 1944, the Guomindang Army Command for the war against Japan moved from Shangnan County to Longjusai's Chenjia village. At the time it was directed by Guo Jijiao, an Anhui native (*Danfeng xianzhi* 1994: 23–24). Either Bai or Li might have brought Guangxi troops with them to the vicinity, and the presence of the Army Command might also have brought southern soldiers to Village Z and its surroundings.

124. Interview with Li Duoduo 1999.

125. Interview with Xiao Gaiye 1999. The generalized sense of sexual menace that pervades so many tales of militarists, bandits, and the Guomindang forces is strikingly absent from stories of the Communist forces. The one sexual overtone we heard in connection with PLA forces was from a woman who spent the civil war years in Chishan, far to the southwest of the province, bordering Sichuan, in an area where Communist troops stayed in her house. She recalls the PLA soldiers singing a song that included the lyrics "As long as the revolution succeeds, everyone [meaning, perhaps, every man?] will be sent a girl student." But in the next breath she explains that the main salutary change that the Communists produced after 1949 was the liberation of women (interview with Ouyang Xiu 2004).

126. Interview with Liu Dongmei 1999.

127. On the military history of the Civil War in Shaanxi, see Westad 2003: 150–54, 254–55.

128. Local histories of Tongguan record that in mid-September 1947, troops of the Communist People's Liberation Army under the command of Chen Geng and Xie Fuzhi moved west into Tongguan from Henan to prevent the Guomindang troops from moving east. The PLA forces attacked Guomindang troops commanded by Hu Zongnan, and Hu tried to prevent them from moving west. On the evening of September 15, the PLA surrounded Shanchekou village from the east, south, and north, eliminating part of the enemy forces and then withdrawing from their position. Shanchekou was less than two kilometers south of Shangmadian village, where Xiuzhen lived, and it was probably this battle that resulted in the destruction of her neighbor's pomegranate tree and privy (*Tongguan juan* 1997: 16; Tongguan xianzhi bianzuan weiyuan hui 1992: 20). For the location of Shangmadian in relation to Shanchekou, see Tongguan xianzhi bianzuan weiyuan hui 1992: frontispiece map.

129. Interview with Li Duoduo 1999.

130. Danfeng xianzhi bianji weiyuan hui 1994: 24–25.

131. Ibid., 20–21; Liu 1981: 240–43; Xu 1982: 35–42, 78–97, 130–31; Zhang 1982: 153–84.

132. Xu 1982: 51–57, 135; Zhang 1982: 260–88.

133. Interview with He Gaizhen 1999.

134. For the history of 1940s conflicts led by the local non-Communist "guerrilla" leader Xiao Tongfu in the Village Z area, see Danfeng xianzhi bianji weiyuan hui 1994: 480. Zhang Kui emerged as a leader of one of Xiao's detachments in the early 1940s. In 1945, the underground Communist Party sought unsuccessfully to recruit the entire group; soon thereafter,

the group suffered a concerted assault from local Guomindang forces, who seized Xiao and the family members of Zhang Kui and other detachment commanders. Zhang was one of two detachment commanders who did not surrender; he subsequently joined up with Communist forces and became "one of the armed backbone cadres of the revolution in the Shangluo district."

135. Interview with He Gaizhen 1999.

136. Interview with Zheng Xiuhua 1999.

137. Ibid. The struggle for the area around Village Z was protracted and intense, but ultimately Zhang Kui's forces prevailed. Details of battles in the area are given in Danfeng xianzhi bianji weiyuan hui 1994: 488–90. Zhang Kui looms less large in this official account than in the stories of Village Z residents. A story He Gaizhen told about Zhang Kui made him out to be far less disciplined and benevolent than the Eighth Route Army's regular soldiers; instead she described him as a local man who knew how to hold a grudge. During the back-and-forth fighting, it is said, he ate a pig at the house of a well-off peasant and left, promising to pay later. When the GMD troops returned, the peasant and his wife attacked and cursed Zhang Kui's wife (or possibly his concubine). Later still, Zhang Kui came back and apparently killed the peasant's wife and son, although the details are somewhat murky (interview with He Gaizhen 1999).

138. Heyang xianzhi bianzuan weiyuan hui 1996: 14–15; Zhang Tie 1982; Weinan diqu difang zhi bianji weiyuan hui 1996: 309–11. *Heyang wenshi ziliao* 2 (Oct. 1988), a special issue devoted to the fortieth anniversary of the liberation of Heyang, includes memoirs by guerrillas who fought in the county. Village G is not mentioned, nor is anyone from the village included in a detailed list of revolutionary martyrs from this period.

139. For an explanation of *laochi,* see Dai 1977: 9.

140. For accounts of the victory of the Communists in the Wei River Valley in June 1949, see Hooton 1991: 166; Weinan diqu difang zhi bianji weiyuan hui 1996: 312–13.

141. Interview with Cao Zhuxiang 1996.

142. Ibid. Of the villages where we interviewed, only Village T in Nanzheng changed hands without immediate fighting in the vicinity, perhaps because the county was not liberated until early December 1949, more than two months after the establishment of the People's Republic of China (Nanzheng xian difang zhi bianji weiyuan hui 1990: 16).

143. PLA troops had begun to move back toward the area in April, and during May they successfully established control over all of Shanxi Province to the north, the city of Xi'an to the west, and the western tip of Henan bordering Tongguan to the east. Xiuzhen does not mention a violent incident that happened on June 25–26, when remnant GMD forces attacked several district governments, including that of Taiyao Township, not far from her village, and killed six Communists (Tongguan xianzhi bianzuan weiyuan hui 1992: 20).

144. FL 178-106-005, June 20, 1949. This report by the newly established Women's Federation was published less than three weeks after Shaanxi was liberated. The putative attitude about labor being shameful bears closer examination. In her study of Hangzhou silk workers, Lisa Rofel (1999: 72) points out, as did Mann (1997) for the imperial era, that the inside/outside dichotomy did not map onto "an American middle-class cultural dichotomy of domestic versus public" and that "inside/outside was not based on a misrecognition of activities within the household as nonlabor." Women in Hangzhou before 1949 produced

silk alongside male family members inside domestic workshops, and this did not challenge the accepted notions of gendered activity. It was only when women went "outside" to work among non-kin that they fell beyond the pale of respectability, and Rofel notes that older women workers' memories of pre-1949 times are still tinged with shame. Rofel argues that Liberation entailed for these women workers not a change of venue (they were already "outside"), but a destigmatizing of "outside" activity (64–80).

145. Some negotiate with the norm even as they reject it, claiming respectability by redefining the boundaries of "going out." Zhang Chaofeng (interview 2001), whose story of the burning banknotes began this book, declares that she did not leave the house after she was married: *I didn't go out. Aside from going to his relatives' houses, his older sister's house, going to the fields to pick cotton, or harvest the wheat. We usually harvested the wheat. I didn't go to the market.*

146. Xiuzhen and her neighbors in western Shaanxi were most likely to have fled their homes during the 1928 drought. Henan natives like Guyu and Cunyu entered eastern Shaanxi during the 1942 famine. Hiding from bandits and soldiers was most common in Village Z, located in a particularly volatile area in the southeast of the province. More women seem to have sold their own thread and cloth and needlework at markets in the south than in the central region. Li Liujin (interview 1997) and Li Xiulan (interview 1997) talk about markets in the south. On marketing in Village G, in east central Shaanxi, see Yang Guishi (interview 2004) on his widowed mother selling cloth at the market with a group of other women, and Lei Caiwa (interview 2001) on going to the market with her mother.

147. Interview with Cao Zhuxiang 1996.

3. WIDOW (OR, THE VIRTUE OF LEADERSHIP)

1. Interview with Shan Xiuzhen 1997; Zhongguo renmin zhengzhi xieshang huiyi Shaanxi sheng Tongguan xian weiyuan hui wenshi ziliao weiyuan hui 1999: 4.

2. Interview with Shan Xiuzhen 1997. On her entry into the Party, see also Weinan diqu nongye hezuo shi bianwei hui bian 1993: 512.

3. On stigmatized women cotton mill workers in Shanghai and Tianjin, see Honig 1986 and Hershatter 1986, respectively.

4. A compelling fictional account of this period in central Shaanxi is Liu Qing 1996, translated into English as Liu Ching 1977.

5. On campaigns, see Bennett 1976. Some campaigns were characterized by considerable coercion and physical violence, but the ones under discussion here, with the exception of the land reform, were largely a matter of political, social, and economic persuasion and pressure.

6. Nora 1996, 1997, 1998.

7. Timothy Mitchell (1991, 1999) has suggested that one should not draw a precise boundary between state and society, nor think of the state as a "free-standing agent issuing orders" (1991: 93). Mitchell wants to begin with the "uncertain boundary" between the state and society and to ask, "How is the effect created that certain aspects of what occurs pertain to society, while others stand apart as the state?" (89). He argues that we should "examine the detailed political processes through which the uncertain yet powerful distinction between

state and society is produced." This distinction is not "the boundary between two discrete entities," but rather "a line drawn internally within the network of institutional mechanisms through which a social and political order is maintained" (78).

Mitchell's analysis is aimed at the postwar capitalist state, with interlocking connections between state and "private" institutions on the one hand, and a naturalized separation between "state and society" or "state and economy" on the other. Although I have wrenched it from its original context, I find his work useful for thinking about the socialist Party-state and the production of an internally differentiated entity known as "the masses," among whom women (or "woman-as-state-subject," in Tani Barlow's [1994] formulation) were an important constitutive part.

8. Mitchell 1999: 89. He continues, "We should examine it [the state effect] not as an actual structure, but as the powerful, apparently metaphysical effect of practices that make such structures appear to exist."

9. Ibid., 76.

10. Here and throughout, women give their ages according to Chinese reckoning, which adds a year to one's age at birth and at every Spring Festival thereafter.

Village B, now part of Red Star Village, was located in what is now Baiyang Township, in the western suburbs of Weinan city, at the southwest corner of Weinan District. Weinan city is about sixty kilometers northeast of Xian. Village B was one of nine "natural villages" (*ziran cun*) that became part of the Red Star Agricultural Producers' Cooperative. The co-op encompassed different villages at different times, making it difficult to estimate the size of the constituent villages. In 1955, the Red Star Advanced Producers' Cooperative comprised 224 households, according to one source (Weinan diqu nongye hezuo shi bianwei hui bian 1993: 368) and 294 according to another ("Cao Zhuxiang mofan" 1957). In 1959 or 1960 Village B split into north and south villages, and the south village, where Cao Zhuxiang lived, became the second production team (*erdui*) under the Red Star Production Brigade of the Baiyang Commune (Village B briefing 1996). Judging from the size of early mutual aid teams centered in the village (see below), it appears to have consisted of fewer than forty households in the 1950s.

11. Interview with Cao Zhuxiang 1996.

12. Ibid.

13. Cao Zhuxiang's area had never been occupied by the Japanese, so she is speaking here from an understanding of history probably acquired after the time she is describing. For a description of Republican-era governance at the village level, based on a 1933 government survey and including four villages in Weinan, see Xu 2006. The village head was selected from a village's propertied families (297), and his expenses were generally met by the villagers (298–99). Abuses of power by local officials were not unknown; for one particularly egregious Weinan County case, see 304–5.

14. Interview with Cao Zhuxiang 1996. Zhuxiang's brothers played an important role at major turning points in her life. Her older brother supported her decision not to remarry after her husband's death, discussed later in this chapter. He opposed her taking on political office. He may have been quite conservative in his notions of proper womanly conduct, but he also taught her to plow, helped her with farmwork, and became a village head in the People's Republic. The younger brother later became a Party secretary.

15. The county Women's Federation was established on August 25, 1949 (Weinan xianzhi bianji weiyuan hui 1987: 21). The provincial organization was formally inaugurated in October 1950, with a province-wide meeting of 247 women's representatives (Shaanxi sheng funü lianhe hui, 1994: 3–5; FL 178–107–016 1950). On early Federation activities in Weinan Prefecture, see Weinan diqu difang zhi bianji weiyuan hui 1996: 271–73.

16. Interview with Cao Zhuxiang 1996. For a Women's Federation report on troop support in Weinan County, see FL 178–102–015 (Oct.–Dec. 1949).

17. Shaanxi sheng funü lianhe hui, 1994: 2. The boiled water amount was 77,900 *dan*, at fifty kilograms per *dan* (*dan* here being a measure of the amount carried by shoulder pole).

18. FL 178–97–011 (Oct. 15, 1949). On similar activities in Xianyang County, see FL 178–100–013 (Oct. 19, 1949).

19. FL 178–97–011 (Oct. 15, 1949). For similar complaints about shoemaking in Chang'an County, see FL 178–102–006 (Oct.–Dec. 1949).

20. Weinan xianzhi bianji weiyuan hui 1987: 21.

21. FL 178–97–011 (Oct. 15, 1949); Shaanxi sheng funü lianhe hui, 1994: 2. Vermeer (1988: 296) cites a *Qunzhong ribao* report to the effect that "between Dec. 1949 and May 1950, 12,651 'bandits' were put to death, a category which included active resistants, left-behind Guomindang agents, landlords' militia, highway robbers and other active criminals." Cao Zhuxiang (interview 1996) also mentions that just after Liberation, men in Village B who engaged in petty thievery to finance their gambling debts (and in one case an opium habit) were detained for labor reform, some for brief periods, reducing the local crime level.

22. Except where otherwise noted, the account that follows draws upon our interview with Cao Zhuxiang 1996; Cao Zhuxiang huzhuzu 1952; Cao Zhuxiang mofan 1957; Weinan diqu nongye hezuo shi bianwei hui bian 1993: 367. Vermeer (1988: 297, 503 n14) notes that in spring 1950, "Some 700,000 people were calamity-stricken.... There were refugees from north and east China."

23. County cadres met in early March to plan for spring plowing and shortage relief work (Weinan xianzhi bianji weiyuan hui 1987: 22).

24. Interview with Liu Fengqin 1996.

25. Interview with Cao Zhuxiang 1996. The seventh woman was the aunt of Wang Xiqin's husband and the mother-in-law of Zhuang Xiaoxia, two of our interviewees (Wang Xiqin 1996; Zhuang Xiaoxia 1996).

26. Interview with Cao Zhuxiang 1996.

27. Interviews with Liu Fengqin 1996; Cao Zhuxiang 1996. Also see Weinan diqu nongye hezuo shi bianwei hui bian 1993: 367.

28. FL 178–209–009 1953. A *dou* was equal to thirty to forty *jin*.

29. Interview with Cao Zhuxiang 1996.

30. FL 178–209–009 1953. After 1949, labor model materials on Cao Zhuxiang routinely included statements such as "Her laboring habits were discriminated against in the old society" (FL 178–27–025 1952). This may be merely postrevolutionary puffery. Such sources never specify the concrete form of that discrimination, and the women we interviewed never mentioned it in retelling their memories of the period before the revolution. The reference to freeing men up to work as seasonal hired laborers elsewhere suggests that the practice of

men leaving home to seek work, detailed in chapter 2, continued into the collective period, when such workers were paid in work points credited to their home production team.

31. For the same sort of measures in Xianyang County, see FL 178–100–013 (Oct. 19, 1949); for a preliminary province-wide survey, see FL 178–106–005 (Jan. 19, 1949).

32. FL 178–103–010 1950.

33. Interviews with Zhou Guizhen 1996; Cao Zhuxiang 1996.

34. Interview with Ma Ruyun 1996. A 1952 Women's Federation report showed that the majority of Federation cadres in Baoji and Suide districts (136 of 179 in Baoji and 88 of 103 in Suide) had gone "down" to the countryside (*xiaxiang*) to stay for periods from fifty to ninety days. At that point, about 85 percent of the townships in the province had Women's Federation branches (FL 178–117–008 1952). Yet the process of building up local organizations through the work of *dundian* cadres was slow. Two years later, the Danfeng County Women's Federation fretted in a report that these township organizations held meetings only at the beginning and end of every movement, and did little follow-up work with the masses and with Party members (Danfeng xian Fulian 1954, "Danfeng xian Fulian guanyu yinian ban de lai" [Aug. 27]).

35. Interview with Xu Nini 1997.

36. Interviews with Liu Zhaofeng 1996; Zheng Caigui 1996.

37. Interview with Li Xiuwa 1996.

38. Interviews with Zheng Caigui 1996; Zhang Xiuyu 1996.

39. Wang Meihua (interview 1996) had been a substitute math teacher at a girls' high school in Xi'an. She was recruited by Cao Guanqun, who headed the provincial Federation from 1950 to early 1953. On Cao Guanqun, see Shaanxi sheng funü lianhe hui 1994: frontispiece, 3–5. Other women among our interviewees who had received some schooling were Liu Zhaofeng (1996); Zhao Feng'e (1996); Xu Nini (1997).

40. This history caused her intermittent political trouble throughout her career, and I was warned not to bring it up in my interview with her.

41. Interview with Zhao Feng'e 1996. A report on one new group of thirty-eight cadres commented that most of them had taken part in the training "because of their personal problems, such as marriage that provided little freedom, mistreatment by the mother-in-law, or desire to live with the husband separately from his parents' house" (FL 178–100–013, Oct. 19, 1949).

42. Interview with Li Xiuwa 1996.

43. Interviews with Zhang Xiuyu 1996; Liu Zhaofeng 1996; Wang Meihua 1996. Much evidence suggests that the national leadership of the Women's Federation worked inside the broader Party-state apparatus during this period to secure more resources for raising the status of women by convincing the largely male leadership that this would be helpful for "bigger" state projects. See, for example, Kang Keqing's explanation of how women's welfare work would be crucial to national productive capacity in Zhonghua quanguo minzhu funü lianhe hui 1952: 17–26. The political efforts of the Women's Federation during this period have been analyzed in Zhang 1996 and Wang 2006.

44. Interview with Zhao Feng'e 1996.

45. Ibid.

46. Interview with Ma Ruyun 1996.

314 NOTES TO PAGES 74–77

47. Another version ran, *The Party committee has power, the government has money, but the Women's Federation has neither* (interview with Li Xiuwa 1996).

48. Interview with Wang Guihua 1997. The process by which nonlocal women acquired enough credibility to be effective is not completely clear, since both *dundian* cadres and village women now speak of the relationship as cordial and uncomplicated.

49. FL 178-110-032 1950.

50. Interviews with Liu Zhaofeng 1996; Lu Yulian 1999; Ma Ruyun 1996. For a 1951 speech by Cao Guanqun on mobilizing rural women to participate in the land reform, see Shanghai shi minzhu funü lianhe hui xuanjiao bu 1951. A summary account of the land reform campaign, mutual aid groups, and the cooperative movement in Weinan Prefecture is Weinan diqu difang zhi bianji weiyuan hui 1996: 401–5. For contemporaneous national-level reporting on mobilizing women to participate in agricultural production, the land reform, and mutual aid groups, some of which includes frank and detailed descriptions of bad cadre attitudes and practices, see *Xin Zhongguo funü* 5 (Nov. 1949): 12–13; 7 (Jan. 1950): 12; 8 (Feb. 1950): 16–18; 9 (Mar. 1950): 22–25, 44; 10 (Apr. 1950): 50–51; 11 (May 1950): 33; 13 (Aug. 1950): 30–32; 14 (Sept. 1950): 6–7; 15 (Oct. 1950): 34–35; 16 (Nov. 1950): 24–25; 20 (Mar. 1951): 12–13; 21 (Apr. 1951): 26–27; 25–26 (Dec. 1951): 16–17; 4 (Apr. 1952): 28–29; 5–6 (May–June 1952): 38–39; 9 (Sept. 1952): 6, 21; *Renmin ribao*, Mar. 11, 1953. For similar reports from various places in Shaanxi, see *Qunzhong ribao* Apr. 12 and Aug. 27, 1950; Jan. 22, Mar. 7, and Dec. 12, 1951; *Funü gongzuo jianxun* 13 (June 1952): 1–17, 22–23; 14 (July 1952): 8–12; 16 (Oct. 1952): 1–11, 19–28, 44–49, 59–60.

51. Interview with Liu Zhaofeng 1996.

52. Ibid.

53. Ibid.; interview with Lu Guilan 1996.

54. Interview with Wang Guihua 1997.

55. Interview with Zhao Feng'e 1996.

56. Interview with Liu Zhaofeng 1996.

57. Interview with Xu Nini 1997.

58. Interviews with Zhang Xiuyu 1996; Ma Ruyun 1996; Liu Zhaofeng 1996; Lu Yulian 1999.

59. Interview with Liu Zhaofeng 1996.

60. Interview with Li Xiuwa 1996. Many *dundian* cadres went on to long careers in the Federation or other government agencies (interviews with Liu Zhaofeng 1996; Wang Meihua 1996; Wang Guihua 1997; Xu Nini 1997).

61. Shaanxi sheng funü lianhe hui, 1994: 4–5; FL 178-107-016 1950.

62. Weinan diqu nongye hezuo shi bianwei hui bian 1993: 54; Weinan xianzhi bianji weiyuan hui 1987: 22.

63. MZT 198-290 1951: 88–96.

64. Ibid. This drought is not listed with other natural disasters in Weinan xianzhi bianji weiyuan hui 1987, but it is mentioned in Shaanxi nongye dili (1978, cited by Vermeer 1988, 187, 489 n9). Promising repayment of loans to wealthier families was a reversal of measures from the previous fall, when the Party-state conducted propaganda against high-interest loans and actively prevented creditors from collecting either the principal or the interest (interview with Cao Zhuxiang 1996).

65. Weinan diqu nongye hezuo shi bianwei hui bian 1993: 5455; Weinan xianzhi bianji weiyuan hui 1987: 22–23; Shaanxi sheng funü lianhe hui, 1994: 5–6. The only benefit of the conjuncture was that eventually, small amounts of grain confiscated from landlords became available for district governments to distribute to those in need (MZT 198–290 1951: 88–96).

66. Vermeer 1988: 298, 503 n16; Weinan xianzhi bianji weiyuan hui 1987: 22–23. A year later the process was repeated in south Shaanxi, which had not come under Communist control until late in 1949 (Nanzheng xian difang zhi bianji weiyuan hui 1990: 17; interview with Feng Gaixia 1997). In Shaannan, a pilot project to reduce rents and oppose local despots in February 1950 led to a fall 1950 campaign, concluded in May 1951. Land reform began experimentally in March 1951, was formally inaugurated in November, and concluded in May 1952, a full year later than in Guanzhong (Shaanxi sheng funü lianhe hui, 1994: 5; Nanzheng xian difang zhi bianji weiyuan hui 1990: 17; see also FL 178–104–004 August 1950). Nanzheng, home of Village T, was also a center of opium cultivation, and much government effort in 1951 was spent putting an end to this (MZT 198–287 1951).

67. Classic accounts of this process in other provinces are Hinton 1997 [1966]; Crook and Crook 1979. For a detailed Republican-era survey of land tenure and related matters in four Weinan villages and several other counties, see Xingzheng yuan nongcun fuxing weiyuan hui 1934.

68. Interview with Liu Zhaofeng 1996.

69. Interview with Peng Guimin 2004. Others, for example Lu Yulian (interview 1999), give variations on these categories, including "half-landlord" and other terms. The official categories laid out in the Agrarian Law are given in Hinton 1997 [1966]: 623–26. Moïse (1983) offers an account comparing land reform in China and Vietnam, with some attention to regional differences within China. For an analysis of land relations in Guanzhong from the Qing to just prior to land reform, see Qin 2001a, 2001b; Qin and Wen 1996.

70. Guo and Sun (2002) observe that the practice of speaking bitterness in Ji village in northern Shaanxi was an important mechanism in producing peasant national consciousness.

71. Interview with Feng Gaixia 1997.

72. FL 178–110–032 1950. Guo and Sun (2002) describe the difficulties of inducing peasants to think and speak bitterness in terms of class rather than rich and poor, blood ties, and virtue. They argue that the mediating category of class helped to link peasants to the larger discourse of state and society.

73. FL 178–110–032 1950; interview with Feng Gaixia 1997. In 1950, several meetings of representatives from various walks of life were held in Guanzhong. At the first, 221 men and 25 women were present; of those 25, 21 were listed as "women's representatives" (rather than workers, peasants, educators, youth, merchants, Party, army, etc.). At a second meeting, the numbers were 226 men and 29 women, of whom 26 were "women's representatives" (MZT 198–37 1950; see also MZT 198–64 1950). The corresponding numbers in Nanzheng County were 192 representatives, 20 representing women (MZT 198–68 1950). In Danfeng in 1950, there were 113 representatives, 7 of them representing women (MZT 198–70 1950). For similar 1951 statistics on Weinan, see MZT 198–218 1951; on Danfeng, see MZT 198–221 1951. For 1952 statistics for Heyang County (214 representatives, 21 women, 14 of whom were women's representatives, but one-quarter of township representatives in the county were

women), see MZT 198–380 1952. By 1952, the Women's Federation reported that Weinan County had 555 women activists (FL 178–117–008 1952). On balance, women were under-represented at all levels, but more so at higher levels (county rather than township), and when they did appear, it was overwhelmingly as representatives of women. Other categories that might well have included women—worker, peasant, educator, youth—were almost invari-ably represented by men. Reports of these representative meetings generally do not include anything specific on "woman-work," which was the province of the Women's Federation. The meetings seem to have been largely devoted to the transmission of Party-state policy, rather than conditions in individual counties.

74. *Ni you tian, ni you di, ni you zhuangjia zai nali? Meiyou qiongren lai laodong, guang kao zhuangjia, chi goupi. Ni jia nanren bu zuo huo, ni jia nüren bu fangxian, ni jia qian cong nali lai? Jintian gei wo jiangchulai* (interview with Feng Gaixia 1997). "To struggle" someone meant to make that person the object of political criticism, accusations, ridicule, and some-times physical violence in a public meeting.

75. Interview with Wang Guihua 1997.

76. FL 178–104–004 1950.

77. Interview with Xu Nini 1997.

78. Interview with Wang Guihua 1997.

79. Interview with Liu Zhaofeng 1996.

80. Interview with Zhao Feng'e 1996.

81. FL 178–107–016 1950.

82. The national campaign against the Yi Guan Dao overlapped with the land reform, with countywide activities in October 1950 and an exhibit on the group's "crimes" in late March 1951 (Weinan xianzhi bianji weiyuan hui 1987: 22; Shaanxi sheng funü lianhe hui, 1994: 7; Lieberthal 1980). On rural unrest in this period, see also Perry 2002.

83. Interview with Cao Zhuxiang 1996. When asked what sort of activities, Cao replied in vague terms: *They propagandized calling people to* ketou *[perform ritual prostrating bows], and develop an organization.*

84. Ibid.

85. Ibid.

86. Interview with Liu Dongmei 1999.

87. Vermeer 1988: 10, 170, 298, 322, 487n94. Citing government sources, Vermeer writes, "Landlords owned 8 percent of all farmland, rich peasants 5 percent. 223,700 ha or 12 per-cent (including also land owned by temples, churches, schools and societies) was confiscated. It was distributed to 460,000 households with 2,020,000 people, viz. 82 percent of the land-less rural laborers, 49 percent of the poor peasants and 7 percent of the 'middle peasants.' After that, the poorest 44.2 percent of the rural population owned 34.6 percent of all farm-land, with an average 1 ha per household. The other farmers owned an average 1.5 ha per households" (Shaanxi sheng renmin zhengfu tudi gaige weiyuan hui, ed., *Shaanxi sheng tudi gaige ziliao huibian*, vol. 1, pp. 4 and 23, cited in Vermeer 1988: 487n94). For Weinan Prefec-ture in particular (one of three prefectures in Guanzhong, the other two being Xianyang and Baoji), poor peasants and laborers were 39.4 percent of the population. Before land reform, as a group they owned 25.6 percent of the land, or 2 to 2.8 *mu* per capita. After the land re-

form, the percentage of land owned by this group increased to 32 percent and the average holding was 3.5 *mu* per capita (Vermeer 1988: 299).

88. Interview with Cao Zhuxiang 1996. In Village G in Heyang, of more than three hundred households, four were classified as landlords, eight as rich peasants, and twenty-four as upper-middle peasants (Village G briefing 2001). In the Shaannan village where women learned to sing about dog farts, only one small-scale landlord was identified. Cadres organized a children's league to serenade him with the land reform songs they had learned (interview with Feng Gaixia 1997).

89. Interview with Liu Dongmei 1999.

90. Interview with Yang Guishi 2004.

91. Later they were relabeled lower-middle peasants (interview with Shan Xiuzhen 1997).

92. First, all the land in the village had to be surveyed, boundaries staked, and quality sorted into grades, a process requiring much discussion (interview with Wang Zhaoru 2004). In Village Z, both level and mountainous land was sorted into good, middle, and bad, with different production quotas assigned to each (interviews with Lu Yulian 1999; Yan Panwa 1999). Peng Guimin (interview 2004) describes this process, known as *chatian dingchan* (investigate the fields and set output), as follows: *We decided the yield according to the quality of the land. Take the yield of three years, add them up, get an average, then decide the yield. Qunzhong luxian [the mass line], people decide. You decide if this piece of land is first grade or third grade. The masses also were in favor of the* chatian dingchan. *If the decision was reasonable and the burden of the part for state purchase was balanced, they would be satisfied. If the decision was unreasonable, of course they disagreed. In this task, the mass work was very important.*

Along with land deeds, peasants were issued contracts specifying how much tax grain they were expected to deliver to the state. This process was largely completed in Weinan County (Village B) by late 1951, but continued in other Guanzhong counties for almost another year (Weinan xianzhi bianji weiyuan hui 1987: 23; Weinan diqu nongye hezuo shi bianwei hui bian 1993: 55). In Shaannan, this work went on well into 1953 (FL 178–124–010 1953–1954). Peng Guimin (interview 2004) participated in a second round of *chatian dingchan* in 1955–56, during the process of cooperativization. According to Vermeer (1988: 301n28), 1952 regulations for Northwest China based the agricultural tax on per capita annual income (calculated in food grain) per household, with rates ranging from 5 to 30 percent. He finds (426) that Shaanxi reduced its annual grain tax from 1951 (480,000 tons) to 1956 (406,000 tons). Nationally, Domes (1980: 10) cites a land tax figure of 13 to 15 percent of the annual crop.

93. One interviewee lamented that her daughter was born several months too late to be allotted land. Her own mother's comment on this situation suggests that the Communist explanations of exploitation were not the only narratives with local purchase. Of the landless child, she said, *She has no fate. The land god is in her way* (interview with Qian Taohua 1997). On the land rights of women before and after marriage, see *Qunzhong ribao,* Nov. 7, 1950.

94. Here He Gaizhen, speaking in 1999, uses language that would not have been available to her in the early 1950s. The slogan "Women hold up half the sky" was published in 1968, although variations appeared in print as early as 1956 (Honig 2010).

95. Interview with He Gaizhen 1999.

96. Shaanxi sheng funü lianhe hui, 1994: 11. In another 1952 directive, however, Women's Federation cadres were cautioned, "Do not emphasize giving women individual property deeds [*dandu fa zheng*], because this will cause the majority of the masses to be dissatisfied" (FL 178–117–008 1952). Nevertheless a 1954 report noted that women who had suffered ill-treatment, widows, and young women who planned to be married soon had asked for separate land deeds. In four Guanzhong counties, including Heyang, 10,829 women asked for separate land deeds, but only 309 received them. The report does not offer particulars on any of these cases, but does note that some areas "didn't handle well problems such as ill-treated women asking for separate land certificates" (FL 178–124–010 1953–54).

97. In spite of the province-wide arguments over land deeds, however, women did get the idea that they were entitled to land. One teenage daughter of a man who had died fighting with the guerrillas even went to court in the early 1950s to assert her inheritance rights as a daughter when her uncle tried to sell the family's land. She did so, she says, influenced by all the propaganda about the equality of women (interview with Xiao Gaiye 1999).

98. FL 178–110–032 1950; FL 178–107–016 1950; FL 178–104–004 1950 (Aug.).

99. Interview with Liu Zhaofeng 1996.

100. In 1949, at the ceremony establishing the People's Republic, Mao Zedong proclaimed, "The Chinese people have stood up."

101. Interview with Shan Xiuzhen 1997.

102. Village B briefing 1996; Domes (1980: 12–13) provides a brief national chronology of this process.

103. Shan Xiuzhen encountered similar attitudes on the part of men about women's ability to do farmwork: *Men were all unwilling and afraid of our hoeing the wheat. I said we could hoe my land first. I led them. Each person took three rows. I was very careful hoeing the weeds. It was very easy to damage the wheat roots if you hoed too deeply. My husband was worried. He followed me and after I hoed, he looked at it. After taking a look, he thought it was not bad. My work couldn't be compared with an experienced farmer, but I hoed better than some careless man* (interview 1997).

104. Interview with Cao Zhuxiang 1996; FL 178–209–009 1953; FL 178–27–025 1952. The numbers of people and households are from FL 178–27–025 1952. The difficulty in getting gender arrangements right was not confined to Zhuxiang's group. A 1949 Women's Federation survey of forms of labor organization found that all-women work units worked well, but were not easy to organize. When men and women worked together, women learned new agricultural skills, but both men and women reportedly felt uncomfortable and gossip proliferated. When men and women were in the same unit but worked separately in single-gender subgroups, quarrels about calculating labor points were common (FL 178–106–005 1949). In Weinan, as in many other communities, the men in mutual aid groups were often kin, but there is no evidence that this decreased disagreements. On the role of male kinship in consolidating rural collectives, see Diamond 1975.

105. The associated group produced an average of 394 *jin* of wheat per *mu*, compared with the village average of 150 *jin*. (But note that production in the area by the early twenty-first century was almost a thousand *jin* per *mu*; Gao Xiaoxian, personal communication.) Improvements in the cotton crop resulted from increasing fertilizer (including chaff from oil pressing and bean cake dregs), weeding, modification of thinning techniques, and use of

waste water from salt making to kill off bugs. On one *mu* of experimental cotton field, Zhu-xiang grew 350 *jin* of cotton, compared to the local average of 254 *jin*. Livestock fared well in her group: they never drank cold water and were given a salt block every two weeks. Men and women were each paid ten points per day, a far more egalitarian system than the gen-der-specific work-point allocation that replaced it a few years later (FL 178-27-025 1952; FL 178-27-026 1952). The God of Wealth comment is from the latter document. For a com-plaint that women in other mutual aid groups were not getting equal pay for equal work, see FL 178-117-008 1952. For directions on how men and women should be organized to work together in mutual aid groups, and what gendered division of tasks is appropriate, see FL 178-117-008 1952. Writing in 1952, the Women's Federation authors set the following goals: "Next year 30–40% of female labor should be in temporary seasonal mutual aid groups. In Shaanbei, 15–30%, in Guanzhong, 30–50% (Baoji should exceed 50%), Shaannan should be 20–40%. 5–15% of these should be in year-round mutual aid groups."

106. FL 178-27-025 1952.

107. A fictional account of how a family benefits from early mutual aid groups in west-ern Henan is Bai Wei's *The Chus Reach Haven*, written in 1950. The main message seems to be that mutual aid improves general welfare and ameliorates family relations. There is still a very pronounced gender division of labor, but women are already moving into more field work because the men are off dredging the river (1950), a pattern that turns out to hold for Weinan as well (Bai 1951; Pai 1954).

108. A 1952 Women's Federation survey of Guanzhong counties found that about 40 per-cent of women had joined in the harvest, and that the number of women in (mostly tem-porary) mutual aid groups was rising above the one-third mark (FL 178-117-008 1952). According to Weinan County population statistics, in September 1952 the county comprised 108 townships (*xiang*; a *xiang* typically encompassed a number of villages), 459 adminis-trative villages, 1,480 natural villages, 26 *zhen* (towns), and 334,502 people, of whom 176,546 were male and 157,956 female (MZT 198-380 1952). Danfeng County in 1954 had about half that number of people: 38,252 households, 90,713 men and 74,254 women, 169,972 to-tal population (Danfeng xian Fulian 1954).

109. FL 178-209-009 1953. Similar material on Shan Xiuzhen is found in FL 178-17-023 1951; FL 178-27-023 1952; FL 178-27-024 1952; FL 178-209-036 1954. Of sixteen model mutual aid groups listed in a 1951 government document, eleven were led by middle peasants, suggesting that it was not always the poorest peasants who produced the most ef-fective local leadership (NYT 194-8 1951). A similar pattern of middle peasant leadership among women shows up in accounts of model mutual aid group leaders in Danfeng County (Danfeng di yi qu Xihe xiang renmin zhengfu 1955; Danfeng Fulian hui 1955).

110. A 1953 Danfeng County report found 156 year-round groups and 2,815 seasonal groups consisting of both men and women. In one group every laborer was paid four *jin* of corn plus meals or six *jin* of corn with no meals for each day of labor (Danfeng xian Fulian 1953a).

111. FL 178-209-009 1953; interview with Cao Zhuxiang 1996. For a typology of mu-tual aid groups and the importance of model groups in promoting them, see *Mutual Aid* 1953.

112. Weinan diqu nongye hezuo shi bianwei hui bian 1993: 367.

113. Weinan xianzhi 1987: 23. Uncertainty about what to do with recently expropriated

landlords was one problem. In April 1952, the Weinan district Party committee forbade land-lords and rich peasants from joining, adding that if rich peasants had already joined, they could stay but not take a leadership role (Weinan diqu nongye hezuo shi bianwei hui bian 1993: 55).

114. Weinan diqu nongye hezuo shi bianwei hui bian 1993: 55.

115. Ibid., 55–56.

116. Interview with Zhuang Xiaoxia 1996. Across the province, sideline production was important, raising incomes and making peasants more enthusiastic about joining mutual aid groups. In Danfeng County, sidelines included collecting wild medicinal plants from the nearby mountains, weaving straw hats and sandals and rope, raising pigs and chickens and silkworms, spinning and weaving, and selling labor to other mutual aid groups (Danfeng xian Fulian 1953a, 1954). Shan Xiuzhen's group made bean curd, bean thread noodles, and sweet potato starch. They also raised pigs (interview with Shan Xiuzhen 1997).

117. Interview with Cao Zhuxiang 1996.

118. Interview with Liu Zhenxi 2006.

119. Interview with Zhou Guizhen 2006.

120. The Central Committee directive, dated October 16, 1953, reflected the ideas of Chen Yun. For a brief explanation, see http://zh.wikipedia.org/wiki/%E7%BB%9F%E8%B4%AD% E7%BB%9F%E9%94%80. The complete text is in Guojia nongye weiyuanhui 1981: 212–14. Domes (1980: 11–12) points out that nationally, private grain traders in mid-1953 offered prices up to 40 percent higher than the state grain procurement system, and that the state monopoly was set up partly in order to stave off further price increases. He discusses peas-ant disgruntlement and black market activity nationally. More extended discussions of the policy and its reception are Oi 1989: 43- 65; Shue 1980; Wang 2005; Chen 2006. For an in-depth study of resistance to the policy in two Jiangsu counties, see Li 2006. For a reform-era political analysis of the policy, see Wen 2000: 157–69.

121. Domes 1980: 11. On attempts by the Nationalist government to implement grain control policies in unoccupied China from 1941 on, which quickly degenerated into forced donations, see Jin 2001.

122. State trading companies collected the grain and paid for it, then transferred it to a state grain depot, which paid the trading companies a commission and sold the grain to those who needed it (interview with Peng Guimin 2004). On resales to the peasants, see Li 2006: 146; Domes 1980: 11. On Shaanxi, see Vermeer 1988: 426.

123. Even before its adoption as a national policy, the Shaanxi provincial authorities were having trouble purchasing enough wheat from farmers. In 1952 the provincial plan had called for the procurement of more than 506 million *jin* of wheat, but in June the province suc-ceeded in taking in only 870,000 *jin*. In Weinan officials declined to mobilize the peasants to sell their grain, because the province had not given them proper notification. See *Neibu cankao* 8, no. 148 (July 2, 1952): 19–20.

124. Ibid. An internal publication for cadres and Party members reported, "The state-owned companies do not have sufficient understanding of the use of the co-ops. For instance, the grain company, when it purchased wheat, did not establish a purchasing relationship with the co-ops" (*Neibu cankao* 8, no. 221 [Sept. 25, 1952]: 389–91).

125. Interview with Lu Yulian 1999.

126. Interview with Feng Gaixia 1997.

127. Interview with He Gaizhen 1999.

128. Interview with Xu Nini 1997. By early 1954, the Women's Federation was deeply involved in promoting the grain purchase policy (Shaanxi sheng funü lianhe hui, 1994: 13). A 1954 Women's Federation report from Danfeng County mentioned the reluctance of many women to sell their surplus grain under the policy (Danfeng xian Fulian 1954). Mao later concluded that in 1954–55 the state had made excessive claims on peasant grain, a situation remedied by the 3-Fix policy (fixed production, fixed purchasing, fixed marketing) put in place in 1955. These regulations said that surplus producers were to sell 80 to 90 percent of the surplus, and that if the state sought to purchase more to offset calamities elsewhere, purchases would be limited to 40 percent of additional output. What counted as "surplus" was to be determined according to "normal" harvest levels. For details on the 3-Fix policy, see Bernstein 1984: 340–41, 352–53. In 1953, Shaanxi ranked eighth among all the provinces in average grain produced per person: 595.1 jin (Cao 2005: 23).

129. Interview with Cao Zhuxiang 1996.

130. Weinan xianzhi bianji weiyuan hui 1987: 617. Shan Xiuzhen became a labor model at a December 1950 provincial meeting, one of six women named in a list of seventeen agricultural labor models from Weinan Prefecture (NYT 194-8 1951). Cao Zhuxiang is listed as a member of a model group in this document.

131. Weinan diqu nongye hezuo shi bianwei hui bian 1993: 367; interview with Cao Zhuxiang 1996.

132. Interview with Cao Zhuxiang 1996.

133. FL 178–116–009 1952; FL 178–122–012 1953.

134. Interview with Cao Zhuxiang 1996.

135. "Cao Zhuxiang mofan" 1957.

136. Interview with Cao Zhuxiang 1996.

137. Interview with Zhang Xiuyu 1996.

138. "Cao Zhuxiang mofan" 1957; FL 178–27–025 1952; Weinan xian minzhu funü lianhe hui 1952b; Weinan xian Baiyang gongshe 1962. For a general account of Women's Federation work in Shaanxi mobilizing women in the Resist America Aid Korea movement, see Xibei minzhu funü lianhe hui xuanchuan bu 1952. Many women labor models were lauded for their work persuading peasants to sell grain to the state. See, for example, Danfeng xian Fulian 1954 Danfeng disan qu Maoping xiang renmin zhengfu 1955.

139. "Cao Zhuxiang danxing cailiao," n.d. For coverage on Shaanxi rural women and the Korean War effort, see Qunzhong ribao, June 16, 1951.

140. Matter-of-fact in tone, full of technical detail, and selective in its deployment of reconstructed dialogue and cinematic description, this six-page document contains in compressed form all the important elements of a labor model narrative ("Cao Zhuxiang danxing cailiao," n.d.). For other examples, see FL 178–27–025 1952; Weinan xian minzhu fulian hui 1952; FL 178–209–009 1953; Xibei funü huabao, May 1, 1953; "Cao Zhuxiang mofan" 1957; Weinan xian Baiyang gongshe 1962.

141. FL 178–209–009 1953. How this remark was allowed to remain without comment in an otherwise optimistic report is an interesting but unanswerable question.

142. Women with living husbands also had their conduct scrutinized when cadres eval-

uated their potential as leaders. One former cadre offered the assessment of Shan Xiuzhen that she was very moral in her conduct, had no irregular relationships with men, and was very intelligent (interview with Zhao Feng'e 1996).

143. Mann 1987.

144. Examples of virtuous widows in the late imperial era who raised their children and/or supported their in-laws through industry and thrift (often spinning and weaving to make ends meet) can be found in gazetteers throughout the areas where we interviewed, interspersed with other tales of heroically virtuous womanly conduct. For Weinan County (where Zhuxiang lived), see Yan and Jiao 1969 [1892]: vol. 3, 860–987. For Nanzheng County (the Village T area), see Wang Xingjian 1968 [1794]: 311–30 (this section also includes some faithful maidens and others); Guo and Lan 1969 [1921]: vol. 2, 527–84. Among the Nanzheng tales are those of women widowed during the mid-nineteenth-century rebellions who supported their families in conditions of flight and other extreme duress. For Village G's Heyang County, see *Heyang xian quanzhi* 1970 [1769]: 267–86, 294–97, 299–306. For cases in Tongguan County, home of Shan Xiuzhen, see Yang Duanben 1967 [1685, rep. 1931]: 137–41, 221–23; Xiang and Wang 1969 [1817]: 163–219, 237–38.

145. Yan and Jiao 1969 [1892]: vol. 3, 860–987, yields 1,375 names at a cursory count. For memorial arches, see vol. 1: 275–77.

146. Interview with Cao Zhuxiang 1996.

147. Interview with Li Xiuwa 1996. Ma Ruyun (interview 1996), another retired Women's Federation cadre, spoke of other widows whom she had trained as women leaders, describing how she had encouraged them: *As long as she was capable, we would support her. Some people said that there would be so many troubles and rumors in front of the doors of widows. We weren't afraid of that. Some people said that a widow ran after others, and who knew what she was up to? We said, "Don't be afraid. As long as you do well, nothing will happen."*

148. Draft material written in the early 1950s by the village leadership reworks the widowhood story in the following way: Zhuxiang's husband dies, his death brings terrible economic and spiritual hardship to her, her natal family pressures her to remarry (something that simply didn't happen), she heroically refuses on the grounds that the family needs her, she regards herself as a determined person who can labor with her own two hands, and why should she depend upon a man? ("Cao Zhuxiang mofan" 1957). This odd amalgam of praise for widow chastity and female independence was crossed out in the draft essay.

149. Interviews with Cao Zhuxiang 1996; Wang Jiji 2006; Zhou Guizhen 2006.

150. Interview with Cao Zhuxiang 1996. She tells another chilling story which makes it clear that before Liberation widow remarriage was often accomplished by family coercion. A woman in her village had been bought as a concubine. The principal wife and her husband both died. The widowed concubine had good relations with the children of her deceased husband. *It so happened that her husband's brother was bad. He wanted to sell the widow and get the money. He sold the wife to Baiyang to be a concubine to someone. Several young fellows carried her off. The cart was placed outside the village at the corner of the wall. They forced her into a cart, and several people closed the curtain. They blocked the opening of the cart with their arms. She kept crying in the cart, calling, calling her grandsons, calling her sons. They put her belongings on the cart and left.*

151. Reports tended to list the domestic achievements of married model laborers side by side with evidence of high production and advanced political consciousness. A 1952 report on Shan Xiuzhen, for instance, included in her Plan for Patriotic Activities her intention to promote women's literacy, organize labor for field work, console soldiers' families, donate grain to the state, produce cloth for her whole family, attend to her child's studies, and not quarrel with her husband (FL 178–27–023 1952).

4. ACTIVIST

1. A *zhang* is 3.3333 meters.

2. Interview with Feng Gaixia 1997.

3. A report on Lintong County in 1950 mentioned a spate of underage marriages planned by rural parents who hoped that increasing the number of people in their household would increase their land allotment. See *Neibu cankao* 2, no. 170 (June 30, 1950): 115–16.

4. For a version of this narrative by an American reporter who spent time in newly liberated areas of rural China in the late 1940s, see Belden 1970: 275–307.

5. On the May Fourth movement, see, among other works, Schwarcz 1986. Ko (2005) offers critical questions about the place that May Fourth holds in national and scholarly narratives about Chinese women.

6. Kay Ann Johnson (1983: 93–153) argues that the Party-state advanced its marriage reform agenda very tentatively, only when it was considered not to conflict with the priorities of land reform and collectivization. See also Stacey 1983. Neil Diamant's (2000) work on the Marriage Law in practice finds that peasants made active use of the law, whose implementation was both more extended and more disruptive of social order than previously understood. For further discussion of this point, see Hershatter 2007c: 17. Diamant's research, which extends into the Cultural Revolution period, focuses mainly on people who took their cases to court, not so much on general popular attitudes.

7. Interviews with Li Liujin 1997; Zhang Qiuxiang 1996; Liu Zhaofeng 1996; Lu Yulian 1999. On similar attitudes in Heyang County, see *Qunzhong ribao,* Oct. 29, 1950, and Mar. 7 and Nov. 14, 1951.

8. Interview with Cao Zhuxiang 1996.

9. Interview with Feng Gaixia 1997.

10. Guizhen successfully mediated a running conflict the woman had with her mother-in-law. But when the county radio station came to do a story about Guizhen's success at promoting family harmony, the daughter-in-law threatened suicide and summoned members of her natal family to beat up Guizhen. Cao Zhuxiang and others intervened, but it was three years before the offended woman would speak to Guizhen again (interview with Zhou Guizhen 1996).

11. In Heyang County in 1940, village elementary schools ran two hours of literacy classes for young women each afternoon. How many people attended is unclear (Heyang xian jiaoyu ju 1998: 148).

12. Interviews with Ma Li 1999; Feng Gaixia 1997; Qian Taohua 1997; Li Liujin 1997; Xiao Gaiye 1999; Wang Nilan 2006; Wang Youna 1997; Qu Guiyue 1999; Yu Xiaoli 2001;

Wang Zhaoru 2004; Zhang Chaofeng 2001. In Mengzhuang Township, near Village G, four girls were among the two hundred students who took the elementary school entrance exam in 1945. Of 180 students who enrolled in 1946–47, only two were girls, both from better-off families (Village G briefing 2001).

13. Cao Zhuxiang's children, ages eleven and nine, went to school for the first time after 1949 (interview with Cao Zhuxiang 1996). Many families, particularly fathers, continued to resist sending their girl children to school (interviews with Feng Sumei 1997; Zhang Qiurong 2004; Xiang Jinwa 2001; Wang Zhaoru 2004). In Village G's intensive literacy class, which taught people to read eight hundred characters, thirty-four of the forty-three students were women (Village G briefing 2001). On the establishment of winter schools in Heyang County as early as 1949, see Heyang xian jiaoyu ju 1998: 149. Countywide, more than fourteen thousand students attended, more than half of them women. Women did not predominate in literacy schools across the province, however. In 1950, the provincial Women's Federation set a goal of having one-quarter of all winter school students in Guanzhong be women; the goal for Shaannan was one-fifth (FL 178–111–026 1950). Women's Federation statistics from 1951 found 700,000 women in literacy classes across the province, with 202,509 of them in Guanzhong (FL 178–117–008 1952). On the winter school movement in the Shaanganning base area from 1939 to 1945, see Shaanganning bianqu funü yundong dashi jishu 1987: 50–54; Shaanganning bianqu funü yundong wenxian ziliao (xuji) 1985: 364–66.

14. Interview with Wang Meihua 1996. The Women's Federation of each prefecture developed their own literacy material, with contents drawn from everyday life, such as the characters chu mai (hoe wheat; interview with Xu Nini 1997). On national reporting about women in winter schools, see Xin Zhongguo funü 7 (Jan. 1950): 13–14; 5–6 (May–June 1952): 14–16; 3 (Mar. 1953): 12–13; Funü gongzuo jianxun 17 (Nov. 1952); 18 (Dec. 1952): 8–14.

15. When the Northwest Women's Federation was dissolved in 1954, the Northwest Women's Pictorial was taken over by the provincial Women's Federation and published as the Shaanxi Women's Pictorial. Like its predecessor, it was distributed free to grassroots cadres (interview with Wang Meihua 1996).

16. Interview with Zhou Guizhen 1996.

17. FL 178–110–032 1950.

18. FL 178–119–017 1952.

19. Interview with Liu Zhaofeng 1996.

20. FL 178–110–032 1950.

21. Interview with Zhao Feng'e 1996.

22. FL 178–117–008 1952.

23. Interview with Liu Zhaofeng 1996.

24. Interview with Shan Xiuzhen 1997.

25. Interview with Li Liujin 1997.

26. Interview with Cao Zhuxiang 1996.

27. Interview with Yang Anxiu 1997; these problems were confirmed in interviews with Qian Taohua 1997; Feng Sumei 1997; Qiao Yindi 2001; Liu Fengqin 1996.

28. Renmin ribao, Jan. 2, 1956; Danfeng Fulian hui 1956, 1957; Danfeng xian Fulian 1957a; "Wu yi she funü jiti mofan danxing cailiao" 1958. Great Leap Forward efforts involved a provincial attempt to mobilize 250,000 people into winter schools and to make sure that

every cadre at the township level and above was literate (FL 178–189–010 1958; FL 178–208–064 1958).

29. Interview with He Gaizhen 1999.

30. Xi 1988, for instance, reprints a land reform song lyric collected in an oral history with a Heyang peasant, explicitly linking women to struggles against the landlords.

31. Interview with Cao Zhuxiang 1996.

32. Interview with He Gaizhen 1999.

33. On Party use of *yangge* in 1940s Yan'an, see Holm 1991.

34. Interviews with Liu Dongmei and He Gaizhen 1999; He Gaizhen 1999; Feng Sumei 1997.

35. Heyang County had previously produced several famous professional women performers. After 1949, amateur drama troupes of all sorts began to flourish, with 133 of them countywide by 1953. See Heyang xianzhi bianzuan weiyuan hui 1996: 652–53; also see Zhongguo renmin zhengzhi xieshang huiyi Heyang xian weiyuan hui wenshi xuexi zuguo tongyi weiyuan hui 2004 for an account of pre- and post-Liberation varieties of opera, singing techniques, troupes, and achievements in the county. On ritual theater, a related but distinct form, and its recent decline in Heyang, see Holm 2003.

36. Interview with Lei Caiwa 2001.

37. Interview with Zhang Qiurong 2004.

38. In the first piece Wang Baochuan, daughter of the prime minister, chooses her groom by throwing her bouquet, which hits the beggar Xue Pinggui on the head. She insists on marrying him, even after her father banishes them from the house. Li Fenglian, whom we interviewed in 2004, sang the part of Wang Baochuan. Although this story is set in the Tang Dynasty (618–907 C.E.), the theme of free-choice marriage and love without regard for riches would have had contemporary resonances for young 1950s performers. The opera's full plot, however, is less compatible with 1950s themes. It has Xue subsequently disappearing for eighteen years in search of fame and fortune, and marrying a high-ranking "barbarian" woman while Wang waits faithfully at home—hardly a model 1950s love story. The story of Wang Baochuan and Xue Pinggui remains popular with a new generation of state tourism entrepreneurs, who have opened a theme park in Xi'an based on their story; see Lu Hongyan, "Qujiang in Xi'an Named Park for Cultural Sector." *China Daily,* Aug. 13, 2007, www.chinadaily.com.cn/china/2007–08/13/content_6024102.htm. Zhang Qiurong (interview 2004) performed in a version of the White Snake story known as *Duan Qiao* (Broken Bridge). For an English translation of a *yangge* version of *The White Snake,* recorded in Hebei in the late 1920s, see Gamble 1970: 704–61. Gamble also offers a description of rural performances (xvii–xxix).

39. Interview with Zhang Qiurong 2004. Clapper talks, a form of oral performance accompanied by bamboo clappers and closely related to Shaanxi opera, were also adapted for political purposes during the mid-1950s (interview with Yang Guishi 2004). The village was also famous for puppet operas; a local artist named Wang Xiaoqian performed for Premier Zhou Enlai in 1956 (Village G briefing 2001). On shadow plays, which were popular in Huayin and other Guanzhong counties, see Chen 2004.

40. Interview with Lei Caiwa 2001.

41. Interviews with Zhang Qiurong 2001, 2004. Some women sang until they married

or had children and became too busy with domestic tasks. Although this particular cohort of women no longer performs, opera remains a major popular activity in Village G, with frequent local performances.

42. For the text of a musical performance describing a woman's participation in rural elections, published in Xi'an in 1953, see Han Qixiang 1953. Women's Federation work on such elections, not otherwise described in the present study, is summarized in Shaanxi sheng Fulian bangong shi 1954.

43. Liu Hulan was a teenage Communist Party member executed by the Guomindang in Shanxi at the age of fourteen, during the civil war. Mao Zedong first mentioned her as a model for youth several months after her death, and after 1949 she was variously the subject of books, a play, a movie, and TV programs.

44. Interview with Feng Gaixia 1997. *Sparkling Red Star,* originally a novel by Li Xintian, was made into a film in 1974, several decades after the events Gaixia is describing. It focused on the adventures of a young boy who accompanies the Red Army in the 1930s. A 2007 children's animated film of the same title, full of revolutionary nostalgia, is described in www .sparklingredstarmovie.com/.

45. Interviews with Ma Li 1999; Lu Yulian 1999.

46. Interview with Lu Yulian 1999.

47. Interview with Feng Gaixia 1997.

48. The complete text of the 1950 Marriage Law can be found, among other places, in Wang 1976: 383–394; www.international.ucla.edu/eas/restricted/marriage.htm. See also *Xin Zhongguo funü* 11 (May 1950): 7–8; Meijer 1971. For critiques of feudal marriage in pre-1949 Shaanxi, including practices within the Communist base areas, see *Shaanxi funü yundong (1919–1937)* 1996: 77–80, 96–106. For marriage regulations and investigations before 1949 in the Shaanganning base area, see *Shaanganning bianqu funü yundong wenxian ziliao xuanbian* 1982: 54–56, 155–56, 192–94; *Shaanganning bianqu funü yundong wenxian ziliao (xuji)* 1985: 334–36, 367–84, 422–24. Yang (1969, vol. 1: 22–85, 197–207) provides a thoughtful discussion of marriage practices and the campaign to change them, written almost contemporaneously with the events and first published in 1959. For national-level reporting on the law and its implementation, see *Xin Zhongguo funü* 11 (May 1950): 5–6, 9–17; 18 (Jan. 1951): 26–27; 22 (May 1951): 12–13; 24 (Oct. 1951): 9–17; 25–26 (Dec. 1951): 22. For reports on implementation in Shaanxi, see *Funü gongzuo jianxun* 15 (Aug. 1952); 16 (Oct. 1952): 11–18; 18 (Dec. 1952): 1–7.

49. For a brief summary of the scholarship on marriage law in the Nationalist period and its limited geographic scope, see Hershatter 2007c: 15.

50. *Hunyinfa tujie* (1951) popularized the Marriage Law in illustrated form. For a popular textbook published just in advance of the Marriage Law campaign of 1953, discussed below, see Renmin chubanshe 1953. For descriptions of pre-1949 engagement and marriage rituals in areas of rural Shaanxi covered by the present study, gleaned from gazetteers and other sources and sometimes recounted in a nostalgic mode, see Wu 1995: 219–34; Weinan diqu difang zhi bianji weiyuan hui 1996: 774–76; Shi 1999: 186–202; Zhang 2000a: 11–17, 242–43; 2000b: 3–4; Zhongguo renmin zhengzhi xieshang huiyi Shaanxi sheng Nanzheng xian weiyuan hui wenshi ziliao 1990: 97–99; Ding and Zhao 1997: 3–4, 44.

51. Peng Guimin (interview 2004), for instance, recounts that his parents betrothed him

when he was still a child to a seven-year-old girl, selling seven *mu* of land to purchase seven *dan* of wheat to give the girl's family. *To marry the daughter-in-law, one* dan *of wheat for one year of age. So it cost us seven* dan *of wheat for the engagement. When I wanted to cancel the arrangement, my parents had already sold the seven* mu *of land. Her family refused to return anything to us. So we had a great loss.* Women reported brideprices ranging from twenty-four yuan in the 1930s (interview with Cao Zhuxiang 1996) to twenty times that amount in the late 1940s (interview with Liu Dongmei 1999, speaking of other villagers), but with the variety and fluctuation of currencies during that time, it is difficult to say anything consistent about the marriage market value of women.

52. On situations of this type in Danfeng County, see MZT 198–381 1951: 139–46.

53. Interviews with Li Liujin 1997; Yang Anxiu 1997.

54. Interviews with Wang Xiqin 1996; Zhuang Xiaoxia 1996.

55. Both Village Z and Village G had cases of uxorilocal marriage, and in Village G, endogamous marriage was also common. On women marrying close to their mothers, see interview with Ma Li 1999.

56. Interview with Yang Anxiu 1997.

57. Zhongguo renmin zhengzhi xieshang huiyi Shaanxi sheng Nanzheng xian weiyuan hui wenshi ziliao 1987: 50; interviews with Yang Anxiu 1997; Qian Taohua 1997.

58. Zhongguo renmin zhengzhi xieshang huiyi Shaanxi sheng Nanzheng xian weiyuan hui wenshi ziliao 1987: 50.

Picking the right wedding day was crucial. In Village G the story is told of a man whose wife kept running away because they had married on an inauspicious day. He picked a more auspicious day and married her again, and she no longer fled (Village G briefing 2001).

59. Interviews with Li Xiulan 1997; Yang Anxiu 1997; Qian Taohua 1997; Cao Zhuxiang 1996; Wang Youna 1997; Liu Dongmei 1999; Qu Guiyue 1999; Qiao Yindi 2001; Zhou Guizhen 1996; Li Liujin 1997; Lei Caiwa 2001.

60. Interviews with Qian Taohua 1997; Yuan Xi 2001; Qiao Yindi 2001; Jiang Qiuwa 2001; Zhang Qiurong 2004; Lei Caiwa 2001; Yang Guishi 2004. This is a composite portrait; variations in dress were common. Some of this elaborate dress and conveyance continued into the 1950s and 1960s, stopping only with the Cultural Revolution, in spite of the propaganda and new practices introduced by activists. People explain the absence of the bride's mother by saying that her presence would require a round of gifts, and that if she left her own home for a day there would be no one to cook for her own family. It is still not the custom for the bride's mother to attend her daughter's wedding (interview with Yang Guishi 2004).

61. On bridal laments in the Yangzi delta, see McLaren 2008. For a brief discussion of a similar practice in Shaannan, see Zhang 2000b: 3–4. On distance between the home village of brides and grooms in the reform era, see Gao 2000: 184–87.

62. Interview with Cao Zhuxiang 1996.

63. Interviews with Qian Taohua 1997; Cao Zhuxiang 1996; Qiao Yindi 2001; Jiang Qiuwa 2001; Lei Caiwa 2001. Versions of this practice have continued into the present, although the overtones of violence have been criticized (Honig and Hershatter 1988: 146–47).

64. Interview with Yuan Xi 2001.

65. Wolf 1972, 1975.

66. Interviews with Wang Youna 1997; Zhang Chaofeng 2001; Qiao Yindi 2001.

67. Interview with He Gaizhen 1999; see also interviews with Jiang Qiuwa 2001; Yang Shulian 2001. On continuing contact between a married woman and her natal family, see Stafford 2000: 110–26. On postmarital dual residence in North China, see Judd 1989.

68. Interviews with Qiao Yindi 2001; Yu Xiaoli 2001; Lei Caiwa 2001.

69. Interview with Li Xiuwa 1996.

70. The law, announced nationally on May 1, 1950, was distributed by the Shaanxi Civil Administration Office (Minzheng ting) to each district in mid-May 1950. On May 27 the office asked each prefecture to report on what the local response had been. In an anxious series of questions that are not characteristic of later central government documents, the national Ministry of Internal Affairs also wanted to know on May 31 if cadres had studied and understood the law, what problems they had encountered in their study and implementation, how they had solved these problems, and how the masses, especially women, workers, and peasants, had reacted. On June 5 the provincial office reminded each district to submit their reports; on June 12 the Northwest District pressured the province to report; this is followed by other notices from the province hectoring the prefectures to turn in their paperwork by the end of June. On August 26 the Ministry of Internal Affairs reminded Shaanxi Province that its report was still not in, and on September 20 the provincial office reminded prefectures that only a handful had reported on implementation. A provincial report was finally issued on September 27 and forwarded up to the national level on October 21. Between March and December, directives also appeared from the Northwest District and the provincial government on such specific topics as suicides caused by unhappy family relations (Sept. 19, Oct. 7 and 10), cadre divorce when the spouse was in another province and only one party wanted the divorce (Dec. 16), and the question of intermarriage between different nationalities, which was permitted with the proviso that people should respect one another's customs (Dec. 26; MZT 198–71 1950). In 1951 central government directives from the Government Administration Council (Zhengwuyuan), the forerunner of the State Council, ordered national inspections to see how well implementation of the law was proceeding (Sept. 26), instructed local leadership to take measures to protect the lives of women who had asked for a divorce (Nov. 1), and pushed for implementation of the law in the armed forces (Sept. 30). Northwest Region and Shaanxi provincial directives on the subject in November 1951 also repeatedly advocated implementation, and case records from Weinan Prefecture discussed a suicide case by an abused daughter-in-law and a letter from a cadre asking for divorce (MZT 198–185 1951; MZT 198–203 1951). All this activity shows a serious central and provincial attempt to implement the Marriage Law starting in 1950, as well as a sluggish response at the grassroots level. For reports on local misunderstandings of the Marriage Law, see also *Neibu cankao* 5, no. 186 (Oct. 12, 1951): 26–8; 5, no. 231 (Dec. 15, 1951): 68.

71. MZT 198–381 1951: 139–46. According to this report, filed by the Danfeng People's Court (whose jurisdiction included Village Z), the county had 163,141 people: 85,451 men and 77,690 women. The report comments that although this was not a terrible gender imbalance, some people found it hard to get married in 1951 because of the high death rate of women and the polygamy practiced among some bureaucrats and landlords before 1949.

72. MZT 198–71 1950 (Sept. 27); MZT 198–381 1951: 139–46. Local governments

seemed particularly vexed by cases involving soldiers, submitting questions such as "If a revolutionary soldier's fiancé is above 20 and the man is serving in the army, and he can't leave his post to return home for marriage although he sends letters back home sometimes, and if the woman takes as a reason that she can't wait any longer and wants to be freed from the engagement, she should wait for another half a year and notify the man about it after government mediation. But if the man doesn't come back after the time limit, can she break off the engagement? Also, if a wife of a wounded soldier who is still in the hospital proposes to divorce for the reason that she can't 'keep the pot boiling,' and mediations don't work after several attempts, how shall we handle such cases?" (MZT 198–71 1950 [Sept. 27]). Article 19 of the Marriage Law read, "The spouse of a member of the revolutionary army on active service who maintains correspondence with his (or her) family must first obtain his (or her) consent before he (or she) can ask for divorce. As from the date of the promulgation of this law, divorce may be granted to the spouse of a member of the revolutionary army who does not correspond with his (or her) family for a period of two years. Divorce may also be granted to the spouse of a member of the revolutionary army who has not maintained correspondence with his (or her) family for a further period of one year subsequent to the promulgation of the present law" (http://www.international.ucla.edu/eas/restricted/marriage.htm).

73. FL 178–106–038 1950. In Guanzhong, the Federation found instances in which divorced women were attacked and sometimes murdered by angry ex-husbands, or seized by the man's relatives. In Shaannan, which had been liberated only recently, implementation of the Marriage Law had not yet begun. Even in Shaanbei, the old Communist base area in the north of the province, women's consciousness of their rights was said to be higher, but violence against divorce-seeking women continued. A 1950 report on Zheng County, near the heart of the old Communist base area, found eleven marriage-related deaths in a nine-month period. Some involved wives committing suicide, others women murdering their husbands. The report placed equal blame on the old marriage system and on cadres with conservative views and "backward feudal ideas" who were unwilling to implement the Marriage Law (FL 178–110–032 1950; FL 178–5–029 1950). Implementation of the Marriage Law in Shaannan's Nanzheng County, where Village T was located, did not begin until February 1953, less than a month before the national campaign (Nanzheng xian difang zhi bianji weiyuan hui 1990: 18). This makes Feng Gaixia's early assertion of her marriage rights all the more extraordinary—although breaking off an engagement was less socially controversial than demanding a divorce.

74. FL 178–106–003 1950. Diamant (2000: 326–27) finds evidence that precisely this pattern emerged in rural areas.

75. FL 178–106–003 1950. This report focuses on Shangluo District in Shaannan, and on Yijun County, just north of Weinan Prefecture. Although Women's Federation documents were clearly critical of such attitudes, the Civil Administration Office and the provincial courts directed that when cadres put forward a unilateral request for divorce, the courts must adjudicate it (MZT 198–185 [June 19, 1951]). For descriptions of similar cadre behavior in other provinces, see Diamant 2000. By late 1952, the Danfeng Women's Federation was requesting that local branches report cases in which cadres themselves were vi-

olating the Marriage Law. Problematic cadre behavior included arranging marriages for their own children, letting children marry while underage, or interfering with children's freedom of marriage; obstructing divorces; beating, scolding, struggling, and locking up women who wanted to divorce; using marriage problems to acquire property; covering up for other relatives who disobeyed the Marriage Law; and personally engaging in mercenary and early marriages themselves, or abusing their wives. The county organization asked district Women's Federations to provide simple reports of the name, gender, age, and occupation of these cadres, the time and place of violation, the resolution, and reflections from the masses. For serious violations, they were asked to prepare a complete report (Danfeng xian Fulian 1952b).

76. FL 178-5-029 1950. For exhaustively detailed reports of similar attitudes from across the province, see FL 178-112-003 1951; *Qunzhong ribao*, Oct. 18, 1951. For a lurid case from Henan that was discussed in the national press as well, also centering on cadre misconduct, see *Qunzhong ribao*, Dec. 10, 1951. For a case from Danfeng County in which a widow who wanted to remarry was hung up and beaten by a coalition of local officials and her deceased husband's relatives (who had a more lucrative remarriage in mind for her), see *Qunzhong ribao*, Apr. 11, 1953.

77. Interview with Liu Zhaofeng 1996.

78. Interview with Zheng Caigui 1996.

79. Interview with Liu Zhaofeng 1996.

80. This Marriage Problems Propaganda and Investigation Group spent twenty-three days in March 1952 in a township of 2,398 people. Except where otherwise noted, all the material in this paragraph and the three that follow is drawn from Shaanxi sheng hunyin wenti xuanchuan diaocha zu 1952b.

The strengths of this particular report deserve comment. In the early years of the People's Republic, before every government unit had its own stationery, reports were scrawled on all sizes and qualities of paper in every imaginable handwriting. As the stationery improved, the language of reportage became more uniform and the incorporation of anecdotal material grew increasingly formulaic: one sentence per anecdote, three to four anecdotes to illustrate a point, all points clearly numbered. Before this format was fully consolidated, documents such as this 1952 report often included material of local interest, such as the aphorisms discussed and the meticulous counting of marriage cases and audience size described below. For similar reports from neighboring locations, see Shaanxi sheng hunyin wenti xuanchuan diaocha zu 1952a; Zhongguo gongchandang Weinan difang weiyuan hui 1953.

The terms used in the document are *zhaofu yangda*, "calling in a husband to support a father," and *zhaofu yangzi*, "calling in a husband to support a son." In the Qing, these were terms for widow remarriage. My thanks to Matthew Sommer for helping to clarify these terms. It is not clear whose father and whose son is the referent here, but since the Marriage Law contained no objection to widow remarriage, but outlawed bigamy, I surmise that these terms actually refer to the form of polyandry known in Qing documents as *zhaofu yangfu*, "calling in a husband to support a husband." See Sommer 2005.

81. The full content of the exam, which was given orally to those who could not write, was as follows:

Exam (cadres should mainly be tested on the first five questions):

1. According to the principle of marriage freedom, is engagement part of the necessary procedure for marriage?
2. When one side insists on divorce, when mediation is not effective there should be a judgment. What does this mean?
3. Why does the Marriage Law say that men should be over 20 and women over 18 for marriage?
4. Why protect children born out of wedlock?
5. What are the procedures for divorce and marriage?
6. How should weddings be held after publication of the Marriage Law?
7. Can women inherit? Why?
8. Is it an offense to interfere with a widow's marriage freedom?
9. What's the procedure for divorce with revolutionary soldiers?
10. Does the Marriage Law lift women's rights too high?
11. What are the disadvantages of arranged, purchased, and early marriages?
12. Some say, "The Marriage Law is a law to disadvantage poor young people." Is this correct? Why?
13. Some say, "If marriage is free, the blind, the crippled, and the mute . . . will be left." Is this correct? Why?
14. Question for teachers: What's your understanding of the Marriage Law? (Shaanxi sheng hunyin wenti xuanchuan diaocha zu 1952b.)

82. Of thirty-nine engaged couples in one village in the township, in twenty-nine each had now met the other party. A small but unspecified number ended the engagement, but most seemed pleased. As an added benefit of their rising political consciousness, women were said to be taking a more active role in attending literacy classes, hoeing the wheat fields, and planting trees. The report commented, "In the first six days after we got here, we only propagated the Marriage Law. This did not satisfy the masses and cadres. Later we corrected this in time. We helped to organize mutual aid groups and propagate the relations between marriage problems and production. After that, the masses and cadres became friendly to our work and became clear in their thinking and understanding" (Shaanxi sheng hunyin wenti xuanchuan diaocha zu 1952b).

83. They did continue to try to enforce the law, however. Civil Administration directives from 1952 called on people to register marriages and divorces with the appropriate authorities (March). The provincial government called for putting a strict halt to irregular deaths associated with marriage cases (June 22). Case reports from around the province showed continued serious effort to address enforcement before the Marriage Law Month campaign of 1953, with instruction on topics such as how to handle cases in which the husband had disappeared during the Korean War, suicides, and murders of women who sought divorce (MZT 198–245 1952; MZT 198–252 1952; MZT 198–254 1952).

84. Shaanxi sheng funü lianhe hui, 1994: 11–12. For announcements from the Northwest District, the Shaanxi provincial government, the Civil Administration Office, and the Marriage Law implementation committee, see MZT 198–338 1953. In this and subsequent years, the provincial governor or vice governor headed an annual leadership group for

Marriage Law implementation, with a Marriage Law propaganda office under that group (interview with Liu Zhaofeng 1996). In addition to Women's Federation workers, cadres from the Youth League and the offices of law, civil administration, the inspectorate, news organizations, propaganda, and culture took part in the campaign (FL 178-117-008 1952). In Weinan County alone, more than five hundred cadres were assigned to conduct propaganda activities during the month (Weinan xianzhi bianji weiyuan hui 1987: 24). At the provincial level, the campaign had two major components: a Marriage Law exhibit in Xi'an that was seen by 440,000 people, and the training of more than 300,000 grassroots cadres and activists in the tenets of the Law (Shaanxi sheng funü lianhe hui, 1994: 12). For reports on the month's activities in Weinan County, see Weinan xian guanche hunyinfa yundong weiyuan hui 1953b, 1953c, 1953d. For Danfeng County, see Danfeng xian Fulian 1953a, 1954; Danfeng xian minzhu funü lianhe hui 1953. Many of the propagandists sent out to do Marriage Law training, many of the cadres who received training, and many women's chairs at the prefectural and township levels were men, although at the village level women activists predominated (interview with Peng Guimin 2004).

85. FL 178-127-004 1953.

86. Pants made frequent appearances in such stories. In a case in Tongguan, a woman refugee from Henan who had been married to a hired laborer wore all her pairs of pants to bed to prevent her husband's sexual advances. In this case, the Women's Federation approved of the woman's right to divorce, but most of the community criticized them for this stance (interview with Zhao Feng'e 1996).

87. FL 178-127-004 1953. If the Women's Federation cadres discovered adulterous affairs in the course of their work, they were told by higher levels of the organization, they should only issue general propaganda saying that such activities were immoral, but not publicize the details, in order to prevent catering to listeners with "vulgar interests" (diji yiwei; Danfeng xian Fulian 1953b). Cadres of other government organizations apparently devoted more attention to adultery investigations than the provincial government had intended. In one telling instance, the Shaanxi provincial government delivered a stinging rebuke to the Weinan County government for concentrating on adultery rather than education about all the provisions of the law (MZT 198-338 1953).

88. Interview with Li Xiuwa 1996. For a summary of Federation activities in implementing the Marriage Law in Weinan Prefecture, see Weinan diqu difang zhi bianji weiyuan hui 1996: 272.

89. Interview with Feng Gaixia 1997. In Village G and other rural communities, blackboard newspapers were also an important means of publicizing the Marriage Law (interview with Yu Xiaoli 2001).

90. Feng Gaixia sang us a truncated version of this song. A published version can be found, among many other places, in Han 1989: 118. The translation is mine, with assistance from Xiaoping Sun. Chinese lyrics are in the glossary under "Lan Huahua." "Elder brother" is a conventional way of referring to a love interest.

> Black threads and blue threads, bluer than blue,
> Lan Huahua was born, and loved by all.
> Of the five grains sprouting in the fields, the sorghum is tallest.

Of all the girls in the 13 provinces, Lan Huahua is the best.
In the first month of the year, the matchmaker comes.
In the second month, the engagement is settled.
In the third month, big money changes hands.
In the fourth month, they welcome the bride.
Three troupes of musicians blow their horns, two troupes beat their drums.
Casting off my beloved elder brother,
I am carried on a sedan chair into the Zhou household.
Lan Huahua stepped down from the sedan chair, looking east and glancing west.
She saw the monkey-faced old man, and it felt like the grave.
"If you want to die, die early.
In the morning your death approaches, in the afternoon I, Lan Huahua, leave.
In my hand I carry lamb meat, in my arm I hold a cake.
I risk my life to run to my elder brother's home.
When I see my beloved elder brother, I have so much to say to him.
The two of us will be together, in life and in death."

Mai (1984: 19–20) gives a free translation of the lyrics (without the original) as follows:

Threads of black and threads of blue, bluer than the sky.
Sewed for baby Lan Huahua, apple of her mother's eye.
Shooting up like the sorghum tall, beauty brings her fame.
In every village in the land, everybody knows her name.
New Year brought the matchmaker, fixed the bridegroom's price.
After the payment's made in March, in April she'll become his wife.
Wedding music fills the air, drums and whistles sound.
She is torn from her own true love and carried to the Zhou compound.
Lan Huahua steps from the wedding chair, there espies the groom.
Old and wizened, eyes half-blind, one foot already in the tomb.
You don't have long to live, old man! You'll soon meet your end.
When you're dead and gone, old man, I'll leave this cursed house again.
Gifts of meat still in my hand, cake tucked in my blouse.
I have risked my life and soul to flee here to my lover's house.
When I saw my lover there, words flowed from my heart.
Living, dying, come what may, we'll ne'er again be torn apart.

A recent online discussion of this song gives three versions: an original collected in the Republican era, with more ribald and ambiguous lyrics; the above version, which circulated in the early 1950s; and a still more sanitized version, absent the landlord, popular in the early twenty-first century. Unfortunately this very entertaining discussion gives no sources for the three versions. See www.tianya.cn/publicforum/Content/music/1/147036.shtml. Blake (1979) discusses the continued importance of traditional love songs, as well as the addition of erotically charged songs about socialist construction from the Great Leap period.

91. The opera was entitled *Liang Qiuyan*. Liang Meiye became a model figure during the Marriage Law campaign, and the opera based on her story was performed for China's top

leadership in 1958. For a story about Liang Meiye in her impoverished old age, living in circumstances similar to those of the labor models who are the subject of chapter 8, see http://
shaanxi.cnwest.com/content/2007-01/17/content_405559.htm.

Ultimately Feng Gaixia's (interview 1997) own story became the subject of a play developed by the regional opera troupe from Hanzhong. Members of the troupe stayed in her
house for several months, interviewing her and accompanying her while she publicized the
Marriage Law. She was given a copy of the script, which was included in a book, but she is
not sure whether the play was ever performed. For pre-1949 CCP songs celebrating marriage reform, some of which made their way into the Marriage Law campaigns of the 1950s,
see *Shaanganning bianqu funü yundong dashi jishu* 1987: 111–13.

92. FL 178-117-008 1952. This was a focus even before Marriage Law Month, as part of
a larger attempt to extend state presence in villages and, in this case, to make sure that marriages met the minimum requirements of the law.

93. FL 178-117-008 1952. The practice of sending child daughters-in-law home intensified with the Marriage Law campaign (interviews with Lu Yulian 1999; Qiao Yindi 2001).
The Women's Federation also stepped in to protect a child daughter-in-law, age about twelve,
whose future father-in-law was attempting to have sexual relations with her. The marriage
arrangement was ended and the father-in-law "seriously reprimanded" (interview with Ma
Ruyun 1996). A report on child brides in the Shaannan districts of Ankang and Shangluo
stated that in twenty-three counties, 15,487 child brides were liberated, and that 4,905 of
these received land in their natal families (FL 178-124-023 1953).

94. Interviews with Liu Guyu 2001; Liu Cunyu 2001.

95. Interview with Cao Zhuxiang 1996.

96. Interview with He Gaizhen 1999.

97. Interview with Liu Zhaofeng 1996.

98. Interview with Feng Gaixia 1997.

99. Ibid.

100. Ibid.; interview with Zhou Guizhen 1996.

101. Interview with Feng Gaixia 1997; also see interviews with Qian Taohua 1997; Ma
Li 1999.

102. Interview with Ma Li 1999.

103. Interview with Feng Sumei 1997.

104. Shan Xiuzhen (interview 1997), as noted above, says there were no divorces in her
village. Cao Zhuxiang (interview 1996) remembers a handful of divorces in Village B. In Village Z, He Gaizhen (interview 1999) recalls only four divorces: a woman who left because
her mother-in-law was unreasonable, another young couple, and two former child daughters-in-law, one of whom had married into a family where the mother-in-law was "stone-
board blind," that is, had no eyes and one nostril.

105. Weinan County, for instance, with a 1954 population of 338,322 in 73,521 households, reported a mere 98 divorces for the year. Heyang, with a smaller population of 193,165
in 47,090 households, had 246 divorces. Nanzheng County had 310 divorces for 313,251
people and 73,400 households, and Danfeng a mere 64 divorces in a population of 168,200
people and 38,200 households. Sources for these divorce statistics are given in Table 2. For
overall population statistics, see Weinan xianzhi bianji weiyuan hui 1987: 24 (Apr. 1954);

Heyang xianzhi bianzuan weiyuan hui 1996: 16, 134 (July 1, 1953); Nanzheng xian difang zhi bianji weiyuan hui 1990: 18, 157 (Oct. 1953; p. 157 gives a total population of 313,400 for 1953, month unspecified); Danfeng xianzhi bianji weiyuan hui 1994: 30 (July 1953).

106. Interview with Lu Yulian 1999; fieldnotes 2001. In Village G's home county of Heyang, registered divorces outnumbered registered marriages in 1950 (though the numbers of people registering any marriage transaction at that point were small; Weinan diqu difang zhi bianji weiyuan hui 1996: 90).

107. Interview with Li Liujin 1997. In Danfeng County, home of Village Z, Women's Federation cadres issued a long report on the divorce and remarriage of Shi Duozi, who was physically abused by her in-laws and husband from her marriage in 1938 until 1951, punctuated by an unsuccessful suicide attempt in 1945 ("Shi Duozi" 1953).

108. *The Marriage Law* 1975; Danfeng xian Fulian 1953b.

109. Interview with Li Liujin 1997. She lived in Nanzheng County, near Village T.

110. Interview 1996. Name withheld in accordance with the considerations outlined in chapter 1. In a 1962 pamphlet about Shan Xiuzhen, a similar story was told. See *Shan Xiuzhen, guangrong de wuchan jieji zhanshi* 1962: 9–10.

111. Interview 1996.

112. For a reference more than three years later to the support the Party gave her in dealings with her husband, see FL 178–162–072 1956 (Nov. 15): 4.

113. The term Chaofeng used was *pianzi* (which may be a mistranscription). *Pianzhui* in Chinese medicine is linked to hernia, orchitis, and other conditions.

114. Pledging sisterhood with other young women was not uncommon in some rural settings, although the degree of formality involved in this case is not clear.

115. Interviews with Zhang Chaofeng 2001, 2004.

116. See, for instance, FL 178–209–009 1953.

117. Article 5A of the Marriage Law reads in part, "The question of prohibiting marriage between collateral relatives by blood within the fifth degree of relationship is to be determined by custom" (www.international.ucla.edu/eas/restricted/marriage.htm.)

118. Interview with Zhuang Xiaoxia 1996.

119. See, for instance, *Renmin ribao*, Mar. 7, 1957. In 1957, the Marriage Law publicity was to be combined with "socialist moral education." "In some families," the announcement declared, "since men are afraid of women's threats of divorce, they indulge their wives too much and allow their wives to manipulate them; in some other families, men abuse women, and don't let women participate in social activities." In the context of rural collectivization, capitalist attitudes joined feudal remnants as the target of criticism. Cadres were instructed to "point out that it is a capitalist point of view to love money and status, love pleasure and hate work, unilaterally despise peasants because of their appearance, and rashly get married and divorced." In a suggestion that elder abuse and neglect were becoming a problem, the support of parents was declared to be "a natural sentiment among family members, the responsibility of daughters-in-law, the traditional virtue of our nation, the moral standard of the new society, and an obligation written into the Marriage Law" (FL 178–171–002 1957).

120. Cross talks were fast-paced humorous dialogues. The national document cited in note 119 was circulated by the provincial Women's Federation on January 29, 1957. In the Danfeng County archives, we can see this directive moving down the chain of command by

February, when the county Women's Federation issued an announcement with the same title, large sections of boilerplate from the provincial announcement, and three pages of county-specific plans for implementing this campaign before and after March 8. Very little of the county announcement had to do with local content (Danfeng xian Fulian 1957b).

121. Details on marriage registration initiatives by the national and provincial government are found in MZT 198–513 (1956); Weinan diqu difang zhi bianji weiyuan hui 1996: 91.

122. Across the province the number of divorce cases apparently fell in each successive year, but spotty reporting for particular counties makes it difficult to be very precise about overall trends or local dynamics. The fact that many counties were missing some of their quarterly divorce report deadlines by 1956 suggests that pressure from higher levels to attend to marriage reform may have abated, or that other projects such as collectivization may have taken priority.

123. On subsequent Women's Federation work to implement the Marriage Law, with a full catalogue of continuing violations and problems, see "Lan Zhuren baogao guanche hunyinfa de zhixing qingkuang ji huihou yijian" 1955. For an account of 1990s marriage practices in a county adjacent to Heyang, see Liu 2000: 58–81.

124. Gao 2000: 80; Gao Xiaoxian, personal communication, Nov. 7, 2008.

125. Yang (1969, vol. 2: 176–77) makes similar observations for a village in south China. On North China, see Cohen 2005: 84–118.

126. On the continued but reconfigured possibilities for social mobility through marriage in the collective period, see Lavely 1991.

127. Interviews with Ma Li 1999; Jiang Qiuwa 2001.

128. For a similar observation based on interviews in North China, see Judd 1998.

5. FARMER

1. In Qiao Yindi's (interview 2001) account, land reform was completed in 1953 and mutual aid groups were not formed until 1954. According to the county gazetteer, however, land reform began in November 1950 in the county and was completed in May 1952. The process of forming mutual aid groups was well under way (although not universal) by August 1952, and the first lower co-op was founded in February 1953. Work on mutual aid and cooperativization was still ongoing in mid-1954, when the first county meeting of people's representatives was held, accelerated further toward the end of 1954, and by early 1956, there were 1,036 lower co-ops in the county. At the same time the county's first higher co-op was founded. By the spring of 1957, 99 percent of the county's farming households had been organized into 217 higher co-ops (Heyang xianzhi bianzuan weiyuan hui 1996: 16–17).

2. Bossen (2002) provides important comparisons of the gendered division of labor in Yunnan in the 1930s and 1990, showing that women were continuously involved in farming but that appropriate tasks and amount of time in the fields shifted over time. Her focus, however, is not the 1950s.

3. *Mutual Aid* 1953: 2–3. Mutual aid groups were formed on an experimental basis by the Party's Central Committee in December 1951, and a revised version of the decision mandating them was issued in February 1953 (1).

4. Weinan diqu nongye hezuo shi bianwei hui bian 1993: 56. Some of the characteristics

of such co-ops had already been described as an advanced form developing out of mutual aid teams. See, for example, *Mutual Aid* 1953: 5–6. Prior to this period, agricultural cooperatives had emerged in small numbers on an experimental basis, but a national movement to organize them began in December 1953 (Domes 1980: 13). These were also known as "land cooperatives," because peasants joined with their land as shares (*Mutual Aid* 1953: 5). For an overall description of the collectivization movement, see Luo 2004.

5. One newly established co-op developed from a mutual aid group with fourteen men and thirteen women laborers; the lower co-op had thirty-one men and twenty-one women laborers. The total number of people involved went from 75 to 124 (FL 178-131-008 [May 1954]). Domes (1980: 13) says that on average twenty-seven households comprised a lower co-op in 1955, and in 1956 the number of households grew to fifty.

6. *Mutual Aid* 1953: 35; *Model Regulations* 1956. For the agrarian reform law and co-op regulations, see also Wang 1976: 395–532.

7. *Model Regulations* 1956: 40, 47–51.

8. *Mutual Aid* 1953: 5–6, 9, 13, 16. On the 70/30 ratio, see Domes 1980: 13. When they wanted to sell their products, obtain loans of seed or fertilizer, or purchase equipment, lower co-ops were supposed to turn to the supply and marketing cooperatives established in the rural areas, which acted as the link between rural producers and state enterprises (*Mutual Aid* 1953: 19–20).

9. On continuing resistance to this policy in the 1950s, see Perry 2002: 282. Tian (2006) offers a case study of Henan.

10. Interviews with Cao Zhuxiang 1996; Liu Zhenxi 2006. A more usual return to land and labor under the lower co-ops was half and half, or four parts labor and six parts land. See, for example, interviews with Lu Guilan 1996; Li Liujin 1997.

11. One of the other lower co-ops was Shuang Wang, home of Zhang Qiuxiang, whose labor model activities are described in chapter 8 (Weinan xianzhi bianji weiyuan hui 1987: 24).

12. On the history of Bima No. 1's development in the 1940s, see Vermeer 1988: 252. Its yield was one-third higher than other varieties, and by 1957, Vermeer says, more than 70 percent of Guanzhong's wheat fields were using it. On other varieties of wheat grown in the 1950s in Guanzhong, see 252–53.

13. Interview with Shan Xiuzhen 1997.

14. Weinan diqu nongye hezuo 1993: 56; Shaanxi sheng funü lianhe hui, 1994: 14. In mid-1954, Shaanxi Province as a whole had 983 co-ops, a number that doubled two months later. The provincial Party Committee aimed to establish another twenty-one thousand co-ops in 1955 (Vermeer 1988: 304). Vermeer cites an April 25, 1955, editorial in *Shaanxi ribao* noting that only 16 percent of rural households in Shaanxi were in co-ops (305). As with earlier policies, lower co-op establishment appears to have begun somewhat later in Shaannan than in Guanzhong, with the transition from mutual aid groups occurring mainly in 1955 (interview with Li Liujin 1997).

15. Weinan diqu nongye hezuo shi bianwei hui bian 1993: 56–58. A year into the campaign, the Party Committee of Weinan Prefecture, mired in planning meetings and training sessions for co-op chairs and district Party secretaries, wearily asked county cadres to "devise more realistic methods that the masses can accept." Friedman et al. (1991: 160–84) describe similar problems in a Hebei community.

16. FL 178–132–019 1954 (May 15).

17. Cadres exchanged tips for mobilizing women: seat women co-op supporters together at registration meetings for mutual support, and include equal pay and childcare guarantees in the formal co-op regulations (FL 178–131–013 1954 [Apr. 23]; FL 178–131–008 1954 [May]; FL 178–132–019 1954 [May 15]; FL 178–131–032 1954 [Dec. 4]; interview with Liu Zhaofeng 1996). *Model Regulations* (1956: 47) suggested, "As production develops, the cooperative should . . . organize nurseries during the busy seasons to help women members over their household difficulties." For national-level reporting and commentary from the Women's Federation on the benefits of socialist transformation for women's liberation, and the work of mobilizing women to join co-ops, see *Xin Zhongguo funü* 1 (Jan. 1954): 8, 10–11; 2 (Feb. 1954): 8–9; 12 (Dec. 1954): 16–17; 7 (July 1955): 11; 12 (Dec. 1955): 2–4, 7; 5 (May 1956): 9; *Renmin ribao,* Nov. 5, 1955. For reporting centered on women and collectivization in Shaanxi province, see *Shaanxi ribao,* Aug. 13, 1955, and Jan. 8, 1956.

18. FL 178–132–019 1954 (May 15). This report was based on surveys in the Guanzhong and Shaannan counties of Weinan, Baoji, Shangluo, Chang'an, and Zhashui.

19. *Model Regulations* 1956: 10–11, 29, 47, 51.

20. FL 178–146–006 1956 (Jan. 15). A joint notice from the Shaanxi Women's Federation and the provincial Agriculture Bureau instructed each county government to include women in agricultural extension classes in seed selection, insect control, corn pollination, and cotton cultivation (FL 178–150–008 1956 [Feb. 1]).

21. Weinan diqu nongye hezuo shi bianwei hui bian 1993: 57.

22. FL 178–131–008 1954 (May).

23. Interview with Zhuang Xiaoxia 1996.

24. Interview with Cao Zhuxiang 1996.

25. Ibid.

26. Interview with Feng Sumei 1997.

27. Interview with Shan Xiuzhen 1997.

28. Interviews with Ma Ruhua 1996; Lu Guilan 1996.

29. Interview with Feng Sumei 1997.

30. Aware that peasants were concealing grain from the state and that collectivization was stalled, "Mao Zedong decided to pursue a strategy of defence by aggression. He saw a solution of the existing problems not in delay, but rather in the acceleration of collectivization." In July 1955, at a meeting of provincial Party leaders, he pushed to intensify the collectivization drive, an approach that was reinforced by the Central Committee in October (Domes 1980: 15). In August the county Party secretaries in Weinan Prefecture were called together to hear a report from Mao and listen to warnings about the "right-leaning line" on collectivization (Weinan diqu nongye hezuo shi bianwei hui bian 1993: 57–59).

31. Mao 1977: 184. His extended thoughts on the topic of cooperative transformation in agriculture can be found on 211–41. For a comprehensive survey of political debates in the top leadership about collectivization in this period, see MacFarquhar 1974.

32. Calls followed for a new push to found co-ops across Weinan Prefecture. A November 1955 plan envisioned almost half of rural households in co-ops before the 1956 fall harvest, suggesting that efforts up until this point had enjoyed only limited success. Even this

ambitious plan estimated that by 1958 fewer than 90 percent of the prefecture's households would be in lower co-ops (Weinan diqu nongye hezuo shi bianwei hui bian 1993: 59).

33. The national percentage of peasant households in higher co-ops is said to have reached 97.3 in 1956 (Domes 1980: 14). In Shaanxi, a provincial report noted that the number of peasants in cooperatives grew from 15 percent in August 1955 to 92 percent in August 1956, with 64 percent of peasants in "completely socialist co-ops" (Zhonggong Shaanxi sheng wei bangong ting 1956: ii). Vermeer (1988: 305) cites newspaper reports of twenty-four thousand higher co-ops and twenty-seven thousand lower co-ops in mid-1956. Because the higher co-ops were bigger, 62 percent of the population was found in those. Vermeer adds that although the move to higher co-ops was slowed in early 1957, Mao's June speech "On the Problem of Correctly Handling Contradictions among the People" put an end to further debate, and that by September reluctant holdout farmers had been forced into higher co-ops (306–7).

34. Domes (1980: 13–14) finds that nationally, by summer 1957 each higher co-op had an average of 156 households, and that the number had expanded so rapidly that "nearly everywhere a large village or a cluster of hamlets could be identified by an APC [higher co-op]."

35. Interview with Feng Zaicai and Wang Fugui 2001. Village G was in Heyang County; as noted above (n1), the county went from 1,036 lower co-ops in September 1955 to 217 higher co-ops in spring 1957 (Heyang xianzhi bianzuan weiyuan hui 1966: 17).

36. Interview with Shan Xiuzhen 1997.

37. *Model Regulations* 1956: 7, 14. Many of these regulations referred to lower co-ops as well.

38. Interview with Cao Zhuxiang 1996. Vermeer (1988: 278, 154) notes that tractors were introduced in 1954 in Guanzhong, but that they became more generally available in the Guanzhong plains only after 1970. In 1965, the entire province still had only eighteen hundred tractors, with the number rising to three thousand in 1970.

39. *Model Regulations* 1956: 31–32. Vermeer (1988: 171) reports that a size of twenty to thirty households was recommended for higher co-ops in early 1957, although the sizes sometimes grew much larger. The province reportedly had fifty-two thousand co-ops in 1956 and thirty-two thousand higher co-ops in 1957 (487–88, n96).

40. *Model Regulations* 1956: 7–8, 29–30, 35.

41. Vermeer 1988: 306.

42. Interviews with Wang Youna 1997; Xiao Gaiye 1999; Jiang Qiuwa 2001; Feng Sumei 1997; Gao Xiaoxian, personal communication, Nov. 11, 2008. Sometimes the staple provided by the collective as "eating grain" was actually sweet potatoes (interview with Feng Zaicai and Wang Fugui 2001). Article 66 of the *Model Regulations* allowed co-ops to advance money to members who were in difficulty, but added, "Advances so made to a member should not, as a rule, exceed the estimated value of work-days already credited to him" (*Model Regulations* 1956: 43–44). Friedman et al. (1991: 185–213) discuss friction caused by the higher co-op arrangements in a Hebei village.

43. In Weinan, a serious drought at the end of 1955 was followed by continuous rain the following June. Much of the wheat crop in 1956 in Villages B and G sprouted or developed

mold. Flash storms in the Village B area flooded the county seat, submerging hundreds of *mu* of farmland (Weinan xianzhi bianji weiyuan hui 1987: 146, 143; Heyang xianzhi bianzuan weiyuan hui 1996: 97). On recurring drought and flooding in Guanzhong, see Vermeer 1988: 185–89.

44. Nanzheng xian difang zhi bianji weiyuan hui 1990: 141, 146–7.

45. Danfeng xianzhi bianji weiyuan hui 1994: 32, 91, 95.

46. Interview with Gao Yuzhong 2004; Heyang xianzhi bianzuan weiyuan hui 1996: 93.

47. Interview with Yang Guishi 2004. For reservations about the higher co-ops expressed by farmers in north Shaanxi, see Guo 2004: 3.

48. Interview with Lu Yulian 1999.

49. Interview with Xu Nini 1997.

50. In Shaanxi, the average yield of wheat per hectare fell from 1,479 kilograms in 1956 to 1,177 in 1957, before rebounding in 1958 (Vermeer 1988: 240). Vermeer notes that in 1956, pressured by officials, farmers expanded double-cropping in dry areas, resulting in a reduced grain output that was, in turn, tied to a limited amount of fertilizer (244). Nationally, agricultural production decreased about 10 percent in 1956, but by the following year it had rebounded, for the first time exceeding 1930s levels (Domes 1980: 16).

51. Interview with Cao Zhuxiang 1996.

52. Interview with Shan Xiuzhen 1997. For a written account of this incident, in which her opponents accused her of having taken food grain belonging to co-op members, see *Shan Xiuzhen* 1962: 7–8.

53. A 1956 Danfeng report mentions that ten women co-op members had been caught stealing wheat from the co-op after the summer harvest (Danfeng xian Fulian 1957a). Vermeer (1988: 240) reports that in Guanzhong, "according to investigations made in 1957, about 10 percent of the harvested summer grains were not reported to the authorities, but privately distributed."

54. Zhonggong zhongyang bangong ting 1956. The six stories about Shaanxi in the national collection emphasized the need to learn from the masses' spontaneous tendencies toward collectivization in the face of timorous higher levels of leadership. Other themes included the importance of local leadership, the need for political education to inculcate socialist consciousness, and concrete problems such as the optimal deployment of draft animals (vol. 3: 1195–231).

55. Zhonggong Shaanxi sheng wei bangong ting 1956.

56. Ibid., 5–6.

57. Ibid., 216–17.

58. It was in this period that Zhang Qiuxiang and some of the other cotton-growing champions profiled in chapter 8 first achieved renown. See, for instance, FL 178–162–072 1956 (Nov. 15); FL 178–153–088 1957 (Mar. 9). In spite of such campaigns, Vermeer (1988: 156) reports that in 1958 the provincial Party Committee found that the average number of labor days per year for all rural laborers was below two hundred. Even in the 1970s, he notes, after the wheat harvest in June, many northern and western Guanzhong farmers left their fields fallow, partly because there was not enough irrigation available to compensate for summer drought. He also notes that December through March remained a slack season enforced by frost and snow (222–24). The Guanzhong growing season was 190 to 210 frost-free days (250).

59. Annual reports from county Women's Federation branches carefully enumerated the number of women who were co-op heads (small), vice heads (larger), and team leaders or cadres (largest). See, for example, Danfeng xian Fulian 1957a, which lists two women co-op directors, 218 vice directors, 502 management committee members, and 612 team leaders.

60. Interview with Liu Dongmei 1999.

61. Reports on the November 1956 activist conference are found in FL 178–154–083 1956 and FL 178–162–073 1956.

62. In one co-op, 40 percent of the work women performed was counted as required corvée work on state construction projects (*yiwu gong*), and was not compensated at all. In response, the district Women's Federation suggested that although men were required to do ten days of such corvée work per year, women should not have to carry this burden (FL 178–137–046 1956 [June 16]).

63. On a similar point made by women recalling collectivization in northern Shaanxi, see Guo 2003: 53–58; Guo 2004: 7–11.

64. Interview with Feng Zaicai and Wang Fugui 2001.

65. Interview with Zhou Guizhen 1996.

66. Interview with Zhang Chaofeng 2001.

67. Interview with Liu Fengqin 1996.

68. Interview with Gao Yuzhong 2004.

69. Group interview with Lei Caiwa, Li Fenglian et al. 2001.

70. Interview with Xiao Gaiye 1999. Article 66 of the *Model Regulations* (1956: 43) for co-ops reads in part, "Farm products harvested in the spring and summer should be distributed as an advance among members in accordance with the number of work-days each is entitled to and with their actual needs; the final settlement may be made when the year's harvest has been brought in."

71. Interview with Song Yufen 1997. For similar observations from northern Shaanxi, see Guo 2004: 4.

72. Interview with Kang Ruqing 1997.

73. Even after the establishment of the co-ops, members were guaranteed the right to engage in sideline production if it did not interfere with the work of the co-op (*Model Regulations* 1956: 12, 28–29). As late as 1956, Cao Guanqun of the provincial Women's Federation argued that family-owned sidelines should be regarded as social production and that women's sideline labor should be counted as part of their participation in agricultural development (FL 178–146–085 1956 [Dec. 25]).

74. Interview with Zhang Chaofeng 2001. One woman in Village G, born in 1912, refused to do field work during the collective period, pleading ill health, but clearly also upset that the land her family received in the land reform had been folded into the collective. *The team objected to the fact that I didn't do field work, and wouldn't let me weave. So I would hide in the back and weave*, she told us. She also earned money bowing cotton for others. This could possibly be understood as an interesting form of resistance (interview with Feng Na 2001).

75. Interview with He Gaizhen 1999. Aside from occasional comments by Women's Federation officials, it is unclear if other state authorities paid attention to how closing down markets affected women's sidelines. Nor is it clear that they took the measure of women's

sidelines as an important contribution to the household economy, or the household economy as an important support to the collective economy rather than a hindrance.

76. Interview with Cao Zhuxiang 1996. Shan Xiuzhen's (interview 1997) lower and higher co-op had a bamboo garden and an orchard.

77. Interview with He Gaizhen 1999. The major collection of higher co-op reports from Shaanxi contained only one account of quota setting and collective management of sidelines. The editors noted that it was the sole submission on this topic among almost three hundred articles (Zhonggong Shaanxi sheng wei bangong ting 1956: 80). On the need to develop collective sidelines, see 105-9. Citing 1956 press reports, Vermeer (1988: 306) says, "As co-ops concentrated on agriculture, many subsidiary undertakings were abandoned. In the plain areas [of Guanzhong], these had previously accounted for over 15 percent of rural income, and in some mountain areas for over half. Problems arose with material supplies, with outlets, with unreasonably low state purchase prices, with cadres' discrimination against such undertakings etc."

78. Interview with Ma Li 1999. On a similar situation in northern Shaanxi, see Guo 2003: 51.

79. Interview with Wang Youna 1997. Li Xiaomei (interview 1997) and Li Liujin (interview 1997) made similar comments. Yuan Xiaoli (interview 1997), however, remembers that when women had their periods they would not go into the paddies, and the women's cadre arranged other work for them.

80. Among many others, Wang Youna (interview 1997) and Li Xiaomei (interview 1997) speak to this point.

81. Interview with Ma Li 1999.

82. This was the dominant practice, but there were local and temporal variations. Some co-ops used a piecework system for certain tasks. In Village G, for instance, the early co-ops adopted a system whereby laborers would be paid five points for each *mu* of wheat they cut. Paid according to a daily labor rate, this job would have yielded nine points, but a man who could cut three *mu* of wheat could make fifteen points. For jobs where a piecework rate could not be set, people were paid according to labor power. People liked the piecework method, and it was in use some of the time in some places for some tasks right up until the economic reforms (interview with Gao Yuzhong 2004).

83. *Model Regulations* 1956: 32-33.

84. Ten of these work points (*gong fen*) equaled a *gong,* or workday; it was the *gong* that was used in calculating income distribution at the end of the year. Obviously the fewer *gong fen* one earned per day, the fewer *gong* one had to show at the end of the year.

85. *Model Regulations* 1956: 34, 9. Children, too, could earn work points, although we did not gather enough information about this to say anything systematic. One woman reported that her son, who did not like school, stopped going at age thirteen and became a cowherd in the co-op for three or four points per day (interview with Wang Youna 1997). Another woman quit school after the fifth grade and began to earn four points a day for field work (interview with Li Duoduo 1999).

86. "[The co-op] should do its best to help women members overcome whatever obstacles or difficulties they meet with in taking part in production; it should give consideration to their special abilities and qualities when allotting them work" (*Model Regulations* 1956: 29).

87. Group interview with Lei Caiwa, Li Fenglian et al. 2001.

88. Interviews with He Gaizhen 1999; Zheng Xiuhua 1999.

89. At a speech to the national Women's Federation conference on rural work in 1956, a former Shaanxi provincial Federation director, Cao Guanqun, cautioned against two tendencies: wasting women's labor and overusing it (FL 178-146-085 1956 [Dec. 25]).

90. FL 178-105-037 1956 (June 11).

91. A brief summary of these issues can be found in Freedman 2002: 176-78, 182-83.

92. *Model Regulations* 1956: 34.

93. Danfeng xian Fulian 1957a. For a reiteration of the need to pay attention to "women's physiological characteristics, physical strength, housework load, and number of children," see FL 178-162-072 (Nov. 15, 1956). Likewise editors of the Shaanxi collection on the socialist "high tide" cautioned that it was extremely important to take into account women's biological circumstances (*shengli tiaojian*), childcare burden, and domestic labor in making work assignments (Zhonggong Shaanxi sheng wei bangong ting 1956: 216-17).

94. The most complete analysis and criticism of these practices in English is Wolf 1985: 79-111. As collective labor was replaced by the household contract system in the late 1970s and early 1980s, remuneration by work points disappeared.

95. Ibid., 83-84.

96. Interview with Cao Zhuxiang 2006.

97. Interviews with Shan Xiuzhen 1997; Wang Youna 1997; Ma Li 1997.

98. Interview with Shan Xiuzhen 1997. In a pamphlet biography of Xiuzhen published in 1962, the story is told somewhat differently: that many women asked to go cut grass in the hills just like men did, but that Xiuzhen went herself and found that the slope was too steep for women and it would be more efficient for them to stay home searching for fertilizer (*Shan Xiuzhen* 1962: 6).

99. Interview with Ma Li 1999.

100. Interview with He Gaizhen 1999.

101. Interview with Ma Li 1999.

102. Interviews with Li Liujin 1997; Wang Youna 1997. Some Village T women made much less: two hundred or so *gong* per year (interview with Kang Ruqing 1997). Reported rates for both men and women in Village B were much lower than in Village T: two hundred to three hundred *gong* per year for men, but less than two hundred even for the highest-earning women (interview with Zhou Guizhen 1996). Shan Xiuzhen (interview 1997), several counties away, says that women could earn between two hundred and three hundred *gong* per year, while men earned 370 or 380. Like other model workers with cadre responsibilities, Xiuzhen herself earned work points both for farm labor and attendance at meetings; one year she earned four hundred *gong*. Such differences may reflect local variations in women's field work participation as well as in work-point rates.

103. Interview with Li Liujin 1997. It appears that at some points in Village G, a similar system prevailed (interviews with Li Fenglian 2004; Gao Yuzhong 2004).

104. A full history of the work-point system has yet to be written. Women's Federation cadres told us that they pushed for work points according to actual work done, but that they ran into resistance from farmers: *This kind of discussion was very detailed, but later people felt it too troublesome, so they changed to some fixed evaluative points. Then men could work*

very easily and get more work points, while women did the same job, but got fewer work points (interview with Wang Meihua 1996). Dissatisfaction with the work-point system contributed to the rapid dissolution of collectives in the late 1970s and early 1980s.

105. Interview with Li Liujin 1997.

106. Interview with Feng Sumei 1997. A former Women's Federation cadre in Shaannan notes that when men and women attended cadre meetings, men were paid ten points and women eight, because they were being paid according to their work-point rate in the fields. The equal pay for equal work policy, she says, put an end to this (interview with Wang Guihua 1997).

107. See, for example, Danfeng xian Fulian 1957a. The issue of equal pay for equal work was discussed again in the wake of the Great Leap Forward. See *Shaanxi ribao*, Aug. 2 and Aug. 22, 1961.

108. The formulation "proclaimed by the state" glosses over a number of questions that require further exploration. By declaring women equal, the state rendered inequality unspeakable, or at least difficult to articulate. Inequality was thus masked and reproduced, even elaborated. Thanks to Judith Butler for raising this troubling issue.

109. The classic discussion of this problem is Evans 1997.

110. This problem is seldom addressed directly in government documents, but a 1956 Women's Federation report from Danfeng County suggests the scope of the shortfall: "In order to improve agricultural production, the county set up workday indexes for women. Each women laborer should work 120–150 days in a year. . . . In collectives where it is the custom for women to work, more than 150 days may be set up for work. Generally women should work 120–130 days. At least women should work more than 80 days. On average, each female worker should work 120 days. There are some women who haven't finished their work for the whole year" (Danfeng xian Fulian 1957a). The place of officially invisible domestic labor in memories of the 1950s is taken up in chapter 7. Li (2005), drawing on material from a village in Jiangsu Province in the 1970s, argues that women at different life-cycle stages were differentially disadvantaged by the work-point system, with unmarried women and women whose children were older showing less of a gender gap in pay because they were able to work for the collective more regularly. Prior to marriage, he finds, unmarried women worked hard to accumulate a dowry. During peak childbearing years, women had an absence rate almost four times that for adult men (295).

111. Interview with Feng Sumei 1997. Village T is in Shaannan. For a similar round of agricultural tasks in Guanzhong, dating from the 1970s, see Vermeer 1988: 288–89.

112. Interview with Feng Sumei 1997.

113. Interview with Liu Dongmei 1999. County archival records on the work done by the model woman cadre Tang Qiufang suggest that some of the work on the embankments may have been done in the summer of 1956, during a season of heavy rain. Pregnant, Tang led women to reinforce the riverbank structures so that the production brigade could harvest the wheat (Zhongguo gongchandang Danfeng xian Zhulinguan qu weiyuan hui 1956). Archival records also indicate that in the years prior to the embankment work, frequent flooding made it necessary for women to work removing sand deposited on the fields, one shoulder-pole load at a time, before the winter planting could take place (Danfeng xian Fulian 1953a). In Village T, farther south and west, women worked in the 1970s building reservoirs

(Qiangjiawan), a dam (Hongsi), and irrigation canals, as well as reclaiming farmland (interview with Feng Sumei 1997). For similar memories of dam building from northern Shaanxi, see Guo 2003: 51.

114. Interview with Shan Xiuzhen 1997.

115. Zhonggong Shaanxi sheng wei bangong ting 1956: 217–22.

116. Ibid., 227–29.

117. Interview with He Gaizhen 1999. For similar observations on the gendered division of labor at the close of the collective era, see Wolf 1985. On the early reform era, see Jacka 1997.

118. Interviews with Xu Nini 1997; Gao Zhenxian 1997.

119. According to a 1956 report, 169 women in five teams in the Danjiang co-op of Village Z made 64,775 pairs of straw shoes and could earn 3,238.78 yuan from the shoes. This is five cents per pair. The total production averages out to 383 pairs of shoes per woman, or more than one per day. For this each woman would net on average slightly more than nineteen yuan per year (Danfeng xian Fulian 1957a).

120. Interviews with Zheng Xiuhua 1999; He Gaizhen 1999.

121. Interview with Feng Sumei 1997.

122. Interview with Wang Zhaoru 2001.

123. Vermeer 1988: 99–100, 110. In early 1957, Vermeer reports, many temporary workers were sent home. Another construction boom in summer 1957 was followed by the ejection of 130,000 temporary workers and others from Xi'an, and then by another construction boom in late 1958 during the Great Leap Forward. In the crisis following the Great Leap, temporary workers were again sent back to their counties of origin. In the early years of collectivization, many traders and handicraftsmen also found the cities a more congenial work environment than the countryside, where sidelines of all kinds were increasingly restricted (Vermeer 1988: 133–34). In sum, he says, in the 1950s "there was a great influx of semi-skilled rural labor into the cities" (419).

124. Interview with Wang Zhaoru 2004.

125. This was true for the husbands of many women we interviewed. The term for waged work, particularly of a white-collar nature, was *gongzuo* (work), as distinguished from the *laodong* (labor) performed by farmers. Men may also have been contracted out to work for other units by the collective, in which case they would be paid in work points. Work-point pay rates for outside work appear to have been higher than those for work in one's home collective, although evidence from our interviewees is spotty. Cao Zhuxiang (interview 1996), who as a leader and model laborer was one of the high earners in her collective, commented, *But I couldn't be compared with the men who went out to work.*

126. Interview with Kang Ruqing 1997. This reservoir was begun in 1955 and finished in the 1960s.

127. Interview with Shan Xiuzhen 1997.

128. Danfeng xian Fulian 1957a.

129. Interview with Wang Xiqin 1996. On the cotton work process, see also interview with Shan Xiuzhen 1997.

130. Interview with Zhuang Xiaoxia 1996. For details about the process by which women moved into cotton cultivation, see Gao 2005, 2006a, and chapter 8 of this volume.

131. Interview with Zhang Qiuxiang 1996.

132. Interview with Xu Nini 1997.

133. The average yield per hectare across Shaanxi rose from 834 kilograms in 1949 to 1,479 kilograms in 1956, before dropping to 1,177 in 1957 (Vermeer 1988: 240–41; detailed figures for each year are given on 240). In Weinan County the figure in 1946 was 580 kilograms, well below the provincial average of 981 for that year, but by 1957 it was well above the provincial average of 1,177, reaching 1,667 kilograms per hectare. In Heyang County, to the north of Weinan and poorer, the yield of 1,105 kilograms was almost twice that of a decade earlier (240, 242). The 1957 levels may have underreported the total grain yield by as much as 10 percent, as farmers concealed part of their grain output from the authorities. Vermeer traces the much higher levels of food grain production in Guanzhong after the early 1960s, including higher wheat yields and the growth of maize production, which doubled between 1957 and 1965 (256–72, 285–86). The GMD government sponsored the construction of two major irrigation canals in 1930s Shaanxi: the Jinghui (finished in 1932) and the Luohui (completed in 1935). By 1947, seven canals had been completed and five others were under construction (Shen 1977: 168, 177–78). Vermeer (1981: 227) says that about 90,000 hectares of Guanzhong land north of the Wei River were irrigated in the 1930s; by the late 1970s, the irrigated area of Guanzhong had increased to 900,000 hectares. See also Wang 1950: 13–28.

134. Vermeer (1988: 275) says that chemical fertilizer was introduced in Guanzhong in about 1957. He dates the rise in chemical fertilizer in irrigated areas of Guanzhong from 1965, when it was very scant, rising rapidly toward the end of the 1970s (155).

135. Interview with Feng Sumei 1997.

136. Interview with Ma Li 1999.

137. The oral historian Alessandro Portelli (1991: 75) comments that when people use the cliché "My life is a novel" they mean that their life is worth telling, and that they tell their life like a novel: "The very act of telling it shapes my identity; my handling of time, point of view, and motivation are not unlike those found in novels (especially contemporary ones)."

138. Interview with Feng Sumei 1997.

139. Interview with Xu Nini 1997. Shan Xiuzhen (interview 1997) and many others date the origins of disaffection later, to the Great Leap Forward and dissatisfaction with the dining halls, a series of events explored in chapter 9.

140. Interview with Li Liujin 1997.

141. Interview with Feng Sumei 1997.

142. Interview with Wang Zhaoru 2004.

143. Interview with Yang Guishi 2004. This does not mean that the quality of life was lower every year. As Vermeer (1988: 411–12) comments about the collective period as a whole, leaving aside the debacle of the Great Leap Forward and its aftermath, "Until 1982, in most areas rural income did not show much increase over the 1930s. However, living conditions had improved beyond comparison. Health, education, relief, a rural infrastructure of roads, electricity and telecommunications were not always tangible, yet these are vital parts of the quality of life. In the provision of these social services, the socialist state took great care to provide an equal distribution to all." Elsewhere he adds that in the 1970s it was partly because industry was supplying chemical fertilizer, pesticides, pumps, tractors, and other costly modern inputs to agriculture, and because the rural labor force was growing, that "there

was little room for improvement of peasant income" (419–20). An additional factor in levels of discontent, difficult to calibrate, is regional difference. Even within Guanzhong, in 1957 the level of income was about twice as high in the Village B area as in the more northern, poorer Village G (431). It may be significant that the particularly sharp comments about lack of enthusiasm for the collective come from men who held local cadre positions in Village G. But it is difficult to make subregional generalizations on such a flimsy basis. Additionally, most interviewees in Village B were profoundly influenced by the presence of Cao Zhuxiang as a regional labor model, which might have made their attitudes toward the collective more positive.

6. MIDWIFE

1. The Chinese measures are one *chi* and one *dou,* respectively.

2. Interview with Yang Anxiu 1997.

3. Ibid.

4. Croll 1994: 183. On women's health as a state priority, see, for instance, *Qunzhong ribao,* June 27, 1950, 2.

5. State documents from this period make no reference to the long tradition of Chinese writing about childbirth, which Charlotte Furth has traced back as far as the twelfth century (1999: 69–106, 120–22, 174–76). The degree to which this knowledge circulated in rural twentieth-century China is unclear; certainly nothing in government writings gives rural midwives any credit for mastery of such knowledge.

6. Banister 1987: 82–83. The figure of three hundred per thousand is based on her analysis of survey data from 1929 to 1931. She discounts as excessively optimistic many of the mid-1950s rural survey results. Her estimate that infant mortality was halved by 1957 includes urban areas. For a summary of local pre-1949 surveys placing infant mortality rates between 30 and 53 percent, see Croll 1994: 182–83.

7. Lim 1959: 375; on the second statistic, see also Zhu 1959: 367; Banister 1987: 58.

8. Gao 2000: 173; interview with Chen Chunhua 2006.

9. Interview with Wang Youna 1997.

10. Interview with Cao Zhuxiang 1996. Rough paper used as sanitary napkins became available in this area in the 1960s, costing about 0.20 yuan per package.

11. Interview with Wang Youna 1997; see also interviews with Kang Ruqing 1997; Liu Dongmei 1999.

12. FL 178–106–038 1950; "Shaanxi sheng 51 nian fuyou weisheng cailiao" 1951.

13. Interview with Cao Zhuxiang 1996.

14. The attitudes and practices described here are of very long standing, with no meaningful break between pre- and post-1949 norms. On similar attitudes from the Song Dynasty, see Furth 1999: 110.

15. Zhongguo renmin zhengzhi xieshang huiyi Shaanxi sheng Nanzheng xian weiyuan hui wenshi ziliao yanjiu weiyuan hui 4 (Sept. 1987): 15.

16. "Fuying weisheng gongzuo diaocha gongzuo" 1950: 3–4. "Shaanxi sheng 1950 nian fuying weisheng diaocha zongjie" 1950 contains an even more disturbing description of a labor gone wrong in the Nanzheng County seat near Village T: "A midwife was called, who

touched and grabbed randomly for a while. On the second day, another midwife was called, who could not reach the baby. When the third midwife was called, one of them pulled the woman's left arm, another pulled her right arm, and her husband pressed her waist. The third midwife took a razor and cut open her abdomen down to the pubis and still failed to take out the baby. At that time, the woman was in so much pain that she bit through two fingers and died in pain shortly thereafter."

17. "Fuying weisheng gongzuo diaocha gongzuo" 1950: 4.

18. Ibid.

19. Ibid., 5.

20. Ibid. Additional graphic descriptions are found in "Shaanxi sheng 1950 nian fuying weisheng diaocha zongjie" 1950 and "Shaanxi sheng 51 nian fuyou weisheng cailiao" 1951. On similar criticisms of midwives in medical texts from the Song and Qing periods, see Wu 2010.

21. Interview with Shi Cuiyu 2001.

22. On this concept in imperial obstetrical writings, see Furth 1999: 110.

23. Gao 2000: 173. One woman, who gave a particularly detailed account of how important it was for a woman to wash her genital area daily in order to avoid gynecological diseases, also commented that a woman should wait forty or more days after giving birth to a boy before resuming sexual relations, and two months after giving birth to a girl. Because boys developed more quickly, she said, the uterus returned to its normal shape more quickly after a boy was born (interview with Kang Ruqing 1997).

24. Zhongguo renmin zhengzhi xieshang huiyi Shaanxi sheng Nanzheng xian weiyuan hui wenshi ziliao yanjiu weiyuan hui 4 (Sept. 1987): 17.

25. Interviews with Wang Youna 1997; Jiang Qiuwa 2001; Ouyang Xiu 2004.

26. Only after the month of postpartum confinement was successfully concluded did a woman leave her mother-in-law's home and visit her natal family (interviews with Qiao Yindi 2001; Cao Zhuxiang 1996; Wang Youna 1997; Ouyang Xiu 2004; Yuan Xi 2001). *Huamo* are made using a scissors, a file, cast-off parts of ballpoint pens, and other unlikely makeshift tools. *Zuo yuezi* customs in Heyang County, home of Village G, are described in detail in Shi 1999: 177–80. For a list of *zuo yuezi* rituals and taboos in Shaanxi, with some attention to regional variation, see Zhang 2000a: 9–11. The postpartum month was a time of status transition for grandparents and the new father as well. On the custom in parts of Guanzhong in which friends rub the faces of a newborn's paternal grandparents black with the soot from the bottom of a wok as part of a raucous celebration when the child is a month old, see Zhang 2000a: 34; on a version of the same practice in Shaannan, performed on new fathers within three days after a child's birth and symbolizing the transition from carefree young man to responsible father, see Zhou 1971.

27. On criticisms of old-style midwives in Shaanbei, see Qin and Yue 1997: 191–94. Similar criticisms appear in a 1951 Women's Federation survey, see "Shaanxi sheng 51 nian fuyou weisheng cailiao" 1951.

28. "Fuying weisheng gongzuo diaocha gongzuo" 1950: 5–6.

29. Ibid., 7.

30. Ibid., 6–7.

31. "Shaanxi sheng 1950 nian fuying weisheng diaocha zongjie" 1950: 29–34.

32. "Fuying weisheng gongzuo diaocha gongzuo" 1950: 7.

33. Interview with Shi Cuiyu 2001.

34. "Shaanxi sheng 1950 nian fuying weisheng diaocha zongjie" 1950: 29–34; "Fuying weisheng gongzuo diaocha gongzuo" 1950; interview with Shi Cuiyu 2004; FL 178-106-038 1950.

35. The Ministry of Health, founded by the new Nationalist government in 1928, issued regulations requiring midwives to undergo a two-year training course or its equivalent in order to be registered with the government. Old-style midwives were supposed to undergo two months of training and register as well (Yip 1995: 58–59; see also Yang 1928: 774–75; "Editorial: Midwifery Training in Peking"). The Ministry's National Midwifery Board reorganized or opened midwifery schools in Beiping and Nanjing to train new midwives and retrain old ones. In 1935, the Commission on Medical Education, which included representatives from the government, proposed to expand the training of village midwives (Yip 1995: 165–72). For a comprehensive description of midwifery reform efforts in Republican China, see Phillips Johnson 2006. Lucas (1982: 1–13) argues for continuity in state medical policies from the late 1920s to the early 1980s, profoundly influenced by transnationally circulated concepts of medical modernization. On the place of midwifery in Nationalist health plans of the 1930s, see Lucas 1982: 72–73, 86.

36. Yip (1995: 167) summarizes a survey in Nanchang, Jiangxi on this point. Charlotte Furth notes, "The twentieth-century public health reformer Marion Yang estimated in 1930 that there were 200,000 old-style midwives needing retraining" (Yang 1930, cited in Furth 1999: 298, n68). In an earlier article Yang estimated their number at 400,000 (1928: 774). On Marion Yang, see also Yang 2006: 159.

37. The hostility to midwives had an even older pedigree: in the Ming Dynasty (1368–1911), midwives had already emerged in the writing of doctors as figures of criticism (Furth 1999: 278, 281).

38. Yip 1995: 10, 167. The rural health specialist cited on reversion to traditional methods was Li Ting'an.

39. Yang 1928: illustration between pp. 768 and 769. Yang cited a maternal mortality rate of fifteen per thousand births in China and an infant mortality rate of 250 to 300 per thousand (769). Ka-che Yip (1995: 120) observes of the Nationalist effort to retrain these women, "Midwifery was never considered a profession; old women usually became midwives because of the number of children they had borne. Thus, the transition to modern maternity and childcare would mean overcoming old customs and philosophy, the acceptance of modern medical practices, a gradual change in the conception of adequate care of pregnant women during the complete cycle of pregnancy, and the provision of care—preventive and clinical—for all infant births. It was a formidable task."

40. Yip (1995: 134) reports that in 1928, an estimated 240,000 midwives were practicing, but as of 1929, "only 385 modern midwives were registered with the government." The number of registered midwives increased to 3,174 in 1936 and 3,694 in 1937 (166).

41. Li (1935: 25) notes that in Dingxian, 90.7 percent of births were delivered by old-style midwives, 10 percent by new-style midwives, and 0.3 percent with no assistance at all, in spite of a long-running rural health program. For a brief catalogue of common birth complications, causes of postpartum infection, and the need for trained midwives, see 65–68.

Chen (1989: 1), who worked in Dingxian, also discusses the particular difficulties his team encountered in bringing in a trained midwife, retraining old-style midwives, and training a younger relative of the old-style midwives, including mistrust of techniques and young outsiders, intransigence, and professional jealousy. He concludes, "This lurching back and forth on such an urgent problem as the need for qualified midwifery was very frustrating, but experience has reinforced our belief that there is no easy solution to this question. Changing attitudes in this area may take more than one generation."

42. Yip 1995: 59. On Health Bureau attempts in the 1930s to supervise and eliminate old-style midwifery in the city of Beijing, see Yang 2006: 150–59. On public health work in rural Dingxian in the early 1930s, including a discussion of tetanus neonatorum as "the leading cause of death among infants," see Chen 1989: 72–99. Shaanxi established a midwifery school in 1934 and each year recruited thirty unmarried woman between the ages of eighteen and twenty-five to study for three years, including a one-year practicum. The school had little influence on rural health practices (Qin and Yue 1997: 190).

43. "Proposed Program of Child Health and Welfare for China" 1948, File 372.40, Number 2 Archives. This report estimated maternal mortality at fifteen per thousand. This document also contains a 1943 survey of 4,973 births over a one-year period in the city of Chengdu, Sichuan. There, 219 or 235 infant deaths occurred in births attended by old-style midwives and others. Of these, 193 were caused by umbilical tetanus. In Bishan, a rural area in Sichuan, of 901 infants born in a two-year period, the mortality rate was 170 per thousand, with umbilical tetanus accounting for 22 percent of all deaths.

44. The Health Department established a goal of adding three new-style midwives to each county of more than 100,000 people, and two new-style midwives to each smaller county. It proposed as well the retraining of old-style midwives, noting that 630 had been retrained but that a far greater number was needed ("Shaanxi sheng weisheng chu gongzuo baogao" 1946, File 372.19, Number 2 Archives: 00019, 00009). Within the same file, item 372.82 contains statistics on deliveries by individual midwives in Shanxi and Guangdong during 1948 and 1949, but no such statistics have been preserved for Shaanxi.

45. The need for women's health work and midwife reform is documented in *Shaanganning bianqu funü yundong wenxian ziliao (xuji)* 1985: 165–66, 356; see also Qin and Yue 1997: 179–205. On the women's health campaign that began in the Shaanganning base area in April 1944, see *Shaanganning bianqu funü yundong dashi jishu* 1987: 166–70. For a description of the work of one new-style midwife in Shaanganning who later became a representative to the first Women's Congress in 1949, see Zhonghua quanguo minzhu funü lianhe hui xuanchuan jiaoyu bu 1949: 137–41.

46. For an astute comparison of the attempts to reform midwifery under the GMD and the CCP, see Ahn 2005.

47. This undated document is filed by the Shaanxi Provincial Archives with documents from the year 1950: "Fuying weisheng gongzuo diaocha gongzuo," FL 178–106–002, (1950?). Newspaper accounts corroborate a drive to survey women's health conditions in April and May 1950; see *Qunzhong ribao,* June 27, 1950, 2.

48. Land reform was promulgated nationally in June 1950. Consolidation of even rudimentary state control was a protracted process in many parts of China, and so it is striking

that this type of health work was made a priority so early in the process of social transformation. In Weinan Special District, just northeast of Chang'an County, widespread land reform did not even begin until October 1950 (Weinan diqu nongye hezuo shi bianwei hui bian 1993: 7–8). The first Women's Congress in Weinan County, however, was held in May 1950, founding the county-level Women's Federation (Weinan xianzhi bianji weiyuan hui 1987: 491). If Chang'an County was following a similar timetable, and if the surveyors were working for the Women's Federation, then a survey of women's and children's health and childbirth practices was one of the first actions undertaken by the new organization.

49. "Fuying weisheng gongzuo diaocha gongzuo" 1950: 1–2, 9.

50. In Tang and Song writings, Furth (1999: 177) notes, those assisting at a birth were instructed to gnaw the umbilical cord rather than cut it with a knife or scissors, a procedure that might well have been effective at preventing umbilical tetanus. In East Weiqu, eighty-four of the 522 babies midwives remembered delivering died of tetanus neonatorum—43 percent of all infant deaths reported ("Fuying weisheng gongzuo diaocha gongzuo" 1950: 8). The month before, three work teams on a similar mission in Baoji, Lantian, and the rural areas just outside Xi'an found that 50 percent of all newborn deaths (total number unclear) were from tetanus neonatorum, and many deaths of women in childbirth resulted from excessive bleeding or puerperal fever (*chanrure; Qunzhong ribao,* June 27, 1950, 2).

51. Of 522 children born in the village, 62 percent had survived. Of the infant deaths, eighty-four (43 percent) were attributed to tetanus neonatorum and 111 to unspecified other causes. It is unclear how long a period is represented by the total of 522 births. Of these 522 births, 278 male and 243 female were "normal" (*pingchan*), and one male birth was "difficult" (*nanchan; "Fuying weisheng gongzuo diaocha gongzuo"* 1950). A provincial-level report from the same period says that of 522 births in the village, 514 were old-style deliveries, and that of these, 314 died—a radically different total that raises questions about the accuracy of counting in all such reports ("Shaanxi sheng 1950 nian fuying weisheng diaocha zongjie" 1950: 29–34).

In 1928, national infant mortality was estimated at 250 per thousand live births, with many of the deaths attributed to tetanus neonatorum (Yang 1928: 769, also cited in Yip 1995: 10). The death rate in rural areas was likely higher. A 1951 government survey done by the Central Women's and Children's Health team estimated that of more than 830,000 children born each year in the northwest (Shaanxi, Gansu, Ningxia, Qinghai, and Xinjiang), the mortality rate was 285 per thousand, or more than 238,000 children per year (*Qunzhong ribao,* Dec. 1, 1951, 3). Nationally, the head of the women's and children's health department of the Ministry of Health estimated in 1952 that seventeen million women gave birth each year, with a maternal death rate of fifteen per thousand, half from puerperal fever, and a 20 percent infant death rate, one-third of those from umbilical tetanus (Zhonghua quanguo minzhu funü lianhe hui 1952: 29–30).

52. *Qunzhong ribao,* December 1, 1951, 3.

53. Shaanxi sheng 1950 nian fuying weisheng diaocha zongjie" 1950: 29–34.

54. This survey gives the number of children born recently in the village as 521 or 522, at two different points in the report. Of these, eight had been delivered by the new-style method (six to one mother and one each to two others; "Fuying weisheng gongzuo diaocha gongzuo" 1950).

55. It appears that this new-style midwife must have been trained before the Communists arrived in 1949, since she had already delivered her sister's six children by 1950.

56. "Fuying weisheng gongzuo diaocha gongzuo" 1950: 2.

57. FL 178–106–038, 1950; Lim 1959: 375.

58. Zhonghua quanguo minzhu funü lianhe hui 1952: 29.

59. Goldstein 1998: 163, 162. For articles in the same journal that strike a less antagonistic tone, particularly with respect to retrained midwives, see *Xin Zhongguo funü,* Oct. 1952, 26, and June 1953, 24–25. Joshua Goldstein has described the campaign to train new-style midwives as an attempt by the Party-state to "dislodge women's reproductive practices from local networks and institutions in order to restructure them within a new state system." Opposing feudalism to science, he says, "prenatal health care workers were mobilized to dismantle" previously existing practices (1998: 154, 156). In a slightly more positive assessment of the old-style midwives, Delia Davin (1975: 257) suggests that the state was to supply the science, while the midwives contributed grassroots presence and labor: "Many of the 'students' were village midwives who, though they had infected countless women with their unwashed hands and long fingernails, had years of practical experience, which when combined with a little theoretical knowledge, turned them into useful medical workers." See also Davin 1976: 131–32. Science was dominant, however; ignorant midwives had to be retrained in scientific methods, or they would pose a menace to women's health.

60. Liu 1950.

61. Goldstein 1998: 153. On the broader campaign to train workers in women's and children's health, under the leadership of the Ministry of Health, see *Renmin ribao,* Feb. 3, 1951 and Nov. 5, 1951. The latter article reports the establishment of 9,464 midwifery stations nationwide.

62. *Qunzhong ribao,* Dec. 1, 1951, 3.

63. Except as otherwise noted, the information in this paragraph is drawn from "Shaanxi sheng 51 nian fuyou weisheng cailiao" 1951. This was a modest and realistic goal; by November 1951, it was reported that 2,045 old-style midwives had already been retrained in the Northwest Region, of which Shaanxi was a part, although the numbers in northern and northeastern China were much higher (*Renmin ribao,* Nov. 5, 1951).

64. Visitors to public exhibits on women's health in county towns throughout central and south Shaanxi were said to number as many as several thousand. In a national directive, Kang Keqing also mentions temple fairs and home interviews as means for teaching women on this issue (Zhonghua quanguo minzhu funü lianhe hui 1952: 2). For a published version of a slide show on pregnancy health and hygiene, directed at rural audiences and with instructions in rhyme, see *Weisheng xuanchuan gongzuo,* Aug. 25, 1951, 63–65. For the text of a clapper talk on childbirth and the lyrics and music to a "Women's Hygiene Song," see 73, 75. Thanks to Miriam Gross for bringing these to my attention. For a cartoon-style illustrated account of the benefit of new midwifery, see *Xibei funü huabao,* May 1, 1953.

65. "Shaanxi sheng 51 nian fuyou weisheng cailiao" 1951.

66. Wang 1949: 1. We seldom encountered reticence on this subject among the older women we interviewed, but there is no way of knowing how they might have responded earlier in their lives had we asked them about childbirth.

67. *Qunzhong ribao,* June 27, 1950, 2.

68. "Shaanxi sheng 51 nian fuyou weisheng cailiao" 1951.

69. See, for example, Shaanxi sheng fulian fuli bu 1954: 3–7.

70. Lu 1951: 8.

71. Ibid., 18–19. An illustrated essay on the virtues of new midwifery explaining many of these points was published in *Weisheng xuanchuan gongzuo,* Aug. 25, 1951, 66–69.

72. "Shaanxi sheng 51 nian fuyou weisheng cailiao" 1951. For a nationally publicized story of a model fourth-generation old-style midwife from Pingyuan Province (later parts of Henan and Shandong), who underwent a week of retraining in 1949, learned about umbilical tetanus, and became an assiduous proponent of new-style midwifery and a trainer of other midwives, see *Weisheng xuanchuan gongzuo,* Aug. 25, 1951, 57.

73. The actual level of contact with government agencies, and the thoroughness of retraining, is difficult to ascertain in the enthusiastic planning sections of these early work reports. See, for instance, "Shaanxi sheng 51 nian fuyou weisheng cailiao" 1951.

74. Shaanxi sheng fulian fuli bu 1954: 1–3.

75. The Women's Federation instructed its local branches to count the old-style midwives in each village and calculate how many training classes would be required to accommodate all of them, while also adding sufficient new-style midwives to meet local needs (Zhonghua quanguo minzhu funü lianhe hui 1952: 1, 12–13). The figure of 100,000 retrained midwives, given by Kang Keqing in a report in this collection, is somewhat higher than the 91,224 reported by the Ministry of Health in November 1951 (*Renmin ribao,* Nov. 5, 1951).

76. FL 178–122–012 1953.

77. Her father had been an advocate of natural feet, and her nephew's wife remembers that *her feet were really big, like a man's* (interviews with Wang Xiqin 1996, 2006).

78. Interview with Zhuang Xiaoxia 1996.

79. Interviews with Wang Xiqin 2006; Zhuang Xiaoxia 1996.

80. For a model case from Shandong publicized by the Ministry of Health, see *Weisheng xuanchuan gongzuo* 3, no. 11 (1952): 230–31.

81. Interview with Yang Anxiu 1997.

82. Ibid. On continuing training, see also interview with Shi Cuiyu 2001.

83. Interview with Yang Anxiu 1997.

84. Interview with Shi Cuiyu 2001.

85. Interview with Yang Anxiu 1997. This reluctance during the reform period to go to the hospital created a dilemma for Anxiu, who often found herself pressured by families to take responsibility for extremely high-risk deliveries. On the reluctance of women in mountain districts to go to the hospital for childbirth, and the reluctance of nonrelatives to transport them for fear of childbirth-associated pollution, see Gao 2002: 62. A recurring theme in the stories of several midwives involves assisting at hospital births when the trained personnel there did not know what to do. Speaking of the reform period, Dong Guizhi (interview 1999) comments, *After the land was distributed to households, if there was a difficult delivery they would go to the hospital. Then the hospital would call me. One of the most difficult cases went to the hospital, and no one there could handle it. They called a doctor from the county. Qu Guiyue's daughter-in-law called me in. The uterus had come down* [xia lai le]. *I pushed it back up, and then put my hand in and pulled the child out.* Ma Li (interview 1999) told a similar story. She had gone to the hospital herself for medical treatment, and while there cor-

rectly diagnosed a difficult delivery: *I was sick that year and I was in hospital. There was a difficult labor in the hospital. There were a young man and a woman. They couldn't tell what was going on and just pressed on the woman. It seemed soft. I said, "The bottom of the baby is coming out first. It is hard. The soft thing you touched is the anus." The doctor scolded me, "What do you know about this!" That baby was like that when it came out. They said, "How did you know it is like this?" I smiled and said, "I learned it. See how puzzled you were! You pressed here and there."*

86. For a sample textbook addressed to midwives, see Wang 1949, which offers detailed descriptions of female anatomy, each stage of pregnancy, symptoms of miscarriage at various stages, normal delivery, midwifery techniques for normal and difficult births, and healthy conditions of postpartum confinement. The audience of midwives may have been rural; p. 24, for instance, directs the midwife, when the baby's head is crowning, to place her fingers on either side of the vaginal opening with the place between the thumb and index finger "at the distance of two chive leaves from the vaginal opening." Briefer instructions about pregnancy, delivery, and postpartum care, apparently directed to rural health care workers, are found in Gu 1951: 63–75.

87. Interview with Shi Cuiyu 2001.

88. Ibid.

89. Gao (2000: 172) finds that very few rural Shaanxi women had prenatal checkups in hospitals before the 1980s.

90. Interview with Shi Cuiyu 2004.

91. For a summary of such comparisons, drawing on birth customs in Shaanbei, see Qin and Yue 1997: 191–94. A 1951 Shaanxi survey deplored the situation in which women had no set place to give birth, instead squatting in outhouses, corrals, or corners ("Shaanxi sheng 51 nian fuyou weisheng cailiao" 1951). Li Xiuwa (interview 1996), who worked for the Women's Federation in the 1950s, reports that Federation cadres composed a verse to be used in public education that said in part, "You will bleed less if you give birth to a child lying down. Both the adult and the child will be healthy."

92. Interview with Ma Li 1999.

93. Interview with He Gaizhen 1999. A 1954 collection of stories about model midwives holds the opposite view, saying that in old-style midwifery, it was believed that lying down to deliver would allow blood to flood the heart (*xue yan xin;* Shaanxi sheng fulian fuli bu 1954: 5, 10). See also Zhonghua quanguo minzhu funü lianhe hui xuanchuan jiaoyu bu 1949: 137–40. The passionate belief that a prone position was the most modern stance for a woman in labor corresponds to similar attitudes in the 1950s in the United States. The 1970s and 1980s birthing movement in the United States, which questioned the authority of doctors and helped popularize the work of midwives, advocated exactly the opposite, instructing women to move around and squat so that gravity could assist them.

94. Interview with Shi Cuiyu 2001. Banister (1987: 67) reports that gynecological diseases such as prolapse and vaginal infections were addressed on a large scale by women barefoot doctors in the 1970s.

95. *Xin Zhongguo funü,* June 1953, 6, cited in Goldstein 1998: 166.

96. Interview with Kang Xingfen 1999.

97. Interview with Ma Li 1999.

98. Interviews with Ma Li 1999; Shi Cuiyu 2004; Li Xiulan 1997.

99. Interviews with Li Xiumei 1999; Kang Ruqing 1997.

100. This could lead to a more equitable division of domestic labor than was the norm in farming households. In Yang Anxiu's (interview 1997) house, her husband took over the cooking, washing, and childcare, at least while she was off delivering babies.

101. Interview with Shi Cuiyu 2001.

102. Ibid.

103. Interview with Cao Zhuxiang 1996.

104. Interview with Yu Xiaoli 2001.

105. The *Model Regulations* (1956: 47) for co-ops noted, "As production develops, the-co-operative . . . should give suitable help to women members before and after childbirth."

106. "Shaanxi sheng 51 nian fuyou weisheng cailiao" 1951. In Danfeng County, for instance, a 1952 Women's Federation work report noted that during the previous year, the health office had run two sets of training classes for eighty-five old-style midwives (Danfeng xian Fulian 1952a). By the autumn of 1953 thirteen midwife stations were scattered around the county (Danfeng xian Fulian 1953a). In Weibin Township, Xianyang County, the forty midwives associated with three stations were actually scattered across twenty-seven villages ("Xianyang xian Weibin xiang yinian lai fuyou weisheng gongzuo qingkuang" 1956).

107. "Xianyang xian Weibin xiang yinian lai fuyou weisheng gongzuo qingkuang" 1956. Procedures varied from place to place. In Village T during the lower co-op period, midwives charged 1.5 yuan per birth directly to the family, keeping the fee for themselves rather than being paid work points; four midwives bought medicine as a group and coordinated their activities (interview with Yang Anxiu 1997).

108. Interview with Shi Cuiyu 2001. Li Xiulan (interview 1997), from the Village T area, says that delivering one baby was worth seven days of work points in the collective era. In Village G, midwives were paid ten points (one workday at the prevailing rate for men) for delivering a child, no matter how long the delivery took. The normal daily rate for them, when they were busy with tasks other than childbirth, was eight points a day (interview with Shi Cuiyu 2001). In Village Z, the rate was two workdays for a birth.

109. Interviews with Yang Anxiu 1997; Shi Cuiyu 2001. Dong Guizhi (interview 1999) of Village Z, like Yang Anxiu in Village T, performed ten to twenty deliveries a month in the 1960s.

110. Weinan xian renmin weiyuan hui 1957. Projected goals for 1957, ranging from 40 to 98 percent, are given in this publication. In Shaanxi Province as a whole, the Women's Federation goal for 1956 was to train six thousand midwives and to have the rate of new-style deliveries reach an average of 40 percent across the province: more than 50 percent for developed areas, more than 30 percent for other plains regions, and more than 15 percent for the mountainous areas (FL 178–164–018 1956 [Mar. 29]). For similar statistics for 1957, see FL 178–175–030 1957.

111. The provincial Women's Federation Social Welfare Office delineated these problems in a 1956 report and promised to help straighten them out. See "Xianyang xian Weibin xiang yinian lai fuyou weisheng gongzuo qingkuang" 1956; see also "1957 nian 7–12 yue fen fuyou weisheng gongzuo anpai yijian" 1958.

112. Weinan xian renmin weiyuan hui 1957; "1957 nian 7–12 yue fen fuyou weisheng

gongzuo anpai yijian" 1958. A 1956 plan for Weinan County stipulated that midwives should attend a five-day course during the slack season in late November, or a three-day refresher course if they had already been trained once. In addition to six hours of lectures each day, women had two hours of individual study and two hours of discussion. The main focus of the course was proper sterilization technique. The county government supplied 0.5 yuan per trainee per day, 0.4 of it for food (prepared by hired cooks) and 0.1 for heating, as well as supplying textbooks. The township nearest Village B, with a total population of 13,018, was slated to train twenty-five new midwives and offer refresher courses to another twenty-five. Countywide, 570 midwives were to be trained or retrained (Weinan xian renmin weiyuan hui 1956; see also "Weinan xian 1957 nian fuxun jiesheng yuan gongzuo jihua" 1956).

113. Weinan xian renmin weiyuan hui 1957. One provincial Women's Federation report noted with dismay that the numbers of people delivering with new-style midwives had actually declined in some places in 1957 (FL 178-175-030 1957). The Women's Federation aimed to make sure that each township had a midwifery station, and that each brigade and newly established small commune had a midwife assigned to it (FL 178-189-010 1958 [Aug. 18–23]).

114. The provincial Party committee sent representatives, signaling that this project was too important to be shunted off to the Women's Federation and the Health Bureau.

115. FL 178-207-067 1958 (Aug. 18–23). See also *Shaanxi ribao*, Aug. 31, 1958; *Weinan ribao*, May 21, 1960. A secondary goal of the conference was to plan the expansion of rural childcare centers so that more women could work in the fields. This topic is addressed more fully in chapters 7 and 9.

116. FL 178-207-067 1958 (Aug. 18–23). The district was Hanzhong.

117. Interview with Yang Anxiu 1997. Li Xiulan (interview 1997), a midwife in the same area, says that women stayed in the birthing center where she worked for seven days, ate one *jin* of rice per day provided by the brigade, and were also provided with oil and eggs. She worked in the fields when her midwife services were not required. Lu Yulian (interview 1999), who helped to set up the Village Z birthing center, comments that the food for postpartum women was provided by the dining halls, and that as soon as the dining halls were disbanded in 1960, the birth station was also closed. On the dining halls, see chapter 9.

118. FL 178-211-005 1959.

119. Interview with Shi Cuiyu 2001. In Village T, a woman could get access to this ration only by having a new-style midwife deliver her baby, although the delivery could take place at home (interview with Qian Taohua 1997).

120. Interview with Feng Sumei 1997.

121. Gao Xiaoxian, personal communication, Nov. 9, 2008; interview with Yang Anxiu 1997. Li Xiulan (interview 1997) reports the cost for a birth as 0.7 yuan for someone from the brigade and one yuan for someone from outside. According to Anxiu, this price remained stable from the higher co-op period to the early years of the reform era. At that time, the price rose to two yuan, to be kept by the midwife, then began an accelerating rise: three yuan for several years, then five yuan until the early 1990s, then ten, and finally fifty by 1995, with an additional charge of twenty to thirty yuan if injections were necessary to stop the bleeding. Hospital births in 1997 (about 40 percent of the total, in Yang Anxiu's estimation) in the Village T area were said to cost between four hundred and six hundred yuan. At the same

time, the number of midwives in the brigade rose from two to seven or eight, and the number of births per family declined in the 1990s because of the birth planning strictures. Even as the price per birth rose, however, continuing medical education for midwives ceased (interview with Yang Anxiu 1997).

122. Interview with Zhou Guizhen 1996.

123. "Xianyang xian Weibin xiang yinian lai fuyou weisheng gongzuo qingkuang" 1956; Danfeng xian Fulian 1957a; interviews with Qian Taohua 1997; He Gaizhen 1999.

124. Interview with Wang Meihua 1996. On how this policy was worked out locally and what tasks women were assigned to perform in Danfeng County in 1956, see Danfeng xian Fulian 1958.

125. Danfeng xian Fulian 1957a. Some county Women's Federations made finer distinctions, dividing women into three groups: (1) young and strong, without much housework, childless or with few children; (2) strong, with housework burden and children, or in the early stages of pregnancy; (3) old or weak, with significant housework burden or many children, mild illnesses, or pregnant (Weinan xian minzhu funü lianhe hui 1958). See also FL 178–164–018 1956 (Mar. 29); FL 178–175–030 1957 (Dec. 31). For national-level commentary on this subject, see also *Renmin ribao,* Aug. 12, 1956. In its provincial plan for 1958, the Shaanxi Women's Federation reiterated the need for the "three transfers, three nontransfers," also mentioning the slogan "Big feet go to the mountains and small feet stay on the plains" (FL 178–189–010 1958 [Mar. 11]).

126. Interview with Yang Anxiu 1997. A provincial Women's Federation work report for 1957 confirms that some places had pregnancy registration forms and menstrual period cards, to aid women team and group leaders in making work assignments (FL 178–175–030 1957 [Dec. 31]).

127. Three excellent recent analyses of birth planning in China are White 2006, Greenhalgh and Winckler 2005, and Greenhalgh 2008. White gives an overview of the origins of birth planning in chapter 2, 19–41, as well as in White 1994. Greenhalgh and Winckler trace the formation of population policy from the Mao era to the early twenty-first century, and its social and political consequences. Greenhalgh focuses on how the one-child policy was developed by improbably empowered missile scientists in the early post-Mao years. For accounts of how this policy played out and the conflicts it engendered in rural China, with substantial data drawn from fieldwork in rural Shaanxi, see also Greenhalgh 1990, 1993, 1994, and Greenhalgh and Li 1995.

128. Interview with Ma Li 1999.

129. Gao 2000: 172.

130. Interview with Yang Anxiu 1997.

131. Interviews with Zhou Guizhen 1996; Feng Na 2001; Liu Cunyu 2001.

132. The Ministry of Health issued a circular that was transmitted by Shaanxi provincial authorities on September 11, 1956, stating, "Contraception is the people's democratic right [*renmin minzhu quanli*], and the government should do everything it can to direct and help the masses with their birth control needs" (Shaanxi sheng weisheng ting 1957).

133. Interviews with Zhang Chaofeng 2001, 2004. The provincial Health Bureau trained fifty-three health workers in 1956 to instruct others in the use of birth control (Shaanxi sheng weisheng ting 1957).

134. Shaanxi sheng weisheng ting 1957.

135. "1957 nian 7-12 yue fen fuyou weisheng gongzuo anpai yijian" 1958; Shaanxi sheng weisheng ting 1957.

136. FL 178-189-010 1958. On the argument within the Party in the early 1950s over whether to encourage birth control at all, and the move from encouraging individual birth control in the mid-1950s to state birth planning in 1956-57 to suspension of birth planning during the Great Leap, see White 1994, 1996: 5-7, 19-41; Greenhalgh 2008: 53, 56-58.

137. Shaanxi sheng weisheng ting 1957.

138. Ibid.

139. Interviews with Zhang Chaofeng 2001, 2004.

140. Interviews with Zhou Guizhen 1996; Kang Ruqing 1997; Qian Taohua 1997; He Gaizhen 1999; Liu Guyu 2001.

141. Interview with Liu Guyu 2001.

142. Interview with Ma Li 1999.

143. Interview with Zhao Feng'e 1996.

144. Interview with Qiao Yindi 2001.

145. Interview with Yang Anxiu 1997.

146. Interview with He Gaizhen 1999.

147. Interviews with Zhou Guizhen 1996; Wang Xiqin 1996.

148. Interview with Li Liujin 1997. This second child died of "summer pox" (*xia mazi*) at eleven months. When Li Liujin later divorced, as recounted in chapter 4, she had one surviving daughter.

149. Interview with Feng Sumei 1997.

150. On reproductive culture in reform-era rural China, see Li 1993; Gao 2002.

151. Danfeng xian minzhu funü lianhe hui 1955. On the number of midwives retrained and stations around the county, see Danfeng xian Fulian 1952a, 1953a.

152. Interview with He Gaizhen 1999.

153. Danfeng xian minzhu funü lianhe hui 1955; interview with He Gaizhen 1999.

154. Danfeng xian minzhu funü lianhe hui 1955.

155. Interview with Ma Li 1999. On beliefs about the pollution of postpartum discharge, see also Ahern 1975.

156. Interview with He Gaizhen 1999.

157. Furth (1999: 107) notes that in Song Dynasty beliefs, pregnancy and ghosts were closely linked: "For pregnant women in particular, the spirit world was populated with ghostly fetuses, those which had miscarried or aborted or been stillborn or killed at birth. These might haunt the gestating woman . . . inflicting agony in labor or delivering monsters." Wu (2002: 188-95) traces the classical Chinese medical discourse of the Ghost Fetus, a false pregnancy thought to result from intercourse with ghosts or frustrated female sexuality.

158. Interview with He Gaizhen 1999.

159. Ibid.

160. Yu Hua incorporates a version of this theme, in which a midwife delivers a ghost baby and subsequently dies, into his short story "World Like Mist" (1996: 87-93, 104, 109-10). He himself may be drawing on ghost story themes dating back to the Tang Dynasty (618-

907 C.E.). Profound thanks to Andrew Jones for reminding me why Liu Xihan's story sounded so familiar. On the recurring theme of "a fertile union between human male and female ghost" in seventeenth-century Chinese fiction, see Zeitlin 2007, especially chapter 1. White (2000b: 19) comments, "When people take circulating stories and transform them into personal narratives, they don't make them up: they deploy powerful and shared vocabularies in their accusations and confessions. That the vocabularies are shared gives them their power. Their truth or falsity is not the relevant factor here."

161. My aim here is modest: to explore what work the ghosts and ghost stories were doing in Liu Xihan's life and death, and in the lives of those who remember her. For a discussion of similar issues in Kenya, see White 2000b. Depending upon when Liu Xihan died—a date we were not able to determine with confidence—the presence of ghosts in the story about her may also reflect conditions in the early 1960s, when Village Z was recovering from the post–Great Leap famine (see chapter 9). As Erik Mueggler (2001) has noted for Yi minority areas in Yunnan, "wild ghosts" and the need to pacify them after famine-related deaths continued to preoccupy villagers into the 1990s. Steve Smith (2006), in a study of rumors in the early 1960s, notes that many urban rumors in China concerned ghosts wandering in the human world. He suggests that when many ghosts are reported, this "indicates that social control of the dead is failing, that the boundary between this world and the supernatural world is unstable" (419), and that the recent famine might have exacerbated the power of stories about wandering ghosts.

162. Something similar might be said of our research assistant, at the time a graduate student at Beijing University, who had trouble sleeping for days after she heard this story.

7. MOTHER

1. Interviews with Liu Dongmei 1999; Feng Xiaoqin 1999.

2. For a similar argument based on interviews with women in northern Shaanxi, see Guo 2003: 50.

3. Interview with Zhang Chaofeng 2001.

4. Mann 1997: 143–65. Statecraft writings should not be taken as a straightforward account of practices in the political economy. Mann notes that even while statecraft writers were touting the beneficial effects of women's cotton and silk production—for household income and the prevention of female indolence alike—proto-industry and the growth of guilds were making women's work in China's most advanced areas less important. Nevertheless, she argues, the assiduous promotion of women's household labor by officials, combined with family practice that kept young married women at home serving their in-laws, may have "reduced the number of women available to work in China's factories on the eve of industrialization" (176).

5. Patriarchs of elite families, many of whom held official posts, also emphasized the family-state linkage in written instructions to their families about appropriate domestic conduct. See, for instance, Furth 1990.

6. Schwarcz 1986: 107–17; Karl 2002.

7. The retrospective creation of a coherent (and eventually reviled) body of thought la-

beled "Confucian" has been explored by Jensen (1997). Ko (1994, 2005) has critically examined this May Fourth–era story about women and national weakness.

8. Glosser 2003.

9. Mao 1975: 44.

10. Mao and Thompson 1990: 212–13.

11. Croll 1980: 189.

12. The 1954 Constitution of the PRC, chapter 3, "Fundamental Rights and Duties of Citizens," listed as Article 96: "Women in the People's Republic of China enjoy equal rights with men in all spheres of political, economic, cultural, social and domestic life. The State protects marriage, the family, and the mother and child." The 1975 and 1978 Constitutions reiterated this provision, although the article number changed. (The 1975 version referred to "equal rights with men in all respects" rather than specifying realms, but the 1978 version restored the original language. The 1978 Constitution also added, "The state advocates and encourages family planning.") See Qi et al 1979: 182, 198, 226. Chapter 3 of the 1950 Marriage Law, "Rights and Duties of Husband and Wife," guaranteed equal status in the home; exhorted husband and wife to love each other, work together, and care for their children; specified that both had free choice of occupation; and guaranteed equal rights in the possession and inheritance of family property. Chapter 4, "Relations between Parents and Children," prohibited maltreatment or desertion of children by parents and vice versa. All of these provisions, especially if they had been enforced (or been enforceable), would certainly have reconfigured family relations substantially. When read against the specificity and detail of other contemporaneous laws, such as the Agrarian Reform Law (1950) or the Model Regulations for producers' cooperatives, however, the provisions about the family are striking for their lack of attention to domestic labor, both productive and reproductive. The 1950 Marriage Law comprises twelve pages of English text; the Agrarian Reform law eighty-seven pages. For the text of the Marriage Law, see Wang 1976: 383–94. For the agrarian reform law and the co-op regulations, see Wang 1976: 395–532.

13. Barlow 1994.

14. Rural people give various accounts of when women stopped producing cloth for the market: some say after land reform, some say the era of the lower co-ops (interviews with Cao Zhuxiang 2006; Liu Zhenxi 2006). In Shaannan, which was not an important cotton-producing region before 1949, people spun and wove for their own use only, in contrast with Guanzhong (interview with Xu Nini 1997). Nicholas Lardy has written that rural handicraft cotton production "was suppressed by the price and marketing policies adopted in the mid-1950s, substantially curtailing the income earning opportunities traditionally open to peasants in cotton-producing areas. The state simultaneously became the monopsonist purchaser of raw cotton and the monopolist seller of cotton textile products. Moreover, the state set the prices of raw cotton and of finished textile products in such as way as to further tax the farming sector" ("State Planning and Marketing Policy and Peasant Opportunities," unpublished paper, 1983, cited in Vermeer 1988: 352). Vermeer goes on to delineate the tug of war between the state and peasants over how much raw cotton they could keep for their own use (352, 354–55). By 1957, textile mills were short of raw cotton, and the state pressured co-ops to abandon cotton handicraft production and sell to the state. "Local cotton cloth and cotton yarn produced by peasants could no longer be sold freely," and were characterized as

a threat to unified purchase and marketing and a sign of incipient capitalism (357). Most of Vermeer's account is based on material published in the *Shaanxi ribao.*

15. For an early view of how the city-country relationship should be constructed, including the role of sidelines, see Lu 1950. For a brief summary of policy on sidelines at various points during the collective era, without particular attention to the gendered division of labor, see Sun and Wu 1982.

16. Croll (1994: 19) argues eloquently that although the household was rendered invisible under the collective, it remained an important economic unit.

17. This arrangement persisted well into the reform period. See Gao 2000: 168–70.

18. Interviews with Zhou Guizhen 1996; Wang Youna 1997; Zhuang Xiaoxia 1996; Yang Anxiu 1997; Cao Zhuxiang 1996; Ma Li 1999. As Harriet Evans (1997) points out, this gendered character of household management, assumed by men and women to be women's proper responsibility, was also rationalized by the state on the grounds of women's physiological characteristics.

19. Interview with Shan Xiuzhen 1997.

20. Interview with Ma Li 1999. Here Ma Li did not question the household division of labor; rather, she regarded women's performance of household tasks as a sign that they were capable.

21. Interview with Wang Xiqin 1996.

22. Zhongguo renmin zhengzhi xieshang huiyi Shaanxi sheng Nanzheng xian weiyuan hui wenshi ziliao yanjiu weiyuan hui 1987: 33. In Village T and much of the rest of Shaannan, housing in the collective era gradually improved, with framed houses of earth and wood and tile roofs replacing daub and wattle houses (34). During the reform period some families who earned money as migrant workers built vastly expanded houses faced with white tiling. In Village Z, on the eastern end of Shaannan, most families lived in households of plastered mud, with front and back courtyards, a kitchen in back, and a privy against the back wall. In northern Guanzhong's Village G, which I visited in 2001 and 2004, much of the old 1960s and 1970s housing stock, of daubed wattle, had still not been replaced. Houses built in the 1980s were made of brick and laid out around a long courtyard, the entrance to which was protected by a spirit screen. The few houses built in the 1990s were lined with white tile but tended not to be multistory, unlike those in the better-off Village B (in central Guanzhong) and Village T (in Shaannan). Of the four houses in four different villages in which we stayed from 1996 to 2004, only those in Village B and Village T had a cold-water tap in the front courtyard. Village G had no running water in any house.

23. Interviews with Peng Guimin 2001; Jiang Qiuwa 2001; Lei Caiwa 2001. Village G's problems with water are ongoing. In 1971, machine-dug wells brought water from the nearby gorge up to the village, at the level of the plain. This solved the drinking water problem for people and livestock, and also provided some water for irrigation. But in 1985, tests by the state revealed that the fluorine content of the water was dangerously high, and the village began purchasing water from neighboring villages for eighteen yuan per cubic meter. In the early 2000s, the village remained too short of cash to pipe in safe water from a more distant well drilled in 1991 (interview with Peng Guimin 2001; see also Shaanxi shida dili xi "Weinan diqu di li zhi" bianxie zu, 1990: 351–52).

24. Interview with Li Liujin 1997. See also interviews with Zhou Guizhen 1996, Wang

Xiqin 1996, Ma Li 1999, Liu Dongmei 1999, Jiang Qiuwa 2001, Zhang Qiurong 2004, Shi Cuiyu 2001.

25. Interview with Liu Dongmei 1999.

26. Interview with Kang Ruqing 1997.

27. Interview with Xiao Gaiye 1999.

28. For a thorough analysis of reciprocity and social networks in a north China village, see Yan 1996.

29. Interview with Ma Li 1999.

30. Interview with Liu Dongmei 1999.

31. Interview with Ma Li 1999.

32. Interview with Liu Dongmei 1999.

33. Interview with Feng Sumei 1997.

34. Thanks to Susan Mann for thoughtful observations about imperial writings. And thanks to Harriet Evans for pointing out that Mann's own 2007 work demonstrates the close ties of filiality, responsibility, and affection between mothers and daughters in the late imperial period, both before and after the daughters married.

35. For a history of household separation (*fenjia*) in the Qing and Republican periods, see Wakefield (1998), as well as an anthropological literature too vast to include here. On a comparison of Shaanxi household structure in 1949 and 1982, see Gao 2000: 164–67.

36. Gao Xiaoxian, personal communication, Nov. 9, 2008.

37. Interview with Kang Xingfen 1999.

38. Interview with Qiao Yindi 2001.

39. Interview with He Shuangyan 1999. On family division contracts in north China families in the reform era, see Cohen 2005: 118–32.

40. Interview with Qiao Yindi 2001. If there was substantial property or a conflict, the maternal uncle's family customarily presided over a division. Cadres participated only if invited, but the team had to be notified, because household division affected how grain was distributed to households after the harvest. Unless there were serious conflicts, a family usually waited until all the brothers had brought in wives before separating (interview with Shi Ranwa 1999).

41. Later, in the reform era, some of these women became mothers-in-law and made the same decision themselves. Asked why she chose to live separately from her sons in the 1990s, Qian Taohua (interview 1997) replied, *I would have had a bitter lot for my whole life* [na ba wo kule yi beizi]. *If you lived with them, you would still have a lot to do. I didn't want to do it. I wanted to rest for several years. I said, "Each of you leave a room for me. I can live wherever I want."*

Gao Xiaoxian: You don't eat together with your youngest son?

Qian Taohua: And eat what he cooks? I cook on the stove. Whenever I am hungry, I cook. If I eat with them, I have to wash dishes for them. I said I wanted to rest for several years. I have thought it through.

42. FL 178-171-002 1957 (Jan. 28), Fulian Archives.

43. Women say much less about the lighter side of needlework—the girls' festival held on the seventh day of the seventh lunar month, celebrating needlework skill and the astral union of the Cowherd and Weaving Girl stars—although it figures in compendia of local

customs. See, for instance, Zhongguo renmin zhenghzhi xieshang huiyi Shaanxi sheng Nanzheng xian weiyuan hui wenshi ziliao yanjiu weiyuan hui 1990: 97–99.

44. Interview with Zhou Guizhen 2006.

45. Interviews with Zhuang Xiaoxia 1996; Ma Li 1999; Wang Youna 1997.

46. Interviews with Yang Anxiu 1997; Zhou Guizhen 2006; Xiao Gaiye 1999. We heard many different accounts of when women stopped spinning and weaving at home, which usually corresponded to the growing availability of store-bought cloth. In Village B, people variously fix the date that their own weaving ended in the early 1960s (interview with Wang Xiqin 2006) or the early 1970s (interview with Zhou Guizhen 2006). In Village Z, women say they stopped spinning in the 1950s (interview with Liu Dongmei 1999) or slightly later (interview with He Gaizhen 1999). Only in Village G did women keep weaving straight through until the present (interview with Yu Xiaoli 2001), although even there people born in the 1980s or later did not learn to weave (interview with Liu Guyu 2004).

47. Interview with Shan Xiuzhen 1997. For similar memories in northern Shaanxi, see Guo 2004: 8.

48. Yuan Xi 2001.

49. Four *jin* of cotton could produce five *zhang* of cloth (interviews with Liu Guyu 2001, 2004). Private plots in Village G were typically seven to eight *fen* (ten *fen* = one *mu*; interview with Jiang Qiuwa 2001).

50. Interviews with He Gaizhen 1999; Song Yufen 1997.

51. Village G briefing 2001; interview with Wang Youna 1997.

52. Interview with Xiao Gaiye 1999.

53. Interview with Shi Ranwa 1999.

54. Interview with Jiang Qiuwa 2001.

55. Interview with Ma Li 1999.

56. Interview with Liu Fengqin 2006.

57. Interview with Wang Youna 1997.

58. Interview with Feng Sumei 1997.

59. Interview with Li Xiaomei 1997.

60. Interview with He Gaizhen 1999.

61. Interview with Zhuang Xiaoxia 2006.

62. Interview with Qian Taohua 1997.

63. Interview with Zhou Guizhen 2006.

64. Interview with Ma Li 1999.

65. On embroidery as a practice with both moral and aesthetic dimensions for elite women in the late imperial period, and its transformation in the early Republican era into a craft providing livelihood for poorer women, see Fong 2004.

66. A pair of embroidered pillows sold for five yuan during the collective period, but when the cost of material was deducted, the net was less than four yuan (interview with Liu Dongmei 1999). These pillows fell out of fashion in the 1980s and were replaced by flat "foreign" pillows that could hold clothing and sheets. In 1999 the old-fashioned pillows were selling for fifteen yuan for a set of four end-pieces (to fit two pillows). Embroidered door curtains were selling for ten yuan (interviews with He Gaizhen 1999; Liu Dongmei 1999).

67. Interview with He Gaizhen 1999.

68. Interview with Zheng Xiuhua 1999. On learning to embroider from Zheng, see Kang Xingfen (interview 1999). Embroidery is a subregional tradition in Village Z. In Village B, Cao Zhuxiang (interview 1996) comments, no one embroidered: *If you wore those kinds of clothes, people would laugh at you. People would laugh at you if you made embroidered shoes for your kids. Nobody did it.*

69. Interview with Liu Dongmei 1999.

70. In 2006, Cao Zhuxiang told us that she had been thinking of taking out her spinning wheel and cleaning it up to do some spinning. Her son, meanwhile, suggested burning it, which she refused to do. But when Gao Xiaoxian remarked that Zhuxiang should donate her spinning wheel to a museum, she expressed surprise: *Whatever use would there be in a museum taking that?* Gao explained that the Women's Federation was collecting artifacts used by women, and that Zhuxiang's old spinning wheel was of particular interest because it had been used in the very early mutual aid group she organized. Zhuxiang remained bemused that anyone would want such an item (interviews with Cao Zhuxiang 2006; Wang Jiji 2006). In Village Z, He Gaizhen (interview 1999) reported, women burned their own looms during the collective period, because they no longer had time to weave.

71. Interview with Yu Xiaoli 2001. She comments that people who were better off used the ration tickets to buy cloth, whereas people who were worse off sold their cloth ration tickets and used the money to buy raw cotton and weave cloth. Today women express preferences for handwoven pure cotton sheets, finding them more comfortable and easier to keep clean-looking (if not actually clean) than store-bought sheets (interview with Cao Zhuxiang 2006). In Village G, women produce plaid sheets and fine woolen throws, as well as handkerchiefs known as *shou papa* that are given to guests at weddings. The family of the bride is responsible for these. Demanding a handkerchief from the bride has become a new form of wedding-day teasing. Where a dowry used to show off the needlework skills of the bride, Gao Xiaoxian comments, now it shows off the needlework skill of the bride's mother, and it is not clear that any of these skills are being passed on. In Village G, Liu Guyu (interview 2004) commented that two of her four daughters can weave, but her granddaughters, now in their late twenties, cannot spin or weave, and buy all their clothing.

72. Interview with Li Fenglian 2001.

73. *Xin Zhongguo funü* 9 (Sept. 1953): 10.

74. FL 178–146–085 1956 (Dec. 12): 8.

75. Weinan xian minzhu funü lianhe hui 1958: 3.

76. Interview with Zhou Guizhen 2006.

77. One Women's Federation work report noted, for instance, that in a village in Chang'an County there were twenty-five mutual aid groups with 126 women members. Among them they had eighty children under the age of four. Fifty-four of these children had someone to watch them, leaving twenty-six in need of childcare (*Funü gongzuo jianxun* 13 (June 1952): 18.

78. Childcare was always somewhere on the agenda of the Women's Federation, although rarely at the top. In a 1949 national compendium giving brief biographies of women attending the first Chinese women's all-China representative meeting, the last of twenty-eight profiles was devoted to a group of Shandong women childcare workers who had heroically cared for

the children of cadres throughout the civil war period (Zhonghua quanguo minzhu funü lianhe hui xuanchuan jiaoyu bu 1949: 164–71).

79. Interview with Wang Meihua 1996. Publications across the county from the very early years of the PRC made the link between women's participation in agricultural production, accidents and deaths of unsupervised infants and children, and the need for organized child-care during the farming busy seasons. See, for instance, Fujian sheng minzhu funü lianhe hui fuli bu 1956: 3–4; *Xin Zhongguo funü* 22 (May 1951): 26, which emphasized the need for popular support for the childcare centers rather than top-down organizing by the Women's Federation. See also *Xin Zhongguo funü* 9 (Sept. 1953): 11; 11 (Nov. 1954): 15; *Renmin ribao,* Aug. 12, 1956, 3.

80. See, for example, FL 178–112–016 1951 (Sept. 25); FL 178–119–012 1952 (June); *Funü gongzuo jianxun* 13 (June 1952): 18–22; 16 (Oct. 1952): 37–43. News stories and pamphlets appeared across the country on how to organize busy-season childcare groups, often edited by the Women's Federation and illustrated with pictures of happy children waving goodbye as their mothers headed off to work in the fields. See, for instance, *Renmin ribao,* Nov. 5, 1951; Sept. 7, 1952; May 30, 1953; May 31, 1953; Zhou 1952 (drawing examples from Anhui and northern Jiangsu); Xinjiang sheng minzhu funü lianhe hui 1953; Fujian sheng minzhu funü lianhe hui fuli bu 1956. The Fujian pamphlet (1956: 1), published several years later than the others, puts the development of childcare in the context of the national plan for agricultural development scheduled to run from 1956 to 1967, mentioning that women's labor would be key to the plan's success.

81. See, for example , Danfeng xian Fulian 1957a; Zhou 1952: 7–8. In 1952 the Shaanxi provincial Women's Federation reported a total of 220 *tuoer suo* and 8,837 *baowa zu,* in which 14,890 childcare workers looked after 43,971 children (*Funü gongzuo jianxun* 16 [Oct. 1952]: 37). The corresponding numbers for Weinan district in 1953 (including eleven cities and counties) were extremely modest: 17 *tuoer suo,* 520 *baowa zu,* and 1,906 children (Weinan diqu difang zhi bianji weiyuan hui 1996: 275). These numbers raise doubts about the province-wide numbers, since Weinan District was one of the most populated and "advanced" areas of the province.

82. Zhou 1952: 15–16.

83. Interview with Liu Zhaofeng 1996.

84. Interview with Zheng Xiuhua 1999.

85. Interviews with Liu Zhaofeng 1996; Yuan Xiaoli 1997. Nevertheless, in some areas women continued to pay childcare workers directly. A 1956 Women's Federation report about Hanzhong District, where Nanzheng County is located, mentioned that some mothers were paying childcare workers half to two-thirds of their work points per day; if this was not enough, some co-op leaders deducted work points earned by the fathers of the children. Faced with this situation, some women decided just to take their children to the fields with them (FL 178–137–046 1956 [June 16]).

86. FL 178–164–018 1956 (Mar. 29).

87. Weinan xian funü lianhe hui 1956. The goal for this county (where Village B was located) in 1956 was for women to spend 150 workdays in the fields per year. See also Weinan xian minzhu funü lianhe hui 1958: 6, which calls daycare "the shared demand of men and women peasants." For other reports on training classes for childcare workers, see FL 178–156–032 1956.

88. *Funü gongzuo jianxun* 16 (Oct. 1952,): 43; interviews with Zhou Guizhen 2006; Zhang Xiuli 1997; Lu Yulian 1999; Zhang Chaofeng 2001.

89. Interview with Zhou Guizhen 2006.

90. Interview with Kang Xingfen 1999.

91. Interview with Zhang Xiuli 1997.

92. Evans 2008.

93. Filial sons, like virtuous widows, can draw on a rich social script. Late imperial county gazetteers for many of the places where we interviewed recorded cases of outstanding filial sons who tended to their gravely ill mothers day and night. For a sampling of such cases in Qing-era Nanzheng County, home of Village T, see Wang 1968 [1794]: 284–88; Guo and Lan 1969 [1921]: vol. 2, 424–26.

94. Interview with Yang Guishi 2004.

95. Interview 1996. Name withheld.

96. Interview with Zheng Xiuhua 1999.

97. Interview with Ma Li 1999.

98. Interview with Cao Zhuxiang 1996. Shan Xiuzhen (interview 1997), too, made a point of saying that she had no time to make elaborate preparations for the 1961 wedding of her adopted son, because she was busy at meetings. *She was a girl from Xibaozhang. Her mother was like me, also one of the first Party members in my village. . . . There was no sedan chair. There was nothing. She walked here. I was at home that day. The wedding was very simple. I didn't invite guests. There was only a ceremony. I wasn't at home before the wedding. I came back on that day. My neighbors helped tidy the house and get ready for the wedding. My neighbors told me, "Getting married is a special day for your son. You must come back." So I came back on that day. Originally, she would have worn colorful clothes and a flowered phoenix headdress. You could rent them. But I didn't rent those things. I thought, I am a Party member. How can I do those things? The natal family didn't ask for anything either. I gave her nothing. My son was in black coarse cloth. My daughter-in-law wore a colorful jacket and blue trousers.*

99. Interview with Zhuang Xiaoxia 1996.

100. Elsewhere (Hershatter 1993, 1997: 24–27) I have argued, in reaction to Gayatri Spivak's declaration that "the subaltern cannot speak," that we can hear the traces of subaltern voices in historical discourse. Perhaps this encounter with Cao Zhuxiang falls in the category of "Be careful what you wish for." When the subaltern speaks, the historian may end up more puzzled than ever.

101. For a discussion of this assumption of equality in a later, urban context, see Honig and Hershatter 1988: chapter 1.

102. Interview with Wang Guihua 1997.

103. As Gao Xiaoxian and I talked about these accounts, she brought up, not for the first time in our friendship, the story of her own mother, surnamed Li. At the age of eleven, Li had come as a beggar from Henan to Shaanxi in 1942, a victim of the famine that ravaged Henan that year. (For an eyewitness account of the devastation wrought by that famine, see Service 1974: 9–19.) Li's mother died in the Luoyang train station before they got out of Henan, and Li and her aunt rolled the body in a mat and threw it in a pit with the bodies of others who had died. Four years after her arrival in the city of Xi'an, Li married at age fifteen

in a free-choice marriage, and gave birth to Gao Xiaoxian at sixteen. Two years later, Xi'an was liberated. Li began to work at a nursery school. Xiaoxian, now a toddler, was placed in another nursery school, since children of daycare workers were not allowed in the centers where their parents worked. There she fell down a flight of stairs, and afterwards reportedly became timid and afraid to speak. Meanwhile Xiaoxian's younger sister was sent to a wet nurse who failed to feed her, taking the supplemental foods Li brought and feeding them to her own children. The younger sister's teeth didn't grow in, and she was shriveled and yellow. Eventually Xiaoxian's father sent the two girls to his mother in the countryside, and she raised them until Xiaoxian was in third grade. Xiaoxian's mother visited periodically, bringing books and clothing unavailable in the countryside; Xiaoxian understands those gifts as the way she expressed her love and concern for the children she saw several times a year. By the time Xiaoxian returned to Xi'an, she had four siblings, and she helped care for the younger ones while going to school. Her mother meanwhile had worked her way through primary school, continuing until she graduated from senior middle school, working all the while as a childcare teacher and administrator. Only during the Cultural Revolution, when (like virtually everyone in charge of a work unit) she endured a period of political disgrace, did she stay at home and cook for her own family. Gao Xiaoxian's mother, like the Women's Federation cadres, is of the generation that felt the revolution liberated them from terrible privation.

104. Interview with Xu Nini 1997.

105. Interview with Zhao Feng'e 1996.

106. Interview with Qian Taohua 1997.

107. Interview with Zhou Guizhen 1996.

108. Interview with Liu Dongmei 1999.

109. Interview with Zhuang Xiaoxia 1996. One connection she does not make in this anecdote is that in 1963, by her own account at another point in the interview, the county was just starting to emerge from several years of food shortages in the wake of the Great Leap Forward.

110. For a thoughtful ethnography about diverse attitudes toward abortion in contemporary China, which unfortunately does not explore the collective era, see Nie 2005.

111. Birth planning was reinstated nationally with the support of Premier Zhou Enlai in the early 1970s (White 2006: 42–61; Greenhalgh 2008: 53, 58–61). In Shaannan's Village T, village cadres began to mobilize women for tubal ligations in 1972 and 1973 (interview with Feng Sumei 1997). In Village Z, tubal ligations became available in 1970 (interview with Li Duoduo 1999).

112. Interview with Zhang Xiuli 1997. Judith Banister (1987: 51) writes, "Until after the Cultural Revolution of 1966–69 the rural network of contraceptive supply and medical skill for birth control operations was too weak to meet the latent demand generated by more receptive attitudes toward birth control. Besides, in many villages, local family planning campaigns did not begin until the late 1960s or the early 1970s."

113. Among the best scholarly treatments of this campaign are White 2006 (on the policy itself, mobilization, and resistance) and Greenhalgh 2008 (on the origins of the policy and what Greenhalgh calls the "dangers of scientism in the political arena" [317]).

Beginning in 1977, birth-planning cadres were responsible for making sure that women with many children had tubal ligations. Beginning in 1982, in at least some villages, the tubal ligation requirement extended to women who had a second pregnancy. As one former local cadre told us (her name and village are withheld here because the birth-planning policy, although it now permits a second child in rural areas under most circumstances, is still a politically sensitive subject), *At that time in our village, over one hundred tubal ligations were done, and not one of them was done without me. On the day of the tubal ligation, I had to go there. The person who had the operation could ask me to put her shoes on for her or put on her pants. As soon as they said the operation was finished, I would hurry into the room, first put on her shoes, slowly help her to stand up and then slowly put on her pants. Her husband was at home. But I was the one who helped her get her clothes on, waited on her until she went to bed, gave her medicine and something to drink, and made sure she was comfortable until she fell asleep. Only then did I stop worrying.* By the late 1990s, although the policy varied locally, we found many families with three children who paid a fine on the third.

114. Writing about Mussolini's Italy, Passerini (1987: 182) has called birth control, which was withheld or punished by the fascist regime but practiced nonetheless, "a kind of practical critique of women's oppression." In rural China, in contrast, birth control was provided by the state, tentatively in 1956 and more actively from the late 1960s on. Nevertheless, in China as in Italy, the heartfelt desire among a particular generation of women for no more children can perhaps be understood as a "practical critique of women's oppression."

115. Interview with Feng Sumei 1997.

116. Interview with Li Liujin 1997.

117. Interview with Feng Sumei 1997.

8. MODEL

1. Published materials include brief biographies, newspaper reports, photographs, pictorial texts, speeches, archival meeting minutes, and (in the 1980s and 1990s) retrospective mention in gazetteers. Archival materials include meeting minutes and Women's Federation work reports. Beyond the paper trail are interviews with former labor models, their fellow villagers, and Women's Federation cadres who worked with them. For a biography of a Shanxi rural woman labor model, see Tian 1999.

2. Official biographical information on Zhang Qiuxiang and attempts to emulate her cotton production achievements can be found, in addition to the sources cited in this chapter, in Weinan diqu nongye hezuo shi bianwei hui bian 1993: 385–91, 511; Weinan diqu difang zhi bianji weiyuan hui 1996: 273–74, 418–20, 960; Shaanxi sheng nongye hezuo shi bianwei hui bian 1994: 482–87; *Funü huabao* 6 (Mar. 16, 1958:); 15 (Aug. 1, 1958); 18 (Sept. 20, 1958); 20 (Oct. 16, 1958); 21 (Nov. 1, 1958); 22 (Nov. 16, 1958); 8 (Apr. 16, 1959); 9 (May 1, 1959); 14 (July 15, 1959); 15 (Aug. 1, 1959); 16 (Aug. 16, 1959); 18 (Sept. 15, 1959); 5 (Mar. 1, 1960); FL 1958: 190–025; National Women's Federation 1960: n.p.; Jiang and Cheng 1958.

3. Official biographical information on Shan Xiuzhen, including lists of major posts she held at the provincial and national level, can be found in Weinan diqu nongye hezuo shi bianwei hui bian 1993: 512; Shaanxi sheng nongye hezuo shi bianwei hui bian 1994: 504–9; Zhongguo renmin zhengzhi xieshang huiyi Shaanxi sheng Tongguan xian weiyuan hui wenshi ziliao weiyuan hui 1999: 3–6; Zhang et al. 1992; *Xibei funü huabao* 14 (Sept. 1, 1952); Zhong-

gong Tongguan xianwei dangshi yanjiu shi 2001: 87–88, 90, 98–100, 106, 109, 116–18, 123–
26, 136–37, 139; Tongguan xianzhi bianzuan weiyuan hui 1992: 154, 528.

4. Official biographical information on Cao Zhuxiang and her collective can be found,
in addition to the sources cited elsewhere in this chapter and chapter 3, in Shaanxi sheng
nongye hezuo shi bianwei hui bian 1994: 182–89; *Xibei funü huabao*, May 1, 1953; *Funü
huabao* 16 (Aug. 15, 1958).

5. Official biographical information on Lu Guilan can be found, in addition to the sources
cited elsewhere in this chapter, in Shaanxi sheng nongye hezuo shi bianwei hui bian 1994:
510–19; *Funü huabao* 17 (Sept. 1, 1958).

6. Differences between late imperial and early socialist women models were also, of
course, significant. Labor models in the 1950s were not explicitly praised for their chastity,
even when, as with Cao Zhuxiang, widowhood and modelhood were linked. Labor models,
unlike some earlier paragons of virtue, did not have shrines set up to their memory, nor were
they understood to have supernatural powers after death. Thanks to Susan Mann and Emily
Honig for raising questions about these differences.

7. "Labor model movement development and problems," NYT 194–8 (n.d., sometime
in 1950–51). On labor models in Yan'an, see also Stranahan 1983a, 1983b.

8. On the mass line, see Selden 1995: 212–13.

9. A 1951 report mentioned twelve such models by name, among them two women, who
were lauded specifically for leading other groups of women to participate in agricultural production ("Labor model movement development and problems," NYT 194–8). In 1952, a
woman from Baoji County, Wang Aiying, was written up as a labor model for her work on
a bumper wheat harvest (*Funü gongzuo jianxun* 14 [July 1952]: 12–15).

10. See, for instance, FL 178–130–030 1954 (Sept. 22).

11. Raphals 1998.

12. The Party-state did make extensive use of dead models after 1949: Liu Hulan (mentioned in chapter 4) and the Canadian doctor Norman Bethune were both lauded for having sacrificed their lives for the revolution, and Lei Feng, who died in 1962, was praised for
his fealty to Chairman Mao's thought and his desire to be a cog in the revolutionary machine. To be a *labor* model, however, a person had to be alive to perform the labor, preferably without having the task lead directly to his or her death.

13. Bossler 2002: 509.

14. "Labor model movement development and problems," NYT 194–8 (sometime in
1950–1951).

15. Ibid.

16. Interview with Liu Zhaofeng 1996.

17. Ibid.

18. FL 178–116–009 1952.

19. Vermeer (1988: 324–25) estimates that it accounted for 12 to 15 percent of all cultivated land in the area, and up to twice as much in irrigated areas. Vermeer's otherwise comprehensive history of cotton cultivation and textile production in Guanzhong (324–82) makes
only brief mention of the fact that peasant women were encouraged to organize cotton field
management groups (359) .

20. Ibid., 346–47. It reached a high in 1957 (317,000 hectares and more than 110,000

tons of cotton) that during the collective period was equaled again only in 1973 and 1982. Widely varying estimates of the area sown to cotton and total cotton output in the 1950s are given in Committee on the Economy of China 1969: tables 20-B, 20-C, and in Weinan diqu difang zhi bianji weiyuan hui 1996: 420.

21. Gao 2006a: 595. Cotton production before 1949 was an important and enduring part of the central Shaanxi (Guanzhong) economy (Nichols 1902: 248–49). Rui (1955: 15–16) notes that before 1949, more than 80 percent of the cotton crop was routinely shipped to Shanghai, Qingdao, and other east coast cities for processing, because of the lack of mechanized spindles and looms in the province. In 1953, Shaanxi, chiefly Guanzhong, produced about 90 percent of the cotton grown in the northwest. By 1955, the Party-state had opened and expanded a number of cotton mills, including five large-scale state-owned mills.

22. FL 178–216–002 1960 (Jan. 17): 1.

23. Vermeer 1988: 347. In 1954, he adds, "producing cotton for the State was depicted as a civic duty and economic benefits (loans, seeds, fertilizer) were to accrue to cooperatives which planted cotton" (352). In September 1955, compulsory quotas were established for cotton, and shortly thereafter, cotton growers were no longer permitted to keep cotton wool for their own use or private sale. Beginning in 1955, all cotton purchases by the state were made in advance, with higher prices paid to co-ops than to individuals. In response, in 1955 many cotton farmers began to grow grain instead, or to grow cotton on illegal plots to escape the required purchasing. Many also retained cotton illegally and sold it on the black market in the mid-1950s, finally leading the government to allow rural state-controlled free markets where cotton could be sold legally. Vermeer bases his account of these conflicts on articles published in the *Shaanxi ribao* (352–54). On low cotton cloth rations in rural areas in 1957 and rationing's "boost to local handicraft cloth production, legal or illegal," see 355.

24. Interview with Liu Zhenxi 2006. The association of women with cotton was a long one in Shaanxi, but historically it was focused more on processing than cultivation. See, for example, Nichols 1902: 129.

25. For a discussion of this transition, see Gao 2005, 2006a: 608.

26. This was part of the broader feminization of agriculture discussed in chapters 5 and 9. As Gao Xiaoxian puts it, *When women began cotton picking* [shi mianhua], *they also talked about "same pay, same work." Men would get less if they picked less, but men didn't do this work. They didn't want to do it. They went off to do higher-paying work. So women were still paid at the lower end. This is also related to the feminization of agriculture. Women entered, men were pulled out* (personal communication, Nov. 10, 2008).

27. Interview with Cao Zhuxiang 1996.

28. Interview with Zhang Qiuxiang 1996. Central Shaanxi cotton cultivation suffered from a lack of fertilizer, which Vermeer (1988: 358) attributes to "insufficient pigbreeding" and the limited availability of chemical fertilizers until the early 1970s.

29. FL 178–216–002 1960 (Jan. 17): 1. Zhang Qiuxiang herself commented that in the past (date unspecified) local yields had averaged about fifty *jin* of ginned cotton (*pimian*) per *mu*, but in 1955, she and eight others started to cultivate nine *mu* of high-yield fields (*fengchan tian*) and slightly more than one *mu* of very high-yield fields (*gao'e fengchan tian*).

In 1955 and 1956, the high-yield fields were producing about seven hundred *jin* of unginned cotton (*zimian*). The very high-yield fields produced 1,225 *jin* in 1955, 1,104 in 1956, and 940 in the drought year of 1957 (all figures in unginned cotton; *Shaanxi ribao*, Mar. 20, 1958). Slightly different figures for those years (1,225, 1,102, and 874.5 *jin* of unginned cotton per *mu*) are given in Zhongguo renmin yinhang 1958: 60.

30. Interview with Li Xiuwa 1996.

31. Interview with Wang Meihua and Li Xiuwa 1996.

32. Interview with Zhang Qiuxiang 1996.

33. Weinan diqu nongye hezuo shi bianwei hui bian 1993: 387; Weinan xianzhi bianji weiyuan hui 1987: 617.

34. Interview with Liu Zhaofeng 1996.

35. Ibid.

36. Interviews with Zhang Qiuxiang 1996; Wang Meihua and Li Xiuwa 1996. For a use of this phrase in print in 1963, when provincial authorities were working to restart the cotton economy after the weather and political problems of the years after the Great Leap Forward, see *Shaanxi ribao*, Apr. 10, 1963, 1.

37. Interview with Li Xiuwa 1996. This account, rendered forty years after the fact, is also an attempt by a Women's Federation cadre to validate the work of her own youth. Gao (2006a: 601) observes, "Women cadres and rural laboring women were co-producers of labor models whose 'experiences' were both grounded in rural women's working environment and shaped by the socialist state project."

38. *Shaanxi ribao*, Mar. 20, 1958.

39. Interview with Wang Meihua 1996.

40. Interview with Li Xiuwa 1996. On the importance of this conference, see Gao 2006a: 596–97. For contemporaneous reports on the meeting, see *Shaanxi ribao*, Apr. 19, 20, 21, and 22, 1956; FL 1956: 154–039.

41. Interview with Zhang Qiuxiang 1996.

42. Ibid. Zhongguo renmin yinhang (1958: 60) gives 1957 as the date of her selection as a national labor model.

43. NYT 194–748 (July 13, 1961), 47–49.

44. Gao 2005, 2006a.

45. On Cao Zhuxiang's activities in support of soldiers in Korea, see FL 178–27–026 1952. I do not want to make overblown claims for these care packages. It is doubtful that rural women woke up in the morning meditating about their link in the chain of international solidarity. Still, in the 1950s, "America" and "Korea" became part of their daily vocabulary.

46. On Shan Xiuzhen donating grain to the state, see FL 178–209–036 1954. On Cao Zhuxiang taking the lead in selling grain to the state, see FL 178–27–026 1952.

47. Like the concealment of grain production, this was a recurring problem. The Women's Federation cadre Zhang Xiuyu (interview 1996) describes her "patriotic education" work as follows: *In order to prevent cotton from being sold on the free market, we educated them to hand in more cotton and good cotton to the nation, educated them that our lives were getting better because of the nation, so we could not be ungrateful, could not forget the nation. During the difficult years, you should not be furtive, and you should hand in patriotic cotton. We*

worked in a village in Dali County, and the effect was very good. The team we worked in handed in more than a thousand jin *that day, and the whole county might have handed in some hundreds of thousands of* jin *that day. I cannot remember the exact figure. This shows that during the flowering season, the loss of cotton was very huge.*

48. On Shaanxi women activists during the co-op transformation, see Shaanxi sheng minzhu funü lianhe hui xuanchuan bu 1957; Zhongguo gongchandang Danfeng xian Zhulinguan qu weiyuan hui 1956.

49. On a competition initiated by Shan Xiuzhen in 1952, see Xibei minzhu funü lianhe hui shengchan bu 1952: 11–13.

50. The following account of the Five Silver Flowers contest, except as otherwise noted, is drawn from Gao 2005, 2006a, who provides a discussion of the broader economic context in which the contest was initiated. She points out that the provincial Party Committee took the lead in such contests, the agricultural departments provided technical support, and the Women's Federation had the bulk of the organizing responsibility (2006a: 597).

51. Interview with Wang Meihua 1996. The other two were Xue Junxiu and Gao Zhenxian. Beyond these five famous women, more than a hundred others were designated labor models in the course of this contest, and a total of 17,665 teams took part in the contest in 1958 (Gao 2006a: 597, 604).

52. Gao 2006a: 599. For contemporary reporting on women in cotton production, see *Shaanxi ribao*, Apr. 29, May 12, 1956; *Shaanxi ribao*, Mar. 8, 1958.

53. Interview with Cao Zhuxiang 1996.

54. Interview with Shan Xiuzhen 1997.

55. The thinking and techniques of these labor models changed over time. In a 1965 interview, looking back on ten years of champion cotton cultivation, Zhang Qiuxiang reflected that in her early years as a model too much time was spent on raising the yields on very small experimental plots. By 1965, she had turned her attention to techniques appropriate for the collective's larger cotton fields (*Shaanxi ribao*, Feb. 7, 1965).

56. More than half of this (2,078 yuan) was used for pesticide applicators, some of the remainder for fertilizer. The bank report furthers notes that in 1955 it lent the co-op 1,219 yuan for fertilizer and pesticides for Qiuxiang's and the co-op's high-yield fields. By 1957, it had worked with Qiuxiang's co-op to plan out their anticipated funding needs ahead of time. And in 1958, the bank stated its willingness to make loans to support the co-op in its goal of producing two thousand *jin* of unginned cotton per *mu* (Zhongguo renmin yinhang 1958: 59–62). Insects were a recurring problem in cotton cultivation during the 1950s; Vermeer (1988: 358–59) details losses from bollworms, aphids, red spiders, and cotton bugs.

57. Gao 2005, 2006a; interviews with Zhang Xiuyu 1996; Cao Zhuxiang 1996.

58. Zhonggong Shaanxi shengwei bangong ting bian 1956: 224.

59. Gao 2006a: 602–3. She concludes, "The feminization of cotton production, though increasing women's participation in farming, did not result in eliminating gender hierarchy in the division of labor" (604).

60. For typical statements about the suitability of women for cotton cultivation, see FL 178–27–012 1958 (Mar.).

61. Interview with Zhang Xiuyu 1996. Cao Zhuxiang (interview 1996) comments that this freed men for large-scale land improvement projects and road building.

62. Interview with Shan Xiuzhen 1997.

63. The term translated here as "champion," *zhuangyuan*, was the title bestowed upon the man who scored highest on the imperial civil service examinations in the late imperial period. In the Great Leap story of women's triumphant emergence into the workforce, women reportedly stopped gossiping and began to discuss production, or stopped competing about whose husband was more capable and whose cloth was more beautiful and started to compete over production skills (FL 178–216–002 1960 [Jan. 17]: 2, 8).

64. FL 178–45–006 1961 (July 31).

65. FL 178–216–002 1960: 3.

66. Interview with Shan Xiuzhen 1997.

67. "Labor model movement development and problems," NYT 194–8 (n.d., sometime in 1950–1951).

68. FL 178–185–057 1958 (Dec.). Xue began to "learn from Zhang Qiuxiang" in 1957. In January 1959 it was reported that Xue Junxiu's group had produced 3,100 *jin* of unginned cotton per *mu*, surpassing Qiuxiang's output, and that her group was preparing to "launch a great satellite of 10,000 *jin* of unginned cotton per *mu*." Qiuxiang's group was reported to have produced 1,002.7 *jin* of ginned (not unginned) cotton per *mu*, with one very high-yield field reaching 1,440.3 *jin* of ginned cotton. County authorities noted that Xue had the highest average output, but that Zhang's very high-yield plot produced more than other high-yield plots (*Shaanxi ribao*, Jan. 5, 1959, 2). For Xue Junxiu's account of how happy Qiuxiang was to be bested in this contest, and her admonition to Junxiu to help others best her in turn, see *Shaanxi ribao*, Mar. 13, 1959.

69. *Shaanxi ribao*, Mar. 23, Apr. 6, 1959; *Weinan ribao*, Apr. 5, 1959. A subsequent story had Shan Xiuzhen explaining how she was inspired by Qiuxiang to work ever harder on her group's cotton plot, achieving an output of eight hundred *jin* per *mu*, very high for her relatively dry area. It also described the hard work of Cao Zhuxiang (*Shaanxi ribao*, Mar. 18, 1959).

70. *Shaanxi ribao*, Nov. 12, 1959.

71. FL 178–216–002 1960 (Jan. 17): 8.

72. NYT 194–8 (Oct. 30, 1951), 26–27.

73. At the beginning of a typical labor model file is a form giving the model's name, gender, age, whether he or she represents his or her own achievements or those of a collective, and the name of his or her work unit. Below this grid is a space for the abstract of stories about the model, followed by a space for noting the type of award (collective first degree, second degree, etc.) that he or she is to receive (NYT 194–534 [3–4, 1956], 81–85).

74. FL 178–83–043 1956.

75. NYT 194–534 (3–4, 1956), 81–85. For brief evaluations of Zhang Qiuxiang, Shan Xiuzhen, Lu Guilan, and Cao Zhuxiang as rural women activists, see FL 178–161–074 1956 (Nov.). Lu received a first-class designation, Cao a second-class designation.

76. A similar type of introduction to the Danfeng County model pig-raiser Liu Xianzhen mentioned, "She establishes deep relations with the pigs she raised. When they sell the pig, several people cannot bind the pig. But she can drive the pigs to the supply and marketing cooperative by herself. On the road, she sat down and rested three times, while the pigs lay down three times too" ("Yang zhu nengshou Liu Xianzhen cailiao" n.d.).

77. FL 178-78-062 1956 (Aug. 29-Sept. 30). She was assiduous as well in training younger women to be activists and co-op officials, encouraging them to speak out and criticize the mistakes of male leaders when appropriate (FL 178-185-058 1958 [Dec.]).

78. Shaanxi sheng minzhu funü lianhe hui 1956, 33-40. A 1958 booklet directed at cotton-growing villagers described organization tasks facing Zhang and her cotton-growing group: overcoming conservative thinking about how much a field could produce and devising an appropriate means of recording work points (Shaanxi sheng nonglin ting 1958). For another example, with a few more rhetorical flourishes, see Shaanxi sheng nongye zhanlan hui 1958.

79. For reports about and speeches by Zhang Qiuxiang that discuss deep plowing, meticulous seed selection, early sowing, thinning and singling of seedlings, generous use of fertilizer (including manure, old earthen bricks, oil residue, calcium phosphate [lin suan gai], and other substances), intertilling (zhonggeng), intensive weeding, pruning, combating insect pests such as cotton aphids with potent insecticides, and improved picking techniques, see Shaanxi ribao, Mar. 20, 1958; NYT 194-519 (Dec. 1959); Weinan ribao, May 15, 1960, 4; Shaanxi ribao, July 11, 1960, 1; Weinan ribao, Mar. 7, 1961, 3; NYT 194-748 (July 1961); Shaanxi ribao, Nov. 15, 1962; Shaanxi ribao, Apr. 10, 1963. In the 1958 article in Shaanxi ribao, Zhang Qiuxiang explicitly gives male co-op members credit for preparing the fields. Such articles continued even after the end of the crisis following the Great Leap, as the province moved to reinvigorate cotton production in 1963. On the production techniques of all five Silver Flowers, see Qingkuang fanying, June 26, 1964.

80. With other advanced producers in industry and agriculture, her picture appeared on the front page of the Shaanxi ribao on March 20, 1958, and several stories on inside pages detailed her achievements. Zhang Qiuxiang (interview 1996) remembers her highest annual cotton yield as dating from that year: 250 jin per mu, produced on an experimental plot by a team of about ten women of various ages. Official documents from that period, however, refer to her "thousand-jin model," in which each mu of Qiuxiang fields was to produce one thousand jin of unginned cotton. See, for example, FL 178-27-012 1958 (Mar.); FL 178-45-006 1961 (Jul. 31).

81. NYT 194-407 1958 (Mar.).

82. Zhonggong Shaanxi shengwei 1958; FL 178-27-012, 3. The text of the directive was reprinted in Shaanxi ribao, Apr. 1, 1958.

83. FL 178-216-002 1960 (Jan. 17): 2. Another version was "Study Qiuxiang, catch up with Qiuxiang, surpass Qiuxiang." See, for instance, Weinan ribao, Apr. 5, 1959. On the Great Leap Forward, see MacFarquhar 1983.

84. On Shan Xiuzhen's work in creating Qiuxiang fields in her commune, see Shan Xiuzhen 1962; FL 178-313-001.

85. Lei Caiwa (interview 2001) of Village G was in a Qiuxiang cotton-growing group in Heyang County, on the northern edge of the cotton belt. Yields in that area were much lower than in groups farther south: forty or fifty jin per mu (interview with Ouyang Xiu 2004). Cao Zhuxiang founded a cotton-growing group in Village B that ran for about three years, yielding about 120 jin per mu (interview with Zhou Guizhen 2006). The Women's Federation also requested in its 1958 work plan that "counties producing cotton enthusiastically spread the

experiences of the Zhang Qiuxiang group and set up flags of extraordinary cotton harvest,"
and proposed the training of women technicians and the establishment of experimental fields
in each brigade (FL 178–189–010 1958 [Mar. 11]).

86. Zhonggong Weinan xianwei bianzhu xiaozu 1959a, 1959b. She was also credited with
inspiring women in non-cotton-growing areas to start experimental high-yield corn fields,
which they tended "just like mothers straightening up their own children" (*Shaanxi ribao,*
Aug. 11, 1958). For accounts in the press by or about Qiuxiang and members of her group,
see also *Weinan ribao,* Mar. 6 and 7, 1959.

87. Jiang and Cheng 1958, 6–7. See also *Shaanxi ribao,* Jun. 27, 1958; *Gongren ribao,*
Sept. 22, 1959, 6; Chen 2003: 276. Similar valorizations of women's affinity for science and
machinery abounded during the Great Leap. For a Danfeng County group of women who
invented more than twenty kinds of new agricultural implements (and several hundred other
items, including one model car for children), see "Nü zhuangyuan nü Zhuge da xian shengcai" 1958 (or 1959?). A project led by Shan Xiuzhen to establish women-run bacterial fertilizer factories is described in a 1958 speech by Shan in FL 178–198–040 1958.

88. See, for instance, *Shaanxi ribao,* Aug. 2, 1958, in which Qiuxiang names a new goal
for the year: that the 282 *mu* of cotton fields in her commune should each produce one thousand *jin* of unginned cotton, and that the 4.3 *mu* cultivated by her and ten other women should
produce three thousand *jin* of unginned cotton per *mu.*

89. *Shaanxi ribao,* Jun. 23, 1959.

90. NYT 194–673 1960 (Feb. 9): 6–13. Many top labor models also held political posts.
Lu Guilan was a member of the Chinese People's Political Consultative Conference and the
executive committee of the provincial Women's Federation, a deputy of the city and provincial People's Congress, and a researcher of the provincial agricultural scientific academy (NYT
194–673 1960 [Feb. 18], 17–24). Shan Xiuzhen was a member of the provincial people's congress (NYT 194–534 1956, 81–85).

91. *Shaanxi ribao,* July 5, 1958.

92. *Shaanxi ribao,* Nov. 7, 1958.

93. *Shaanxi ribao,* Jan. 1, 1959. The General Line (for Socialist Construction) refers to a set
of goals and priorities promulgated by the Communist Party before and during the Great Leap.

94. NYT 194–673 1960 (Feb. 9): 6–13. A similar document in the same folder, in the
form of a capsule biography rather than a speech, was devoted to Lu Guilan and her determination to learn from Zhang Qiuxiang and other models: "They set a record for corn and
cotton output, and their hard work and will power stirred up her heart. During the day she
concentrated on the meetings, but at night she could not fall asleep. She blamed herself, 'Lu
Guilan, Lu Guilan! Other people can do it, why couldn't you? Do you lack arms or legs?' The
more she thought the worse she felt. She wiped away her tears with the corner of the quilt. 'It's
no use crying. You should make up your mind: work! We must make some achievements in
agricultural production!' . . . She worked on her cotton farm like an industrious and careful
mother, raising her 'children' cautiously and conscientiously" (NYT 194–673 1060 [Feb. 18],
17–24). Looking at a sheaf of labor model speeches gleaned from the archives, Gao Xiaoxian (personal communication, April 2001) pronounced herself uninterested in them: *Each
of them was probably written by a different person from the Women's Federation. Maybe this*

one added this sentence, that one put things a bit differently, to put their own stamp on things. So the differences between one speech and the next don't tell me much about Zhang Qiuxiang, only about the individuals who wrote her speeches. I myself did write-ups on labor models when I first came to the Women's Federation. I know how it is done. Of course, the work of local cadres in producing labor models also had to take account of local understandings and desires; a labor model whose achievements were puffed up by state authorities but who did not connect to local social arrangements would not have been effective.

95. See, for instance, *Weinan ribao,* Sept. 2, 1959.

96. In a 1960 article, Cao Zhuxiang claimed that in 1959 her group produced an average of 1,688.5 *jin* of unginned cotton per *mu* of high-yield fields, with a high of 1,815.2 *jin* on its highest field, forty *jin* more than Qiuxiang that year. Shan Xiuzhen, growing cotton in a semimountainous district in Tongguan, reported her yield as 1,265 *jin,* meaning that she had caught up with Qiuxiang. She hoped for two thousand to three thousand *jin* in 1960 (*Shaanxi ribao,* Apr. 24, 1960).

97. Qiuxiang's brigade, it said, had 1,150 *mu* sown to cotton. If each *mu* yielded one hundred *jin* of ginned cotton, this would bring 92,000 yuan in income to the brigade, an average of 206 yuan per household, or 40.7 yuan per person. Since the state awarded thirty-five *jin* of grain for each thousand *jin* of ginned cotton sold, the brigade could earn 40,250 *jin* of grain, or about ninety *jin* per household (FL 178–45–006 1961 [July 31]).

98. FL 178–45–006 1961 (July 31); for this jingle, see also FL 178–216–002 1960 (Jan. 17): 9, and *Shaanxi ribao,* Apr. 2, 1960, which is a revised version of the January 17 report.

99. In early 1960, Cao Zhuxiang's planting group was given a March 8 Red Flag Award for their work in emulating Qiuxiang, protecting the cotton crop from the 1959 cold and drought—and, the citation said, resisting the ridicule of conservative elements (FL 178–244–015 1960 [Mar. 2]).

100. *Weinan ribao,* Mar. 7, 1961, 3.

101. *Weinan ribao,* Apr. 5, 1961, 1.

102. NYT 194–747 1961 (July 14). Subsequent references to peasants preferring grain cultivation to cotton growing can be found in an interview with Shan Xiuzhen in the *Shaanxi ribao,* Mar. 6, 1963,3. Vermeer (1988: 348; see also 510 n98) finds that "nationwide, the cotton acreage fell from 5.5 million hectares in 1959 to a low of 3.5 million hectares in 1962," a clear response by peasants to the shortage of food grain.

103. *Weinan ribao,* May 5, 1960. This new emphasis may be related to the increased attention to rural women's literacy during the Great Leap Forward, but the article makes no explicit link.

104. *Shaanxi ribao,* Dec. 11, 1961. Vermeer (1988: 348) notes than from 1953 until the 1970s, cotton prices were kept low, figured at a ratio of one kilogram of cotton to 6.25 kilograms of wheat. He argues that "state price control and cooperative sales were not conducive to quality improvements in varieties, cultivation and processing."

105. *Shan Xiuzhen* 1962. This piece was also published in the *Shaanxi ribao,* Jan. 25, 1962, 1–2. In a follow-up report using this study material, various localities reported that they should first give positive comments on the local work before studying the materials about Xiuzhen, and then inspire people to make comparisons. Otherwise, the report warned, some women cadres might feel that they could never live up to the Xiuzhen standard, while other,

older cadres might adopt the arrogant attitude that they had nothing to learn from her. Some communes, the report noted, were even requiring men cadres to study Xiuzhen's example (FL 178-313-009 1962 [June 4]). *Shaanxi ribao*, Mar. 7, 1962, 2, reported that the Five Silver Flowers greeted International Women's Day with a combination of support for national cotton policy and practical cultivation advice.

106. *Shaanxi ribao*, Mar. 7, 1962, 3. For other pieces by or about Shan Xiuzhen in this period, see *Shaanxi ribao*, Mar. 6, 1963, and Apr. 25, 1964. According to the March 6 article, the province also held a cotton production meeting in 1963. For similar statements of political determination from Zhang Qiuxiang in the years after the Great Leap, sometimes combined with technical cultivation advice, see *Shaanxi ribao*, Feb. 27, Mar. 19, Apr. 10, May 31, July 29, 1963. In 1964, Zhang and a younger colleague traveled to Zhejiang to speak to agricultural workers there (*Shaanxi ribao*, Apr. 4, 1964).

107. *Shaanxi ribao*, Apr. 25, 1964, 1. For Shan Xiuzhen on goat dung, see *Shaanxi ribao*, Mar. 6, 1963, 3.

108. For a Yuan example, see Bossler 2002: 510.

109. Cotton cultivation did not continue to expand. Vermeer (1988: 371–75) notes that in the 1960s and 1970s "the low prices of cotton did not make it attractive for the farmers to devote more collective land to cotton than the acreage assigned by the State." Peasants also did not grow cotton on their private plots. Meanwhile production costs rose with the introduction of chemical fertilizer, pesticides, and other inputs. Farmers came to prefer wheat, maize, and other crops. Vermeer notes that although the state could require peasants to devote a certain amount of acreage to cotton, its low return meant that "farmers were likely to be reluctant in allocating prime land and scarce material resources to it" (374). Loss of farmland to roads, housing, and factories was another factor in the stagnation of cotton production. Finally, in the early 1980s, "as soon as the responsibility system had given peasants far greater freedom in their choice of crops to be cultivated, cotton cultivation was reduced in most areas of Guanzhong" (379).

110. According to a former provincial Women's Federation cadre, twenty-five women were designated provincial labor models during this period, comprising 22 percent of the total (interview with Li Xiuwa 1996). Gao (2006a: 600) notes that statements "about equal pay for equal work that appeared in the initial promotion materials (for cotton production contests) later disappeared," and that in the writings about Zhang Qiuxiang it was "difficult to identify any content related to women's rights and interests, women's development, women's status and women's liberation. . . . 'Learn from Zhang Qiuxiang' became a movement purely for promoting cotton-planting technique. 'Women's liberation' and its impact vanished, or were entirely embodied by women's participation in labor." Gao goes on to observe that gaining technical skills through these campaigns was an important experience for Zhang and other women (601), and that they were committed less to building a remote socialist state than to being "able to attain social respectability previously only enjoyed by men" (605).

111. Interview with Cao Zhuxiang 1996.

112. Interview with Wang Jiji 2006.

113. Interview with Zhang Qiuxiang 1996. For an official account of Zhou Enlai's concern for Zhang Qiuxiang, see Guo 1993. Both her memories of Zhou and the 1993 account

may well have been shaped by the discourse on his heroic qualities that emerged after his death and particularly after the death of Mao Zedong. My thanks to Harriet Evans for making this link.

114. Interview with Zhang Qiuxiang 1996.

115. Ibid.

116. Gao Xiaoxian, personal communication, Nov. 10, 2008. These observations, and our inability to address contextual factors on the basis of a single interview, also point to a limitation of oral history in comparison to long-term ethnographic research.

117. Zhang Qiuxiang died in 2000. According to an account published in a local newspaper, she asked her son if her funeral clothes (*laoyi*) were ready. He said yes, they were all prepared and stored in a chest. She said, "All right, you go to sleep now, and I am going to sleep too, because I am tired." She died during the night, of old age, with no apparent illness.

118. Interviewing Indonesians who had been domestic workers for the Dutch, Ann Stoler and Karen Strassler (2002) found that their stories were curiously empty of affect. They did not sound like the lushly sentimental accounts that former Dutch colonials wrote about their servants, nor did they sound like heroic tales of anticolonial subaltern resistance. Stoler and Strassler surmise that this is partly because official narratives of the past provided by the repressive Suharto Indonesian state of the late 1990s were ambiguous about the Dutch. "To tell of one's experiences during the Dutch period conferred neither glory nor legitimacy or 'recognition,'" they tell us (176). "Subtle shifts, evasions, and formulaic responses located the fault lines of memory, the places of discomfort and disinterest as well as those of safety and concern" (175).

119. For background on the teenage Communist martyr Liu Hulan, who was invoked by many activists, see chapter 4, n43. The reference to death being heavier than Mount Tai is drawn from a phrase coined by the Han Dynasty historian Sima Qian, that the significance of a person's death (and by extension the significance of the person's life) can be either lighter than a feather or weightier than Mount Tai. The phrase was used by Chairman Mao in his 1944 speech "Serve the People" (1967: 177).

120. Interview with Lu Guilan 1996.

121. Ibid.

122. According to an official biography of Shan Xiuzhen, she went to Beijing eight times and was received by Mao Zedong and Zhou Enlai four times (Zhongguo renmin zhengzhi xieshang huiyi Shaanxi sheng Tongguan xian weiyuan hui wenshi ziliao weiyuan hui 1999: 3). Feng Gaixia (interview 1997), the young marriage rights activist whose story opens chapter 4, was also at this meeting; she recalls being instructed by Deng Yingchao, Zhou Enlai's wife and a senior Party leader herself, not to imperil Chairman Mao's health by shaking hands with him. *I was in the thirteenth row, four or five rows away. Chairman Mao came, and everybody sat down. Chairman Mao arrived and waved. All of a sudden, no one was sitting down. Some of them even went up to the table. Zhang Qiuxiang sat together with me. She crawled under the table to go shake hands with Chairman Mao. I was standing on my chair. But I was timid, because Sister Deng had already told us what to do. . . . All the people in the front were sitting on the table and some were crawling under the table. I couldn't really get to where I wanted to be. I was too short and at that time I was only eighteen. So I was not able to press to the front. That is a lifelong regret. That was the most unforgettable day of my life. At that time, I didn't*

have the pictures developed, because my [monthly] salary was only twenty yuan. It would have cost fifteen yuan, three-fourths of my salary.

9. LABORER

1. Chan 2001: 54–60. For a chronology of events before, during, and after the Great Leap Forward, covering the period 1955–62, see Teiwes and Sun 1999: xv–xxvii.

In late 1957, Mao first put forward the goal of overtaking Great Britain economically within fifteen years. By the summer of 1958, he was predicting that in 1962, China would equal or surpass the United States in steel production (MacFarquhar 1983: 17, 90). Initial goals of overtaking the United Kingdom in fifteen years and the United States in twenty were soon adjusted downward, to seven and fifteen years (Lü 2000: 75). By June 1, the Shaanxi Women's Federation was echoing the Shaanxi Party Committee's call for "three years of bitter warfare to change the face of the entire province" (Shaanxi sheng funü lianhe hui, 1994: 26).

2. To my knowledge, the only other scholar who uses women's memories as a primary source for understanding the Leap is Kimberley Manning, whose work has been centered in Henan and Jiangsu. Manning labels the CCP's approach to mobilizing women "Marxist maternalist," which she says "combined Engelsian principles of sexual equality with a republican maternalist concern for protecting reproductive health and maintaining the family at the centre of the national project" (2005: 87). She explores the tensions between this conception, which emphasized physiological difference and was promoted by the Women's Federation, and what she calls "a revolutionary Maoist ethic according to which all were expected to struggle equally" (2006a: 350–51), subscribed to by grassroots rural women leaders who often abused women under their supervision (2006a; also see 2006b, 2007). Manning argues that the Great Leap is remembered differently (and more fondly) by "women who had the formal and informal support of party institutions" than by those who did not, and that the Marxist maternalist vision failed "to enable the majority of rural women to realize themselves as liberated *funü* [women] throughout the Maoist era" (2005: 85, 90). Manning's main concern in these essays is to disentangle how state discourses of women's liberation were embodied, sorted out, or neglected at the grassroots level, both among women cadres and among ordinary women farmers. Whether because of differences in location, interviewees, or the ears of the interviewer, I have not discerned such a clear conflict among state discourses, or for that matter such clear discourses at all, in the Shaanxi villages where I interviewed with Gao Xiaoxian.

3. Banister (1987: 59) calls the Great Leap an "attempt to substitute increased physical labor by the peasants for all the agricultural inputs in short supply." Anglophone scholarship on the Great Leap mixes fine-grained analysis of national politics, regional studies, and works on a particular village. Schurmann (1968: 464–97) describes the emergence and organization of the communes. On the national political scene, MacFarquhar (1983: 334) sees Mao's "sheer personal dominance" as the crucial force in the launching of the Great Leap. For political decisions and their consequences in this period, see also Cong 1996; Li 1996a, 1996b; Xie 1990. Bachman (1991) focuses on the period just before the Leap, tracing a struggle between a group that favored the development of heavy industry and one that concerned it-

self with balancing revenue and expenditure. He regards institutional interests as primary, rather than Mao's thinking on economic development, and sees Mao as moving his support from one group to another. Chan (2001: 6–8) focuses on the origins of the Leap and on 1958 as the most important time of policy innovation. He allies himself with Teiwes and Sun (1999: 13) in regarding Mao's leadership role as crucial to the development of the Leap. Chan (2001: 8–9, 11) concedes, however, that Mao was not able to control the outcomes of policies he had set in motion, while Teiwes and Sun (1999: 19) suggest that Mao's own ambivalence and changes of course, coupled with the unwillingness of other leaders to confront him, allowed the crisis to develop into disaster. Xiaobo Lü (2000) focuses on Party policy and cadre behavior, arguing that the Great Leap marked the beginning of "involution" in the CCP. This is his term for the party's choice to deal with popular dissatisfaction with low-level officials via "a return to the old ways of organizational integration that had been effective during wartime and . . . by devising new techniques to remedy bureaucratic problems" (73). He sees the resulting lack of rules for cadre actions, and the substitution of revolutionary goals for rules, as the root cause of the Great Leap disaster (111). Chan (2001: 280) makes a related argument that extends beyond the bureaucracy: "Without physical resources commensurate with the tasks at hand, mass mobilization and exhortation were the only option, and increasingly, mass mobilization became the only means toward the goal of output maximization, and then ultimately became an end in itself." Domes (1980: 20–60) focuses on the people's communes. Provincial studies include Chan (2001: 198–279) on Guangdong, Chan (1992) on Liaoning, and Domenach (1995) on Henan. Lin (1990) uses game theory to analyze peasant commitment to the communes as a case of the failure of a self-enforcing contract. Becker (1996) offers an impassioned account of the famine. Dali Yang (1996) develops an intriguing analysis of the relationship between the recovery from the Great Leap famine and the post-Mao economic reforms. Thaxton (2008) brings the discussion of state extraction and brutal local cadre behavior down to the village level in one Henan location. Wang and Yang (1989: 164–203) offer a county-level perspective from Anhui. Other local studies are cited elsewhere in this chapter. Li (1994: 263–355) offers a Mao-centered account of the Great Leap. For contemporaneous criticisms of the communes and the Leap by a local Hebei cadre, see Pickowicz 1994, 2007.

4. Schoenhals 1987: 26–27; interview with Feng Zaicai and Wang Fugui 2001. Schoenhals notes that in fall 1957, the Rural Work Department recommended that co-ops be reduced in size, rather than enlarged. The conference also set new limits on household handicraft production, lest it encourage spontaneous capitalism (26).

5. Chan 2001: 54–60. This was the meeting at which Mao "pronounced the new goal of catching up with Britain in *seven* years, and the USA in fifteen to seventeen years" (55).

6. Schoenhals 1987: 74.

7. Communes were intended to combine production and governmental administrative functions in one entity. For details on which provinces took up this call and when, and on Mao's endorsement of the trend, see Chan 2001: 67–71, 78–84. For policy implementation nationally by the Ministry of Agriculture, see 109–57. For the formation of communes and their development during the Great Leap era and its immediate aftermath, see also Ling 1997: 1093; Luo Pinghan 2006: 1–288.

8. Weinan diqu nongye hezuo shi bianwei hui bian 1993: 40. The communes were divided into 3,797 production brigades, suggesting that the brigades were on average slightly larger than the higher co-ops had been. See also Weinan diqu difang zhi bianji weiyuan hui 1996: 405–7. Counties, too, were amalgamated. Heyang County (home of Village G) was folded into Hancheng County for several years (interview with Zhang Chaofeng 2001), and Danfeng County (home of Village Z) became part of Shan County between late 1958 and October 1961 (Shaanxi sheng Danfeng xian jiaotong ju 1990: 76).

9. Weinan Prefecture had eighteen counties. From early 1959 to 1961, three of them (Tongguan, Huayin, and Hua) were absorbed into Weinan County. The resulting enlarged county had ten communes, divided into eighty-two management districts, 844 brigades, and 4,512 teams (Weinan xianzhi bianji weiyuan hui 1987: 65).

10. Weinan diqu nongye hezuo shi bianwei hui bian 1993: 20–21, 61, 368.

11. Interview with Liu Zhaofeng 1996. For folk songs composed in Shaanxi celebrating the Leap, see *Shi kan she* 1958a: 14, 24–26, 31–32, 44–45, 51–52, 55, 57, 68; 1958b: 48; 1959: 27.

12. Interview with Li Liujin 1997; He Gaizhen (interview 1999) supplied the last two phrases. In Danfeng County, the Great Leap period did in fact bring electricity to more than two thousand households in the county seat, but Village Z appears not to have had even limited electricity (from riverside hydroelectric stations) until the mid-1960s, with further development from the mid-1970s on (Shaanxi sheng Danfeng xian shuili zhi 1990: 130–31, 134).

13. An extraordinary visual rendition of such a future village, full of consumer goods and services, predates the Great Leap by more than two years. See *Xibei funü huabao*, Apr. 1, 1956.

14. On the origins of the "backyard steel" campaign, see MacFarquhar 1983: 113–16.

15. Interviews with Wang Youna 1997; He Gaizhen 1999; Zhang Chaofeng 2001.

16. Interview with Liu Zhaofeng 1996. In Weinan, the thick pine trees surrounding village burial sites were cut down one by one and sent off to the smelting furnaces (interview with Cao Zhuxiang 1996). Carl Riskin (Columbia University Modern China Seminar, Apr. 2, 2009) comments that the Great Leap followed a period in which resources had been redistributed. This time, however, the requisitioned resources were necessary household goods such as pots and pans.

17. FL 178–197–037 1958 (Oct. 20): 4, 12–14.

18. Interview with Li Liujin 1997.

19. Interview with Cao Zhuxiang 1996.

20. For a similar point about Henan women, see Manning 2005: 96.

21. Interview with Liu Zhenxi 2006.

22. A comprehensive assessment of water control is beyond the scope of this study. Liu Zhenxi (interview 2006) notes that in Weinan, water control slowly improved across the collective period, only to erode during the reform era. Water wheels, worked with belts, dated from the pre-1949 era. These were slowly replaced in the 1960s by pumps attached to pipes, deep wells dug with state support, and electrically powered pumps inside wells. At the same time, regional authorities undertook the repair and construction of large canals in the area.

382 NOTES TO PAGES 240–242

Liu added that in the 1990s, the development district (*kaifa qu*) established during the reforms drew off much of the area's water, cutting off water supply from the canals, and that people have returned to digging wells.

23. FL 178–186–043 1958. Friedman (2006: 43–44) describes a region in eastern Fujian where most labor on public works projects was provided by women, in accordance with a local gendered division of labor that "defined manual labor as women's work" (44).

24. Interview with Liu Zhenxi 2006.

25. Interviews with Qian Taohua 1997; Kang Ruqing 1997; Feng Sumei 1997.

26. Interviews with Ouyang Xiu 2004; Gao Yuzhong 2004.

27. Interviews with Zheng Xiuhua 1999; Liu Dongmei 1999; He Gaizhen 1999; Li Duoduo 1999. Village Z and other locations in Danfeng County had been damaged by floods throughout the Republican period. Village Z was partially flooded in 1953 and almost completely inundated in 1954. For descriptions of floods from the Republican period through the 1970s, see Shaanxi sheng Danfeng xian shuili zhi bianzuan zu 1990: 58–62, 75–78. The Great Leap years were particularly volatile in the county, with flooding in 1958 (61) and periods of drought in each year from 1959 to 1963 (71, 76).

28. Interview with He Gaizhen 1999.

29. Interview with Liu Dongmei 1999.

30. Interview with Zhou Guizhen 1996.

31. Interview with Li Liujin 1997.

32. Interview with Cao Zhuxiang 1996. Provincial plans for the Great Leap Forward included minimum quotas for women leaders. Townships were exhorted to incorporate women into their leadership ranks through grassroots elections, to have women make up 25 percent or more of township representatives and 15 percent of township governing committee members (FL 178–189–010 1958 [Mar. 11]). This initiative does not feature in any of the memories people recounted to us, but women do talk about the experience of being local cadres then.

33. The You River in Weinan historically flooded frequently from gorge runoff. In drought years, it would dry up and more than sixty thousand *mu* of good land would get no irrigation. In the 1950s, the Weinan City Committee and the provincial water bureau decided to construct a comprehensive reservoir to meet the needs of irrigation, city water supply, and flood control. The reservoir extended from Chuankou Wang village five kilometers southward to the mouth of the You River Valley. Work began in December 1959, entailing the labor of ten thousand people by the time of its completion in November 1963 (Huang 2002). On the much larger and disastrous resettlement occasioned by the Sanmenxia reservoir project in Henan, which brought 147,000 people to Dali, Weinan, Pucheng, and other counties, see Vermeer 1981: 23–24; Weinan diqu difang zhi bianji weiyuan hui 1996: 239–41; Jing 1997; Jing and Meng 1999. On a 2010 exposé of this relocation by Xie Chaoping, which led to his detention, see Lee 2010. On a large-scale Great Leap Forward Yanguoxia dam project in Gansu and its deleterious effects on local ecology and rural life, see Jing 1996, 1999, 2001.

34. Interviews with Zhou Guizhen 1996, 2006. In 1964, an investigative team was called in from higher levels. Zhou was cleared of wrongdoing, but her challenger was discovered to have been hoarding grain. See Jing 1997 for a survey of long-term problems among "reser-

voir relocatees" (*shuiku yimin*) displaced by large-scale dam and reservoir projects during the Great Leap, exacerbated by what the author calls "neglect, coercion and suppression" (74) of the relocated populations.

35. Because of the Great Leap labor shortage, the seasonal supply of migrant male farmworkers disappeared: *That time during the great steel smelting, if you wanted to hire someone you couldn't, so women replaced men. From the time of the commune, women were the main labor force* (interview with Liu Zhenxi 2006). Similar statements were also made by Zheng Caigui (interview 1996).

36. Interview with Cao Zhuxiang 1996.

37. Interview with Zhou Guizhen 2006.

38. Interview with Liu Zhaofeng 1996. Wang Youna (interview 1997) spoke about women's active role in rice cultivation and threshing, as well as wheat planting, and Zhou Guizhen (interview 2006) talked about women growing cotton. Lu Yulian (interview 1999) described women's participation in planting.

39. Interviews with Cao Zhuxiang 1996; Zhou Guizhen 1996, 2006.

40. Interview with Feng Sumei 1997.

41. Just prior to the Leap, Women's Federation cadres were still involved in trying to increase the number of days women spent in the fields. In spring 1958, the provincial Federation began a "Two Diligences" campaign, exhorting women to be diligent and thrifty in constructing the nation and managing the household (FL 178–189–010 1958 [Mar. 11]). On the unfolding of this campaign, see Shaanxi sheng funü lianhe hui, 1994: 24–25; FL 178–196–013 1958 (Mar. 28).

42. Interview with Zhou Guizhen 2006. Her phrase "there was no one in the village" (*cunshang dou meiyou ren*), meaning that there were no men, echoes the usage of "no one is home" discussed in chapter 2. This usage has persisted more than half a century after it was first criticized as a feudal remnant.

43. Interview with Zhou Guizhen 1996.

44. FL 178–197–037 1958 (Oct. 20): 7. Wage systems varied during the Great Leap. For an experiment with direct supply of foodstuffs, clothing, and fuel, see *Weinan ribao,* Oct. 13, 1958. For a brief period in 1958, production brigades paid wages, but they soon returned to recording work points and distributing cash at year's end. As with work points, women routinely earned less than men. Brigades did not issue part of the payment in grain, as they had earlier, but by the second year they were distributing about two *jin* of cotton to every brigade member (interviews with Zhuang Xiaoxia 1996; Cao Zhuxiang 1996; Liu Zhenxi 2006).

45. "Funü minbing daibiao Zhang Chunfang tongzhi danxing cailiao" 1958. The enemy in question was not specified, but the liberation of Taiwan was mentioned, and the immediate context appears to have been the second Quemoy-Matsu crisis, which began in August 1958. On the public health campaign to eliminate the "four pests" (rats, flies, mosquitoes, and sparrows), see also FL 178–189–010 1958 (Mar. 11); FL 178–195–001 1958; "Wu yi she funü jiti mofan danxing cailiao" 1958; FL 178–207–067 1958 (Aug. 18–23).

46. FL 178–189–010 1958 (Mar. 11); "Wu yi she funü jiti mofan danxing cailiao" 1958. This piece also addresses the Great Leap–era campaign against rural illiteracy, described briefly in chapter 4.

47. FL 178–197–037 1958 (Oct. 20): 5–6. For a national-level version of this argument, see National Women's Federation 1960.

48. Interview with Zheng Xiuhua 1999.

49. Interview with Liu Dongmei 1999.

50. The feminization of agriculture continued apace, with local variations, throughout the rest of the collective period. Liu Xiuzhen (interview 2004), a woman who served as a team leader from 1971 to 1973 in Village G, estimates that women provided 80 percent of the labor power in the team she led, because many of the men in her team, including her own husband, had gone out to work. She was the only woman team leader in the entire commune, suggesting that leadership positions continued to be held predominantly by men even when women were an important component of the labor force. Speaking of his home village in Jiangxi Province, Mobo Gao (1999: 133) comments that during the Great Leap Forward, "women started to work in the fields like men for the first time in Gao Village."

51. Interview with Li Liujin 1997.

52. FL 178–211–005 1959.

53. Interviews with Gao Yuzhong 2004; Lu Guilan 1996.

54. Xiaobo Lü (2000: 89) renders *fukua feng* as a "tendency toward exaggeration and cheating." On the logic of competition that led to it, see 90–93. Liu Zhaofeng (interview 1996), who spent time in many rural Shaanxi locations during this period, describes the behavior of local cadres: *Some of them were very ambitious for great achievements, and would report good news but not the bad news.* On exaggerated grain production figures from many provinces (not including Shaanxi) in 1958, see Chan 2001: 65–66, 137–38. Teiwes and Sun (1999: 175n148) quote an unnamed Chinese historian as saying that the Shaanxi provincial leader Zhang Desheng was among the more "realistic" leaders. The implication here is that more realistic leadership led to less exaggeration, less extraction, and ultimately to a less severe local famine. Our interviews provide anecdotal support for this line of argument.

55. Thomas Bernstein (1984: 351) reports that nationally, "in the case of the 1958 harvest, grain production was reported in December 1958 at 375 million metric tons, i.e., just about double the 1957 output." After verification in 1959, this was reduced to 250 MMT, and later to 200 MMT. In 1959, the first estimate was 270 MMT, later lowered to 170 MMT. Yields in 1958 were somewhat higher than those from 1957, but 1959 yields were down sharply.

56. Interview with He Gaizhen 1999.

57. Bernstein (1984: 341–42) reports that during the Great Leap, particularly in 1959, "procurement of grain reached extraordinary heights, even while output fell to the level of 1951." He explains official credulousness by citing a confluence of factors: officials feared losing face and being criticized as conservative, particularly in the wake of the Anti-Rightist campaign. The nation's leaders were predisposed to believe the exaggerated figures in spite of the fact that many had spent years in the countryside, a phenomenon that Bernstein calls "absence of learning." He rejects the parallel other scholars have made with Stalin's behavior in the USSR, concluding that the assumption was "that a breakthrough had occurred in agricultural production, a belief, in other words, that increased extraction was compatible with peasant welfare. This assumption turned out to be erroneous; it was part and parcel of the extraordinary mismanagement of the GLF [Great Leap Forward]. Famine was an unanticipated outcome of this mismanagement, an outcome for which Mao Zedong and his associ-

ates are responsible." Even while assigning responsibility, however, in contrast to other scholars writing on the Great Leap famine, he argues that "excessive procurements were thus the result of regime misjudgments rather than of a deliberate policy of harshly squeezing the peasants." Bernstein also offers a meticulous discussion of how regulations limiting extraction were rendered ineffective by the 1958 comprehensive guarantee system (*baogan zhi*), which incorporated planned increases in production into the definition of what counted as a surplus (368–70, 352–55, 345). In a more recent essay he criticizes Mao's refusal to acknowledge that the renewed push for Great Leap economic policies and a new Anti-Rightist campaign after the Lushan Plenum would have disastrous consequences for rural areas, as well as Mao's failure to believe reports of a national disaster (Bernstein 2006).

58. Interview with Cao Zhuxiang 2006.

59. Interview with Zhou Guizhen 2006.

60. Interview with Liu Zhaofeng 1996.

61. Each of these changes was signified by the addition of the character *hua* at the end of the word: *shitanghua, fengrenhua, chanyuanhua, tuoerhua, momian jiagonghua* (FL 178–186–043 1958). Manning (2005: 84) calls the introduction of dining halls and childcare a "remarkable experiment in women's liberation" initiated by the CCP. Schoenhals (1987: 80–81) quotes Zhu De's secretary Liao Gailong as saying that dining halls "would undermine the traditional prerogatives of family heads and contribute to the creation of 'genuinely liberated relationships' between men and women, young and old." Women's Federation and government documents in Shaanxi, however, do not make this argument. For an illustrated account of the virtues of such collective services, see National Women's Federation 1960: n.p.

62. For discussions of this point in the provincial media, see *Shaanxi ribao*, July 7, 1958, which concentrated on the "three changes" of dining halls, childcare, and sewing groups. By August, birthing centers had been added to the list (*Shaanxi ribao*, Aug. 11, 1958). Reiteration by the national leadership that the commune was the best form of organization for the thorough liberation of women was republished in *Shannxi ribao*, Mar. 1, 1960.

63. FL 178–198–040 1958 (Oct. 8).

64. FL 178–186–043 1958.

65. FL 178–189–010 1958 (Mar. 11); "Wu yi she fünü jiti mofan danxing cailiao" 1958. Another collective in the county, comprising 228 families and 1,043 people, established five baby care groups (*boawazu),* in which thirty-six staff cared for sixty-eight children, and five nursery schools for 145 children ("Shangzhen zhen" 1958).

66. FL 178–189–010 1958 (Mar. 11); "Wu yi she fünü jiti mofan danxing cailiao" 1958.

67. FL 178–207–067 1958 (Aug. 18–23). This report was delivered at the conference on birth stations and childcare discussed in chapter 6.

68. Interview with Zhou Guizhen 2006. A 1961 provincial relief report estimated that 4 percent of women of childbearing age (about 140,000) suffered from prolapse, and 5 percent (about 175,000) suffered from amenorrhea. The Health Bureau was ordered to provide free treatment for these diseases with funds supplied by the Civil Administration Bureau, which in turn resolved to ask the central government for more help (MZT 198–768 1961 [Mar. 27]: 80–81; MZT 198–768 1961 [Oct. 26]: 246).

69. Interview with Shi Cuiyu 2004. On uterine prolapse among women in Sichuan, see Ruf 1998: 106.

70. Interview with Lu Yulian 1999.

71. On her official position at this time, see FL 178–244–015 1960 (Mar. 2).

72. Interview with Zhuang Xiaoxia 1996. Li Xiaomei (interview 1997) remembers the price of clothing as forty cents for a pair of pants, fifteen cents for underpants, and 1 yuan for a jacket.

73. FL 178–211–005 1959.

74. The term they used, "household labor" (*jiawu laodong*), rather than simply "household tasks," is significant, elevating the importance of women's domestic production. The Women's Federation was more attuned to this question than were other Party-state entities (FL 178–197–037 1958 [Oct. 20]: 7–8). For a similar discussion in August of that year, see FL 178–207–067 1958 (Aug. 18–23).

75. *Zhongguo funü* 16 (1958): 19. For efforts in Shaanxi, see also FL 178–207–067 (Aug. 18–23).

76. FL 178–207–068 1958 (Aug. 18–23). For reports in the provincial press on childcare centers, see *Shaanxi ribao*, Feb. 21, 1959; *Weinan ribao*, Aug. 27, 1959.

77. In Shaanxi, the provincial Party Committee in June 1958 called for the establishment of rural childcare centers "in order to lighten the burden of women's housework and liberate the labor power of rural women" (FL 178–27–020 1958 [June 3]). The "women's children" phrase is from FL 178–189–010 1958. Other Women's Federation documents in which this project was discussed include FL 178–195–018 1958 (May 24); FL 178–196–029 1958 (July 31); FL 178–193 (2)–050 1958 (Nov. 4).

78. Interview with Feng Xiaoqin 1999.

79. FL 178–189–048 1958 (Dec. 2). Subsequently the Women's Federation launched a campaign in 1959 called "Six Goods and Four Satisfactions," aimed at raising the number and quality of daycare centers and nursery schools. In Weinan County, even as bad news on other fronts mounted, the Federation reported that more and more children were being cared for collectively. The number of children in Weinan County nursery schools had jumped from 737 in 1957 to 68,288 the following year. By 1959, 22,755 children were attending 903 year-round nursery schools, cared for by 2,691 teachers. Meanwhile 19,873 younger children were in 1,470 daycare centers, staffed by 5,767 childcare workers (Wang 1959: 3). Also in 1959, an inspection group found that one childcare group consisted of "one old woman taking care of eight children. The woman also raised two pigs. Sometimes she also helped the dining hall cooks chopping vegetables. The children's hygiene was very bad, not to mention their education" (FL 178–211–005 1959). For the continuation of ambitious childcare plans even as the Great Leap foundered, see FL 178–219–013 1959 (July 9).

80. Interview with Li Liujin 1997. On the inadequacy of childcare facilities in Henan, see Manning 2005: 102–3.

81. Weinan diqu difang zhi bianji weiyuan hui 1996: 275.

82. On similar circumstances in northern Shaanxi, see Guo 2003: 51–52, 2004: 5–6.

83. Interview with Yuan Xiaoli 1997.

84. Interview with Kang Ruqing 1997.

85. Interview with Liu Guyu 2004.

86. Carl Riskin (Columbia University Modern China Seminar, Apr. 2, 2009) comments that during the Great Leap Forward, women's labor time was reallocated to the fields as if no

opportunity costs were attached, but in fact the cost with regard to neglected children was very high. Ruf (1998: 103–9) describes the Great Leap railroad construction and water control projects on which men worked in Sichuan, commenting that many in the 1990s were nostalgic for those experiences (104). He notes that women were left to do the farming in a situation of labor shortage, exacerbated by domestic chores and the requirement that they attend many political meetings, and that their memories of this period were considerably less rosy (104–5).

87. Interview with Liu Dongmei 1999.

88. Interview with Yang Anxiu 1997.

89. FL 178–282–010 1961 (Mar.–Dec.).

90. By October 1958, the national *People's Daily* reported that more than 80 percent of the peasants in north and northeast China were eating in dining halls (*Renmin ribao*, Oct. 25, 1958, cited in Schoenhals 1987: 100). For a general history of the dining halls, see Luo 2001. In Shaanxi, more than seven hundred communes had established dining halls by November 1958 (*Shaanxi ribao*, Nov. 12, 1958; for adjustments to and arguments about their operation, see also *Shaanxi ribao*, Nov. 22, 1958, Nov. 8 and Dec. 30, 1959, Feb. 5, 1961).

91. Interview with He Gaizhen 1999.

92. Interview with Ma Fangxian 1999; see also interview with Zheng Xiuhua 1999. This was the case in Village Z; in Village G, people retained their pots and were sometimes able to bring flour back from the dining hall and cook at home (interviews with Qiao Yindi 2001; Zhang Qiurong 2004).

93. Interviews with Cao Zhuxiang 1996; Yan Panwa 1999; "Shangzhen zhen" 1958.

94. Interview with Cao Zhuxiang 1996. In Village Z, two teams shared each dining hall, and a special dining hall was provided for youth; cadres also ate there (interview with He Gaizhen 1999).

95. Interview with Zhou Guizhen 1996.

96. Interview with Feng Zaicai and Wang Fugui 2001. In the Village T area, each team had a dining hall (interview with Yang Anxiu 1997).

97. Interview with Lu Yulian 1999.

98. Interview with Qiao Yindi 2001; also see interview with Shi Ranwa 1999.

99. Interview with Ouyang Xiu 2004.

100. Interview with Cao Zhuxiang 1996.

101. Interview with Li Duoduo 1999.

102. Ibid.

103. Interview with Zhou Guizhen 2006.

104. For an extended discussion of this point, particularly in the later years of the collective, see Yan 1996.

105. Interview with Shi Ranwa 1999 (Village Z); see also Zhang Qiurong (interview 2004, Village G).

106. Interview with Qian Taohua 1997.

107. Interview with Yang Anxiu 1997.

108. Interview with Cao Zhuxiang 2006.

109. Interviews with Yang Anxiu 1997 (Village T); Yuan Xi 2001 (Village G); Xu Nini 1997 (Village T).

110. Interview with Yuan Xi 2001.

111. Interview with Li Liujin 1997.

112. Interview with Zhang Chaofeng 2001; Ouyang Xiu (interview 2004) also discusses such conflicts.

113. Interview with Lu Yulian 1999.

114. Interview with He Gaizhen 1999.

115. Interview with Liu Zhaofeng 1996. She does not specify the source of her fear, but many national-level histories of the Great Leap discuss the chilling effect of the Anti-Rightist campaign in silencing criticism.

116. Interview with Xu Nini 1997.

117. Interview with Zhou Guizhen 1996.

118. Interview with Shan Xiuzhen 1997. Henan had a reputation in Shaanxi for being "left" in every movement; one Women's Federation cadre who went there to visit her natal family during the Great Leap reported that people had knocked down the walls between their courtyards to communize housing (interview with Liu Guitang 1997). On the course of the Great Leap and the famine in a Henan village, see Thaxton 2008: 118-246. For a village-level critique of Great Leap policies in Henan, and the efforts of a Party secretary to protect his village from the worst consequences of those policies, see Seybolt 1996: 51-58.

119. See, for instance, Becker 1996. Aside from one passing and unsubstantiated mention (213), he does not discuss famine in Shaanxi in the aftermath of the Great Leap, although he provides details on every other province in the northwest. See also Kane 1988.

120. Banister 1987: 233; Cao Shuji 2005: 17.

121. Banister 1987: 59-60. She finds that fertility went back up in 1962, adding that in 1961 the government imported grain and improved distribution, so that in spite of bad crops, starvation must have dropped (233). On grain production levels, see also Riskin 1998: 115.

122. Bernstein 1984: 344. In his study of "abnormal" (excess) deaths as a percentage of the predisaster population, Cao Shuji (2005: 21) names the top six affected provinces as Anhui, Sichuan, Guizhou, Hunan, Gansu, and Henan. Of these, Sichuan, Gansu, and Henan border Shaanxi.

123. Cao 2005: 26-27. Thaxton (2008), in a recent study of a Henan village, links local CCP history during the Japanese occupation and the civil war to commandist and sometimes brutal leadership during the Great Leap Forward. He explores the contributions of Mao, the provincial Party leadership, and the commune leadership in producing a severe local famine. On famine in Sichuan in 1960-61, see Ruf (1998: 106-7).

124. For 1958 reports on flood, drought, hail, and frost, see MZT 198-686 1958: 269-72. In June and July 1961, rain fell in the Village T area for twenty-one days in a row. The counties just to the west were harder hit than Village T's Nanzheng County, as the Han and Jialing Rivers began to breach their banks. Between a fifth and half of the rice and corn crops in some counties around Hanzhong city were damaged, with the total harvest for summer and autumn down about 100 million *jin* because of the flooding. People, cattle, and poultry drowned, houses collapsed, furniture and stored grain floated away, and canals, dikes, and reservoirs were destroyed. In the mountains, wheat and potatoes sprouted and rotted in the fields because the harvest was delayed by the rain. Provincial officials from the Civil Administration Bureau noted that this was only the damage they knew about: because roads

were blocked in some areas, they were unsure of the full extent of the catastrophe. In Hanzhong District, authorities estimated that close to 220,000 people were in immediate need of disaster relief, asking the provincial government for 700,000 to 800,000 yuan in relief funds (MZT 198-768 1961 [July 11]: 164–66). In 1961 and 1962, Village B and much of Guanzhong, in contrast, suffered from drought, affecting the fall cotton and corn harvests and winter wheat (interview with Liu Zhenxi 2006).

125. Cao 2005: 26–27; Johnson 1998; see also sources cited in subsequent footnotes. Han (2003) surveys explanations for the famine and argues that it should not be used as the basis for condemnation of the entire collective period. Dikötter (2010) draws mainly on provincial archives (not, however, including those of Shaanxi) for a detailed and chilling account of the famine.

126. Johnson 1998: 103–4. Schoenhals (1987: 153) observes that Mao assumed, based on such predictions, that the harvest would total 400 million tons of grain, though eventually there were only 200 million, and less than two million tons of cotton.

127. Johnson 1998: 103–4; Riskin 1998: 115. Lin and Yang (1998, 2000) focus on grain exports from some provinces to others and the favoring of urban areas, Chang and Wen (1997, 1998) on the food wasted in the dining halls and reduction in grain output, Yang and Su (1998) on the radicalism of provincial leaders.

128. Riskin 1998: 115, 119.

129. Thaxton (2008: 127, 200–207) argues forcefully that in one Henan village, grain yields remained good from 1958 to 1960, and that the problem was that the center took 60 percent of the harvest in procurement, while an additional 21 percent was taken out for famine relief, public welfare, and administration, so that in the end only about 20 percent of the harvest was left to feed the peasants. He adds that farmers responded by eating the crops in the field before they had ripened and could be taken away. On cases of forcible extortion of grain from peasants in Hebei, Shanxi, and other provinces through arrests, beatings, and other means, see Lü 2000: 93–94. On eating green crops in the field in Shandong and Henan, see Han 2003.

130. Interview with Zhuang Xiaoxia 1996.

131. Interviews with Shan Xiuzhen 1997; Zhuang Xiaoxia 1996.

132. Interview with Zhuang Xiaoxia 2006.

133. Interview with Zhuang Xiaoxia 1996.

134. Interview with Liu Fengqin 1996.

135. Interviews with Zheng Xiuhua 1999; Liu Zhenxi 2006; Liu Fengqin 1996. In Village B, the "dining hall" for the aged was a small stove in the larger dining hall, meant to give the elderly a food supplement in the form of noodles added to the thin corn porridge (interview with Liu Zhenxi 2006).

136. Interview with Kang Xingfen 1999.

137. Interview with Liu Fengqin 1996.

138. Interview with Zheng Xiuhua 1999; Liu Guyu (interview 2001) tells a similar story.

139. Interview with Kang Xingfen 1999.

140. "A gourdful," *yi piao*, was an allusion to Confucius's disciple Yan Hui, by extension referring to one who was happily frugal.

141. Interview with Shi Ranwa 1999.

142. Interview with Gao Yuzhong 2004. Cao Zhuxiang (interview 1996) recalls the daily food allocation in Village B (the most prosperous of the villages where we interviewed) during the three hard years as twenty *jin* per person per month, dipping to a low of sixteen *jin* for several months. In Village T, Li Liujin (interview 1997) gave us the even more disturbing figure of twelve *jin* of rice per month. Relief reports in late 1962 from two Weinan communes described an area, Qiaonan, where the average per capita grain consumption ranged from 163 to 216.2 *jin* annually as a "light" disaster area, and a place where the average per capita grain consumption ranged from 121.2 to 166.2 *jin* annually as a "heavy" disaster area. There were reportedly seventeen light and six heavy disaster areas in Qiaonan. Half of the households in the four production teams studied had only 6.75 to 15 *jin* of consumption grain per person per month. This report described other problems as well: households that had been profligate with grain consumption, cadres besieged by relief requests, and scattered cases of people selling daughters (MZT 198-31 1962 [Dec. 30]: 93–96).

143. Kenneth Pomeranz, personal communication, Nov. 10, 2009.

144. Interview with Shan Xiuzhen 1997.

145. FL 178-211-005 1959.

146. Gao Hua 2005: 162–63. Banister (1987: 60) comments that in the northeastern province of Liaoning, corncobs and marshwater plankton were grain substitutes, while wild plants and paper pulp were used in north China. Relief reports from the Shaanxi Civil Administration Bureau mentioned that some areas only had low standards (i.e., rations) and no grain substitutes (MZT 198-768 1961 [Mar. 27], 77).

147. Interview with Gao Yuzhong 2004.

148. Interview with Wang Fugui 2001.

149. Interview with Liu Zhaofeng 1996.

150. Interview with Xu Nini 1997.

151. Interview with He Gaizhen 1999.

152. Interview with Ouyang Xiu 2004.

153. Interview with Zheng Xiuhua 1999.

154. Interview with Yang Anxiu 1997.

155. Interview with Xiao Gaiye 1999.

156. Interview with Xu Nini 1997.

157. Ibid. According to provincial relief reports from the Civil Administration Bureau, in the winter of 1960 and the spring of 1961, many dining halls were "purified" by the Bureau and their leadership removed (MZT 198-768 1961 [Mar. 27], 73–74).

158. Interview with Li Duoduo 1999. Yan Panwa (interview 1999) gives 1960 as the date of dissolution in Village Z, as does Li Duoduo (interview 1999). Even within the same village, there are different memories about timing. In Village B, Liu Zhenxi (interview 2006) and Cao Zhuxiang (interview 1996) remember that the dining halls were disbanded in 1962 or 1963, but Liu Fengqin (interview 1996) recalls that they started at the end of 1958 and were disbanded after only a bit more than a year. In Village T, Li Liujin (interview 1997) recalls that the dining halls opened in 1958 and disbanded in 1960, though not all at the same time; Qian Taohua (interview 1997) corroborates that 1960 was the year her dining hall disbanded, placing it in memory as just before the birth of her daughter. Nationally some din-

ing halls dissolved in early 1959; the Party officially abolished them in June 1961 (Schoen-hals 1987: 165).

159. Interviews with Qian Taohua 1997; Feng Sumei 1997.

160. Interview with Zheng Xiuhua 1999.

161. Interview with He Gaizhen 1999.

162. Interview with Shi Cuiyu 2004. Total fertility rates in China dropped from 6.405 in 1957 to 5.679 in 1958, continuing to fall in each of the three hard years (4.303, 4.015, 3.287) and only beginning to recover in 1962 (6.023) and 1963 (7.502). China's birth rate may have fallen from forty-three per thousand in 1957 to twenty-two per thousand in 1961 (Banister 1987: 230, 233–34). Riskin (1998: 112–13) notes that the 1982 census shows a drop in births from 1959 to 1961, but adds that it is unclear whether this is because fertility dropped or mortality rose. Infant mortality rose precipitously, from 132.4 per thousand in 1957 to 284 per thousand in 1960. Banister (1987: 116) reconstructs infant mortality rates per one thousand live births, showing a spike beginning in 1958 (146.3), rising in 1959 (159.9), peaking in 1960 (284), and beginning to decline in 1961 (183.4). Greenhalgh (1990: 202) reproduces data on population size and growth rates, which shows less of a dip in Shaanxi for 1959 than the national average. She notes that the crisis there was not as severe as elsewhere. See also Li 1993: 9.

163. Banister 1987: 118.

164. Ibid. Cao Shuji (2005: 14) finds a total abnormal or excess death toll of 32.5 million for 1959–61. Riskin (1998: 113–14) notes that estimates of excess deaths range from an offi-cial figure of 15 million up to scholarly estimates of 16.5, 23, 30, and 43 million, each figure based on a different method of calculation, and that no consensus has yet emerged. Diköt-ter (2010: x), drawing on Public Security and Party reports, puts the number of deaths at 45 million.

165. Riskin (1998: 117, 120) writes that death rates rose starting in 1958 in Sichuan, Gansu, Anhui, Yunnan, and Ningxia. Measured by death rates, he finds that the areas most affected by the famine were, first, west-central China, including Guangxi, Guizhou, Hunan, Sichuan, and Gansu. Sichuan experienced mortality rates of 347 percent above its prefamine level, and Gansu's mortality rate was 273 percent of its earlier level. The second most affected were in east-central China, including Anhui, Henan, Shandong, and Hebei. Of these, Anhui was most severely affected: peak mortality was 7.5 times the prefamine level. Empirically rich descriptions of famine conditions in various parts of China are found in Chu 1996. For a collection of letters from local to higher authorities about the crisis, see Yu Xiguang 2005. Most letters are from Henan, Anhui, and Jiangsu; one is from Hu County in Shaanxi (476–90).

166. Cao 2005: 21, 25. Cao uses gazetteer records, basing his calculation on the Qing Dynasty unit of the *fu* because PRC administrative units shifted so frequently. A 1961 Civil Administration Bureau report for Shaanxi estimated that 57 percent of all peasants in the province were affected by disasters in 1960 (MZT 198–768 1961 [Mar. 27], 73). In an in-triguing, if unsupported argument, Cao (2005: 22–25, 27) uses regional historical memory patterns of exaggeration about productivity. In places that had suffered greatly during late nineteenth-century famines, he believes, local people and local cadres took the grain ques-tion very seriously in 1958, listened to the wishes of the people more closely, and engaged

in very little exaggeration of output. In Shaanxi, for instance, he finds that in the course of the Muslim revolt that began in 1862 and the ensuing drought, the province lost 7.1 million people, or 52 percent of its prewar population, compared to about 1 percent of its population during the famine of 1959–61. An additional three million died in the Guanzhong drought of 1929–30. For Gansu, he finds that the districts that lost the most people in the Muslim revolt lost the fewest in 1959–61. In Cao's account, differences in memory had immediate and tragic consequences: places that exaggerated were taxed more heavily, reducing the grain available for peasant consumption, leading ultimately to regional differences in the death rate.

167. Interview with Yan Panwa 1999. On edema in Hanzhong special district, and attempts to address it through nutrition provided by the Civil Administration Bureau, medical treatment, and rest, see MZT 198-735 1960 (Nov. 26, Dec. 22). On edema in Henan and Gansu, see Manning (2005: 85–86).

168. Interviews with Zhang Qiurong 2004; Ouyang Xiu 2004.

169. Interview with Zhou Guizhen 1996. An additional problem mentioned in government relief reports from this period was the death of livestock (MZT 198-768 1961 [Mar. 27], 81–82). For fragmented seasonal statistics on human deaths and occasionally livestock deaths assembled by the Civil Administration Bureau from 1960–63, see MZT 198-732 1960 (Feb. 13–Oct. 8), which reported 287 deaths for the province, none of them in Weinan County, and MZT 198-821 (1961–63).

170. Weinan diqu difang zhi bianji weiyuan hui 1996: 272. On daughter-selling, see also MZT 198-31 1962 (Dec. 30): 96. Reports in 1961 and 1962 from the provincial Civil Administration Bureau (Minzheng ting) talk about limited government relief efforts. In January 1961, for instance, the Bureau sent winter clothes and quilts to Hanzhong, Weinan, and other districts to help more than fifteen thousand people survive the winter. In Shanghai, near Danfeng, the local government asked for and received money to provide winter clothing. Funds came from the Civil Administration Bureau, as well as city and county social relief funds (MZT 198-768 1961 [Jan. 28], 5–6). Later that spring, the Bureau also attempted to transport grain from Yan'an and Shaannan to areas that were in even worse circumstances, but they were hampered by a lack of vehicles (MZT 198-768 1961 [Mar. 27], 79). None of our interviewees, however, mentioned government relief efforts when describing this period.

171. Interview with Liu Zhenxi 2006.

172. In early 1963, men from neighboring Gansu were writing to the provincial Civil Administration Bureau complaining that their wives had fled to Shaanxi and were living with men there (MZT 198-31 1963 [Jan. 8]).

173. Interview with Li Liujin 1997.

174. Interview with Zhou Guizhen 1996.

175. Ibid.

176. Interview with Li Liujin 1997.

177. Interview with Xiang Jinwa 2001.

178. Interview with Li Fenglian 2001.

179. Interviews with Zhou Guizhen 2006; Liu Zhenxi 2006; Lei Caiwa 2001.

180. Interview with He Gaizhen 1999.

181. Interview with Zhou Guizhen 2006. In his study of a Henan village, Thaxton (2008:

157–98) lists various local survival strategies: foot dragging, remittances, migration (limited), a black market in earth salt, begging, crop theft, gleaning (combined with intentionally sloppy harvesting), and grain concealment. Peasants survived, however, mainly by *chi qing* (eating unripe crops in the fields), which was difficult for outsiders, even at the commune level, to police or prevent (200–207). In the village he studied, the famine killed 128 people, or 8.7 percent of the village population (215). Unresolved grievances against local Party leaders in this period, he argues, shaped subsequent Cultural Revolution conflicts at the village level (253–62). He sees village actions during the recent reform era as expressions of an ongoing determination to secure food entitlements in the wake of the Leap (292–324).

182. Interview with He Gaizhen 1999.

183. In Village Z, for instance, construction of a major irrigation canal was discontinued and has never been completed (Shaanxi sheng Danfeng xian shuili zhi bianzuan zu 1990: 82). For a survey of post-Leap adjustments, see MacFarquhar 1997: 1–71.

184. Interview with Yan Panwa 1999.

185. Interviews with Liu Dongmei 1999; Zheng Xiuhua 1999.

186. Interview with Ouyang Xiu 2004; Banister 1987: 60. Johnson (1998: 106) mentions some possible factors that were not brought up by anyone we interviewed, but that undoubtedly played a role, including a drop in government procurements and grain imports. In 1950 China exported 2.7 million tons of grain; in 1962 it imported 4 million tons. Riskin (1998: 118–19) notes the return of local markets and the fact that net procurement of grain from the countryside went down in 1962 to 16 to 17 percent of output, in contrast to 28 percent in 1959 and 22 percent in 1960. On high rates of adult schizophrenia in Anhui linked to prenatal exposure to famine, see St. Clair et al. 2005. Thanks to Bruce Hershatter for this reference.

187. Interview with Shi Ranwa 1999.

188. I borrow the term "memoryscape" from Lisa Yoneyama (1994: 128), who refers to the effects of urban renewal in Hiroshima after the A-bomb with the phrase "taming the memoryscape."

189. L'Engle 1975 [1962].

190. Yang 1996: 73. In spite of state-directed moves to retrench and undo the major changes put in place by the Great Leap, "the rural population, in its struggle for survival, preferred to return the organization of agricultural production to the household level" (80–81). By 1964, household contracting had been largely suppressed and land recollectivized, although Yang notes that few details about this crackdown are available. On household farming in the early 1960s, see 82–97. On the Leap, the famine, and household farming, see also Yang 1997. Shaanxi does not appear in any of the material cited by Yang.

191. We heard versions of this story (dining halls are disbanded, land is distributed to families, people have enough to eat) from He Gaizhen (interview 1999), Zhang Zizhen (interview 1999), Shi Ranwa (interview 1999, who estimated that four or five years passed between the dining halls and the household contracting system), and others. Lu Yulian (interview 1999), however, said emphatically that there had been no small-scale contracting until the late 1970s or early 1980s.

192. The only village records are from 1967, 1977, and 1984, and they say nothing about household contracting until the 1980s.

193. Writing about memories of life in Turin under fascism, Luisa Passerini (1987) notes

that most people remember 1919–21, and then 1943–45, and put the interwar period in the background: "The mental leap from one great moment of social tension and collective identity to the other, is not, however, just a way of keeping quiet about the 20 years locked away between these two high points. It is already an historical interpretation in its own right, a way of redeeming something from the defeat" (in this case, of Italian leftist working-class politics; 68). Alessandro Portelli (1991: 68) makes a similar observation: when people have difficulty dating particular incidents or descriptions of daily life, there may be a periodization and an interpretation implied.

194. The "wrinkle in time" phenomenon was less pronounced but not utterly absent in other villages, nor was it limited to women. Two men who had been cadres in Village G told us that after the "years of low standard" (the early 1960s) things only got better "after the 1980s, when the land was distributed to households." (interview with Feng Zaicai and Wang Fugui 2001). Since the years of low standard, by every recoverable measure, were significantly worse than the later 1960s and the 1970s, this account should be regarded as a kind of compression, if not an outright wrinkle.

195. Interview with Jiang Qiuwa 2001. Wrinkles in time and moveable political signposts are not the only ways that Chinese villagers have marked and implicitly interpreted the upheavals of the Great Leap and the ensuing famine. Eric Mueggler (2001, 2007) explores how members of the Yi minority in Yunnan have worked their way to understanding the famine deaths and local responsibility for them through encounters with and exorcisms of wild ghosts. Steve Smith (2006) describes a government campaign against rumors from 1962 to 1965; many of the rural rumors that worried the Party-state concerned ritual observances, in which younger people were called upon to feed sugar dumplings and toad-shaped buns to the elderly to avert disaster. Smith sees this as an instance of people reflecting on reasons for the famine as it started to recede, with many people convinced that neglect of rituals had caused the disaster. The rumors, he observes, provided a means for people to talk about how extraordinary recent events had been, and to assert a degree of psychological control over events by talking about them. He sees this not only as resistance to state meanings, but also as an attempt to participate in and enter responses into public discourse.

196. The classic discussion of trauma, Holocaust survivors, and difficulties of self-narration is Felman and Laub (1992). Laub, a psychoanalyst and himself a child survivor, observes, "Massive trauma precludes its registration; the observing and recording mechanisms of the human mind are temporarily knocked out, malfunction" (57). For a discussion of silence and remembrance of the Great Leap and the famine, and their discussion in late twentieth-century novels by Zhi Liang and Yu Hua, see Weigelin-Schwiedrzik (2003). Feuchtwang (2005: 2, 14, 1) observes that in southern Fujian, where "the subject of the famine is still surrounded by fear" and also by self-reproach on the part of cadres, "other ways of transmitting the experience of the famine prevail, in more embodied and unverbalised memories, in habits of overconsumption and in ritual." For an intriguing recent comparison of memories of the Chinese famine and the Ukrainian famine of 1933, which includes a discussion of official explanations for the famine and the exclusion of peasant suffering from official discussion, see Wemheuer (2009).

197. In other regions, the feminization of agriculture began as early as the late nineteenth and early twentieth centuries, especially in the Yangzi delta and areas of north China where

cotton was commercially grown. For a study of the Yangzi delta that makes this point, see Walker (1993, 1999: 192–93). As indicated earlier in the present study, women were working in Shaanxi fields before 1949, but in lesser numbers, usually in circumstances of family catastrophe. The routine full-time participation of women in agricultural labor, and men's partial exit from collective field work, did not begin with the Great Leap but certainly accelerated at that point.

198. For a brief survey of the literature on this point, see Hershatter (2007c: 76). Guo (2003: 51) has a somewhat different finding for Ji village in northern Shaanxi: there men retained responsibility for skilled farming, while women were moved (with some men) into a capital construction group that did "strenuous physical labor all the year round: filling up gullies and building dams and terraced fields."

199. On this point, see also Andors 1983.

200. Interview with Zhang Xiuyu 1996.

201. As Wen (2001: 293) puts it, in an argument that recognizes the accomplishments of the collective period as well as its costs, "Although thousands of peasants perished in the process of the capital-accumulation of state industrialization, China finally crossed this threshold in the shortest time and completed the formation of an industrial infrastructure for the political and economic autonomy of the country." Riskin (Columbia University Modern China Seminar, Apr. 2, 2009) notes that while the First Five Year Plan helped China to move toward crossing this threshold, the Great Leap Forward actually slowed the process down. Wen argues that during the collective period, "China was forced to carry out an unprecedented self-exploitation led by a highly centralized government: In the villages, they implemented the symbiotic system of people's communes and state monopoly for purchase and marketing, while, in the cities, they established a system of planned allocation and bureaucratic institution. By controlling all surplus value produced by both rural and urban labour, the central government redistributed resources to expand heavy-industry based production." For the Chinese text of this article, see Wen (1999); for an extended discussion of debates between Wen and others about the peasantry in postsocialist China, see Day (2007). Wen's analysis of the collective peasant economy is laid out in Wen (2000: 141–271).

202. This is meant as an invitation to those more practiced at economic history than I. The challenges are many: how to quantify the exodus of men from basic agriculture, particularly when many were still registered as "peasants"; how to estimate the value of the products that men produced and women underwrote (particularly during the Great Leap, given the ill-considered nature of many of the enterprises); and how to distinguish the gendered differentiation of "human capital" in more than generally descriptive terms. I thank Kenneth Pomeranz for encouraging me to think about some of these difficulties.

10. NARRATOR

1. Interview with Yang Anxiu 1997.

2. An obituary for Shan Xiuzhen can be found online at the Weinan CCP web site, under "Laodongmo Shan Xiuzhen."

3. Among the helpful discussions of rural reform are Kelliher 1992; Jacka 1997; Liu 2000; Xiong 2000; Oi 1999; Cao 2003; Jiang; Chen and Wu 2006; Gao 2006b.

4. Article 49 of the 1982 Constitution reads in part, "Parents have the duty to rear and educate their children who are minors, and children who have come of age have the duty to support and assist their parents. . . . Violation of the freedom of marriage is prohibited. Maltreatment of old people, women and children is prohibited" (www.constitution.org/cons/china.txt). These provisions remained the same when the Constitution was amended in 1988 and 1993.

5. This chapter does not dwell on physical complaints, but even women who are happy in other respects have something to say on that score, often invoking their youth in the 1950s in contrast with the aches and pains of the present. Jiang Qiuwa (interview 2001) comments, *I was very busy when I was young. But I felt it was interesting. Now I'm old, hao ya ya, I hurt here and I hurt there. I have just found life is not so interesting. In theory, it's easier to live now. I should have nothing to worry about. But when you are old, either here is painful or there is painful. When you were young, you were very busy and waited for your children to grow up. You were afraid the children couldn't grow up. Now they are grown up and you are not busy. But to me, I think now is not as good as the time when I was young. When I was young, I was so happy when I went to the field. Aiya, when we hoed, we sang qinqiang [Shaanxi folk] opera. I loved it so much. At that time, I saw a qinqiang opera every few days and I would be happy for several days. Now I'm old. So boring!*

6. Although they do, sometimes, complain about the collective labor regime in contrast to the present. Asked when she was happiest, He Gaizhen (interview 1999) comments: *After the land was distributed to households.*

Gao Xiaoxian: When you were an activist?

He Gaizhen: Oh. No. After the land was distributed to households, then I was happy.

Gao Xiaoxian: After the responsibility system [zeren zhi]?

He Gaizhen: Yes. You don't have to go to the collective [nongyeshe] to work in the fields. You work in your own family. I can get up early if I want or late if I want. In the old days when we were building terraces, oh mother, if you came late, they put up a small black flag for you. White flags and black flags.

7. Interview with Wang Xiqin 1996.

8. Ibid.

9. On this point see also Yan Yunxiang 2003: 180.

10. Jing 1996: 168. Amin (1995: 118) notes that generating a narrative independent of an official account (in his case, the Chauri Chaura riots of 1922) is difficult for other reasons as well: "The subalterns make their own memories, but they do not make them just as they please. . . . Peasant narratives that I collected were inescapably tainted or vitiated or coloured in varying degrees by the hegemonic master narratives."

11. For a brief account of the Cultural Revolution in Weinan Prefecture, see Weinan diqu difang zhi bianji weiyuan hui 1996: 318–23.

12. Interview with Zhou Guizhen 2006.

13. Interview with Zhang Qiuxiang 1996.

14. Interview with Li Liujin 1997.

15. Interview with Shan Xiuzhen 1997.

16. This was a common Cultural Revolution term.

17. Interview with Shan Xiuzhen 1997.

18. The question of when and how the expectation of progress became so entrenched and widespread among rural women is an interesting and unanswerable question, particularly given the "wrinkle in time" phenomenon noted in chapter 9.

19. One woman, formerly a women's team leader, expressed dismay at the decline of local-level Women's Federation work in the reform era: *The village does not pay attention to it. Neither does the township. In the past, no matter what happened, no matter who came, men were notified, so were women. Now, women are never mentioned. Before the 1970s, all woman-work was successful. Now there is no women's cadre in the village. After I quit, another woman was chosen. I asked her, "What have you done since then?" She said, "What is there to do? In your day, you could help to solve some problems, to help others, to do something. But now you are not asked to. Women are not asked to go."* At that time, it was like this: *if anything happened, if it did not go through women, if anything was to be implemented, you dared not do it if I did not agree.* She adds that this seems to be part of a more general lack of political activity; in the 1960s, the Party branch met every two weeks or once a month, but as of summer 1999 there had been no Party branch meeting for a year, and someone from the village leadership sent a non-Party member around to collect Party membership dues. She demurred, saying that she had no money (interview with Lu Yulian 1999).

20. Interview with Shan Xiuzhen 1997.

21. For a useful introduction to recent rural protest, see O'Brien and Li 2006.

22. Yan Yunxiang 2003.

23. In 1999 in Village Z, actually an amalgamation of sixteen administrative villages, the total population was 17,000 people in 4,231 households. The total number of able-bodied laborers (*laodongli*) was 6,783, almost half of them women. More than a thousand of the households were engaged in embroidery for export, and we could see women crocheting in the lanes and alleyways. More than 2,800 people not counted in the able-bodied laborer total, 30 percent of them women, mostly unmarried, had left the village to work. The village leaders told us that within the village, women took more responsibility than men for farmwork (Village Z briefing 1999).

24. For a Republican-era version of this discourse on the "small household," see Glosser 2003.

25. Yan Yunxiang (2003) offers a compelling introduction to these issues in reform-era rural China.

26. On various dimensions of desire in reform-era China, see Rofel 1999, 2007.

27. Interview with Li Liujin 1997.

28. Interview with Zhuang Xiaoxia 1996.

29. Interview with Zhou Guizhen 1996.

30. On this point, see also Stafford 2000: 110–26; Yan Yunxiang 2003: 178–82.

31. Interview with Kang Ruqing 1997.

32. Interview with Qian Taohua 1997.

33. Interview with Kang Ruqing 1997.

34. Interview with Li Liujin 1997.

35. Interview with He Gaizhen 1999.

36. Interview with Xiao Gaiye 1999.

37. Interview with Ma Li 1999.

38. Interview with Kang Ruqing 1997. Nevertheless Kang maintains that it is her own choice to eat alone, that is, to maintain her own household as an economic unit: *The reason I eat alone is that I feel that life is freer, I am a bit more removed. When they eat lunch, I want to eat rice gruel, but the rice they eat is a bit harder. I want to eat something a bit softer. I have been living alone these seventeen years. When my mother was still alive, she told me to eat alone. Sons and daughters, when you eat together with young people, every year you get a year older, and they like to eat things baked and stewed and fried, you see yourself every year getting a year older, your teeth are no good, and that is how it is when you eat together with others.*

39. Interview with Liu Fengqin 1996. Kang Ruqing (interview 1997) said more directly that having more than one son created conflicts: *If you live with the older one, he will say you gave something to the second one. If you live with the second one, he will say you gave something to the older one.*

40. Interview with Liu Fengqin 2006.

41. This sort of distressing situation is not unique to the central Shaanxi plain. In Village Z, we interviewed a woman with five living sons. The arrangement was that the first and fifth were to support and bury her, while the second and third had supported and buried her husband when he died a decade earlier. The fifth son provided her with grain, but nothing else. Each son had agreed to give her five yuan a month, but none had ever done so. She made a minimal living by selling things at the market and planned to chase her sons for money when she couldn't work anymore. She could not get through her story without crying. In her account, this sort of problem started with the reforms (interview with Hu Layue 1999; also see interview with Xiao Gaiye 1999). The township secretary told us that the problem of children abusing parents is much worse in the mountains, where there are no neighbors around to gossip about what goes on in your house.

In Village G, retired cadres and workers who have returned to the village have formed an Old People's Association, which sponsors a Respect the Old holiday on September 9 of each year. They give awards such as Good Daughter-in-law, Good Mother-in-law, and Good Filial Sons, pay courtesy calls on old people twice a year, and sponsor a local periodic market called the Respect the Old Market, which makes it more convenient for older people to buy things. The association has a four-point program: (1) the family should eat together (*tuan-yuan fan*) on September 9; (2) they should have one family roundtable discussion; (3) old people should set themselves one task within their capabilities; and (4) children should do one thing for their parents. It remains to be seen whether similar forms of community association will emerge elsewhere, or make headway addressing the needs of the rural elderly.

For discussions of the elder care problem in other regions in China, see Guo 2001; Yan Yunxiang 2003: 162–89; Ye and He 2008; Ye and Wu 2008; Huang 2007. Whyte (1997) suggests that the sense of filial obligation in urban China has become stronger during the reform era. On seniors' organizations in the context of the new rural reconstruction movement in Hubei and Henan, see Wang 2009. On the problems of elderly women in both urban and rural China, see Jia 2007; Huang 2007.

42. Interview with He Gaizhen 1999.

43. Articles 31 and 32 of the 1992 Law Safeguarding Women's Rights and Interests of the People's Republic of China specifically protect the rights of widows to inherited property:

"Widowed women have the right to dispose of the property inherited by them, and no one may interfere with the disposition thereof. . . . Widowed women who have made the predominant contributions in maintaining their parents-in-law shall be regarded as the statutory successors first in order, and their rights of succession thereto shall not be affected by inheritance in subrogation" (that is, the right of inheritance of the in-laws' sons and daughters; www.women.org.cn/english/english/laws/02.htm).

44. Interview with He Gaizhen 1999.

45. Ibid. On continued participation of the elderly in both formal and informal labor, and its connection to living arrangements and the decline of elder support, see Pang, de Brauw, and Rozelle 2004.

46. Details on some of the forms this broadening has taken can be found in Hershatter 2004, 2007c.

47. "Across generations," writes Paul Connerton (1989: 3) in *How Societies Remember*, "different sets of memories, frequently in the shape of implicit background narratives, will encounter each other; so that, although physically present to one another in a particular setting, the different generations may remain mentally and emotionally insulated, the memories of one generation locked irretrievably, as it were, in the brains and bodies of that generation." On intergenerational transmission of memories, see Feuchtwang (2000: 65) and the essays in Bertaux and Thompson 1993.

GLOSSARY

airen　爱人

aiye　艾叶

ba ni keliansile　把你可怜死了

baituo le jiawu tuolei　摆脱了家务拖累

bannian xizi, bannian ke　半年媳子, 半年客

baoguan　保管

baowa zu　保娃组

Bima　蓖麻

bu guan le　不管了

bu zenyang　不怎样

buyiding neng wenchulai　不一定能问出来

Cao Zhuxiang　曹竹香

chahua　插花

chan yuan　产院

changgong　长工

chanrure　产褥热

chatian dingchan　查田定产

chi　尺

chi le kui le　吃了亏了

chifan shitang hua, laodong junshihua, chuanyi fengren hua　吃饭食堂化, 劳动军事化,
　穿衣缝纫化

401

chu   锄

chu gong bu chu li   出工不出力

chu mai   锄麦

chuqin tian   出勤天

da buhuan shou, ma buhuan kou   打不还手, 骂不还口

daihua   带花

Dan (River)   丹

dan   担

dan da   胆大

dandu fa zheng   单独发证

Danfeng   丹凤

dang jia ren   当家人

dazaqiang   打砸抢

dei xia ku   得下苦

diandeng dianhua, loushang louxia, tuimo buyao niu, zhaoliang buyao you, zoulu bu yong
   tui, chifan bu yong zui   电灯电话, 楼上楼下, 推磨不要牛, 照亮不要油,
   走路不用腿, 吃饭不用嘴

diji yiwei   低级意味

dingbaosheng   顶包生

dingding guangguang   叮叮咣咣

Dingtian si   顶天寺

diyige nongmin chushen de yanjiuyuan   第一个农民出身的研究员

dou   斗

dundian   蹲点

e'laosheng   饿老生

erbobo   二跛跛

ergan   二敢

Erma   二妈

fangxia baofu, kaidong jiqi   放下包袱, 开动机器

fanshen   翻身

fen   分

fengchan tian   丰产田

fukua feng   浮夸风

funü xiaodui zhang   妇女小队长

furen jiao fuyou, qiongren jie qiongqin   富人交富友, 穷人结穷亲

ganniang   干娘

gao lihai　搞厉害

Gao Zhenxian　高贞贤

gaoʾe fengchan tian　高额丰产田

gen za chang duitai xi　跟咱唱对台戏

genshang zuo guande, zuo niangzi, genshang shazhude, fan changzi　跟上做官的做
　娘子, 跟上杀猪的翻肠子

gong　工

gongzuo　工作

gua cai dai, di biaozhun　瓜菜代, 低标准

gua le　刮了

Guan Gong　关公

guanjiao　管教

guanli qu　管理区

guanming　官名

Guanzhong　关中

gufeng　骨缝

gugan　骨干

Guoji ertong jinji jijin hui　国际儿童紧急基金会

guokui　锅盔

guokui mo　锅盔馍

Guomindang　国民党

guzi　谷子

Heyang　合阳

hong shendan　红身丹

hu pao　胡跑

huamo　花馍

huan qin　换亲

huchoubing　狐臭病

huhu (paste)　糊糊

huihuang　辉煌

huizhuan fa　回转法

huo　活

jiali mei ren　家里没人

jiang　犟

Jiang Jieshi　蒋介石

jiao　角

jiawu huo   家务活

jiefang hou   解放后

jiefang qian   解放前

jiesheng gei sile, ba ming gei songle   接生给死了, 把命给送了

jiesheng zhan   接生站

jin   斤

jingquansheng   井圈生

Jingyang   泾阳

Jiwa   机娃

kaikouxian   开口霰

kan naoke   砍脑壳

kang   炕

kang Mei yuan Chao, guojia ren shao   抗美援朝, 国家人少

kanwa   看娃

ketou   磕头

kouliang   口粮

la bu xia lai   拉不下来

Lan Huahua   蓝花花

青线线那个蓝线线, 蓝个英英采, 生下一个蓝花花, 实实的爱死人.

五谷子那个田苗子, 数上高粱高, 一十三省的女儿, 就数上蓝花花好.

正月里那个说媒, 二月里定, 三月里交大钱, 四月里迎.

三班子那个吹来, 两班子打, 撇下我的情哥哥, 抬进了周家.

蓝花花那个下轿来, 东张西又照, 找见周家的猴老子, 好象一座坟.

你要死来你, 早早地死, 前晌你死来, 后晌我蓝花花走.

手提上那个羊肉, 怀揣上糕, 我拼上个性命, 往哥哥你家跑.

我见到我的情哥哥呀, 有说不完的话, 咱们俩死哟, 长在一搭.

lao niu li di dao jian si   老牛犁地刀尖死

lao tianye   老天爷

laodong   劳动

Laomohai   老魔海

li   犁

li   里

Li Changyou   李长有

Li Qiming   李啓明

lianhuasheng   莲花生

liang   两

Lienü zhuan   烈女传

Liquan   礼泉

Liu Hulan   刘胡兰

Liu Xiang   刘向

lixia   立夏

Lu Guilan   鲁桂兰

luan dong shou   乱动手

Lujing   陆井

Ma   妈

ma ya   妈呀

maigei renjia   卖给人家

maike   麦客

maitou kugan   埋头苦干

majiang   麻将

majiao gan tan   马脚干碳

mangeda   蛮疙瘩

mansheng   慢生

mao   毛

Mao Zedong   毛澤東

mei mingtang   没名堂

mei sha shuiping   没啥水平

Meiguo jidu jiao xietong hui   美国基督教协同会

mo   糢

mo   磨

moyang gong   磨洋工

mu   亩

na ba wo kule yi beizi   那把我苦了一辈子

na dongxi   那东西

na xiaoyue bushi jian shi bao   那小月不是肩是抱

nanchan   难产

nanren shengle qi da poniang, poniang sheng le qi nanren da   男人生了气打婆娘,
    婆娘生了气男人打

Nanzheng   南郑

neibu   内部

ni hai shou le xie zui   你还受了些罪

Ni you tian, ni you di,   你有田, 你有地
    nide zhuangjia zai nali?   你有庄稼在哪里
    Meiyou qiongren lai laodong,   没有穷人来劳动
    guang kao zhuangjia, chi goupi. 光靠庄稼吃狗屁
    Ni jia nanren bu zuo huo,   你家男人不做活
    ni jia nüren bu fangxian,   你家女人不纺线
    ni jia qian cong nali lai?   你家钱从哪里来
    Jintian gei wo jiangchulai.   今天给我讲出来!

nongyeshe   农业社

nü shi xin, er shi gen, za hao de xifu wai xing ren   女是心, 儿是根, 咋好的媳妇外姓人

nüxu   女婿

pa   耙

peiyang   培养

pianzhui   偏坠

pianzi   偏子

pimian   皮棉

pingchan   平产

pingjun zhuyi   平均主义

polan   破烂

qiandan bu huan jian, chuba bu huan shou, gongfen tiantian you   扦担不换肩,
    锄把不换手, 工分天天有

qican   凄惨

qiche zoule dududu, wu [na] litou zuode dafeizhu   汽车走的嘟嘟嘟,
    喔里头坐的大肥猪

qigen fa miao   起根发苗

qingxinwan   清心丸

Qinling   秦岭

qipao   旗袍

qunzhong luxian   群众路线

renjia lao hanr   人家老汉儿

Renmin gongshe yizhi hua   人民公社一枝花
    Huakai shili xiang wanjia   花开十里香万家
    Funü daochu nao jingsai   妇女到处闹竞赛
    Qiuxiang hongqi biandi cha.   秋香红旗遍地插.

sangde   丧德

Shaanbei　陕北

Shaannan　陕南

Shaanxi　陕西

Shan Xiuzhen　山秀珍

Shanchekou　善车口

shang gong　上工

Shangmadian　上马店

shangtou　上头

Shanshan de hongxing (Sparkling Red Star)　闪闪的红星

sheng　生

shengchan　生产

shengchan dadui　生产大队

shengchan dui　生产队

shi cheng　十成

shi mianhua　拾棉花

shua laipi　耍赖皮

si xi li　四喜礼

siliufeng　四六风

song xi tie　送喜帖

suizi　穗子

suozi　梭子

suzhi　素质

tianshang wuyun bu xiayu, shishang wumei bu chengqin　天上无云不下雨, 世上无媒
　不成亲

tigao dao jiejishang lai renshi　提高到阶级上来认识

tingxia zhen, fangxia xian, wu mian zhanxian zheng zhuangyuan　停下针, 放下线,
　务棉战线争状元

tonggou tongxiao　统购统销

Tongguan　潼关

tongyangxi　童养媳

toulu chuanci fa　头颅穿刺法

tufei　土匪

tuoer suo　托儿所

waiqian ren　外前人

waitian ren　外天人

wanyingding　万应锭

Weinan   渭南

wu hua   五化

wuli ren   屋里人

wuli zongshi zuicui lali   屋里总是嘴碎啦哩

Xi'an   西安

xian wu xu hou wu shi   先务虚后务实

xiao du   消毒

xiaoji   消极

xiazhi   夏至

Xibei funü huabao   西北妇女画报

xiguasheng   西瓜生

xihuang   牺惶

xijun   细菌

Xin Zhongguo funü   新中国妇女

xingfu zao   幸福灶

Xu Haidong   徐海东

xue mi xin   血迷心

Yan'an   延安

Yang wawa   养娃娃

yangge   秧歌

yashen nü   押身女

Yi Guan Dao   一贯道

yi xu dai shi   以虚带实

Yinhua   银花

yishu   艺术

yongkou   咏口

youcai   油菜

youeryuan   幼儿园

yuan   元

yunyong bianzheng fa, kantian kandi, wu mianhua   运用辩证法,看天看地务棉花

yushu   榆树

zai hao de a jia you wang fa   再好的阿家有王法

zai shuo   再说

zaonie   造孽

zei wa dan   贼娃胆

zeren zhi   责任制

zhang   丈

Zhang Qiuxiang   张秋香

zhaofu yangda   招夫养大

zhaofu yangzi   招夫养子

zheng jizi lao ba   争鸡子老八

zher shi mei ren   这儿是没人

Zhou Enlai   周恩来

zhua wa   抓娃

zhuasile, esile, kusile   抓死了, 饿死了, 苦死了

zimian   籽棉

Zong luxian shi dengta   总路线是灯塔

    Zhaode renxin kaile hua   照得人心开了花

    Jinnian youle zong luxian   今年有了总路线

    Yao mianhua kaifang bi yun da.   要棉花开放比云大.

zunpo aixi   尊婆爱媳

zuo yuezi   坐月子

zuobude cuo   做不得错

zuofeng wenti   作风问题

REFERENCES

"1957 nian 7–12 yue fen fuyou weisheng gongzuo anpai yijian" [An opinion about the arrangements for health care work among women and children, July–December 1957]. 1958. Report (printed). Weinan County Archives.

Abram, Jan, and Knud Hjulmand. 2007. *The Language of Winnicott: A Dictionary of Winnicott's Use of Words.* London: Karnac Books.

Ahern, Emily [Martin]. 1975. "The Power and Pollution of Chinese Women." In *Women in Chinese Society,* ed. Margery Wolf and Roxane Witke, pp. 193–214. Stanford, CA: Stanford University Press.

Ahn, Byungil. 2005. "Midwifery Reform, Modernization and Revolution in Twentieth-Century China." Unpublished paper, cited by permission.

Amin, Shahid. 1995. *Event, Metaphor, Memory: Chauri Chaura 1922–1992.* Berkeley: University of California Press.

Anagnost, Ann. 1997. *National Past-Times: Narrative, Representation, and Power in Modern China.* Durham, NC: Duke University Press.

Andors, Phyllis. 1983. *The Unfinished Liberation of Chinese Women, 1949–1980.* Bloomington: Indiana University Press.

Bachman, David M. 1991. *Bureaucracy, Economy, and Leadership in China: The Institutional Origins of the Great Leap Forward.* Cambridge: Cambridge University Press.

Bai Wei. 1951. *Du huang* [Pulling Through the Famine]. Shanghai: Xin wenyi chubanshe.

Banister, Judith. 1987. *China's Changing Population.* Stanford, CA: Stanford University Press.

Barlow, Tani E. 1994. "Theorizing Woman: *Funü, Guojia, Jiating.*" In *Body, Subject and Power in China,* ed. Angela Zito and Tani E. Barlow, pp. 253–89. Chicago: University of Chicago Press.

Becker, Jasper. 1996. *Hungry Ghosts.* New York: Free Press.

Belden, Jack. 1970. *China Shakes the World.* New York: Monthly Review Press.

Bennett, Gordon A. 1976. *Yundong: Mass Campaigns in Chinese Communist Leadership.* Berkeley: Center for Chinese Studies, University of California.

Bernstein, Thomas P. 1984. "Stalinism, Famine, and Chinese Peasants: Grain Procurements during the Great Leap Forward." *Theory and Society* 13, no. 3 (May): 339–77.

———. 2006. "Mao Zedong and the Famine of 1959–60: A Study in Willfulness." *China Quarterly,* no. 186 (June): 421–45.

Bertaux, Daniel, and Paul Thompson, eds. 1993. *Between Generations.* Vol. 2 of *International Yearbook of Oral History and Life Stories.* Oxford: Oxford University Press.

Billingsley, Phil. 1988. *Bandits in Republican China.* Stanford, CA: Stanford University Press.

Blake, C. Fred. 1979. "Love Songs and the Great Leap: The Role of a Youth Culture in the Revolutionary Phase of China's Economic Development." *American Ethnologist* 6, no. 1 (February): 41–54.

Bloch, Maurice. 1996. "Internal and External Memory: Different Ways of Being in History." In *Tense Past: Cultural Essays in Trauma and Memory,* ed. Paul Antze and Michael Lambek, pp. 215–33. New York: Routledge.

Bohannon, John Neil, III, and Victoria Louise Symons. 1992. "Flashbulb Memories: Confidence, Consistency, and Quantity." In *Affect and Accuracy in Recall: Studies of "Flashbulb" Memories,* ed. Eugene Winograd and Ulric Neisser, pp. 65–91. Cambridge: Cambridge University Press.

Bossen, Laurel. 2002. *Chinese Women and Rural Development: 60 Years of Change in Lu Village, Yunnan.* Lanham, MD: Rowman and Littlefield.

Bossler, Beverly. 2002. "Faithful Wives and Heroic Martyrs: State, Society and Discourse in the Song and Yuan." In *Chūgoku no rekishi sekai, tōgō no shisutemu to tagenteki hatten* [China's Historical World: Unified System and Diverse Developments], ed. Chūgokushi gakkai, pp. 507–56. Tokyo: Tokyo Metropolitan University Press.

Boyarin, Jonathan, ed. 1994a. *Remapping Memory: The Politics of TimeSpace.* Minneapolis: University of Minnesota Press.

———. 1994b. "Space, Time, and the Politics of Memory." In *Remapping Memory: The Politics of TimeSpace,* ed. Jonathan Boyarin, pp. 1–37. Minneapolis: University of Minnesota Press.

Bradley, Harriet. 1999. "The Seductions of the Archive: Voices Lost and Found." *History of the Human Sciences* 12, no. 2: 107–22.

Brown, Roger, and James Kulik. 2000. "Flashbulb Memories." In *Memory Observed: Remembering in Natural Contexts,* 2nd ed., ed. and comp. Ulric Neisser and Ira E. Hyman Jr., pp. 50–65. New York: Worth Publishers.

Brücker, Eva. 1996. "Clubmen and Functionaries: Male Memory in Two Berlin Working-Class Neighbourhoods from the 1920s to the 1980s." In *Gender and Memory.* Vol. 4 of *International Yearbook of Oral History and Life Stories,* ed. Selma Leydesdorff, Luisa Passerini, and Paul Thompson, pp. 45–58. Oxford: Oxford University Press.

Buck, John Lossing. 1964 [1937]. *Land Utilization in China.* New York: Paragon Book Reprint Corp.

Cao Jinqing. 2003. *Huanghe bian de Zhongguo: Yige xuezhe dui xiangcun shehui de guancha yu sikao* [China on the Banks of the Yellow River: A Scholar's Observations and Thoughts about Rural Society]. Shanghai: Shanghai wenyi chubanshe.

Cao Shuji. 2005. "1959–1961 nian Zhongguo de renkou siwang jiqi chengyin" [Population

Deaths in China 1959–1961 and Their Causes]. *Zhongguo renkou kexue* [Chinese Journal of Population Science], no. 1: 14–28.

"Cao Zhuxiang danxing cailiao [Individual Material on Cao Zhuxiang]. N.d. Women's Federation Archives, Shaanxi Provincial Archives, Xi'an.

"Cao Zhuxiang huzhu lianzu danxing cailiao" [Individual Material on the Cao Zhuxiang United Mutual Aid Group]. 1953. 178–209–009. Women's Federation Archives, Shaanxi Provincial Archives, Xi'an.

"Cao Zhuxiang huzhuzu mofan shijian danxing cailiao" [Individual Material on Model Incidents in the Cao Zhuxiang Mutual Aid Group]. 1952. 178–27–025. Women's Federation Archives, Shaanxi Provincial Archives, Xi'an.

"Cao Zhuxiang mofan shiji danxing cailiao" [Individual Material on the Model Activities of Cao Zhuxiang]. 1957. Records of Village B, Weinan. Handwritten ms.

Chan, Alfred L. 1992. "The Campaign for Agricultural Development in the Great Leap Forward: A Study of Policy-making and Implementation in Liaoning." *China Quarterly*, no. 129 (March): 52–71.

———. 2001. *Mao's Crusade: Politics and Policy Implementation in China's Great Leap Forward*. Oxford: Oxford University Press.

Chan, Anita, Richard Madsen, and Jonathan Unger. 2009. *Chen Village: Revolution to Globalization*. 3rd ed. Berkeley: University of California Press.

Chang, Gene Hsin, and Guanzhong James Wen. 1997. "Communal Dining and the Chinese Famine of 1958–1961." *Economic Development and Cultural Change* 46, no. 1 (October): 1–34.

———. 1998. "Food Availability versus Consumption Efficiency: Causes of the Chinese Famine." *China Economic Review* 9, no. 2 (Autumn): 157–65.

Chen, C. C. 1989. *Medicine in Rural China: A Personal Account*. Ed. Frederica M. Bunge. Berkeley: University of California Press.

Chen, Fan Pen Li. 2004. *Visions for the Masses: Chinese Shadow Plays from Shaanxi and Shanxi*. Ithaca, NY: East Asia Program, Cornell University.

Chen, Tina Mai. 2003. "Female Icons, Feminist Iconography? Socialist Rhetoric and Women's Agency in 1950s China." *Gender and History* 15, no. 2 (August): 268–95.

Chen Guidi and Wu Chuntao. 2006. *Will the Boat Sink the Water? The Life of China's Peasants*. New York: Public Affairs.

Chen Yiyuan. 2006. *Geming yu xiangcun: Jianguo chuqi nongcun jiceng zhengquan jianshe yanjiu, 1949–1957* [Revolution and the Countryside: Research on the Construction of Rural Grassroots Political Power in the Early Period of National Construction, 1949–1957]. Shanghai: Shanghai shehui kexue yuan chubanshe.

Chen Zhongshi. 1993. *Bai lu yuan* [White Deer Plain]. Beijing: Renmin wenxue chubanshe.

Chu Han. 1996. *Zhongguo 1959–1961: Sannian ziran zaihai changbian jishi* [China 1959–1961: A Draft Account of the Three Years of Natural Disaster]. Chengdu: Sichuan renmin chubanshe.

Chuan Shaan geming genjudi shiliao xuanji [Selection of Historical Material on the Sichuan-Shaanxi Revolutionary Base Area]. 1986. N.p.: Renmin chubanshe.

Cohen, Myron L. 2005. *Kinship, Contract, Community, and State: Anthropological Perspectives on China*. Stanford, CA: Stanford University Press.

Committee on the Economy of China. 1969. *Provincial Agricultural Statistics for Communist China*. Ithaca, NY: Social Science Research Council.

Confino, Alon. 1997. "Collective Memory and Cultural History: Problems of Method." *American Historical Review* 102, no. 5 (December): 1386–403.

Cong Jin. 1996. *Quzhe fazhan de suiye* [English title: The Stage of Winding Development]. Vol. 7 of *20 shiji de Zhongguo* [China in the Twentieth Century]. Zhengzhou: Henan renmin chubanshe.

Connerton, Paul. 1989. *How Societies Remember*. Cambridge: Cambridge University Press.

Conway, Martin A. 1997. "The Inventory of Experience: Memory and Identity." In *Collective Memory of Political Events: Social Psychological Perspectives*, ed. James W. Pennebaker, Dario Paez, and Bernard Rimé, pp. 21–45. Mahwah, NJ: Lawrence Erlbaum.

Crane, Susan A. 1997. "Writing the Individual Back into Collective Memory." *American Historical Review* 102, no. 5 (December): 1372–85.

Croll, Elisabeth. 1980. *Feminism and Socialism in China*. New York: Schocken Books.

———. 1994. *From Heaven to Earth: Images and Experiences of Development in China*. London: Routledge.

———. 1996. "Gendered Moments and Inscripted Memories: Girlhood in Twentieth-Century Chinese Autobiography." In *Gender and Memory*, ed. Selma Leydesdorff, Luisa Passerini, and Paul Thompson, pp. 117–31. Vol. 4 of *International Yearbook of Oral History and Life Stories*. Oxford: Oxford University Press.

Crook, Isabel, and David Crook. 1979. *Ten Mile Inn: Mass Movement in a Chinese Village*. New York: Pantheon Books.

Cruikshank, Julie, and Kitty Smith, in collaboration with Angela Sidney and Annie Ned. 1990. *Life Lived Like a Story*. Lincoln: University of Nebraska Press.

Dai Yingxin. 1977. *Guanzhong shuili shihua* [A Historical Account of Guanzhong Water Conservancy]. Xi'an: Shaanxi renmin chubanshe.

Danfeng disan qu Maoping xiang renmin zhengfu. 1955. "Danfeng xian disan qu Maoping xiang Chang Qinglian danxing cailiao" [Individual Material on Chang Qinglian from Maoping Township, the Third District of Danfeng County]. Danfeng County Archives.

Danfeng diyi qu Xihe xiang renmin zhengfu. 1955. "Danfeng xian diyi qu Xihe xiang Fulian zhuren Zhai Chunmei danxing cailiao" [Individual Material on Zhai Chunmei, the Women's Chair from Xihe Township in the First District of Danfeng County]. Danfeng County Archives.

Danfeng Fulian hui. 1955. "Danfeng xian dijiu qu Beiludao xiang gongzuo mofan Yang Chunlan danxing cailiao" [Individual Material of Work Model Yang Chunlan from Beiludao Township, Ninth District, Danfeng County]. Danfeng County Archives.

———. 1956. "Lianhe tongzhi" [Joint Announcement]. Danfeng County Archives.

———. 1957. "Guanyu saomang gongzuo" [On the Work of Sweeping Away Illiteracy]. Danfeng County Archives.

Danfeng xian Fulian. 1952a. "Danfeng xian funü gongzuo yinian lai de zongjie" [Summary of the Past Year of Women's Work in Danfeng County]. Danfeng County Archives.

———. 1952b. "Tongzhi" [Notice]. Nov. 3, Danfeng County Archives.

———. 1953a. "Danfeng xian yinian lai de funü gongzuo zongjie baogao" [Summary Report of the Past Year of Women's Work in Danfeng County]. Danfeng County Archives.

————. 1953b. "Guanche hunyinfa yundong yue zhong funü gongzuo de jidian yijian" [A Few Opinions on Woman's Work in the Course of Implementing Marriage Law Movement Month]. Mar. 1. Danfeng County Archives.

————. 1954. "Danfeng xian Fulian guanyu yinian ban de lai de funü gongzuo baogao" [Danfeng County Women's Federation Report on the Past Year and a Half of Woman's Work]. Aug. 27. Danfeng County Archives.

————. 1957a. "Danfeng xian Fulian yinian lai de funü gongzuo zongjie" [Danfeng County Women's Federation Summary on the Past Year of Woman's Work]. Jan. 27. Danfeng County Archives.

————. 1957b. "Guanyu jixu xuanchuan guanche hunyinfa yu jinxing shehuizhuyi daode pinzhi jiaoyu de lianhe tongzhi" [Unified Announcement on Continuing to Propagandize the Implementation of the Marriage Law and Conducting Socialist Moral Character Education]. Danfeng County Archives.

————. 1958. "Danfeng xian Fulian 57 nian funü gongzuo zongjie ji 58 nian yuan zhi san yue fen gongzuo yijian" [Danfeng County Women's Federation Summary of 1957 Woman's Work and a Look at Work for the First Three Months of 1958]. Jan. 16. Danfeng County Archives.

Danfeng xian minzhu funü lianhe hui. 1953. "Sanqu guanche hunyinfa yundong yi, er jieduan gongzuo baogao" [Report on First- and Second-Stage Implementation Work of the Marriage Law Movement]. Danfeng County Archives.

————. 1955. "Danfeng xian disi qu Zhulinguan xiang Liu Xihan mofan danxing cailiao" [Individual Material on Liu Xihan of Zhulinguan Township, the Fourth District, Danfeng County]. Danfeng County Archives.

Danfeng xianzhi bianji weiyuan hui. 1994. *Danfeng xianzhi* [Danfeng County Gazetteer]. Xi'an: Shaanxi renmin chubanshe.

Davin, Delia. 1975. "Women in the Countryside of China." In *Women in Chinese Society*, ed. Margery Wolf and Roxane Witke, pp. 243–73. Stanford, CA: Stanford University Press.

————. 1976. *Woman-Work: Women and the Party in Revolutionary China*. Oxford: Oxford University Press.

Day, Alexander F. 2007. "Return of the Peasant: History, Politics, and the Peasantry in Post-socialist China." Ph.D. diss., University of California, Santa Cruz.

Derrida, Jacques. 1995. *Archive Fever*. Chicago: University of Chicago Press.

Diamant, Neil J. 2000. *Revolutionizing the Family: Politics, Love, and Divorce in Urban and Rural China, 1949–1968*. Berkeley: University of California Press.

Diamant, Neil J., Stanley B. Lubman, and Kevin J. O'Brien, eds. 2005. *Engaging the Law in China: State, Society, and Possibilities for Justice*. Stanford, CA: Stanford University Press.

Diamond, Norma. 1975. "Collectivization, Kinship, and the Status of Women in Rural China." In *Toward an Anthropology of Women*, ed. Reyna R. Reiter, pp. 372–95. New York: Monthly Review Press.

Dikötter, Frank. 2010. *Mao's Great Famine: The History of China's Most Devastating Catastrophe, 1958–62*. London: Bloomsbury.

Ding Shiliang and Fang Zhao, eds. 1997. *Zhongguo difangzhi minsu ziliao huibian: Xibei juan* [Collection of Material on Folk Customs from Chinese Local Gazetteers: Northwest Volume]. Beijing: Beijing tushuguan chubanshe.

Domenach, Jean-Luc. 1995. *The Origins of the Great Leap Forward: The Case of One Chinese Province*. Boulder, CO: Westview Press.

Domes, Jurgen. 1980. *Socialism in the Chinese Countryside: Rural Societal Policies in the People's Republic of China, 1949–1979*. Trans. Margitta Wendling. London: C. Hurst.

Du Fangqin, ed. 1998. *Da shan de nüer: Jingyan, xinsheng, he xuyao* [Daughters of the Great Mountains: Experiences, Inner Voices, and Needs]. *Shanqu funü koushu* [Oral Histories of Mountain District Women]. Guiyang: Guizhou minzu chubanshe.

Dudley, Kathryn Marie. 1998. "In the Archive, in the Field: What Kind of Document Is an 'Oral History'?" In *Narrative and Genre*, ed. Mary Chamberlain and Paul Thompson, pp. 160–66. London: Routledge.

Dutton, Michael. 2005. *Policing Chinese Politics*. Durham, NC: Duke University Press.

"Editorial: Midwifery Training in Peking." 1928. *China Medical Journal* 42: 782–84.

Evans, Harriet. 1997. *Women and Sexuality in China: Dominant Discourses of Female Sexuality and Gender Since 1949*. London: Blackwell.

———. 2008. *The Subject of Gender: Daughters and Mothers in Urban China*. Lanham, MD: Rowman and Littlefield.

Felman, Shoshana, and Dori Laub. 1992. *Testimony: Crises of Witnessing in Literature, Psychoanalysis, and History*. New York: Routledge.

Feuchtwang, Stephan. 1998. "Distant Homes, Our Genre: Recognizing Chinese Lives as an Anthropologist." In *Narrative and Genre*, ed. Mary Chamberlain and Paul Thompson, pp. 126–41. London: Routledge.

———. 2000. "Reinscriptions: Commemoration, Restoration and the Interpersonal Transmission of Histories and Memories under Modern States in Asia and Europe." In *Memory and Methodology*, ed. Susannah Radstone, pp. 59–77. Oxford: Berg.

———. 2005. "Remembering Terror: The Great Leap Famine in Official Discourse and in Personal Accounts." Unpublished draft, cited by permission.

FL. Fulian [Women's Federation]. 1950s–1960s. Archival materials held at the Shaanxi Provincial Archives, Xi'an, Shaanxi.

Fong, Grace S. 2004. "Female Hands: Embroidery as a Knowledge Field in Women's Everyday Life in Late Imperial and Early Republican China." *Late Imperial China* 25, no. 1 (June): 1–58.

Freedman, Estelle B. 2002. *No Turning Back: The History of Feminism and the Future of Women*. New York: Ballantine Books.

Friedman, Edward, Paul G. Pickowicz, and Mark Selden. 2005. *Revolution, Resistance, and Reform in Village China*. New Haven, CT: Yale University Press.

Friedman, Edward, Paul G. Pickowicz, Mark Selden, with Kay Ann Johnson. 1991. *Chinese Village, Socialist State*. New Haven, CT: Yale University Press.

Friedman, Sara L. 2006. *Intimate Politics: Marriage, the Market, and State Power in Southeastern China*. Cambridge, MA: Harvard University Asia Center and Harvard University Press.

Fujian sheng minzhu funü lianhe hui fuli bu (comp.). 1956. *Zenyang ban nongcun tuoer zuzhi* [How to Run Village Childcare Organizations]. Fuzhou: Fujian renmin chubanshe.

Funü huabao [Women's Pictorial]. 1957–59. Xi'an.

"Funü minbing daibiao Zhang Chunfang tongzhi danxing cailiao" [Individual Material on Women's Militia Representative Zhang Chunfang]. 1958. Danfeng County Archives.

Furth, Charlotte. 1990. "The Patriarch's Legacy: Household Instructions and the Transmission of Orthodox Values." In *Orthodoxy in Late Imperial China,* ed. Kwang-ching Liu, pp. 187–211. Berkeley: University of California Press.

———. 1999. *A Flourishing Yin: Gender in China's Medical History, 960–1665.* Berkeley: University of California Press.

"Fuying weisheng gongzuo diaocha gongzuo" [Investigation and Work on Women and Children's Health Work]. Women's Federation Archives, n.d. (1950?).

Gamble, Sidney. 1970. *Chinese Village Plays from the Ting Hsien Region (Yang Ke Hsüan).* Amsterdam: Philo Press.

Gao, Mobo C. F. 1999. *Gao Village: A Portrait of Rural Life in Modern China.* London: Hurst.

Gao Hua. 2005. *Zai lishi de Fengling dukou* [English title: At the Fengling Du Ferry Crossing of the History]. Xianggang: Shidai guoji chuban youxian gongsi.

Gao Xiaoxian. 2000. "Hunyin, jiating, funü" [Marriage, Family, Women]. In *Jinru 21 shiji de Zhongguo nongcun* [English title: Come into Chinese Country of Twenty-one Century], ed. Xiong Jingming, pp. 164–206. Beijing: Guangming ribao chubanshe.

———. 2002. "Pinkun diqu funü yunchanqi baojian fuwu fenxi" [An Analysis of Health Care Services for Pregnancy and Childbirth in Poor Districts]. *Funü yanjiu,* no. 4: 59–62.

———. 2005. "'Yinhua sai': 1950 niandai nongcun funü yu xingbie fengong" ["The Silver Flower Contest": Rural Women in the 1950s and the Gendered Division of Labor]. In *Bainian Zhongguo nüquan sichao yanjiu* [Research on 100 Years of Feminist Thought], ed. Wang Zheng and Chen Yan, pp. 259–77. Shanghai: Fudan daxue chubanshe.

———. 2006a. "'The Silver Flower Contest': Rural Women in 1950s China and the Gendered Division of Labour." Trans. Yuanxi Ma. *Gender and History* 18, no. 3 (Nov.): 594–612.

———. 2006b. *Zhongguo shehui zhuanxing: nongcun funü yanjiu* [Chinese Social Transformation: Research on Rural Women]. Xi'an: Shaanxi renmin chubanshe.

Glosser, Susan L. 2003. *Chinese Visions of Family and State, 1915–1953.* Berkeley: University of California Press.

Goldstein, Joshua. 1998. "Scissors, Surveys, and Psycho-Prophylactics: Prenatal Health Care Campaigns and State Building in China, 1949–1954." *Journal of Historical Sociology* 11, no. 2 (June): 153–84.

Gongren ribao [Workers' Daily]. Beijing. 1959.

Greenhalgh, Susan. 1990. "The Evolution of the One-Child Policy in Shaanxi, 1979–88." *China Quarterly,* no. 122 (June): 191–229.

———. 1993. "The Peasantization of the One-Child Policy in Shaanxi." In *Chinese Families in the Post-Mao Era,* ed. Deborah Davis and Stevan Harrell, pp. 219–50. Berkeley: University of California Press.

———. 1994 "Controlling Births and Bodies in Village China." *American Ethnologist* 21, no. 1: 3–30.

———. 2008. *Just One Child: Science and Policy in Deng's China.* Berkeley: University of California Press.

Greenhalgh, Susan, and Jiali Li. 1995. "Engendering Reproductive Policy and Practice in Peasant China: For a Feminist Demography of Reproduction." *Signs* 20, no. 3 (Spring): 601–41.

Greenhalgh, Susan, and Edwin A. Winckler. 2005. *Governing China's Population: From Leninist to Neoliberal Biopolitics*. Stanford, CA: Stanford University Press.

Grele, Ronald J., ed. 1991. *Envelopes of Sound: The Art of Oral History*. New York: Praeger.

Gu Ximing. 1951. *Nongcun dazhong weisheng* [Public Health in Rural Areas]. Shanghai: Zhonghua shuju.

Gu Zhizhong. 1932. *Xixing ji* [Record of a Western Journey]. Shanghai: Lixing she.

Gu Zhizhong and Lu Yi. 1937. *Dao Qinghai qu* [To Qinghai]. Shanghai: Shangwu yinshu guan.

Guo Butao. 1932. *Xibei lüxing riji* [Diary of a Trip through the Northwest]. Shanghai: Dadong shuju.

Guo Fengzhou and Peiyuan Lan, eds. and comps. 1969 [1921]. *Xuxiu Nanzheng xianzhi* [Continuation of the Nanzheng Gazetteer]. 3 vols. Taipei: Chengwen chubanshe.

Guo Runzi. 1992. *Shaanxi minguo zhanzheng shi* [A Military History of Republican-era Shaanxi]. Vol. 1. Xi'an: Sanqin chubanshe.

Guo Yuhua. 2001. "Daiji guanxi zhong de gongping luoji jiqi bianqian: dui Hebei nongcun yanglao shijian de fenxi" [The Logic of Fairness and Its Change in Cross-generational Relations: An Analysis of Cases of Elderly Support in Rural Hebei]. *Zhongguo xueshu*, no. 4: 221–54.

———. 2003. "Psychological Collectivization: Cooperative Transformation of Agriculture in Jichun Village, Northern Shaanxi, as in [sic] the Memory of the Women." *Social Sciences in China*, no. 4: 48–61.

———. 2004. "Xinling de jitihua: Shaanbei Ji cun nongye hezuohua de nüxing jiyi [Collectivization of the Soul: Women's Memories of Agricultural Collectivization in Ji Village, Shaanbei]. Paper prepared for the conference Feminism in China since the Women's Bell, Fudan University, Shanghai.

Guo Yuhua and Liping Sun. 2002. "Suku: Yizhong nongmin guojia guannian xingcheng de zhongjie jizhi" [Pouring Out Grievances: A Mediated Mechanism for the Shaping of the Peasants' Idea of the State]. *Zhongguo xueshu*, no. 4: 130–57.

Guo Zhihua. 1993. "Zhou Zongli yu Zhang Qiuxiang [Premier Zhou and Zhang Qiuxiang]. *Weinan shi wenshi ziliao*, no. 5: 165–70.

Guojia nongye weiyuan hui. 1981. *Nongye jitihua zhongyao wenjian huibian 1949–57* [Compendium of Important Documents on Agricultural Collectivization, 1949–57]. Beijing: Zhongguo zhongyang dangxiao chubanshe.

Gupta, Akhil. 1994. "The Reincarnation of Souls and the Rebirth of Commodities: Representations of Time in 'East' and 'West.'" In *Remapping Memory: The Politics of TimeSpace*, ed. Jonathan Boyarin, pp. 161–83. Minneapolis: University of Minnesota Press.

Haaken, Janice. 1998. *Pillar of Salt: Gender, Memory, and the Perils of Looking Back*. New Brunswick, NJ: Rutgers University Press.

Halbwachs, Maurice. 1992. *On Collective Memory*. Ed. Lewis A. Coser. Chicago: University of Chicago Press.

Hamilton, Carrie. 2003. "Memories of Violence in Interviews with Basque Nationalist

Women." In *Contested Pasts: The Politics of Memory*, ed. Katharine Hodgkin and Susannah Radstone, pp. 120–35. London: Routledge.

Han, Kuo-Huang. 1989. "Chinese Music Theory." *Asian Music* 20.2 (Summer): 107–28.

Han Dongping. 2003. "The Great Leap Famine, the Cultural Revolution and Post Mao Rural Reform: The Lessons of Rural Development in Contemporary China." Apr. 1. http://chinastudygroup.net/2003/04/the-great-leap-famine-the-cultural-revolution-and-post-mao-rural-reform-the-lessons-of-rural-development-in-contemporary-china/.

Han Qixiang (performer) and Lin Shan (recorder/writer). 1953. *Zhang Yulan canjia xuanju hui* [Zhang Yulan Participates in the Election Meeting]. Xi'an: Xibei renmin chubanshe, July.

He Hanwei. 1980. *Guangxu chu nian (1876–79) Huabei de da han zai* [The Great Drought Disaster in North China, 1876–1879]. Xianggang: Zhongwen daxue chubanshe.

Heehs, Peter. 2000 "Shaped Like Themselves." *History and Theory*, no. 39 (October): 417–28.

Hershatter, Gail. 1986. *The Workers of Tianjin, 1900–1949*. Stanford, CA: Stanford University Press.

———. 1993. "The Subaltern Talks Back: Reflections on Subaltern Theory and Chinese History." *positions: east asia cultures critique* 1, no. 1 (Spring): 103–30.

———. 1997. *Dangerous Pleasures: Prostitution and Modernity in Twentieth-Century Shanghai*. Berkeley: University of California Press.

———. 2000. "Local Meanings of Gender and Work in Rural Shaanxi in the 1950s." In *Re-Drawing Boundaries: Work, Households, and Gender in China*, ed. Barbara Entwisle and Gail E. Henderson, pp. 79–96. Berkeley: University of California Press.

———. 2002. "The Gender of Memory: Rural Chinese Women and the 1950s." *Signs* 28, no. 1 (Fall): 43–70.

———. 2003. "Making the Visible Invisible: The Fate of 'the Private' in Revolutionary China." In *Wusheng zhi sheng: Jindai Zhongguo de funü yu guojia (1600–1950)* [Voices amid Silence: Women and the Nation in Modern China (1600–1950)], ed. Lü Fang-sheng, pp. 257–81. Taiwan: Zhongyang yanjiu yuan, Zhongguo jindaishi yanjiu suo [Institute of Modern History, Academia Sinica].

———. 2004. "State of the Field: Women in China's Long Twentieth Century." *Journal of Asian Studies* 63, no. 4 (November): 991–1065.

———. 2005. "Virtue at Work: Rural Shaanxi Women Remember the 1950s." In *Gender in Motion: Divisions of Labor and Cultural Change in Late Imperial and Modern China*, ed. Bryna Goodman and Wendy Larson, pp. 309–28. Lanham, MD: Rowman and Littlefield.

———. 2007a. "Birthing Stories: Rural Midwives in 1950s China." In *Dilemmas of Victory: The Early Years of the People's Republic of China*, ed. Jeremy Brown and Paul G. Pickowicz, pp. 337–58. Cambridge, MA: Harvard University Press.

———. 2007b. "Forget Remembering: Rural Women's Narratives of China's Collective Past." In *Re-envisioning the Chinese Revolution: The Politics and Poetics of Collective Memories in Reform China*, ed. Ching Kwan Lee and Guobin Yang, pp. 69–92. Washington, D.C., and Stanford, CA: Woodrow Wilson Center Press and Stanford University Press.

———. 2007c. *Women in China's Long Twentieth Century*. Berkeley: University of California Press.

———. 2011. "Getting a Life: The Production of 1950s Women Labor Models in Rural

Shaanxi." In *Beyond Exemplar Tales: Women's Biography in Chinese History,* ed. Hu Ying and Joan Judge. Berkeley: University of California Global, Area, and International Archive. http://escholarship.org. Print ed. University of California Press.

Heyang wenshi ziliao. Heyang. 1988.

Heyang xian jiaoyu ju jiaoyu zhi bianzuan bangong shi, ed. *Heyang xian jiaoyu zhi* [Heyang County Education Gazetteer]. 1998. Xi'an: Sanqin chubanshe.

Heyang xian quanzhi. 1970 [1769]. Zhongguo fangzhi congshu [China Gazetteers Series]. Taibei: Chengwen chubanshe.

Heyang xianzhi bianzuan weiyuan hui, ed. 1996. *Heyang xianzhi* [Heyang County Gazetteer]. Xi'an: Shaanxi renmin chubanshe.

Hinton, William. 1997 [1966]. *Fanshen: A Documentary of Revolution in a Chinese Village.* Berkeley: University of California Press.

Ho, Wing Chung. 2004. "The (Un-)Making of the Shanghai Socialist 'Model Community': From the Monolithic to Heterogeneous Appropriations(s) of the Past." *Journal of Asian and African Studies* 39, no. 5: 379–405.

———. 2006. "From Resistance to Collective Action in a Shanghai Socialist 'Model Community': From the Late 1940s to Early 1970s." *Journal of Social History* 40, no. 1: 86–117.

Hodgkin, Katharine, and Susannah Radstone. 2003. "Introduction: Contested Pasts." In *Contested Pasts: The Politics of Memory,* ed. Katharine Hodgkin and Susannah Radstone, pp. 1–21. London: Routledge.

Holm, David. 1991. *Art and Ideology in Revolutionary China.* Studies in Contemporary China, no.1. Oxford: Oxford University Press.

———. 2003. "The Death of *Tiaoxi* (the 'Leaping Play'): Ritual Theatre in the Northwest of China." *Modern Asian Studies* 37, no. 4: 863–84.

Honig, Emily. 1986. *Sisters and Strangers: Women in the Shanghai Cotton Mills, 1919–1949.* Stanford, CA: Stanford University Press.

———. 1997. "Getting to the Source: Striking Lives: Oral History and the Politics of Memory." *Journal of Women's History* 9, no. 1 (Spring): 139–57.

———. 2010. "The Life of a Slogan: Maoism, Gender, and the Cultural Revolution." Unpublished paper, cited by permission.

Honig, Emily, and Gail Hershatter. 1988. *Personal Voices: Chinese Women in the 1980s.* Stanford, CA: Stanford University Press.

Hooton, E. R. 1991. *The Greatest Tumult: The Chinese Civil War, 1936–49.* London: Brassey's.

Huang Lianshe. 2002. "Youhe shuiku zhan xinmao" [The You River Reservoir Gets a New Look]. *Weinan wenshi ziliao (Sanhe zhuanji)* [Three Rivers, special issue], no. 1: 191–93.

Huang Peng. 2007. "Guanzhu laonian funü wenti: Yi Anhui wei li fenxi" [Close Attention to the Problem of Older Women: An Analysis Using Anhui as an Example]. *Funü yanjiu,* no. 6: 38–41.

Hunyinfa tujie tongsu ben [The Marriage Law in Illustrations]. 1951. Shanghai: Huadong renmin chubanshe.

Huyssen, Andreas. 1995. *Twilight Memories: Marking Time in a Culture of Amnesia.* New York: Routledge.

Jacka, Tamara. 1997. *Women's Work in Rural China: Change and Continuity in an Era of Reform.* Cambridge: Cambridge University Press.

Jaschok, Maria, and Jingjun Shui. 2000. " 'Outsider Within': Speaking to Excursions across Cultures." *Feminist Theory* 1, no. 1: 33–58.

Jensen, Lionel M. 1997. *Manufacturing Confucianism: Chinese Traditions and Universal Civilization*. Durham, NC: Duke University Press.

Jia Yunzhu. 2007. "Zhongguo laonian funü de jingji diwei zhuangkuang fenxi" [An Analysis of the Circumstances of the Economic Status of Older Women in China]. *Funü yanjiu*, no. 2: 43–50.

Jiang Xinghan and Cheng Wanli. 1958. "Diyige nongmin chushen de nü yanjiuyuan Zhang Qiuxiang" [Zhang Qiuxiang, the First Woman Researcher of Peasant Origin]. *Zhongguo funü*, October: 6–7.

Jiang Zexian. 2005. *Zhongguo nongmin shengsi baogao* [Report on the Life and Death of Chinese Peasants]. Nanchang: Jiangxi renmin chubanshe.

Jin Pusen. 2001. "To Feed a Country at War: China's Supply and Consumption of Grain During the War of Resistance." In *China in the Anti-Japanese War, 1937–1945: Politics, Culture, and Society*, ed. David P. Barrett and Larry N. Shyu, pp. 157–69. New York: Peter Lang.

Jing, Jun. 1996. *The Temple of Memories: History, Power, and Morality in a Chinese Village*. Stanford, CA: Stanford University Press.

———. 1997. "Rural Resettlement: Past Lessons for the Three Gorges Project." *China Journal*, no. 38 (July): 65–92.

———. 1999. "Villages Dammed, Villages Repossessed: A Memorial Movement in Northwest China." *American Ethnologist* 26, no. 2: 324–43.

———. 2001. "Male Ancestors and Female Deities: Finding Memories of Trauma in a Chinese Village." In *Disturbing Remains: Memory, History, and Crisis in the Twentieth Century*, ed. Michael S. Roth and Charles G. Salas, pp. 207–26. Los Angeles: Getty Research Institute.

Jing, Jun, and Meng Leng. 1999. "From China's Big Dams to the Battle of Sanmenxia." *Chinese Sociology and Anthropology* 31, no. 3 (Spring): 3–68.

Johnson, D. Gale. 1998. "China's Great Famine: Introductory Remarks." *China Economic Review* 9, no. 2 (Autumn): 103–9.

Johnson, Kay Ann. 1983. *Women, the Family, and Peasant Revolution in China*. Chicago: University of Chicago Press.

Judd, Ellen R. 1989. "Niangjia: Chinese Women and Their Natal Families." *Journal of Asian Studies* 48, no. 3 (August): 525–44.

———. 1998. "Reconsidering China's Marriage Law Campaign: Toward a De-Orientalized Feminist Perspective." *Asian Journal of Women's Studies* 4, no. 2 (June): 525–44, gw.proquest.com.

Kane, Penny. 1988. *Famine in China, 1959–1961: Demographic and Social Implications*. New York: St. Martin's Press.

Kaneff, Deema. 2004. *Who Owns the Past? The Politics of Time in a "Model" Bulgarian Village*. New York: Berghahn Books.

Kaplan Murray, Laura May. 1985. "New World Food Crops in China: Farms, Food, and Families in the Wei River Valley, 1650–1910." Ph.D. diss., University of Pennsylvania.

Karl, Rebecca E. 2002. " 'Slavery,' Citizenship, and Gender in Late Qing China's Global Context." In *Rethinking the 1898 Reform Period: Political and Cultural Change in Late Qing China*, ed. Rebecca E. Karl and Peter Zarrow, pp. 212–44. Cambridge, MA: Harvard University Asia Center and Harvard University Press.

Kelliher, Daniel. 1992. *Peasant Power in China: The Era of Rural Reform, 1979–1989*. New Haven, CT: Yale University Press.

Kelly, Joan. 1984. *Women, History, and Theory: The Essays of Joan Kelly*. Women in Culture and Society Series. Chicago: University of Chicago Press.

Ko, Dorothy. 1994. *Teachers of the Inner Chambers: Women and Culture in Seventeenth-Century China*. Stanford, CA: Stanford University Press.

———. 2005. *Cinderella's Sisters: A Revisionist History of Footbinding*. Berkeley: University of California Press.

Kopijn, Yvette J. 1998. "The Oral History Interview in a Cross-Cultural Setting." In *Narrative and Genre*, ed. Mary Chamberlain and Paul Thompson, pp. 142–59. London: Routledge.

Kovács, András. 1992. "The Abduction of Imre Nagy and His Group: The 'Rashomon' Effect." In *Memory and Totalitarianism*. Vol. 1 of *International Yearbook of Oral History and Life Stories*, ed. Luisa Passerini, pp. 117–24. Oxford: Oxford University Press.

Lambek, Michael. 1996. "The Past Imperfect: Remembering as Moral Practice." In *Tense Past: Cultural Essays in Trauma and Memory*, ed. Paul Antze and Michael Lambek, pp. 235–55. New York: Routledge.

———. 2003. "Memory in a Maussian Universe." In *Regimes of Memory*, ed. Susannah Radstone and Katharine Hodgkin, pp. 202–16. London: Routledge.

"Lan Zhuren baogao guanche hunyinfa de zhixing qingkuang ji huihou yijian" [Director Lan's Report on the Circumstances of Marriage Law Implementation and Suggestions by Those Meeting]. 1955. July 13. Danfeng County Archives.

"Laodongmo Shan Xiuzhen" [Labor Model Shan Xiuzhen]. 2006. Weinan dang jianwang. http://wndj.org.cn/xgcl/2006/12/0108201812.html.

Larsen, Steen F. 1992. "Potential Flashbulbs: Memories of Ordinary News as the Baseline." In *Affect and Accuracy in Recall: Studies of "Flashbulb" Memories*, ed. Eugene Winograd and Ulric Neisser, pp. 32–64. Cambridge: Cambridge University Press.

Lavely, William. 1991. "Marriage and Mobility under Rural Collectivism." In *Marriage and Inequality in Chinese Society*, ed. Rubie S. Watson and Patricia Buckley Ebrey, pp. 286–312. Berkeley: University of California Press.

Le Goff, Jacques. 1992. *History and Memory*. Trans. Steven Rendall and Elizabeth Claman. New York: Columbia University Press.

Lee, Peter. 2010. "China's Sorrow, China's Embarrassment: The Great Relocation That Failed." *Asia Times*, Oct. 13. http://atimes.com/atimes/China/LJ13Ad02.html, http://atimes.com/atimes/China/LJ13Ad03.html.

L'Engle, Madeleine. 1975 [1962]. *A Wrinkle in Time*. New York: Dell.

Leydesdorff, Selma, Luisa Passerini, and Paul Thompson, eds. 1996. *Gender and Memory*. Vol. 4 of *International Yearbook of Oral History and Life Stories*. Oxford: Oxford University Press,

Li, Huaiyin. 2005. "Life Cycle, Labour Remuneration, and Gender Inequality in a Chinese Agrarian Collective." *Journal of Peasant Studies* 32, no. 3 (Apr.): 277–303.

————. 2006. "The First Encounter: Peasant Resistance to State Control of Grain in East China in the Mid-1950s." *China Quarterly* 185 (Mar.): 145–62.

Li, Zhisui. 1994. *The Private Life of Chairman Mao.* Trans. Hung-chao Tai, with the editorial assistance of Anne F. Thurston. New York: Random House.

Li Rui. 1996a. *"Da yuejin" qinli ji* [A Personal Record of the Great Leap Forward]. Haikou: Nanfang chubanshe.

————. 1996b. *Lushan huiyi shilu* [A Veritable Record of the Lushan Plenum]. Zhengzhou: Henan sheng renmin chubanshe.

Li Ting'an. 1935. *Zhongguo xiangcun weisheng wenti* [Problems of Rural Health in China]. Shanghai: Shangwu yinshuguan.

Li Xiaojiang. 2003. *Rang nüren ziji shuohua* [Let Women Speak for Themselves]. 3 vols. Beijing: Sanlian shudian.

Li Yinhe. 1993. *Shengyu yu Zhongguo cunluo wenhua* [Reproduction and Chinese Village Culture]. Hong Kong: Oxford University Press.

Li Yunfeng and Wenwei Yuan. 2006. "Minguo shiqi de Xibei tufei yu xiangcun shehui weiji" [Northwest Bandits in the Republican Period and the Social Crisis in the Countryside]. In *Jindai Zhongguo de chengshi yu xiangcun* [City and Country in Modern China], ed. Li Changli and Zuo Yuhe, pp. 448–64. Beijing: Shehui kexue wenxian chubanshe.

Lieberthal, Kenneth G. 1980. *Revolution and Tradition in Tientsin, 1949–1952.* Stanford, CA: Stanford University Press.

Lim, Kahti. 1959. "Obstetrics and Gynecology in Past Ten Years." *Chinese Medical Journal* 79, no. 5 (Nov.): 375–83.

Lin, Justin Yifu. 1990. "Collectivization and China's Agricultural Crisis in 1959–1961." *Journal of Political Economy* 98, no. 6 (Dec.): 1228–52.

Lin, Justin Yifu, and Dennis Tao Yang. 1998. "On the Causes of China's Agricultural Crisis and the Great Leap Famine." *China Economic Review* 9, no. 2 (Autumn): 125–40.

————. 2000. "Food Availability, Entitlements, and the Chinese Famine of 1959–1961." *Economic Journal* 110, no. 460 (Jan.): 136–58.

Lin Chao, ed. 1982. *Chuanshaan geming genjudi lishi changbian* [Draft History of the Sichuan-Shaanxi Revolutionary Base Area]. Chengdu: Sichuan renmin chubanshe.

Ling Zhijun. 1997. *Lishi buzai paihuai: Renmin gongshe zai Zhongguo de xingqi he shibai* [History No Longer Hesitates: The Rise and Fall of People's Communes in China]. Beijing: Renmin chubanshe.

Liquan xian difang zhi bianzuan weihui, ed. 1999. *Liquan xianzhi* [Liquan County Gazetteer]. Shaanxi difang zhi congshu [Shaanxi Local Gazetteer Series]. Xi'an: Sanqin chubanshe.

Liu, Ching [Liu Qing]. 1977. *Builders of a New Life.* Trans. Sidney Shapiro. Peking: Foreign Languages Press.

Liu, Xin. 2000. *In One's Own Shadow: An Ethnographic Account of the Condition of Postreform Rural China.* Berkeley: University of California Press.

Liu Qing. 1996. *Chuangye shi* [The Builders]. Xi'an: Shaanxi renmin chubanshe.

Liu Yanzhou. 1950. *Yang wawa* [Childbirth]. Shanghai: Xinhua shudian.

Liu Ziqian. 1981. "Di shiqilu jun yu hong si fangmian jun zai Shangluo zhanyi zhi huiyi" [Reminiscences of the Battle between the (Guomindang) 17th Route Army and the Red Fourth Front Army in Shangluo]. *Shaanxi wenshi ziliao,* no. 11 (Sept.): 240–43.

Lü, Xiaobo. 2000. *Cadres and Corruption: The Organizational Involution of the Chinese Communist Party*. Stanford, CA: Stanford University Press.

Lu Hong (ed.). 1950. *Lun cheng xiang hezuo* [On Cooperation between City and Countryside]. Beijing: Sanlian shudian.

Lu Hongyan. 2007. "Qujiang in Xi'an named park for cultural sector." *China Daily* (Aug. 13). http://www.chinadaily.com.cn/china/2007–08/13/content_6024102.htm.

Lu Xia. 1951. *Gaizao jiu chanpo jingyan jieshao* [Introduction to the Experience of Reforming Old Midwives]. Jinan: Shandong renmin chubanshe.

Lucas, AnElissa. 1982. *Chinese Medical Modernization: Comparative Policy Continuities, 1930–1980s*. New York: Praeger.

Luo Pinghan. 2001. *"Da guo fan": Gonggong shitang shimo* [One Big Pot: The Whole Story of the Public Dining Halls]. Nanning: Guangxi renmin chubanshe.

———. 2004. *Nongye hezuoshe yundong shi* [A History of the Agricultural Collectives]. Fuzhou: Fujian renmin chubanshe.

———. 2006 [2003]. *Nongcun renmin gongshe* shi [A History of the Rural People's Communes]. 2nd ed. Fuzhou: Fujian renmin chubanshe.

MacFarquhar, Roderick. 1974. *Contradictions among the People, 1956–1957*. Vol. 1 of *The Origins of the Cultural Revolution*. New York: Columbia University Press.

———. 1983. *The Great Leap Forward, 1958–1960*. Vol. 2 of *The Origins of the Cultural Revolution*. New York: Columbia University Press.

———. 1997. *The Coming of the Cataclysm, 1961–1966*. Vol. 3 of *The Origins of the Cultural Revolution*. New York: Columbia University Press.

Mai, Ding, comp. 1984. *Chinese Folk Songs: An Anthology of 25 Favorites with Piano Accompaniment*. Beijing: New World Press.

Malysheva, Marina, and Daniel Bertaux. 1996. "The Social Experiences of a Countrywoman in Soviet Russia." In *Gender and Memory*, vol. 4 of *International Yearbook of Oral History and Life Stories*, ed. Selma Leydesdorff, Luisa Passerini, and Paul Thompson, pp. 31–44. Oxford: Oxford University Press.

Mann, Susan. 1987. "Widows in the Kinship, Class, and Community Structures of Qing Dynasty China." *Journal of Asian Studies* 46, no. 1 (Feb.): 37–56.

———. 1997. *Precious Records: Women in China's Long Eighteenth Century*. Stanford, CA: Stanford University Press.

———. 2007. *The Talented Women of the Zhang Family*. Berkeley: University of California Press.

Manning, Kimberley Ens. 2005. "Marxist Maternalism, Memory, and the Mobilization of Women in the Great Leap Forward." *China Review* 5, no. 1 (Spring): 83–110.

———. 2006a. "The Gendered Politics of Woman-Work: Rethinking Radicalism in the Great Leap Forward." *Modern China* 32, no. 3 (July): 349–84.

———. 2006b. "Making a Great Leap Forward? The Politics of Women's Liberation in Maoist China." *Gender and History* 18, no. 3 (Nov.): 574–93.

———. 2007. "Communes, Canteens, and Creches: The Gendered Politics of Remembering the Great Leap Forward." In *Re-envisioning the Chinese Revolution: The Politics and Poetics of Collective Memories in Reform China*, ed. Ching Kwan Lee and Guobin Yang, pp. 93–118. Washington, D.C., and Stanford, CA: Woodrow Wilson Center Press and Stanford University Press.

Mao Zedong [Tse-tung]. 1967. *Selected Works of Mao Tse-tung.* Vol. 3. Beijing: Foreign Languages Press.

———. 1975. *Selected Works of Mao Tse-tung.* Vol. 1. Beijing: Foreign Languages Press.

———. 1977. *Selected Works of Mao Tse-tung.* Vol. 5. Beijing: Foreign Languages Press.

Mao Zedong and Roger R. Thompson. 1990. *Report from Xunwu.* Stanford, CA: Stanford University Press.

The Marriage Law of the People's Republic of China. 1975 [1950]. Peking: Foreign Languages Press.

McLaren, Anne E. 2000. "The Grievance Rhetoric of Chinese Women: From Lamentation to Revolution." *Intersections,* no. 4 (Sept.), wwwsshe.murdoch.edu.au/intersections/issue4/mclaren.html.

———. 2008. *Performing Grief: Bridal Laments in Rural China.* Honolulu: University of Hawai'i Press.

Meijer, Marinus Johan. 1971. *Marriage Law and Policy in the Chinese People's Republic.* Hong Kong: Hong Kong University Press.

Meng Yue and Dai Jinhua. 1989. *Fuchu lishi dibiao: Xiandai funü wenxue yanjiu* [Emerging onto the Horizon of History: Research on Modern Women's Literature]. Zhengzhou: Henan renmin chubanshe.

Mitchell, Timothy. 1991. "The Limits of the State: Beyond Statist Approaches and Their Critics." *American Political Science Review* 85, no. 1 (Mar.): 77–96.

———. 1999. "Society, Economy, and the State Effect." In *State/Culture: State-Formation after the Cultural Turn,* ed. George Steinmetz, pp. 76–97. Ithaca, NY: Cornell University Press.

Model Regulations for an Agricultural Producers' Co-operative. 1956. Beijing: Foreign Languages Press.

Moïse, Edwin E. 1983. *Land Reform in China and North Vietnam: Consolidating the Revolution at the Village Level.* Chapel Hill: University of North Carolina Press.

Mueggler, Erik. 2001. *The Age Of Wild Ghosts: Memory, Violence, and Place in Southwest China.* Berkeley: University of California Press.

———. 2007. "Spectral Chains: Remembering the Great Leap Forward Famine." In *Re-envisioning the Chinese Revolution: The Politics and Poetics of Collective Memories in Reform China,* ed. Ching-Kwan Lee and Guobin Yang, pp. 50–68. Washington, D.C., and Stanford, CA: Woodrow Wilson Center Press and Stanford University Press.

Mutual Aid and Cooperation in China's Agricultural Production. 1953. Beijing: Foreign Languages Press.

Myrdal, Jan. 1967. *Report from a Chinese Village.* Trans. Maurice Michael. Harmondsworth U.K.: Penguin Books.

MZT. *Mingzheng ting* [Civil Administration Office]. 1950s–1960s. Archival materials held at the Shaanxi Provincial Archives, Xi'an, Shaanxi.

Nanzheng xian difang zhi bianji weiyuan hui. 1990. *Nanzheng xianzhi* [Nanzheng County Gazetteer]. Beijing: Zhongguo renmin gong'an daxue chubanshe.

National Women's Federation of the People's Republic of China, ed. 1960. *Women in the People's Communes.* Beijing: Foreign Languages Press.

Neibu cankao [Internal Reference]. 1949–1952. Beijing: Zhonghua she cankao xiaoxi.

Neisser, Ulric. 1988. "What Is Ordinary Memory the Memory Of?" In *Remembering Re-*

considered: Ecological and Traditional Approaches to the Study of Memory, ed. Ulric Neisser and Eugene Winograd, pp. 356–73. New York: Cambridge University Press.

———. 2000a. "John Dean's Memory." In *Memory Observed: Remembering in Natural Contexts*, 2nd ed., ed. and comp. Ulric Neisser and Ira E. Hyman Jr., pp. 263–86. New York: Worth Publishers.

———. 2000b. "Memory: What Are the Important Questions?" In *Memory Observed: Remembering in Natural Contexts*, 2nd ed., ed. and comp. Ulric Neisser and Ira E. Hyman Jr., pp. 1–17. New York: Worth Publishers.

Neisser, Ulric, and Nicole Harsch. 1992. "Phantom Flashbulbs: False Recollections of Hearing the News about *Challenger*." In *Affect and Accuracy in Recall: Studies of "Flashbulb" Memories*, ed. Eugene Winograd and Ulric Neisser, pp. 9–31. Cambridge: Cambridge University Press.

Neisser, Ulric, and Lisa K. Libby. 2000. "Remembering Life Experiences." In *The Oxford Handbook of Memory*, ed. Endel Tulving and Fergus I. M. Craik, pp. 315–32. New York: Oxford University Press.

Nichols, Francis H. 1902. *Through Hidden Shensi*. New York: Charles Scribner's Sons.

Nie, Jing-Bao. 2005. *Behind the Silence: Chinese Voices on Abortion*. Lanham, MD: Rowman and Littlefield.

Nora, Pierre. 1996. *Realms of Memory: The Construction of the French Past*. Vol. 1: *Conflicts and Divisions*. Ed. Lawrence D. Kritzman. Trans. Arthur Goldhammer. New York: Columbia University Press.

———. 1997. *Realms of Memory: The Construction of the French Past*. Vol. 2: *Traditions*. Ed. Lawrence D. Kritzman. Trans. Arthur Goldhammer. New York: Columbia University Press.

———. 1998. *Realms of Memory: The Construction of the French Past*. Vol. 3: *Symbols*. Ed. Lawrence D. Kritzman. Trans. Arthur Goldhammer. New York: Columbia University Press.

———. 2001. *Rethinking France: Les Lieux De Mémoire*. Trans. Mary Trouille. Chicago: University of Chicago Press.

"Nü zhuangyuan nü Zhuge da xian shengcai" [Women First-Ranked Scholars and Strategists Show Their Stature]. 1958 (or 1959?). Danfeng County Archives.

NYT. *Nongye ting* [Agriculture Office]. 1950s–1960s. Archival materials held at the Shaanxi Provincial Archives, Xi'an, Shaanxi.

Oakley, Ann. 1981. "Interviewing Women: A Contradiction in Terms." In *Doing Feminist Research*, ed. Helen Roberts, pp. 30–61. London: Routledge and Kegan Paul.

O'Brien, Kevin J., and Lianjiang Li. 2006. *Rightful Resistance in Rural China*. New York: Cambridge University Press.

Oi, Jean C. 1989. *State and Peasant in Contemporary China: The Political Economy of Village Government*. Berkeley: University of California Press.

———. 1999. *Rural China Takes Off: Institutional Foundations of Economic Reform*. Berkeley: University of California Press.

Osborne, Thomas. 1999. "The Ordinariness of the Archive." *History of the Human Sciences* 12, no. 2: 51–64.

Pai, Wei [Bai Wei]. 1954 (Chinese version 1950). *The Chus Reach Haven*. Trans. Yang Hsien-yi and Gladys Yang. Beijing: Foreign Languages Press.

Pang, Lihua, Alan de Brauw, and Scott Rozelle. 2004. "Working until You Drop: The Elderly of Rural China." *China Journal,* no. 52 (July): 73–94.

Passerini, Luisa. 1987. *Fascism in Popular Memory: The Cultural Experience of the Turin Working Class.* Trans. Robert Lumley and Jude Bloomfield. Cambridge: Cambridge University Press.

———. 2003. "Memories between Silence and Oblivion." In *Contested Pasts: The Politics of Memory,* ed. Katharine Hodgkin and Susannah Radstone, pp. 238–54. London: Routledge.

Pennebaker, James W. 1997. Introduction to *Collective Memory of Political Events: Social Psychological Perspectives,* ed. James W. Pennebaker, Dario Paez, and Bernard Rimé, pp. vii–xi. Mahwah, NJ: Lawrence Erlbaum.

Pennebaker, James W., and Becky L. Banasik. 1997. "On the Creation and Maintenance of Collective Memories: History as Social Psychology." In *Collective Memory of Political Events: Social Psychological Perspectives,* ed. James W. Pennebaker, Dario Paez, and Bernard Rimé, pp. 3–19. Mahwah, NJ: Lawrence Erlbaum.

Perelli, Carina. 1994. "*Memoria de Sangre:* Fear, Hope, and Disenchantment in Argentina." In *Remapping Memory: The Politics of TimeSpace,* ed. Jonathan Boyarin, pp. 39–66. Minneapolis: University of Minnesota Press.

Perry, Elizabeth J. 1994. "Trends in the Study of Chinese Politics: State-Society Relations." *China Quarterly,* no. 139 (Sept.): 704–13.

———. 2002. *Challenging the Mandate of Heaven: Social Protest and State Power in China.* Armonk, NY: M. E. Sharpe.

Phillips Johnson, Tina. 2006. "Building the Nation through Women's Health: Modern Midwifery in Early Twentieth-Century China." Ph.D. diss., University of Pittsburgh.

Pickowicz, Paul G. 1994. "Memories of Revolution and Collectivization in China: The Unauthorized Reminiscences of a Rural Intellectual." In *Memory, History, and Opposition under State Socialism,* ed. Rubie S. Watson, pp. 127–47. Santa Fe, NM: School of American Research Press.

———. 2007. "Rural Protest Letters: Local Perspectives on the State's Revolutionary War on Tillers, 1960–1990." In *Re-envisioning the Chinese Revolution: The Politics and Poetics of Collective Memories in Reform China,* ed. Ching Kwan Lee and Guobin Yang, pp. 21–49. Washington, D.C., and Stanford, CA: Woodrow Wilson Center Press and Stanford University Press.

Pillemer, David B. 1998. *Momentous Events, Vivid Memories.* Cambridge, MA: Harvard University Press.

———. 2000. "Personal Event Memories." In *Memory Observed: Remembering in Natural Contexts,* 2nd ed., ed. and comp. Ulric Neisser and Ira E. Hyman Jr., pp. 35–40. New York: Worth Publishers.

Piscitelli, Adriana. 1996. "Love and Ambition: Gender, Memory, and Stories from Brazilian Coffee Plantation Families." In *Gender and Memory,* vol. 4 of *International Yearbook of Oral History and Life Stories,* ed. Selma Leydesdorff, Luisa Passerini, and Paul Thompson, pp. 89–104. Oxford: Oxford University Press.

Pohlandt-McCormick, Helena. 2000. " 'I Saw a Nightmare': Violence and the Construction of Memory (Soweto, June 16, 1976)." *History and Theory* 39 (Dec.): 23–44.

Portelli, Alessandro. 1991. *The Death of Luigi Trastulli and Other Stories*. Albany: State University of New York Press.

———. 1997. *The Battle of Valle Giulia: Oral History and the Art of Dialogue*. Madison: University of Wisconsin Press.

———. 1998. "Oral History as Genre." In *Narrative and Genre*, ed. Mary Chamberlain and Paul Thompson, pp. 23–45. London: Routledge.

———. 2003. "The Massacre at the Fosse Ardeatine: History, Myth, Ritual and Symbol." In *Contested Pasts: The Politics of Memory*, ed. Katharine Hodgkin and Susannah Radstone, pp. 29–41. London: Routledge.

"Proposed Program of Child Health and Welfare for China." 1948. Guoji ertong jinji jijin hui guanyu Zhongguo fuyou gongzuo de gezhong jihua he youguan cailiao [Plans and Related Material about Women's and Children's Health Work in China by the International Children's Emergency Foundation]. File 372.40, Number 2 Archives [Zhongguo di er lishi dang'an guan]. Nanjing.

Qi, Xin, et al. 1979. *China's New Democracy*. Hong Kong: Cosmos Books.

Qin Hui. 2001a. "Fengjian shehui de 'Guanzhong moshi' " [The "Guanzhong Model" in Feudal Society]. In *Kongjian, jiyi, shehui zhuanxing: "Xin shehui shi" yanjiu lunwen jingxuan ji* [Space, Memory, Social Transformation: Selected Essays on "New Social History" Research], ed. Yang Nianqun, pp. 284–308. Shanghai: Shanghai renmin chubanshe.

———. 2001b. " 'Guanzhong moshi' de shehui lishi yuanyuan: Qingchu zhi minguo—Guanzhong nongcun jingji yu shehui shi yanxi" [The Historical Origins of the Social History of the "Guanzhong Model": Early Qing to Republican Period—A Study of Guanzhong Village Economic and Social History]. In *Kongjian, jiyi, shehui zhuanxing: "Xin shehui shi" yanjiu lunwen jingxuan ji* [Space, Memory, Social Transformation: Selected Essays on "New Social History" Research], ed. Yang Nianqun, pp. 309–45. Shanghai: Shanghai renmin chubanshe.

Qin Hui and Su Wen. 1996. *Tianyuan shi yu kuangxiang qu: Guanzhong moshi yu qian jindai shehui de zai renshi* [English title: Pastorals and Rhapsodies: A Research for Peasant Societies and Peasant Culture]. Beijing: Zhongyang bianyi chubanshe.

Qin Yan and Yue Long. 1997. *Zouqu fengbi: Shaanbei funü hunyin yu shengyu 1900–1949* [Leaving Enclosure: Marriage and Childbirth among Women in North Shaanxi, 1900–1949]. Xian: Shaanxi renmin chubanshe.

Qingkuang fanying [Report on the Situation]. 1964, June 26. Weinan: Zhonggong Weinan diwei bangong shi.

Qingnian chengren yong guomin changshi keben (xia) [Textbook on Common Knowledge for Citizens, for the Use of Youths and Adults. Vol. 2]. 1947. N.p.: Zhonghua pingmin jiaoyu cujin hui.

Qunzhong ribao [Masses Daily]. 1950–53. Xi'an.

Radstone, Susannah, and Katharine Hodgkin. 2003. "Regimes of Memory: An Introduction." In *Regimes of Memory*, ed. Susannah Radstone and Katharine Hodgkin, pp. 1–22. London: Routledge.

Ran Guanghai. 1995. *Zhongguo tufei* [Chinese Bandits]. Chongqing: Chongqing chubanshe.

Raphals, Lisa. 1998. *Sharing the Light: Representations of Women and Virtue in Early China*. Albany: State University of New York Press.

Renmin chubanshe, ed. 1953. *Hunyinfa tongsu jiangjie cailiao* [Popular Explanation Material on the Marriage Law]. Beijing: Renmin chubanshe.

Renmin ribao [People's Daily]. 1951–57. Beijing.

Riskin, Carl. 1998. "Seven Questions about the Chinese Famine of 1959–61." *China Economic Review* 9, no. 2 (Autumn): 111–24.

———. 2009. Commentary, Columbia Modern China Seminar. Apr. 2.

Rofel, Lisa. 1999. *Other Modernities: Gendered Yearnings in China after Socialism*. Berkeley: University of California Press.

———. 2007. *Desiring China: Experiments in Neoliberalism, Sexuality, and Public Culture.* Durham, NC: Duke University Press.

Ruf, Gregory. 1998. *Cadres and Kin: Making a Socialist Village in West China, 1921–1991.* Stanford, CA: Stanford University Press.

Rui Qiaosong. 1955. *Zuguo de da xibei* [The Motherland's Great Northwest]. Beijing: Zhonghua quanguo kexue jishu puji xiehui.

Rutz, Henry J. 1992. "The Idea of a Politics of Time." In *The Politics of Time*, ed. Henry J. Rutz, pp. 1–17. Washington, D.C.: American Anthropological Association.

Schoenhals, Michael. 1987. *Saltationist Socialism: Mao Zedong and the Great Leap Forward, 1958.* Stockholm: JINAB.

Schurmann, Franz. 1968. *Ideology and Organization in Communist China*. Berkeley: University of California Press.

Schwarcz, Vera. 1986. *The Chinese Enlightenment: Intellectuals and the Legacy of the May Fourth Movement of 1919.* Berkeley: University of California Press.

Schwarz, Bill. 2003. "'Already the Past': Memory and Historical Time." In *Regimes of Memory,* ed. Susannah Radstone and Katharine Hodgkin, pp. 135–51. London: Routledge.

Selden, Mark. 1995. *China in Revolution: The Yenan Way Revisited.* Armonk, NY: M. E. Sharpe.

Service, John S. 1974. *Lost Chance in China: The World War II Despatches of John S. Service.* Ed. Joseph W. Esherick. New York: Random House.

Seybolt, Peter J. 1996. *Throwing the Emperor from His Horse: Portrait of a Village Leader in China, 1923–1995.* Boulder, CO: Westview Press.

Shaanganning bianqu funü yundong dashi jishu [Record of Major Events in the Shaanganning Border Region Women's Movement]. 1987. N.p.: Shaanganning sanshengqu fulian.

Shaanganning bianqu funü yundong wenxian ziliao xuanbian [Selected Documentary Material on the Shaanganning Border Region Women's Movement]. 1982. N.p.: Shaanxi sheng funü lianhe hui.

Shaanganning bianqu funü yundong wenxian ziliao (xuji) [Documentary Material on the Shaanganning Border Region Women's Movement (cont.)]. 1985. N.p.: Shaanxi sheng funü lianhe hui.

Shaanxi funü yundong (1919–1937) [The Shaanxi Women's Movement (1919–1937)]. 1996. N.p.: Shaanxi renmin chubanshe.

Shaanxi ribao [Shaanxi Daily]. 1950s. Xi'an.

"Shaanxi sheng 1950 nian fuying weisheng diaocha zongjie" [Summary of an Investigation of Women's and Children's Health in Shaanxi Province in 1950]. 1950. Minzheng ting [Civil Administration] files, Shaanxi Provincial Archives, Xi'an.

"Shaanxi sheng 51 nian fuyou weisheng cailiao" [Material on Women's and Children's Health in Shaanxi Province, 1951]. 1951. Women's Federation Archives, Shaanxi Provincial Archives, Xi'an.

Shaanxi sheng Danfeng xian jiaotong ju, ed. 1990. *Danfeng jiaotong zhi* [Danfeng Transportation Gazetteer]. Shaanxi: Shaanxi sheng Danfeng xian jiaotong ju.

Shaanxi sheng Danfeng xian shuili zhi bianzuan zu, ed. 1990. *Danfeng Xian shuili zhi* [Gazetteer of Water Conservancy in Danfeng County]. Shaanxi difang zhi shuili zhi congshu [Shaanxi Local Gazetteer Water Conservancy Series]. Danfeng xian: Danfeng xian shuidian shui tu baochi ju.

Shaanxi sheng ditu ce [Mapbook of Shaanxi Province]. 1991. Xi'an: Xi'an ditu chubanshe.

Shaanxi sheng fulian bangong shi, ed. 1954. *Shaanxi sheng jiceng xuanju zhong funü gongzuo zongjie* [Summary of Womanwork during the Basic-Level Elections in Shaanxi Province]. Women's Federation Xibei sheng fulian bangong shi, Aug.

Shaanxi sheng fulian fuli bu. 1954. *Fuying weisheng gongzuo jingyan jieshao* [Introduction to the Experience of Work on Women's and Children's Health]. N.p.: N.p., Sept. Women's Federation Archives, Shaanxi Provincial Archives, Xi'an.

Shaanxi sheng funü lianhe hui, ed. 1994. *Shaanxi funü yundong 40 nian dashi ji 1949–1989.* [Major Events in the Past 40 Years of the Shaanxi Women's Movement, 1949–1989]. Xi'an: Shaanxi sheng funü lianhe hui.

Shaanxi sheng hunyin wenti xuanchuan diaocha zu [Shaanxi Provincial Marriage Problems Propaganda and Investigation Group]. 1952a. "Weinan xian dier qu Yin cun xiang hunyin wenti xuanchuan diaocha gongzuo zongjie baogao" [Summary Report of Propaganda and Investigative Work on Marriage Problems in Yin Village and Township, District 2, Weinan County]. May 26. Ms. no. 213. Weinan County Archives.

———. 1952b. "Weinan xian Xinyi qu de liu xiang gongzuo zongjie [Work Summary for Sixth Township, Xinyi District, Weinan County]. Report (handwritten), Apr. 1. Weinan County Archives.

Shaanxi sheng minzheng ting. 1940. *Shaanxi sheng zhengli baojia zong baogao* [General Report on the Reorganization of the Baojia System in Shaanxi Province]. Shaanxi sheng: Minzheng ting.

Shaanxi sheng minzhu fulian hui (ed.). 1952. *Funü gongzuo jianxun* [Women's Work Newsletter], nos. 13–18.

Shaanxi sheng minzhu funü lianhe hui (ed.). 1956. *Shaanxi sheng funü miantian guanli jingyan jiaoliu dahui zhuanji* [Special Collection on the Shaanxi Province Women's Meeting to Exchange Experiences of Cotton Field Management]. N.p. [Xian]: Shaanxi sheng minzhu funü lianhe hui, May.

Shaanxi sheng minzhu funü lianhe hui xuanchuan bu (ed.). 1957. *Nongcun funü de hao bangyang* [Good Models for Village Women]. Xi'an: Shaanxi renmin chubanshe, May.

Shaanxi sheng nonglin ting (ed.). 1958. *Jiuyuan nüjiang wumian liqi gong: Weinan xian Shuangwang xiang Bali dian she Zhang Qiuxiang wumian xiaozu jingyan* [The Immediate Outstanding Service of Nine Women Commanders Growing Cotton: The Experience of Zhang Qiuxiang's Cotton Growing Group in Bali dian Collective, Shuang Wang Township, Weinan County]. Xi'an: Shaanxi renmin chubanshe, April.

Shaanxi sheng nongye hezuo shi bianwei hui bian. 1993. *Shaanxi sheng nongye hezuo zhong-*

yao wenxian xuanbian [Selected Compilation of Documents on Shaanxi Province Agricultural Cooperatives]. In *Shaanxi sheng nongye hezuozhi shiliao congshu* [Collection of Historical Materials on the Agricultural Cooperative System in Shaanxi Province]. Xi'an: Shaanxi renmin chubanshe.

———. 1994. *Shaanxi sheng nongye hezuo dianxing cailiao xuanbian* [Selected Compilation of Representative Materials on Shaanxi Province Agricultural Cooperatives]. *Shaanxi sheng nongye hezuozhi shiliao congshu* [Collection of Historical Materials on the Agricultural Cooperative System in Shaanxi Province]. Xi'an: Shaanxi renmin chubanshe.

Shaanxi sheng nongye zhanlan hui (ed.). 1958. *Mianhua fengchan yimian hongqi: Weinan xian Zhang Qiuxiang zhimian xiaozu* [A Red Flag in the Cotton Bumper Crop: Zhang Qiuxiang's Cotton Growing Group in Weinan County]. N.p.: N.p., Nov. Women's Federation Archives, Shaanxi Provincial Archives, Xi'an.

"Shaanxi sheng weisheng chu gongzuo baogao" [Work Report of the Shaanxi Provincial Department of Health]. 1946. In *Guanyu Shaanxi, Gansu, Qinghai weisheng chu, Xibei yiyuan, Zhongshi yuan Sibei fenyuan zai quanguo weisheng huiyi shang tigong de gongzuo baogao cailiao* [Work Report Material Supplied to the National Health Congress by the Health Departments of Shaanxi, Gansu, and Qinghai, and the Xibei Hospital and Xibei Branch of the Zhongshi Hospital]. File 372.19, Number 2 Archives [Zhongguo di er lishi dang'an guan]. Nanjing.

Shaanxi sheng weisheng ting. 1957. "Guanyu jiji kaizhan biyun gongzuo de tongzhi" [Communiqué on Actively Developing Birth Control Work]. Weinan County Archives.

Shaanxi shida dili xi "Weinan diqu dili zhi" bianxie zu, ed. 1990. *Shaanxi sheng Weinan diqu dili zhi* [Geography Gazetteer for Weinan District, Shaanxi Province]. Xi'an: Shaanxi renmin chubanshe.

Shan Xiuzhen, guangrong de wuchan jieji zhanshi: jiceng funü ganbu xuexi ziliao [Shan Xiuzhen, Glorious Proletarian Fighter: Study Material for Grassroots Women's Cadres]. 1962. Pamphlet. N.p.: Shaanxi Fulian ying, Jan. 27. Women's Federation Archives 178–313–001 Shaanxi Provincial Archives, Xi'an.

Shanghai shi minzhu funü lianhe hui xuanjiao bu, ed. 1951. *Funü gongzuo shouce* [Handbook for Women-Work]. Shanghai: Xinhua shudian Huadong zongfen dian.

"Shangzhen zhen Shangshan she mofan danwei cailiao" [Individual Material on the Model Unit of Shangzhen Township, Shangshan Commune]. 1958. Danfeng County Archives.

Shen, Tsung-han. 1977. "Food Production and Distribution for Civilian and Military Needs in Wartime China, 1937–1945." In *Nationalist China During the Sino-Japanese War, 1937–45*, ed. Paul K. T. Sih, pp. 167–201. Hicksville, NY: Exposition Press.

"Shi Duozi." 1953. Danfeng County Archives.

Shi kan she [Poetry Magazine], ed. 1958a. *Da yuejin minge xuan yibai shou* [Selection of 100 Folk Songs from the Great Leap Forward]. Vol. 1 of *Xin minge bai shou* [One Hundred New Folk Songs]. Beijing: Zhongguo qingnian chubanshe.

———, ed. 1958b. *Xin minge bai shou* [One Hundred New Folk Songs], vol. 2. Beijing: Zhongguo qingnian chubanshe.

———, ed. 1959. *Xin minge bai shou* [One Hundred New Folk Songs], vol. 3. Beijing: Zhongguo qingnian chubanshe.

Shi Yaozeng. 1999. *Heyang fengqing* [Heyang Customs]. Xian: Shaanxi lüyou chubanshe.

Shue, Vivienne. 1980. *Peasant China in Transition: The Dynamics of Development toward Socialism, 1949–1956.* Berkeley: University of California Press.

———. 1988. *The Reach of the State: Sketches of the Chinese Body Politic.* Stanford, CA: Stanford University Press.

———. 1990. "Emerging State-Society Relations in Rural China." In *Remaking Peasant China: Problems of Rural Development and Institutions at the Start of the 1990s,* ed. Jørgen Delman, Clemens Stubbe Østeraard, and Flemming Christiansen, pp. 60–80. Aarhus, Denmark: Aarhus University Press.

Singer, Wendy. 1997. *Creating Histories: Oral Narratives and the Politics of History-Making.* Delhi: Oxford University Press.

Skultans, Vieda. 1998. *The Testimony of Lives: Narrative and Memory in Post-Soviet Latvia.* London: Routledge.

Smith, Arthur H. 1894. *Chinese Characteristics.* New York: Fleming H. Revell.

Smith, S[tephen]. A. 2006. "Talking Toads and Chinese Ghosts: The Politics of 'Superstitious' Rumors in the People's Republic of China, 1961–1965." *American Historical Review* 111, no. 2 (Apr.): 405–27.

Solinger, Dorothy J. 1984. *Chinese Business under Socialism: The Politics of Domestic Commerce, 1949–1980.* Berkeley: University of California Press.

Sommer, Matthew H. 2005. "Making Sex Work: Polyandry as a Survival Strategy in Qing Dynasty China." In *Gender in Motion,* ed. Bryna Goodman and Wendy Larson, pp. 29–54. Lanham, MD: Rowman and Littlefield.

St. Clair, David, Xu Mingqing, Wang Peng, Yu Yaqin, Fang Yourong, Zheng Feng, Zheng Xiaoying, Gu Niufan, Feng Guoyin, Sham Pak, and He Lin. 2005. "Rates of Adult Schizophrenia Following Prenatal Exposure to the Chinese Famine of 1959–1961." *Journal of the American Medical Association* 294, no. 5 (Aug.): 557–62.

Stacey, Judith. 1983. *Patriarchy and Socialist Revolution in China.* Berkeley: University of California Press.

Stafford, Charles. 2000. *Separation and Reunion in Modern China.* Cambridge: Cambridge University Press.

Steedman, Carolyn. 1998. "The Space of Memory: In an Archive." *History of the Human Sciences* 11, no. 4: 65–83.

———. 2002. *Dust: The Archive and Cultural History.* New Brunswick, NJ: Rutgers University Press.

Stoler, Ann Laura, with Karen Strassler. 2002. "Memory-Work in Java: A Cautionary Tale." In Ann Laura Stoler, *Carnal Knowledge and Imperial Power: Race and the Intimate in Colonial Rule,* pp. 162–203. Berkeley: University of California Press.

Stranahan, Patricia. 1983a. "Labor Heroines of Yan'an." *Modern China* 9, no. 2 (Apr.): 228–52.

———. 1983b. *Yan'an Women and the Communist Party.* Berkeley: Institute of East Asian Studies, University of California, Berkeley.

Sun Deshan and Wu Yan. 1982. *Sheyuan jiating fuye he jishi maoyi* [Commune Members' Household Sidelines and Trade and Periodic Markets]. Beijing: Nongye chubanshe.

Tai, Hue-Tam Ho, ed. 2001a. *The Country of Memory: Remaking the Past in Late Socialist Vietnam.* Berkeley: University of California Press.

————. 2001b. "Faces of Remembrance and Forgetting." In *The Country of Memory: Remaking the Past in Late Socialist Vietnam*, ed. Hue-Tam Ho Tai, pp. 167–95. Berkeley: University of California Press.

Teichman, Eric. 1921. *Travels of a Consular Officer in North-West China: With Original Maps of Shensi and Kansu and Illustrated by Photographs Taken by the Author.* Cambridge: Cambridge University Press.

Teiwes, Frederick C., with Warren Sun. 1999. *China's Road to Disaster: Mao, Central Politicians, and Provincial Leaders in the Unfolding of the Great Leap Forward 1955–1959.* Armonk, NY: M. E. Sharpe.

Thaxton, Ralph A., Jr. 1997. *Salt of the Earth: The Political Origins of Peasant Protest and Communist Revolution in China.* Berkeley: University of California Press.

————. 2008. *Catastrophe and Contention in Rural China: Mao's Great Leap Forward Famine and the Origins of Righteous Resistance in Da Fo Village.* Cambridge Studies in Contentious Politics. Cambridge: Cambridge University Press.

Tian He. 1999. *Hongse ren sheng: Laomo Shen Jilan* [The Life of a Red (Revolutionary): Labor Model Shen Jilan]. Taiyuan: Shanxi jiaoyu chubanshe.

Tian Xiquan. 2006. *Geming yu xiangcun: Guojia, sheng, xian yu liangshi tonggou tongxiao zhidu, 1953–1957* [Revolution and the Countryside: Nation, Province, County, and the System of Unified Purchase and Sale of Grain, 1953–1957]. Shanghai: Shanghai shehui kexue yuan chubanshe.

Tongguan juan [Tongguan Volume]. 1997. Zhongguo guoqing congshu—bai xian shi jingji shehui diaocha [Series on China's National Situation—Economic and Social Investigation of 100 Counties and Cities]. Beijing: Zhongguo da baike quanshu chubanshe.

Tongguan xianzhi bianzuan weiyuan hui. 1992. *Tongguan xianzhi* [Tongguan County Gazetteer]. Shaanxi sheng difang zhi congshu. Xi'an: Shaanxi renmin chubanshe.

Tonkin, Elizabeth. 1992. *Narrating Our Pasts: The Social Construction of Oral History.* Cambridge: Cambridge University Press.

Van de Ven, Hans J. 2003. *War and Nationalism in China, 1925–1945.* London: Routledge Curzon.

Vansina, Jan. 1965. *Oral Tradition: A Study in Historical Methodology.* Trans. H. M. Wright. Chicago: Aldine. [French edition 1961].

————. 1985. *Oral Tradition as History.* Madison: University of Wisconsin Press.

Verdery, Katherine. 1992. "The 'Etatization' of Time in Ceausescu's Romania." In *The Politics of Time*, ed. Henry J. Rutz, pp. 37–61. Washington, D.C.: American Anthropological Association.

Vermeer, Eduard. 1981. "Population and Agriculture in Guanzhong [Kuan-chung], 1935–1980." In *Leyden Studies in Sinology: Papers Presented at the Conference Held in Celebration of the Fiftieth Anniversary of the Sinological Institute of Leyden University, December 8–12, 1980*, ed. W. L. Idema, pp. 214–34. Leiden, Netherlands: Brill.

————. 1988. *Economic Development in Provincial China: The Central Shaanxi since 1930.* Cambridge: Cambridge University Press.

Village B briefing. 1996. Aug. 6. Current village leaders. Author's notes.

Village G briefing. 2001. Mar. 23. Party secretary and officials of the Senior Citizens Association. Author's notes.

Village T briefing. 1997. July 3. Current and former Party secretaries, township cadres, former village women's chairs, county Women's Federation representatives. Author's notes.

Village Z briefing. 1999. July 25. Township and village heads. Author's notes.

Visweswaran, Kamala. 1994. *Fictions of Feminist Ethnography*. Minneapolis: University of Minnesota Press.

Vogel, Ezra F. 1971. *Canton under Communism: Programs and Politics in a Provincial Capital, 1949–1968*. New York: Harper and Row.

Wakefield, David. 1998. *Fenjia: Household Division and Inheritance in Qing and Republican China*. Honolulu: University of Hawai'i Press.

Walker, Kathy Le Mons. 1993. "Economic Growth, Peasant Marginalization, and the Sexual Division of Labor in Early Twentieth-Century China." *Modern China* 19, no. 3 (July): 354–86.

———. 1999. *Chinese Modernity and the Peasant Path: Semicolonialism in the Northern Yangzi Delta*. Stanford, CA: Stanford University Press.

Wang, Joseph En-pao. 1976. *Selected Legal Documents of the People's Republic of China*. Arlington, VA: University Press of America.

Wang, Ximing. 2009. "Seniors' Organizations in China's New Rural Reconstruction: Experiments in Hubei and Henan." Trans. Matthew A. Hale. *Inter-Asia Cultural Studies* 10, no. 1: 138–53.

Wang, Zheng. 2006. "Dilemmas of Inside Agitators: Chinese State Feminists in 1957." *China Quarterly* 188 (Dec.): 913–32.

Wang Chengjing. 1950. *Xibei de nongtian shuili* [Irrigation and Water Conservancy in the Northwest]. Shanghai: Zhonghua shuju.

Wang Deyi. 1949. *Zhuchan changshi* [Elementary Knowledge of Midwifery]. Dalian: Dazhong shudian.

Wang Gengjin, Yang Xun, Wang Ziping, Liang Xiaodong, and Yang Guansan. 1989. *Xiangcun sanshi nian: Fengyang nongcun shehui jingji fazhan shilu (1949–1983 nian)* [Thirty Years in the Countryside: A Faithful Record of the Development of the Social Economy in the Villages of Fengyang, 1949–1983]. Beijing: Nongcun duwu chubanshe.

Wang Guohong. 1993. Personal interviews, Liquan, Wugong, and Xingping Counties, Shaanxi Province. Unpublished interview transcripts.

Wang Li. 1959. "Weinan xian funü lianhe hui xiang funü di wujie daibiao dahui de gongzuo baogao" [Weinan County Women's Federation Work Report to the Fifth Representative Congress of Women]. Weinan County Archives.

Wang Ruifang. 2005. "Chen Yun yu liangshi tonggou tongxiao" [Chen Yun and the Unified Purchase and Sale of Grain]. *Zhongguo jingji shi luntan* [China Economic History Forum], no. 4 (28 Oct.), http://economy.guoxue.com/article.php/6770.

Wang Xingjian, ed. and comp. 1968 [1794]. *Nanzheng xianzhi* [Nanzheng County Gazetteer]. Taipei: Taiwan xuesheng shuju.

Weigelin-Schwiedrzik, Susanne. 2003. "Trauma and Memory: The Case of the Great Famine in the People's Republic of China (1959–1961)." *Historiography East and West* 1, no. 1: 1–67.

Weinan diqu difang zhi bianji weiyuan hui. 1996. *Weinan diqu zhi* [Gazetteer of Weinan District]. Shaanxi difang zhi congshu [Shaanxi Gazetteer Series]. Xi'an: Sanqin chubanshe.

Weinan diqu nongye hezuo shi bianwei hui bian [Editorial Committee on the History of Agricultural Cooperation in Weinan District]. Li Xiyuan, chair. 1993. *Weinan diqu nongye hezuo shiliao* [Historical Material on Agricultural Cooperation in Weinan District]. Xi'an: Shaanxi renmin chubanshe.

Weinan ribao [Weinan Daily]. Weinan.

"Weinan xian 1957 nian fuxun jiesheng yuan gongzuo jihua" [Plans for the Work of Retraining Midwives in Weinan County in 1957]. 1956. Weinan County Archives.

"Weinan xian Baiyang gongshe Hongxing shengchan dadui dang zhibu shuji Cao Zhuxiang mofan shiji danxing cailiao" [Individual Material on the Model Activities of Party Branch Secretary Cao Zhuxiang, Red Star Production Brigade, Baiyang Commune, Weinan County]. 1962. Records of Village B, Weinan.

Weinan xian funü lianhe hui. 1956. "Weinan xian Fulian guanyu xunlian tuoer huzhu gugan de qingkuang zongjie baogao" [Weinan County Women's Federation Summary Report on the Circumstances of Training Childcare Mutual Aid Backbone Cadres]. May 25. Weinan County Archives.

Weinan xian guanche hunyinfa yundong weiyuan hui [Weinan County Committee on the Campaign to Carry Out the Marriage Law]. 1953a. "Weinan xian guanche hunyinfa yundong" [Weinan County Movment to Carry Out the Marriage Law]. Weinan County Archives.

———. 1953b. "Weinan xian guanche hunyinfa yundong shouci baogao" [Initial Report on the Movement to Carry Out the Marriage Law in Weinan County]. Weinan County Archives.

———. 1953c. "Weinan xian guanche hunyinfa yundong erci baogao" [Second Report on the Movement to Carry Out the Marriage Law in Weinan County]. Weinan County Archives.

———. 1953d. "Weinan xian guanche hunyinfa yundong zongjie" [Summary Report on the Movement to Carry Out the Marriage Law in Weinan County]. Weinan County Archives.

Weinan xian minzhu funü lianhe hui. 1952a. "Weinan xian diwu qu liu xiang Cao Zhuxiang pingwei xian mianhua fengchan hu danxing cailiao" [Individual Material on Cao Zhuxiang of the Sixth Township, Fifth District, Weinan County, Being Chosen as a Bumper Cotton Crop Household]. 178-27-026. Women's Federation Archives, Shaanxi Provincial Archives, Xi'an.

———. 1952b. "Weinan xian diyi jie funü daibiao da hui zongjie baogao" [Summary Report of the First Representative Congress of Weinan County Women]. Weinan County Archives.

———. 1958. "Weinan xian 1957 nian funü gongzuo zongjie baogao" [Weinan County Summary Report on Women-Work in 1957]. Feb. 11. Weinan County Archives.

Weinan xian renmin weiyuan hui. 1956. "Guanyu gei nongyeshe xunlian weisheng yuan he jiesheng yuan de tongzhi" [Communiqué on Training Health Personnel and Midwives for the Agricultural Collectives]. Nov. 26. Weinan County Archives.

———. 1957. "1957 nian 1 zhi 6 yue fen fuyou weisheng gongzuo jihua" [Plan of Women's and Children's Health Work, January–June 1957]. Report (handwritten). Weinan County Archives.

Weinan xian [Weinan County]. *Weinan xian dang'an guan* [Weinan County Archives]. Weinan, Shaanxi.

Weinan xianzhi bianji weiyuan hui. 1987. *Weinan xianzhi* [Weinan County Gazetteer]. Shaanxi: Sanqin chubanshe.

Weisheng xuanchuan gongzuo [Hygiene Propaganda Work]. 1951–52. Beijing: Zhongyang renmin zhengfu weisheng bu weisheng xuanchuan chu.

Wemheuer, Felix. 2009. "Regime Changes of Memory: Creating the Official History of the Ukrainian and Chinese Famines under State Socialism and after the Cold War." *Kritika: Explorations in Russian and Eurasian History* 10, no. 1 (Winter): 31–59.

Wen Tiejun. 1999. "'Sannong wenti': Shiji mo de fansi" [Reflections at Century's End on the "Threefold Problem of the Rural Areas"]. *Dushu*, no. 12 (Dec.): 3–11.

———. 2000. *Zhongguo nongcun jiben jingji zhidu yanjiu: "Sannong" wenti de shiji fansi* [Research on the Basic Economic System of China's Rural Areas: Centenary Reflections on the "Threefold Problem of the Rural Areas"]. Beijing: Zhongguo jingji chubanshe.

———. 2001. "Centenary Reflections on the 'Three Dimensional Problem' of Rural China." Trans. Petrus Liu. *Inter-Asia Cultural Studies* 2, no. 2: 287–95.

Wen Xianmei, ed. 1987. *Chuan Shaan geming genjudi luncong* [Collected Essays on the Sichuan-Shaanxi Revolutionary Base Area]. Chengdu: Sichuan daxue chubanshe.

Wertsch, James V. 2002. *Voices of Collective Remembering.* Cambridge: Cambridge University Press.

Westad, Odd Arne. 2003. *Decisive Encounters: The Chinese Civil War, 1946–1950.* Stanford, CA: Stanford University Press.

White, Luise. 2000a. *Speaking with Vampires: Rumor and History in Colonial Africa.* Berkeley: University of California Press.

———. 2000b. "Telling More: Lies, Secrets, and History." *History and Theory* 39 (Dec.): 11–22.

———. 2004. "True Confessions." *Journal of Women's History* 15, no. 4 (Winter): 142–44.

White, Luise, Stephan F. Miescher, and David William Cohen, eds. 2001. *African Words, African Voices: Critical Practices in Oral History.* Bloomington: Indiana University Press.

White, Richard. 1998. *Remembering Ahanagran: Storytelling in a Family's Past.* New York: Hill and Wang.

White, Tyrene. 1994. "The Origins of China's Birth Planning Policy." In *Engendering China: Women, Culture, and the State*, ed. Christina K. Gilmartin, Gail Hershatter, Lisa Rofel, and Tyrene White, pp. 250–78. Cambridge, MA: Harvard University Press.

———. 2006. *China's Longest Campaign: Birth Planning in the People's Republic, 1949–2005.* Ithaca, NY: Cornell University Press.

Whyte, Martin King. 1997. "The Fate of Filial Obligations in Urban China." *China Journal*, no. 38 (July): 1–31.

Wolf, Margery. 1972. *Women and the Family in Rural Taiwan.* Stanford, CA: Stanford University Press.

———. 1975. "Women and Suicide in China." In *Women in Chinese Society*, ed. Margery Wolf and Roxane Witke, pp. 111–41. Stanford, CA: Stanford University Press.

———. 1985. *Revolution Postponed: Women in Contemporary China.* Stanford, CA: Stanford University Press.

Wu, Yi-Li. 2002. "Ghost Fetuses, False Pregnancies, and the Parameters of Medical Uncertainty in Classical Chinese Gynecology." *Nan Nü* 4, no. 2: 170–206.

———. 2010. *Reproducing Women: Medicine, Metaphor, and Childbirth in Late Imperial China*. Berkeley: University of California Press.

Wu Wen. 1995. *Yong bu banjie de huang tudi—Qinlong wenhua lun* [Yellow Earth That Never Hardens: On the Culture of Qinlong]. Beijing: Renmin chubanshe.

"Wu yi she funü jiti mofan danxing cailiao" [Individual Material on the Model Women's Collective from May First Commune]. 1958. Sept. 15. Danfeng County Archives.

Xi Jianfang [oral history]. 1988. "Da dizhu" [Strike the Landlords]. *Heyang wenshi ziliao* 2 (Oct.): 46.

Xia Mingfang. 2000. *Minguo shiqi ziran zaihai yu xiangcun shehui* [Republican-era Natural Disasters and Village Society]. Beijing: Zhonghua shuju.

Xiang Hui and Wang Senwen, eds. and comps. 1969. *Xu Tongguan xianzhi* [Continuation of Tongguan Gazetteer]. Taipei: Chengwen chubanshe.

"Xianyang xian Weibin xiang yinian lai fuyou weisheng gongzuo qingkuang [Conditions of Women's and Children's Health Work in the Past Year in Xianyang County, Weibin Township]. 1956. 178-153-081. Women's Federation Archives, Shaanxi Provincial Archives, Xi'an.

Xibei funü huabao [Northwest Women's Pictorial]. 1953–56 Xi'an Xibei minzhu funü lianhe hui shengchan bu, ed. 1952. *Xibei funü shengchan jianxun* [News in Brief on Production by Women in the Northwest], no. 6, Nov. Xibei minzhu funü lianhe hui shengchan bu.

Xibei minzhu funü lianhe hui xuanchuan bu, ed. 1952. *Yinian lai Xibei funü zai kang Mei yuan Chao zhong de huodong* [The Activities of Northwest Women During the Past Year in Resisting America and Aiding Korea]. Feb. Xibei minzhu funü lianhe hui shengchan bu.

Xibei xiangdao [Guide to the Northwest]. 1936. June-Dec. Xi'an Xie Chuntao. 1990. *Da yuejin kuanglan* [Raging Waves of the Great Leap Forward]. Henan: Henan renmin chubanshe.

Xin Zhongguo funü [Women of New China]. 1949–55. Beijing.

Xingzheng yuan nongcun fuxing weiyuan hui [Rural Rehabilitation Committee of the Executive Yuan], ed. 1934. *Shaanxi sheng nongcun diaocha* [Investigation of Shaanxi Rural Areas]. Shanghai: Shangwu yinshu guan.

Xinjiang sheng minzhu funü lianhe hui, ed. 1953. *Funü canjia shengchan wawa zenmaban* [What to Do with the Children When Women Join in Production]. May. Dihua: Xinjiang renmin chubanshe.

Xiong Jingming, ed. 2000. *Jinru 21 shiji de Zhongguo nongcun* [English title: Come into Chinese Country of Twenty-one Century]. Beijing: Guangming ribao chubanshe.

Xu Haidong. 1982. *Shengping zishu* [My Life in My Own Words]. Beijing: Shenghuo dushu xinzhi sanlian shudian.

Xu Xiuli. 2006. "20 shiji 30 niandai de xiangcun gongwu renyuan—jianzhiyu nongcun fuxing weiyuan hui de diaocha" [Government Functionaries in the Countryside in the 1930s, as Seen from the Investigations of the Village Revitalization Committee]. In *Jindai Zhongguo de chengshi yu xiangcun* [City and Country in Modern China], ed. Li Changli and Zuo Yuhe, pp. 263–306. Beijing: Shehui kexue wenxian chubanshe.

Yan, Hairong. 2003. "Spectralization of the Rural: Reinterpreting the Labor Mobility of Rural Young Women in Post-Mao China." *American Ethnologist* 30, no. 4 (Nov.): 578–96.

Yan, Yunxiang. 1996. *The Flow of Gifts: Reciprocity and Social Networks in a Chinese Village*. Stanford, CA: Stanford University Press.

———. 2003. *Private Life under Socialism: Love, Intimacy, and Family Change in a Chinese Village, 1949–1999.* Stanford, CA: Stanford University Press.

Yan Shulin and Jiao Lianjia, eds. and comps. 1969. *Xinxu Weinan xianzhi* [New Continuation of Weinan Gazetteer]. 3 vols. Taipei: Chengwen chubanshe.

Yang, C. K. 1969. *Chinese Communist Society: The Family and the Village.* Cambridge, MA: MIT Press.

Yang, Dali L. 1996. *Calamity and Reform in China: State, Rural Society, and Institutional Change since the Great Leap Famine.* Stanford, CA: Stanford University Press.

———. 1997. "Surviving the Great Leap Famine: The Struggle over Rural Policy, 1958–1962." In *New Perspectives on State Socialism in China,* ed. Timothy Cheek and Tony Saich, pp. 262–302. Armonk, NY: M. E. Sharpe.

Yang, Dali L., and Fubing Su. 1998. "The Politics of Famine and Reform in Rural China." *China Economic Review* 9, no. 2: 141–55.

Yang, Marion. 1928. "Midwifery Training in China." *China Medical Journal* 42: 768–75.

———. 1930. "Control of Practicing Midwives in China." *China Medical Journal* 44, no. 5: 428–31.

Yang Duanben, ed. and comp. 1967 [1685, rep. 1931]. *Tongguan xianzhi* [Tongguan Gazetteer]. Taipei: Chengwen chubanshe.

Yang Nianqun. 2006. *Zaizao "bingren": Zhong xi yi chongtu xia de kongjian zhengzhi (1832–1985)* [Remaking "Patients": Spatial Politics in the Conflict between Chinese and Western Medicine, 1832–1985]. Beijing: Zhongguo renmin daxue chubanshe.

"Yang zhu nengshou Liu Xianzhen cailiao" [Material on Pig-Raising Expert Liu Xianzhen]. N.d. Danfeng County Archives.

Ye Jingzhong and He Congzhi. 2008. *Jingmo xiyang: Zhongguo nongcun liushou laoren* [English title: Lonely Sunsets: Old People Left Behind in Rural China]. Beijing: Shehui kexue wenxian chubanshe.

Ye Jingzhong and Wu Huifang. 2008. *Qianmo duwu: Zhongguo nongcun liushou funü* [English title: Dancing Solo: Women Left Behind in Rural China]. Beijing: Shehui kexue wenxian chubanshe.

Yip, Ka-che. 1995. *Health and National Reconstruction in Nationalist China: The Development of Modern Health Services, 1928–1937.* Ann Arbor, MI: Association for Asian Studies.

Yoneyama, Lisa. 1994. "Taming the Memoryscape: Hiroshima's Urban Renewal." In *Remapping Memory: The Politics of TimeSpace,* ed. Jonathan Boyarin, pp. 99–134. Minneapolis: University of Minnesota Press.

Yu, Hua. 1996. *The Past and the Punishments.* Trans. Andrew F. Jones. Honolulu: University of Hawaii.

Yu Xiguang, ed. 2005. *Da yuejin, ku rizi shang shu ji* [Great Leap Forward, Days of Privation: Collection of Statements Submitted to the Higher Authorities]. Xianggang: Shidai chaoliu chubanshe.

Zeitlin, Judith. 2007. *The Phantom Heroine: Ghosts and Gender in Seventeenth-Century Chinese Literature.* Honolulu: University of Hawai'i Press.

Zhang, Naihua. 1996. "The All-China Women's Federation, Chinese Women and the Women's Movement, 1949–1993." Ph.D. diss., Michigan State University.

Zhang Jianzhong, ed. 2000a. *Guanzhong. Shaanxi minsu caifeng* [Collecting Folk Customs of Shaanxi: Guanzhong]. Vol. 1. Xi'an: Xi'an ditu chubanshe.

———, ed. 2000b. *Shaannan, Shaanbei. Shaanxi minsu caifeng* [Collecting Folk Customs of Shaanxi: Shaannan, Shaanbei]. Vol. 2. Xi'an: Xi'an ditu chubanshe.

Zhang Lin. 1982. *Xu Haidong jiangjun zhuan* [Biography of General Xu Haidong]. Beijing: Jiefang jun wenyi chubanshe.

Zhang Ruyun, Zhang Ziqian, and Zhao Guoxi. 1992. "Dang zhengjiu he peiyang le wo: Fang quanguo laomo Shan Xiuzhen tongzhi" [The Party Saved and Trained Me: An Interview with National Labor Model Comrade Shan Xiuzhen]. *Tongguan wenshi ziliao,* no. 6 (June): 12–31.

Zhang Shao. 1997. *Xijiang miaozu funü koushushi yanjiu* [A Study of Oral Histories of Miao Women from West River]. Guiyang: Guozhou renmin chubanshe.

Zhang Tie. 1982. "Huiyi dongfu wugong dui de chengli he Heyang deng xian youjidui de geming huodong" [Remembering the Founding of the Armed Worker Corps of Dongfu and the Revolutionary Activities of the Guerrilla Corps in Heyang and Other Counties]. *Shaanxi wenshi ziliao* 13 (July): 36–48.

Zhonggong Heyang xianwei zuzhi bu. 2000. *Zhongguo gongchandang Shaanxi sheng Heyang xian zuzhi shi ziliao* [Historical Materials on the Organization of the CCP in Heyang County, Shaanxi]. Vol. 2. 1987.11–1993.5. Xi'an: Shaanxi renmin chubanshe.

Zhonggong Shaanxi shengwei. 1958. "Zhonggong Shaanxi shengwei guanyu zuohao mianhua bozhong he tuiguang Zhang Qiuxiang zhimian jingyan de zhishi" [Directive by the Shaanxi Provincial Committee of the CCP on Doing a Good Job of Sowing Cotton Seeds and Promoting the Cotton-Growing Experience of Zhang Qiuxiang]. Mar. 25. 178–27-012. Women's Federation Archives, Shaanxi Provincial Archives, Xi'an.

Zhonggong Shaanxi shengwei bangong ting bian, ed. 1956. *Shaanxi nongcun de shehuizhuyi jianshe* [Socialist Construction in Shaanxi Villages]. Vol. 1. Xi'an: Shaanxi renmin chubanshe.

Zhonggong Tongguan xianwei dangshi yanjiu shi. 2001. *Zhongguo gongchandang Tongguan xian lishi dashiji (1919.5–2000.12)* [Major Events in the History of the CCP in Tongguan County (1919.5–2000.12)]. Xi'an: Shaanxi renmin chubanshe.

Zhonggong Weinan xianwei bianzhu xiaozu, ed. 1959a. *"Huangmao nüzi" fangchu le "mianhua weixing"* ["Silly Girls" Launch a "Cotton Satellite"]. May. Xi'an: Shaanxi renmin chubanshe.

———. 1959b. *Women ganshangle Zhang Qiuxiang* [We Caught Up with Zhang Qiuxiang]. May. Xi'an: Shaanxi renmin chubanshe.

Zhonggong zhongyang bangong ting, ed. 1956. *Zhongguo nongcun de shehui zhuyi gaochao* [The High Tide of Socialism in the Chinese Countryside]. 3 vols. Beijing: Renmin chubanshe.

Zhongguo funü [Women of China]. 1956–58. Beijing: Zhongguo funüshe.

Zhongguo gongchandang Danfeng xian Zhulinguan qu weiyuan hui. 1956. "Danfeng xian Zhulinguan qu fenhui Tang Qiufang danxing cailiao danxing cailiao" [Individual Material on Tang Qiufang of Zhulinguan District Branch, Danfeng County]. Danfeng County Archives.

Zhongguo gongchandang Weinan difang weiyuan hui [Chinese Communist Party Weinan Local Party Committee]. 1953. "Weinan zhuanqu guanche hunyinfa shiban gongzuo jiben zongjie" [Basic Summary of Pilot Work in Carrying Through the Marriage Law in Weinan Special District]. Weinan County Archives.

Zhongguo renmin yinhang Shaanxi sheng fenhang, ed. 1958. *Weinan he Chaoyi liang xian nongcun jinrong gongzuo jingyan huibian* [Compilation on Experience of Rural Financial Work in Weinan and Chaoyi Counties]. Beijing: Jinrong chubanshe.

Zhongguo renmin zhengzhi xieshang huiyi Heyang xian weiyuan hui wenshi xuexi zuguo tongyi weiyuan hui, ed. 2004. *Heyang wenshi ziliao,* 8: *xiqu zhuanji* [Heyang Materials on Culture and History, no. 8: Special Issue on Traditional Opera]. Aug.

Zhongguo renmin zhengzhi xieshang huiyi Shaanxi sheng Nanzheng xian weiyuan hui wenshi ziliao yanjiu weiyuan hui, ed. 1987. *Nanzheng xian wenshi ziliao* [Nanzheng County Materials on Culture and History] 4 (Sept.): 15–50.

———, ed. 1990. *Nanzheng xian wenshi ziliao* [Nanzheng County Materials on Culture and History] 7 (Feb.): 97–99.

Zhongguo renmin zhengzhi xieshang huiyi Shaanxi sheng Tongguan xian weiyuan hui wenshi ziliao weiyuan hui, ed. 1999. "Qindong dadi de yike mingzhu" [A Bright Pearl from the Vast Earth of Eastern Shaanxi]. In *Xiongguan zhuhun* [Impregnable Pass, Molder of Souls]. *Tongguan wenshi ziliao,* 9: 3–6.

Zhonghua quanguo minzhu funü lianhe hui [All-China Democratic Women's Federation], ed. 1952. *Funü ertong fuli gongzuo jingyan* [Experience in Women's and Children's Welfare Work]. Beijing: Zhonghua quanguo minzhu funü lianhe hui.

Zhonghua quanguo minzhu funü lianhe hui xuanchuan jiaoyu bu [All-China Democratic Women's Federation Propaganda and Education Department], ed. 1949. *Xin Zhongguo de xin funü: Zhongguo funü diyici quanguo daibiao dahui daibiaotuan ji dianxing renwu jieshao* [The New Women of New China: An Introduction to the Delegation and Exemplary Characters of the First Chinese Women's All-China Representative Meeting]. N.p.: Zhongguo quanguo minzhu funü lianhe hui. Aug. Distributed by Xinhua shudian.

Zhou Gunian, comp. 1952. *Nongmang tuoer suo* [Childcare for the Busy Agricultural Season]. Shanghai: Huadong renmin chubanshe. Dec.

Zhou Lishun. 1971. "Shaannan qisu 'mohei' " [The Strange Shaannan Custom of "Smearing Black"]. *Shaanxi wenxian,* no. 6 (July): 23.

Zhu Futang. 1959. "Jianguo shinian lai ertong baojian shiye de chengjiu" [Achievements in the Enterprise of Children's Health in the Past Ten Years Since the Founding of the PRC]. *Zhonghua erke zazhi* [Chinese Journal of Pediatrics] 10, no. 5 (Oct.): 367–73.

ONLINE RESOURCES

http://aes.iupui.edu/rwise/banknotes/china/chi079_f.jpg.
http://aes.iupui.edu/rwise/banknotes/china/ChinaP73–10Yuan-1934-donated_f.jpg.
http://aes.iupui.edu/rwise/banknotes/china/ChinaP218d-10Yuan-1936_f.jpg.
http://aes.iupui.edu/rwise/banknotes/china/ChinaP460–50Cents-1936_f.jpg.
http://shaanxi.cnwest.com/content/2007–01/17/content_405559.htm.

http://zh.wikipedia.org/wiki/%E7%BB%9F%E8%B4%AD%E7%BB%9F%E9%94%80.
www.constitution.org/cons/china.txt.
www.international.ucla.edu/eas/restricted/marriage.htm.
www.sparklingredstarmovie.com/.
www.tianya.cn/publicforum/Content/music/1/147036.shtml.
www.women.org.cn/english/english/laws/02.htm.

shame, 44–45, 63; women's entry into, 10, 67, 72, 129, 138, 140, 143, 183, 186, 219, 268; women's tasks, 8, 42–44, 62, 140, 191, 198, 227, 265
First Five Year Plan, 171, 395n201
Five Changes, 238, 246–50, 385n61
Five Silver Flowers, 89, 219, 221, 226
floods, 14, 17, 77, 217, 226, 254; and labor models, 222, 225; in Village B, 135; in Village T, 135, 388n24; in Village Z, 135, 146
food shortages, 254–57. *See also* famine; Great Leap famine
footbinding, 35, 41–42, 44, 100, 134, 184, 189

Gansu, 58
Gan Yifei, 111–12
Gao Xiaoxian, 2, 3, 6, 7, 17, 203, 235, 236, 262, 375n94; and Cao Zhuxiang, 91–93; comments on archives, 19; and He Gaizhen, 285; as interviewer, 18, 28; on labor models, 218; and mother, 366n102; status as urban woman, 21; and Zhang Qiuxiang, 229–32
Gao Yuzhong, 255, 256
Gao Zhenxian, 226
gazetteers, 16, 91, 212, 234
gender, 4, 13; as contingent practices, 286; difference, 8, 13, 145; equality, 5; and generational differences, 287; at heart of story, 265; meanings of, 287; of memory, 13, 24–31, 270; and normative behavior, 13; and revolution, 287; and virtue, 287
gendered division of labor, 8, 10, 24, 44, 66–67, 83, 183; and collectivization, 129–30; constant shifts in, 140; and cotton cultivation, 214; and domestic labor, 186–87; and Great Leap Forward, 237; and shame, 309n144; and sideline production, 214; in Village T, 145–46; in Village Z, 140, 146–47; and Women's Federation, 140
ghosts, 38, 178, 180–81, 187, 358n160, 359n161; and pregnancy, 358n157; and rumors, 394n195
good-enough story, 3, 15, 31, 293n7
Great Leap famine, 25, 26, 199–200, 216, 225, 236–37, 254–58, 271, 272, 279; and exaggeration wind, 254–55; and fertility, 258; regional variation in, 254, 258, 391n165, 391n166; in Henan, 254; as human-made disaster, 254; and infant mortality, 258; and memory, 123, 260, 261, 264, 265, 280; and mortality, 258; official explanation for, 254;

recovery from, 260; and Shaanxi, 258; and state procurement, 245, 254–55; survival strategies, 191, 258–60
Great Leap Forward, 3, 4, 6, 11, 16, 26, 28, 123, 153, 236–66, 271; assessment of, 227; and birthing clinics, 157, 172, 246; and campaign time, 236; and Cao Zhuxiang, 238; and childcare, 197; and chronology, 236–37; and cotton cultivation, 220–21, 243; and dining halls, 250–58; and domestic time, 236; and dredging for iron, 240; and exaggeration wind, 245–46; and feminization of agriculture, 147, 220, 226, 236, 237, 238, 242–44; and Five Changes, 238; and gendered division of labor, 237; and grain production, 254; and intensive cultivation, 244–45; and labor models, 228, 243; and labor shortage, 238–39; and literacy, 102; and Mao Zedong, 237; and memory, 237, 272; midwife training after, 167; and new-style midwifery, 170; and Party-state goals, 238; and reproductive health, 171–72; resistance to, 240; scholarship on, 379n3; and socialization of domestic labor, 186; and state procurement, 384n57; and survival strategies, 236; and women's initial enthusiasm, 238; and women's social worlds, 240; and work assignments, 240; and Zhang Qiuxiang, 243
gua cai dai, di biaozhun, 26, 256, 394n94
Guanzhong, 7, 14, 66; and cholera, 49; and cotton cultivation, 137, 214, 219, 220; and crops, 42–43, 48; and footbinding, 42; and Great Leap famine, 258–59; land reform in, 77, 81; and lower producers' co-ops, 131; men working outside village, 147, 215; mutual aid groups in, 84–85; and spinning, 194; and troop support, 70–71; and women's field work participation, 62, 137

Hai Tao, 205
Halbwachs, Maurice, 23
He Gaizhen, 88, 142; as activist, 285; brother as Communist guerrilla, 59; and childbearing, 168–69; and childbirth, 177; and creativity, 193–94; and daughter-in-law, 278, 283–86; death of newborn son, 179; on dining halls, 250, 253, 256–57; and elder neglect, 283–86; on exaggeration wind, 245; and family property, 285; and Gao Xiaoxian, 285; husband's suicide, 284; and legal conflict with son, 284; and literacy, 283; and Liu Xihan, 179;

227; and exaggeration wind, 245–46; and fertilizer, 220; and Five Silver Flowers, 219; and footbinding, 41; and Great Leap famine, 225–26; and Great Leap Forward, 221, 224–25, 243; and interviewing, 229–32; and Kang Keqing, 224; as labor model, 211, 215, 217, 222–26, 243; learning to speak, 215–17; and Mao Zedong, 226; as medium for technical message, 223; in post-Mao years, 230; and "Qiuxiang groups," 222; selling shoes at market, 48; and Soviet official, 224; and state purchase of cotton, 226–27; and Three Hard Years, 226; woman researcher of peasant origin, 224; and Women's Federation, 230; and Women's Federation cadres, 215–17, 223–24; writing about, 222–25; and Xue Junxiu, 221–22; and Zhou Enlai, 229, 272

Zhao Feng'e, 74; and death of twins, 205–6

Zheng Xiuhua, 48, 59; and childcare, 197; on dining halls, 257; on food shortages, 255; and sideline embroidery, 193, 194

Zhou Enlai, 205, 212; and labor model meetings, 233; and Zhang Qiuxiang, 229, 272

Zhou Guizhen, 87; on Cao Zhuxiang, 245; and childcare, 197; and Cultural Revolution, 272; on dining halls, 251, 253; and feudal remnants, 100; and literacy training, 101; and machine-woven cloth, 191; mentored by Cao Zhuxiang, 241; and mobilization of women for field work, 242–43; and remittances, 260; and resettlement of villagers, 241–42; suicide of father, 50–51; on survival strategies, 258–59; and transfer of men out of agriculture, 241

Zhuang Xiaoxia, 86; and abortion, 207; on contemporary women, 277; and contraception, 207; on co-ops, 132–33; on food shortages, 255; marriage of, 125–26; and shoemaking, 193; on state procurement, 255

zodiac cycle: as marker of memory, 27–28, 87, 183

zuo yuezi (month of confinement), 156, 348n26; customary practices, 159–60; and reproductive health, 247; in Village G, 160; in Village T, 159–60; and women's health in old age, 175; and work points, 174–75

TEXT
10/12.5 Minion Pro

DISPLAY
Minion Pro

COMPOSITOR
Integrated Composition Systems

PRINTER AND BINDER
Maple-Vail Book Manufacturing Group